QBasic
for Students

QBASIC FOR STUDENTS

Michael Trombetta

Mitchell McGRAW-HILL

New York St. Louis San Francisco Auckland Bogotá Caracas
Lisbon London Madrid Mexico Milan Montreal New Delhi Paris
San Juan Singapore Sydney Tokyo Toronto Watsonville

To Gary Popkin and Steve Switzer—
for friendship measured in decades.

Mitchell **McGRAW-HILL**
Watsonville, CA 95076

QBASIC FOR STUDENTS

4 5 6 7 8 9 0 SEM SEM 9 0 9 8 7 6 5

ISBN 0-07-065261-9

Sponsoring editor: *Dean Barton*
Director of production: *Jane Somers*
Project manager: *Jane Granoff*
Compositor: *Jonathan Peck Typographers, LTD.*
Cover/interior designer: *John Edeen*
Printer and binder: *Semline, Inc.*

Library of Congress Card Catalog No. 93-79182

CONTENTS IN BRIEF

CONTENTS IN DETAIL

PREFACE TO THE INSTRUCTOR

QBasic for Students is designed for the first course in computer programming at two-year, four-year and vocational institutions. It teaches fundamental concepts using a modern, easy-to-learn programming language. Although the text emphasizes QBasic, it can also be used to teach QuickBASIC. The additional commands available in QuickBASIC are listed in Appendix C.

QBasic for Students provides a student-oriented approach to teaching programming; because programming can be tedious, challenging and complicated, this text does the following:

- Assumes no prerequisites and begins with computer basics.
- Develops user confidence by guiding students step-by-step through new procedures before adding complexity, in small increments.
- Motivates students by teaching new programming concepts within the context of solving real-world business problems.

Features and Benefits

The key features of *QBasic for Students* include:

1. **Structured, seven-step procedure.** Introduced in Chapter 2 and used throughout the text, this procedure provides a framework for developing programs.
2. **Thorough discussion of debugging.** Early discussion of syntax, run-time, and logic errors—and how they are debugged—equips students early in the book to detect and correct errors in their programs.
3. **Emphasis on good programming style.** Choosing meaningful variable names, thorough documentation, and proper indention of statements, loops, and subprograms are emphasized throughout the text.
4. **Problem-solving approach.** To motivate students, most chapters begin with the statement of a problem that students cannot yet program. Within the context of solving this problem, students are taught new QBasic statements and concepts; students not only learn the syntax of statements, but also how the statements work within a program.
5. **Integrated discussion of the QBasic environment.** Students learn how to effectively use the QBasic environment from discussions

integrated in the first few chapters, rather than referring to an appendix.

6. **Structured design.** Top-down design and hierarchy charts are used to develop algorithms, but only after students learn how to do arithmetic, code loops, and make decisions. When these design tools are introduced, the programs are sufficiently complex to make meaningful use of them. Subprograms are introduced at the same time.

7. **Numerous learning aids.** Each chapter includes Learning Objectives, extensive screen displays, annotated program listings, flowcharts and pseudocode, Review Exercises, Self-Check Questions, and Programming Assignments (which include problems for more advanced students).

8. **Extensive reference section.** Five appendices form a reference section that contains the answers to exercises marked with a star, important tables presented in the text, summaries of QBasic *and* QuickBASIC menu commands, DOS commands, and syntax of all statements presented in the book. A glossary and index are also included.

This book contains more material than can be covered in a one-semester programming course. The first eight chapters must be covered in order, but the remaining chapters are independent and may be covered in any order.

Approach

Like any book, this text reflects its author's views. Since the computer's power derives from its ability to process many cases, I introduce repetition as soon as reasonable—before decisions. I take advantage of the flexibility of QBasic's DO...LOOP statement by using both pretest and posttest loops, and by using both WHILE and UNTIL conditions—choosing whichever construction logically fits the problem. Many authors, reflecting the limitations of Pascal, use only pretest WHILE and posttest UNTIL loops. When I do discuss decisions, I discuss both simple and nested IF statements, IF statements with ELSEIF clauses, and the SELECT CASE statement. Some authors present the SELECT CASE statement simply as an alternative to IF statements with ELSEIF clauses—but of course, that is not true. To help students see the differences, I illustrate the ELSEIF clause using an example that cannot be coded using a SELECT CASE statement. I do not confuse students by discussing the one-line IF statement, which was retained in QBasic only to maintain compatibility with programs written in BASIC.

A great deal of thought was given to the question of exactly when to introduce procedures. Although procedures should be introduced early, students should have the pleasure of successfully writing some simple programs before facing the complications of local variables and passing variables. One solution to this dilemma is to use global variables, but that's a cure that is worse than the disease—using global variables is not good programming practice, and should be discouraged. Finally, I decided to introduce procedures in Chapter 6, after repetition and decisions. By that time, the programs that students can write are sufficiently complicated so students can see the advantages of using top-down design and procedures. GOSUB-type subroutines, which were retained in QBasic only to maintain compatibility with BASIC, are not discussed at all.

Instructor Support

1. **Instructor's Manual.** Contains answers to all of the Review Exercises and Self-Check Questions, teaching tips for each chapter, and sample course syllabi.

2. **Instructor's Solutions Disk.** Packaged with the Instructor's Manual, this disk contains every example program in the text, as well as answers to all of the Programming Assignments. The disk also includes files to supply data for several Programming Assignments, programs, and files specifically for use with the Programming Assignments in Chapters 9 and 10.

Acknowledgments

Many of my colleagues at Queensborough Community College taught from my earlier books and gave me the benefit of their experience. I would like to thank: Barry Appel, Edward Berlin, Stephen Berlin, Layne Bonaparte, Charles Fromme, Melchiore LaSala, Emil Parinello, Arlene Podos, Marie Rummo, Daniel Tsang, and John Zipfel. Lowell Lifschultz provided valuable assistance when it was critical.

My project manager, Jane Granoff, kept all the wheels running smoothly; copy editor Karen Richardson eliminated dozens of embarrassing errors. My gratitude to them both.

I would also like to thank the following reviewers for their thoughtful comments:

Kathy Cupp, Oklahoma City Community College
Kathy Schmidt, Mars Hill College
Timothy Vaughn, Northern Illinois University

Michael Trombetta

PREFACE TO THE STUDENT

Boy, are you in for a good time! Writing computer programs has always been exciting and challenging—but in the past, the exciting part was accompanied by a certain amount of tedious detail. QBasic provides a modern language—with all the features you could want in a programming language—and an environment that reduces the tedium to a minimum. When you use QBasic, you can have the fun of writing programs, without the drudgery.

You may be wondering why you should learn QBasic. There are several reasons. First, QBasic is easy to learn; BASIC, the grandparent of QBasic, was specifically designed to be easy to learn. Second, after learning QBasic, you can graduate to VisualBASIC, which is used by corporations to write Windows-based applications. Furthermore, several leading vendors of microcomputer applications programs use dialects of VisualBASIC to write macros, which are programs that enhance applications. The ability to write macros will be valuable to you in both your personal and professional life. Finally, even if you eventually intend to study other languages, like C, it is much easier to first learn the principles of programming in a friendly language like QBasic.

This book reflects the principles I have developed in 20 years of teaching various dialects of BASIC and in writing three earlier books about BASIC programming. Those principles involve starting at the beginning and discussing each topic carefully and thoroughly. The following features will help you in your study of programming:

- **Learning Objectives.** Each chapter begins with a list of learning objectives and a brief overview of the chapter.
- **Syntax Summaries.** Present each new statement's syntax, provide an example of how to use the statement, and explain what the statement does.
- **Annotated Programs.** Clearly point out important parts of the code.
- **Key Terms/Glossary.** Important terms introduced in the chapter are printed in **bold type** (like this) the first time they appear and are defined in the margin. A list of these terms appears at the end of the chapter. A comprehensive glossary at the end of the book repeats these definitions.
- **Chapter Summaries.** Highlight major points and recap the use of new QBasic statements.
- **Exercises and Self-Check Questions.** At the end of each section, a set of exercises allows you to test your understanding of the material just covered by writing QBasic statements and analyzing small programs. At the end of each chapter, Self-Check Questions test your knowledge of QBasic statements and commands and your understanding of key terms. Appendix A contains the answers to starred exercises.

xviii Preface

- **Programming Assignments.** The programming assignments involve simple applications that you can immediately understand. Examples include calculating gross pay, average gas mileage, and translating English into pig Latin. More complicated applications are thoroughly explained.

When programming in QBasic, statements need to be typed on one line. Occasionally in this book, space limitations require that a statement be printed on two lines. Such statements are shown with the continuation symbol (↵). For example:

```
AvgSales = (JanSales + FebSales + ↵
  MarSales) / 3
```

That's enough background for now. Let's start learning about personal computers and QBasic!

Michael Trombetta

AN INTRODUCTION TO PERSONAL COMPUTERS AND QBASIC

LEARNING OBJECTIVES

After reading this chapter, you will be able to:

- Name the components and functions of a computer system.

- Understand the difference between hardware and software.

- Use the keyboard of a personal computer (PC).

- Explain the concept of programming languages.

- Name the parts of the QBasic screen.

- Use the Run menu commands Start and Continue.

- Use the View menu command Output Screen.

- Use the File menu commands New, Open, Save, Save As, Print, and Exit.

- Use dialog boxes.

- Use the Options menu commands Display, Help Path, and Syntax Checking.

We begin this chapter by discussing the components of computer systems. Since you will be using the keyboard to enter your programs and data, we explain how to use it in some detail. We then discuss the concept of a programming language. Finally, we explain the parts of the QBasic screen, and how to use menus and dialog boxes.

1.1   THE COMPONENTS OF A COMPUTER SYSTEM

It's easy to see that computers are widely used. They are used as word processors, to prepare our pay checks, and to play games. But what exactly is a computer? A **computer** is an electronic device that can follow our instructions and process data. **Data** are the values we give the computer to process. For example, in a student grading system, the data consist of each student's name and test scores, and the processing consists of calculating the average test score for each student.

A computer system consists of both hardware and software. **Hardware** refers to the physical components of a computer system—the parts of the computer you can physically touch. **Software** refers to the instructions that the computer follows. A set of instructions to perform a particular task is called a **computer program**. Computer programs are written in one of several programming languages. The objective of this book is to teach you how to write programs in the QBasic language.

The best way to learn how to write programs is to actually plan, write, and execute them—and for that, you will need a computer. In this book, you will learn how to write programs for the IBM Personal Computer, which comes in several models, and for computers that work like IBMs (called IBM compatibles), but are manufactured by other companies. Programs are written the same way for all of these computers, so we will refer to each of them as a **personal computer (PC)**. Figure 1.1 shows a typical PC.

computer
An electronic device that can accept data, process the data according to your instructions, and display results.

data
Values in the form of numbers or words that the computer processes.

hardware
The physical components of a computer system—the parts of the computer you can physically touch.

software
The instructions that the computer follows.

computer program
A set of instructions followed by a computer to solve a problem.

personal computer (PC)
A single-user computer made by IBM (and many other companies).

FIGURE 1.1   A personal computer.
Courtesy of International Business Machines Corporation.

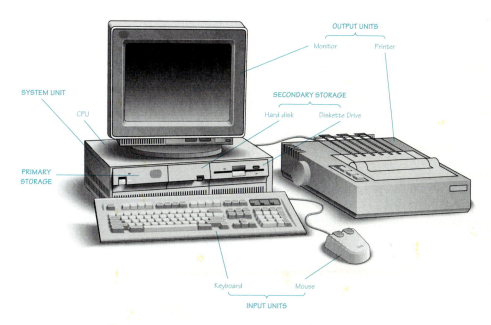

FIGURE 1.2 The major components of a personal computer system.

Hardware

Figure 1.2 shows the five major hardware components common to all personal computers.

1. The **input unit** allows you to enter data and instructions into the computer. On a PC, the keyboard is the main input unit. We will discuss the keyboard in more detail later in this chapter. Many PCs also use a mouse for input. A **mouse** is a device that fits under your hand. To move a pointer on the screen, you roll the mouse around on your desktop. A mouse also contains two (or sometimes three) buttons that you press to perform certain operations. We will explain how a mouse is used with QBasic later in this chapter.

2. The **output unit** displays the computer's results. On a PC, both the monitor and printer serve as output units. The **monitor** is a display device that looks like a television set. The monitor typically displays 25 lines on a screen and 80 characters (letters, digits, and special characters such as commas and dollar signs) on a line. A short flashing line, called the **cursor**, shows where the next character you type will appear on the screen.

   Some monitors can display information in several colors, while others use only one color. Also, some monitors can display graphics (such as pie charts), while other monitors can display only text. For most of this book, the QBasic programs run on computers with any kind of monitor. Only Chapters 11 and 12, which deal with graphics, require a monitor that can display multiple colors and graphics.

   When the computer is turned off, the information on the screen disappears. But often, you will want a permanent copy of your output; for this, you will need a printer. Printed output is called **hard copy**—in contrast to output on the monitor, which is called **soft copy**.

3. The **system unit** houses the **central processing unit (CPU)**. The CPU, which can be considered the "brains" of the computer,

input unit
The component of a computer system that allows you to enter data and instructions into the computer.

mouse
A device that you roll around on the desktop in order to move a pointer on the screen.

output unit
The component of a computer system that displays the computer's results.

monitor
A television-like display device.

cursor
A short flashing line that indicates where the next character you type will appear on the screen.

hard copy
Printed output.

soft copy
Output displayed on the monitor's screen.

system unit
The case that houses the CPU, primary storage, hard disk, and diskette drives.

central processing unit (CPU)
The computer component that executes program instructions, such as adding two numbers or printing results.

executes program instructions, such as adding two numbers or printing an answer.

4. Also inside the system unit is the **primary storage**, which is sometimes called **main memory**. The two kinds of primary storage are ROM and RAM. **ROM**, which stands for **read only memory**, permanently stores the instructions that the computer requires for its operation. As the name implies, you can only read the information in ROM; you cannot change it. **RAM**, which stands for **random access memory**, stores programs and data while the computer is working on them. The information stored in RAM is not permanent, and it can be changed.

   Primary storage consists of microscopic electronic components that can be in one of two states—like a switch that can be on or off. One of the states is represented by the digit 0 and the other by the digit 1. 0 and 1 are the two digits used in the binary number system, so each electronic component is called a **bit**, which is short for binary digit. Eight bits form a **byte**, which is the unit of storage that can store one character; for example, a single letter or digit.

   The size of primary storage is measured in bytes. PCs come with about 40 **kilobytes** of ROM, which is abbreviated 40K. (One kilobyte is 1024 bytes, so 40K is 40,960 bytes.) The amount of RAM installed varies, but values between 640K and 4 megabytes are typical. (One **megabyte** is approximately one million bytes and is abbreviated 1**M**.)

5. When you finish working on a problem and tell the computer to begin a new one, or when you turn the computer off, the data and instructions you entered up to that point are erased from RAM. To save your data and programs for future use, you need the last component of the computer system—a **secondary storage device**.

   The most common secondary storage devices are **diskette drives** and **hard disks**. A typical configuration is one diskette drive and a hard disk or two diskette drives. If a PC has only one diskette drive, it is called drive A. The hard disk is usually called drive C. If a PC has two diskette drives, the one on the left (or sometimes on the top) is called drive A, while the drive on the right (or on the bottom) is called drive B.

   A **diskette**, often called a **floppy disk**, is used with a diskette drive. A diskette consists of a thin layer of magnetic material on a plastic support. Programs and data are stored in the form of tiny magnetized spots that represent bits. Diskettes come in two sizes, which are shown in Figure 1.3. The older style is 5¼ inches in diameter, is easily bent, and can store either 360K or 1.2M of data. The newer style is 3½ inches in diameter, is rigid, and can store either 720K, 1.44M, or 2.88M. The capacity of a diskette depends on how the diskette was manufactured and on the design of the diskette drive that is installed in the PC.

   Diskettes are delicate and should be handled with care. On 5¼-inch diskettes, you should never touch the recording surface that can be seen through the head access window. Protect the diskette from dust by putting it back into its protective envelope as soon as you remove it from the drive. The 3½-inch diskettes are protected by a hard plastic cover and have a metal shutter that covers the recording surface when the diskette is removed from the drive, so they are not as fragile as the 5¼-inch diskettes. However, all diskettes should be kept away from extremes of hot and cold and from strong magnets. When a label is already on the disk, it is best to use a felt-tip pen to write on it.

---

primary storage (main memory)
The computer component in which data and instructions that are being processed are stored.

read only memory (ROM)
The part of primary storage with contents that cannot be changed (permanent storage).

random access memory (RAM)
The part of primary storage that stores programs and data while the computer is working on them. The contents are erased when the computer is turned off (temporary storage).

bit
Binary digit.

byte
The unit of storage, consisting of eight bits, that can store one character.

kilobyte (K)
1024 bytes.

megabyte (M)
Approximately 1 million bytes (exactly 1,048,576 bytes).

secondary storage device
A computer component, such as a diskette drive, that supplements primary storage—allowing data and programs to be stored permanently.

diskette drive
A secondary storage device that can read and write data on diskettes.

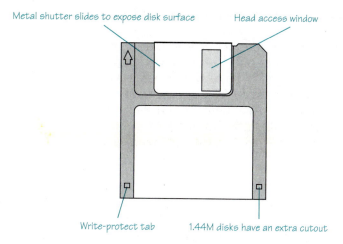

Metal shutter slides to expose disk surface   Head access window

Write-protect tab   1.44M disks have an extra cutout

(a)   3½-inch diskette.

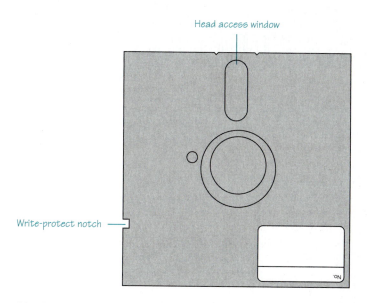

Head access window

Write-protect notch

(b)   5¼-inch diskette.

FIGURE 1.3   3½- and 5¼-inch diskettes.

Before most new diskettes can be used to store programs and data, they must be formatted. The procedure for formatting diskettes is explained in Appendix D.

To insert a 3½-inch diskette into a drive, turn the diskette so that the metal shutter faces the drive (the arrow stamped on the disk should be on the top left side of the disk). Slide the diskette into the drive until the diskette clicks into place. To insert a 5¼-inch diskette into a drive, turn the diskette so that the head access window faces the drive (the write-protect notch should be on the left side of the diskette). Slide the diskette into the drive until the diskette is inserted all the way. Some drives have a lever that you must push down to lock the diskette in place.

A hard disk typically stores between 20M and 250M. One advantage of a hard disk is that reading and writing are much faster than with a floppy diskette. Another advantage is that you can use it to store all the programs you routinely use—for

hard disk
A high-capacity, fast-access, secondary storage device.

diskette (floppy disk)
A magnetic-coated plastic disk that is used to store programs and data.

example, QBasic, word processors, spreadsheets, and databases.
In contrast, if your PC has only diskette drives, you have to search
through a box of diskettes looking for the one with the program
you want to execute.

The PC's Keyboard

You will be using your PC's keyboard to type programs and data into the computer. Different computers use slightly different keyboards, but two are typical: the standard keyboard, shown in Figure 1.4(a)—and the newer, enhanced key-

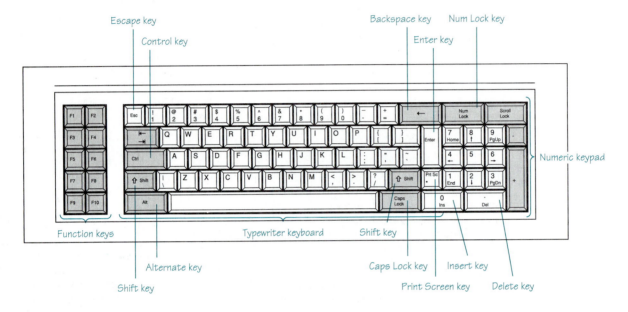

(a) The standard keyboard.

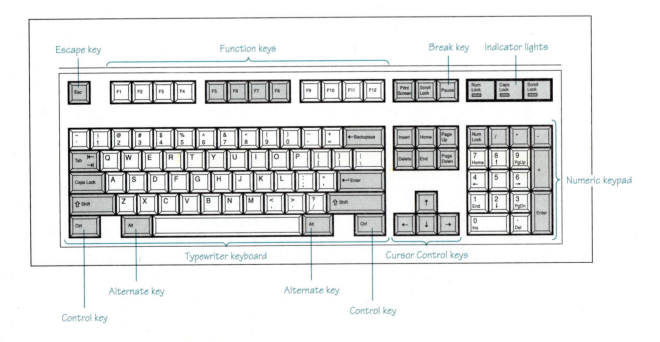

(b) The enhanced keyboard.

FIGURE 1.4   Two typical types of keyboards.

board, shown in Figure 1.4(b). On both keyboards, all the keys—including the Spacebar—repeat automatically if they are held down. This means that when you type, you must be careful not to hold down a key too long. When you want to repeat a key, the automatic repeat feature is very convenient.

All keyboards have **function keys** labeled F1, F2, and so on. The inside front cover lists the special tasks that these keys perform. Depending on the make and model of your keyboard, you may have 10 or 12 function keys located at the far left of the keyboard or across its top.

function keys
Any of the keys labeled F1 through F12.

The Typewriter Keys.   In the center of all keyboards are letter and number keys similar to those found on a typewriter. As on a typewriter, you can use these keys together with one of the two Shift keys (marked with large upward pointing arrows) to type capital letters and special symbols such as $ and %. However, typewriter and PC keyboards differ in important ways. For example, to type zero, you must use the number 0 key—not the letter O key. Similarly, to type the number one, you must use the number 1 key—not the letter l. PC keyboards also include keys not found on most typewriters, as shown in the following list.

1.   Alternate key. The Alternate key (Alt) is used in combination with another key. Sometimes you press and hold the Alt key and then press another key, and other times you press and release the Alt key and then press another key. The function performed by the Alt key depends on the software you are using.

2.   Backspace key. Each time you press it, the Backspace key erases one character to the left, allowing you to correct typing errors.

3.   Caps Lock key. The Caps Lock key does not stay down when you press it (as it does on a typewriter). Instead, the Caps Lock key acts as a **toggle** switch. One press turns Caps Lock on, and a second press turns it off. When a PC is first turned on, the letter keys are set for lower case. After you press the Caps Lock key, the letter keys type capital letters. When you press it again, Caps Lock is turned off. On the enhanced keyboard, a green light indicates that Caps Lock is on. The Caps Lock key affects only the letter keys; it does not give you the special symbols printed on the tops of keys. To type those, you must use one of the two Shift keys. To type a $, for example, you must hold down a Shift key and press the number 4 key.

toggle
A key that alternately turns on and off when pressed.

When you press a Shift key, you reverse the condition set by the Caps Lock key. If Caps Lock is on (that is, typing capital letters), holding down the Shift key produces lower case letters, and vice versa.

4.   Control key. The Control key (Ctrl) functions by pressing and holding it while you press another key. Like the Alt key, the function performed by the Ctrl key depends on the software you are using.

5.   Enter key. In QBasic, when you finish typing a line, you must press the Enter key to indicate that the line is finished. Generally, the PC does not act on anything you type until you press the Enter key.

6.   Escape key. The Escape key (Esc) usually backs you out of (provides an escape from) a situation you entered by mistake. That sounds cryptic, but you will see an example of the Escape key later in this chapter.

7.   Print Screen key. The Print Screen key (Print Screen) prints whatever is displayed on the screen. To get the Print Screen function on a standard keyboard, hold down the Shift key while you press the PrtSc key. Of course, the printer must be turned on and have paper in it.

The Numeric Keypad.   On the far right of the keyboard is the numeric keypad, which can be used either to type numbers or to move the cursor around the screen.

The Num Lock key toggles between these two modes. When you start a computer that has a standard keyboard, these keys are set to be used as cursor movement keys—you must press Num Lock if you want to use them to type numbers. In contrast, when you start a computer that has an enhanced keyboard, these keys are set in number mode—you must press Num Lock if you want to use them as cursor movement keys. On enhanced keyboards, a green light indicates that these keys are in number mode. The enhanced keyboard also has a separate group of cursor movement keys, located between the typewriter keys and the numeric keypad.

Software

Software may be divided into three categories: operating system software, programming languages, and applications software. Applications software refers to programs like the word processing, spreadsheet, and database packages you may have learned in other courses.

The most common operating system software used on the PC is called **DOS** (**disk operating system**), which was developed by the Microsoft Corporation. DOS is a collection of programs. Some of these programs control the PC, while others—called "utility" programs—make it easier for you to use the computer. Appendix D discusses DOS in more detail. Periodically, new versions of DOS are released. These new versions usually incorporate improvements in the form of new instructions and enhancements to existing instructions. As of this book's writing, the current version of DOS is 6.0.

When you turn on the PC, the DOS control programs are read from the hard disk or a floppy diskette into RAM. This process is called **booting** the PC. With a hard disk system, booting DOS is automatic if you remember not to put a diskette into drive A until the PC is booted. With a diskette-based system, you must remember to put a DOS diskette into drive A *before* you turn on the PC. Appendix D gives instructions for making a DOS diskette.

If the PC is already on, pressing and holding the Ctrl and Alt keys, and then pressing the Delete key, causes a **warm boot**. A warm boot produces the same effect as turning the PC off and then on; the PC restarts itself from scratch. A warm boot takes less time than turning the PC off and on; it also causes less wear and tear on the computer.

When you perform a warm boot, the program in RAM is erased. That can be an advantage, particularly when you are first learning, because sometimes a PC may freeze so that it doesn't respond to any of your instructions. On rare occasions, a PC won't respond to a warm boot; in those cases, you must turn the PC off, wait a few seconds, and turn it on again.

disk operating system (DOS)
A collection of programs that control the PC and make it easier for you to use it.

booting
Reading DOS from a disk into RAM.

warm boot
An action equivalent to turning the computer off and then on. Accomplished by pressing the Ctrl+Alt+Delete keys.

Programming Languages and QBasic

By itself, computer hardware is not useful. Before a computer can do anything useful, someone must write a program. When you use applications software, you are working with a program written by someone else. This book will teach you how to write programs. You can write programs in a number of programming languages, such as BASIC, Pascal, C, COBOL, and FORTRAN. In this book, you will learn **QBasic**, which was developed by the Microsoft Corporation.

BASIC, which stands for beginner's all-purpose symbolic instruction code, was developed by John Kemeny and Thomas Kurtz at Dartmouth College in the early 1960s. BASIC was designed to help beginners learn to program. In the mid-

QBasic
A modern version of the BASIC language, QBasic is distributed with DOS versions 5.0 and later.

1980s, Microsoft introduced QuickBASIC, which is similar to BASIC, but contains additional features that make it more powerful and even easier to use. In 1991, Microsoft distributed QBasic with DOS 5.0. QBasic is similar to QuickBASIC, but lacks some of QuickBASIC's advanced features. Because these advanced features are not crucial for students, and because QBasic is distributed with DOS 5.0 and later versions at no additional cost, this book concentrates on teaching you QBasic. Appendix C describes the additional features available with QuickBASIC.

Before the instructions in a program can be executed on a computer, they must be translated into **machine language**, which is the only language the computer understands. A computer program does this translation. Two kinds of translator programs exist: interpreters and compilers. **Interpreters** translate and execute program statements one at a time. If a program statement is executed more than once, as they usually are, that statement must be translated more than once. This repeated translation results in programs that execute slowly. The advantage of interpreters is that they make correcting and changing programs convenient.

Compilers, on the other hand, translate a complete program into machine language before any statements are executed. Programs that are compiled execute more quickly than programs that are interpreted, but correcting errors and changing programs is not as convenient when using a compiler as it is when using an interpreter. QBasic uses an interpreter, while QuickBASIC, getting the best of both possibilities, can use either an interpreter or a compiler.

machine language
The only language the computer understands without translation.

interpreter
A program that translates a program into machine language one statement at a time.

compiler
A program that translates a program into machine language before any statements are executed.

1.1 EXERCISES

Answers to questions marked with a star are given in Appendix A.

1. What is the difference between RAM and ROM?

★2. What does the abbreviation CPU stand for?

3. Would a computer whose primary storage contains 500 bytes be useful? What about one with 500K bytes?

★4. What is output on the screen called? What is output on the printer called?

5. What is the difference between primary storage and secondary storage?

1.2   THE QBASIC ENVIRONMENT

The method used to start QBasic depends on whether your PC has a hard disk or only diskette drives, and how the PC was set up. Typically, you just type QBASIC. However, for the exact steps used at your school, you should follow the instructions provided by your instructor.

The QBasic Screen

The opening QBasic screen is shown in Figure 1.5. If you follow the instructions on the screen and press the Enter key to see the Survival Guide, QBasic displays a screen of information on how to use menus and the help system. That information is presented in more detail in the following pages, so for now, press the Escape

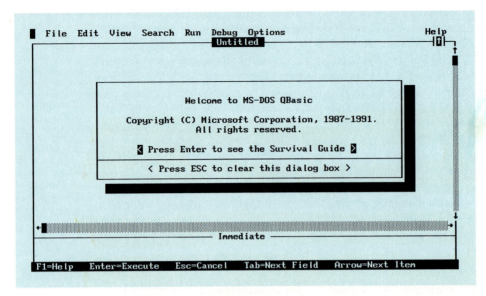

```
        Welcome to MS-DOS QBasic

Copyright (C) Microsoft Corporation, 1987-1991.
         All rights reserved.

   Press Enter to see the Survival Guide

   < Press ESC to clear this dialog box >
```

Immediate

F1=Help   Enter=Execute   Esc=Cancel   Tab=Next Field   Arrow=Next Item

FIGURE 1.5
The opening
QBasic screen.

key (Esc) to get Figure 1.6, which shows the QBasic screen with the important parts identified.

Across the top of the screen is the **Menu bar**. The Menu bar shows the names of the QBasic menus (File, Edit, and so on) that you will use to perform operations such as executing and saving your program. A **menu** is a list of choices from which you make a selection.

Along the bottom of the screen is the **Reference bar**. The Reference bar shows you keys that you can use to perform various operations. This information changes, depending on what you are doing. In Figure 1.6's Reference bar, the notation <Shift+F1=Help> means that pressing and holding the Shift key and pressing function key F1 displays a help screen. (In QBasic and in this text, a + between two keys means that you should press and hold down the first key while you press the second key. Do *not* type the +.) On the right end of the Reference bar are numbers that show the row and column position of the cursor. The Reference bar displays a C if Caps Lock is on, and an N if Num Lock is on. As you can see, Figure 1.6 has Num Lock on.

The main part of the screen is divided into two rectangular areas called windows. The larger window is the **View window**, which is where you type your programs. The QBasic statements you type in the View window are not executed until you decide to execute (run) them. The smaller window is the **Immediate window**. The QBasic statements you type in the Immediate window are executed as soon as you press the Enter key. Both windows have a title bar. The title bar in the View window displays the name of the program you are working on. It displays Untitled until you give your program a name. (How you name a program is explained later.) The title bar in the Immediate window always displays Immediate.

When you start QBasic, the View window is the active window. The active window is the one that contains the cursor and whose title bar is highlighted. The Reference bar shows that function key F6 is the Window key. Pressing F6 makes the Immediate window active. Pressing it again makes the View window active.

If a mouse is connected to your PC, you will see the mouse pointer in the upper-left corner of the screen. The **mouse pointer** is a rectangle that moves when you roll the mouse. With a mouse, you can change the active window by moving the mouse pointer to the window you want to be active and **clicking** it (that is, quickly pressing and releasing the left mouse button).

You can increase the size of the active window one line by pressing the Alt+Plus keys; you decrease the size of the active window one line by pressing the

Menu bar
The bar at the top of the QBasic screen that contains the names of the menus.

menu
A list of choices from which you make a selection.

Reference bar
The bar at the bottom of the QBasic screen that shows the operations that the function keys will perform, the keyboard status, and the cursor position.

View window
The area of the QBasic screen where you type your programs.

Immediate window
The area of the QBasic screen where statements are executed when they are entered.

mouse pointer
The rectangle that moves around the screen when you roll the mouse around the desktop.

clicking
Pressing and quickly releasing a mouse button.

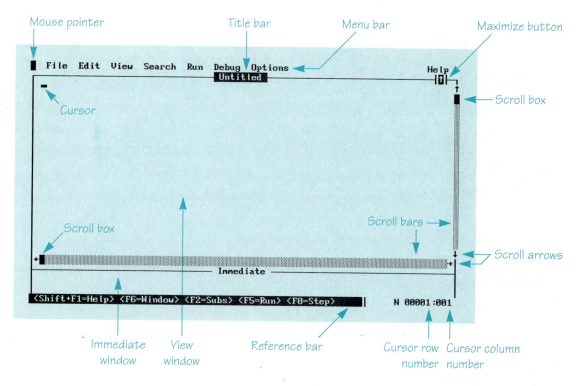

FIGURE 1.6   The QBasic screen.

Alt+Minus keys. In these operations, you must use the Plus and Minus keys in the numeric keypad. With a mouse, you can change the size of the windows by dragging the Immediate window title bar. You **drag** an object by moving the mouse pointer to the object, then pressing and holding down the left mouse button while you move the mouse.

You can expand the active window so that it fills the whole screen by using the Ctrl+F10 keys. Pressing the Ctrl+F10 keys again returns the active window to its original size. With a mouse, you can expand the View window by moving the mouse pointer over the maximize button in the upper-right corner of the screen and clicking. Clicking on the maximize button again returns the View window to its original size.

Often, all of your program won't fit in the View window. To see parts of the program that are not visible, you can move the text up, down, right, and left—a process known as **scrolling**. The arrow keys are used to scroll the program one line up or down, and one character right or left. The Page Up and Page Down keys will scroll a screen at a time, which moves you through the program faster. These and other cursor movement keys are summarized in Table 1.1.

With a mouse, you can scroll the program using either the scroll bars, the scroll arrows, or the scroll boxes on the right and bottom of the View window. To scroll a line or character at a time, click on a scroll arrow. To scroll a screen at a time, position the mouse pointer on the scroll bar between the scroll box and the end of the scroll bar and click. You can also drag the scroll box to a position on the scroll bar that roughly corresponds to the position in the file you want to see.

drag
To move the mouse pointer to an object, press the left mouse button, and move the mouse pointer while holding down the button.

scrolling
To move text up, down, right, and left so that you can see parts that aren't visible.

Using Menus

The best way to learn how to use QBasic's menus is to enter and execute a simple program. Figure 1.7 shows a three-statement program as it would look in the View window. Chapter 2 provides a full explanation of the statements in this program. For now, all you need to know is that when this program is executed, the

TABLE 1.1
The cursor movement and editing keys

Key	Function
→	Move right one character
←	Move left one character
Ctrl+→	Move right one word
Ctrl+←	Move left one word
↑	Move up one line
↓	Move down one line
Home	Move to first character in line
End	Move to last character in line
Page Up (PgUp)	Scroll up one screen
Page Down (PgDn)	Scroll down one screen
Ctrl+Home	Move to start of program
Ctrl+End	Move to end of program
Ctrl+Page Up	Scroll left one screen
Ctrl+Page Down	Scroll right one screen
Backspace	Erase the character to the left of the cursor
Delete (Del)	Delete character at cursor
Insert (Ins)	Toggle between insert and overtype

first statement (CLS) clears the screen and the second statement (PRINT "Happy Birthday, Harry") displays Happy Birthday, Harry on the screen. The third statement (END) marks the end of the program.

You should start QBasic by following your instructor's directions and then entering the program shown in Figure 1.7. Type the statements carefully, paying particular attention to the quotation marks in the PRINT statement, and remembering to press the Enter key at the end of each line.

When you press the Enter key, the QBasic "smart" editor reformats the statement so that the QBasic reserved words—CLS, PRINT, and END—are capitalized. The editor also checks the statement to see if you typed it properly. For now, we will assume that no errors were made, but the next section shows how you can correct errors.

Most statements are relatively short, like the ones in this program, and they easily fit within the screen. But occasionally, long statements may extend beyond the right edge of the screen. Don't let that bother you. Just keep typing—the screen will shift so that you can see what you are typing, although you will not see the beginning of the line anymore. QBasic statements can be up to 255 characters long, but lines that extend beyond the edge of the screen are difficult to read, and print peculiarly, so we will avoid them in this book.

The Run Menu

As mentioned earlier, to have QBasic actually carry out the statements you type in the View window, you must execute your program. This is done by selecting the Start command from the Run menu.

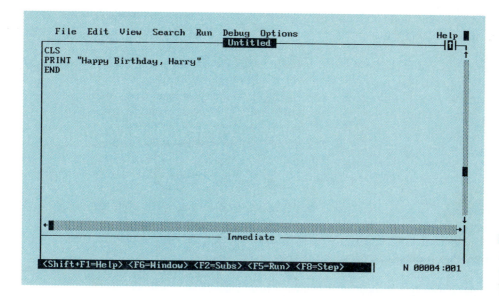

FIGURE 1.7
A sample pro-
gram in the View
window.

First, you must access the Run menu. Begin by pressing and releasing the Alt key. This highlights the first letter of each menu name. Then, you can press the first letter of the menu's name (for example, R for the Run menu). This causes the Run menu, shown in Figure 1.8, to be displayed. Alternatively, you can use the right and left arrow keys to highlight the menu name and press Enter. (If the computer beeps when you press an arrow key, it is because these keys are in their number mode. Press the Num Lock key to change to arrow mode.) When you press and release the Alt key, the Reference bar displays information on how to access the menus.

Next, select the Start command from the menu. You select a command by typing the letter highlighted in the command. The highlighted letter is usually the first letter of the command. Alternatively, you can use the up and down arrow keys to highlight the desired command and then press the Enter key. Since Start is already highlighted, you select it by just pressing Enter.

If you access the wrong menu, you can move to another menu by pressing the left or right arrow keys. You can clear a menu from the screen by pressing the Escape key.

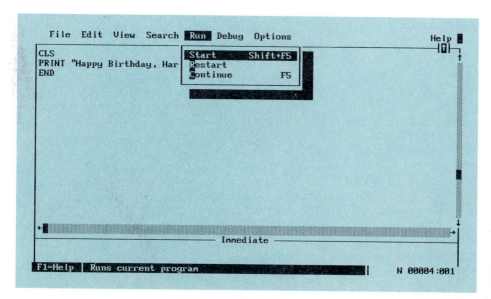

FIGURE 1.8
The Run menu.

With a mouse, selecting a command is much simpler. First, move the mouse pointer to the appropriate menu name on the menu bar and click the left mouse button. This causes the menu to be displayed. Then, move the mouse pointer to the desired command and click the left mouse button. You can clear a menu from the screen by clicking outside the menu.

When a command is highlighted, the reference bar displays a brief description of the command's function. For instance, in Figure 1.8, the Start command is highlighted and the reference bar displays Runs current program.

Notice that the Run menu in Figure 1.8 shows that the shortcut keys for the Start command are Shift+F5. This means that instead of accessing the Run menu, you can save time and execute your program by pressing and holding down the Shift key and then pressing function key F5. The menu commands and their shortcut keys are listed in Appendix C and on the inside front cover.

Looking back at Figure 1.7, it might seem odd that the Reference bar shows that to run your program, you can simply press function key F5. The Run menu in Figure 1.8 shows that function key F5 is the shortcut key for the Continue command. The Start command executes the program from the beginning, while the Continue command resumes execution from a stopping point. We will discuss stopping points—and the third Run menu command, Restart—in Chapter 4. Until then, you should use the Start command (Shift+F5) to execute your programs.

When you select the Start or Continue command, QBasic executes the program statements one at a time—starting with the first statement. When it executes the first statement,

```
CLS
```

the Output screen (not the View window) is cleared. When the second statement

```
PRINT "Happy Birthday, Harry"
```

is executed, the message Happy Birthday, Harry is displayed on the Output screen, as Figure 1.9 shows. When the third statement

```
END
```

is executed, the program stops and QBasic displays the message Press any key to continue in the lower left corner of the Output screen. When you press a key, you are returned to the View window. Now you understand that the View window shows your instructions, while the Output screen shows the result of executing those instructions.

You can switch back to the Output screen by selecting the Output Screen command from the View menu, which is shown in Figure 1.10. The View menu shows that the shortcut key to switch to the Output screen is function key F4.

```
Happy Birthday, Harry




Press any key to continue
```

FIGURE 1.9.
The output screen.

Pressing any key returns you to the View window. The other View menu commands are discussed in later chapters.

Editing the Program

The QBasic editor makes it easy to change a program. If you accidentally leave out one or more characters, use the cursor movement keys to move the cursor to where the missing characters belong, and simply type them. The characters you type are inserted at the cursor's position, and characters to the right of the cursor are moved to the right.

Suppose you want to change the message in the program in Figure 1.7 to Happy Birthday, Sally. You would use the cursor movement keys to move the cursor under the H in Harry. Then press the Delete key five times. The Delete key deletes the character above the cursor. The characters to the right of the cursor move to the left to fill the hole. Alternatively, you could move the cursor to the right of the y in Harry, and press the Backspace key five times. The Backspace key deletes the characters to the left of the cursor. Be careful when you use these keys, because—like all keys—they repeat; if you hold them down too long, you may delete more than you intended. After Harry is deleted, you can type Sally.

Because Harry and Sally both have five letters, in this case, you might prefer to use the editor's overtype mode. When the editor is in overtype mode, the characters you type replace the ones on the screen. The editor is put into overtype mode by pressing the Insert key. To remind you that the editor is in overtype mode, the cursor changes to a large blinking box. Move the cursor under the H of Harry, press the Insert key, and type Sally. To return to insert mode, press the Insert key again.

Sometimes, you may want to delete a whole line. To do this, use the Home key to move the cursor to the beginning of the line you want to delete, then press and hold down the Delete key. One after another, you will see the characters being deleted. A faster way to delete a line is to use the Ctrl+Y keys while the cursor is anywhere on the line.

At other times, you may want to add a statement. To do so, move the cursor either to the beginning of the line below where you want to add the new statement, or to the end of the line above where you want to add the new statement, and press Enter. The two lines will separate, leaving you a blank line in which to type the new statement.

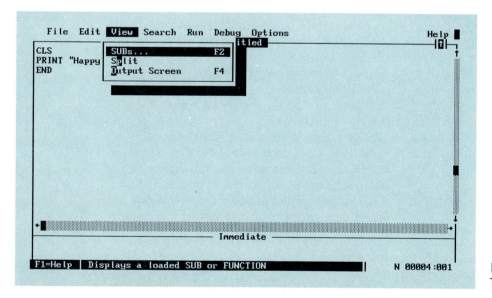

FIGURE 1.10
The View menu.

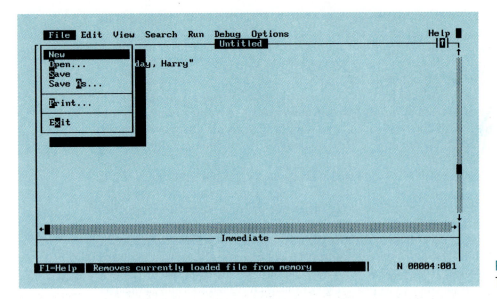

FIGURE 1.11
The File menu.

The File Menu

The File menu, shown in Figure 1.11, contains several important commands that you'll need to learn. Next, we'll cover the Save, Save As, Open, New, Print, and Exit commands.

The Save Command

Suppose you have a program that you would like to use in the future. When you exit QBasic, or if you simply turn off the computer, the program in the View window is erased from RAM. To execute the program later, you would have to laboriously retype it. You can avoid retyping the program by using the Save command from the File menu to save the program on a diskette or on a hard disk.

When QBasic needs more information before it can execute a command, it displays a **dialog box**. All dialog boxes have similar features. The first time you save a program, QBasic presents you with the dialog box shown in Figure 1.12, which has its parts labeled. The Save command dialog box contains three areas:

dialog box
A box that QBasic displays when it needs additional information to execute a command.

Text box	You type information in the text box. In the Save dialog box, you type the name you want to give the program when it is saved.
List box	You select one of the items in the list box. In the Save dialog box, the list box shows the drives where you can save the program.
Command buttons	Command buttons are enclosed with angle brackets: <>. You use command buttons to execute the command, cancel it, or get help. The command buttons are primarily used with a mouse because with the keyboard, you can execute the command by pressing the Enter key, cancel the command by pressing the Escape key, and display a help screen by pressing function key F1.

Initially, the cursor is in the File Name text box. You move the cursor from one area to the next by pressing the Tab key. You move backwards by pressing the Shift+Tab keys. Within an area, you select an item by pressing the arrow keys.

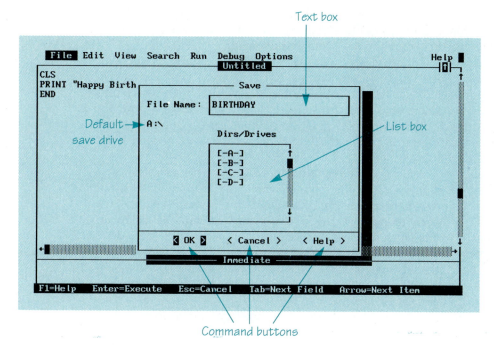

FIGURE 1.12
The Save command dialog box.

When the desired item is selected, you can use the Tab key to move to the next area. You don't have to remember all of this information because the Reference bar displays it. Using a mouse is much simpler; you select an item simply by clicking on it.

When a program is saved on disk, it is called a **file**. When you use the Save command, you must type the **filename** that you want to have associated with the file in the File Name text box. You will use the same name later when you want to retrieve the file. The name you choose for the file must contain 1–8 characters, which may include letters, digits, and the special characters ( ) { } @ # $ % & ! - _ and / . A name *must not* contain a blank space and *should not* contain a period. You should choose a name that is meaningful so that you will remember what the program does. As you can see in Figure 1.12, I chose the name BIRTHDAY. (You can type the name by using any combination of upper and lower case letters; when the program is saved, all the letters are changed to upper case.)

QBasic saves the file with the name BIRTHDAY.BAS. The three letters, BAS, are called the **filename extension**. They and the period are automatically added by QBasic.

The Save dialog box also shows the default save drive; in Figure 1.12, it is A:\ (the A drive). A **default** is an automatic setting. You want to save your program on the diskette in drive A or B, so that you can take the program with you. The instructions you followed to start QBasic should have made either drive A or B the default save drive. If the dialog box shows that the default drive is not A or B, you can use the Dirs/Drives list box to select A or B as the default drive.

To change the default drive, press the Tab key to move the cursor to the Dirs/Drives list box. Use the down arrow key to highlight the drive you want to make the default drive, and then press the Enter key. With a mouse, you can click on the drive you want to make the default drive, and then click the OK command button.

When the Enter key is pressed, or the OK command button is clicked, QBasic copies the program in the View window to the disk in the default save drive. You will see the light on the disk drive go on. Never insert or remove a diskette while the light is on because you may damage the diskette or drive. Of course, to save a program, you must have a formatted diskette in the diskette

file
A program, or other data, stored on a diskette or hard disk.

filename
The name of a file. Can be up to eight characters and is composed of letters, digits, and selected special characters.

filename extension
One to three characters that may be added to the end of a filename. QBasic automatically uses BAS as the filename extension.

default
The value you get automatically (used if you don't specify a different value).

drive. As mentioned earlier, instructions for formatting a diskette are given in Appendix D. If you forget to put a diskette in the drive, a "Disk not ready" dialog box appears. Correct the error and reexecute the command.

After the program is saved, you will see that QBasic changed the name in the title bar of the View window from Untitled to the filename you used. If you save the program again, QBasic automatically uses the name in the title bar and doesn't display the dialog box. A typical sequence is that you enter a program and save it. Then you discover that the program contains errors. You correct the errors and save the program again. On the disk, the new (corrected) version of the program replaces the old version.

Sometimes you want to use a different name, so that you have two versions of the program saved on the disk—the original version and a modified version. The two programs might have names like BRTHDAY1 and BRTHDAY2. To save a program with a different name, select the Save As command from the file menu. This command, plus the Open and Print commands, are followed by three dots. The three dots mean that these commands always display a dialog box when they are selected. The Save As dialog box is the same as the Save dialog box shown in Figure 1.12. To save the program with a new name, type the new name in the File Name text box and press the Enter key.

You don't have to wait until a program is completely entered to save it. A power interruption will erase the program in the View window, but a program that was saved to disk is safe. Therefore, as your programs get longer, you should develop the habit of saving every 10–15 minutes—and after you type something especially complicated. It's also a good idea to save your program before you execute it.

The Open Command

Before a program that was saved on a diskette can be executed, it must be read into RAM by using the Open command from the File menu. The Open command dialog box is shown in Figure 1.13. The File Name text box initially contains *.BAS. The asterisk stands for any number of characters, and is called a wild card. The name *.BAS means that the Files list box shows the names of all files with the extension BAS; that is, the names of all the QBasic programs.

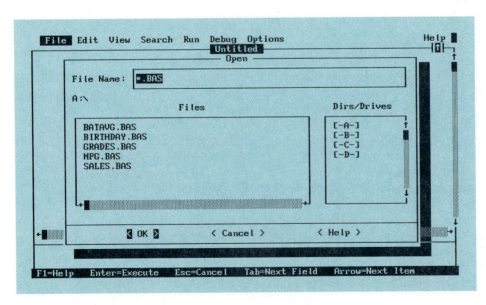

FIGURE 1.13
The Open command dialog box.

The Open command dialog box contains two list boxes: a Dirs/Drives list box (like the one in the Save dialog box) and a Files list box that shows the QBasic programs that you may open.

To open a file, press the Tab key to move to the Files list box, then use the arrow keys to highlight the file you want to open. As you highlight different filenames, that filename replaces *.BAS in the File Name text box. When the filename you want is highlighted, press the Enter key to open the file. With a mouse, just click on the file you want to open, and then click on the OK command button, or double-click on the filename. (You double-click by clicking twice quickly.)

Opening a program does not alter the program on disk; the program is still stored on the disk and can be opened as many times as you want. However, when you open a file, the program in the View window is erased from RAM, so you should save that program before opening a file. If you forget to save the program in the View window, QBasic displays the dialog box shown in Figure 1.14, giving you a chance to save it before it is erased. If you want to save the program, simply press Enter. If you do not want to save the program, press N—or use the Tab key to highlight the No button and then press Enter. You can also press Escape to cancel the command, or F1 to get help.

The New Command

The New command from the File menu removes the current program from RAM and clears the View window so that you can start working on a new program.

If you forget to save the program in the View window before you execute the New command, QBasic displays the same dialog box we just saw in connection with the Open command (Figure 1.14). This gives you a chance to save the program before it is erased.

The Print Command

To get a hard copy of your program, use the Print command from the File menu. The Print command and the QBasic PRINT statement are different, and should not be confused. When you select the Print command, it presents a dialog box asking if you want to print all or part of the program. Usually, you will just press Enter to print the whole program.

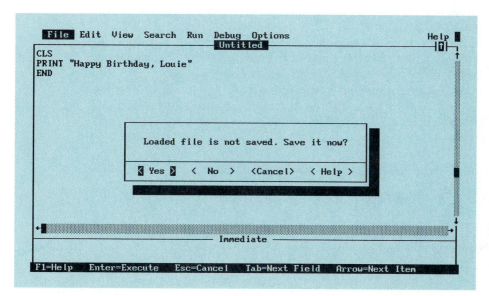

FIGURE 1.14
Dialog box displayed when program in View window was not saved.

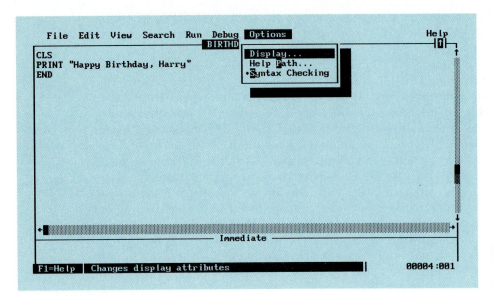

```
     File  Edit  View  Search  Run  Debug  Options                    Help
                              BIRTHD                                   [↕]
CLS                                   Display...                              ↑
PRINT "Happy Birthday, Harry"         Help Path...
END                                  •Syntax Checking




















←░                                                                        →
                             Immediate
F1=Help │ Changes display attributes                        00004:001
```

FIGURE 1.15
The Options
menu.

If the printer is off or the On Line indicator is not on, a "Device fault" dialog box appears. Turn on the printer or the On Line indicator and reexecute the command.

The Exit Command

You should always use the Exit command from the File menu to end a QBasic session. If you forgot to save the program you were working on, QBasic displays the same dialog box we saw in Figure 1.14—giving you a chance to save the program before you exit.

The Options Menu

Figure 1.15 shows the Options menu. The Display command provides a dialog box that allows you to change the screen colors. The dialog box also lets you display or remove the scroll bars. If you do not use a mouse, removing the scroll bars gives you more room to see your program. Finally, the dialog box allows you to change the number of spaces the cursor advances when you press the Tab key. The default setting is 8, which is too large. If it hasn't already been changed, you should change the tab setting to 4.

The Help Path command is used to tell QBasic where the help files are stored. You probably won't need this command. If you must use this command, your instructor will tell you where the help files are stored.

The Syntax Checking command is a toggle that turns the editor's syntax checking on and off. If syntax checking is on, a dot appears next to the command, as in Figure 1.15. You want syntax checking turned on.

1.2 EXERCISES

★**1.**   List the steps to execute a program.

2.   List the steps to print a program.

★**3.**   Why is it important to save a program?

4.   List the steps to save a program on the diskette in the default save drive, using the filename PGM.

5. List the steps to retrieve a program called FIRSTPGM, which is stored on the default drive.

6. List the steps to clear the View window so that you can work on a new program.

7. Enter the program shown in Figure 1.7 (page 13) into your computer. Execute the program. Edit the program to print any message you like.

WHAT YOU HAVE LEARNED

In this chapter, you learned that:

- All computer systems contain major five components: input units, output units, a central processing unit (CPU), primary storage, and secondary storage.
- The input units send data and instructions from the outside world to the computer. On a typical PC, the input units are the keyboard and the mouse.
- The output units send the computer's answers to the outside world. On a typical PC, the output units are the monitor and the printer.
- The CPU executes instructions.
- Random access memory stores programs that are being executed and data that are being processed.
- Secondary storage devices enable you to store programs and data when they are not being used and when the computer is turned off. On PCs, the most common secondary storage devices are diskette drives and hard disks.
- PCs typically have a hard disk and one diskette drive or two diskette drives.
- A PC's keyboard is similar to a typewriter's, but it is divided into three sections: the function keys, the alphanumeric keys, and the numeric keypad. The enhanced keyboard has separate cursor movement keys.
- Pressing the Ctrl+Alt+Delete keys causes a warm boot. A warm boot is equivalent to turning the computer off and then on, but it is faster and causes less wear and tear on the computer.
- Software is composed of instructions that the computer follows.
- The most common operating system used on the PC is called DOS.
- Programs written in QBasic are translated into machine language by an interpreter before they are executed.
- The main parts of the QBasic screen are **1)** the menu bar, which contains the menu names; **2)** the View window, where you type your programs; **3)** the Immediate window, where commands are executed when you press the Enter key; and **4)** the reference bar, which tells you what the function keys will do.
- To access a menu, press and release the Alt key, then press the first (highlighted) letter of the menu's name. Alternately, after pressing and

releasing the Alt key, use the right and left arrow keys to highlight the menu's name and press Enter. With a mouse, just click on the menu's name.
- To select a command from a menu, press the letter that is highlighted in the command. Alternatively, use the up and down arrow keys to highlight the command and press Enter. With a mouse, click on the command.
- The Start or Continue command in the Run menu executes a program.
- The Output Screen command in the View menu switches to the Output screen.
- The Save command in the File menu saves a program on a hard disk or a floppy diskette.
- The Save As command in the File menu saves a program on a hard disk or a floppy diskette with a new (different) name.
- The Open command in the File menu retrieves a program from a floppy diskette or a hard disk.
- The New command in the File menu removes the current program from RAM and clears the View window before starting a new program.
- The Print command in the File menu prints the program in the View window.
- The Exit command in the File menu ends a QBasic session.
- The Display command in the Options menu changes the screen colors, displays or removes the scroll bars, and sets the size of the tab stops.
- The Syntax Checking command in the Options menu toggles the editor's syntax checking on and off.
- A dialog box appears when QBasic needs additional information to execute a command.
- In a dialog box, pressing the Tab key moves the cursor from one area to the next. Pressing Shift+Tab moves the cursor to the previous area. Within an area, pressing the arrow keys moves the cursor from one item to the next. The command is executed by pressing the Enter key, and the dialog box is cleared from the screen. Pressing the Escape key cancels the command and clears the dialog box from the screen. With a mouse, items are highlighted by clicking on them. The command is executed by clicking on the OK command button, and the dialog box is cleared from the screen. Clicking on the Cancel command button cancels the command and clears the dialog box from the screen.

KEY TERMS

bit
booting
byte
central processing unit (CPU)
clicking
compiler
computer
computer program
cursor
data
default
dialog box
disk operating system (DOS)
diskette drive
diskette (floppy disk)
drag
file

filename
filename extension
function keys
hard copy
hard disk
hardware
Immediate window
input unit
interpreter
kilobyte (K)
machine language
main memory
megabyte (M)
menu
Menu bar
monitor
mouse

mouse pointer
output unit
personal computer (PC)
primary storage
QBasic
random access memory (RAM)
read only memory (ROM)
Reference bar
scrolling
secondary storage device
soft copy
software
system unit
toggle
View window
warm boot

REVIEW EXERCISES

SELF-CHECK

1. Complete the following sentences:
   a) Pressing the Ctrl, Alt, and Delete keys at the same time causes a(n) _____.
   b) The unit of storage that can hold one character is a(n) _____.
   c) The _____ shows where the next character you type will appear on the screen.
   d) To access a menu, you first press the _____ key.
   e) To move from one area to the next in a dialog box, press the _____ key.
   f) The part of the QBasic screen where you type your programs is called the _____.

2. When QBasic needs additional information to execute a command, it displays a(n) _____.

3. Name the five major hardware components of a computer.

4. You must end every line you type by pressing the _____ key.

5. Which key is used to move the cursor from the View window to the Immediate window?

6. What is the name of the operating system used on the PC?

7. What does an interpreter do?

8. What devices are most frequently used as output units?

9. How do you access a menu when using a mouse?

10. Which command is used to store the program in the View window on a floppy diskette or a hard disk?

11. Which command is used to execute a program? What is the shortcut key for that command?

12. Which command is used to print a program?

13. What does the New command in the File menu do? When should you use it?

14. Which command is used to retrieve a program from a diskette or a hard disk?

15. How many characters may a filename contain?

16. Which command is used to view the Output screen? What is the shortcut key for that command?

17. Which command is used to leave QBasic?

18. Which command is used to change the size of the tab stops?

STRUCTURED PROGRAMMING AND QBASIC

LEARNING OBJECTIVES

After reading this chapter, you will be able to:

- Follow a structured procedure for solving problems using a computer.
- Draw a flowchart.
- Write, enter, and execute a QBasic program.
- Trace a program.
- Debug a program.
- Use the QBasic help system.
- Use the QBasic statements LET, PRINT, END, REM, and CLS.

Now that you are familiar with the workings of a PC, you're ready to write QBasic programs. To help you write correct programs, you'll learn a seven-step procedure that you should follow when developing a program. You will learn your first QBasic statements, plus how to detect and eliminate errors from programs.

We will begin our study of programming by solving a simple problem.

EXAMPLE 1

A PROGRAM THAT CALCULATES A PAYCHECK

Problem Statement

Suppose you make $6.25 an hour working part time at a local drugstore. Last week you worked 25 hours. Write a QBasic program that calculates your pay.

Writing QBasic programs requires two skills. First, you must learn the QBasic instructions to perform operations such as adding numbers and printing results. Second, you must learn how to put the QBasic instructions together to solve a problem.

To help you learn how to put the QBasic instructions together, we use a seven-step procedure:

1. Identify the variables required by the problem and choose names for them.
2. Develop an algorithm to solve the problem.
3. Check the algorithm by calculating an answer to the problem by hand.
4. Write a QBasic program.
5. Enter the program and correct syntax errors if necessary.
6. Execute the program and correct run-time errors if necessary.
7. Compare the computer's answer against the answer you calculated in step 3, and correct logic errors if necessary.

The meanings of "syntax error" and "run-time error" are clarified later in this chapter. You should follow this procedure whenever you write QBasic programs. Don't be intimidated by the thought of having to follow seven steps every time you want to solve a problem. Some of the steps are easy, and they all contribute to a successful program.

STEP 1   Variable Names

The first step is to identify variables in the problem and choose names for them. Variables represent quantities in problems whose values may change. When you are trying to identify the variables in a problem, think about what data you are given and what answers you want to calculate. In this problem, you are given the pay rate and hours worked, and you want to calculate gross pay. So pay rate, hours worked, and gross pay are the variables in this problem.

Now that we have identified the variables in our problem, we must choose names for them. A **variable name** is the name of a storage location in primary storage where QBasic stores the value of the variable.

When choosing variable names, you must follow these QBasic rules:

- A variable name may contain only letters, digits, and the period.
- A variable name may not contain a blank space.
- A variable name must start with a letter and may contain up to 40 characters.
- A variable name must not be a QBasic reserved word.

Although the first rule states that a variable name may contain a period, the period is used for special purposes; we will not use variable names that contain a

variable name
The name of a storage location in primary storage where data is stored.

period until Chapter 9. The last rule mentions **reserved words**, which are words that have special meaning in QBasic. Some reserved words are LET, PRINT, and END. A complete list of QBasic reserved words is shown on the inside back cover.

Here is a list of some valid and invalid variable names.

reserved word

A word that has a special meaning in QBasic.

Proposed Variable Name	Status
A	Valid
4Sale	Invalid—a variable name must start with a letter
Test1	Valid
Rumpelstiltskin	Valid
%Interest	Invalid—a variable name must start with a letter
Gross Pay	Invalid—a variable name may not contain a blank space
Grosspay	Valid
GrossPay	Valid—using a capital letter where a new word begins makes this easier to read than Grosspay
Beep	Invalid—Beep is a reserved word, which may not be used as a variable name
Beeper	Valid—although you cannot use a reserved word as a variable name, a reserved word may be part of a variable name

As we said earlier, when you use a variable name in a program, QBasic assigns a location in the computer's RAM where it stores the value of that variable. QBasic does not distinguish between upper and lower case letters, so it considers TOTALPAY, totalpay, and TotalPay to be three different forms of the same variable name. In other words, all three forms refer to the same storage location in the computer's RAM. Normally, we will capitalize only the first letter of a variable name. However, when a variable name consists of more than one word, we will capitalize the first letter of each word (for example, TotalPay is easier to read than TOTALPAY or totalpay).

Now that you know how to choose variable names, let's choose names for the three variables in our problem: pay rate, hours worked, and gross pay. You could choose A, B, and C, but it is better to use meaningful variable names that help you remember what they mean. So we will use:

Variable	Variable Name
Pay rate	PayRate
Hours worked	Hours
Gross pay	GrossPay

When you choose variable names, you have to strike a balance between variable names that are too short to help you remember what they mean and variable names that are so long they increase the chance that you'll make a mistake when typing them. In this case, P, H, and G are too short—but HourlyPayRate and TotalWeeklyGrossPay are too long.

QBasic uses two kinds of variables: numeric variables and string variables. The value of a **numeric variable** is a number. The three variables we are using in our program are numeric variables. A **string** is a sequence of letters, numbers, or other characters. The value of a **string variable** is a string. In this chapter, we will use only numeric variables. You will learn about string variables in Chapter 3.

numeric variable

A variable whose value is a number.

string

A sequence of letters, numbers, or other characters.

string variable

A variable whose value is a string.

STEP 2   Algorithm

The second step of our systematic procedure is to develop a plan to solve the problem. In computer terminology, the step-by-step procedure to solve a problem is called an **algorithm**. Some people are surprised that we need a plan to solve the problem. They think the computer solves the problem. But remember, the computer does not know anything about your problem. It just follows the instructions you give it. *If you do not know how to solve a problem by hand, you won't be able to solve it with a computer, either.*

Don't be intimidated by the requirement of developing an algorithm—you've done it most of your life. For example, whether you use it or not, the algorithm for recording programs on a VCR is:

1. Insert a tape in the VCR.
2. If the tape is not rewound, rewind it.
3. Repeat steps 4 through 7 for each program you want to record.
4. Set the date.
5. Set the start time.
6. Set the stop time.
7. Set the channel.
8. Set the VCR to timer mode.

These steps illustrate features that are found in most algorithms. Step 2 involves a decision; if the tape is not rewound, you must rewind it. If it is rewound, you don't have to do anything. Step 3 involves repetition; you must perform steps 4–7 for each program you want to record. To make the steps that are repeated stand out clearly, you can indent them. Steps 4, 5, 6, and 7 illustrate sequence; the steps are executed one after another. Sequence, decision, and repetition are the constructions we use in all of our algorithms. In this chapter, we cover only sequence; later chapters use decision and repetition.

The order of some steps is important, while the order of others is not. For instance, step 2 (rewind the tape) must follow step 1 (insert the tape). On the other hand, on many VCRs, step 7 (set the channel) can be done either before or after step 4 (set the date). When you develop an algorithm for the computer, you must also consider the order in which the steps are done.

An algorithm to calculate your paycheck from the drugstore is

1. Assign 6.25 to the variable PayRate.
2. Assign 25 to the variable Hours.
3. Multiply the variables PayRate and Hours and assign the result to the variable GrossPay.
4. Print the value of the variable GrossPay.

In this algorithm, the order of steps 1 and 2 is not important. However, step 3 must follow steps 1 and 2, and step 4 must follow step 3.

Flowcharts.   Several techniques are available to help you develop an algorithm. One technique is to draw a flowchart. A **flowchart** pictorially represents an algorithm to show its logical structure more clearly. It is often easier to develop and understand an algorithm when it is in the form of a flowchart than when it is in a series of English sentences. Figure 2.1 shows a flowchart for the paycheck algorithm.

As Figure 2.1 illustrates, a flowchart consists of symbols connected by lines. These lines are called flowlines. Flowlines end in arrows, which show their direction. Table 2.1 contains the symbols used to draw flowcharts, plus their names and meanings. The flowchart in Figure 2.1 uses only the terminal symbol, the processing symbol, and the input/output (I/O) symbol. In later chapters, you will see flowcharts that use the other symbols.

---

algorithm
A step-by-step procedure to solve a problem.

flowchart
A pictorial representation of an algorithm that shows its logical structure more clearly.

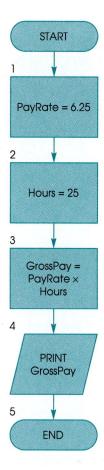

FIGURE 2.1 Flowchart for a program that calculates a paycheck.

Notice that, except for the terminal symbols, the symbols in the flowchart correspond to the steps in the algorithm. The three processing symbols correspond to the first three steps, and the input/output symbol corresponds to the fourth step.

Notice also that the symbols in Figure 2.1 are numbered. These numbers allow me to refer unambiguously to a particular symbol. They also match the numbers on the statements in the QBasic program that we will write soon. These matching numbers help you see the relationship between the flowchart and the program.

STEP 3 Hand-Calculated Answer

The third step in our systematic procedure is to calculate the answer to the problem by hand. For the paycheck problem, we can easily calculate that the gross pay should be

```
$6.25 × 25 = $156.25.
```

Only by comparing the program's solution to the solution you calculate by hand can you be sure that your program is correct. You might argue that if you must calculate the answer to a problem by hand, you do not need a program. However, in later chapters, we will use the program's ability to repeat the same calculations; we will solve a problem many times, but use different initial data. For example, we can have the program calculate the pay for all the employees at the store. In those cases, we will still calculate an answer by hand for only one case (or a small number of cases). If the program's answer agrees with the hand-

TABLE 2.1
Flowchart symbols and their meanings

Symbol	Name	Meaning
Terminal	Terminal	Marks the start and end of a program. Contains the words START or END.
Processing	Processing	Shows a calculation.
Input/Output	Input/Output	Shows an input or output process.
Decision	Decision	Shows a decision step in which one of several alternative paths is to be followed.
Predefined Process	Predefined Process	Shows the execution of a subprogram or function.
Connector	Connector	Shows the exit from one part of a flowchart and entry to another part. Also used where two flowlines meet.

calculated answer for that sample case, the program's answers are probably correct for all the other cases.

STEP 4   QBasic Program

The fourth step in developing a program is to write a QBasic program based on the algorithm and the flowchart. A QBasic program consists of a set of QBasic statements that the computer follows to solve a problem. Program 2.1 shows a QBasic program that calculates a paycheck.

QBasic is so straightforward that even without an explanation, you can probably see that the first three lines correspond to the first three steps of the algorithm and that the fourth line corresponds to the fourth step.

Constants and Arithmetic Operations.   A **constant** is a value—either a number or a string—that does not change when a program is executed. Program 2.1 uses two numeric constants: 6.25 in the first line and 25 in the second line. When you write a numeric constant, you may use only digits, a decimal point, and a plus or

constant
A value—either a number or a string—that does not change when a program is executed.

```
LET PayRate = 6.25
LET Hours = 25
LET GrossPay = PayRate * Hours
PRINT GrossPay
END
```

PROGRAM 2.1
A program that
calculates a
paycheck.

minus sign. Therefore, although 6.25 represents $6.25 an hour, you write it as the number 6.25—without the dollar sign. QBasic always uses numbers without any units like dollars, inches, or gallons. You need to know that the 6.25 stands for dollars per hour to interpret the output. Similarly, you never use commas in numbers (write 4352, not 4,352).

Notice the asterisk (*) in the third line of the program. You use an asterisk for multiplication. Do not use the usual X for multiplication because QBasic won't know if the X stands for multiplication or a variable named X. You use + for addition, – for subtraction, and / for division.

QBasic Statements.   A QBasic **statement** is an instruction to the computer. In Program 2.1, we need three different QBasic statements: the LET statement, the PRINT statement, and the END statement. The words LET, PRINT, and END—which begin each statement—are QBasic reserved words. Every QBasic statement begins with a reserved word.

statement
An instruction to the computer.

The rules that specify the correct way to write each kind of statement are called the statement's **syntax**. One general syntax rule is that QBasic reserved words must be separated from other parts of a QBasic statement. Most often, a space is used as a separator—but in some cases, a comma or parentheses may be used. The syntax of each statement shows which separators may be used. This means that

syntax
The rules that must be followed when writing a statement.

```
PRINTGrossPay
```

is wrong because there is no separator between the reserved word PRINT and the variable name GrossPay.

The LET Statement.   You use the LET statement, which is also called the assignment statement, when you want QBasic to assign the value of an expression to a variable. An **expression** is a combination of variables, numbers, and arithmetic operation symbols (+, –, *, /, and three others you will learn later in this chapter) that can be evaluated to produce a number. Expressions may be as simple as a constant (such as 6.25) or a variable (such as Sales)—or they can be more complex (such as Miles / Gallons). When you study string variables, you will learn that some expressions produce a string when they are evaluated.

expression
A combination of variables, numbers, and arithmetic operation symbols that can be evaluated to produce a number.

In Program 2.1, the first three lines are examples of LET statements.

```
LET PayRate = 6.25
LET Hours = 25
LET GrossPay = PayRate * Hours
```

The QBasic help system displays a model that shows briefly and clearly the syntax of each statement. Because the method is so effective, and because you should learn how to read the help screens, we will use a slightly simplified version of the same method. Appendix E shows the syntax for all the statements discussed in this book.

The syntax of the LET statement is

```
[LET] variable = expression
```

In model statements, words printed in capital letters are QBasic reserved words and must be typed as shown. In this case, the word LET is a QBasic reserved word. Words and letters in lower case stand for items supplied by you, the programmer. When you write a LET statement, you must replace the words variable and expression with values required by your problem. The equals sign and other punctuation shown in the model statement—such as commas, semicolons, and parentheses—must be included when you write the QBasic statement.

Square brackets—[ ]—are not part of the statement. They are never typed. Square brackets enclose parts of the statement that are optional; in this case, the word LET. The form

```
variable = expression
```

is an alternate form of a LET statement. To reduce typing, we will not use LET in any future programs in this book. The LET statement is the only exception to the rule that every QBasic statement must begin with a reserved word.

When a LET statement is executed, the computer first evaluates the expression in order to arrive at a number. That number is then put in the storage location for the variable. For example, when the LET statement

```
LET GrossPay = PayRate * Hours
```

is executed, the expression is evaluated by multiplying the value in the storage location for PayRate (6.25) by the value in the storage location for Hours (25) and the result (156.25) is stored in the storage location for GrossPay. When a new value is put in a storage location, the old value is erased.

When a value from a storage location is used to evaluate an expression, the value does not change. So after this LET statement is executed, the PayRate storage location still contains 6.25, and the Hours storage location still contains 25.

The syntax of the LET statement says that the variable must be on the left side of the equals sign and the expression must be on the right side. Therefore, the following two LET statements are *incorrect*:

```
6.25 = PayRate
PayRate * Hours = GrossPay
```

We will discuss the LET statement in more detail later in this chapter; in the meantime, make sure you understand the following simple LET statements:

ILLUSTRATIONS

LET Statement	Effect
Seconds = 60 * Minutes	Multiplies the number in the Minutes storage location by 60 and puts the answer in the Seconds storage location. (Converts minutes to seconds.)
Total = N1 + N2 + N3	Adds the numbers in the N1, N2, and N3 storage locations and puts the answer in the Total storage location.
Change = Paid - Price	Subtracts the number in the Price storage location from the number in the Paid storage location and puts the answer in the Change storage location.

The PRINT Statement. Calculating an answer doesn't do us any good unless that answer is displayed. The PRINT statement in Program 2.1

```
PRINT GrossPay
```

displays on the screen the number in the GrossPay storage location. It is important to realize that the words GrossPay are *not* printed; the number in the Gross-Pay storage location is displayed.

The syntax of the PRINT statement is

```
PRINT expressionlist
```

where expressionlist is a list of expressions separated by commas or semicolons. (In Chapter 3, you'll learn the difference between using commas and semicolons in an expressionlist. Until then, use commas.) In Program 2.1, the expression printed is the variable GrossPay. The syntax shows that we could print more than one expression. For example, the PRINT statement could be written as

```
PRINT PayRate, Hours, GrossPay
```

This statement displays the numbers in the PayRate storage location, the Hours storage location, and the GrossPay storage location—in that order. Be careful to follow the form shown exactly, putting a comma between the variable names, but not after PRINT or GrossPay.

Because it is legal to print expressions, the PRINT statement could also be written as

```
PRINT PayRate * Hours
```

or

```
PRINT PayRate, Hours, PayRate * Hours
```

In this case, the expression is evaluated and the calculated result is displayed. For clarity, however, in this text we will usually calculate a value, assign that value to a variable (as we did with GrossPay), and then print that variable.

The END Statement. The last statement in a QBasic program is the END statement. Its syntax is simply

```
END
```

END tells QBasic to stop executing a program. The END statement is not required at the end of your program, but it helps you see the end of the program. We will write it in all examples in this book and you should use it in all of your programs.

STEP 5 Enter the Program

The fifth step in our structured procedure is to enter the program into the computer and, if necessary, correct syntax errors. We explained in Chapter 1 that you start QBasic by typing QBASIC, or by following the procedure your instructor gives you. When your PC displays the opening QBasic screen shown in Figure 1.6 (page 11), you may begin typing.

Type Program 2.1 just as we wrote it, one statement on a line. When you finish typing each line, press the Enter key. When you press Enter, the QBasic "smart" editor reformats the line into its standard form. In this form, QBasic reserved words are capitalized, and equals signs and arithmetic operators (+, −, *, /, ^, and \) are separated from surrounding text by one space. The editor examines the capitalization you use when you type variable names. If you use a different capitalization than you used earlier, the editor changes the earlier capitalization to agree with the current capitalization. So if you type a variable name

Line numbers

```
1 | LET PayRate = 6.25
2 | LET Hours = 25
3 | LET GrossPay = PayRate * Hours
4 | PRINT GrossPay
5 | END
```
                                                        View window
```
  156.25                                                Output screen
```
                              ────Answer, displayed by PRINT statement

PROGRAM 2.2   The paycheck program as it appears in the computer.

as payrate and later type it as PayRate, the editor will change the earlier payrate to PayRate.

The editor also checks the syntax of the statement to see if you made an error. For now, we assume that no errors were made, but in the next section, we will see how the editor responds when you make an error.

Program 2.2 shows how the paycheck program looks after it is entered into the View window. The line numbers at the left *are not part of the program and are not typed.* They are included in the figure so you can easily locate specific lines and also so you can see the connection between the flowchart symbols and the QBasic statements. To emphasize that they are not part of the program, the line numbers are separated from the program by a vertical line.

STEP 6   Execute the Program

The sixth step of our structured procedure is to execute the program and, if necessary, correct run-time errors. As you learned in Chapter 1, you execute your program by selecting the Start command from the Run menu, or by pressing Shift+F5. For now, we will assume that the program is correct and does not produce any run-time errors; in the next section, you will learn how to correct these errors.

When you execute the program, the answer—156.25—is displayed in the Output screen. In this and all future programs, we will use a horizontal line to separate the View window from the Output screen. Furthermore, we will not show the message Press any key to continue. As you saw in Figure 1.9 (page 14), this message is displayed on the last line of the Output screen.

If you entered and executed Program 2.2, you found that besides the answer (156.25), the Output screen also showed the commands you typed when you turned on the PC and started QBasic. I cleared that extraneous output from the screen, and later in this chapter you will learn how to erase this extra material from your screen.

STEP 7   Compare Hand-Calculated Answer

The seventh and last step of our structured procedure is to compare the computer's answer against your hand-calculated answer and, if necessary, correct logic errors. In this case, both answers are 156.25, so we conclude that the program does not contain any logic errors. Our work on this program is complete. In the next section, you will learn how to correct logic errors.

Tracing the Program.   Now that our program is finished, let's consider exactly what happened when QBasic executed it. The best way of doing that is to execute the program, line by line, just the way QBasic does. We call this **tracing** the program. Figure 2.2 shows a trace of the program. Each statement shown in the left

tracing
Executing a program by hand, line by line, and keeping track of the changing values of the variables.

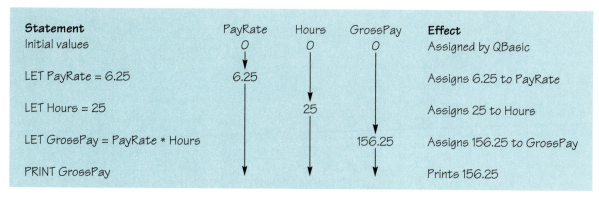

Statement	PayRate	Hours	GrossPay	Effect
Initial values	0	0	0	Assigned by QBasic
LET PayRate = 6.25	6.25			Assigns 6.25 to PayRate
LET Hours = 25		25		Assigns 25 to Hours
LET GrossPay = PayRate * Hours			156.25	Assigns 156.25 to GrossPay
PRINT GrossPay				Prints 156.25

FIGURE 2.2 Tracing Program 2.2.

column is in the order that it is executed. The middle section shows the contents of the storage locations for the three variables after the statement in the left column is executed. The last column explains the effect of the statement.

Before any statements are executed, QBasic assigns the value 0 to all numeric variables. That is why the first line in Figure 2.2 shows 0 as the contents of the storage locations for all three variables.

When the first statement

```
LET PayRate = 6.25
```

is executed, its effect is to assign 6.25 to PayRate. Therefore, Figure 2.2 shows 6.25 replacing 0 as the contents of the PayRate storage location. The vertical line drawn from the 6.25 indicates that for the rest of the program, that value doesn't change.

Continuing, the figure shows that when the second LET statement

```
LET Hours = 25
```

is executed, 25 is put into the Hours storage location, erasing the 0 originally there.

The next line shows that when the third LET statement

```
LET GrossPay = PayRate * Hours
```

is executed, the number in the PayRate storage location (6.25) is multiplied by the number in the Hours storage location (25). The answer (156.25) is put in the GrossPay storage location, erasing the 0 originally there. When the PRINT statement

```
PRINT GrossPay
```

is executed, it displays the number that is in the GrossPay storage location (156.25).

Tracing is valuable because it helps you understand how a QBasic program is executed. ■

Correcting Errors

When we discussed steps 5, 6, and 7, we assumed that no errors were made. Unfortunately, when you write QBasic programs, you will frequently make errors—so it is important to know how to correct them. Errors are often called **bugs**, and the process of correcting errors is called **debugging**.

The simplest but most common errors are in typing. If you press the wrong character, you can use Backspace to delete the character to the left of the cursor, type the correct character, and continue.

bugs
Errors in a program.

debugging
Eliminating errors (bugs) in a program.

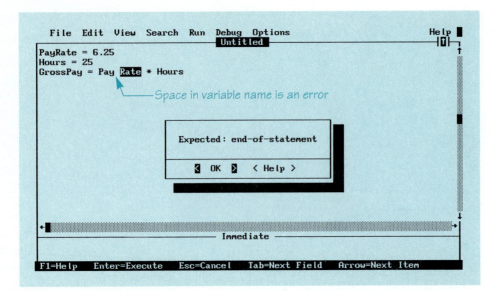

PROGRAM 2.3
QBasic finds a
syntax error—
a space in a
variable name.

Syntax Errors

The fifth step of our systematic procedure is to enter the program and correct syntax errors. When you type a line and press Enter (or an up or down arrow key), the QBasic smart editor checks the syntax of the line. If it finds a **syntax error**, it displays a dialog box similar to that shown in Program 2.3. A syntax error occurs when you don't follow the rules for writing QBasic statements. In Program 2.3, the error is the space between Pay and Rate. The editor caught the error and highlighted Rate, but the error message—Expected: end-of-statement—is not very helpful. The editor finds most syntax errors, but it doesn't always correctly identify the cause of the error—that's your job.

> **syntax error**
> A violation of the
> rules for writing
> QBasic statements.

To get more information on the probable cause of the error, you could press the F1 function key (or click the mouse on the Help button) to display a Help screen. In this case, the Help screen is not particularly enlightening, so it is not shown. When you press Enter or click the OK button to clear the dialog box, QBasic places the cursor on the line with the error, near where it thinks the error occurred. To correct the error, move the cursor to the exact position in the line where the error occurred.

In this case, to delete the space between Pay and Rate, move the cursor to the space and press the Delete key. Alternatively, you could move the cursor to the R and press the Backspace key. After you correct the error, either choose the Start command to execute the program again, or use the arrow keys to move to a different part of the program. Do *not* press the Enter key. Pressing Enter in the middle of a line splits the line in two. If you accidently press the Enter key, you can rejoin the two parts by pressing the Backspace key immediately.

Most of the time, your syntax errors will result from simple typing errors, and you will spot the mistake as soon as you look at the statement—as we did in Program 2.3. Sometimes, however, the error occurs because you did not follow the correct syntax rules, and won't be immediately obvious. In that case, you should compare your statement with the correct syntax of the statement given in the text or in Appendix E. You can also have QBasic's help system display the statement's syntax, as explained later. If you still can't locate the error, you should suspect that you used a reserved word as a variable name. A list of reserved words appears on the inside back cover.

Run-Time Errors

Unfortunately, the smart editor does not find one of the most common syntax errors—misspelling a QBasic keyword. This means that if you type PRINT as

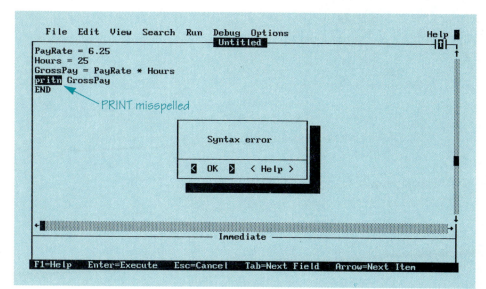

```
    File  Edit  View  Search  Run  Debug  Options                Help
                          Untitled
PayRate = 6.25
Hours = 25
GrossPay = PayRate * Hours
pritn GrossPay
END
            PRINT misspelled


                    ┌──────────────────────────┐
                    │                          │
                    │      Syntax error        │
                    │                          │
                    │   ◄  OK  ►   < Help >     │
                    │                          │
                    └──────────────────────────┘



    ←                                                             ↓
    ─────────────────────── Immediate ───────────────────────

  F1=Help    Enter=Execute    Esc=Cancel    Tab=Next Field    Arrow=Next Item
```

PROGRAM 2.4
QBasic finds a run-time error— a misspelled word.

pritn, as shown in line 4 of Program 2.4, the editor will not warn you. (Chapter 6 explains the reason why the editor does not find keyword misspellings.) That kind of error is detected only when the program is executed. The alert student might notice that something is wrong because the editor did not change pritn to capitals. (That's why it's wise to type QBasic reserved words in lower case.) If you don't notice the error, and execute the program anyway, QBasic stops, highlights the misspelling, and displays a dialog box similar to that shown in Program 2.4. An error that causes QBasic to stop execution is called a **run-time error**.

When you press Enter to clear the dialog box, QBasic positions the cursor on the line with the error. Correct the error by moving the cursor to the error and using the Delete, Insert, and typewriter keys, as you learned earlier.

Misspelled keywords are not the only mistakes that cause run-time errors. For example, you might write an expression in a LET statement that results in division by zero. As you learn new QBasic statements, you will observe new kinds of run-time errors.

run-time error
An error that causes QBasic to stop execution.

Logic Errors

The seventh step of our systematic procedure required you to make sure the answer produced by the program is correct. To do so, you must compare the answer you hand-calculated in step 3 with the values displayed by the computer. If the results agree, your program is free of logic errors and you are finished.

You may find, however, that the results do not agree. If so, your program gave a wrong answer. A program that executes but gives a wrong answer is said to contain a **logic error**.

How can a program give a wrong answer? Easily enough. Suppose, for example, that you incorrectly typed line 3 as

```
GrossPay = PayRate + Hours
```

Program 2.5 contains this incorrect line. Notice that QBasic does not print any messages about this line containing a syntax error. Why not? Because the expression PayRate + Hours is perfectly legal in QBasic. Of course, adding PayRate and Hours does not make any sense if you are trying to calculate Gross-Pay, but QBasic does not know that. If you tell it to add PayRate and Hours, that is what it will do. We know, though, that the program has a logic error because its answer, 31.25, does not agree with the 156.25 we calculated by hand.

If your program contains a logic error, you must find and correct it. Because QBasic does not indicate which line is wrong, as it does with syntax errors, logic

logic error
An error in a program that lets the program execute— but it produces a wrong answer.

+ typed instead of *

```
1 | PayRate = 6.25
2 | Hours = 25
3 | GrossPay = PayRate + Hours
4 | PRINT GrossPay
5 | END
```

31.25

PROGRAM 2.5   A program with a logic error—an incorrect mathematical operation.

errors are more difficult to find and correct. QBasic does offer some sophisticated debugging aids that are covered in later chapters. But for now, the best way of discovering logic errors is to trace the program as we did earlier.

Another kind of logic error is shown in Program 2.6. We know the program has a logic error because it printed 0 as the value of GrossPay. The source of the error is the misspelling of Hours as Hour in line 3. This misspelling caused QBasic to set aside a new storage location in RAM named Hour. When QBasic evaluated the expression in line 3, it used the number in the Hour storage location. Since we never put a number there (when line 2 was executed, 25 was put in the Hours storage location), QBasic used 0 for Hour. As we said earlier, when you execute a program, QBasic assigns an initial value of zero to all numeric variables.

This kind of error is called using an **uninitialized variable** because a variable is used before it is assigned a value. Unfortunately, QBasic does not stop and print an error message to warn you that an uninitialized variable was used. If a program produces 0 as an incorrect answer, you should suspect that you used an uninitialized variable—probably because you misspelled a variable name.

uninitialized variable
A variable to which a value was not assigned.

In a long, complicated program, finding uninitialized variables can be particularly difficult. That is why the first step of our procedure, identifying and choosing names for variables, is so important. If you write down the variable names you choose and keep the list handy as you write the program, you will be less likely to use two different names for a variable.

Using QBasic's Help System

QBasic has an extensive on-line help system that you can easily access. To get help on a QBasic menu command, highlight the command (as though you were about to execute it) and press the F1 function key. To get help on a QBasic statement, move the cursor to the reserved word and press the F1 function key. (To get help on the LET statement, you have to type the LET reserved word.) With a

Hours misspelled

```
1 | PayRate = 6.25
2 | Hours = 25
3 | GrossPay = PayRate * Hour
4 | PRINT GrossPay
5 | END
```

0

PROGRAM 2.6   A program with a logic error—an uninitialized variable.

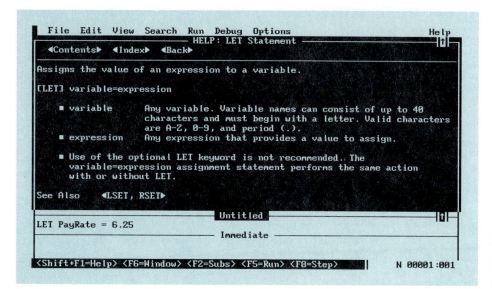

```
 File  Edit  View  Search  Run  Debug  Options              Help
┌──────────────────── HELP: LET Statement ──────────────────┐↑│
│ ◄Contents►  ◄Index►  ◄Back►                                 │ │
│───────────────────────────────────────────────────────────│
│ Assigns the value of an expression to a variable.          │
│                                                             │
│ [LET] variable=expression                                  │
│                                                             │
│   ■ variable      Any variable. Variable names can consist of up to 40 │
│                   characters and must begin with a letter. Valid characters │
│                   are A-Z, 0-9, and period (.).            │
│   ■ expression    Any expression that provides a value to assign. │
│                                                             │
│   ■ Use of the optional LET keyword is not recommended.. The │
│     variable=expression assignment statement performs the same action │
│     with or without LET.                                   │
│                                                             │
│ See Also     ◄LSET, RSET►                                  │
│                                                             │
├──────────────────────── Untitled ─────────────────────────┤↑│
│ LET PayRate = 6.25                                         │ │
│─────────────────────── Immediate ──────────────────────────│
│                                                             │
│<Shift+F1=Help> <F6=Window> <F2=Subs> <F5=Run> <F8=Step>    │    N 00001:001
└─────────────────────────────────────────────────────────────┘
```

FIGURE 2.3
The LET statement help screen.

mouse, move the mouse pointer to the reserved word and click the right mouse button. QBasic displays a help screen that shows the statement's syntax and a short explanation of the statement. Figure 2.3 shows the help screen for the LET statement.

The help screen can be used to obtain additional help. Notice the terms across the top of the Help window inside highlighted arrowheads (◄ ►): ◄Contents►, ◄Index►, and ◄Back►. These are **hyperlinks**—ways of getting deeper into the help system. To use a hyperlink, move the cursor to it and press the Enter key. To do this, you must first move the cursor to the Help window. The F6 function key moves the cursor between windows. Press it once and the cursor moves to the Immediate window; press it again and the cursor moves to the Contents hyperlink in the Help window. Alternately, Shift+F6 moves directly from the View window to the Contents hyperlink. With a mouse, you activate a hyperlink by moving the pointer to the hyperlink and clicking the right mouse button.

With the cursor on the Contents hyperlink, press Enter to display a screen listing many QBasic topics. These topics are also hyperlinks, so to display help information on any of them, use the Tab key to move to the topic and press Enter. To erase the Help screen, press the Escape key.

The Index hyperlink displays a screen with an alphabetical listing of all the QBasic statements as hyperlinks. To get help on any statement, move the cursor to the statement and press Enter. The help you get is identical to the help obtained by moving the cursor to the keyword in the View screen and pressing the F1 function key. The Back hyperlink displays the previous help screen.

Most Help screens display the names of related statements as hyperlinks. In the LET Help screen, the hyperlinks are the LSET and RSET statements, which are shown at the bottom of the Help screen in Figure 2.3. To get information about one of these related statements, use the Tab key to move the cursor to it and press Enter.

You can also use the Help menu to get general help about QBasic. The Help menu has five commands: Index, Contents, Topic, Using Help, and About. Selecting Topic gives you help on the reserved word the cursor is on, just like pressing F1. Selecting Using Help displays a general introduction on how to use the Help system. You can also display the Using Help screen by pressing the shortcut keys Shift+F1. The Index and Contents commands display the screens previously mentioned. Selecting About displays a dialog box showing the version of QBasic you are using.

hyperlink
A term that may be used as an entry point into the QBasic help system.

Syntax Summary

LET Statement

Form: `[LET] variable = expression`
Example: `Area = Height * Base`
Explanation: Evaluates the expression on the right of the equals sign and assigns the resulting value to the variable on the left of the equals sign.

PRINT Statement

Form: `PRINT expressionlist`
Example: `PRINT Height, Base, Area`
Explanation: Displays the values of the variables and/or expressions on the screen.

END Statement

Form: `END`
Example: `END`
Explanation: Indicates the end of the program and causes the program to stop executing.

2.1 EXERCISES

1. Which of the following variable names are legal and which are illegal? For those that are illegal, explain why.
   a) NumberTallerThanTenFeet
   b) 1StClass
   c) FourSale
   ★d) Overtime-Pay
   e) Final Grade
   ★f) Width
   g) EndOfData

2. Which of the following numeric constants are legal and which are illegal?
   ★a) $81
   ★b) 16.4
   c) 21,643
   d) −46.25
   e) 90 ozs

3. Which of the following LET statements contain errors? Rewrite the incorrect statement(s) correctly.
   ★a) `B = 6,500`
   b) `T = S / V`
   ★c) `P3 = -12`
   d) `M * C * C = E`
   e) `Length = 30 Feet`
   f) `A = A + 5`

4. If A = 7, B = 8, and C = 12, what values are assigned by the following LET statements?
   a) `G = A + B + C`
   b) `H = C / 3`
   ★c) `B = B + 1`

5. Which of the following PRINT statements contains errors? Rewrite the incorrect statement(s) correctly.
    a) `PRINT Phi, Beta, Kappa`
    b) `PRINT RegularPay, OvertimePay, and TotalPay`

6. What would be printed by this one-line program?
    ```
    PRINT A, B, C, D
    ```

7. Write the statement to display the values of the variables Weight, Volume, and Density.

★8. Let Speed stand for speed in miles per hour, Time for time in hours, and Distance for total distance in miles. Does the following program calculate and print the distance traveled by a car going 40 miles per hour for 3 hours? If not, correct the program.
    ```
    Speed = 40
    Time = 3
    PRINT Distance
    Distance = Speed * Time
    END
    ```

9. In Program 2.2 (page 34), suppose we used PR to stand for pay rate and wrote the first line as
    ```
    PR = 6.25
    ```
    What other changes in the program, if any, would be required?

10. We said that when you write a numeric value, you should write just the number—without any units. Yet in line 2 of Program 2.2, we used the word Hours. Explain.

★11. In Program 2.2, interchange the order of lines 1 and 2. Trace the program to determine what the output will be.

12. In Program 2.2, interchange the order of lines 4 and 5. Trace the program to determine what the output will be.

13. Several students are trying to correct the logic error in Program 2.6 (page 38). Huey says you must change Hour in line 3 to Hours. Louie says you must change Hours in line 2 to Hour. Dewey says it doesn't matter as long as you spell the variable the same in both lines. Who is correct?

★14. Trace the following program to determine the output:
    ```
    A = 6
    B = 8
    C = A + B
    D = A - B
    PRINT A, B, C, D
    END
    ```

15. Trace the following program to determine the output:
    ```
    P = 24
    M = P / 4
    R = 2 * M
    PRINT P, M, R
    END
    ```

16. How do you know if a statement contains a syntax error?

★17. How do you know if a program contains a logic error?

18. List the steps to take if you want to get help on a QBasic statement.

2.2 THE LET STATEMENT

In the previous section, we studied a simplified form of the LET statement. In this section, we present a complete discussion of the LET statement.

First, you must understand that although a LET statement looks like an algebraic equation, it is not. Instead, a LET statement assigns a value to a variable. For example, the algebraic equation $a = a + 1$ is meaningless; nothing is equal to itself plus 1. But the LET statement

```
A = A + 1
```

makes perfect sense. It means that the number in the A storage location is added to 1 and the result is put back in the A storage location.

Additional Arithmetic Operations

exponentiation Raising a numeric value to a power.

Besides adding, subtracting, multiplying, and dividing—which we discussed earlier—three other arithmetic operations are also possible in QBasic. Raising a numeric value to a power, or **exponentiation**, is indicated by the caret symbol (^), which is the upper shift character on the 6 key. Thus, A^4, the algebraic notation raising A to the fourth power (equal to A * A * A * A), is written as A ^ 4 in QBasic.

integer division Division that yields as its answer only the integer (whole number) part of the quotient. Specified by the backslash: \.

Two other arithmetic operations are sometimes useful. The backslash, \, specifies **integer division**. Don't confuse the backslash, \, with the ordinary forward slash, /, which is used for usual division. Integer division gives the integer (whole number) part of a quotient. For example, the statement

```
A = 14 \ 4
```

assigns the whole number 3 (rather than 3.5) to A. If the values to be divided are not themselves integers, they are rounded to the nearest integer *before* they are divided. Hence,

```
B = 11.3 \ 5.7
```

assigns the value 1 to B. The 11.3 is rounded down to 11, the 5.7 is rounded up to 6, and then the answer, 1.8333, is converted to 1.

modulo arithmetic Arithmetic in which the answer is the integer that is the remainder of an integer division. Specified by the operator MOD.

The word MOD specifies **modulo arithmetic**. Modulo arithmetic gives the integer value that is the remainder of an integer division. That is, the statement

```
C = 14 MOD 4
```

assigns the value 2 to C because when 14 is divided by 4, the remainder is 2. (When checking remainders, do the division by hand; ordinary calculators do not give you remainders.) Again, if the values involved are not integers, they are rounded to the nearest integer *before* they are divided. Therefore,

```
D = 11.3 MOD 5.7
```

assigns the value 5 to D because when 11 is divided by 6, the remainder is 5.

You might wonder when integer division and the MOD operator would be useful. Actually, there are many such occasions. For example, suppose you measure a distance of Length in inches, and you want to convert that measurement to feet and inches. The number of feet is

```
Feet = Length \ 12
```

and the number of inches remaining is

```
Inches = Length MOD 12
```

Another situation in which MOD is useful is when you want to know if one variable divides into another variable evenly. Since the MOD operator gives the remainder, if the second variable divides into the first variable evenly, the MOD operator gives a value of zero. For example, the value of 6 MOD 2 would be 0 because 2 divides into 6 evenly. If we use the LET statement

```
Remainder = A MOD B
```

to assign a value to the variable Remainder, then if Remainder equals 0, you know that B divides into A evenly. (In Chapter 5, you will learn how to test if Remainder equals 0.)

Hierarchy of Operations

You now have the tools to write expressions with more than one operator, but you still do not know how they are evaluated. For example, suppose that A equals 2 and B equals 3. What value is assigned to C when the following LET statement is executed?

```
C = A + 4 * B
```

Some students first add A and 4 to get 6, then multiply by B and assume that C equals 18. Other students multiply B by 4 to get 12, then add A, so that C equals 14. Only one answer is correct. To know which value C has, you must understand the **hierarchy of operations** that determines the order in which the operations are performed.

The operations are done from left to right according to the following hierarchy:

1. Exponentiation (^)
2. Multiplication and division (* and /)
3. Integer division (\)
4. Modulo arithmetic (MOD)
5. Addition and subtraction (+ and –)

hierarchy of operations
The order in which the operations are performed when expressions are evaluated.

Now we can see that when the expression A + 4 * B is evaluated, the multiplication is done first, and then the addition is done, giving a value of 14.

Note that when step 2 is performed, the multiplications are *not* all done before the divisions. Instead, multiplications and divisions are performed as they are encountered while the expression is scanned from left to right. Suppose A equals 12 and B equals 2. What is the value of the expression A / 3 * B? Since there is no exponentiation, nothing happens during step 1. During step 2, as the expression is scanned from left to right, the division is encountered first. 3 is divided into A, giving 4. At this point, the expression is 4 * B. Then 4 and B are multiplied to give 8 as the value of the expression.

Similarly, when step 5 is done, additions and subtractions are performed as they are encountered while the expression is scanned from left to right. So if A equals 20, B equals 5, and C equals 3, the expression A – B + C equals 18.

It is particularly easy to make mistakes with expressions in which an arithmetic step follows division. For example, consider the expression A / B + 1, with A equal to 12 and B equal to 2. When this expression is evaluated, first A is divided by B to get 6, and then 6 and 1 are added to get 7. Many students mistakenly add B and 1 to get 3, and then divide A by 3 to get the wrong answer, 4.

Use of Parentheses

Suppose you want to add A and 4, then multiply the sum by B. You couldn't use the expression A + 4 * B because the hierarchy of operations causes the multiplication to be done before the addition. The solution is to use parentheses. In fact, the hierarchy of operations really includes a zero step to add to our previous ones:

0.   Evaluate expressions inside parentheses.

Inside the parentheses, the operations are performed by following the usual hierarchy of operations.

Therefore, if you want A and 4 to be added before the multiplication, you must write the expression as (A + 4) * B. The parentheses force QBasic to add A and 4 before it multiplies by B. In this expression, notice that the asterisk indicating multiplication must be present. In algebra, multiplication is often implied simply by writing two terms together; for example, (A+4)B. In QBasic, this is wrong; if you want to indicate multiplication, you must use an asterisk.

Whenever you use parentheses, remember that you must have the same number of right parentheses as left parentheses. You must also be careful to use the correct keys when you are typing; (is the upper shift character on the 9 key, and) is the upper shift character on the 0 (zero) key. Do not use square brackets, [ ], or curly braces, { }; they are illegal in QBasic. You may use as many parentheses as you want. It is often helpful to include unnecessary parentheses to make the expression clearer to anyone who reads the program. QBasic simply ignores unnecessary parentheses.

The following examples illustrate how expressions with multiple operators are evaluated.

Expression	Evaluation
4 + 6 / 2	Divide 6 by 2 to give 3, then add 4 and 3 to give the answer 7.
(4 + 6) / 2	Add 4 and 6 to give 10, then divide 10 by 2 to give the answer 5.
6 + 15 / 3 + 2	Divide 15 by 3 to give 5, then add 6, 5, and 2 to give the answer 13.
6 + 15 / (3 + 2)	Add 3 and 2 to give 5, divide 15 by 5 to give 3, then add 6 and 3 to give the answer 9.
2 ^ 3 + 5	Raise 2 to the third power to give 8, then add 8 and 5 to give the answer 13.
2 ^ (3 + 1)	Add 3 and 1 to give 4, then raise 2 to the fourth power to give the answer 16.

Make sure you understand how the LET statements are evaluated in the following examples.

ILLUSTRATIONS

LET Statement	Effect
AvgSales = (JanSales +↵ FebSales + MarSales) / 3	Adds the numbers in the JanSales, FebSales, and MarSales storage locations, divides the sum by 3, and puts the answer in the AvgSales storage location. This is the correct way to calculate an average.

```
C = (A ^ 2 + B ^ 2) ^ .5          Raises the numbers in the A and B
                                  storage locations to the second power,
                                  adds the results, and raises the sum to .5
                                  power (square root). The answer is put
                                  in the C storage location. (Uses the
                                  Pythagorean theorem to calculate the
                                  hypotenuse of a right triangle.)
```

EXAMPLE 2

A PROGRAM THAT USES EXPONENTIATION

Let's write a program that requires a more complex expression.

Problem Statement

Suppose you make a deposit of $1000 into a savings account at the Loansome Bank, which pays an interest rate of 6%. Write a program that calculates your balance if your money stays in the bank for 5 years.

STEP 1   **Variable Names**

The variables in this problem are the amount of the deposit, the interest rate paid, the number of years the deposit stays in the bank, and the balance in the account at the end of that time. We will use the following variable names:

Variable	Variable Name
Amount deposited	Deposit
Interest rate	Rate
Number of years	Years
Balance in account	Balance

STEP 2   **Algorithm**

The balance can be calculated by using the compound interest formula:

```
Balance = Deposit * (1 + Rate) ^ Years
```

In this formula, Rate must be a decimal, not a percent. The algorithm we will use is

1. Assign 1000 to Deposit.
2. Assign .06 to Rate.
3. Assign 5 to Years.
4. Calculate Balance by using the compound interest formula.
5. Print Balance.

Pseudocode.   In addition to flowcharts, which we used for the paycheck problem, programmers use several other techniques to help develop algorithms. One such technique is to write the program first in pseudocode. **Pseudocode** refers to a way of writing program steps using a language somewhere between English and QBasic. You might wonder why you should use pseudocode at all; why not simply write the program statements in QBasic, since that is what you must do eventually? The answer is that by using pseudocode, you postpone having to think about the details of how to code QBasic instructions and can concentrate on developing the algorithm. This is similar to starting a difficult term paper by writing a rough draft first—without worrying about spelling or other details. After the algorithm is fully developed, you can translate it easily into QBasic

pseudocode
A language somewhere between English and QBasic that is used to develop the algorithm for a program.

statements. Often, individual pseudocode statements translate directly into individual QBasic statements.

There are no specific rules for pseudocode; anything that helps make it easy to write and understand will work. So when writing pseudocode for a problem, we put the problem name on the first line. We will also use the variable names we chose for the problem. The pseudocode description for the savings account problem is

> Calculate Balance in Savings Account
> Assign 1,000 to Deposit
> Assign .06 to Rate
> Assign 5 to Years
> Calculate Balance
> PRINT Balance
> End

You know that "Calculate Balance" is not a QBasic statement. In the actual program, we must write a valid LET statement. We use a simplified statement here because, at this point, we want to concentrate on how to solve the problem. We do not want to get bogged down in the details of exactly how we will calculate Balance. Fortunately, in this case, the pseudocode is very similar to the algorithm; in other problems, the two will not be so similar.

STEP 3 Hand-Calculated Answer

Look at the compound interest formula given previously in step 2. If we substitute the values of 1000 for Deposit, .06 for Rate, and 5 for Years, we get a Balance of 1,338.23.

STEP 4 QBasic Program

The QBasic program based on this algorithm is shown in Program 2.7. This program contains two new statements: a remark statement and a CLS statement.

The Remark Statement. The remark statement is used to include comments in your program that will be helpful to you and anyone else who reads it. Including comments in your program is called **documenting** the program. The syntax of the remark statement is

```
REM any comment you like
```

You can use an apostrophe (') instead of the word REM, as in

```
'any comment you like
```

Since an apostrophe is easier to type than the word REM, all the programs in this book use apostrophes instead of REM. Remark statements are used in Program 2.7 (lines 1–9) to include the title of the program and the list of variable names. Every program you write should contain similar remark statements. In addition, you should include a remark statement with your name. Your instructor may require that you include additional remark statements with information such as your class code and the date.

You can also use an apostrophe to include a comment at the end of a statement. For example, in Program 2.7, line 15 could be written as

```
Balance = Deposit * (1 + Rate) ^ Years  'Compound interest formula
```

When QBasic translates your program into machine language, it completely ignores remark statements. Thus, remark statements have no effect on the answers produced by the program. You can use as many remark statements as you like and place them anywhere in the program. Since remark statements are

documenting
Adding comments to a program to explain what the program does and how it does it.

```
 1 | '    *** LOANSOME BANK PROBLEM ***
 2 | '    Calculate compound interest
 3 |
 4 | '    Variables used
 5 |
 6 | '    Balance          Balance in the account
 7 | '    Deposit          Amount deposited
 8 | '    Rate             Interest rate
 9 | '    Years            Number of years
10 |
11 | CLS
12 | Deposit = 1000
13 | Rate = .06
14 | Years = 5
15 | Balance = Deposit * (1 + Rate) ^ Years
16 | PRINT Balance
17 | END
```

```
1338.226
```

PROGRAM 2.7 A program that uses exponentiation to calculate compound interest.

not part of the logic of the program, they are not shown in the algorithm, flow-chart, or pseudocode.

By choosing meaningful variable names, you make your program self-documenting, reducing the number of remark statements required. Beginners often underestimate the importance of documenting programs. Experience shows that programs are almost always modified. It's extremely frustrating to begin modifying a program you wrote (even recently), only to discover that you don't understand it anymore. You can easily spend as much time trying to understand the program as you did originally developing it.

To improve readability, Program 2.7 uses several blank lines (see lines 3, 5, and 10). To enter a blank line, simply press the Enter key when the cursor is at the beginning of a line.

The CLS Statement.   As you may have noticed, the Output screen is not cleared when a program is executed, making it difficult to see the output you want. To clear the Output screen, use the CLS statement as the first executable statement in your program. As shown on line 11, the syntax of the CLS statement is simply

```
CLS
```

In every program in this book, the first statement after the remark statements is a CLS statement. Since the CLS statement is not an important part of the program's logic, we will generally not include the CLS statement in the algorithm, flowchart, or pseudocode.

When you follow our systematic procedure, steps five, six, and seven require you to enter and execute the program—correcting syntax, run-time, and logic errors. Starting with this program, we will assume that no errors were made. So we will not continue to discuss these last three steps, except to point out that the program's answer agrees with the hand-calculated answer.

Program 2.7 displays a value for Balance of 1338.226. This should have been rounded to 1338.23, in which case it would have agreed with our hand-calculated answer exactly. We will learn how to have answers rounded in Chapter 3. ∎

Reviewing the Seven-Step Procedure

Now that we have completely solved two problems using our seven-step procedure, let's review it (see page 26). When solving a problem on a computer, most people are tempted to jump immediately to step 5 (Enter the program and correct syntax errors if necessary). *Resist this temptation.* Step 2 (Develop an algorithm to solve the problem) is the most important step. If you don't have a correct algorithm, then everything else you do will be a waste of time. Typically, step 2 requires up to 75 percent of the total time spent solving the problem. Algorithms are not specific to any particular computer language, and the skills you acquire developing algorithms will be useful if you study other computer languages.

The second most important step is step 4 (Write the QBasic program). When you write a program, you should carefully check the syntax of the statements you use. It is far better to avoid syntax errors from the start than to have to find and correct them later. The first four steps do not require a computer: they require human thought. If you have thoroughly and carefully completed steps 1–4, then you will significantly reduce the time spent finding and correcting syntax, run-time, and logic errors.

Although the procedure is presented here as seven sequential steps, in practice, you may have to backtrack occasionally. For example, you may develop an algorithm (step 2), but when you calculate an answer by hand (step 3), you discover that the algorithm is incorrect. You then must return to step 2 and further develop the algorithm. Similarly, when you write the program (step 4), you may discover that you omitted a variable. In that case, you would return to step 1 and add that variable to your list of variable names.

Syntax Summary

Remark Statement

Form: `REM any comment you like`
or   `' any comment you like`
Example: `' This program calculates sales commissions`
Explanation: Adds a comment to your program.

CLS Statement

Form: `CLS`
Example: `CLS`
Explanation: Clears the Output screen.

2.2 EXERCISES

1. Which of the following LET statements contain errors? Rewrite the incorrect statement(s) correctly.
   a) `M = 5 (N - S)`
   ★b) `W = R * ((S + T) * V - P / N`
   c) `A = B * ((1 + C) ^ (E - F) + G) / (H + 1)`

2. Calculate the value assigned to A by the following LET statements if B = 2, C = 12, D = 3, and E = 1.
   a) `A = B + C / D + E`
   b) `A = (B + C) / D + E`

★c)   A = (B + C) / (D + E)
★d)   A = B + 3 * C / D ^ 2 + E
 e)   A = (B + 3 * C) / (D ^ 2 + E)

3. Calculate the value assigned to A by the following LET statements if B = 28, C = 8, D = 37, and E = 9.
    ★a)   A = B \ C
     b)   A = D \ E
    ★c)   A = B MOD C
     d)   A = D MOD E

4. Translate the following algebraic equations into LET statements.

    a) $a = \dfrac{b+c+d}{3}$

    ★b) $g = \dfrac{b+2c+3d}{6e}$

    ★c) $t = \dfrac{d\left(\left(1+r^n\right)-1\right)}{r}$

    d) $p = \dfrac{mr}{1+\left(1+r\right)^{-n}}$

5. Write a statement to add the following comment to a program:

    ```
    Programmer: Roy G. Biv
    ```

6. If Test1 is 70, Test2 is 80, and Test3 is 90, what value is calculated for AverageTest by the following LET statement?

    ```
    AverageTest = Test1 + Test2 + Test3 / 3
    ```

7. Program 2.8 shows a solution to Programming Assignment 2.4 (see page 52). However, it contains a logic error. How would you fix the error?

```
1  '     *** CONVERTING OUNCES TO GRAMS ***
2
3  '     Converting a weight given in ounces to grams
4
5  '     Variables used
6
7  '     Grams        Weight in grams
8  '     Ounces       Weight in ounces
9
10   CLS
11   Ounces = 13
12   PRINT Grams
13   END
```

0

PROGRAM 2.8   An incorrect solution to Programming Assignment 2.4.

WHAT YOU HAVE LEARNED

In this chapter, you learned that:

- The following seven-step structured procedure helps you solve problems by using a computer:
  1. Identify the variables required by the problem and choose names for them.
  2. Develop an algorithm to solve the problem.
  3. Calculate an answer to the problem by hand.
  4. Write a QBasic program.
  5. Enter the program and correct syntax errors if necessary.
  6. Execute the program and correct run-time errors if necessary.
  7. Compare the computer's answer against the answer you calculated by hand in step 3, and correct logic errors if necessary.
- Variable names may consist of letters, digits, and the period. A variable name must start with a letter, may contain up to 40 characters, and may not contain a blank space. A reserved word may not be used as a variable name.
- Flowcharts are helpful when you are developing an algorithm and when you are trying to understand someone else's algorithm because they show the logic of an algorithm more clearly.
- Both flowcharts and pseudocode are helpful when you are developing an algorithm because they allow you to concentrate on the problem—rather than on the syntax rules of QBasic.
- Every QBasic statement begins with a reserved word. However, in the LET statement, the reserved word is optional.
- In the model statement that shows the syntax of a statement, words in upper case represent QBasic reserved words and must be typed as shown; words in lower case letters represent values supplied by the programmer. Square brackets—[ ]—enclose optional parts of the statement.
- A LET statement is used to assign a value to a variable.
- In an expression, use + for addition, – for subtraction, * for multiplication, / for division, ^ for exponentiation, \ for integer division, and MOD for modulo arithmetic.
- When expressions are evaluated, operations are performed in the following order: exponentiation, multiplication and division, integer division, modulo arithmetic, and addition and subtraction. Expressions inside parentheses are evaluated first.
- A PRINT statement displays answers.
- An END statement marks the end of a QBasic program.
- A remark statement, using either REM or ', adds a comment to a program.
- A CLS statement clears the Output screen.
- If you use a numeric variable without assigning it a value, QBasic gives it the value zero.
- To trace a program, first set up columns (on paper) that correspond to the storage locations that QBasic assigns to each variable. Then execute each line in the program, putting values in the columns—just as QBasic puts values in the storage locations. Tracing is helpful in understanding how a program works and in correcting logic errors.
- When you press Enter to end a line, the QBasic editor checks the line's syntax. If it finds an error, a dialog box with an error message is displayed.
- If QBasic discovers an error when running a program, it stops execution and displays a dialog box with an error message.
- The QBasic help system displays help on statements, commands, and dialog boxes. The help system is accessed by pressing function key F1.

NEW QBASIC STATEMENTS

STATEMENT	EFFECT
LET	
`Area = Height * Base`	Multiplies Height by Base, and assigns the answer to Area.
PRINT	
`PRINT Height, Base, Area`	Displays the values of Height, Base, and Area on the screen.
END	
`END`	Indicates the end of the program and causes the program to stop executing.

Remark

`'Written by M. Trombetta`   Adds a comment to your program.

CLS

`CLS`   Clears the Output screen.

KEY TERMS

algorithm	hyperlink	statement
bugs	integer division	string
constant	logic error	string variable
debugging	modulo arithmetic	syntax
documenting	numeric variable	syntax error
exponentiation	pseudocode	tracing
expression	reserved word	uninitialized variable
flowchart	run-time error	variable name
hierarchy of operations		

REVIEW EXERCISES

SELF-CHECK

1. Which statement is used to display answers on the screen?

2. What is the name of the following flowchart symbol:

3. Indicate which of the following LET statements contain errors. Rewrite the incorrect statement(s) correctly.

   a) `B4 = C + E`
   b) `N = $625.00`
   c) `A = Y Minus Q`
   d) `Key = 415 / Door`

4. What is the difference between ordinary division and integer division?

5. If A and B are integers, what is the value of

   `B * (A \ B) + A MOD B`

6. When QBasic evaluates an expression, which does it do first: multiplication or division?

7. True or false: When writing a program in pseudocode, it is essential to follow QBasic syntax rules exactly.

8. When a new value is put into a storage location, what happens to the value that was there?

9. In a model statement that shows the syntax of a statement, what do square brackets mean? What do words printed in upper case letters represent?

10. Which characters may be used in a variable name?

11. What is debugging?

12. What is a logic error?

13. Which statement is used to include documentation in a program?

14. What happens if you use a reserved word as a variable name?

15. What is a syntax error?

16. How do you get help on a QBasic statement?

PROGRAMMING ASSIGNMENTS

You should choose variable names to stand for the variables in the problem and assign values to the variables—just as we did in this chapter's sample programs. To help you get started, the variables that you should choose names for are already specified. You should save your programs so that you can use them later. Select a filename that will help you remember which assignment belongs to which program. For example, the solution to the first programming assignment could be saved with the filename P2-1. (Do not use a filename like P2.1 because QBasic will not be able to add the filename extension BAS, making it difficult to retrieve the file later.)

Section 2.1

1. Suppose you traveled 335 miles and your car used 9.8 gallons of gasoline. Write a program to calculate and print average gas mileage by dividing miles traveled by gasoline used. Choose names to stand for miles traveled, gasoline used, and average gas mileage.

2. Twice Sold Tales, a used-book store, is having a sale; everything is reduced 20 percent. An unabridged dictionary regularly costs $19.98. Write a program to calculate and print the sale price of that dictionary. Choose variable names to stand for the usual price, the discount amount, and the sale price.

3. You got 18 questions correct on a 25-question multiple-choice test. Write a program to calculate and print your percentage grade. Choose variable names to stand for the total number of questions, the number you got correct, and your percentage grade.

4. Write a program to calculate and print the number of grams in 13 ounces. You can convert from ounces to grams by using this formula: grams = 28.4 * ounces. Choose variable names to stand for ounces and grams.

5. Mark O. Polo is traveling in Japan and wants to buy a VCR that costs 30,000 yen. Write a program to calculate and print the cost of the VCR in dollars. Choose variable names to stand for the price in yen and the price in dollars. To convert yen to dollars, divide the price in yen by 131.46.

6. Casey Batt made 42 hits in 228 times at bat. Write a program to calculate and print her batting average. To calculate batting average, divide hits by at bats and multiply the quotient by 1000. Choose variable names to stand for the number of hits, the number of at bats, and the batting average.

7. An interior designer wants to cover a room that is 4 yards wide and 5.3 yards long with a rug that costs $18 a square yard. Write a program to calculate and print the rug's cost. Choose variable names to stand for the width, height, and area of the room and the cost of the rug.

Section 2.2

8. Scientists estimate that each hour spent watching the TV program "Loving Hospitals" causes 1/4 cubic centimeter of the human brain to turn to oatmeal. The average human brain contains 1456 cubic centimeters. Suppose you have watched "Loving Hospitals" for 250 hours. Write a program to calculate and print the percent of your brain that has turned to oatmeal. Choose variable names to stand for the hours watched and the percent of your brain that is now oatmeal.

9. The equation used in Program 2.7 (page 47) assumes that the interest is compounded once a year. If the interest is compounded M times a year, the correct equation is

```
Balance = Deposit *↵
   (1 + Rate / M) ^ (Years * M)
```

Modify Program 2.7 so that it will use this equation and utilize M as an additional variable. Run the program with M = 1, which should give the same answers as the unmodified program; with M = 2, which is semiannual compounding; with M = 4, which is quarterly compounding; with M = 12, which is monthly compounding; and with M = 365, which is daily compounding. When M = 4, the computer should print 1346.855 for Balance.

10. Scientists estimate that the greenhouse effect causes the earth's average temperature to increase .08 degree each year. Suppose that Year stands for the year. If the average temperature in 1990 were 72 degrees, the temperature in Year would be given by the equation

```
Temp = 72 + .08 * (Year - 1990)
```

Write a program that calculates and prints the average temperature in the year 2010.

11. Renting a car costs $40 plus a mileage charge. The first 25 miles are free, but after that, the charge is 18 cents a mile. Write a program that calculates and prints the bill if you drive the car 60 miles. Choose variable names for the miles driven and the bill.

12. The area of a circle is πR^2 and the volume of a sphere is $4/3\pi R^3$, where π is the numeric constant 3.14159 and R is the radius. Write a program that calculates and prints the area of a circle and the volume of a sphere with a radius of 10. Choose variable names for the radius, area, and volume.

13. If Height represents the distance (measured in feet) you are standing above sea level, the distance to the horizon, in miles, is given by

```
Horizon = 1.23 Height ^ .5
```

Write a program that calculates and prints the distance to the horizon if the height above sea level is 5 feet.

14. A company has 4390 feet of video tape on hand. Write a program that calculates and prints the number of cassettes it can manufacture. Also calculate the number of feet of tape left over after all the cassettes are made. Assume that a video cassette contains 275 feet of tape. Choose variable names for the number of feet of tape on hand, the number of cassettes manufactured, and the number of feet of tape left over.

15. If an object is dropped from a height, the time it takes to reach the ground is given by

```
Time = (Height / 16.1) ^ .5
```

and its final velocity is

```
Velocity = (64.4 * Height) ^ .5
```

(These equations ignore air resistance.) In the equations above, Height is in feet, Time is in seconds, and Velocity is in feet per second. Write a program that calculates and prints Time and Velocity for an object dropped from the World Trade Center towers, which are 1350 feet tall.

16. **a)** Given an arithmetic progression,

$$a, a+d, a+2d, \text{K}$$

where a is the first term and d is the common difference, the sum of the first n terms is

$$S = \frac{n}{2}\left[2a + (n-1)d\right]$$

Write a program that calculates and prints the sum of the arithmetic progression when a is 10, d is 4, and n is 6.

b) Given a geometric progression

$$a, ar, ar^2, \text{K}$$

where a is the first term and r is the common ratio, the sum of the first n terms is

$$S = a\left(\frac{r^n - 1}{r - 1}\right)$$

Write a program that calculates and prints the sum of the geometric progression when a is 3, r is 2, and n is 5.

17. A bakery packs 12 cookies in a box and 20 boxes in a carton. Write a program that calculates and prints the number of cartons produced, the number of boxes left over, and the number of cookies left over when the number of cookies baked is 1,000.

BEYOND THE BASICS

18. If the three sides of a triangle are represented by A, B, and C, the area of the triangle is given by the equation

```
Area = (S * (S - A) * (S - B) *
       (S - C)) ^ .5
```

where S is defined as

```
S = (A + B + C) / 2
```

Write a program that calculates and prints the area of the triangle when the sides are 3, 4, and 5. The area should be 6.

19. Help Yourself vending machines sell items that cost less than $1.00. They also accept a dollar as payment, giving correct change as needed. Write a program to calculate the number of half-dollars, quarters, dimes, nickels, and pennies required to make change if the cost of the item is 9 cents.

20. Write a program that adds two durations given in terms of hours, minutes, and seconds—and that prints their sum (also in terms of hours, minutes, and seconds).

3

STRINGS, INPUT, AND PRINTING

LEARNING OBJECTIVES

After reading this chapter, you will be able to:

- Use string variables.

- Use the QBasic statements INPUT, LPRINT, PRINT USING, LPRINT USING, and CONST.

- Use the QBasic functions TAB and SPC.

- Use the Edit menu commands Cut, Copy, Paste, and Clear.

- Use the Search menu commands Find, Repeat Last Find, and Change.

In Chapter 2, we calculated gross pay for one employee—you. To use that program to calculate gross pay for a different employee, we would have to retype lines 1 and 2 in Program 2.2 (page 34), using the new employee's pay rate and hours worked. That is obviously inconvenient. In this chapter, you will learn an easy way to have a computer calculate gross pay for different employees. You will also learn how to write programs that process data that consist of strings, how to make your output more attractive, and how to use the commands on the Edit and Search menus.

STRING VARIABLES

In Chapter 2, our programs used only numbers as input and produced only numbers as output. But no doubt you have received computer-prepared checks and bills with your name and address on them. These labels are possible because computers can process string data (or simply, strings). Strings can contain letters, numbers, and special characters—as the following examples show:

```
"Please enter your name"
"14 Elm Street"
"5A!@#$%&7Z"
```

Notice that string data must be enclosed in quotation marks, and that within strings, blank spaces are treated the same as other characters.

QBasic uses quotation marks to determine the beginning and the ending of a string, but the quotation marks are not part of the string. In fact, the one character you cannot include in a string is a quotation mark; QBasic would be unable to tell which quotation marks indicate the beginning and the ending of the string and which are actual parts of the string.

Variables that store strings are called, naturally enough, string variables. A legal name for a string variable is created by adding a $ to the end of a legal name for a numeric variable. You can also create a legal string variable name by adding a $ to the end of a reserved word. This means that—although Name is *not* a legal numeric variable name because NAME is a reserved word—Name$ *is* a legal string variable name. Since DATE$ and INPUT$ are reserved words (see the inside back cover), they may not be used as variable names.

When we talk about string variables, we pronounce the $ as the word "string"; that is, Name$ is pronounced "Name-string." The following is a list of valid and invalid string variable names. For the invalid names, the reason they are not valid is given.

Proposed Variable Name	Status
A$	Valid
$A	Invalid—a string variable name must end with a dollar sign, not begin with one
City$	Valid
Time$	Invalid—Time$ is a reserved word and may not be used as a variable name
StartingTime$	Valid

The last two examples illustrate that although you may not use a reserved word as a variable name (Time$), a reserved word may be part of a variable name (StartingTime$).

When QBasic encounters a string variable in your program, it sets up a storage location for that variable—just as it does for numeric variables. A maximum of 32,767 characters can fit in one of these storage locations. Each letter, number, special symbol, and blank space counts as one character.

Just as QBasic assigns zero as the initial value for all numeric variables, it similarly assigns the null string as the initial value for all string variables. The **null string** is the string that contains no characters; two quotation marks next to each other—""—represent it.

null string
The string that contains no characters.

Using String Variables

String variables may be used just like numeric variables—although, of course, you cannot perform arithmetic with them. So if Address$ stands for an address, and we want to assign the string 14 Elm Street to Address$, we could use the LET statement

```
Address$ = "14 Elm Street"
```

After this LET statement is executed, Address$ contains 14 Elm Street. The statement

```
PRINT Address$
```

would display 14 Elm Street on the screen.

A string variable may be set equal to another string variable, as in the LET statement

```
Q$ = P$
```

When QBasic executes this statement, it copies the string in the storage location for P$ into the storage location for Q$.

Numbers and strings are stored differently in RAM. In particular, although they look alike, 4 is stored as a number and "4" is stored as a string. You must be careful to assign string expressions to string variables and numeric expressions to numeric variables. The following LET statements are therefore *illegal*:

LET Statement	Why It Is Illegal
A$ = P	A string variable cannot be set equal to a numeric variable
A$ = 4	A string variable cannot be set equal to a number
A = "4"	A numeric variable cannot be set equal to a string
F = L$	A numeric variable cannot be set equal to a string variable
Day = "July 4"	A numeric variable cannot be set equal to a string
C$ = A$ * B$	Strings cannot be multiplied

These statements cause a run-time error, and QBasic displays the error message Type mismatch. As you will learn in Chapter 7, it is possible to "add" strings and string variables in a special way.

3.1 EXERCISES

1. Which of the following are legal and which are illegal variable names for string variables? For those that are illegal, explain why.
    a) Address
    ★b) Answer$
    c) 1StName$
    d) LastName$
    ★e) Left$

2. Write the LET statement to assign the string Button Gwinnett to the string variable Signer$.

3. Which of the following LET statements contain errors? Rewrite the incorrect statement(s) correctly.
    a) `Number$ = "123"`
    ★b) `ZipCode = "10050"`
    c) `Month = "April"`
    ★d) `Flower$ = Rose`
    e) `String$ = "anything"`
    f) `FruitSalad = Apples * Oranges`

3.2   THE INPUT STATEMENT

In Program 2.2 (page 34), we calculated the gross pay for an employee. If we wanted to use that program to calculate the gross pay for a different employee, we would have to change the constants in lines 1 and 2 to the new employee's pay rate and hours worked. That is inconvenient. The INPUT statement offers a convenient way to change the data that a program uses.

In Program 3.1, lines 11 and 12 show how the first two LET statements in Program 2.2 could be replaced by the following two INPUT statements:

```
INPUT "Enter Pay Rate: ", PayRate
INPUT "Enter Hours Worked: ", Hours
```

The strings "Enter Pay Rate: " and "Enter Hours Worked: " are prompts. A **prompt** is a message the computer displays to indicate that it is waiting for the user to enter data or an instruction. When the first INPUT statement is executed, Enter pay rate: is displayed on the screen and execution pauses. The user must type a number and press the Enter key for execution to resume. Program 3.1 shows that the user typed 6.75 and pressed the Enter key. 6.75 was then assigned to the variable PayRate and execution continued. In response to the second prompt, the user typed 40, which was assigned to Hours. The LET statement in line 13 used these values to calculate a GrossPay of 270, and the PRINT statement in line 14 printed 270.

The syntax of the INPUT statement is

```
INPUT [;] ["prompt"{; | ,}] variablelist
```

where variablelist is a list of variables separated by commas. In model statements, curly braces—{ }—enclose items from which you must choose; the choices are separated by a vertical line. In the model statement for the INPUT statement, {; | ,} means that following the prompt, you must choose either a semicolon or a comma. If you choose a semicolon, QBasic adds a space and a question mark at the end of the prompt. If the prompt is a question—for example, Are there more employees—you would choose the semicolon because you want the question mark. In Chapter 4, you will see an example of using a semicolon. Most of the time, the prompt is not a question, and you would choose the comma, as we did in Program 3.1 (lines 11 and 12).

The syntax shows that the prompt is optional. If you omit the prompt, only a question mark is printed when the INPUT statement is executed. Although the prompt is optional, you should always include one when you code an INPUT statement. If you don't, another user of the program (or even you, several weeks after the program is written) will not know what values should be entered.

prompt
A message displayed by the computer indicating that it is waiting for you to enter instructions or data.

```
 1 | '      *** PAYCHECK PROGRAM ***
 2 | '      Calculate gross pay
 3 |
 4 | '      Variables used
 5 |
 6 | '      GrossPay          Gross pay
 7 | '      Hours             Hours worked
 8 | '      PayRate           Hourly pay rate
 9 |
10 | CLS
11 | INPUT "Enter Pay Rate: ", PayRate
12 | INPUT "Enter Hours Worked: ", Hours
13 | GrossPay = PayRate * Hours
14 | PRINT GrossPay
15 | END
```

```
Enter Pay Rate: 6.75                    ───────Prompt displayed by line 11
Enter Hours Worked: 40          Values entered by user
  270                                   ───────Prompt displayed by line 12
                                ───────Answer printed by line 14
```

PROGRAM 3.1   Using INPUT statements to provide data to the paycheck program.

If you code the optional semicolon directly after the word INPUT, the cursor stays on the same line when the user presses the Enter key. Chapter 6 will explain why you would want to do that.

If an INPUT statement's variable list contains more than one variable, you must enter a value for each variable in the list when the program is executed, using commas to separate the values. When you press Enter, the first value is assigned to the first variable, the second value to the second variable, and so on. It is much easier for the user to enter only one value at a time, and because we want our programs to be user-friendly, we will generally use only one variable with INPUT statements. When a program requires values for more than one variable, as Program 3.1 does, we will use more than one INPUT statement.

If—in response to an input prompt for a numeric variable—you enter non-numeric data (for example, typing a $ or a comma as part of a number), QBasic displays an error message: Redo from start. You must then reenter the number correctly. Similarly, if you enter too many or too few values, QBasic displays the Redo from start error message.

Inputting String Variables

You can also use an INPUT statement to assign values to string variables. An especially nice feature of the INPUT statement is that if the string value you enter does not contain a comma, it does not have to be enclosed in quotation marks. (However, the INPUT statement ignores spaces you type before or after a string, so if you want such spaces to be included as part of the string data, you must enclose the whole string in quotation marks.) For example, a program could obtain an employee's name with the following INPUT statement:

```
INPUT "Enter name: ", EmpName$
```

Then, when Enter name: is displayed and execution pauses, you could type

```
Mary Jones
```

Mary Jones would be put in the EmpName$ storage location. However, to type the name as Jones, Mary, you must use quotation marks, as in

```
"Jones, Mary"
```

If you do not use quotation marks in this case, QBasic assumes that the comma is a separator and that you typed two values: Jones and Mary. Since the INPUT statement expects only one value, QBasic displays the error message Redo from start.

ILLUSTRATIONS

INPUT Statement	**Effect**
`INPUT "Enter shipping`↵ `    weight: ", Weight`	Accepts the value entered and assigns it to weight.
`INPUT "Enter gallons and`↵ `    price: ", Gallons, Price`	Accepts the first value entered and assigns it to Gallons; then accepts the second value entered and assigns it to Price.
`INPUT "Enter name of`↵ `    city: ", City$`	Accepts the value entered and assigns it to City$.

Syntax Summary

INPUT Statement

Form:	`INPUT [;] ["prompt"{;	,}] variablelist`
Example:	`INPUT "Enter height: ", Height`
Explanation:	The prompt is displayed and the program waits for value(s) to be entered from the keyboard. The value(s) entered are assigned to the variable(s) listed.

3.2 EXERCISES

1. Which of the following INPUT statements contain errors? Rewrite the incorrect statement(s) correctly.
    ★**a)** `INPUT Enter number sold: Sold`
    b) `INPUT "Do you want to play again (Y/N)"; Response$`
    c) `INPUT "Enter name of spouse: ", Name`

2. What will happen if in response to the following INPUT statement,

    ```
    INPUT "Enter your phone number: ", Phone
    ```

    the user enters (212) 627-8952?

3. For the following problems, write the INPUT statement(s) to accept the specified data. Invent any legal data names you want and print prompts.
   ★**a)** Accept the amount of a check.
   b) Accept a student's name and three test scores.
   c) Accept date of birth in the form October 9, 1972.

3.3	MORE ABOUT PRINTING

Our programs use the PRINT statement to display answers on the screen (soft copy). Often, you want a permanent copy of your answers to be printed on a printer (hard copy). The LPRINT statement does that.

The LPRINT Statement

An LPRINT statement functions just like a PRINT statement, except that it sends the output to the printer instead of to the screen.
The syntax of the LPRINT statement is

```
LPRINT expressionlist
```

Notice that the syntax of the LPRINT statement is the same as that of the PRINT statement.

When you develop your programs, you should use PRINT statements instead of LPRINT statements. While you are debugging, it is more convenient to have your answers displayed on the screen, rather than on the printer. When your program is completely debugged, you can change the PRINT statements to LPRINT statements to get a permanent copy of your answers.

More About the PRINT and LPRINT Statements

We have used PRINT and LPRINT statements in our programs to print answers, but we have not yet explained exactly how these statements work.

Printing Numeric Variables

QBasic divides the monitor screen and printer paper into zones that are 14 characters wide, with any remaining characters forming a short zone. The standard screens and printers, which contain 80 characters on a line, are divided into five full zones and one short zone; the short zone is not used.

When commas are used to separate the variables in PRINT and LPRINT statements, QBasic prints one value in each zone. If you specify more than five variables to be printed, QBasic prints the values of five variables on a line and uses as many lines as necessary to print the values of all the variables. So if the statement were

```
PRINT A, B, C, D, E, F, G, H
```

the values of A, B, C, D, and E would be printed on the first line, and the values of F, G, and H on the second.

Use of Semicolons

Often, we want to print more than five values on a line. QBasic makes that very easy; just separate the variables with semicolons instead of commas. A legal PRINT (or LPRINT) statement would be

```
PRINT A; B; C; D; E; F; G; H
```

This PRINT statement causes all eight values to be printed on one line. If you leave one or more spaces between variables, QBasic inserts semicolons for you.

When semicolons are used to separate the variables in a print list, the values are printed next to each other. Numbers are printed with a space before and after. The space before the number is used to show the sign of the number. If the number is positive, the space is left blank; if the number is negative, a minus sign is printed. The space after the number is always left blank, so there will be at least one blank space between numbers.

You might wonder how many values will be printed on a line when semicolons are used. Unfortunately, there is no simple answer—different values take different numbers of columns to print. For example, the number 1 requires only three columns to print (including the spaces before and after), while the number 16976 requires seven columns.

Printing String Variables and Strings

Like numeric variables, string variables are printed one to a zone. If you print a string or a string variable that contains 14 or more characters, it will occupy more than one print zone, and the next variable will be printed at the start of the next zone. For example, if N$ contains 18 characters, the statement

```
PRINT N$, A
```

causes the value of N$ to fill all of print zone 1 and the first four columns of print zone 2. The value of A is printed in print zone 3.

Program 3.2 is a modification of Program 3.1 that uses a new variable, Emp-Name$, to accept and print the employee's name. It also uses an LPRINT statement to print the answers. As in Chapter 2, the first horizontal line separates the View window from the Output screen. In this and subsequent programs, the second horizontal line separates the Output screen from the printed output produced by the LPRINT statement.

To have the program accept the employee's name, we simply add a new INPUT statement in line 12:

```
INPUT "Enter Name: ", EmpName$
```

We also change the PRINT statement to

```
LPRINT EmpName$, PayRate, Hours, GrossPay
```

to print EmpName$, PayRate, and Hours—as well as GrossPay. Because this program will calculate GrossPay for different employees, it is helpful to print the input data as well as GrossPay. That way, we have a permanent record of which GrossPay goes with which EmpName$, PayRate, and Hours.

Printing the input data also helps you locate and eliminate logic errors. Suppose the program prints an incorrect value for GrossPay. We know we have a logic error, but we do not know where it is. You can easily check the printed values of PayRate and Hours against their input values. If they are correct, you know that the logic error must be in the calculation of GrossPay. If they are incorrect, the error must be in the INPUT statements for PayRate and Hours.

```
 1 | '    *** PAYCHECK PROGRAM ***
 2 | '    Calculate gross pay
 3 |
 4 | '    Variables used
 5 |
 6 | '    EmpName$        Employee's name
 7 | '    GrossPay        Gross pay
 8 | '    Hours           Hours worked
 9 | '    PayRate         Hourly pay rate
10 |
11 | CLS
12 | INPUT "Enter Name: ", EmpName$
13 | INPUT "Enter Pay Rate: ", PayRate
14 | INPUT "Enter Hours Worked: ", Hours
15 | GrossPay = PayRate * Hours
16 | LPRINT EmpName$, PayRate, Hours, GrossPay
17 | END
```

View window

```
Enter Name: Joe Tinker
Enter Pay Rate: 6.75          }——User enters data for an employee
Enter Hours Worked: 40
```
Output screen

Printed output
```
Joe Tinker      6.75                40               270
```
Values printed by line 16

PROGRAM 3.2   The paycheck program with a string variable.

You can also mix strings and variables in the same PRINT statement. For example, the LPRINT statement in Program 3.2 could be

```
LPRINT EmpName$, "earned", GrossPay, "dollars last week."
```

This statement would print

```
Joe Tinker    earned          270             dollars last week.
```

To make this statement read better, you may want to use semicolons so the values are printed closer together. The statement

```
LPRINT EmpName$; "earned"; GrossPay; "dollars last week."
```

prints as

```
Joe Tinkerearned 270 dollars last week.
```

Obviously, Tinkerearned should not be one word. This problem occurs because when strings or string variables are printed with semicolons, they are printed right next to each other. The easiest way to correct the error is to add a space at the beginning of the string "earned", as in the following statement:

```
LPRINT EmpName$; " earned"; GrossPay; "dollars last week."
```

This statement finally prints the line correctly:

```
Joe Tinker earned 270 dollars last week.
```

When you print a string, everything between the quotation marks—including spaces and special characters—is printed exactly as it appears in the PRINT or LPRINT statement.

Hanging Punctuation

In the examples we saw so far, whenever a PRINT or LPRINT statement was executed, it started printing on a new line. That's fine; usually, you want to keep the output for each case on its own line. But if you put a comma or a semicolon after the last variable in a PRINT or LPRINT statement (**hanging punctuation**), the next PRINT or LPRINT statement executed will not start on a new line. Instead, it begins printing where the previous printing stopped. Sometimes that is desirable, but most of the time, hanging punctuation is undesirable because the output for different cases becomes mixed on the same line.

One further comment: You should be able to see now why the quotation marks are important—they make the difference between printing a numerical variable and printing a string. The statement

```
PRINT Rate
```

prints the value of the variable Rate, which could be any number and might be a different number each time the statement is executed. In contrast, the statement

```
PRINT "Rate"
```

always prints the word Rate.

hanging punctuation

A comma or a semicolon that is coded after the last variable in a PRINT or LPRINT statement.

3.3 EXERCISES

1. You want to print the values of the variables R, M, L, W, Z, P, and G. Write the statement(s) that will print them all on one line. Write the statement(s) that will print one on each line.

2. What output is produced by Program 3.2 (page 63) if the following changes are made? Assume the same data are entered, and that the program is restored to its original condition before each change is made.
   ★a) Lines 14 and 15 are interchanged.
   b) Lines 15 and 16 are interchanged.
   c) The LPRINT statement is omitted.

3. If A is 5 and B is 10, what output is produced by the following statements?
   a) `PRINT A, B`
   b) `PRINT A; B`
   c) `PRINT A,`
      `PRINT B`

★4. What output is produced by the following program?
   ```
   A = 6
   PRINT "A"
   END
   ```

3.4 ADVANCED PRINTING

Now that you know a little more about printing, let's look at some advanced printing features. So far, the control we've exercised over the appearance of our output is fairly crude. To get wide spacing between values, we used commas to separate the variables in the print list; to get narrow spacing, we used semicolons. The functions TAB and SPC, which are used with the PRINT and LPRINT statements, can give you the exact spacing you want on the screen or printer. And two new statements, PRINT USING and LPRINT USING, can give you exact spacing and control exactly how each variable is printed.

The TAB and SPC Functions

The TAB function works like the tab key on a typewriter. It can be used with both the PRINT and LPRINT statements. Consider the statement

```
PRINT TAB(5); A; TAB(14); B; TAB(46); C$
```

This statement tells QBasic to move the print position to column 5 and print the value of A, then move the print position to column 14 and print the value of B, and finally to move the print position to column 46 and print the value of C$. As discussed previously, QBasic inserts a space to the left of a number to allow for easier reading and also for a possible minus sign. Therefore, the first digit of A will actually start printing in column 6, and the first digit of B in column 15. However, the first character of C$ prints in column 46 because QBasic does not insert a space before it prints a string.

Notice that you must use semicolons, not commas, to separate the items in the list of expressions. A comma causes QBasic to space over to the start of the next print zone and destroys the spacing you tried to achieve by using TAB. If you already printed beyond the column specified in the TAB function, QBasic advances to the next line and starts printing at the specified column. For example,

```
PRINT TAB(30); A$; TAB(5); B$
```

prints A$ starting in column 30, and B$ starting in column 5 on the *next* line.

TAB is the first function we have studied. **Functions** are a part of QBasic that perform a specific operation. In effect, they are like the function keys on many calculators. For example, many calculators have a square root function key. If you enter a number into the calculator and press the square root key, the calculator displays, or returns, the square root of the number you entered. The number you entered is called the **argument**. In QBasic, the argument (sometimes there is more than one) is enclosed in parentheses immediately after the function's name. The function returns a value. The TAB function returns the new print position.

The syntax of the TAB function is

```
TAB(column)
```

TAB moves the print position to the column specified by its argument column. The argument column may be a number, as in our examples, or a numerical expression. The statement

```
PRINT TAB(PrintPos); "A Moveable String"
```

will print A Moveable String starting in the column equal to the value of PrintPos.

The SPC function is used in a PRINT or LPRINT statement to specify the number of spaces to skip. For example, if you wanted to print column headings with eight spaces between each heading, you could use

```
PRINT SPC(8); "Name"; SPC(8); "Room"; SPC(8); "Phone"
```

The syntax for the SPC function is

```
SPC(spaces)
```

SPC skips the number of spaces specified by its argument spaces. The argument spaces may be a number or a numeric expression. As with the TAB function, semicolons must separate the variables.

Students often wonder when to use TAB instead of SPC and vice versa. There are no hard and fast rules. Your choice of TAB or SPC depends on which is more convenient for the problem at hand.

function
A part of QBasic that operates on one or more arguments and returns a value.

argument
A constant, variable, or expression supplied to a function—and used by the function to determine a result.

The PRINT USING and LPRINT USING Statements

The TAB and SPC functions are useful in positioning output on the screen or printer, but sometimes you want to control other aspects of your output. For example, in Program 3.2 (page 63), Joe Tinker's pay is $270.00, but is printed as 270. Numerically, 270.00 and 270 are equivalent, so QBasic does not print the two zeros. But since this number represents dollars and cents, we would like it to be printed as $270.00. You may also recall that in Program 2.7 (page 47), the balance was printed as 1338.226. The balance should be rounded to $1,338.23. The PRINT USING and LPRINT USING statements give you control over such situations. Except for the difference that PRINT USING sends its output to the screen and LPRINT USING sends its output to the printer, the two statements work identically. We will use PRINT USING statements in the following examples, but you should understand that everything applies equally to the LPRINT USING statement.

A typical PRINT USING statement is

```
PRINT USING " #,###.##"; BalanceDue
```

The string " #,###.##" is called the **format string**. The format string contains formatting characters, such as #, that specify how you want the variables printed.

The syntax of the PRINT USING statement is

```
PRINT USING formatstring; expressionlist
```

where formatstring may be either a string that is written as part of the PRINT USING statement or a separately defined string variable. As in an ordinary PRINT statement, expressionlist contains the numeric or string expressions that are to be printed, separated by semicolons. If you separate the expressions with commas, QBasic changes them to semicolons. As with the ordinary PRINT statement, you may print expressions, although you will usually print variables.

To learn how to use the PRINT USING statement, you just have to learn how to code the format string. This is most easily done by studying the next four programs and their outputs.

Printing Numeric Variables

Line 9 in Program 3.3 shows the coding for the format string Fmt1$:

```
Fmt1$ = "  ####         ##.##     ##,###.##    ##"
```

This statement specifies the format for four numeric fields: ###, ##.##, ##,###.##, and ##. Each numeric field specifies how and where you want a numeric variable printed. So for each numeric variable in the expression list, you must specify a numeric field in the format string. As you can see, numeric fields are specified by using one or more # symbols, together with decimal points and commas if needed. Each # corresponds to one digit. Numeric fields may be placed anywhere in a format string; the only rule is that they must be separated from each other by at least one space. To help you clearly see the relationship between the format string and the values printed, line 10 in Program 3.3 prints the format string; of course, normally you would not print the format string.

When the PRINT USING statement in line 11 is executed, the numeric values of the variables replace the #s in the format string. The variable A prints using the first numeric field, B prints using the second numeric field, C using the third, and D using the fourth.

If the numeric field does not contain a decimal point, the numeric value is **right-justified**. That is, the numeric value is printed as far to the right in the field as possible. If the numeric field contains more #s than the number of digits in the value being printed, the extra #s on the left are replaced by spaces.

format string
A string that specifies the placement and format of output produced by a PRINT USING or LPRINT USING statement.

right-justified
Printed as far to the right in a field as possible.

```
 1 |   '      *** DEMONSTRATING THE PRINT USING STATEMENT ***
 2 | CLS
 3 |   '                  Printing numbers
 4 | A = 1
 5 | B = 4.2
 6 | C = 5328.268
 7 | D = 213
 8 |
 9 | Fmt1$ = "   ####          ##.##          ##,####.##      ##"
10 | PRINT Fmt1$
11 | PRINT USING Fmt1$; A; B; C; D
12 | END
```

```
      ####              ##.##            ##,####.##        ##  ◄──Format string
        1                4.20             5,328.27         %213  ◄──Values displayed by line 11
        ▲                  ▲                   ▲            ▲
   Number right-      Trailing zero      Comma added    Value too large
   justified          printed                           for field
```

PROGRAM 3.3   Printing numbers with the PRINT USING statement.

Let's see how this works in Program 3.3. Line 11 prints A using the numeric field ###. A is set equal to 1 in line 4, so the 1 is printed in the position of the rightmost #, and the first two #s are replaced by spaces. If you examine the output in Program 3.3, you will see that the 1 is printed in the same column as the rightmost #.

If the numeric field contains a decimal point, extra #s to the right of the decimal point are replaced by zeros. This feature allows us to force QBasic to print two decimal positions for cents. Line 11 prints B using the second numeric field, ##.##. Since the value of B is 4.2, the last # is replaced by 0. Notice how the decimal point in 4.20 is printed in the same column as the decimal point in ##.##. This feature allows you to produce columns of output with the decimal points lined up, which makes the output much easier to read.

The third numeric field, ##,###.##, shows how commas may be inserted when values larger than 999 are printed; just put a comma in the numeric field where the comma should print. If the number printed is not greater than 999, the comma in the field is replaced by a space. Notice also that when line 11 prints C using this numeric field, the comma is inserted and the value of C, 5328.268, is rounded and printed as 5,328.27.

In fact, all values are rounded before they are printed. The following new examples show how A, which is assumed to have the value 10.674, is printed by the statement

```
    PRINT USING Format$; A
```

when different Format$ are used.

Format$	Value Printed
##	11
##.#	10.7
##.##	10.67

What happens if you print a value that is too large to fit in a numeric field? The value still prints, but the alignment is spoiled; as a warning, the number is preceded with a %. For example, look again at Program 3.3. There, line 11 prints D using the numeric field ## and that field allows for only two digits. Since the value of D is 213, it can't fit in that field. Accordingly, D prints as %213, spoiling the column alignment.

This example illustrates an important point. When you design a numeric field, you must consider the size of the numbers that will be printed in it. How many digits will they have to the left of the decimal point? Since the disadvantage of making a numeric field too large is printing extra spaces, while the disadvantage of making a numeric field too small is spoiling the column alignment, it is better to make the numeric field one or two digits larger than you think you need. Adding an extra space or two is often not noticeable, while misaligning numbers clearly is wrong.

Note, however, that for the digits to the *right* of the decimal point, use only as many #s as you want to print. A value that has more digits than that will not cause QBasic to print a %. Instead, as we saw in the printing of C, the value will be rounded, which is often desirable.

Printing String Variables

String variables may also be printed with the PRINT USING statement. In Program 3.4, line 8 shows the coding for a format string to print four string variables:

```
Fmt2$ = "   \          \      \          \      !    &"
```

Backslashes, \, are used to specify string fields. The first backslash indicates the start of the string field and the second backslash, the end of the field. The number of characters printed is equal to the number of spaces between the backslashes plus 2. So two backslashes next to each other, \\, print two characters; two backslashes separated by one space, \ \, print three characters, and so on.

String variables are always **left-justified**, which means that the string is printed as far to the left as possible in the field. If the string variable to be printed contains fewer characters than the field provides, spaces are printed at the right end. If the string variable contains more characters than the field provides, as many characters as will fit are printed and the extra characters are not printed.

left-justified
Printed as far to the left in a field as possible.

```
 1  |  '    *** DEMONSTRATING THE PRINT USING STATEMENT ***
 2  |  CLS
 3  |  '                    Printing strings
 4  |  A$ = "STRING"
 5  |  B$ = "VERY BIG STRING"
 6  |  C$ = "ANOTHER STRING"
 7  |
 8  |  Fmt2$ = "   \          \      \          \      !    &"
 9  |  PRINT Fmt2$
10  |  PRINT USING Fmt2$; A$; B$; A$; C$
11  |  END
```

```
\◄8 spaces►\        \◄8 spaces►\        !   & ◄──Format string
   STRING              VERY BIG S        S   ANOTHER STRING ◄──Values displayed by line 10
     ▲                     ▲             ▲        ▲
String right-          String      First character   Complete string
justified              truncated   printed           printed
```

PROGRAM 3.4   Printing strings with the PRINT USING statement.

For example, the first two fields in line 8 have 8 spaces between the back-slashes, so they will print 8 + 2 = 10 characters. Line 10 prints A$ using this field. Since A$ contains the 6 characters STRING, it is left-justified in the field, and spaces are printed in the remaining 4 columns. Line 10 also prints B$ using an identical field. But B$, which is assigned the value VERY BIG STRING in line 5, contains 15 characters, so only the first 10 characters—VERY BIG S—are printed. Notice that unlike the % that prints when a number is too large for its field, QBasic does not indicate that only part of B$ was printed.

In addition to backslashes, two other characters may be used to define string fields. You use an exclamation point—!—when you want to print only the first character of a string. (Remember that the smallest field you can specify using backslashes, \\, prints two characters.) Line 10 prints A$ using !; you can see how only the first character of A$, an S, was printed. You can use ! if you want to print initials. Suppose GivenName$ is equal to John, MidName$ is equal to Fitzgerald, and LastName$ is equal to Kennedy. The statement

```
PRINT USING "!!!"; GivenName$; MidName$; LastName$
```

prints JFK.

The ampersand, &, prints the complete string. Line 10 prints C$ using an &, and you can see that all of C$ is printed. Printing a string variable using an ampersand field gives the same output you would get if you used an ordinary PRINT statement. That is, the ampersand prints a variable number of characters.

One place you would use an ampersand is if you want to print sentence-like output that contains a variable length string. For example, suppose you want to print employees' names and pay rates, and suppose the longest employee's name contains 15 characters. You might use the following statement:

```
PRINT USING "\              \'s pay rate is $##.##"; EmpName$; PayRate
```

allowing 15 characters for the employees' names. This would be fine for the employee whose name contains 15 characters, but for an employee whose name is shorter—for example, Tom Mix— this statement prints

```
Tom Mix         's pay rate is $ 7.95
```

which is not satisfactory. Instead, we can use an ampersand in the format string

```
PRINT USING "&'s pay rate is $##.##"; EmpName$; PayRate
```

which would give us

```
Tom Mix's pay rate is $ 7.95
```

for the employee with the short name, and

```
George Anderson's pay rate is $ 6.60
```

for the employee whose name contains 15 characters.

Other Format Characters

In Program 3.5, the output produced by the first numeric field defined in line 7, $####.##, shows that to print a $ in front of a number, you simply code a $ at the beginning of the numeric field. But sometimes, especially on checks, spaces between the $ and the first digit are not desirable (this enables forgers to add extra digits). The output produced by the second numeric field in line 7, $$####.##, shows that to eliminate that space, you code two dollar signs, $$, at the beginning of the numeric field. This causes the $ to be printed next to the first digit. A dollar sign that prints next to the first digit is called a **floating dollar sign**. One of the $s in the field represents a position for a digit, so the field $$####.## could correctly print numbers as large as 99999.99.

floating dollar sign
A dollar sign that prints next to the first digit.

```
 1 |  '    *** DEMONSTRATING THE PRINT USING STATEMENT ***
 2 | CLS
 3 | '              Additional Formatting Characters
 4 | A = 150
 5 | B = 20.25
 6 |
 7 | Fmt1$ = "   $#####.##    $$#####.##"
 8 | PRINT Fmt1$
 9 | PRINT USING Fmt1$; A; B
10 |
11 | Fmt2$ = "   **#####.##   **$#####.##"
12 | PRINT Fmt2$
13 | PRINT USING Fmt2$; A; B
14 |
15 | Fmt3$ = "  Total Sales This Month    $$###.##"
16 | PRINT Fmt3$
17 | PRINT USING Fmt3$; B
18 | END
```

```
                 $#####.##     $$#####.##  ◄──────Format string
       Fixed $─► $ 150.00          $20.25  ◄──────Values printed by line 9
    Floating $──────────────────────┘

                 **#####.##    **$#####.##  ◄──────Format string
 Asterisk fill─►***150.00     ****$20.25  ◄──────Values printed by line 13
 Asterisk fill────────────────────┘
 with $

          Total Sales This Month    $$###.##  ◄──────Format string
          Total Sales This Month       $20.25  ◄──────Values printed by line 17
```

PROGRAM 3.5 Demonstrating the PRINT USING statement with additional formatting characters.

Another way to eliminate spaces when numbers are printed is to code two asterisks, **, at the beginning of the numeric field. This is shown in the first numeric field defined in line 11, **####.##. Coding ** at the beginning of the numeric field causes asterisks to replace leading spaces in the printed numeric field, which is called asterisk fill. You can get asterisk fill and a dollar sign by coding **$ at the beginning of the numeric field, as the second numeric field defined in line 11, **$####.##, indicates. The output shows that this combination causes the dollar sign to be printed next to the first digit and the leading spaces to be replaced by asterisks.

When a PRINT USING statement is executed, only the characters used to specify numeric and string fields in the format string are replaced by numbers and characters. All other characters are printed exactly as they appear in the format string. This is illustrated in the format string defined in line 15:

```
Fmt3$ =  "  Total Sales This Month    $$###.##"
```

The output shows that the whole string constant Total Sales This Month was printed, as well as the edited number.

Sometimes, you might want to print a character that is used to specify a format string. For example, suppose you want to print the words Student Id# followed by the actual number. If you write the PRINT USING statement as

```
PRINT USING "Student ID# ####"; StudNum
```

QBasic assumes that you defined two numeric fields, # and ####. If the value of StudNum is 1234, this statement prints as

```
Student Id%1234
```

which is not what you want. The solution is to use an underscore character (_) in the format string, as follows:

```
PRINT USING "Student ID_# ####"; StudNum
```

The underscore character tells QBasic to print the next character as it stands and not to interpret it as part of a field definition. This statement prints what you want:

```
Student Id# 1234
```

Controlling Plus and Minus Signs

As we saw in these examples, the PRINT USING statement prints positive numbers with no sign. It prints negative numbers with a leading minus sign. For example, line 8 in Program 3.6 defines Fmt1$ as

```
Fmt1$ = "  ###.#  +####.#  +####.#  ###.#+  ###.#+"
```

Line 10 prints C (which is set equal to –14.7 in line 4) using the first format field in Fmt1$, ###.#. The value printed is –14.7.

We can control how QBasic prints the sign of the number by using plus and minus signs in the format field. A plus sign, +, may be coded at the beginning or the end of the format field, as shown in the last four format fields defined in Fmt1$ (line 8). Line 10 uses these format fields to print D (which is set equal to 39.4 in line 5) and E (which is set equal to –23.9 in line 6). The output produced

```
 1 |  '    *** DEMONSTRATING THE PRINT USING STATEMENT ***
 2 | CLS
 3 |  '              Plus  and  Minus  Signs
 4 | C = -14.7
 5 | D = 39.4
 6 | E = -23.9
 7 |
 8 | Fmt1$ = "  ###.#  +####.#  +####.#  ###.#+  ###.#+"
 9 | PRINT Fmt1$
10 | PRINT USING Fmt1$; C; D; E; D; E
11 |
12 | Fmt2$ = "   ###.#-  ###.#-"
13 | PRINT Fmt2$
14 | PRINT USING Fmt2$; C; D
15 | END
```

PROGRAM 3.6 Demonstrating the PRINT USING statement with plus and minus signs.

shows that a plus sign in the format field causes a positive number to be printed with a plus sign and a negative number to be printed with a minus sign. The sign is printed before or after the number, depending on whether the plus sign is coded at the beginning or the end of the format field.

A minus sign, −, may be coded only at the end of a numeric field, as shown in line 12:

```
Fmt2$ = "  ###.#-   ###.#-"
```

Line 14 prints C and D using this format string. The output produced shows that negative numbers are printed with a minus sign and positive numbers are printed with no sign.

You can mix string and numeric field definitions in the same format field; for example,

```
PRINT USING "\        \ ###"; PatientName$; Age
```

When you do so, though, you must be careful to print string variables using string format fields and numbers using numeric format fields. If you mistakenly try to print a numeric variable using a string format field or a string variable using a numeric format field, QBasic displays a Type mismatch error message.

Additional Notes

Format strings do not always need to appear in the order and style you just saw. For example, it is not necessary to define a format string in the line just before the line in which it is used. A format string may be defined anywhere in the program; the only requirement is that the line in which it is defined must be executed before the line in which it is used is executed.

It is not necessary that the number of fields defined in the format string be the same as the number of variables in the print list. For example, consider the statement:

```
PRINT USING " ###   ##.###"; A; B; C; D
```

The print list contains four variables, but the format string defines only two numeric fields. Under these conditions, the format string is reused from the beginning. In this example, A and C are printed by using the first number field, ###; B and D are printed by using the second number field, ##.###.

If you try to print by using a field that does not contain any field definitions, QBasic displays an Illegal function call message. The probable cause of this error is that you used a slash, /, instead of a backslash, \, to define a string field.

Table 3.1 summarizes the functions of the formatting characters we just discussed.

TABLE 3.1
Formatting Characters Used with PRINT USING

Character	Description
	String-Printing Characters
!	Prints only the first character of the string.
\ \	Prints 2 + the number of spaces between the two backslashes. The string is left-justified in the field; if the string is longer than the field, it is truncated.
&	Prints the whole string.

TABLE 3.1 *(continued)*

Character	Description
	Number Printing Characters
####	Specifies a numeric field. Each # represents a digit position. The number is right-justified in the field. If the number is larger than the number of digits allowed, a % is printed.
.	Specifies the position of the decimal point in the numeric field. The decimal point in the numeric value is aligned with the decimal point in the field.
$	Prints as a $ in a fixed position.
$$	Prints a single $ that floats to the immediate left of the number.
**	Prints asterisks in the leading spaces of the numeric field.
**$	Combines the effects of $$ and **. Leading spaces of the numeric field are filled with asterisks, and a $ is printed to the immediate left of the numeric field.
+	Prints the sign of the number. The sign is printed either before the number (if the + is at the beginning of the numeric field) or after the number (if the + is at the end of the field).
−	Prints a minus sign if the number is negative and nothing if the number is positive. Must be used at the end of a numeric field.
	Miscellaneous Characters
_ (underscore)	Causes the following character to be printed as is, and not to be interpreted as part of a field definition.

EXAMPLE 1

A PROGRAM THAT PRINTS HEADINGS

Let's put what we learned about printing to print headings and improve the output for a variation of Program 3.2 (page 63).

Problem Statement

Write a program that accepts values for employee name, pay rate, and hours worked—and that calculates and prints gross pay, income tax, and net pay. Income tax is 18% of gross pay, and net pay is gross pay minus income tax. The program should print headings and use a PRINT USING statement to make the output easy to read.

STEP 1 **Variable Names**

Following our seven-step procedure, we begin by identifying and naming the variables. We can use the same names we used in Program 3.2, and add names for income tax and net pay.

Variable	Variable Name
Employee name	`EmpName$`
Pay rate	`PayRate`
Hours worked	`Hours`
Gross pay	`GrossPay`
Income tax	`IncomeTax`
Net pay	`NetPay`

STEP 2   Algorithm

The second step is to develop an algorithm. We can modify the algorithm we used for the paycheck problem in Chapter 2.

1. Print headings.
2. Accept a value for EmpName$.
3. Accept a value for PayRate.
4. Accept a value for Hours.
5. Calculate GrossPay by multiplying PayRate by Hours.
6. Calculate IncomeTax by multiplying GrossPay by .18.
7. Calculate NetPay by subtracting IncomeTax from GrossPay.
8. Print EmpName$, PayRate, Hours, GrossPay, IncomeTax, and NetPay.

STEP 3   Hand-Calculated Answer

Next, we must calculate an answer by hand. As in Program 3.2, we use 6.75 for PayRate and 40 for Hours. We find

$$GrossPay = 6.75 \times 40 = 270$$
$$IncomeTax = 270 \times .18 = 48.60$$
$$NetPay = 270 - 48.60 = 221.40$$

STEP 4   QBasic Program

The next step in our structured procedure is to write a QBasic program. A program that solves this problem is shown in Program 3.7.

The CONST Statement.   The only new statement in Program 3.7 is the CONST statement in line 13:

```
CONST TaxRate = .18          'Income tax rate assumed to be 18%
```

The CONST statement allows you to define symbolic constants to be used in your program. In Program 3.7, TaxRate is defined to have the value .18. As the name implies, symbolic constants cannot be changed. For example, you cannot use TaxRate on the left side of a LET or in an INPUT statement. You may have as many CONST statements as you want. Since symbolic constants must be defined before they may be used, it is customary to place all the CONST statements near the beginning of the program.

The most important advantage of using symbolic constants—rather than variables—is that symbolic constants cannot be inadvertently changed. Using symbolic constants instead of their numerical values also makes your programs easier to understand and modify. The statement in line 28

```
IncomeTax = TaxRate * GrossPay
```

```
 1 |  '    *** PAYCHECK PROGRAM ***
 2 |  '    Calculate gross pay, income tax, and net pay
 3 |
 4 |  '    Variables used
 5 |
 6 |  '    EmpName$          Employee's name
 7 |  '    GrossPay          Gross pay
 8 |  '    Hours             Hours worked
 9 |  '    IncomeTax         Income tax
10 |  '    NetPay            Net pay
11 |  '    PayRate           Hourly pay rate
12 |
13 |  CONST TaxRate = .18              'Income tax rate assumed to be 18%
14 |
15 |  CLS
16 |
17 |  ' Print heading and define format string
18 |  LPRINT "                         Payroll Report"
19 |  LPRINT
20 |  LPRINT "              Pay              Gross    Income      Net"
21 |  LPRINT "  Name        Rate   Hours     Pay       Tax        Pay"
22 |  Frmt$ = "\              \   ##.##    ##   $###.##   $##.##   $###.##"
23 |
24 |  INPUT "Enter Name: ", EmpName$
25 |  INPUT "Enter Pay Rate: ", PayRate
26 |  INPUT "Enter Hours Worked: ", Hours
27 |  GrossPay = PayRate * Hours
28 |  IncomeTax = TaxRate * GrossPay
29 |  NetPay = GrossPay - IncomeTax
30 |  LPRINT USING Frmt$; EmpName$; PayRate; Hours; GrossPay; IncomeTax; NetPay
31 |  END
```

(handwritten annotation: data dictionary (documentation))

```
Enter Name: Joe Tinker
Enter Pay Rate: 6.75
Enter Hours Worked: 40
```

```
                          Payroll Report

                Pay              Gross    Income      Net
  Name          Rate   Hours     Pay       Tax        Pay
Joe Tinker      6.75    40      $270.00   $48.60    $221.40
```

PROGRAM 3.7 Paycheck program with headings and the PRINT USING statement.

is much more meaningful than

```
IncomeTax = .18 * GrossPay
```

Furthermore, if the tax rate changes, you can update your program by simply changing the CONST statement, rather than searching through the whole program to change all the .18s to the new rate, and perhaps mistakenly changing a .18 that represents a different quantity.

The syntax of the CONST statement is

```
CONST ConstantName = expression
```

Study the following CONST statements.

ILLUSTRATIONS

CONST Statement	Effect
`CONST NumStudents = 40`	NumStudents is defined to be a symbolic constant and given the value 40.
`CONST Message$ = "Your ↵` `  account is overdrawn"`	Message$ is defined to be a symbolic constant, and given the value Your account is overdrawn.

Printing Headings. Before you can print a heading, you have to design it; for that, a **spacing chart**—like the one shown in Figure 3.1—is helpful. Your instructor may supply spacing charts, or you may be able to buy them in the bookstore.

Figure 3.1 shows a title, column headings, and format string that could be used for this program. After designing column headings, you should design the format string on the spacing chart to make sure that values will be printed under their column headings. When the spacing chart is complete, the title, column headings, and format string can be translated into heading and format strings.

The title, column headings, and format string from Figure 3.1 were translated into lines 18–22 of Program 3.7. Line 19 shows that to print a blank line, all you do is include an empty LPRINT statement.

Program 3.7 also uses a little trick that you may find helpful. Notice that the LPRINT statements in lines 18, 20, and 21 are indented so that their left quotation marks line up with the quotation marks in the LET statement in line 22. With this

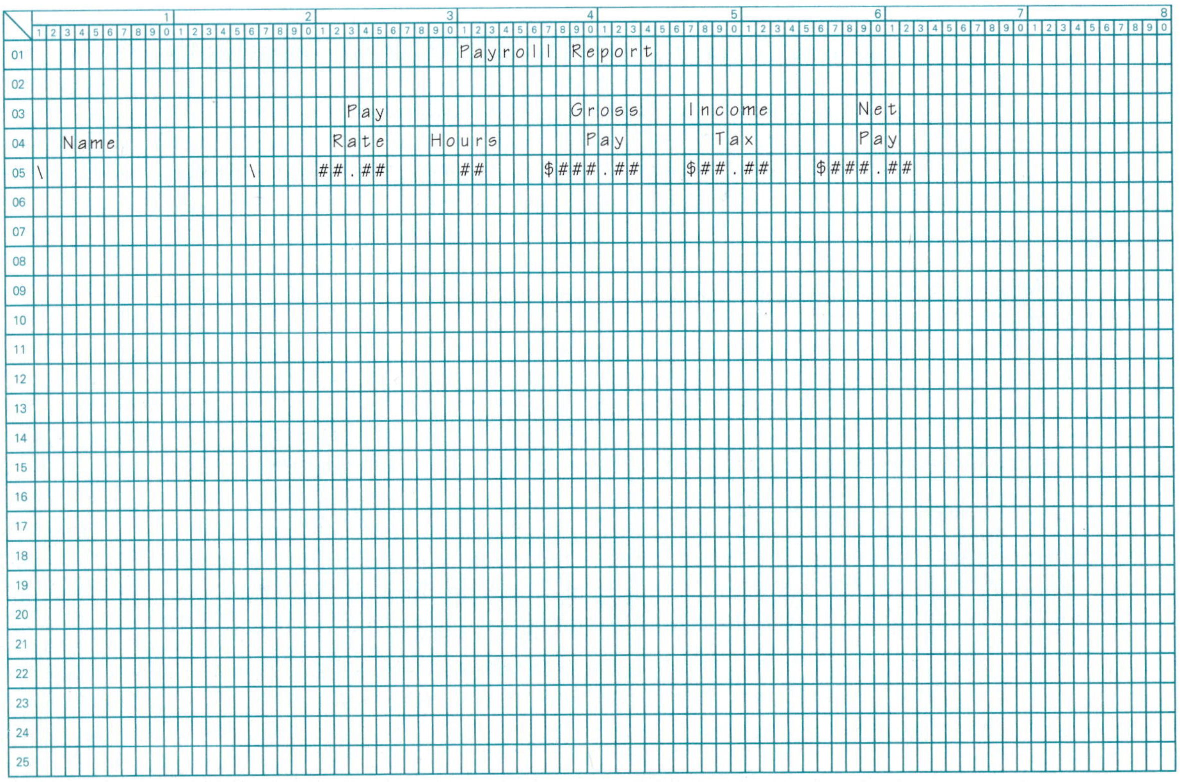

spacing chart
A chart used to design printed reports and screens.

FIGURE 3.1 A printer spacing chart for the paycheck program.

alignment, after you carefully type Frmt$, counting spaces between symbols to match Figure 3.1, you can easily type the other lines by aligning them with Frmt$.

Notice how attractive the output produced by Program 3.7 looks and that it agrees with our hand-calculated answers. The only problem with Program 3.7 is that every time we run the program to print the pay for a different employee, the heading also prints. It would be much nicer if the heading just printed once, and the output for each employee lined up under the heading. You will learn how to do that in the next chapter.

Syntax Summary

PRINT USING Statement

Form: `PRINT USING formatstring; expressionlist`
Example: `PRINT USING "\ \ ###.### sq. miles"; State$; Area`
Explanation: The values of the expressions are displayed on the screen as specified in formatstring. For a description of the formatting string characters, see Table 3.1 on page 72. (Note: The LPRINT USING statement functions exactly the same way, but sends the output to the printer instead of to the screen.)

CONST Statement

Form: `CONST ConstantName = expression`
Example: `CONST Dashes$ = "—————————"`
Explanation: Defines a symbolic constant.

3.4 EXERCISES

1. Explain the difference between the TAB and SPC functions.

★2. Write a PRINT statement with a TAB function to print the message Please enter your name starting in column 40.

3. Write a LPRINT statement to print a blank line.

★4. Consider the following PRINT USING statement:

```
PRINT USING "\          \   $##.##"; Item$; Price
```

(There are nine spaces between the \s—backslashes—and three spaces between the right \ and the $.) What output will this statement produce if Item$ = Peaches and Price = 1.35? Indicate blank spaces on the output by the letter "b."

5. Consider the following PRINT USING statement:

```
PRINT USING Fmt$; StudentName$, CourseCredits; GPA
```

StudentName$ may have up to 25 characters, CourseCredits is a whole number in the range 0 to 200, and GPA has two decimal positions and is in the range 0.00 to 4.00. Write the LET statement to define Fmt$.

6. Write the format string to print Amount. Amount may be as large as $99,999.99, and should be printed with a comma and a dollar sign next to the leading digit.

7. Consider the following PRINT USING statement:

```
PRINT USING PriceFmt$; Price
```

Price will be in the range 5,000 to 35,000. Write the LET statement to define PriceFmt$ so that, for example, if Price = 8632 the statement prints

```
Sticker price . . . . . . $ 8,632.00
```

★8. **(a)** Define a symbolic constant named OvertimeLimit that has the value 40.
(b) Define a symbolic constant that has the value The check is in the mail.

3.5	THE QBASIC ENVIRONMENT

We continue our discussion of the QBasic environment by turning next to the Edit and Search menus. Using commands on the Edit menu, you can move or copy a part of your program from one place to another. Using commands on the Search menu, you can find a string anywhere in your program and, if you want, change it to a different string.

The Edit Menu

Before you can use the commands on the Edit menu to move or copy part of your program, you must first select the text you want to work on. Let's next discuss how you select text.

Selecting Text

To select text, move the cursor to the first character you want to select. While you press and hold the Shift key, move the cursor to the last character you want to select. You can move the cursor by using the arrow keys—or any of the other keys covered in Chapter 1 that move the cursor a large distance: Home, End, Page Up, Page Down, and so on. For example, the fastest way to select a whole line is to use the Home key to move the cursor to the beginning of the line, press and hold the Shift key, and press the End key. When you select text, it is highlighted.

To select text with a mouse, move the mouse pointer to the first character you want to select. Press and hold the left mouse button while you move the mouse pointer to the last character you want to select. Finally, release the mouse button. Alternatively, move the mouse pointer to the first character you want to select and click the left mouse button. Then move the mouse pointer to the last character you want to select. Press and hold the Shift key and click the left mouse button. To select a word, move the mouse pointer to the word, and double click the left mouse button.

You must be careful when text is selected, because any character you type will replace all of the selected text. If you find that you selected the wrong text, you can cancel the selection by pressing the Escape key or any cursor control key (such as an arrow key). With a mouse, click the left mouse button.

After text is selected, you can tab it, move it, copy it, or delete it. To tab selected text, press the Tab key. You can even remove indention from selected text by pressing Shift+Tab.

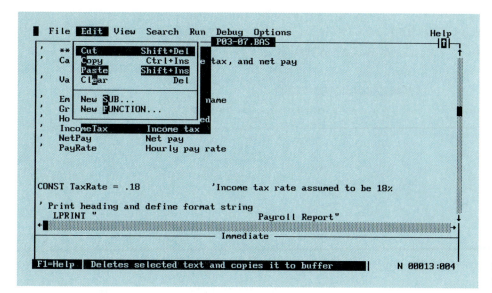

FIGURE 3.2
The Edit menu.

Moving Text

To move or copy the selected text, you must use the Edit menu, which is shown in Figure 3.2. The Edit menu lists six commands, but for now, we are concerned with only the first four: Cut, Copy, Paste, and Clear.

Moving selected text is a two-step operation. You must first cut the selected text, and then paste it. After you select the text you want to move, access the Edit menu and choose the Cut command. The Cut command deletes the selected text from the screen, but saves it in a temporary storage area called the **clipboard**. Next, move the cursor to the location where you want the text to appear. Access the Edit menu again, and this time choose the Paste command. You will see the text appear as though it were just typed. Choosing the Paste command does not empty the clipboard, so you can Paste the same text as many times as you want. Figure 3.2 shows that the shortcut keys for cutting text are Shift+Delete, and for pasting text are Shift+Insert. If you remember those shortcut keys, you don't have to use the Edit menu.

clipboard
A temporary storage area that holds text you are copying or moving.

Copying Text

Copying selected text is similar to cutting and pasting, except that in the first step, you choose the Copy command instead of the Cut command (or use the shortcut keys Ctrl+Insert). Like the Cut command, the Copy command also saves selected text to the clipboard; unlike the Cut command, the Copy command does not delete the selected text from the screen. When you later paste the text from the clipboard, your program will contain two copies of the selected text (one in the original location and one in the area where you just pasted text).

You can even copy the example programs in the Help screens. When you have displayed help on a statement, press function key F6 twice to move the cursor to the Help screen. You can then move the cursor to any of the examples, select it, and copy it to the View screen.

To delete selected text, choose the Clear command (or use the shortcut key Delete). If you access the Edit menu when no text is selected, the Cut, Copy, and Clear commands are displayed in gray, showing that they cannot be chosen. Similarly, if the clipboard is empty, the Paste command is gray. You can use them again as soon as you perform the first step of the process they help complete (after you select text, cut text, and so on).

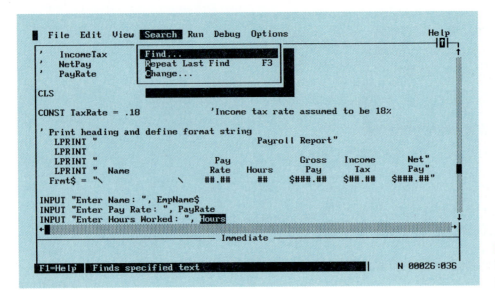

FIGURE 3.3
The Search
menu.

The Search Menu

The commands in the Search menu (shown in Figure 3.3) allow you to find specific text in your program and, if you want, to replace it with other text.

The Find Command

The Find command allows you to find specific text anywhere in your program. When you select the Find command, the Find dialog box is displayed, as shown in Figure 3.4. The Find What text box contains the word that the cursor was on when you invoked the command. If that is the text you want to search for, just press the Enter key. If you want to search for different text, type it, and then press the Enter key.

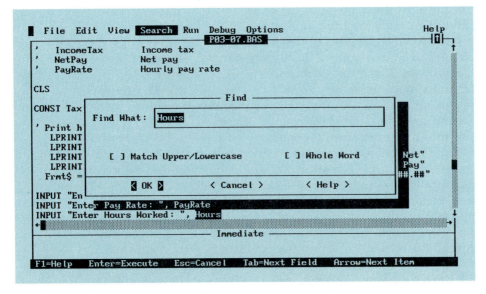

FIGURE 3.4
The Find dialog
box.

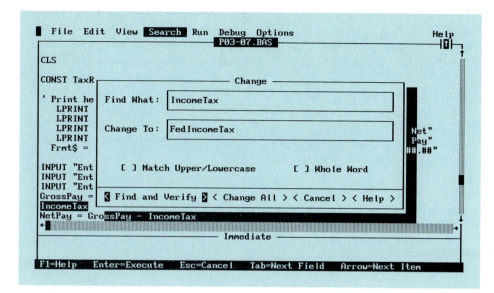

FIGURE 3.5
The Change
dialog box.

The search starts from the current cursor position. When QBasic finds the text, it stops and highlights the text. You can find the next occurrence of the text by choosing the Repeat Last Find command from the Search menu or by pressing function key F3 (see Figure 3.3). When the search reaches the end of the program, it continues at the beginning of the program.

By default, the search is not case sensitive; that is, the search text Hours finds HOURS, as well as Hours and hours. If you want the search to be case sensitive, use the Tab key to move the cursor to the Match Upper/Lowercase option box, and press the arrow keys or the space bar until an X appears in the option box. With a mouse, click on the Match Upper/Lowercase option box.

Similarly, by default, the search finds all occurrences of the search text; that is, the search text PUT finds INPUT, as well as PUT. If you want to find only whole words, use the Tab key to move the cursor to the Whole Word option box, and press the arrow keys or space bar until an X appears in the option box. With a mouse, click on the Whole Word option box.

The Change Command

The Change command from the Search menu (see Figure 3.3) allows you to change specified text to different text. When you select the Change command, the Change dialog box is displayed, as shown in Figure 3.5. If you selected text before you invoked the Change command, that text will be in the Find What text box. If you haven't selected any text, the Find What text box will be empty the first time you use the Change command—or it will contain the text you used the last time you executed the Change command.

If necessary, type the text you want to change in the Find What box, but *don't press Enter!* If you press Enter, you will replace the text in the Find What box with nothing. Instead, press the Tab key or use the mouse to move to the Change To text box, and enter the replacement text. In Figure 3.5, we want to change IncomeTax to FedIncomeTax.

You can then execute the command by choosing either the Find and Verify or Change All command buttons. You can also cancel the command or get help. If you choose Find and Verify, each time the Find What text is found, QBasic displays four more command buttons: Change, Skip, Cancel, and Help. The Change button makes the change and the Skip button skips this occurrence of the Find What text. In either case, QBasic moves to the next occurrence of the Find What text, and the same four command buttons are displayed. The command ends when all the occurrences of the Find What text are found or if you cancel the process at any point.

The Change All command button changes all the occurrences of the Find What text, but without asking for confirmation. Just as with the Find command, you can put restrictions on the Change command by activating the Match Upper/Lowercase and Whole Word options. Also note that the Change command offers a convenient way to change PRINT to LPRINT.

3.5 EXERCISES

★1. If you find that you have selected the wrong text, how can you unselect it?

2. What is the difference between moving text and copying it?

3. List the steps needed to copy a line.

★4. You can execute the Change command by choosing either the Find and Verify command button or the Change All command button. What is the difference between these two choices?

5. Program 3.8 shows an attempt to execute a solution to Programming Assignment 3.13 (on page 85). As you can see, QBasic displayed the error message Redo from start. What went wrong?

```
1  '    *** PROGRAMMING ASSIGNMENT 3.13 ***
2
3  CONST YenInDollar = 131.46
4
5  CLS
6  INPUT "Enter name of item: ", ItemName$
7  INPUT "Enter price: ", PriceYen
8  PriceDollars = PriceYen / YenInDollar
9  PRINT ItemName$, PriceYen, PriceDollars
10 END
```

```
Enter name of item: Camera
Enter price: 30,000

Redo from start
Enter price:
```

PROGRAM 3.8   Trying to execute a solution to Programming Assignment 3.13.

WHAT YOU HAVE LEARNED

In this chapter, you have learned that:

- Strings must be enclosed in quotation marks and may contain a maximum of 32,767 characters.
- String variable names are formed by adding a $ to the end of a legal numeric variable name or a reserved word.
- The INPUT statement is used to prompt the user and to accept data entered from the keyboard.
- In model statements, curly braces, {}, enclose items from which you must choose. A vertical line separates the choices.
- Prompts are used to tell the user what data must be entered. Prompts should be clear, thorough, and user-friendly.
- An LPRINT statement is used to print output on the printer.
- When semicolons are used in a print list, the values are printed close together. Each numeric value is printed with a space before it, which will contain a minus sign if the value is negative, and a blank space after it. Strings and string variables are printed with no spaces between them.
- A comma or a semicolon at the end of a print list is called hanging punctuation. Hanging punctuation causes the next PRINT or LPRINT statement to begin printing where the last PRINT or LPRINT statement stopped.
- Strings may be printed by surrounding them by quotation marks and including them in a print list.

- The TAB and SPC functions are used with a PRINT or LPRINT statement. TAB skips to the specified column, while SPC skips the specified number of columns.
- The PRINT USING and LPRINT USING statements require a format string. In a format string, number signs (#) are used to specify numeric fields. Numeric fields may also contain periods, commas, and dollar signs as well as plus and minus signs. Backslashes (\) are generally used to specify string fields, but an ampersand (&) prints the complete string and an exclamation point (!) prints just the first character of a string.
- The CONST statement is used to define symbolic constants.
- A spacing chart is used to design a screen and to help devise appropriate spacing for titles, column headings, and format strings in a printed report.
- Text is selected by holding down the Shift key and moving the cursor. With a mouse, text is selected by holding the left mouse button and moving the mouse cursor.
- Selected text is moved by using the Cut and Paste commands from the Edit menu.
- Selected text is copied by using the Copy and Paste commands from the Edit menu.
- The Search menu Find command allows you to find a specified string anywhere in your program.
- The Search menu Change command allows you to replace a specified string by another string.

NEW QBASIC STATEMENTS

STATEMENT	EFFECT

INPUT

```
INPUT "Enter height: ", Height
```

Displays the prompt Enter height:, and assigns the value entered at the keyboard to Height.

LPRINT

```
LPRINT Height, Base, Area
```

Prints the values of Height, Base, and Area on the printer.

PRINT USING

```
Fmt$ = "\        \ ###,### sq. miles"
PRINT USING Fmt$; State$; Area
```

Displays the value of State$ according to the field \   \, and the value of Area according to the field ###,###. (*Note*: The LPRINT USING statement functions exactly the same way, but sends the output to the printer instead of to the screen.)

CONST

```
CONST Pi = 3.14159
```

Defines a symbolic constant.

KEY TERMS

argument
clipboard
floating dollar sign
format string

function
hanging punctuation
left-justified
null string

prompt
right-justified
spacing chart

REVIEW EXERCISES

SELF-CHECK

1. True or false: A string may contain both upper and lower case letters.

2. What is the maximum number of characters that a string variable can hold?

3. Name two statements that may be used to assign a value to a variable.

4. Give two reasons why it is useful to print the input data along with the answer to a problem.

5. How wide are print zones?

6. When do you have to enclose in quotation marks a string that is entered in response to an INPUT statement?

7. What is the purpose of printing a prompt with an INPUT statement?

8. True or false: When semicolons are used in a print list, exactly eight values are printed on a line.

9. True or false: It is legal to print string variables and numeric variables in the same PRINT statement.

10. A comma at the end of a print list causes the next output to be printed _____.

11. True or false: In a format string, the field $$####.## causes two $s to be printed.

12. In the format string of a PRINT USING statement, which character is used to indicate the printing of numeric variables? Which characters are used to indicate the printing of string variables?

13. In a PRINT USING statement, what punctuation must separate the format string from the list of variables to be printed?

14. Headings are designed using a(n) _____.

15. In a format string, if there are five spaces between two \s (backslashes), how many characters can be printed?

16. What statement is used to define symbolic constants?

17. What commands are used to move selected text?

18. When the Search menu Find command stops at the search string, how can you continue the command to find the next occurrence of the search string?

19. What is the difference between executing the Search menu Change command with the Match Upper/Lowercase option activated and with it not activated?

PROGRAMMING ASSIGNMENTS

Most of these assignments are modifications of assignments in Chapter 2. If the earlier assignment number is not clear from the statement of the problem, it is given in parentheses at the end of the assignment, as in (PA 2.2).

Section 3.2

1. Rewrite your solution to Programming Assignment 2.1, using INPUT statements to accept miles driven and gas used.

2. Rewrite your solution to Programming Assignment 2.3, using INPUT statements to accept the student's name, the number of questions on the test, and the number of questions the student got correct.

3. Write a program that accepts three numbers and prints them in reverse order.

4. All the used books at Twice Sold Tales are reduced 20 percent. Accept as input the original price of a book. Write a program to calculate and print the sale price of the book. (PA 2.2)

5. Each chocolate bar uses three quarters of an ounce of nuts, and nuts cost $.12 per ounce. Write a program that accepts the number of chocolate bars manufactured, then calculates and prints the cost of the nuts.

Section 3.3

6. a) Write a program that accepts the name of a food and the amount of cholesterol it contains and produces a report like the following:

```
CHOLESTEROL CONTENT OF FOODS
Food            Cholesterol
Hamburger         375
```

b) Modify the program to print the output in the following format (all on one line):

```
Hamburger contains 375 mg of
   cholesterol.
```

7. Write a program that accepts a name and prints a message like the following:

```
Good Morning, George
Have a good day
```

8. Modify your solution to Programming Assignment 2.10 to accept a year in which to calculate the average temperature, and whose output is in the form (on one line):

```
In 2030 the average temperature
   will be 75.2 degrees.
```

Section 3.4

9. Make Program 3.7 (page 75) more realistic by deducting social security tax and medical insurance premiums—as well as income tax—from gross pay to get net pay. Assume that the social security tax rate is 8%, and medical insurance is $15. Print name, pay rate, hours worked, gross pay, income tax, social security tax, and net pay. Use a PRINT USING statement to make your output attractive, and use symbolic constants for the social security tax rate and the medical insurance premium. If you use the data in Program 3.7, you should find that Joe Tinker's social security tax is $21.60, and his net pay is $184.80.

10. Write a program to print the following rectangle:

```
**********
*        *
*        *
*        *
*        *
**********
```

Let the user enter a number to specify the column in which to print the left edge of the rectangle. (*Hint*: Use the TAB and SPC functions.)

11. Write a program that accepts two whole numbers—A and B—and performs the following calculations:

```
C = (B + 1) / A
D = (C + 1) / B
E = (D + 1) / C
F = (E + 1) / D
```

Print A, B, and F using a PRINT USING statement with a format string that prints these variables as whole numbers. Run the program with different values of A and B. What do your answers tell you?

12. Accept as input a baseball player's name, the number of times at bat and the number of hits made. Write a program to calculate and print the batting average. Use a PRINT USING statement to print your output. (PA 2.6)

ADDITIONAL PROGRAMMING ASSIGNMENTS

13. Mark O. Polo is traveling in Japan and wants to buy a gift. Write a program that accepts the name and price (in yen) of a gift and prints the name and price in dollars. To convert from yen to dollars, divide the price in yen by 131.46. Use a symbolic constant for the conversion factor. (PA 2.5)

14. Accept as input the length and width of a room (in yards). Write a program to calculate and print the cost of a rug for the room. Assume the rug costs $18 a square yard. Use a symbolic constant for the rug cost per square yard. (PA 2.7)

15. Scientists estimate that each hour spent watching "Loving Hospitals" causes ¼ cubic centimeter of the human brain to turn to oatmeal. The average human brain contains 1456 cubic centimeters. Write a program to accept as input a person's name and the number of hours that person has watched this soap opera. Calculate and print the percent of that person's brain that has turned to oatmeal. (PA 2.8)

16. Write a program to convert inches to yards, feet, and inches. For example, if the input is 94, the output should be (all on one line)

```
94 inches is 2 yards 1 feet and
   10 inches
```

17. Modify Program 3.2 (page 63) to use the PRINT USING statement to print the information for the employee in the following format:

```
Name            JoeTinker
Pay Rate        6.75
Hours Worked    40
Gross Pay       $270.00
```

18. Suppose that each cigarette smoked reduces a person's life span by 14 minutes. Write a program that accepts a person's name, the number of packs per day the person smokes, and the number of years that person has smoked. Write a program to calculate and print the number of days that person's life span has been reduced. (A pack contains 20 cigarettes.) Use a symbolic constant for the number of minutes each cigarette reduces a person's life span.

19. Accept as input a salesperson's name and sales. Write a program to calculate and print the salesperson's commission. Commission is calculated as 12% of sales. Use a symbolic constant for the commission rate.

BEYOND THE BASICS

20. If your house has a mortgage of M dollars that must be paid off in Y years, and the bank charges R annual interest rate, then the monthly payment, P, is given by

$$p = M \frac{i}{1 - (1+i)^{-n}}$$

where n is the number of monthly payments (which is equal to $12Y$) and i is the monthly interest rate (which is equal to $R/12$). Write a program to calculate your monthly payment, the total amount to be paid to the bank, and the total amount of interest to be paid. Calculate the percent of the total paid to the bank that repaid the loan, and the percent that paid the interest on the loan. Report your results in the following form:

```
Amount of mortgage      $100,000
Annual interest rate    8%
Years mortgage runs     25
Monthly payment         $ 771.82
Total paid to bank      $231,545
Total interest          $131,545
Percent to pay loan     43.2%
Percent to pay interest 56.8%
```

21. Drew Draper, interior decorator, wants to order carpet for a room. The amount of carpet must be specified in square yards, but the length and width of the room are given in terms of yards, feet, and inches. For example, the width might be 3 yards, 2 feet, 9 inches. Write a program that accepts the length and width in this form and calculates and prints the area in square yards. Your output should be in the form:

```
Length  4 yards, 1 feet, 7 inches
Width   3 yards, 2 feet, 9 inches
Area    17.73 square yards
```

REPETITION

LEARNING OBJECTIVES

After reading this chapter, you will be able to:

- Use the QBasic statements DO...LOOP, READ, DATA, and RESTORE.

- Calculate totals and averages using accumulators and counters.

- Write programs that process many cases.

- Use the QBasic function UCASE$.

- Use trailer data to end program execution.

- Use the Debug menu commands Step, Trace On, Toggle Breakpoint, Clear All Breakpoints, and Set Next Statement.

- Use the Immediate window.

- Use the Run menu commands Continue and Restart.

In the previous chapters, we wrote programs that solved one case. For example, the paycheck program calculated gross pay for only one employee. To calculate the gross pay for a different employee we would have to execute the program again. But one of the most powerful features of a computer is its ability to repeat calculations—in this example, to calculate the gross pay for *all* employees. To repeat calculations, you must learn how to program a loop: a series of statements that is executed repeatedly. You also have to learn how to exit from a loop; to do that, you must learn about conditions.

Programs that repeat calculations for many cases often calculate totals, and in this chapter, you will learn how to calculate totals and averages. You will also learn how to use the READ and DATA statements (instead of the INPUT statement) to provide data to a program. Finally, you will learn how to use the debugging commands available on the Debug and Run menus.

4.1 CONDITIONS

In the next section, you will learn how to create a loop. A **loop** is a set of statements that is executed repeatedly. Clearly, we don't want to repeat those statements forever; eventually, all the cases will be processed, and we'll need some way to exit from the loop. To exit from a loop, you use a condition, which we will study now.

> **loop**
> A set of statements that is executed repeatedly.

A **condition** is a logical expression in which two numeric or two string expressions are compared. A condition is either true or false. Although expressions can be compared, usually we compare a variable with either another variable or with a constant. Typically, conditions are written as either

> **condition**
> A logical expression in which two numeric or two string expressions are compared. A condition is either true or false.

```
variable relational-operator variable
```

or

```
variable relational-operator constant
```

Relational operators are used to compare two expressions. The relational operators that may be used in a condition are listed in the following table.

> **relational operator**
> One of the six symbols =, <, >, <=, >=, and <> used in writing conditions.

Relational Operator	Meaning
=	Equal to
<	Less than
>	Greater than
<=	Less than or equal to
>=	Greater than or equal to
<>	Not equal to

(Note that to express the last three comparisons, you must type the two symbols next to each other.) These six symbols are called relational operators because they indicate a relation (such as "less than" or "equal to").

A typical condition is

```
Total = 100
```

A condition is read as a question and is either true or false. The condition Total = 100 is read, "Is Total equal to 100?" Only when Total is equal to 100 is the condition true; otherwise, the condition is false. Notice that the condition Total = 100 is very different from the LET statement Total = 100. In a LET statement, you *tell* the computer to assign 100 to Total. In a condition, you *ask* the computer to determine if Total is equal to 100.

Some other conditions are examined below.

Condition	Explanation
`GPA > 3.0`	True if GPA is greater than 3.0, false otherwise
`MPH < 55`	True if MPH is less than 55, false otherwise
`Age >= 21`	True if Age is greater than or equal to 21, false otherwise
`Sales <= 1000`	True if Sales is less than or equal to 1000, false otherwise
`Length <> 1`	True if Length is not equal to 1, false otherwise

Using String Variables in Conditions

As we said earlier, string expressions may also be compared in conditions. The meaning of the condition

```
Response$ = "N"
```

is easily understood. The condition is true if the variable Response$ contains the string N; false otherwise. But the conditions U$ < V$ and R$ > S$ are also legal, and the meaning of these conditions is not as obvious. What does it mean to say one string is "more" or "less" than another?

Strings are compared according to their **ASCII codes,** which is the code used by the computer to store data. (ASCII stands for American Standard Code for Information Interchange.) In the ASCII code, each character is associated with a numeric value; strings are compared according to their numeric values. The ASCII codes are shown in Appendix B. For example, the table in Appendix B shows that the ASCII code of a space is 32, that of the digit 1 is 49, that of the letter A is 65, and that of the letter a is 97. Therefore, a space is less than the digit 1, which in turn is less than the letter A, which is less than the letter a. Digits have lower ASCII values than capital letters, which have lower values than lower case letters.

ASCII code
American Standard Code for Information Interchange. The code used to store data in the computer.

QBasic compares strings from left to right, taking one character at a time from each string and comparing their ASCII values. If the values are unequal, the string containing the character with the lower value is considered to be less than the other string, and the comparison is finished. If the values are equal, the next pair of characters is compared, and so on. If all the characters are equal in value, the strings are considered to be equal. However, if the end of one string is reached before the end of the other string, and all values up to that point are equal, QBasic considers the longer string to be greater than the shorter string. The following examples illustrate this point.

Condition	Explanation
`"ANDERSON" < "BAKER"`	A has a lower ASCII code than B
`"7 Oak Street"↵` `  < "Five Fifth Avenue"`	7 has a lower ASCII code than F
`"no" > "NO"`	n has a higher ASCII code than N
`"Zen"< "apples"`	Z has a lower ASCII code than a
`"YES " > "YES"`	The first three characters of both strings are equal, and the space at the end of "YES " makes "YES " greater than "YES"

Notice that the number of characters in a string is significant only if the two strings are equal through the length of the smaller string. So, even though Anderson has more characters than Baker, Anderson is less than Baker because A has a lower ASCII code than B.

4.1 EXERCISES

1. Assume that A = 6, B = 19, and C = 19. Which of the following conditions are true and which are false?
   a) `A > C`
   ★**b)** `B > C`
   c) `C <= B`
   d) `B <> C`

2. Assume that W$ = "NO", X$ = "no", Y$ = "Sixteen Hundred Pennsylvania Avenue", and Z$ = "1600 Pennsylvania Avenue". Which of the following conditions are true and which are false?
   ★**a)** `W$ = X$`
   b) `W$ < X$`
   c) `Y$ <> Z$`
   ★**d)** `Y$ >= Z$`

3. Use the ASCII table in Appendix B to put the following characters in ascending order: x, 1, P, $, =.

4.2 THE DO...LOOP STATEMENT

As we mentioned earlier, loops repeat a set of statements. One way to create a loop in QBasic is to use the DO statement and the LOOP statement. The DO and LOOP statements are *always* used together. The DO statement indicates the top of the loop, and the LOOP statement indicates the bottom of the loop. Coding a DO statement without a LOOP statement, or a LOOP statement without a DO statement, causes a run-time error.

DO WHILE Loops

The DO and LOOP statements can be written in several ways. One common way is shown below:

```
DO WHILE condition
   .
   .
   statement(s)
   .
   .
LOOP
```

This coding creates what is called a DO WHILE loop. The easiest way to understand the DO WHILE loop is to examine the flowchart in Figure 4.1(a). The loop is shown by the flowline that returns to the circle. This flowchart also shows a decision symbol, which is shaped like a diamond. Inside the decision symbol, we write a condition. Figure 4.1(a) shows two flowlines, or branches, leaving the

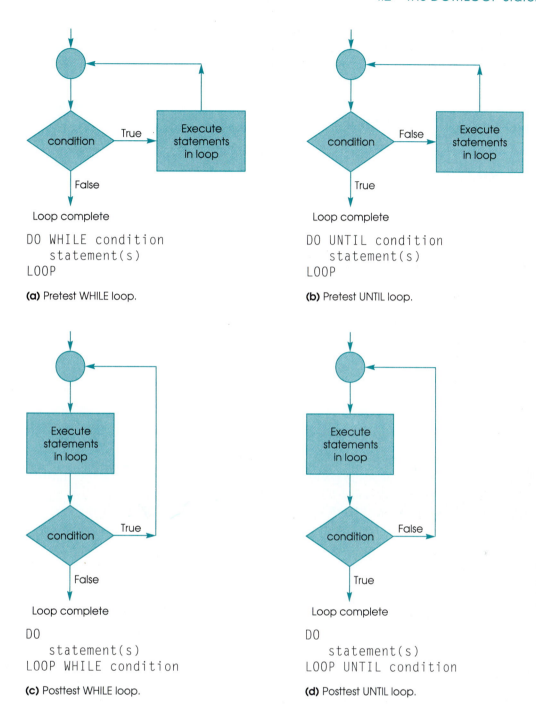

```
DO WHILE condition
    statement(s)
LOOP
```

(a) Pretest WHILE loop.

```
DO UNTIL condition
    statement(s)
LOOP
```

(b) Pretest UNTIL loop.

```
DO
    statement(s)
LOOP WHILE condition
```

(c) Posttest WHILE loop.

```
DO
    statement(s)
LOOP UNTIL condition
```

(d) Posttest UNTIL loop.

FIGURE 4.1   The four ways to write DO loops.

decision symbol. One of the branches is labeled "True," the other "False." If the condition is true, we leave the decision symbol along the true branch. If the condition is false, we leave the decision symbol along the false branch.

If the condition is true, the statements in the loop are executed, and the condition is tested again. If the condition is still true, the statements in the loop are executed again. If the program was written correctly, eventually the condition becomes false, and instead of executing the statements in the loop, the program branches to the statement following the LOOP statement.

Figure 4.1(a) shows that the condition is tested *before* the statements in the loop are executed. A loop in which the condition is tested before the loop is executed is called a **pretest loop**. Because the condition is coded using the word WHILE, this loop is called a pretest WHILE loop.

As an example, the following program uses a pretest WHILE loop to print the numbers 1, 2, and 3, and then print We're finished.

```
N = 1
DO  WHILE N <= 3
      PRINT N
      N = N + 1
LOOP
PRINT "We're finished"
```

Figure 4.2 traces the execution of this program. Each program statement is listed on the left in the order of its execution. The value of N after the statement is executed is shown in the next column, and the effect of the statement is shown on the right.

The first statement

```
N = 1
```

assigns 1 to N. The next statement

```
DO WHILE N <= 3
```

marks the top of the loop. Because N is less than 3, the condition is true and the loop is entered. Then the statement

```
PRINT N
```

displays 1. The next statement

```
N = N + 1
```

is different from other LET statements we have seen because N appears on both sides of the equals sign. To understand this statement, remember that when it is executed, the expression on the right is evaluated first, and then the number that was calculated is assigned to the variable on the left. In this case, when the expression N + 1 is evaluated, it yields 1 + 1 = 2. Then 2 is assigned to N.

> **pretest loop**
> A loop in which the condition is tested before the statements in the loop are executed. In QBasic, such loops are coded by including a condition on the DO statement.

Statement	N	Effect
Initial values	0	Assigned by QBasic
N = 1	1	Assigns 1 to N
DO WHILE N <= 3		Condition is true; executes loop
PRINT N		Prints 1
N = N + 1	2	Assigns 1 + 1 = 2 to N
LOOP		Branches back to the DO statement
DO WHILE N <= 3		Condition is true; executes loop
PRINT N		Prints 2
N = N + 1	3	Assigns 2 + 1 = 3 to N
LOOP		Branches back to the DO statement
DO WHILE N <= 3		Condition is true; executes loop
PRINT N		Prints 3
N = N + 1	4	Assigns 3 + 1 = 4 to N
LOOP		Branches back to the DO statement
DO WHILE N <= 3		Condition is false; exits loop
PRINT "We're finished"		Prints "We're finished"

FIGURE 4.2   Tracing a DO WHILE loop.

In this statement, the variable N is used as a counter. A **counter** is a variable that counts the number of times some action is performed. In our example, N counts the number of times that the loop is executed. The LET statement for a counter is always

```
counter = counter + increment
```

In the LET statement for a counter, the counter appears on both sides of the equals sign. Each time this statement is executed, the value of counter increases by the value of increment. Most often, as in our example, the increment is 1.

Returning to our example, the next statement

```
LOOP
```

marks the end of the loop, and returns control to the DO statement at the top of the loop.

You can follow the rest of the execution in Figure 4.2 on your own. Eventually, N becomes 4, and the condition on the DO statement

```
N <= 3
```

is false. Control is then transferred to the statement that follows the LOOP statement:

```
PRINT "We're finished"
```

This program illustrates the features that are common to all programs using the DO and LOOP statements to create loops. The variable that is tested in the condition is given an initial value before the DO statement is executed. Somewhere in the loop, usually the last statement, that variable changes. Eventually, the change causes the condition to become false, and the loop is exited.

If the condition in a pretest WHILE loop is false the first time the DO statement is executed, the statements in the loop will not be executed at all. Sometimes, that is exactly what you want. Consider the next example:

```
INPUT "Enter a number less than 100: ", Number
DO WHILE Number >= 100
    PRINT "The number must be less than 100"
    INPUT "Enter a number less than 100: ", Number
LOOP
```

If the user follows the instructions and enters a number less than 100, the condition Number >= 100 is false, and the statements in the loop are not executed. However, if the user does not follow the instructions and enters a number that is not less than 100, the condition is true, and the program enters the loop and prints the message

```
The number must be less than 100
```

and requests input again. The program stays in the loop until the user enters a number less than 100. This is one way to ensure that before the program continues, the user enters a valid value for Number.

Notice in these examples that the statements between DO and LOOP are indented. QBasic doesn't require this indention, but the indention helps show the loop more clearly and makes the program easier to read. This convention is used in all the programs in this book, and you should follow the same convention in your own programs. To indent a statement, just press the Tab key before you start typing the statement.

If a line was indented, QBasic maintains the same indention on the next line after you press the Enter key. This means that to get uniform indention, you must press the Tab key only once. After you type the last line that you want indented and press the Enter key, press the Backspace key to move the cursor back one level of indention.

counter
A variable that is used to keep track of some number, such as the number of times that a loop is executed.

DO UNTIL Loops

It is also possible to write the DO statement using the word UNTIL:

```
DO UNTIL condition
    .
    .
    statement(s)
    .
    .
LOOP
```

This kind of loop is called a DO UNTIL loop or a pretest UNTIL loop. Figure 4.1(b) on page 91 is a flowchart for a pretest UNTIL loop. It shows that in a pretest UNTIL loop, the statements in the loop are executed until the condition becomes true. Figures 4.1(a) and (b) show that the only difference between a WHILE and an UNTIL loop is that in the WHILE loop, the loop is executed *while* the condition is true; in the UNTIL loop, the loop is executed *until* the condition becomes true.

You can always convert from a WHILE to an UNTIL loop simply by coding the negative of the relational operator. The negatives of the six relational operators are shown in the following table.

Relational Operator	Negative Relational Operator
>	<=
<	>=
=	<>
<=	>
>=	<
<>	=

Since the negative of <= is >, the example we studied on page 92 could be written as

```
N = 1
DO  UNTIL N > 3
      PRINT N
      N = N + 1
LOOP
PRINT "We're finished"
```

When you are deciding whether to use a WHILE or an UNTIL loop, you should choose the one that is clearer. In these examples, it doesn't matter whether the loop is continued WHILE N <= 3 or UNTIL N > 3—but in other problems, one construction may be preferable.

Conditions on the LOOP Statement

Another variation of the DO loop puts the condition on the LOOP statement. You can code WHILE on the LOOP statement:

```
DO
    .
    .
    statement(s)
    .
    .
LOOP WHILE condition
```

or you can code UNTIL on the LOOP statement:

```
DO
      .
      .
      statement(s)
      .
      .
LOOP UNTIL condition
```

The flowcharts for these loops are shown in Figure 4.1(c) and (d) on page 91. In these flowcharts, the circles represent the DO statement at the top of the loop. Both flowcharts show that the statements in the loop are executed first, and then the condition is tested. Because the condition is tested *after* the loop is executed, this kind of loop is called a **posttest loop**.

The examples we studied earlier could use a posttest loop as follows:

```
N = 1
DO
      PRINT N
      N = N + 1
LOOP WHILE N <= 3
PRINT "We're finished"
```

We could get the same output by changing the LOOP statement to

```
LOOP UNTIL N > 3
```

One major difference between pretest and posttest loops is that posttest loops are executed at least once. As you saw earlier, and as the illustrations show, a pretest loop may not be executed at all.

posttest loop
A loop in which the condition is tested after the statements in the loop are executed. In QBasic, such loops are coded by including a condition on the LOOP statement.

ILLUSTRATIONS

Pretest WHILE Loop
```
A = 1
DO WHILE A < 5
     PRINT "Go Team"
     A = A + 1
LOOP
```
Effect
Go Team is printed 4 times: when A is equal to 1, 2, 3, and 4. When A is 5, the condition is false, and QBasic branches to the statement following LOOP.

Pretest UNTIL Loop
```
A = 1
DO UNTIL A < 5
     PRINT "Go Team"
     A = A + 1
LOOP
```
Effect
Go Team is not printed at all. When the DO statement is executed, A is 1, so the condition is true; QBasic branches to the statement following LOOP.

Posttest WHILE Loop
```
A = 5
DO
     PRINT "Go Team"
     A = A + 1
LOOP WHILE A < 5
```
Effect
Go Team is printed once. When the LOOP statement is executed, A is 6, so the condition is false; QBasic branches to the statement following LOOP.

(continued)

Posttest UNTIL Loop	Effect

``
A = 1
DO
    PRINT "Go Team"
    A = A + 1
LOOP UNTIL A >= 5
``
	Go Team is printed 4 times: when A is equal to 1, 2, 3, and 4. When A is 5, the condition is true, and QBasic branches to the statement following LOOP.

Pretest WHILE Loop	**Effect**
``` A = 1 DO WHILE A < 5 PRINT "Go Team" LOOP ```	Go Team is printed forever because there are no statements inside the loop that will make the condition become false. A loop that doesn't stop is called an **endless loop**.

endless loop
A loop that doesn't stop executing.

This last example illustrates an important point. It is the programmer's responsibility to make sure that the loop eventually terminates. If you make a logic error so that the loop never ends, you can break execution by holding down the Ctrl key and pressing the Break key on the upper right side of the keyboard.

EXAMPLE 1

USING A DO LOOP TO CALCULATE PAY FOR MORE THAN ONE EMPLOYEE

Let's put what you have learned about DO loops to use by writing a program that calculates the paychecks for several employees.

Problem Statement

Modify Program 3.2 (page 63) to calculate and print the gross pay for the three employees of the Bat-O Boat Company. Their pay rates and hours worked last week are as follows.

Employee Name	Pay Rate	Hours Worked
Joe Tinker	6.75	40
Joan Evers	6.00	30
Frank Chance	5.75	25

STEP 1 **Variable Names**

Following our structured procedure, you first identify the variables in the problem and select names for them. In addition to the variables used in Program 3.2, this problem uses a variable for the user's response when we ask if there are more employees to process.

In this and future problems, we will indicate which variables are input variables and which are output variables. The input variables are the variables whose values we know in advance. Input variables are given values, for example, with INPUT statements. The output variables are the variables whose values we do not know, and which the program is supposed to calculate. The variable names then look like the following:

Variable	Variable Name
Input Variables	
Employee's name	EmpName$
Pay rate	PayRate
Hours worked	Hours
User's response	Response$
Output Variable	
Gross pay	GrossPay

Although each employee has a different name, we define only one Emp-Name$, which is used for all three employees. Similarly, we define only one PayRate, one Hours, and one GrossPay. You will see how Response$ is used when we examine the program.

STEP 2   Algorithm

The second step is to develop an algorithm. The algorithm for this problem is similar to that used in Chapter 3.

1. Print headings.
2. Execute steps 3 through 5 for each employee.
3.   Input values for EmpName$, PayRate, and Hours for an employee.
4.   Calculate GrossPay by multiplying PayRate by Hours.
5.   Print EmpName$, PayRate, Hours, and GrossPay.

A flowchart illustrating this algorithm is shown in Figure 4.3. If you compare this flowchart with Figure 4.1 (page 91), you will recognize that the loop from symbols 21 to 28 is a posttest UNTIL loop. Notice the input/output symbol 14–18, which contains the statement "Print Headings." Print Headings is not a legal QBasic statement. We are just reminding ourselves to print the headings at that point in the flowchart. We don't put all the details in a flowchart because that makes the flowchart more complex and less useful. Notice also that symbol 14–18 is outside the loop because we want to print headings only once. In input/output symbol 27, we ask the user if there are more employees to process. When the user enters N, the program stops.

This flowchart shows the structure that is found in many computer programs:

1. *Input step*: Get the data for a case. (A case might be an employee, an inventory item, and so on.)
2. *Process step*: Calculate the answer for the case.
3. *Output step*: Print the answer for the case.

The three steps are repeated for all the cases of interest.

STEP 3   Hand-Calculated Answer

Next, calculate an answer by hand. For employee number 1 (Joe Tinker), Gross-Pay is 6.75 × 40 = 270. That's all you have to do. You do not need to calculate GrossPay for the other two employees. If the computer's answer agrees with your hand-calculated answer for one employee, you can assume that the program is correct and need not check the answers for the other employees.

Now you can see why computers are useful for problem solving, even though it is necessary to calculate a sample answer by hand. If you can prove that a program is correct for one case, you can then use that program to calculate two, two thousand, or even two million additional cases and be confident that the answers for these additional cases are correct. (In Chapter 5, you will learn that in more complicated problems, it is necessary to check more than one case. But the

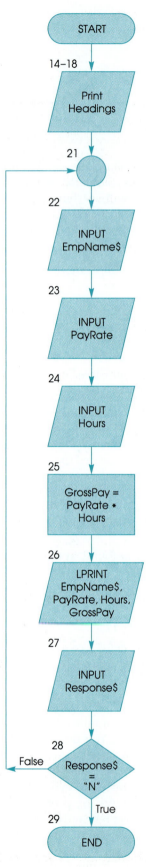

FIGURE 4.3   Flowchart for payroll with more than one employee using a posttest UNTIL loop.

basic idea remains the same: You prove that a program is correct by checking a limited number of cases, and then use that program to calculate many additional cases.)

STEP 4   QBasic Program

The next step of our structured procedure is to write a QBasic program. Program 4.1 shows a program based on the flowchart in Figure 4.3. The DO and LOOP statements in lines 21 and 28 create a posttest UNTIL loop that executes until the condition in line 28 becomes true.

The Output screen shows the user entering the data for the three employees. In addition, the user entered Y the first two times that the question Any more employees (Y/N)? was asked, and N the third time it was asked. Entering N caused the program to stop executing, just as it was supposed to.

In addition to the headings, the printed output contains one line for each employee. Such lines are called **detail lines**. The detail line for Joe Tinker shows that his gross pay is $270.00. Since this agrees with the hand-calculated answer, we conclude that the program is correct.

detail line
A line that is printed for each case or record processed.

The UCASE$ Function.   As we saw, the program exits from the loop when the user enters N in response to the INPUT statement in line 27:

```
INPUT "Any more employees (Y/N)"; Response$
```

This INPUT statement uses a semicolon to separate the prompt from the variable. The semicolon causes QBasic to add a question mark and a space when it displays the prompt, as you can see in Program 4.1's Output screen.

In string comparisons, upper and lower case letters are different. That is, N and n are different, so if the condition on line 28 were

```
LOOP UNTIL Response$ = "N"
```

and the user entered n instead of N, the condition would not be true, and the loop would continue. However, we want our program to be user-friendly and exit from the loop even if the user mistakenly enters n instead of N. The condition on line 28

```
LOOP UNTIL UCASE$(Response$) = "N"
```

uses the QBasic function UCASE$ to accomplish this.

The syntax of the UCASE$ function is

```
UCASE$(string)
```

where the argument, string, may be string data or a string variable. The UCASE$ function returns a string in which all the lower case letters of its argument are converted to upper case. UCASE$ has no effect on upper case letters, digits, or punctuation marks. So for example,

```
UCASE$(july 4, 1776)
```

returns JULY 4, 1776.

Now you can understand how the UCASE$ function in Program 4.1 works. Even if a user enters n for Response$, UCASE$(Response$) returns N, the condition in line 28 is true, and the program stops executing.

Tracing the Program

Now that you know the program works, let's trace it and see *how* it works. Figure 4.4 shows a trace of the program, assuming that the user enters the data shown in Program 4.1. As usual, each statement is shown in the left column in the order

```
 1 |  '     *** BAT-O PROGRAM ***
 2 |  '     Calculate gross pay for all employees
 3 |
 4 |  '     Variables used
 5 |
 6 |  '     EmpName$          Employee's name
 7 |  '     GrossPay          Gross pay
 8 |  '     Hours             Hours worked
 9 |  '     PayRate           Hourly pay rate
10 |  '     Response$         User's response to continue; Y or N
11 |
12 |  CLS
13 |  ' Print heading and define format string
14 |      LPRINT "                    Payroll Report"
15 |      LPRINT
16 |      LPRINT "                              Pay                 Gross"
17 |      LPRINT "   Name                       Rate     Hours       Pay"
18 |  Format$ = "\                    \    ##.##       ##     $###.##"
19 |
20 |  ' Process employees
21 |  DO
22 |      INPUT "Enter Name: ", EmpName$
23 |      INPUT "Enter Pay Rate: ", PayRate
24 |      INPUT "Enter Hours Worked: ", Hours
25 |      GrossPay = PayRate * Hours
26 |      LPRINT USING Format$; EmpName$; PayRate; Hours; GrossPay
27 |      INPUT "Any more employees (Y/N)"; Response$
28 |  LOOP UNTIL UCASE$(Response$) = "N"
29 |  END
```

```
Enter Name: Joe Tinker ⎫
Enter Pay Rate: 6.75    ⎬ ◄── Data entered for first employee
Enter Hours Worked: 40 ⎭
Any more employees (Y/N)? Y ◄── Continue
Enter Name: Joan Evers ⎫
Enter Pay Rate: 6        ⎬ ◄── Data entered for second employee
Enter Hours Worked: 30 ⎭
Any more employees (Y/N)? Y ◄── Continue
Enter Name: Frank Chance ⎫
Enter Pay Rate: 5.75     ⎬ ◄── Data entered for third employee
Enter Hours Worked: 25 ⎭
Any more employees (Y/N)? N ◄── Stop
```

```
                  Payroll Report

                          Pay              Gross
   Name                   Rate    Hours      Pay
Joe Tinker                6.75      40    $270.00
Joan Evers                6.00      30    $180.00
Frank Chance              5.75      25    $143.75
```

PROGRAM 4.1   Using a DO...LOOP UNTIL loop to calculate pay for more than one employee.

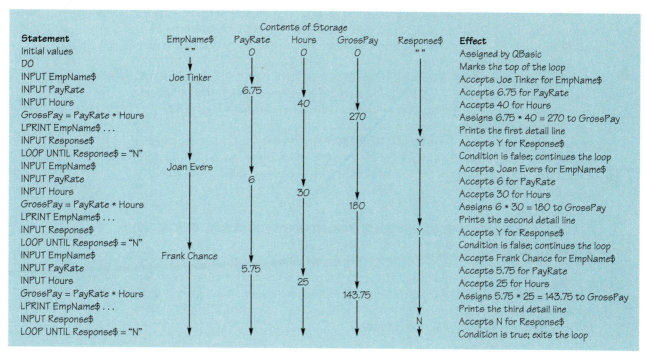

FIGURE 4.4   Tracing Program 4.1.

that it is executed. The next columns show the contents of storage after the statement is executed, and the column on the right explains the effect of the statement. The statements that clear the screen and print the headings are not shown.

The statement in line 21 of Program 4.1

```
DO
```

marks the top of the loop. The statement in line 22

```
INPUT "Enter Name: ", EmpName$
```

accepts Joe Tinker for EmpName$. The next statement

```
INPUT "Enter Pay Rate: ", PayRate
```

accepts 6.75 for PayRate, and the statement after that

```
INPUT "Enter Hours Worked: ", Hours
```

accepts 40 for Hours. When the LET statement in line 25

```
GrossPay = PayRate * Hours
```

is executed, it multiplies 6.75 by 40 and assigns the result, 270, to GrossPay. The LPRINT statement

```
LPRINT USING Format$; EmpName$; PayRate; Hours; GrossPay
```

prints the values of EmpName$, PayRate, Hours, and GrossPay, giving the first detail line shown in Program 4.1. The statement in line 27

```
INPUT "Any more employees (Y/N)"; Response$
```

accepts Y for Response$. The condition in line 28

```
LOOP UNTIL UCASE$(Response$) = "N"
```

is false, so the program returns to the DO statement in line 21.

The three INPUT statements in lines 22, 23, and 24 then accept Joan Evers for EmpName$, 6 for PayRate, and 30 for Hours. Remember that the storage locations can hold only one value at a time. So when these values are put in the storage locations, the old values are erased.

Now when the LET statement in line 25 is executed, it multiplies 6 by 30 and assigns 180 to GrossPay. The LPRINT statement produces the second detail line shown in Program 4.1. You can follow the rest of the execution in Figure 4.4.

We developed this program to calculate and print gross pay for three employees. It should be clear that this program could be used for any number of employees. You need only enter Y for Response$ and values for name, pay rate, and hours for each employee; the program will keep calculating and printing gross pay. ∎

EXAMPLE 2

USING TRAILER DATA TO STOP EXECUTION

Asking the user if more cases need to be processed is not the only way to control execution of a loop. Another way is to enter imaginary data after all the real data are entered and have the program stop when it encounters this imaginary data. Because these imaginary data are entered after all the real data, they are called **trailer data** (or sometimes, **sentinel values**).

trailer data or sentinel value
Extra data entered after all the real data to indicate that all the real data were entered.

Problem Statement

Write a program that accepts values of deposit into a bank account, the interest rate the bank pays, and the number of years the account is held; it should then calculate and print the final balance in the account. This is the same problem we solved in Program 2.7 (page 47) except that this program should process as many sets of data as we want.

STEP 1 Variable Names

This program uses the same variables as Program 2.7, so we can also use the same variable names.

Variable	Variable Name
Input Variables	
Amount deposited	Deposit
Interest rate	Rate
Number of years held	Years
Output Variable	
Balance in the account	Balance

STEP 2 Algorithm

Balance can be calculated by using the compound interest formula

```
Balance = Deposit * (1 + Rate) ^ Years
```

We want to use trailer data to stop execution. Trailer data must be so peculiar—so wildly outside of possibility—that the program cannot mistake them for real data. For instance, a real Deposit could never be 0, so 0 is a good choice for the trailer data.

The algorithm is then:

1. Execute steps 2 through 4 until the trailer data is entered.
2. Accept values for Deposit, Rate, and Years.
3. Calculate Balance using the compound interest formula.
4. Print Deposit, Rate, Years, and Balance.

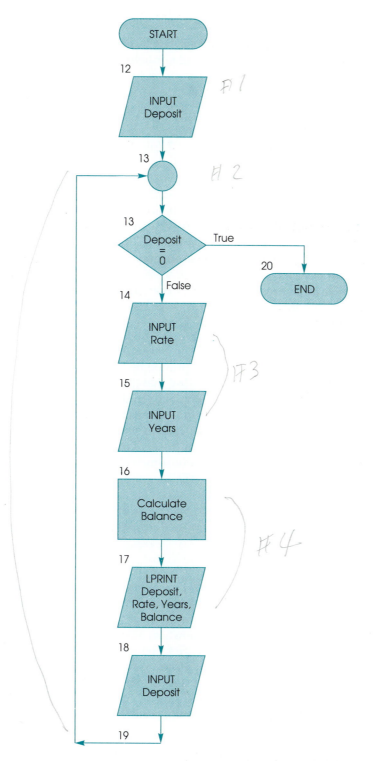

FIGURE 4.5   Flowchart for compound interest that uses a pretest UNTIL loop with trailer data to stop execution.

Figure 4.5 shows the flowchart for this algorithm that uses a pretest UNTIL loop and trailer data to control execution of the loop. The reason we input Deposit twice, in I/O symbols 12 and 18, is explained later when we examine the program.

STEP 3   **Hand-Calculated Answer**

We could use the same input values we used in Chapter 2, but instead, let's use $10,000 for Deposit, .06 for Rate, and 50 for Years. A calculator helps us figure a Balance of $184,201.54.

STEP 4   **QBasic Program**

The program based on this algorithm is shown in Program 4.2. Like the flowchart, the program contains two INPUT statements for Deposit (lines 12 and 18). The INPUT statement in line 12 accepts just the first value of Deposit, so we will have a value of Deposit to test in line 13. Despite the fact that it is an INPUT statement, it is called the **priming read**. The INPUT statement in line 18 accepts the second and all subsequent values of Deposit. This INPUT statement also eventually accepts the trailer data, 0. The trailer data makes the condition in the DO statement true, causing the program to exit the loop and stop executing.

Programs that use trailer data are more convenient for users than programs like Program 4.1 (page 100), which ask users if they want to continue. With trailer data, users have to indicate only once that they want to stop, rather than indicating after each case that they want to continue.

> **priming read**
> The INPUT statement that accepts the first value. It is coded before the start of the loop.

Round-Off Errors.   If you compare the value of Balance printed by the program (184201.5) against the exact answer (184201.54), you will find that the two do not exactly agree. This small difference does not reflect a logic error in the program. Rather, the difference is due to a round-off error. **Round-off errors** are small numeric errors that sometimes occur in computer-calculated answers.

Round-off errors happen because the storage locations that QBasic sets up to store the values of variables can hold only seven digits. But some values require more digits to represent them. For instance, $\frac{1}{3} = .333333333 \ldots$, and the 3s keep going forever. So there is no way to store $\frac{1}{3}$ exactly.[1]

Often, round-off errors have no detectable effect on the final answers. However, sometimes (as in this case), they result in a small error. Notice that the error in this case is only 4 cents in more than $184,000.

> **round-off errors**
> A small numerical error that sometimes occurs in a computer-calculated answer because of the way the computer stores numbers.

Values Printed in Scientific Notation.   The second line of output in Program 4.2 shows the answers calculated when the input data are changed to Deposit = 100000, Interest = .2 (20 percent), and Years = 50. As you can see, the value of Balance is printed as 9.100439E+08. This form of output, known as **scientific notation**, is used when a variable has a value that is too large to be represented in seven digits. The portion after the E tells us how many places to move the decimal point and whether to move it to the left (when the sign is minus) or to the right (when the sign is plus). In this case, the E+08 tells us that to get the value represented by this number, we must shift the decimal point eight places to the right. If you shift the decimal point eight places to the right, you get 910,043,900, which is the value of Balance.

Scientific notation is also used for very small numbers. Suppose a variable has the value 0.000013596426. This value prints as 1.359643E-05. The E-05 tells us that to get the value represented by this number, we must shift the decimal point five places to the left. If you shift the decimal point five places to the left, you get

> **scientific notation**
> A method of printing very large and very small numbers.

---

[1] QBasic can also store values in "double precision" form, in which 17 digits are stored. This method of storage reduces the size of the round-off error, but slows execution. Double precision is discussed further in Chapter 9.

```
 1 | '    *** LOANSOME BANK PROBLEM ***
 2 | '    Calculate compound interest
 3 |
 4 | '    Variables used
 5 |
 6 | '    Balance          Balance in the Account
 7 | '    Deposit          Amount deposited
 8 | '    Rate             Interest rate
 9 | '    Years            Number of years
10 |
11 | CLS
12 | INPUT "Enter deposit, 0 to stop: ", Deposit
13 | DO UNTIL Deposit = 0
14 |     INPUT "Enter rate, decimal: ", Rate
15 |     INPUT "Enter number of years: ", Years
16 |     Balance = Deposit * (1 + Rate) ^ Years
17 |     LPRINT Deposit, Rate, Years, Balance
18 |     INPUT "Enter deposit, 0 to stop: ", Deposit
19 | LOOP
20 | END
```

(handwritten annotations: "condition for sentinel value" pointing to lines 8–9; "#1" by line 12; "#2" by line 13; "#3" by lines 14–15; "#4" by lines 16–17; "#5" by line 18)

```
Enter deposit, 0 to stop: 10000
Enter rate, decimal: .06
Enter number of years: 50
Enter deposit, 0 to stop: 100000
Enter rate, decimal: .20
Enter number of years: 50
Enter deposit, 0 to stop: 0
```

(handwritten annotations: "#12" by first line; "#18" by fourth line)

10000	.06	50	184201.5
100000	.2	50	9.100439E+08

(annotations: "Answer with round-off error" pointing to 184201.5; "Value printed using scientific notation" pointing to 9.100439E+08)

PROGRAM 4.2   A program that uses a pretest UNTIL loop and trailer data to stop execution.

0.00001359643, which is the original value rounded to seven digits. You can avoid having your answers printed in scientific notation if you use a PRINT USING statement to print your answers. In fact, the only reason a PRINT USING statement was not included in Program 4.2, was to show you a value printed in scientific notation.

It is also possible to use scientific notation to define constants. For example, if you want A to equal one million, you could code

```
A = 1E+06
```

DO Loops Reexamined

DO loops are the most complicated construction we have discussed so far, so it is worthwhile to examine them again. Many beginners mistakenly believe that each time any statement in the loop is executed, the condition is checked. That is wrong! As the flowcharts in Figure 4.1 (page 91) show, the condition is checked only at the top or bottom of the loop—depending on the type of loop used.

Because the condition is checked only at the top or bottom of the loop, the statement that affects the condition is almost always the last statement in the loop. For example, in Program 4.1 (page 100), the variable Response$ is tested in the condition, and the INPUT statement for Response$ is the last in the loop.

Similarly, in Program 4.2, Deposit is tested in the condition, and the INPUT statement for Deposit is the last in the loop.

Using Strings as Trailer Data

When a program uses a string variable, we can use string data as trailer data. For example, in Program 4.1, we could use trailer data for EmpName$. In that case, we must use as trailer data a string that couldn't possibly be an employee's name. Often, the strings EOD (End of Data) and EOF (End of File) are used.

If we used trailer data in Program 4.1, we would replace the DO loop in lines 21 through 28 with the following statements:

```
INPUT "Enter Name, EOD to stop: ", EmpName$
DO UNTIL UCASE$(EmpName$) = "EOD"
    INPUT "Enter Pay Rate: ", PayRate
    INPUT "Enter Hours Worked: ", Hours
    GrossPay = PayRate * Hours
    LPRINT USING Format$; EmpName$; PayRate; Hours; GrossPay
    INPUT "Enter Name, EOD to stop: ", EmpName$
LOOP
```

Choosing the Type of Loop

As mentioned earlier, for most problems, you can use any of the four DO loops. For example, to use a posttest UNTIL loop in Program 4.2, you would simply change line 13 to

```
DO
```

and line 19 to

```
LOOP UNTIL Deposit = 0
```

You would still need the two INPUT statements for Deposit in lines 12 and 18.

From the user's point of view, only one difference exists between Program 4.2 (which uses a pretest UNTIL loop) and this modification (which uses a posttest UNTIL loop). With Program 4.2, if the user enters 0 (the trailer data) at the first prompt for Deposit, the program ends. With a posttest UNTIL loop, even if the user enters 0 at the first prompt for Deposit, the loop is executed. The user still has to enter values for Rate and Years, a meaningless Balance is calculated in line 16 and printed in line 17, and the user has to enter 0 again in response to the INPUT statement in line 18. Eliminating unnecessary work is one reason why pretest loops are often more desirable to use than posttest loops with trailer data.

If you know that the statements in the loop must be executed at least once, then the posttest loop is acceptable. Program 4.5, later in this chapter (page 125), is an example of such a situation.

Syntax Summary

DO and LOOP Statements

Form:
```
DO [{WHILE | UNTIL} condition]
        .
    statement(s)
        .
    LOOP
```
or

```
          DO
             .
            statement(s)
             .
          LOOP [{WHILE | UNTIL} condition]
Example:  N = 1
          DO WHILE N <= 10
             PRINT N
             N = N + 1
          LOOP
```

Explanation: If the condition is coded on the DO statement, it is checked *before* the loop is executed; if the condition is coded on the LOOP statement, it is checked *after* the loop is executed. If WHILE is used, the loop is executed *while* the condition is true; if UNTIL is used, the loop is executed *until* the condition becomes true. The square brackets show that WHILE and UNTIL may be omitted. If they are omitted, some other method must be used to exit from the loop. All of our examples will use either WHILE or UNTIL.

4.2 EXERCISES

1. Suppose that Program 4.2 (page 105) were run with 25 sets of data (in addition to the trailer data). How many times would line 12 be executed? How many times would line 18 be executed?

2. Show how you would modify Program 4.2 to use a DO WHILE loop.

3. How many times is Hello printed by the following programs?

   ★a)
   ```
   A = 10
   DO WHILE A < 10
        PRINT "Hello"
        A = A + 1
   LOOP
   END
   ```

   Modify the DO statement to print Hello just once.

   ★b)
   ```
   A = 10
   DO WHILE A >= 10
        PRINT "Hello"
        A = A + 1
   LOOP
   END
   ```

   c)
   ```
   A = 10
   DO UNTIL >= 10
        PRINT "Hello"
        A = A + 1
   LOOP
   END
   ```

d)
```
B = 1
DO
    PRINT "Hello"
    B = B + 1
LOOP UNTIL B > 5
END
```

e)
```
B = 1
DO
    PRINT "Hello"
    B = B + 1
LOOP WHILE B > 5
END
```

4. How many times is Goodbye printed by the following programs?

a)
```
B = 1
DO WHILE B < 5
    PRINT "Goodbye"
LOOP
END
```

Modify the program to print Goodbye five times.

★b)
```
B = 1
DO UNTIL B < 5
    PRINT "Goodbye"
LOOP
END
```

Modify the program to print Goodbye five times.

★5. What output is produced by the following program?

```
M = 2
DO WHILE M < 50
    M = 2 * M
    PRINT M
LOOP
END
```

6. Trace Program 4.1 (page 100) to determine what output is produced if the following changes are made. Before making each change, assume that the program is restored to its original form.
   ★a) The DO and LOOP statements are eliminated.
   b) The INPUT statement in line 27 is moved to between lines 21 and 22.
   c) The INPUT statement in line 27 is moved to between lines 28 and 29.

★7. In Program 4.1, what would happen if we entered the first name as Tinker, Joe?

8. What value is assigned to M$ by the LET statement

```
M$ = UCASE$("apple")
```

9. A companion function to UCASE$ is LCASE$, which converts its string argument to lower case. How would you change line 28 in Program 4.1 to use LCASE$ instead of UCASE$?

10. A student objects to writing the INPUT statement for Deposit twice, so he wrote his version of Program 4.2 (page 105) as follows:

```
DO UNTIL Deposit = 0
    INPUT "Enter deposit, 0 to stop: ", Deposit
    INPUT "Enter rate, decimal: ", Rate
    INPUT "Enter number of years: ", Years
    Balance = Deposit * (1 + Rate) ^ Years
    LPRINT Deposit, Rate, Years, Balance
LOOP
```

Trace this program to determine the output when the following three sets of data are used: 10000, .06, 50; 100000, .20, 50; 0, 0, 0.

11. What is the value of a number that is printed as 1.43826E+08? Of one that is printed as 6.03498E-04?

4.3 THE READ AND DATA STATEMENT

In Program 4.1, we entered the name, pay rate, and hours worked for each employee. But an employee's name rarely changes and if his or her pay rate doesn't change from one week to the next (that is, if the only change is in the hours worked), it is a nuisance to enter these data every time you run the program. In this section, we will discuss how you can use the READ and DATA statements so that when the program is run, you just have to input the hours worked. We will also calculate total gross pay and average gross pay.

EXAMPLE 3
PAYROLL AND TOTALS USING READ AND DATA

Problem Statement

Modify Program 4.1 (page 100) using READ and DATA statements to reduce the amount of data the user must enter. Also calculate and print the total gross pay and the average gross pay.

STEP 1   **Variable Names**

We begin by identifying and naming the following variables.

Variable	Variable Name
Input Variables	
Employee's name	EmpName$
Pay rate	PayRate
Hours worked	Hours
Internal Variable	
Counter for number of employees	Employees

Output Variables

Gross pay	`GrossPay`
Total gross pay	`TotGrossPay`
Average gross pay	`AvgGrossPay`

Notice that we have a new kind of variable: an internal variable. An internal variable is neither read in nor printed out. It is used only in the program. Sometimes, you may not realize that you need an internal variable until you start to develop the algorithm and draw the flowchart. If so, simply come back and add the names of the internal variables to the list of variable names.

STEP 2   Algorithm

The algorithm for this problem is similar to the algorithm for Program 4.1; as you will see, using READ and DATA statements does not affect the logic. What does affect the logic is that now we must calculate the total and average gross pay. Clearly, we cannot print TotGrossPay until GrossPay is calculated for all employees. But how can we then go back and add up all the earlier GrossPays? We cannot wait until the end of processing to add up all the GrossPays, because each GrossPay was erased when the next GrossPay was calculated. Instead, we must add each GrossPay to the total as we go. This totaling process requires a variable to act as an **accumulator**. In this program, we will use TotGrossPay as the accumulator. After we find TotGrossPay, we can find AvgGrossPay by dividing TotGrossPay by the number of employees. To determine the number of employees, we will use the variable Employees as a counter—similar to the counters we used earlier in this chapter.

> **accumulator**
> A variable used to obtain the sum of the values of another variable.

To solve this problem, we can use the following algorithm:

1. Set TotGrossPay and Employees equal to zero.
2. Execute steps 3 through 8 for each employee.
3.   Read EmpName$ and PayRate for an employee.
4.   Input Hours for that employee.
5.   Calculate GrossPay.
6.   Increment Employees.
7.   Accumulate GrossPay into TotGrossPay.
8.   Print EmpName$, PayRate, Hours, and GrossPay.
9. Print TotGrossPay.
10. Calculate and print AvgGrossPay.

We will consider why step 1 is necessary and how step 7 is done when we trace the program. To get ready to write the QBasic program, we can express this algorithm by using pseudocode.

```
Calculate pay with total and average
TotGrossPay = 0
Employees = 0
Read EmpName$, PayRate
Do until trailer data is read
     Input Hours
     Calculate GrossPay
     Add 1 to Employees
     Add GrossPay to TotGrossPay
     Print EmpName$, PayRate, Hours, GrossPay
     Read EmpName$, PayRate
End of loop
Print TotGrossPay
Calculate AvgGrossPay
Print AvgGrossPay
End
```

STEP 3   **Hand-Calculated Answer**

We can use the same data we used in Program 4.1, then calculate the total and average gross pay as shown.

Employee No.	Employee Name	Rate of Pay	Hours Worked	Gross Pay
1	Joe Tinker	6.75	40	270.00
2	Joan Evers	6.00	30	180.00
3	Frank Chance	5.75	25	143.75

Total = 593.75
Average = 197.92

STEP 4   **QBasic Program**

Program 4.3 is based on the current algorithm. The new statements in this program are the READ statements in lines 32 and 40, and the DATA statements in lines 48–51. The READ and DATA statements are always used together. The accumulator TotGrossPay is used in line 38. Let's trace the program to see how these statements work.

Tracing the Program

Figure 4.6 helps you trace the program. Lines 18 and 19 of Program 4.3

```
Employees = 0
TotGrossPay = 0
```

assign 0 to Employees and TotGrossPay. That is, these lines **initialize** Employees and TotGrossPay with the value 0. Then lines 22–28 print headings and define format strings.

initialize
To assign a variable a value at the start of a program or a loop.

When the READ statement in line 32 is executed,

```
READ EmpName$, PayRate
```

two things happen. First, the program searches for a DATA statement. If, as in this case, more than one DATA statement exists, they are used in the order that they occur in the program. Second, the variables listed in the READ statement are assigned the values listed in the DATA statement. In this case, the DATA statement in line 48 is used, and EmpName$ is assigned Joe Tinker and PayRate is assigned 6.75. Joe Tinker and 6.75 are then marked as "used" so they will not be used again. If more variables were listed in the READ statement, this process would continue until all the variables were assigned values.

The statement in line 33

```
DO UNTIL EmpName$ = "EOD"
```

marks the top of the loop. Because the value of EmpName$ is not EOD, the loop is entered. The statement in line 34

```
PRINT "Enter hours worked for employee "; EmpName$;
```

displays the message Enter hours worked for employee and, next to that, the value of EmpName$ (Joe Tinker)—as shown in the Output screen's first line in Program 4.3. We cannot use an INPUT statement prompt to print this line because an INPUT statement prompt only displays a string; it cannot display a variable like EmpName$. The hanging semicolon on this line causes the prompt from the following INPUT statement and the value input for Hours to appear next to the employee's name.

The statement in line 35

```
INPUT ": ", Hours
```

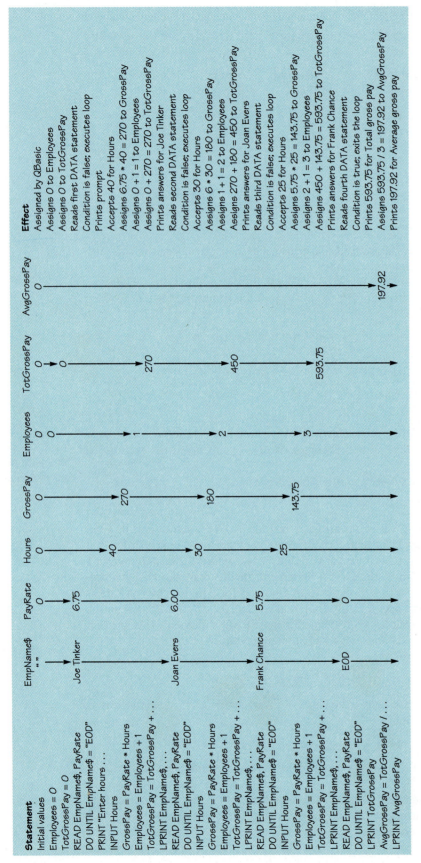

FIGURE 4.6 Tracing Program 4.3.

```
 1  '    *** BAT-O PROGRAM ***
 2  '    Calculate gross using READ and DATA
 3
 4  '    Variables used
 5
 6  '    AvgGrossPay      Average gross pay
 7  '    Employees        Counter for employees
 8  '    EmpName$         Employee's name
 9  '    GrossPay         Gross pay
10  '    Hours            Hours worked
11  '    PayRate          Hourly pay rate
12  '    TotGrossPay      Total gross pay
13
14  CLS
15
16  'Initialize accumulator and counter
17
18  Employees = 0
19  TotGrossPay = 0
20
21  ' Print headings and define format strings
22      LPRINT "                    Payroll Report"
23      LPRINT
24      LPRINT "                        Pay              Gross"
25      LPRINT "   Name                 Rate    Hours     Pay"
26   Format$ = "\                \   ##.##      ##     $###.##"
27  TotalFmt$ = "                    Total gross pay   $#,###.##"
28    AvgFmt$ = "                    Average gross pay $#,###.##"
29
30  ' Process employees
31
32  READ EmpName$, PayRate                      'Data is at end of program
33  DO UNTIL EmpName$ = "EOD"
34      PRINT "Enter hours worked for employee "; EmpName$;
35      INPUT ": ", Hours
36      GrossPay = PayRate * Hours
37      Employees = Employees + 1                'Count employee
38      TotGrossPay = TotGrossPay + GrossPay     'Accumulate gross pay
39      LPRINT USING Format$; EmpName$; PayRate; Hours; GrossPay
40      READ EmpName$, PayRate
41  LOOP
42  LPRINT USING TotalFmt$; TotGrossPay
43  AvgGrossPay = TotGrossPay / Employees
44  LPRINT USING AvgFmt$; AvgGrossPay
45  PRINT "Normal end of program"
46
47  '    Data used in program
48  DATA Joe Tinker, 6.75
49  DATA Joan Evers, 6.00
50  DATA Frank Chance, 5.75
51  DATA EOD, 0                                 : REM Trailer data
52  END
```

PROGRAM 4.3 Payroll program with totals using READ and DATA statement. *(continued on next page)*

```
Enter hours for employee Joe Tinker: 40
Enter hours for employee Joan Evers: 30
Enter hours for employee Frank Chance: 25
Normal end of program
```

```
                        Payroll Report

                        Pay              Gross
        Name            Rate    Hours     Pay
        Joe Tinker      6.75     40     $270.00
        Joan Evers      6.00     30     $180.00
        Frank Chance    5.75     25     $143.75
                        Total gross pay  $  593.75
                        Average gross pay $ 197.92
```

PROGRAM 4.3 *(continued)*

accepts 40 input from the keyboard for Hours that Joe Tinker worked. As you can see, we accomplished our main goal—reducing the amount of data that must be entered. The statement in line 36

```
GrossPay = PayRate * Hours
```

assigns 6.75 * 40 = 270 to GrossPay. The statement in line 37

```
Employees = Employees + 1
```

is the LET statement for a counter—like the ones we studied earlier. It assigns 0 + 1 = 1 to Employees. The statement in line 38

```
TotGrossPay = TotGrossPay + GrossPay
```

is different from any LET statement we've seen before. Recall that when a LET statement is executed, the expression on the right is evaluated first. This LET statement first adds TotGrossPay (0) and GrossPay (270) to get 270. It then assigns 270 to TotGrossPay.

As noted earlier, in this program, TotGrossPay is acting as an accumulator. The LET statement for an accumulator is written as follows:

```
accumulator = accumulator + something else
```

This statement is similar to the LET statement for a counter. In both cases, the same variable appears on both sides of the equals sign. Each time this LET sentence is executed, it accumulates the value of the something else variable. In line 38, the accumulator is TotGrossPay and the something else is GrossPay.

Now you can see why we had to initialize Employees and TotGrossPay in lines 18 and 19. If we want Employees to correctly count the number of employees, and TotGrossPay to correctly accumulate the values of gross pay, these variables must begin at zero. You know that if you didn't initialize these variables, QBasic would initialize them at zero for you. But you should always initialize counters and accumulators yourself. It is poor practice to depend on QBasic to do it for you; later in this chapter, you will see how depending on QBasic for this can give you incorrect answers. Also, other programming languages do not initialize variables.

The statement in line 39

```
LPRINT USING Format$; EmpName$; PayRate; Hours; GrossPay
```

prints the detail line for Joe Tinker. The statement in line 40

```
READ EmpName$, PayRate
```

takes the values from the DATA statement in line 49, then assigns Joan Evers to EmpName$ and 6.00 to PayRate. The statement in line 41

```
LOOP
```

returns to the DO statement at the top of the loop (line 33). You can follow the rest of the execution in Figure 4.6. Here, let's just follow the execution of the accumulator LET statement in line 38 for the next two passes. The next time line 38 is executed, GrossPay is 180. So line 38 assigns 270 + 180 = 450 to TotGrossPay. On the third pass, GrossPay is 143.75, so line 38 assigns 450 + 143.75 = 593.75 to TotGrossPay.

Eventually, the trailer data in line 51 is read. Notice that this DATA statement, like those in lines 48–50, contains values for both EmpName$ (EOD) and PayRate (0). The only function of this DATA statement is to assign EOD to EmpName$. However, we must include a value for PayRate because the READ statement requires two values. If this DATA statement did not have a value for PayRate when the READ statement was executed, the program would stop and QBasic would display the error message Out of DATA. It doesn't matter what value we use for PayRate, because that value is never used.

After the trailer data are read, the condition on line 33

```
DO UNTIL EmpName$ = "EOD"
```

is true. The program then exits from the loop and executes line 42

```
LPRINT USING TotalFmt$; TotGrossPay
```

to print the total gross pay. In line 43,

```
AvgGrossPay = TotGrossPay / Employees
```

average gross pay is calculated, and in line 44,

```
LPRINT USING AvgFmt$; AvgGrossPay
```

it is printed. At this point, all we really must do is stop execution. However, since in this program users do not enter the trailer data (it is in the DATA statements), they might be surprised when the program stops executing. So line 45

```
PRINT "Normal end of program"
```

prints a message explaining that the program ended normally.

In previous programs, we added a comment to the end of a statement simply by beginning the comment with an apostrophe; that technique does not work with DATA statements. Line 51 shows that the proper way to add a comment to the end of a DATA statement is to add a colon followed by REM (: REM) followed by the comment.   ■

More About the READ and DATA Statements

Now that you have seen how the READ and DATA statements work in a program, let's examine them in more detail. The syntax of the READ statement is

```
READ variablelist
```

where, as usual, variablelist is a list of variables separated by commas. The syntax of the DATA statement is

```
DATA constant1 [, constant2]...
```

You may list as many constants as you want. See the following illustrations for some examples of this.

ILLUSTRATIONS

READ and DATA Statements	Effect
`READ Sales, Profit` `DATA 153925, 45619`	Assigns 153925 to Sales and 45619 to Profit. Note that commas are used to separate numeric constants in DATA statements, but *not* within constants that are greater than 999.

`READ StudentName$,`↵
`  Test1, Test2, Test3`
`DATA Jose Carlos,`↵
`  95, 89, 94`
	Assigns Jose Carlos to StudentName$, 95 to Test1, 89 to Test2, and 94 to Test3.

`READ President$,`↵
`  Birthdate$`
`DATA Abraham Lincoln,`↵
`  "Feb. 12, 1809"`
	Assigns Abraham Lincoln to President$ and Feb. 12, 1809 to Birthdate$.

The last example shows that string values in DATA statements, like those in INPUT statements, are enclosed by quotation marks only when a string contains commas or is preceded or followed by blanks that you want to include in the string data.

If a READ statement encounters numeric data when it was expecting string data, the numeric data are converted to a string. For example, when the statements

```
READ Name$
DATA 8
```

are executed, the 8 is converted to "8" and assigned to Name$. Assigning "8" to Name$ doesn't make much sense, but it does not cause an error.

However, if a READ statement encounters string data when it was expecting numeric data, the program stops and QBasic displays the error message: Syntax error. This error is often caused by a missing comma in the DATA statement *before* the one that caused the program to stop.

You can place DATA statements anywhere you want, but the best place to put them is just before the END statement (as in Program 4.3). This placement makes your programs less cluttered, easier to read, and easier to follow.

As stated earlier, if you mistakenly try to execute a READ statement after all the DATA statements are used, the program stops and QBasic displays an Out of DATA message. On the other hand, no error message is displayed if you don't read all the values in all the DATA statements.

Finally, you should know that DATA statements never appear in algorithms, flowcharts, or pseudocode. The reason they don't is that the particular data they represent are not part of the logic of the program. To be useful, the program must work for any values of EmpName$ and PayRate. For example, if Joe Tinker got a raise to $8 an hour, the DATA statement in line 48 would change— but the algorithm, pseudocode, and the rest of the program would still be correct.

The Data Bank

When a program is executed, all the values from all the DATA statements are collected in order in one list that we will call the data bank. When a READ statement is executed, it takes the values it needs from the next available values in the data bank. This means that the four DATA statements in Program 4.3 (page 113) could be written as one long statement:

```
DATA Joe Tinker, 6.75, Joan Evers, 6.00, Frank Chance, 5.75, EOD, 0
```

Your programs will be much clearer if, as in Program 4.3, each DATA statement contains exactly the number of values necessary for one execution of a READ statement. We will make the number of values in the DATA statements agree with the number of variables in the READ statement—except when the READ statement contains just one variable. In that case, we will code several values on each DATA statement.

You saw how the READ and DATA statements reduce the amount of input users must enter, but they are not without drawbacks. If any employee's pay rate changes, the values in the DATA statement must be changed. That presents no problem to you because you know how to edit QBasic statements. So in programs you write for yourself, you can use DATA statements wherever they are convenient.

But suppose you are a professional programmer and you wrote this program for users who do not know QBasic. You don't want someone who doesn't know QBasic to go into your program and change things—he or she might destroy the program. Therefore, in programs written for nonprogrammers, DATA statements should be used only for values that never change; for example, the names of months or states. For values that might change, it is better to use the INPUT statement or data files, which you will learn about in Chapters 9 and 10.

The RESTORE Statement

Sometimes, it is useful to reuse the values in the data bank. The RESTORE statement allows you to do that. The syntax of the RESTORE statement is simply

```
RESTORE
```

After a RESTORE statement is executed, the next READ statement gets its values from the first values in the data bank.

Syntax Summary

READ Statement

Form: `READ variablelist`
Example: `READ State$, Population`
Explanation: The next available values in the data bank are assigned to the variables listed.

DATA Statement

Form: `DATA constant1 [, constant2]. . .`
Example: `DATA Wyoming, 494568`
Explanation: The values are stored in a data bank and used by READ statements.

(continued)

> **RESTORE Statement**
>
> Form: RESTORE
> Example: RESTORE
> Explanation: Causes the next READ statement to obtain its values from
>   the first values in the data bank.

4.3 EXERCISES

1. ★a) Write the READ statement to read a runner's name and time for the
        100-yard dash.
   b)   Write three DATA statements to supply the data for the READ state-
        ment you wrote for part a).

2. In Program 4.3, why do we use LPRINT statements in lines 22–25 and 39,
   but PRINT statements in lines 34 and 45?

★3. Consider the following READ statement:

```
READ A, B$, C
```

Which of the following DATA statements would cause an error when used
with this READ statement?

```
DATA 1, 2, 3
DATA A, B, C
DATA 6, Sunday, 24
```

4. Consider the following program.

```
READ P
DO UNTIL P = -1
    R = P + 4
    PRINT R
    READ P
LOOP
DATA 19, 8, -1
END
```

   ★a) What is the first value assigned to the variable P?
   ★b) What is the first number printed?
    c) What is the second number printed?
    d) What output is produced if the following line is added to the program
        before the READ statement?
        P = 1
    e) Remove the line P = 1 and change the DATA statement to
        DATA -1, 8, 19

What output will be produced?

5. Trace the following program to determine the output.

```
READ Office$, Profit
DO UNTIL Office$ = "EOD"
    PRINT Office$, Profit
    READ Office$, Profit
LOOP
```

```
DATA New York, 213,655
DATA Chicago, 345,123
DTA EOD, 0
END
```

★**6.**   Write the LET statement to accumulate Area into TotalArea.

7.   Trace Program 4.3 to determine what output will be produced if the following changes are made and the same data are entered. Before making each new change, assume that the program is restored back to its original form.
   a)   The DO statement is moved to line 15.
   b)   Line 36 is moved between lines 38 and 39.
   c)   Lines 37 and 38 are interchanged.
   d)   Lines 37 and 38 are moved between lines 39 and 40.

8.   The following four programs are supposed to print the sum of the numbers 1 through 5. Trace the programs to determine their output and comment on your results.

★**a)**
```
Sum = 0
Number = 1
DO WHILE Number <= 5
    Sum = Sum + Number
    Number = Number + 1
LOOP
PRINT Sum
END
```

b)
```
Sum = 0
Number = 1
DO WHILE Number <= 5
    Number = Number + 1
    Sum = Sum + Number
LOOP
PRINT Sum
END
```

c)
```
Sum = 0
Number = 1
DO UNTIL Number >= 5
    Sum = Sum + Number
    Number = Number + 1
LOOP
PRINT Sum
END
```

d)
```
Sum = 0
Number = 1
DO
    Sum = Sum + Number
    Number = Number + 1
LOOP UNTIL Number > 5
PRINT Sum
END
```

4.4 NESTED DO LOOPS

Sometimes, a problem requires one DO loop inside another. Such loops are called **nested loops**. The only requirement of nested loops is that the inner loop must be completely inside the outer loop. The easiest way to understand how nested loops work is to use them in a program.

nested loops
Loops in which an inner loop is enclosed inside an outer loop.

EXAMPLE 4

A PROGRAM WITH NESTED DO LOOPS

Problem Statement

Write a program that allows a user to enter a number, then prints all the integers up to that number. For example, if the user enters a 6, the program should print 1 2 3 4 5 6. Use trailer data to stop the program.

STEP 1 Variable Names

This problem has only two variables:

Variable	Variable Name
Input Variable	
Highest integer printed	Limit
Output Variable	
Counter	N

STEP 2 Algorithm

We will use a value of 0 for Limit as the trailer data. The algorithm for this problem is then:

1. Repeat steps 2 through 6 until the trailer data is entered.
2. Accept a value for Limit.
3. Initialize N at 1.
4. Repeat steps 5 and 6 while N is <= Limit.
5. Print N.
6. Increment N.

The flowchart is shown in Figure 4.7. The outer loop—which includes flowchart symbols 11–19—controls the execution of the program and ends execution when the trailer data is entered. It is similar to the loop in Program 4.2 (page 105). The inner loop—which includes flowchart symbols 13–16—prints and increments N. The program exits from this loop when N is no longer less than or equal to Limit.

STEP 3 Hand-Calculated Answer

There are no hand-calculated answers to this problem.

STEP 4 QBasic Program

The QBasic program is shown in Program 4.4. The indention clearly shows the two loops. After the user enters a value for Limit, the program enters the outer loop. It stays in this loop until the user enters 0 for Limit. In line 12, N is initialized at 1 and the inner loop is entered. The inner loop prints and increments N. The

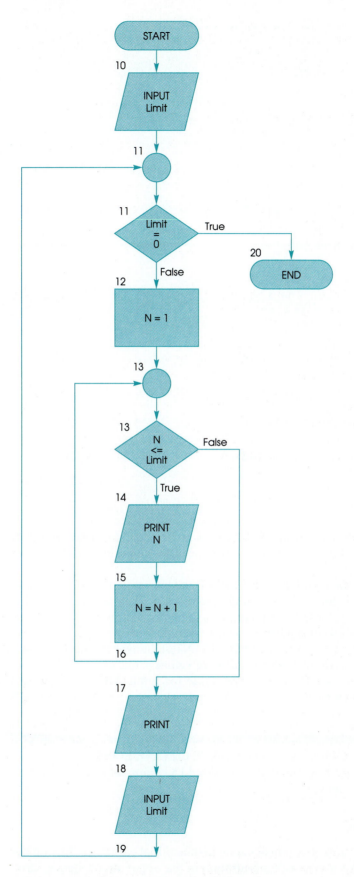

FIGURE 4.7   Using nested DO loops to print integers up to a user-specified limit.

```
 1  |   '     DEMONSTRATING NESTED DO LOOPS
 2  |   '     Print the integers from 1 to user-specified limit
 3  |
 4  |   '     Variables used
 5  |
 6  |   '     Limit          Highest integer to be printed
 7  |   '     N              Counter variable
 8  |
 9  |   CLS
10  |   INPUT "Enter the highest integer to be printed, 0 to stop: ", Limit
11  |   DO UNTIL Limit = 0
12  |       N = 1
13  |       DO WHILE N <= Limit
14  |           PRINT N;
15  |           N = N + 1
16  |       LOOP
17  |       PRINT
18  |       INPUT "Enter the highest integer to be printed, 0 to stop: ", Limit
19  |   LOOP
20  |   END
```

```
Enter the highest integer to be printed, 0 to stop: 6
 1  2  3  4  5  6
Enter the highest integer to be printed, 0 to stop: 2
 1  2
Enter the highest integer to be printed, 0 to stop: 0
```

PROGRAM 4.4   Using nested DO loops to print integers up to a user-specified limit.

program stays in this loop while N is less than or equal to Limit. When N becomes greater than Limit, the program exits from the inner loop and executes line 17.

To understand the function of this PRINT statement, you must notice that the PRINT statement in line 14 uses a hanging semicolon. That hanging semicolon caused the first set of values, the numbers 1–6, to be printed on one line (see the output in Program 4.4). That is what we wanted, but now we want the second set of values to print on a new line. The empty PRINT statement in line 17 doesn't print anything, but ensures that the second set of values prints on a new line.

Line 18 asks the user to enter a new value for Limit. The whole process repeats until the user enters 0.   ■

EXAMPLE 5

USING NESTED LOOPS TO CALCULATE OZONE LOSS

As another example of a program that uses nested DO loops, let's calculate ozone loss in the upper atmosphere.

Problem Statement

Write a program that accepts a rate of ozone loss, and that calculates the number of years it will take for the ozone concentration in the upper atmosphere to drop from 450 parts per million (ppm) to 200 ppm.

STEP 1   **Variable Names**

Variable	Variable Name
Input Variable	
Fraction of ozone lost each year	`LossRate`
Internal Variable	
Amount of ozone lost each year	`Loss`
Output Variables	
Concentration of ozone	`Ozone`
Counter for years	`Year`

STEP 2   **Algorithm**

For any year, we can calculate the loss of ozone by using the equation

```
Loss = LossRate * Ozone
```

Then, the ozone concentration at the end of the year is

```
Ozone = Ozone - Loss
```

To find the number of years for Ozone to drop below 200, we simply use these two LET statements repeatedly until Ozone drops below 200. We can use a Loss-Rate of 0 as trailer data.

The algorithm is

1.   Execute steps 2 through 8 until trailer data is entered.
2.   Accept a value for LossRate.
3.   Initialize Year at 0, and Ozone at 450.
4.   Execute steps 5 through 7 until Ozone is less than 200.
5.   Increment Year.
6.   Calculate Loss.
7.   Calculate Ozone.
8.   Print LossRate, Year, and Ozone.

The pseudocode for this problem is the following:

```
Calculate ozone loss
Input LossRate
Do until trailer data is entered
    Year = 0
    Ozone = 450
    Do
        Increment Year
        Calculate Loss
        Calculate Ozone
    Loop until Ozone is less than 200
    Print LossRate, Year, and Ozone
    Input LossRate
End of loop
```

We coded the inner loop using a posttest loop because we know we must execute the statements in that loop at least once.

STEP 3   **Hand-Calculated Answer**

At this point, we would usually calculate an answer by hand. For this problem, we will delay that step until we examine the program.

STEP 4   **QBasic Program**

The QBasic program is shown in Program 4.5. Line 20 accepts a value for Loss-Rate. The outer loop in lines 21–31 is executed until we enter 0 for LossRate. The inner loop in lines 24–28 is executed until Ozone is less than 200. When Ozone drops below 200, line 29—which prints the answers—is executed.

This program demonstrates forcefully why you must initialize counters and accumulators and not rely on QBasic to do it for you. Suppose line 22

```
Year = 0
```

were omitted. Since QBasic would assign an initial value of 0 to Year, the answers calculated for the first case would be correct. But without line 22 to reset Year to 0, the answers calculated for the second case would be incorrect.

The output shows that when LossRate is .10, it takes 8 years for Ozone to drop to 194. To check this answer by hand, we must repeat the ozone loss calculation 8 times. Fortunately, we don't have do that. If we can be sure that Year, Loss, and Ozone are calculated properly—and if, when we exit from the loop and print the answers, we see that Ozone is in fact less than 200—we can have confidence in our program.

We can be sure that Loss and Ozone are calculated properly by checking the program's calculation against a hand calculation. Let's pick a LossRate of .10 and calculate Loss and Ozone for Years = 1, and Years = 2. That is not very hard, particularly if we use a calculator. The answers are

Year	Loss	Ozone
1	45	405
2	40.5	364.5

But this doesn't do us any good because the program doesn't print Loss and Ozone when Year was 1 or 2. It only prints Year, Loss, and Ozone when Ozone is less than 200. In the next section, you will learn how to print Loss and Ozone when Year is 1 and 2.   ∎

4.4 EXERCISES

1. ★a)   In Program 4.5, rewrite line 21 by using a WHILE clause.
   b)   In Program 4.5, rewrite line 28 by using a WHILE clause.

2. Delete line 22 from Program 4.5. What output is produced if the modified program is run with the same values of LossRate as shown in Program 4.5?

3. Consider the following program:

```
CLS
INPUT P
DO UNTIL P = 0
    S = 0
    N = 1
    DO
        S   S + N
        N = N + 1
    LOOP UNTIL N >= P
    PRINT P, S
    INPUT P
LOOP
END
```

```
 1 | '      *** OZONE LOSS ***
 2 | '     Calculate ozone loss
 3 |
 4 | '     Variables used
 5 |
 6 | '     LossRate           Fraction of ozone lost each year
 7 | '     Loss               Amount of ozone lost each year
 8 | '     Ozone              Concentration of ozone
 9 | '     Year               Counter for years
10 |
11 | CLS
12 |
13 | 'Print headings and define format string
14 | LPRINT "                                    Final"
15 | LPRINT "    Loss Rate          Years      Ozone Concentration"
16 | Fmt$ = "      #.##              ###              ###"
17 |
18 | 'Calculate loss
19 |
20 | INPUT "Enter loss rate, 0 to stop: ", LossRate
21 | DO UNTIL LossRate = 0
22 |     Year = 0                          'Initialize year
23 |     Ozone = 450                       'Initialize ozone concentration
24 |     DO
25 |         Year = Year + 1               'Increment year
26 |         Loss = LossRate * Ozone       'Calculate loss
27 |         Ozone = Ozone - Loss          'New ozone concentration
28 |     LOOP UNTIL Ozone < 200
29 |     LPRINT USING Fmt$; LossRate; Year; Ozone
30 |     INPUT "Enter loss rate, 0 to stop: ", LossRate
31 | LOOP
32 | END
```

```
Enter loss rate, 0 to stop: .10
Enter loss rate, 0 to stop: .20
Enter loss rate, 0 to stop: 0
```

		Final
Loss Rate	Years	Ozone Concentration
0.10	8	194
0.20	4	184

PROGRAM 4.5   A program that uses nested DO loops to calculate ozone loss.

★a) What output is produced by this program if the user enters 3, 5, 0?
 b) Delete the statement S = 0. Now what output is produced when the user enters 3, 5, 0?
 c) Restore the statement S = 0, and change the inner LOOP statement to LOOP UNTIL N > P. Now what output is produced when the user enters 3, 5, 0?

4.5   THE QBASIC ENVIRONMENT

In this section, we discuss the commands on the Debug menu and we complete our discussion of the Run menu. We also explain the use of the Immediate window.

Advanced Debugging Tools

QBasic offers advanced debugging tools that are accessed from the Debug and Run menus.

Program 4.6 shows an incorrect version of Program 4.2 (page 105) that produces no output. Let's see how QBasic's debugging tools can help find the error. To better understand this discussion you should enter or load this program into your computer now.

The Step Command

To find the error, we can trace this program using the Step command from the Debug menu, which is shown in Figure 4.8. As the menu and Reference bar show, the shortcut key for the Step command is function key F8. The Step command executes the program one line at a time, and highlights the next line to be executed. If any output is produced, the Output screen is briefly displayed. You can return to the Output screen for a longer look by pressing function key F4.

The first time you press F8, the CLS statement is highlighted. Press F8 again to execute the CLS statement and highlight the INPUT statement. Press F8 to execute the INPUT statement. When the INPUT statement is executed, the prompt is displayed and execution halts—just as it does under normal execution. After you enter a value for Deposit, QBasic returns to the View window with the DO state-

```
 1  '    *** LOANSOME BANK PROBLEM ***
 2  '    Calculate compound interest
 3
 4  '    Variables used
 5
 6  '    Balance         Balance in the Account
 7  '    Deposit         Amount deposited
 8  '    Rate            Interest rate
 9  '    Years           Number of years
10
11  CLS
12  INPUT "Enter deposit, 0 to stop: ", Deposit
13  DO UNTIL Deposet = 0  ◄──────────────────  Error; Deposit misspelled
14      INPUT "Enter rate, decimal: ", Rate
15      INPUT "Enter number of years: ", Years
16      Balance = Deposit * (1 + Rate) ^ Years
17      LPRINT Deposit, Rate, Years, Balance
18      INPUT "Enter deposit, 0 to stop: ", Deposit
19  LOOP
20  END
```

PROGRAM 4.6   The compound interest program with a logic error.

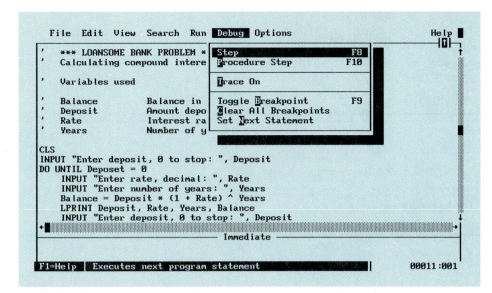

```
   File  Edit  View  Search  Run  Debug  Options                    Help
   ┌─────────────────────────────────────────────────────────────────────┐
   │'   *** LOANSOME BANK PROBLEM *│ Step                          F8 │
   │'   Calculating compound intere│ Procedure Step                F10 │
   │'                              │                                   │
   │'   Variables used             │ Trace On                          │
   │'                              │                                   │
   │'   Balance        Balance in  │ Toggle Breakpoint             F9 │
   │'   Deposit        Amount depo │ Clear All Breakpoints             │
   │'   Rate           Interest ra │ Set Next Statement                │
   │'   Years          Number of y └───────────────────────────────────┘
   │                                                                   │
   │CLS                                                                │
   │INPUT "Enter deposit, 0 to stop: ", Deposit                        │
   │DO UNTIL Deposet = 0                                               │
   │   INPUT "Enter rate, decimal: ", Rate                             │
   │   INPUT "Enter number of years: ", Years                          │
   │   Balance = Deposit * (1 + Rate) ^ Years                          │
   │   LPRINT Deposit, Rate, Years, Balance                            │
   │   INPUT "Enter deposit, 0 to stop: ", Deposit                     │
   │                                                                   │
   ├───────────────────────────── Immediate ──────────────────────────┤
   │                                                                   │
   └─────────────────────────────────────────────────────────────────┘
    F1=Help │ Executes next program statement          │   00011:001
```

FIGURE 4.8
The Debug menu.

ment highlighted. Press F8 and the END statement is highlighted. Jumping directly to the END statement means that the condition in the DO statement was true. With your attention directed to the condition, you can examine it closely, noticing that Deposit was misspelled Deposet. That explains what happened. No matter what value was entered for Deposit, Deposet had the default initial value of 0. Therefore, the condition Deposet = 0 was true, so the loop was not entered and the program stopped.

The Trace On Command

You could also use the Trace On command from the Debug menu to debug this program. The Trace On command is a toggle. The first time you select Trace On, tracing is turned on; the next time you select it, tracing is turned off. When tracing is on, the Debug menu displays a small dot next to the Trace On command. When tracing is on, your program executes in slow motion, and each statement is highlighted as it is executed. In effect, you get step-by-step execution without having to repeatedly press function key F8.

Using Breakpoints

Different errors require different debugging tools. For example, Program 4.7 prints 0 for Balance. You probably already noticed that the error occurs because the LPRINT statement prints Amount instead of Balance. But let's see how we can systematically track down the error. Again, you will understand this discussion better if you can enter or load this program in your computer now.

To debug this program, we will use a breakpoint. A **breakpoint** is a statement in your program where you want execution to pause. To set a breakpoint, move the cursor to the line you want to use as a breakpoint. Then select the Toggle Breakpoint command from the Debug menu or press function key F9. For this program, move the cursor to the LPRINT statement (line 17) and press F9. The line is displayed in red on a color monitor and in reverse video on a monochrome monitor to remind you that it is a breakpoint. Now, run the program as usual. The program executes normally until it reaches the breakpoint, where it stops.

Next, you want to see if Balance was calculated properly. To see the value of Balance, press function key F6 to move the cursor to the Immediate window (or

breakpoint
A statement in a program where execution pauses.

```
 1 |  '    *** LOANSOME BANK PROBLEM ***
 2 |  '    Calculate compound interest
 3 |
 4 |  '    Variables used
 5 |
 6 |  '    Balance          Balance in the Account
 7 |  '    Deposit          Amount deposited
 8 |  '    Rate             Interest rate
 9 |  '    Years            Number of years
10 |
11 |  CLS
12 |  INPUT "Enter deposit, 0 to stop: ", Deposit
13 |  DO UNTIL Deposit = 0
14 |      INPUT "Enter rate, decimal: ", Rate
15 |      INPUT "Enter number of years: ", Years
16 |      Balance = Deposit * (1 + Rate) ^ Years
17 |      LPRINT Deposit, Rate, Years, Amount  ◄──────── Error; Balance
18 |      INPUT "Enter deposit, 0 to stop: ", Deposit       should be printed
19 |  LOOP
20 |  END
```

PROGRAM 4.7   The compound interest program with a logic error.

move the mouse pointer to the Immediate window and click). Now type the statement

```
    PRINT Balance
```

and press the Enter key. The statement is executed, and the Output screen is displayed showing the correct value of Balance. Since this proves that Balance was calculated properly, you can concentrate on the LPRINT statement and discover the error. You must press F6 again to return the cursor to the View window, and then correct the LPRINT statement.

To continue execution, select the Continue command from the Run menu (see Figure 1.8 on page 13) or press F5. Since this is the first time we have suspended execution, this is also the first time that there is a difference between the way the Run menu Start (Shift+F5) and Continue (F5) commands work. The Start command erases the values of all the variables in the program and begins execution at the first statement in the program. The Continue command retains all the values of the variables and resumes execution at the breakpoint.

In a complicated program, you might have several breakpoints. When you select Continue from the Run menu (or press F5), the program executes from one breakpoint to the next. At any breakpoint, you can use F6 to move to the Immediate window. Then, you can enter and execute any PRINT statement that is useful. To remove a breakpoint, move the cursor to the breakpoint and select Toggle Breakpoint from the Debug menu (or press F9). To remove all the breakpoints in a program, select the Clear All Breakpoints command from the Debug menu.

Breakpoints and the Immediate window also allow us to verify that Program 4.5 (page 125) is correct. All we have to do is add a breakpoint to the program at line 28. Execute the program. When it stops at the breakpoint, use the Immediate window to print the value of Year, Loss, and Ozone. If the values agree with the hand-calculated answers, continue execution. When the program stops a second time, use the Immediate window again to print Year, Loss, and Ozone. When you verify that the Year is being incremented and Loss and Ozone are being calculated properly, you can have confidence that the program is correct. You can then remove the breakpoint and continue the program to its normal end.

The Immediate Window

Although PRINT statements are most often used in the Immediate window, you can also use just about any QBasic statement you want. LET statements are often used. For example, suppose you assigned a value of 1000 to Deposit. For some reason, you now want Deposit to have the value of 500. At a breakpoint, you can execute the statement

```
Deposit = 500
```

in the Immediate window. When you resume execution, Deposit has the value 500.

The Immediate window can store up to ten lines. If you enter more than ten lines, the earlier ones are lost. In a complicated program, you can have several PRINT statements—each for a different variable or variables. You can use the arrow keys to move the cursor to the statement you want, then press Enter to execute it.

Additional Debugging Techniques

We haven't discussed two commands on the Debug menu yet. The Procedure Step command (function key F10) is used with procedures; Chapter 6 will cover it.

The Set Next Statement command allows you to continue execution at the statement of your choosing. After a program stops at a breakpoint, move the cursor to the line where you want to begin execution—either before or after the line where you stopped. Then select Set Next Statement. QBasic immediately jumps to and highlights the line that the cursor is on. Execution continues from that line when you press function key F5.

The only Run menu command we haven't discussed yet is Restart. The Restart command erases the values of all the variables and highlights the first executable statement in the program. Restart is useful when a program halts at a breakpoint, you make some changes, and now you want to step through the program from the beginning. In this case, you can't use the Step command from the Debug menu or the Continue command from the Run menu because they will continue from the breakpoint. Nor can you use the Start command from the Run menu because it executes the program at full speed—and you want to step through the program.

Finally, function key F7 performs a function that is not on any menu. Pressing F7 executes your program to the line the cursor is on, where execution pauses. This is equivalent to setting a breakpoint and selecting the Continue command.

4.5 EXERCISES

★**1.**   When you use the Step command, what does it mean if a statement is highlighted?

2.   What is the difference between the Step command and the Trace On command?

3.   How do you resume execution after a program pauses at a breakpoint?

★**4.** What happens when you type a QBasic statement in the Immediate window?

5. Program 4.8 shows an incorrect solution to Programming Assignment 4.2
(page 133). Although the program uses the UCASE$ function, when the
user entered eod for trailer data, the program continued executing. How
would you correct the error?

```
1    '    *** PROGRAMMING ASSIGNMENT 4.2 ***
2    '    Calculate grade on a 25 question test
3
4    '    Variables used
5
6    '    Correct           Number of questions correct
7    '    Grade             Grade on test
8    '    Student$          Student's name
9
10   CLS
11   INPUT "Enter student's name, EOD to end: ", Student$
12   DO UNTIL Student$ = UCASE$("EOD")
13       INPUT "Enter the number of questions correct: ", Correct
14       Grade = (Correct / 25) * 100
15       LPRINT Student$, Correct, Grade
16       INPUT "Enter student's name, EOD to end: ", Student$
17   LOOP
18   END
```

```
Enter student's name, EOD to end: Jill
Enter the number of questions correct: 24
Enter student's name, EOD to end: eod
Enter the number of questions correct
```

```
Jill            24              96
```

PROGRAM 4.8 An incorrect solution to Programming Assignment 4.2.

WHAT YOU HAVE LEARNED

In this chapter, you learned that:

- A condition is used to compare two expressions. Usually, a variable is compared with another variable or with a constant. A condition is either true or false.
- The relational operators used in conditions are
  - =   Equal to
  - <   Less than
  - >   Greater than
  - <=   Less than or equal to
  - >=   Greater than or equal to
  - <>   Not equal to
- When strings and string variables are used in conditions, they are compared according to their ASCII codes.
- The DO and LOOP statements create a loop so that a program can process multiple cases.
- DO loops may be coded by including a WHILE or UNTIL clause on the DO or LOOP statement. When a WHILE clause is used, the statements in the loop are executed *while* the condition is true. When an UNTIL clause is used, the statements in the loop are executed *until* the condition becomes true. When the WHILE or UNTIL clause is coded on the LOOP statement, the loop is called a posttest loop. The statements in a posttest loop are executed at least once. When the WHILE or UNTIL clause is coded on the DO statement, the loop is called a pretest loop. The statements in a pretest loop may not be executed at all.

- The UCASE$ function converts its string argument to upper case.
- Trailer data are used to control the number of times a loop is executed.
- The Ctrl+Break keys may be used to stop execution.
- If a variable has a value that is too large or too small to be printed in seven digits, it is printed in scientific notation.
- The READ statement obtains values from DATA statements and assigns them to variables. DATA statements may be placed anywhere in the main program, but should be placed just before the END statement.
- Counter variables count the number of times a loop is executed.
- Accumulator variables obtain the sum of another variable.
- The Debug menu command Step (or function key F8) allows you to execute your program one step at a time.
- The Debug menu command Toggle Breakpoint (or function key F9) allows you to specify a line where execution will pause.
- When program execution pauses, you can enter PRINT statements in the Immediate window to examine the values of variables.
- The Run menu Continue command (or function key F5) allows you to resume execution.

NEW QBASIC STATEMENTS

STATEMENT	EFFECT

DO...LOOP

```
N = 1
DO WHILE N <= 10
    PRINT N
    N = N + 1
LOOP
```

Executes the statements between DO and LOOP while the condition N <= 10 is true. When the condition becomes false, branches to the statement following LOOP. Other variations include coding UNTIL instead of WHILE, and coding the condition on the LOOP statement.

READ

```
READ State$, Population
```

Gets the next value from the data bank and assigns it to State$, then gets the following value and assigns it to Population.

DATA

```
DATA Wyoming, 494568
```

Stores values in the data bank to be used by READ statements.

RESTORE

```
RESTORE
```

Causes the next READ statement to get its values from the first values in the data bank.

KEY TERMS

accumulator	endless loop	priming read
ASCII code	initialize	relational operator
breakpoint	loop	round-off errors
condition	nested loops	scientific notation
counter	posttest loop	sentinel value
detail line	pretest loop	trailer data

REVIEW EXERCISES

SELF-CHECK

1. True or false: Conditions may not be used to compare string variables.

2. Explain the difference between the equals sign used in a condition and the one used in a LET statement.

3. What is the relational operator that means greater than or equal to?

4. What is the ASCII code for Z? For a?

5. Is "ape" > "Zebra"?

6. True or false: If you code a WHILE clause on a DO statement, you must code an UNTIL clause on the LOOP statement.

7. A DO loop with a WHILE clause is executed as long as the condition is (true/false).

8. What error did you make if a program that contains a DO loop goes into an endless loop?

9. True or false: The statements in a DO loop are always executed at least once.

10. Suppose Program 4.1 (page 100) were used to calculate gross pay for 17 employees. The answers to how many cases would have to be calculated by hand?

11. How do you stop an endless loop?

12. True or false: A DO statement is always used with a LOOP statement.

13. When a variable is assigned a new value, what happens to the value it was previously assigned?

14. What is the purpose of indenting the statements in a loop?

15. True or false: The argument of the UCASE$ function is a string or string variable.

16. Trailer data are entered (before/after) the data for the other cases.

17. Why do round-off errors occur?

18. If an answer is printed as 1.0E+09, what is its value?

19. What punctuation mark separates the values listed in a DATA statement?

20. True or false: DATA statements must be placed before their READ statements.

21. When must string data listed in a DATA statement be enclosed by quotation marks?

22. True or false: If a program contains a READ statement, it must also contain at least one DATA statement.

23. How can you add a comment at the end of a DATA statement?

24. In the following statement, which variable is used as an accumulator?

    ```
    P = P + Q
    ```

25. What is the first thing you must do to an accumulator variable?

26. What is the shortcut key for the Debug menu Step command?

27. What is a breakpoint? How do you set a breakpoint?

28. What is the difference among the Run menu Start, Continue, and Restart commands?

PROGRAMMING ASSIGNMENTS

In each of the following programming assignments, use a loop so your program can process multiple cases. Most of these assignments are modifications of assignments in Chapters 2 or 3. If the earlier assignment number is not clear from the statement of the problem, it is given in parentheses at the end of the assignment, as in (PA 2.2).

Section 4.2

1. Resolve Programming Assignment 3.1. Ask the user if there are more cases to process.

2. Resolve Programming Assignment 3.2, using EOD as trailer data for the student's name.

3. Write a program that accepts a person's name and age, in years, and prints the number of seconds the person has lived. Assume that there are 365 days in a year. Ask the user if there are more cases to process.

4. Resolve Programming Assignment 3.4, using 0 for the original price of the book as trailer data.

5. Resolve Programming Assignment 3.6(a), using EOD for the name of the food as trailer data.

Section 4.3

Now that you know how to use READ and DATA statements, some programming assignments will suggest that you obtain data for your program by using a file of DATA statements. These files, all of which have the filename extension DAT, have the form

```
DATA value, value, ...
```

You must begin by opening the DAT file. Then type your program. (If you begin by typing your program, there will be no way to add the DATA statements to it.) The DAT files will not be listed in the Open dialog box, but they can be retrieved simply by typing their complete name in the File Name text box (for example, PA04-07.DAT).

6. Resolve Programming Assignment 3.19, but this time, read the salesperson's name and enter the sales. Also calculate and print the total and the average sales and the total and average commissions. Use EOD for the salesperson's name as trailer data.

7. Write a program that reads a student's name and the grades that student got on three tests. Calculate and print the student's average grade, plus the class's average grade. Use EOD for the student's name as trailer data. Use PA04-07.DAT to provide the DATA statements.

8. Resolve Programming Assignment 3.15, but this time, read the person's name and enter the number of hours that person has watched "Loving Hospitals." Also calculate and print the total and average amount of brain that has turned to oatmeal. Use EOD for the person's name as trailer data.

Section 4.4

9. If you make an annual deposit of Deposit dollars into a bank account that pays Rate interest rate, and you do this for Years years, the Total amount of money in your account can be calculated by using the equation:

```
Total = Deposit * ((1 + Rate) ^↵
    Years - 1) / Rate
```

In this equation, Rate must be expressed as a fraction, not a percent. Write a program that accepts Deposit and Rate, and which calculates the number of years required for Total to be equal to or greater than 1 million dollars. With Deposit equal to 1,000, and Rate equal to .10, your program should find that in 49 Years, Total will be $1,057,190. Use 0 for Deposit as trailer data.

10. Suppose you have a business deal that doubles your money each month, and further suppose you start with $1. Write a program that determines how many months it will take for your money to grow to more than $1000. (*Hint:* This program requires no input.)

11. Chancy Wynn won $100,000 in a lottery. She put the money in a savings account that pays 8% interest. At the end of each year, she withdraws $15,000 from the account and spends it on a big bash. Write a program to determine how many years she can do this before her account balance is down to or below zero.

   To be sure you understand the problem, let's examine what happens during the first two years. During the first year, the full $100,000 is on deposit, so the interest earned is 0.08 × $100,000 = $8,000. On December 31, therefore, the balance is $100,000 + 8,000 = $108,000. However, Chancy now withdraws $15,000, so her balance goes down to $108,000 – 15,000 = $93,000. During the second year, interest is earned on $93,000 and is only 0.08 × $93,000 = $7,440. When Chancy withdraws her usual $15,000 at the end of the second year, her balance is reduced to $93,000 + 7,440 – 15,000 = $85,440. This process continues until her balance becomes less than or equal to 0.

12. The population of the world is now 3.5 billion (you can write that number in a program as 3.5E9). If the population now is represented by Pop and the rate of increase (as a decimal) as Rate, then the growth in population in one year is

```
Growth = Rate * Pop
```

and the population at the end of the year is

```
Pop = Pop + Growth
```

Write a program that accepts a value for Rate (suggested values are 0.01, 0.02, and 0.03) and determines how long it will take for the population to reach 6 billion people at that Rate. (You can write 6 billion as 6E9.) Use 0 for Rate as trailer data.

ADDITIONAL PROGRAMMING ASSIGNMENTS

13. Suppose the face value of a bond is Face, its coupon is Coupon, and the number of years to maturity is Years. Then for the yield to maturity to be Yield, the current price Price is given by the equation

```
Price = Face * V + Coupon * A
```

where V and A are given by

```
V = (1 + Yield) ^ (-Years)
A = (1 - V) / Yield
```

For example, if Face = 1000, Coupon = 40, Years = 10, and Yield = .08, then V = .4631933, A = 6.710084, and Price = 731.5967. Write a program that accepts Face, Coupon, Years, and Yield— and calculates and prints Price. Use Face = 0 as trailer data.

14. Resolve Programming Assignment 3.9—but this time, read the employee's name and pay rate and enter the hours worked. Also calculate and print the total and average gross pay, income tax withholding, social security tax, and net pay. Use EOD for the name as trailer data.

15. Write a program that calculates the sum of the numbers 1+2+3+... and keeps adding numbers until the sum is greater than 1000. The program should then print the last number added to the sum and the sum.

16. Resolve Programming Assignment 2.11, accepting as input the miles driven. Assume that all renters drive more than 25 miles. Also calculate and print the total and average miles driven and total of all the bills and average bill.

17. Write a program that accepts a number, calls it Max, and then finds the largest integer whose square is less than Max.

18. Write a program that accepts a series of numbers and prints their average. Use 9999 as the trailer data.

BEYOND THE BASICS

19. Seymour's Videos rents video cassettes for $4.50 per day, or $2.75 per day if you pay $35 to join a rental club. Write a program that determines the number of cassettes you have to rent in order to save money by joining the club.

20. A bug is crawling from one end of a rubber band to the other. Initially, the rubber band is 10 inches long, and the bug crawls 1 inch per minute. At the end of the first minute, the rubber band stretches to 20 inches. During the stretching, the bug holds on tightly and is carried along by the stretching. The bug's position after the stretch may be calculated by the equation

```
PositionAfter = PositionBefore *↵
    (Length + 10) / (Length)
```

The bug keeps crawling at the same rate, and at the end of each subsequent minute, the rubber band is stretched an additional 10 inches. The situation after the first few minutes is as follows:

At the End of Minute	Position After Crawling	Position After Stretching	Length of Rubber Band
1	1	2	20
2	3	4.5	30
3	5.5	7.333	40

Write a program to determine how long it takes the bug to reach the end of the rubber band.

5

DECISIONS

LEARNING OBJECTIVES

After reading this chapter, you will be able to:

- Write a program containing simple decisions, nested decisions, and multiple-alternative decisions.
- Use the QBasic statements IF, BEEP, and SELECT CASE.
- Construct compound conditions.
- Use the QBasic function INPUT$.

In the problems considered so far, we treated all cases identically. For example, in the savings account problem in Chapter 4, we paid the same interest rate to every customer. In many problems, however, we would like to treat different accounts differently. For instance, accounts with balances greater than $500 might have an interest rate of 7 percent, while all other accounts have an interest rate of 5 percent. As another example, a store might sell doughnuts for 50 cents each if a customer buys fewer than 12, but for only 35 cents each if the customer buys 12 or more.

To solve these kinds of problems, a program must decide which instructions to execute in each case. In the savings account example, if the balance is greater than $500, the program must execute the statement in which the interest rate is 7 percent. But if the balance is $500 or less, the program must execute the statement in which the interest rate is 5 percent. You already did that in a simple way by testing for trailer data and stopping execution when the trailer data is entered. In this chapter, you will learn how to write programs with different kinds of decisions.

In QBasic, the IF statement is used to make decisions. We will start our discussion with the simple version of the IF statement.

EXAMPLE 1

A SALES PROBLEM THAT USES AN IF STATEMENT

For our first example, we will write a program that calculates customers' bills at a doughnut shop when the cost of a doughnut depends on the number of doughnuts a customer buys.

Problem Statement

Write a program that calculates bills for the Hole-in-One Doughnut Shop. The price for doughnuts is 35 cents each if a customer buys more than 12, but 50 cents each if a customer buys 12 or less.

STEP 1   Variable Names

As always, our first step is to identify the variables and select names for them. Let's use the following:

Variable	Variable Name
Input Variable	
Number of doughnuts purchased	`NumDonuts`
Output Variable	
Customer's bill	`Bill`

Notice especially that the price of the doughnuts is not a variable. The program will determine the correct price to charge for the doughnuts.

STEP 2   Algorithm

Next, we develop an algorithm.

1. Execute steps 2 through 4 for all customers.
2. Input NumDonuts for a customer.
3. Determine whether this customer bought more than 12 doughnuts, and calculate Bill using the appropriate price.
4. Print NumDonuts and Bill.

The only new step in the procedure is step 3, where we must determine if the customer bought more than 12 doughnuts.

The flowchart for this algorithm is shown in Figure 5.1. Notice that in input/output symbol 11, we print a heading—even though the algorithm did not mention headings. Printing headings is a detail that we do not want to be bothered with when we develop the algorithm; when the flowchart is drawn, we can fill in the details.

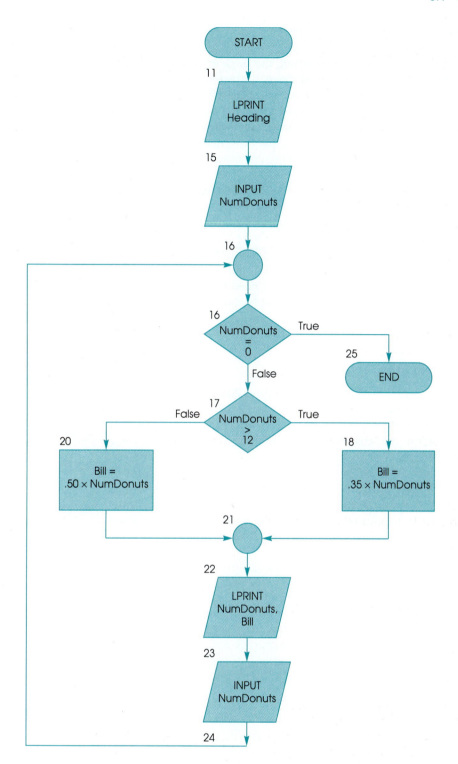

FIGURE 5.1   Flowchart to calculate bills using an IF statement.

The flowchart in Figure 5.1 contains two decision symbols. The one in symbol 16 represents the pretest UNTIL loop that tests for trailer data and is similar to those you studied in Chapter 4. The decision symbol in symbol 17—together with symbols 18, 20, and 21—represents the decision structure, which is new. The decision structure determines whether this customer bought more than 12 doughnuts, and calculates the bill.

If NumDonuts is greater than 12, the condition in symbol 17 is true. The "True" branch leads to process symbol 18, which shows Bill calculated using the equation Bill = .35 * NumDonuts. In this equation, the price of each doughnut is 35 cents, which is the correct price when NumDonuts is greater than 12.

If NumDonuts is 12 or less, the condition is false. The "False" branch leads to process symbol 20, which shows Bill calculated using the equation Bill = .50 * NumDonuts. In this equation, the price of each doughnut is 50 cents, which is the correct price when NumDonuts is 12 or less. Thus, the flowchart shows Bill being calculated by the correct equation whether or not the customer buys more than 12 doughnuts.

The small circle numbered 21 represents the end of the decision structure, where the "True" and "False" branches rejoin. We enter the decision structure, take either the "True" or "False" branch, exit the structure, and continue to the next step in sequence.

When solving these kinds of problems, students sometimes mistakenly use two decision steps: one that tests if NumDonuts > 12, and a second that tests if NumDonuts <= 12. You should realize that we don't need the second test. If the first test, NumDonuts > 12, is false, then we know that NumDonuts <= 12, and we don't need a separate test.

STEP 3 Hand-Calculated Answer

We next calculate an answer by hand. If a customer buys 20 doughnuts, the bill is 20 ×.35 = $7.00. If a customer buys 10 doughnuts, the bill is 10 ×. 50 = $5.00. Notice that for this problem, we must calculate an answer for two cases: customers who buy more than 12 doughnuts and customers who buy 12 or less.

We must calculate an answer for both cases because it is possible for a program to calculate the correct answer for one case, but an incorrect answer for the other case. You can't be sure your program is correct unless the answers calculated for both cases agree with the hand-calculated answers. In more complicated problems, it is possible to have more than two cases; in those problems, it is necessary to calculate answers by hand for each case.

STEP 4 QBasic Program

Now, we are ready to write the QBasic program, which is shown in Program 5.1. Lines 1 through 16 are similar to statements you saw in earlier programs, but line 17 is new. In it, the decision structure in the flowchart is written as an IF statement:

```
IF NumDonuts > 12 THEN
    Bill = .35 * NumDonuts
ELSE
    Bill = .50 * NumDonuts
END IF
```

When QBasic executes this statement, it evaluates the condition NumDonuts > 12. If the condition is true, the statement following the reserved word THEN is executed. If the condition is false, the statement following the reserved word ELSE is executed. This IF statement does exactly what the flowchart specified; it charges .35 per doughnut if more than 12 are bought and .50 per doughnut if 12 or less are bought. In either case, QBasic continues with the statement following END IF—in this case, the LPRINT statement that prints the answers. Notice that the printed results agree with our hand-calculated answers.

```
 1 | '     *** THE HOLE-IN-ONE DOUGHNUT PROBLEM ***
 2 | '     Calculate bills
 3 |
 4 | '     Variables used
 5 |
 6 | '     Bill              Customer's bill
 7 | '     NumDonuts         Number of doughnuts purchased
 8 |
 9 | CLS
10 | '     Print heading and define format string
11 | LPRINT "Doughnuts      Bill"
12 | Fmt$ = "     ##            #.##"
13 |
14 | '     Process customers
15 | INPUT "Enter Number of Doughnuts, 0 to stop : ", NumDonuts
16 | DO UNTIL NumDonuts = 0
17 |     IF NumDonuts > 12 THEN
18 |         Bill = .35 * NumDonuts
19 |     ELSE
20 |         Bill = .50 * NumDonuts
21 |     END IF
22 |     LPRINT USING Fmt$; NumDonuts; Bill
23 |     INPUT "Enter Number of Doughnuts, 0 to stop : ", NumDonuts
24 | LOOP
25 | END
```

```
Enter Number of Doughnuts, 0 to stop : 10
Enter Number of Doughnuts, 0 to stop : 20
Enter Number of Doughnuts, 0 to stop : 0
```

```
Doughnuts      Bill
       10      5.00
       20      7.00
```

PROGRAM 5.1   A program that calculates bills using an IF statement.

IF Statement Syntax

You saw how the IF statement in Program 5.1 works; now, let's examine the syntax of the IF statement. We will study the syntax of the complete IF statement later in this chapter. The syntax of the simple IF statement we are using here is

```
IF condition THEN
    statement(s) to be executed if condition is true
[ELSE
    statement(s) to be executed if condition is false]
END IF
```

The condition coded on an IF statement is the same as the condition coded on the DO and LOOP statements. When an IF statement is executed, the condition is evaluated. If the condition is true, QBasic executes the statements following the word THEN until it comes to the word ELSE. It then skips to the statement following the END IF statement. If the condition is false, QBasic skips to the word ELSE, and then executes the statements between ELSE and END IF. It then continues with the statement following END IF. Both THEN and ELSE clauses may consist of a single QBasic statement (as in Program 5.1) or as many statements as you need.

The square brackets around the ELSE clause indicate that the ELSE clause is optional. If the ELSE clause is omitted and the condition is false, QBasic simply falls through the IF statement and executes the statement following END IF.

The IF statement must be written as shown. IF, condition, and THEN are on one line; the statement(s) you want to execute if the condition is true are on their own lines; ELSE is on its own line, followed by the statement(s) you want to execute if the condition is false; and finally, the IF statement is ended by the END IF statement, on its own line. We call the word THEN and the statements that follow it the THEN clause; the word ELSE and the statements that follow it are the ELSE clause.

QBasic does not require that the statements in the true and false branches be indented, but indenting them makes the program easier to understand. In this book, we always indent the true and false branches. You should indent them in your programs also.

Study the following examples of IF statements.

ILLUSTRATIONS

IF Statement	Effect
| ```
IF Sales > 1000 THEN
    Bonus = 50
    Commission = .20  Sales
ELSE
    Bonus = 0
    Commission = .10 * Sales
END IF
Pay = Bonus + Commission
``` | If Sales is greater than 1000, Bonus is set to 50 and Commission is calculated as .20 times Sales; otherwise, Bonus is set to 0, and Commission is calculated as .10 times Sales. In either case, the LET statement that calculates Pay is then executed. |
| ```
IF Number MOD 2 = 0 THEN
    PRINT "Number is even"
ELSE
    PRINT "Number is odd"
END IF
``` | If Number MOD 2 is 0, Number is even will print; otherwise, Number is odd will print. (Recall that the MOD operator gives the integer remainder of integer division.) |
| ```
IF GPA > 3.0 THEN
    PRINT "DEAN'S LIST"
END IF
``` | If GPA is greater than 3.0, DEAN'S LIST will print; otherwise, nothing will print. |

It is sometimes desirable to execute a QBasic statement or statements only if a condition is false. In that case, do not code any statements between THEN and ELSE. For example, the last IF statement above could be written as

```
IF GPA <= 3.0 THEN
ELSE
    PRINT "DEAN'S LIST"
END IF
```
```

More Complicated Price Schedules

Not all price schedules are as straightforward as these. For example, suppose the charges at a parking lot are

First 2 hours or less	$5.00 an hour
Additional hours	$3.00 an hour

If Hours stands for the number of hours parked and Bill stands for the customer's bill, how would you write the LET statements for this problem? The bill for customers who park for 2 hours or less is straightforward; they are charged a flat $5.00 an hour, so the LET statement is

```
Bill = 5 * Hours
```

The bill for customers who park over 2 hours is slightly more complicated. In such cases, it is helpful to calculate a sample bill for a customer and to use the numeric calculation as an aid in developing the LET statement. For example, let's calculate the bill for a customer who parks for 6 hours. For the first 2 hours, she is charged $5 per hour; for the next 4 hours, she is charged $3 per hour. Her bill is

```
Bill = (5 * 2) + (3 * 4) = 22
```

But we went too fast. We got the 4 in this equation by subtracting 2 hours from the 6 hours she was parked. Let's show that subtraction explicitly:

```
Bill = (5 * 2) + (3 * (6 - 2)) = 22
```

With this numeric equation as a guide, we can write the required LET statement:

```
Bill = (5 * 2) + (3 * (Hours - 2))
```

But according to the hierarchy of operations, QBasic always performs multiplication before addition, so we may drop the outer parentheses:

```
Bill = 5 * 2 + 3 * (Hours - 2)
```

The IF statement is then

```
IF Hours <= 2 THEN
    Bill = 5 * Hours
ELSE
    Bill = 5 * 2 + 3 * (Hours - 2)
END IF
```

Whenever you have difficulty writing a LET statement, do a calculation using numbers. Then use the resulting numeric equation to help you write the required LET statement. This process does not involve any additional work, because you must do a hand calculation anyway to check your program.

Syntax Summary

IF Statement (Simplified Version)

Form:
```
IF condition THEN
    statement(s) to be executed if condition is true
[ELSE
    statement(s) to be executed if condition is false]
END IF
```
(continued)

Example: IF Age >= 65 THEN
                    PRINT "Senior Citizen"
                ELSE
                    PRINT "Not a Senior Citizen"
                END IF
Explanation: If the condition is true, the statement or statements between
                THEN and ELSE are executed. If the condition is false, the
                statement or statements between ELSE and END IF are
                executed.

5.1 EXERCISES

★1. Write the IF statement to test the variables A and B. If A is greater than B, print the sentence A is greater; otherwise, print the sentence A is not greater.

2. Suppose S is 25. What will be printed when the following statements are executed?

```
IF S > 10 THEN
    PRINT "BONUS"
END IF
PRINT "NO BONUS"
```

3. A record store is having a sale. The first three tapes cost $8.98 each. Additional tapes cost $6.98 each. Write the IF statement to calculate customers' bills.

★4. Presidential elections are held in years that are divisible by 4. Write an IF statement that tests the variable Year and prints Election Year if Year is a presidential election year.

5. A student says that it is not necessary to hand-calculate two answers for Program 5.1 (page 139). Show that he is wrong by changing the program so that it calculates the correct bill if a customer buys 12 or more doughnuts, but an incorrect bill if she buys less than 12.

5.2   NESTED IF STATEMENTS

We can use any QBasic statements we want in the true and false branches of an IF statement—including IF statements. When an IF statement includes an IF statement in its true or false branch, we call it a **nested IF statement**. The following problem illustrates a nested IF statement.

nested IF statement
An IF statement that contains another IF statement in either its true or false branches.

EXAMPLE 2
USING A NESTED IF STATEMENT TO FIND THE LARGEST OF THREE NUMBERS

Problem Statement

Write a program that accepts three numbers and prints the largest number. Assume that none of the numbers is equal to another.

STEP 1   **Variable Names**

The variables in this problem are the following.

Variable	Variable Name
Input Variables	
The three numbers	`A, B, C`
Output Variable	
The largest number	`Largest`

STEP 2   **Algorithm**

The algorithm is

1. Execute steps 2 through 3 for all values of A, B, and C.
2. Compare pairs of variables until you can conclude which variable is the largest. Set Largest equal to that variable.
3. Print A, B, C, and Largest.

The heart of the algorithm is step 2, where we compare pairs of variables until we can conclude which is the largest. The flowchart in Figure 5.2 shows the logic involved. Step 2 begins at decision symbol 15, where we compare A and B. If A is greater than B, we know that B cannot be the largest, but we do not know anything about the relative size of A and C. So in the true branch, we compare A and C in decision symbol 16. If A is larger than C, then since A was already larger than B, we conclude that A is the largest—and in process symbol 17, we set Largest = A. If A is not larger than C, then we conclude that C is larger than A and since A was already larger than B, C is the largest—and in process symbol 19, we set Largest = C. Similar logic is implemented in the false branch of decision symbol 15.

STEP 3   **Hand-Calculated Answer**

This problem has no answers to be calculated, but when we plan the test data, we must be sure to choose data that test every path in the flowchart. You can't be sure your program is correct unless you check every path. The following data test the four paths through the nested IF statement; in every case, Largest is 3.

A	B	C
3	1	2
2	1	3
1	3	2
1	2	3

STEP 4   **QBasic Program**

Decision symbols 16 and 22 in the true and false branches of decision symbol 15 in Figure 5.2 lead to the nested IF statement in Program 5.2. The nested IF statement starts at line 15 and ends at line 27. Notice how the indention makes it easy to see the outer IF statement and the two inner IF statements.

Tracing the Program

If the condition in line 15

```
IF A > B THEN
```

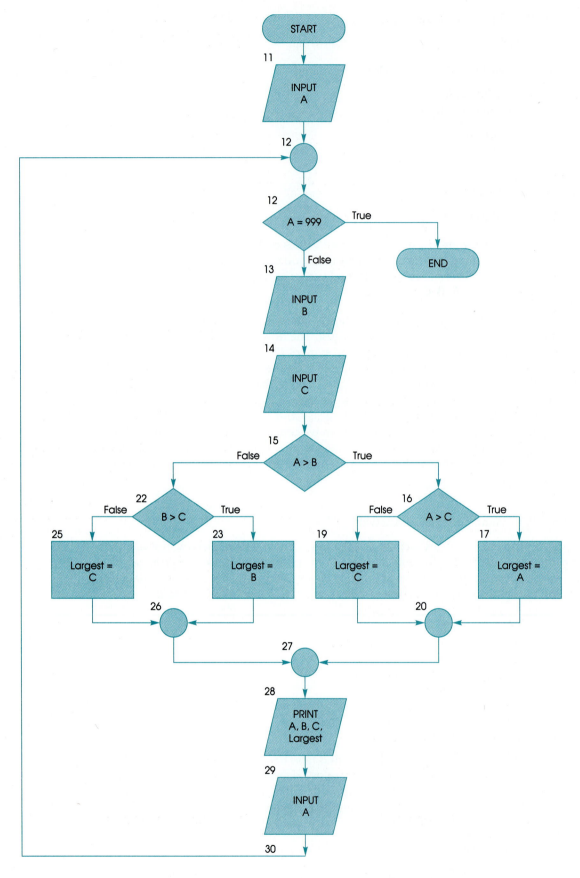

FIGURE 5.2 Flowchart to find the largest of three numbers using a nested IF statement.

```
 1 | '    *** FINDING THE LARGEST OF THREE NUMBERS ***
 2 | '    Find the largest number by successive compares
 3 |
 4 | '    Variables used
 5 |
 6 | '    A, B, and C        Three numbers
 7 | '    Largest            Largest of the three numbers
 8 |
 9 | CLS
10 | '    Process cases
11 | INPUT "Enter a number, 999 to stop: ", A
12 | DO UNTIL A = 999
13 |     INPUT "Enter a second number: ", B
14 |     INPUT "Enter a third number: ", C
15 |     IF A > B THEN
16 |         IF A > C THEN
17 |             Largest = A
18 |         ELSE
19 |             Largest = C
20 |         END IF
21 |     ELSE
22 |         IF B > C THEN
23 |             Largest = B
24 |         ELSE
25 |             Largest = C
26 |         END IF
27 |     END IF
28 |     PRINT "A = "; A; "B = "; B; "C = "; C; "Largest = "; Largest
29 |     INPUT "Enter a number, 999 to stop: ", A
30 | LOOP
31 | END
```

```
Enter a number, 999 to stop: 3
Enter a second number: 1
Enter a third number: 2
A =  3 B =  1 C =  2 Largest =  3
Enter a number, 999 to stop: 2
Enter a second number: 1
Enter a third number: 3
A =  2 B =  1 C =  3 Largest =  3
Enter a number, 999 to stop: 1
Enter a second number: 3
Enter a third number: 2
A =  1 B =  3 C =  2 Largest =  3
Enter a number, 999 to stop: 1
Enter a second number: 2
Enter a third number: 3
A =  1 B =  2 C =  3 Largest =  3
Enter a number, 999 to stop: 999
```

PROGRAM 5.2 A program that finds the largest of three numbers using a nested IF statement.

is true, the IF statement in line 16

```
IF A > C THEN
```

is executed. If this condition is true, line 17

```
Largest = A
```

is executed, setting Largest equal to A. If the condition in line 16 is false, line 19

```
Largest = C
```

is executed, setting Largest equal to C. In either case, QBasic next executes the PRINT statement in line 28, which prints the answer.

That completes the tracing of the true branch of the IF statement in line 15. We next trace the false branch. If the condition in line 15 is false, the IF statement in line 22

```
IF B > C THEN
```

is executed. If this condition is true, line 23

```
Largest = B
```

is executed, setting Largest equal to B. If the condition in line 22 is false, line 25

```
Largest = C
```

is executed, setting Largest equal to C. In either case, QBasic next executes the PRINT statement in line 28, which prints the answer. This processing is exactly what the flowchart illustrates. Notice that no matter which branches we follow, we always arrive at the PRINT statement in line 28.

Because the program contains three IF statements, it also contains three END IF statements. Students frequently leave out END IF statements. The syntax shows that every IF statement needs its own END IF statement. The output shows that in every case, the largest value was printed. ■

As a second example of nested IF statements, let's calculate ticket prices at a theater. The theater has the following schedule of prices:

Weekend
            Orchestra   12
            Balcony   8
Non-Weekend
        Senior Citizen
            Orchestra   7
            Balcony   4
        Non-Senior Citizen
            Orchestra   9
            Balcony   6

To solve this problem, we introduce three variables: Weekend$, Senior$, and Orch$. These variables either have the value Y (meaning that the time is the weekend, the customer is a senior citizen, and the location is the orchestra) or they have the value N (meaning that the time is *not* the weekend, the customer is *not* a senior citizen, and the location is *not* the orchestra). The variable Price is the ticket price.

The flowchart that implements this logic is shown in Figure 5.3. The nested IF statement that determines the ticket price is

```
IF Weekend$ = "Y" THEN
    IF Orch$ = "Y" THEN
        Price = 12
    ELSE
        Price = 8
    END IF
ELSE
    IF Senior$ = "Y" THEN
        IF Orch$ = "Y" THEN
            Price = 7
        ELSE
            Price = 4
        END IF
    ELSE
        IF Orch$ = "Y" THEN
            Price = 9
        ELSE
            Price = 6
        END IF
    END IF
END IF
```

If you draw a flowchart before you start coding, use proper indention, and remember that every IF statement requires its own END IF statement, you will find that nested IF statements are very powerful and not difficult to learn.

Logical Operators

Often a decision depends on two or more conditions. For example, suppose that to encourage people to buy refrigerators that help the environment, the government offers to pay a rebate of $20 to anyone who buys a refrigerator whose efficiency is greater than 80 percent and that does not use CFC (which destroys the ozone layer).

The logic for this decision problem can be simplified by using a compound condition. A **compound condition** is a set of two or more simple conditions, like the ones we have studied so far, that are connected by the reserved words AND or OR. These words, along with the word NOT, are the most common examples of what are known as **logical operators**.

compound condition
A set of two or more simple conditions joined by the reserved words AND or OR.

AND Operator

Let Eff stand for the refrigerator's efficiency and CFC$ indicate whether it uses CFC. Figure 5.4 shows the flowchart for this rebate policy using a compound condition. That flowchart is written as the following IF statement:

logical operator
In this book, one of the reserved words AND, OR, and NOT.

```
IF Eff > 80 AND CFC$ = "NO" THEN
    Rebate = 20
ELSE
    Rebate = 0
END IF
```

The condition

```
Eff > 80 AND CFC$ = "NO"
```

is an example of a compound condition that uses the logical operator AND to join two simple conditions. When two simple conditions are connected by AND, the compound condition is true only if both simple conditions are true. In this case,

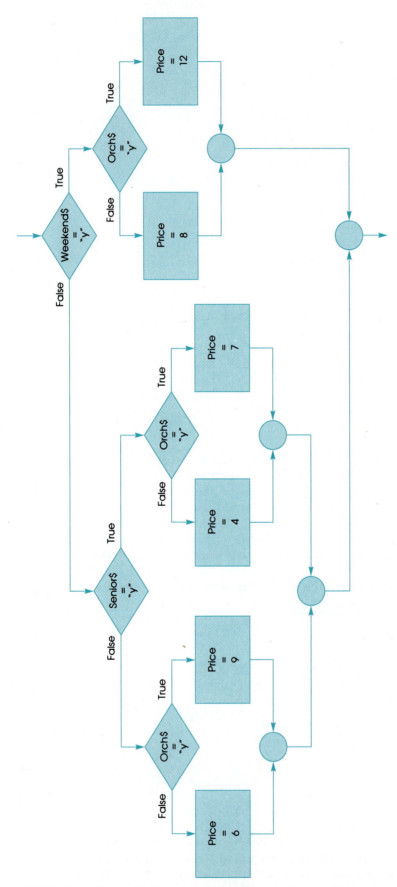

FIGURE 5.3   Flowchart to determine ticket prices using a nested IF statement.

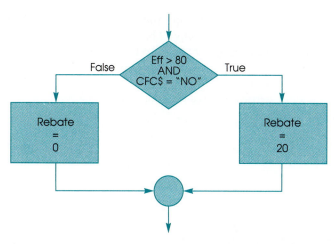

FIGURE 5.4   Flowchart for the first rebate policy using a compound condition.

the compound condition is true if Eff is greater than 80 and CFC$ is equal to NO. When these conditions are true, we want to pay the $20 rebate—so in the true branch, we set Rebate equal to 20. If either one or both of these conditions is false, the compound condition is also false. Under that condition, we do not want to pay the rebate—so in the false branch, we set Rebate equal to 0.

This problem could also be solved using nested IF statements. The advantage of using a compound condition in this case is that the flowchart and the IF statement closely follow the logic of the problem. Remember that we wanted to pay the rebate if Eff was greater than 80 and CFC$ was equal to NO—and those are exactly the conditions we wrote in the IF statement.

Another example of AND used in a compound condition is

```
IF Month$ = "July" AND Day = 4 THEN
    PRINT "Independence Day"
END IF
```

This statement will print Independence Day only if Month$ is equal to July and Day is equal to 4.

Compound conditions can also be used with DO and LOOP statements. Imagine that a user is supposed to enter a number between 10 and 20 (including the end points 10 and 20). We can trap values that are outside the correct range using the following DO loop:

```
INPUT "Enter a number between 10 and 20: ", Number
DO UNTIL Number >= 10 AND Number <= 20
    BEEP
    INPUT "Enter a number between 10 and 20: ", Number
LOOP
```

You must be particularly careful when you write this kind of compound condition. In English it is correct to say "number" only once: "If number is greater than or equal to 10 and less than or equal to 20." Translating that sentence into a condition

```
Number >= 10 AND <= 20
```

is *wrong*. The operator AND must connect two complete conditions. That means that you must include the variable Number in both conditions—even if it seems repetitive—as we did in the example.

If Number is between 10 and 20, the condition will be true and the loop will not be entered. If Number is *not* between 10 and 20, the condition will be false and the loop will be entered. In the loop, we use the BEEP statement to beep the computer's speaker and request input again. The program will stay in the loop until the user enters a value in the correct range.

Beeping the speaker is an effective way of getting the user's attention. The syntax of the BEEP statement is simply

```
BEEP
```

OR Operator

As an alternative rebate policy, suppose the government agrees to pay the $20 rebate to anyone who buys a refrigerator whose efficiency is greater than 80 percent *or* that doesn't use CFC. Figure 5.5 shows the flowchart for this rebate policy. That flowchart is written as the following IF statement:

```
IF Eff > 80 OR CFC$ = "NO" THEN
    Rebate = 20
ELSE
    Rebate = 0
END IF
```

The condition

```
Eff > 80 OR CFC$ = "NO"
```

is an example of a compound condition that uses the logical operator OR to join two simple conditions. When two simple conditions are connected by OR, the compound condition is true if either or both simple conditions are true. In this case, the compound condition is true if Eff is greater than 80 or CFC$ is equal to NO. Because when either of these conditions is true, we want to pay the rebate, in the true branch we set Rebate equal to 20. If both of these conditions are false, the compound condition will be false. Under that condition, we do not want to pay the rebate, so in the false branch we set Rebate equal to 0.

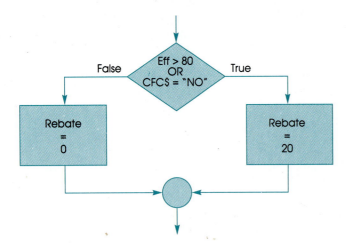

FIGURE 5.5 Flowchart for the second rebate policy using a compound condition.

Another example of OR used in a compound condition is

```
IF Weather$ = "Rain" OR Weather$ = "Snow" THEN
    PRINT "No swimming today."
END IF
```

This statement prints

```
No swimming today
```

if Weather$ is equal to either Rain or Snow.

Earlier, we used the AND operator in a condition to check whether a user entered a value between 10 and 20. We could also use the OR operator to perform that test if we replace >= by < and <= by > and change UNTIL to WHILE. The DO loop becomes

```
INPUT "Enter a number between 10 and 20 ", Number
DO WHILE Number < 10 OR Number > 20
    BEEP
    INPUT "Enter a number between 10 and 20 ", Number
LOOP
```

Notice that in this case, if Number is between 10 and 20, the condition is false, so the loop is not entered. If Number is not between 10 and 20, the loop is entered, which is where the BEEP statement beeps the computer's speaker and the INPUT statement requests input. As with the earlier example, the program stays in the loop until the user enters a value in the correct range.

Sometimes compound conditions are so complicated that we can't be sure what they mean. For example, the condition

```
Yield > 10 OR Maturity < 15 AND TaxFree$ = "Y"
```

can be read two ways. The first way is

```
(Yield > 10 OR Maturity < 15) AND TaxFree$ = "Y"
```

and the second way is

```
Yield > 10 OR (Maturity < 15 AND TaxFree$ = "Y")
```

Just as QBasic follows a hierarchy of operations to evaluate arithmetic expressions, so it also follows a hierarchy of operations to evaluate logical expressions. QBasic evaluates the AND operator before the OR operator, so if you don't code parentheses, QBasic will interpret this condition the second way. Rather than take a chance that your interpretation of a complex compound condition will disagree with QBasic's, it is safer to use parentheses to force the interpretation you want. Using extra parentheses also makes the statement clearer to anyone who reads your program and may simplify future modifications.

NOT Operator

NOT is also a logical operator. NOT negates the condition it operates on. NOT is most useful when it is applied to compound conditions. Suppose we want to print

```
Special Processing
```

if BloodType$ is not A, B, or O. You can write this IF statement in several correct ways (and even more incorrect ways), but the most straightforward correct way is

```
IF NOT (BloodType$ = "A" OR BloodType$ = "B" OR BloodType$ = "O") THEN
    PRINT "Special Processing"
END IF
```

This discussion of logical operators is summarized in the following table.

A	B	A AND B	A OR B	NOT A
True	True	True	True	False
True	False	False	True	False
False	True	False	True	True
False	False	False	False	True

Syntax Summary

BEEP Statement

Form: BEEP
Example: BEEP
Explanation: Causes the computer's speaker to beep.

5.2 EXERCISES

1. Nested IF statements that are not indented properly are hard to understand. Rewrite the following nested IF statement using proper indention, and then answer the questions.

```
IF R > 5 THEN
PRINT "Red"
IF S = 0 THEN
PRINT "Blue"
ELSE
PRINT "Yellow"
END IF
PRINT "Green"
IF T < 10 THEN
PRINT "Black"
ELSE
PRINT "White"
END IF
END IF
```

   ★a) What is printed if R = 8, S = 3, and T > 805?
   b) What is printed if R > 800, S = 0, and T = 0?
   c) What is printed if R = 4, S = 0, and T = 9?

2. A broker recommends stock based on profit, sales, and growth rate. If profit is less than 8 percent, the stock should be sold. If profit is greater than or equal to 8 percent, the stock should be held. However, if profit is greater than or equal to 8 percent and either sales is greater than $2 million or growth rate is greater than 10 percent, the stock should be bought. Write a nested IF statement to implement this logic and display either Sell, Hold, or Buy.

★3. Write the IF statement that prints Lousy Day if Temp and Humidity are both over 90.

4. Write a nested IF statement to implement the following flowcharts.

★**a)**

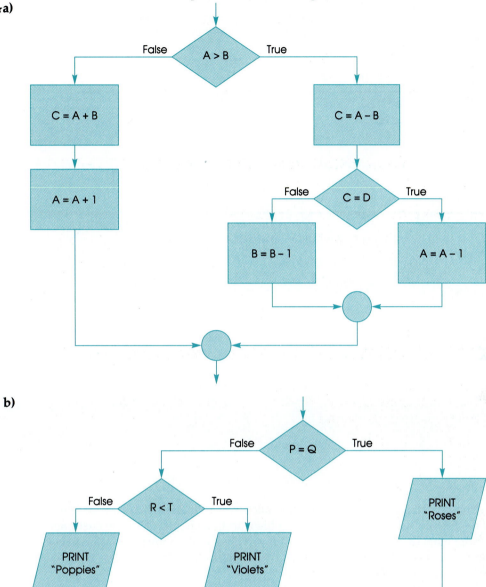

b)

5. Write an IF statement that prints Summer Vacation if Month$ equals June, July, or August.

6. For values of A of 1, 2, 3, and 4, determine whether the following compound conditions are true or false:
   a) `A <> 2 OR A <> 3`
   b) `NOT (A = 2 OR A = 3)`

7. If Make$ = Ford, and Doors = 4, determine if the following compound conditions are true or false:
   ★a) `Make$ = "Ford" OR Doors = 4`
   b) `Make$ = "Honda" OR Doors = 4`
   ★c) `Make$ = "Honda" AND Doors = 4`
   d) `Make$ = "Ford" AND Doors = 4`
   e) `Make$ <> "Honda" OR Doors = 2`
   f) `Make$ <> "Honda" AND Doors >= 2`

8. If A is 25, what is printed by the following IF statement?

```
IF A >= 0 OR <= 20 THEN
    PRINT "A is between 0 and 20"
ELSE
    PRINT "A is less than 0 or greater than 20"
END IF
```

5.3 MULTIPLE-ALTERNATIVE DECISIONS

multiple-alternative decision
A decision in which more than two choices exist.

The simple IF statement we have studied allows us to make a two-way decision, such as the one we made in the first problem in this chapter: Did the customer buy more than 12 doughnuts or not? Often, we must make a **multiple-alternative decision**, a decision in which more than two choices exist. The complete IF statement allows us to make such decisions.

The format of the complete IF statement—which can be used to make multiple-alternative decisions—is

```
IF condition1 THEN
    statements executed if condition1 is true
[ELSEIF condition2 THEN
    statements executed if condition2 is true]
[ELSEIF condition3 THEN
    statements executed if condition3 is true]
    .
    .
    .
[ELSE
    statements executed if all the conditions are false]
END IF
```

The column of three dots indicates that you can have as many ELSEIF clauses as you need. When QBasic executes an IF statement, it first evaluates condition1. If condition1 is true, QBasic executes the statements between THEN and the first ELSEIF, and then branches to the statement following the END IF. If condition1 is false, QBasic evaluates condition2. If condition2 is true, QBasic executes the statements between the second THEN and the second ELSEIF, and then branches to the statement following the END IF. If condition2 is false, QBasic goes to the next ELSEIF, and evaluates its condition. This continues until QBasic finds a condition that is true. If all of the conditions are false, the statements following ELSE are executed. If all of the conditions are false and there is no ELSE clause, then none of the statements is executed, and execution continues at the statement following END IF. Notice that since this is one IF statement, there is only one END IF statement.

These ideas will become clearer if we consider an example. Suppose a user enters values for two strings—A$ and B$—and we want to know if A$ is less than B$, if A$ is equal to B$, or if A$ is greater than B$. This is a three-way decision because three possible outcomes exist: less than, equal to, and greater than. The flowchart for this decision problem is shown in Figure 5.6. This flowchart is represented by the following IF statement:

```
IF A$ < B$ THEN
     PRINT "A$ is less than B$"
ELSEIF A$ = B$ THEN
     PRINT "A$ is equal to B$"
ELSE
     PRINT "A$ is greater than B$"
END IF
```

If the condition A$ < B$ is true, QBasic executes the first PRINT statement, displays A$ is less than B$, and then branches to the statement following the END IF. If the condition A$ < B$ is false, QBasic evaluates the condition A$ = B$. If that

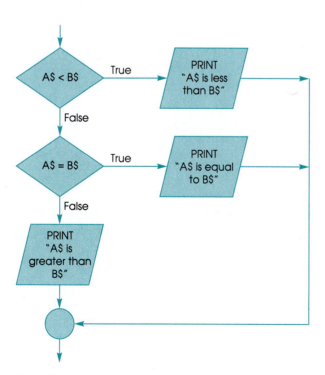

FIGURE 5.6   Flowchart to determine if A$ is less than, equal to, or greater than B$ using a multiple-alternate decision.

condition is true, QBasic executes the second PRINT statement, and displays A\$ is equal to B\$. If that condition is false, QBasic executes the PRINT statement in the ELSE clause, and displays A\$ is greater than B\$. In any case, execution continues with the statement following the END IF.

The ELSE clause could be replaced with an ELSEIF clause:

```
ELSEIF A$ > B$
    PRINT "A$ is greater than B$"
```

This version is less efficient than the earlier version because the computer must evaluate an unnecessary condition, but it is clearer because the condition that leads to the execution of the PRINT statement is shown.

EXAMPLE 3

USING A MULTIPLE-ALTERNATIVE DECISION TO DETERMINE AN INSURANCE PREMIUM

As another example of a problem that requires a multiple-alternative decision, consider the Titanic Insurance Company, which sets its automobile insurance premiums based on whether any young drivers are in the household and whether the car is garaged. The premium is determined as follows:

Case Number	1	2	3	4
Young Driver	Yes	Yes	No	No
Garaged	Yes	No	Yes	No
Premium	470	540	350	385

Problem Statement

Write a program that accepts information about a customer's policy, and calculates and prints the insurance premium.

STEP 1   Variable Names

We begin by identifying and naming the following variables.

Variable	Variable Name
Input Variables	
Are there young drivers	`YoungDriver$`
Is the car garaged	`Garaged$`
Output Variable	
Premium	`Premium`

The variable YoungDriver\$ will have either the value Y (to indicate that there are young drivers) or N (to indicate that there are no young drivers). Similarly, the variable Garaged\$ will have the values Y or N—indicating that the car either is (Y) or is not (N) garaged.

STEP 2   Algorithm

The algorithm is particularly simple:

1. Execute steps 2 through 4 for all customers.
2. Input data for a customer.
3. Determine the premium for this customer.
4. Print the premium for this customer.

We will figure out how to determine the premium when we draw the flowchart.

Figure 5.7 shows the flowchart for this problem. This flowchart uses connectors, which are circles with letters in them. The connector at symbol 19 is an input connector, and the connector at symbol 46 is an output connector. Connectors are used in place of flowlines when drawing the flowlines would make the flowchart cluttered and hard to read, or when the flowchart extends over more than one page. To show which connectors go together, you put the same letter inside them. In Figure 5.7, output connector B simply means that the flowchart continues at input connector B. Input connector A and output connector A show the pretest UNTIL loop.

I/O symbols 17, 21, and 44 show a new statement, INPUT$. We will explain how INPUT$ is used when we examine the program.

Flowchart symbols 24 through 30 determine the premium. They show how you draw a flowchart for a multiple-alternative decision. The true branches lead to a process symbol, and the false branches lead to the next decision symbol. The actual conditions that will be tested are too long to show on the flowchart, so they are represented as condition 1, condition 2, and so on. As you will see when we examine the program, the actual conditions correspond to the four given in the statement of the problem.

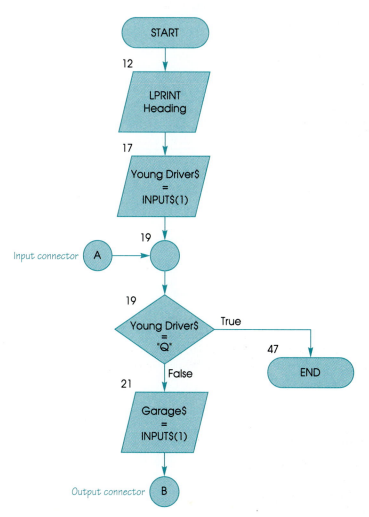

FIGURE 5.7   Flowchart to determine insurance premiums using a multiple-alternate decision. *(continued on next page)*

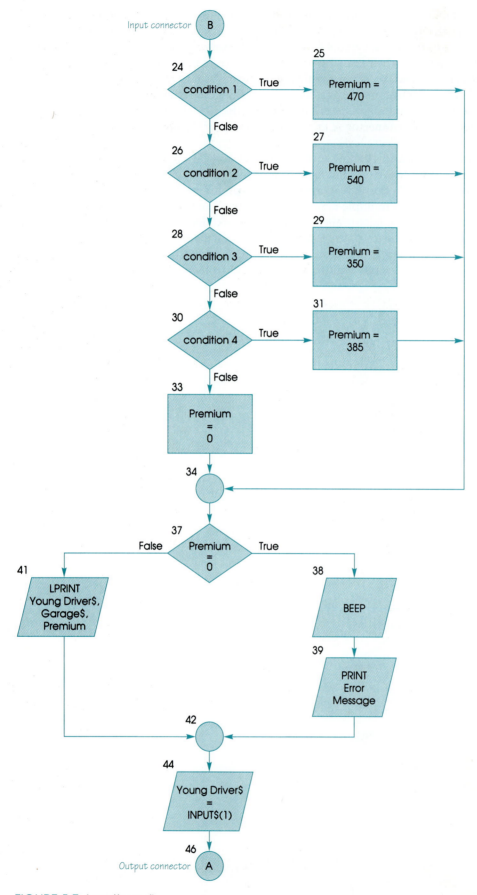

FIGURE 5.7 *(continued)*

Notice the false branch from the last decision, in which we set Premium to 0. This branch is taken if all of the four conditions are false. Since the four conditions include all the possible combinations of Y and N, you may wonder how all four conditions could be false. They could all be false if the user enters invalid data. There is nothing to prevent a user from hitting the wrong key and entering a U when he or she meant to enter a Y. In that case, all of the conditions are false and the Premium is set to 0.

You should understand that we cannot check that the *correct* data were entered. It is still possible for users to enter an N when they should enter a Y instead. All we can do is verify that either a Y or an N was entered.

Whenever possible, you should check that the data entered are valid. In our earlier programs, we did not make this check because we had no way of knowing if the data were valid. When a name or a pay rate is entered, just about any value could be valid, so the program cannot determine whether valid data were entered. In this problem, we can check that the data are valid because the only valid data are Y or N.

In decision symbol 37, we test Premium. If Premium is 0, we beep the speaker and print an error message, telling the user that he or she has entered invalid data, and to try again. If Premium is not 0, we print the input data and the premium.

This flowchart might be criticized because it doesn't test for invalid data until all the data are entered. If the user enters an invalid value, he or she must reenter all the data, including the values that were entered correctly. In Chapter 6, you will see a more sophisticated program that checks each value when it is entered.

This is the most complicated flowchart so far. As your flowcharts get more complicated, you should check them when you finish them. Make sure that every flowchart symbol has a flowline leaving it. Without an exit flowline from a symbol, you haven't specified what you want to do next. The only flowchart symbol that does not require an exit flowline is the terminal symbol.

STEP 3 Hand-Calculated Answer

The answers were given when we specified the premiums. We must check that the program gives the correct premiums for all four cases.

STEP 4 QBasic Program

Instead of using the INPUT statement, Program 5.3 uses the INPUT$ function to obtain input from the keyboard.

The INPUT$ Function

After clearing the screen and printing a heading, in line 17 the program uses the INPUT$ function to obtain data for YoungDriver$. The INPUT$ function accepts data entered from the keyboard, without requiring the user to press the Enter key. The syntax of the INPUT$ function is

```
string-variable = INPUT$(n)
```

Notice that the INPUT$ function returns a string. In this statement, n is the argument of the INPUT$ function. It specifies the number of string characters to be accepted from the keyboard. Thus, line 17, the statement

```
YoungDriver$ = UCASE$(INPUT$(1))
```

specifies the value of n as 1. That is, when a user types one character, that character is accepted by the INPUT$ function, converted to upper case by UCASE$, and assigned to YoungDriver$. We convert the input data to upper case so that later

```
 1 |  '     *** TITANIC AUTOMOBILE INSURANCE PREMIUMS ***
 2 |  '     Calculate insurance premiums
 3 |
 4 |  '     Variables used
 5 |
 6 |  '     Garaged$             Is the car garaged
 7 |  '     Premium              Premium
 8 |  '     YoungDriver$         Are there young drivers
 9 |
10 | CLS
11 |  '     Print heading and define format string
12 | LPRINT "Young Drivers  Garaged  Premium"
13 | Fmt$ = "        !            !        ### "
14 |
15 |  '     Process customers
16 | PRINT "Are there drivers under 25 (Y/N), Q to quit? ";
17 | YoungDriver$ = UCASE$(INPUT$(1))
18 | PRINT YoungDriver$
19 | DO UNTIL YoungDriver$ = "Q"
20 |     PRINT "Is the car garaged (Y/N)? ";
21 |     Garage$ = UCASE$(INPUT$(1))
22 |     PRINT Garage$
23 |     'Calculate the premium
24 |     IF YoungDriver$ = "Y" AND Garage$ = "Y" THEN
25 |         Premium = 470
26 |     ELSEIF YoungDriver$ = "Y" AND Garage$ = "N" THEN
27 |         Premium = 540
28 |     ELSEIF YoungDriver$ = "N" AND Garage$ = "Y" THEN
29 |         Premium = 350
30 |     ELSEIF YoungDriver$ = "N" AND Garage$ = "N" THEN
31 |         Premium = 385
32 |     ELSE
33 |         Premium = 0
34 |     END IF
35 |
36 |     'Print premium
37 |     IF Premium = 0 THEN
38 |         BEEP
39 |         PRINT "Invalid data entered, please try again"
40 |     ELSE
41 |         LPRINT USING Fmt$; YoungDriver$; Garage$; Premium
42 |     END IF
43 |     PRINT "Are there drivers under 25 (Y/N), Q to quit? ";
44 |     YoungDriver$ = UCASE$(INPUT$(1))
45 |     PRINT YoungDriver$
46 | LOOP
47 | END
```

PROGRAM 5.3 A program that determines insurance premiums using a multiple-alternative decision. *(continued on next page)*

```
Are there any drivers under 25 (Y/N), Q to quit? Y      } First case
Is the car garaged (Y/N)? Y
Are there any drivers under 25 (Y/N), Q to quit? Y
Is the car garaged (Y/N)? U      ←—————— Invalid data
Invalid data entered, please try again      ←—————— Error message
Are there any drivers under 25 (Y/N), Q to quit? Y      } Second case
Is the car garaged (Y/N)? N
Are there any drivers under 25 (Y/N), Q to quit? N      } Third case
Is the car garaged (Y/N)? Y
Are there any drivers under 25 (Y/N), Q to quit? N      } Fourth case
Is the car garaged (Y/N)? N
Are there any drivers under 25 (Y/N), Q to quit? Q
```

Young Drivers	Garaged	Premium
Y	Y	470
Y	N	540
N	Y	350
N	N	385

PROGRAM 5.3 *(continued)*

we will determine the correct premium—even if a user disregards the instructions and enters a lower case y or n instead of upper case.

INPUT$ is convenient for the user, who does not have to press the Enter key. But you cannot always use INPUT$. For example, we couldn't use INPUT$ in most of our earlier programs because we didn't know how many characters of data would be entered. We couldn't know whether the user entering data for PayRate would enter one character (such as 5), two characters (such as 12), or perhaps four characters (such as 6.25). When INPUT$ is used, we must specify, by its argument, how many characters of data will be entered.

In addition to the need to specify an argument, the INPUT$ function differs from the INPUT statement in two important ways. First, the INPUT$ function does not provide a way to print a prompt. Second, it does not automatically display the input value on the screen. To achieve those effects, you must add PRINT statements like those in lines 16, 18, 20, and 22. Also, if you want the input value to be displayed next to the prompt—the way it is when the INPUT statement is used—you must end the PRINT statement that prints the prompt with a semicolon (as in lines 16 and 20).

ILLUSTRATIONS

INPUT$ Function	Effect
`Response$ = INPUT$(1)`	Accepts one character and assigns it to Response$.
`StateAbv$ = UCASE$(INPUT$(2))`	Accepts two characters, which are converted to upper case by the UCASE$ function and assigned to StateAbv$.

Determining the Premium

Returning to the program, the Premium is determined in lines 24 through 34. This is a single IF statement with three ELSEIF clauses. QBasic tests each condition in turn. If the user enters valid data, one of the four conditions is true. QBasic executes the LET statement that follows that condition, which sets Premium to the correct value, and then branches to line 37. For example, suppose the user enters Y for YoungDriver$ and N for Garage$. The condition in line 24 is false, but the condition in line 26 is true, so the LET statement in line 27 sets the Premium at 540.

If the user enters invalid data, none of the conditions is true, so QBasic executes the LET statement in the ELSE clause in line 33, which sets Premium to 0.

Premium is then tested in line 37:

```
IF Premium = 0 THEN
    BEEP
    PRINT "Invalid data entered, please try again"
ELSE
    LPRINT USING Fmt$; YoungDriver$; Garage$; Premium
END IF
```

If Premium is 0, the program beeps the speaker and displays an error message. If Premium is not 0, the LPRINT statement prints the input data and Premium.

The program output shows the user entering a U, and the error message that the program displayed. (The speaker also beeped, but you can't hear that.) The output shows four correctly calculated premiums. ∎

Syntax Summary

IF Statement

Form:
```
IF condition1 THEN
    statements executed if condition1 is true
[ELSEIF condition2 THEN
    statements executed if condition2 is true]
[ELSEIF condition3 THEN
    statements executed if condition3 is true]
    .
    .
    .
[ELSE
    statements executed if all the conditions are↵
        false]
END IF
```

Example:
```
IF Number = 1 THEN
    PRINT "Number is 1"
ELSEIF Number = 2 THEN
    PRINT "Number is 2"
ELSEIF Number = 3 THEN
    PRINT "Number is 3"
ELSE
    PRINT "Number is not 1, 2, or 3"
END IF
```

Explanation: QBasic first evaluates condition1. If condition1 is true,
QBasic executes the statements between THEN and the first
ELSEIF, and then branches to the statement following the
END IF. If condition1 is false, QBasic evaluates condition2. If
condition2 is true, QBasic executes the statements between
the second THEN and the second ELSEIF, and then branches
to the statement following the END IF. If condition2 is false,
QBasic goes to the next ELSEIF, and evaluates its condition.
This continues until QBasic finds a condition that is true. If
all of the conditions are false, the statements following ELSE
are executed. If all of the conditions are false and there is no
ELSE clause, then none of the statements is executed, and
execution continues at the statement following END IF.

INPUT$ Function

Form: `string-variable = INPUT$(n)`
Example: `Dept$ = INPUT$(2)`
Explanation: Accepts n characters from the keyboard and assigns them to
the string variable on the left of the equals sign. The user
does not have to press the Enter key.

5.3 EXERCISES

1. In Program 5.3, lines 12 and 41 are LPRINT statements, but lines 16, 18, 20,
    22, 39, 43, and 45 are PRINT statements. Why aren't all of these LPRINT
    statements?

★2. Would Program 5.3 give the same results if lines 26 and 27 were inter-
    changed with lines 28 and 29?

3. Write an IF statement to perform the following logic: If A and B are both 0,
    print A and B are zero. If A is 1 but B is not 1, print A is 1, but B is not. If B
    is 1, but A is not, print B is 1, but A is not. Finally, if none of these cases is
    true, print Special Case.

4. A program accepts the following data:

    a) Address
    b) Gender (M/F)
    c) Social security number
    d) Married (Y/N)

    Which of these values could be accepted using an INPUT$ function?

★5. Write a statement to use INPUT$ to assign four characters to Section$.

5.4 THE SELECT CASE STATEMENT

Often a multiple-alternative decision involves only one variable. In those cases it is clearer to use the SELECT CASE statement instead of an IF statement with ELSEIF clauses.

As an example, suppose a user entered a value for the variable Number and we want to test Number, and print one of the messages: The number is positive, The number is zero, or The number is negative. The flowchart for this decision problem is shown in Figure 5.8. This flowchart shows the symbol used for the SELECT CASE statement. The variable that is tested is put inside a diamond, and each branch is labeled with the value that causes that branch to be taken. The small circle represents the END SELECT statement that marks the end of the SELECT CASE statement.

The SELECT CASE statement that implements this logic is

```
SELECT CASE Number
    CASE IS > 0
        PRINT "The number is positive"
    CASE IS = 0
        PRINT "The number is zero"
    CASE IS < 0
        PRINT "The number is negative"
END SELECT
```

When QBasic executes this statement, it compares Number with the first test, > 0. If this test is true (that is, if Number is greater than 0), QBasic executes the first PRINT statement, displays The number is positive, and then branches to the statement following the END SELECT. If the first test is not true, QBasic compares Number with the second test, = 0. If this test is true, QBasic executes the

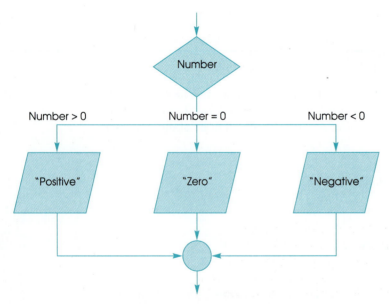

FIGURE 5.8   Flowchart to determine if a number is positive, zero, or negatrive using a SELECT CASE statement.

second PRINT statement, displays The number is zero, and then branches to the statement following the END SELECT. If the second test is not true, QBasic compares Number with the third test, < 0. If this test is true (as it must be since the first two tests were false), QBasic executes the third PRINT statement, displays The number is negative, and branches to the statement following the END SELECT. Each CASE clause may consist of one QBasic statement, as they do here, or as many statements as you need.

EXAMPLE 4

USING A SELECT CASE STATEMENT TO CALCULATE COMMISSION

The SELECT CASE statement can also be used to calculate commissions when commission rate depends on sales.

Problem Statement

Write a program to calculate commission if the commission rate depends on sales, as in the following table.

Sales	Commission Rate
Sales less than $100	10%
Sales greater than or equal to $100 but less than $500	20%
Sales greater than or equal to $500 but less than $1000	30%
Sales greater than or equal to $1000	40%

STEP 1   Variable Names

We identify and name the following variables:

Variable	Variable Name
Input Variables	
Sales	Sales
Salesperson's name	SalesName$
Output Variables	
Rate	Rate
Commission	Commission

STEP 2   Algorithm

The algorithm for this problem is

1. Execute steps 2 through 5 for all salespeople.
2. Input SalesName$ and Sales for a salesperson.
3. Determine this salesperson's commission Rate.
4. Calculate Commission using the appropriate Rate.
5. Print SalesName$, Sales, Rate, and Commission.

Since we used a flowchart for the previous SELECT CASE problem, this time we will use pseudocode:

```
Calculate commission when rate depends on sales
Input SalesName$
Do until trailer data is entered
   Input Sales
   Select case Sales
      Sales between 0 and 99.99
         Rate = 10%
      Sales between 100 and 499.99
         Rate = 20%
      Sales between 500 and 999.99
         Rate = 30%
      Sales greater than or equal to 1000
         Rate = 40%
      None of the previous tests was true
         Rate = 0
   End select
   If Rate = 0
      Print error message
   Else
      Commission = Rate * Sales
      Print SalesName$, Sales, Rate, Commission
   End if
   Input SalesName$
End of loop
End
```

STEP 3   Hand-Calculated Answers

We need four test cases, corresponding to the four categories for commission rate. The four test cases and their answers are as follows.

Case Number	Sales	Rate	Commission
1	50	0.1	5
2	200	0.2	40
3	700	0.3	210
4	2,000	0.4	800

STEP 4   QBasic Program

Program 5.4 shows the QBasic program based on this pseudocode. After printing a heading, the program accepts data for SalesName$ and Sales, in lines 17 and 19. The SELECT CASE statement in lines 20 through 31 uses Sales to determine the Rate:

```
SELECT CASE Sales
    CASE 0 TO 99.99
        Rate = .1
    CASE 100 TO 499.99
        Rate = .2
    CASE 500 TO 999.99
        Rate = .3
    CASE IS >= 1000
        Rate = .4
    CASE ELSE
        Rate = 0
END SELECT
```

```
 1  |  '    *** SALES COMMISSION PROBLEM ***
 2  |  '    Calculate salesperson's commission
 3  |
 4  |  '    Variables used
 5  |
 6  |  '    Commission      Commission
 7  |  '    Rate            Commission rate
 8  |  '    Sales           Sales
 9  |  '    SalesName$      Salesperson's name
10  |
11  |  CLS
12  |  '    Print heading and define format string
13  |  LPRINT "Name            Sales    Rate    Commission"
14  |  Fmt$ = "\            \    #,###    #.##       $###.## "
15  |
16  |  '    Process salespeople
17  |  INPUT "Enter name, EOD to stop: ", SalesName$
18  |  DO UNTIL UCASE$(SalesName$) = "EOD"
19  |      INPUT "Enter sales: ", Sales
20  |      SELECT CASE Sales
21  |          CASE 0 TO 99.99
22  |              Rate = .1
23  |          CASE 100 TO 499.99
24  |              Rate = .2
25  |          CASE 500 TO 999.99
26  |              Rate = .3
27  |          CASE IS >= 1000
28  |              Rate = .4
29  |          CASE ELSE
30  |              Rate = 0
31  |      END SELECT
32  |      IF Rate = 0 THEN
33  |          BEEP
34  |          PRINT Sales; " is not a valid value"
35  |      ELSE
36  |          Commission = Rate * Sales
37  |          LPRINT USING Fmt$; SalesName$; Sales; Rate; Commission
38  |      END IF
39  |      INPUT "Enter name, EOD to stop: ", SalesName$
40  |  LOOP
41  |  END
```

```
Enter name, EOD to stop: George
Enter sales: 50
Enter name, EOD to stop: Maria
Enter sales: 99.995        ◀────────── Invalid data
 99.995  is not a valid value ◀────── Error message
Enter name, EOD to stop: Mei
Enter sales: 200
Enter name, EOD to stop: Paul
Enter sales: 700
Enter name, EOD to stop: Helen
Enter sales: 2000
Enter name, EOD to stop: EOD
```

PROGRAM 5.4   A program that calculates commission using a SELECT CASE statement. *(continued on next page)*

Name	Sales	Rate	Commission
George	50	0.10	$ 5.00
Mei	200	0.20	$ 40.00
Paul	700	0.30	$210.00
Helen	2,000	0.40	$800.00

PROGRAM 5.4   *(continued)*

The first three CASE clauses show how you can specify a range of values against which Sales is to be tested. For example, the first CASE clause uses the range 0 TO 99.99. If Sales is in the range 0 to 99.99 (including the end points), the test will be true, and QBasic will execute the LET statement in the next line, setting Rate to .1. The fourth CASE clause is similar to those we studied earlier, using a relational operator to test if Sales is >= 1000.

Finally, the last clause is a CASE ELSE clause. The statement following a CASE ELSE clause is executed if none of the previous tests was true. In Program 5.4, this could happen if Sales were negative, or if Sales had a meaningless value like 99.995. Of course, Sales should never have such values, but you can't count on users to always enter valid data. It is important to code a CASE ELSE clause to catch invalid data because if none of the CASE tests is true and a SELECT CASE statement doesn't have a CASE ELSE clause, program execution continues normally.

The rest of the program is similar to Program 5.3 (pages 160–161). In line 32, we test Rate:

```
IF Rate = 0 THEN
    BEEP
    PRINT Sales; " is not a valid value"
ELSE
    Commission = Rate * Sales
    LPRINT USING Fmt$; SalesName$; Sales; Rate; Commission
END IF
```

If Rate is 0, we beep the computer's speaker and print an error message. If Rate is not 0, we calculate Commission, then print the input data and the calculated Commission.

The output shows that the correct Commission was calculated for the four test cases, and that an error message was printed when invalid data were entered.

■

Syntax of the SELECT CASE Statement

With these examples behind us, it's time to look at the complete syntax of the SELECT CASE statement.

```
SELECT CASE testexpression
    CASE test1
        statement(s) to be executed if test1 is true
    [CASE test2
        statement(s) to be executed if test2 is true]
        .
        .
        .
    [CASE ELSE
        statement(s) to be executed if all tests are false]
END SELECT
```

The three vertical dots indicate that you can have as many CASE clauses as you need. Each CASE clause may also have as many statements as you need. In the first line, testexpression may be a numeric or string expression, but is usually a variable. QBasic compares testexpression against each of the tests in turn. When it finds a test that is true, it executes the statements that belong to that CASE clause, and then branches to the statement after the END SELECT. If none of the tests is true, QBasic executes the statements following the CASE ELSE statement.

The tests that are coded as part of the CASE clause may have several forms. You can list a value or a series of values, you can use the word IS and a relational operator, and you can use the word TO and a range of values. Assuming that the SELECT CASE clause is

```
SELECT CASE N
```

the following table shows the test, an example, and the conditions under which the test is true.

Test	Example	Meaning
value	2	Test is true if N equals 2.
value,...	2, 4, 6, 8	Test is true if N equals 2, 4, 6, or 8.
expression,...	3, A, B ^ 2	Test is true if N equals 3, A or B ^ 2.
IS relop* expression	IS > 50	Test is true if N is greater than 50.
	IS <= LowLimit	Test is true if N is less than or equal to LowLimit.
expression TO expression	10 TO 20	Test is true if N is between 10 and 20, including the end points.
	Low TO High	Test is true if N is between Low and High, including the end points.

*Note: relop means one of the relational operators =, <, >, <=, >=, or <>.

Notice that the table shows two ways to check if testexpression is equal to a particular value: you can simply list the value, or you can use the IS = test. For example, if you want to check if testexpression is equal to 100, you could code

```
CASE 100
```

or

```
CASE IS = 100
```

When you use the word TO, the lower value must be coded first.

You can even mix the three different types of tests in one CASE clause:

```
CASE D, 32 TO 64, IS > 128
```

However, such complicated tests are rarely required.

The following SELECT CASE statements illustrate these various tests.

ILLUSTRATIONS

SELECT CASE Statement	Effect
| ```
SELECT CASE Year
    CASE 1
        PRINT "You're a Freshman"
    CASE 2
        PRINT "You're a Sophomore"
    CASE 3
        PRINT "You're a Junior"
    CASE 4
        PRINT "You're a Senior"
    CASE ELSE
        PRINT "You're a graduate student"
END SELECT
``` | If Year is 1, You're a Freshman is printed. If Year is 2, You're a Sophomore is printed. If Year is 3, You're a Junior is printed. If Year is 4, You're a Senior is printed. If Year is any other value, You're a graduate student is printed. |
| ```
SELECT CASE UCASE$(Char$)
    CASE "A", "E", "I", "O", "U"
        PRINT "Char$ is a vowel"
    CASE "A" TO "Z"
        PRINT "Char$ is a consonant"
    CASE ELSE
        PRINT "Char$ is not a letter"
END SELECT
``` | UCASE$ is used to change Char$ to upper case, so that the SELECT CASE statement works properly whether Char$ contains an upper or lower case letter. If Char$ is A, E, I, O, or U, Char$ is a vowel will be printed. If Char$ is not a vowel, but is a letter, Char$ is a consonant will be printed. If Char$ is not a letter, Char$ is not a letter will be printed. |

In this last illustration, if Char$ is A, both the first and second tests are true—but only Char$ is a vowel will be printed. When QBasic finds a test that is true, it executes the statements that belong to that CASE clause, and then branches to the statement following the END SELECT statement. So the second test is never made. This shows that if more than one test could be true, you must code the tests in the order that reflects the logic of the problem. In this example, if Char$ is a vowel, you want to print Char$ is a vowel, so you must put the test for a vowel before the test for a letter.

Comparing SELECT CASE and IF Statements

You have seen that a multi-way decision may be coded using either a SELECT CASE statement or an IF-THEN-ELSEIF statement, and you may be wondering which one you should use. In general, if you can use a SELECT CASE statement, you should do so. The limitation on SELECT CASE statements is that they can test the value of only one expression. For example, we could not use a SELECT CASE statement in the automobile insurance program (Program 5.3, pages 160–61) because there, we had to test the values of two variables. But when you must test the value of one variable, or one expression, use a SELECT CASE statement.

Syntax Summary

SELECT CASE Statement

Form:
```
SELECT CASE testexpression
    CASE test1
        statement(s) to be executed if test1 is↲
            true
    [CASE test2
        statement(s) to be executed if test2 is↲
            true]
        .
        .
        .
    [CASE ELSE
        statement(s) to be executed if all↲
            tests are false]
END SELECT
```

Example:
```
SELECT CASE Value
    CASE 1, 3, 5, 7, 9
        PRINT "Value is odd"
    CASE 2, 4, 6, 8, 10
        PRINT "Value is even"
    CASE ELSE
        PRINT "Value should be between 1 and 10"
END SELECT
```

Explanation: You can have as many CASE clauses as you need and each CASE clause may have as many statements as you need. In the first line, testexpression may be a numeric or string expression. QBasic compares testexpression against each of the tests in turn. When it finds a test that is true, it executes the statements that belong to that CASE clause, and then branches to the statement after the END SELECT. If none of the tests is true, QBasic executes the statements following the CASE ELSE statement. If none of the tests is true and a CASE ELSE statement is not coded, execution continues normally.

The tests that are coded as part of the CASE clauses may have three forms:

1. expression1 [,expression2 ...]
2. expression3 TO expression4
3. IS relational-operator expression5

The first type of test is true if testexpression is equal to any of the listed expressions. The second type of test is true if testexpression is in the range expression3 to expression4 (including the end points). In this type of test, it is necessary that expression3 be less than expression4. The third type of test is true if testexpression satisfies the condition.

5.4 EXERCISES

1. Correct the syntax errors in the following SELECT CASE statement:

```
SELECT CASE M
    CASE 0 1 2 3
        PRINT "Small value"
    CASE 8 TO 4
        PRINT "Middle value"
    CASE > 10
        PRINT "Big value"
    CASE ELSE
        PRINT "Negative value"
END CASE
```

2. What will be printed if N has the value 2 when the following SELECT CASE statement is executed?

```
SELECT CASE N
    CASE 1 TO 10
        PRINT "N is between 1 and 10"
    CASE 2, 4, 6, 8, 10
        PRINT "N is an even number"
    CASE ELSE
        PRINT "N should be between 1 and 10"
END SELECT
```

★3. A typing instructor grades his students on the basis of how fast they type. Students who type more than 60 words per minute (wpm) are graded "Excellent," those who type between 40 and 60 are "Good," and those who type less than 40 are "Weak." Write the SELECT CASE statement that tests the variable Wpm and assigns a value to the variable Grade$.

4. The class to which a student belongs depends on the number of credits completed, as shown in the following table. Write the case structure that tests the variable Credits and prints the class.

Credits Completed	Class
0-32	Freshman
33-64	Sophomore
65-96	Junior
97 and above	Senior

★5. A program accepts a three-letter abbreviation for the day of the week—SUN, MON, TUE, and so on—and prints the day in full. Write the SELECT CASE statement to perform this processing and print an error message if the abbreviation does not represent a day of the week.

6. Write a SELECT CASE statement that tests the variable Char$. If Char$ is a lower case letter, print Char$ is a lower case letter. If Char$ is an upper case letter, print Char$ is an upper case letter. If Char$ is a digit (0 to 9), print Char$ is a digit. Finally, if Char$ is none of these, print Char$ is not a letter or a digit.

7. A department store classifies its customers into several categories, and two of those categories receive discounts. Category W members receive a 20 percent discount and category C members receive a 10 percent discount. The other categories receive no discount. Category Q is not used, so it is used as trailer data. Program 5.5 accepts a membership category and a bill, then calculates and prints the discount percent, the discount, and the net bill. As the output shows, the program contains an error. Correct it.

```
1    ' *** DEPARTMENT STORE BILLING ***
2    '    Calculate net bills
3
4    '    Variables used
5
6    '    Bill            Customer's bill
7    '    Category        Customer's category
8    '    Discount        Discount received on bill
9    '    NetBill         Net bill after discount
10   '    FrctDiscount    Fraction discount
11   '    PctDiscount     Percent discount allowed
12
13   CLS
14   '    Print heading and define format string
15   LPRINT "Category     Bill     % Discount    Discount     Net Bill"
16   Fmt$ = "    !        ###.##         ##        ###.##       ###.##"
17
18   '    Process customers
19   INPUT "Enter category, Q to quit: ", Category$
20   DO UNTIL UCASE$(Category$) = "Q"
21        INPUT "Enter bill: ", Bill
22        SELECT CASE UCASE$(Category$)
23            CASE "W"
24                FrctDiscount = .2
25            CASE "C"
26                FrctDiscount = .1
27        END SELECT
28        PctDiscount = 100 * FrctDiscount
29        Discount = FrctDiscount * Bill
30        NetBill = Bill - Discount
31        LPRINT USING Fmt$; Category$; Bill; PctDiscount; Discount; NetBill
32        INPUT "Enter category, Q to quit: ", Category$
33   LOOP
34   END
```

```
Enter category, Q to quit: A
Enter bill: 300
Enter category, Q to quit: W
Enter bill: 200
Enter category, Q to quit: C
Enter bill: 500
Enter category, Q to quit: A
Enter bill: 300
Enter category, Q to quit: Q
```

Category	Bill	% Discount	Discount	Net Bill
A	300.00	0	0.00	300.00
W	200.00	20	40.00	160.00
C	500.00	10	50.00	450.00
A	300.00	10	30.00	270.00

PROGRAM 5.5   An incorrect program for department store billing.

WHAT YOU HAVE LEARNED

In this chapter, you learned that:

- You must make up test data to test *all* the branches in your program.

- An IF statement is used to make a decision. If the condition is true, the statements following the word THEN are executed; if the condition is false, the statements following the word ELSE are executed. The word ELSE and the statements following it are optional.

- You can nest IF statements by including IF statements in either or both the true and false branches of another IF statement.

- The logical operators AND and OR are used to construct compound conditions. The logical operator NOT is used to negate simple and compound conditions.

- The BEEP statement is used to sound a beep through the computer's speaker.
- You can use the ELSEIF clause of the IF statement to make a multiple-alternative decision.
- The INPUT$ function is used to accept input from the keyboard, without requiring the user to press the Enter key.
- The SELECT CASE statement is used to make a multiple-alternative decision when the decision depends on a single variable or expression.
- The tests that may be coded with a SELECT CASE statement are
  1. An expression or a list of expressions separated by commas: expression1 [,expression2...]
  2. A range of values in the form: lowvalue TO highvalue
  3. A condition in the form: IS relational-operator expression

NEW QBASIC STATEMENTS

STATEMENT

EFFECT

IF

```
IF A < B THEN
    PRINT "A is less than B"
ELSEIF A = B THEN
    PRINT "A is equal to B"
ELSE
    PRINT "A is greater than B"
END IF
```

If A is less than B, displays A is less than B; if A is equal to B, displays A is equal to B; otherwise displays A is greater than B.

BEEP

```
BEEP
```

Beeps the computer's speaker.

SELECT CASE

```
SELECT CASE Value
    CASE 1, 3, 5, 7, 9
        PRINT "Value is odd"
    CASE 2, 4, 6, 8, 10
        PRINT "Value is even"
    CASE ELSE
        PRINT "Value out of range"
END SELECT
```

If Value is 1, 3, 5, 7, or 9, displays Value is odd; if Value is 2, 4, 6, or 8, displays Value is even; otherwise, displaysValue should be between 1 and 10.

INPUT$

```
MaritalStatus$ = INPUT$(1)
```

Accepts one character entered at the keyboard and assigns it to MaritalStatus$.

KEY TERMS

compound condition
logical operator
multiple-alternative decision
nested IF statement

REVIEW EXERCISES

SELF-CHECK

1. Which statement is used to make a decision?

2. True or false: In an IF statement, the word THEN must be on a line by itself.

3. What happens if the condition in an IF statement is false and the statement does not have an ELSE clause?

4. How many statements may be included in the THEN clause of an IF statement?

5. True or false: It is legal to code an IF statement in the true branch of another IF statement.

6. AND, OR, and NOT are _____ operators.

7. What is a compound condition?

8. Which statement can be used to make the computer's speaker sound?

9. How many ELSEIF clauses may an IF statement contain?

10. Does the INPUT$ function return a string or a number?

11. True or false: The SELECT CASE statement is used to choose one of two alternatives.

12. Under what conditions are the statements in the CASE ELSE clause executed?

13. Describe the three kinds of tests that may be coded with a SELECT CASE statement.

PROGRAMMING ASSIGNMENTS

In the following programming assignments, follow the standard instructions and make sure you create test data to check all the branches. You will find the Step command on the Debug menu helpful in tracking down logic errors. If the earlier assignment number is not clear from the statement of the problem, it is given in parentheses at the end of the assignment, as in (PA2.11).

Section 5.1

1. Solve the parking lot problem described on page 141.

2. Accept two numbers and print the larger number (assume that the numbers are not equal).

3. Write a program that decides whether students are passing or failing. The program should accept a student's name and three test grades. It should calculate the average of the three test grades and print the student's name, the three test grades, the average, and a message. If the average is less than 60, the message should be Failing; if it is 60 or greater, the message should be Passing.

4. Renting a car costs $40 a day plus a mileage charge. The first 25 miles each day are free, but after that, the charge is 18 cents a mile. Write a program that accepts the number of days rented and the total miles driven, and that calculates the bill. (PA 2.11)

5. An exercise spa charges $20 per month if you join for 12 months or less, and $15 per month if you join for more than 12 months. Write a program that accepts a length of membership and calculates and prints bills. Your program should calculate a bill of $200 for a 10-month membership and $300 for a 20-month membership.

6. A video store rents cassettes for $3 a day—but if you rent more than two, you get a 20 percent discount. Write a program that accepts the number of cassettes rented and calculates and prints customers' bills.

7. A pizzeria sells both 12-inch and 10-inch pizzas. Write a program that accepts the price for both sizes and calculates the price per square inch for both sizes. The program should print either The 12-inch pizza is a better buy or The 10-inch pizza is a better buy. Assume that the price per square inch of the two sizes will not be equal. (*Hint:* Remember that the area of a circle is 3.14 times the radius squared.)

8. A ski shop rents skis for $15 per day if you rent for one or two days, and gives a 20 percent discount if you rent for more than two days. Write a program that accepts the number of days the skis are rented and calculates and prints a bill. Sample data and output are as follows.

Number of Days	Bill
2	$30
5	$60

Section 5.2

9. Write a program that determines whether to pay a rebate based on the policy shown in Figure 5.4 (page 149).

10. Write a program that accepts a salesperson's sales and the number of years he or she has been employed, and that calculates commission. The commission rate is as follows.

Years Employed	Sales Less Than 1000	Sales 1000 and Above
More than 5 years	20 percent	30 percent
5 years or less	10 percent	15 percent

11. An exercise club has special rates for members who are older than 65 years. If members older than 65 years are married, they are charged $5 per month; if they are not married, they are charged $7.50 per month. Members who are not over 65 years are charged $12 per month, regardless of their marital status. Write a program that accepts a person's age, marital status (Y or N), and number of months of membership—and that calculates a bill.

12. Write a program that accepts two numbers. If the smaller number is not zero, divide the larger by the smaller, and print the input values and the quotient. If the smaller number is zero, do not divide—instead, print the input values and zero.

13. Write a program that accepts three numbers and prints the largest one. In your solution, use compound conditions, rather than the nested IF statement used in Program 5.2.

Section 5.3

14. Write a program that accepts three numbers and then prints one of three messages: All three numbers are equal, Two of the numbers are equal, or The numbers are all different.

15. Write a program that accepts information about symptoms and prints a diagnosis. The program should ask the user if he or she has a sore throat and if he or she has a fever, and then print a diagnosis as shown in the table.

Fever	Sore Throat	Diagnosis
N	N	You are healthy.
N	Y	Try gargling.
Y	N	Drink lots of fluids.
Y	Y	See a doctor.

16. The Mount Vesuvius Pizzeria sells pizza with three different toppings: extra cheese, pepperoni, and sausage. Write a program that asks a customer which toppings he or she wants, and calculates and prints a bill according to the following table.

Sausage	Pepperoni	Extra Cheese	Price
N	N	N	8.00
N	N	Y	9.00
N	Y	N	9.50
N	Y	Y	10.00
Y	N	N	10.25
Y	N	Y	10.75
Y	Y	N	11.50
Y	Y	Y	12.25

17. Write a program that accepts the month and day a person was born, and prints that person's Zodiac sign. Zodiac signs are determined from birth date as follows.

Birth Date	Sign
March 21–April 19	Aries
April 20–May 20	Taurus
May 21–June 21	Gemini
June 22–July 22	Cancer
July 23–August 22	Leo
August 23–September 22	Virgo
September 23–October 23	Libra
October 24–November 21	Scorpio
November 22–December 21	Sagittarius
December 22–January 19	Capricorn
January 20–February 18	Aquarius
February 19–March 20	Pisces

Section 5.4

18. Write a program that accepts two numbers—A and B—and uses a SELECT CASE statement to print one of three messages: A is greater than B,

A is less than B, or A and B are equal. (*Hint*: Test the expression A – B.)

19. An electric company measures the amount of electricity its customers use in kilowatt-hours (kwh) and charges them according to the following schedule:

Electricity Used	Charge
First 12 kwh or less	$2.80
Next 78 kwh	$0.08 each kwh
Above 90 kwh	$0.10 each kwh

The minimum bill is $2.80. So if a customer uses 5 kwh, the bill for that customer is $2.80. If a customer uses 50 kwh, the charge is $2.80 for the first 12 kwh and $.08 each for the rest. The bill for that customer is therefore

Bill = 2.80 + .08 * (50 − 12) = 5.84

If a customer uses 120 kwh, the charge is $2.80 for the first 12 kwh, $.08 each for the next 78 kwh, and $.10 each for the rest. The bill for that customer is thus

Bill = 2.80 + .08 * 78 + .10 * (120 − 90) = 12.04

Write a program to calculate and print customers' bills.

20. An airline gives discounts to children according to the following schedule:

Age	Discount
Under 2	100%
2 or older, but under 6	50%
6 or older, but under 12	20%
12 or older	None

Write a program that accepts a ticket price and a child's age, then prints the discount and the discounted ticket price.

21. Write a program like Programming Assignment 5.3—but this time, instead of merely determining if the student is passing or failing, assign letter grades to students. Letter grades are assigned as follows.

Average	Grade
>= 90	A
>= 80, but < 90	B
>= 70, but < 80	C
>= 60, but < 70	D
< 60	F

Hint: Since the calculated average can be any value, it is impractical to use range tests in this program. Instead, use relational tests.

22. If you travel to a different planet, your weight changes because of the different gravity on that planet. The factors by which your earth weight must be multiplied to give your weight on the various planets are given in the following table.

Planet	Factor
Mercury	0.37
Venus	0.90
Mars	0.38
Jupiter	2.54
Saturn	1.16
Uranus	0.92
Neptune	1.19
Pluto	0.06

Write a program that accepts a person's earth weight and the name of a planet, then calculates and prints the person's weight on that planet. Beep the speaker and print an error message if the planet name entered is not valid.

23. The charge for a local telephone call depends on the area to which the call is made and the call's duration. One telephone company's charges are as follows.

Call Area	Charge for First Minute	Charge for Each Additional Minute
A	8.7 cents	0
B	10.6 cents	2.9 cents
C	14.4 cents	4.8 cents
D	18.3 cents	5.8 cents

Write a program that accepts the area to which a call was made and its duration, then calculates and prints the charge for that call. Beep the speaker and print an error message if an invalid area is entered.

ADDITIONAL PROGRAMMING ASSIGNMENTS

24. First class postage is charged according to weight, as follows.

First ounce or less	$0.29
Each additional ounce	$0.23

Write a program that accepts weight, then calculates and prints postage.

25. Write a program that accepts two letters and prints them in alphabetical order. Assume that the two letters are not the same.

26. To encourage fuel conservation, the government has a gas-guzzler's tax on automobiles. The amount of the tax depends on the gas mileage a car delivers, as follows.

Mileage (Mpg)	Tax
21 or higher	0
14 or higher, but less than 21	$500
10 or higher, but less than 14	$1000
Less than 10	$2500

Write a program that accepts the mileage, then calculates and prints the tax.

27. The Have-A-Byte computer store sells floppy disks according to the following schedule.

Number of Disks	Price
9 or fewer	$2.00 each
More than 9	$1.50 each

Write a program that accepts the number of disks purchased and prints the bill. Sample data and output are the following.

Number of Disks	Bill
5	10.00
10	15.00

28. Write a program that accepts a month number and a year and prints the month number and year six months later.

29. In the New York City area, the major television channels are the following.

Channel Number	Station
2	WCBS
4	WNBC
5	WNYW
7	WABC
9	WWOR
11	WPIX
13	WNET

Write a program that accepts a channel number and prints the station's name. If an invalid channel number is entered, beep the speaker and print an error message.

30. A health club has many membership categories, and two of those categories receive discounts. Category G members receive a 20 percent discount, and category S members receive a 10 percent discount. The other membership categories receive no discount. Write a program that accepts a membership category and bill, then calculates and prints the discount percent, discount, and the net bill. Category Q is not used, so you can use that as trailer data.

31. For three numbers to represent the sides of a triangle, it is necessary that the sum of any two of the numbers be greater than the third. For example, 1, 2, and 3 cannot be the sides of a triangle, because 1 + 2 is not greater than 3. Write a program that accepts three numbers and reports either that they do make a triangle or that they do not make a triangle.

32. A company pays its salespeople a 5 percent commission on their first $10,000 of sales, 10 percent on their second $10,000 of sales, and 20 percent on all their sales above $20,000. Write a program that accepts the salesperson's name and sales, then prints the name, sales, and commission.

BEYOND THE BASICS

33. Write a program to accept three numbers and print them in sorted order; that is, in the order smallest, middle, and largest.

34. At one college, a student's academic standing depends on his or her grade point average and the number of credits completed, as follows.

Credits Completed	Grade Point Average Required for		
	Dismissal	Probation	Passing
1–32	< 1.4	>= 1.4 but < 1.6	>= 1.6
33–64	< 1.5	>= 1.5 but < 1.7	>= 1.7
65–96	< 1.6	>= 1.6 but < 1.8	>= 1.8
97 and above	< 1.8	>= 1.8 but < 2.0	>= 2.0

Write a program that accepts a student's grade point average and credits completed, then prints his or her academic standing. (*Hint*: Use a nested SELECT CASE statement.)

35. Write a program to solve the quadratic equation

$$x = ax^2 + bx + c$$

using the quadratic formula

$$x = \frac{-b \pm \sqrt{b^2 - 4ac}}{2a}$$

Your program should handle three cases: 1) the roots are real and different, 2) the two roots are equal, and 3) the roots are complex—in which case, the program should print the real and imaginary parts.

36. Write a "Tomorrow" program that accepts three numbers representing the month, day, and year and that determines the month, day, and year of the next day. You may simplify your program by assuming that the three numbers entered represent a valid date and that any year divisible by 4 is a leap year. (The real rules for leap years are more complicated than that; we will learn them in Chapter 6.)

37. Write a program that accepts three numbers—A, B, and C—and prints the name of the largest. If two or more variables are tied for largest, print all their names. Your output should be Largest number A or Largest numbers are A and B, and so on.

38. The date for Easter Sunday for any Year can be determined as follows: let A be the remainder when Year is divided by 19; let B be the remainder when Year is divided by 4; let C be the remainder when Year is divided by 7; let D be the remainder when $19 * A + 24$ is divided by 30; and let E be the remainder when $2 * B + 4 * C + 6 * D + 5$ is divided by 7. Then the date for Easter Sunday is March $22 + D + E$. If $22 + D + E$ is greater than 31, the date is in April. For example, if $22 + D + E$ is 32, the date is April 1. Write a program that accepts a value for Year, and that calculates the date of Easter Sunday for that Year.

PROCEDURES

LEARNING OBJECTIVES

After reading this chapter, you will be able to:

- Write programs containing subprograms and functions.
- Understand the concepts of local and global variables.
- Write programs that use menus.
- Use the QBasic statements CALL, SUB, END SUB, COMMON SHARED, FUNCTION, END FUNCTION, LOCATE, and COLOR.
- Use the QBasic function SPACE$.
- Use the Edit menu commands New SUB and New FUNCTION.
- Use the View menu commands SUBs and Split.

Some of the problems we solved in Chapter 5 are long enough and complicated enough that we could benefit by using new tools to help us write them. We will study two such tools in this chapter: top-down design (which helps us develop the algorithm) and procedures (which help us write the program).

A **procedure** is a group of self-contained statements that perform a specific task—such as displaying a menu or calculating a value. QBasic has two kinds of procedures: subprograms and functions. Subprograms are designed to perform a particular task. Functions are similar to QBasic's functions—like UCASE$—with the advantage that they can be customized to do whatever you want. We will study both kinds of procedures in this chapter.

procedure
Self-contained statements that perform a specific task—such as displaying a menu or calculating a value.

6.1	SUBPROGRAMS

To illustrate how subprograms are used, we will examine a program that writes a message on the screen. You wouldn't use a subprogram for such a simple problem, but this program will help us see how subprograms are used without extraneous complications.

EXAMPLE 1

A PROGRAM THAT USES A SUBPROGRAM
Program 6.1 prints the message

```
Have a good day
```

on the screen. It consists of a main module (lines 1 through 8) and a subprogram named PrintLine (lines 10 through 14). Names for subprograms follow the same rules as names for variables. In addition, a subprogram name must be different from any variable names and from other procedure names in the program.

The statements in the program that involve subprograms are the DECLARE statement in line 4, the CALL statement in line 7, the SUB statement in line 10, and the END SUB statement in line 14.

A typical DECLARE statement is shown in line 4:

```
DECLARE SUB PrintLine ()
```

You do not have to write the DECLARE statements yourself, because when you save a program that uses subprograms or functions, QBasic automatically inserts DECLARE statements for each subprogram and function as the first lines in your program. I prefer having remark statements with the program's name and purpose as the first lines, so in Program 6.1 (and in all the programs in this book), I used the Edit menu's Cut and Paste commands to move the DECLARE statement(s) after the remark statements. Since you don't have to type DECLARE statements, their syntax is not discussed.

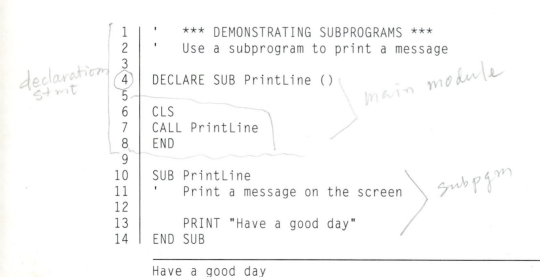

```
 1  '    *** DEMONSTRATING SUBPROGRAMS ***
 2  '    Use a subprogram to print a message
 3
 4  DECLARE SUB PrintLine ()
 5
 6  CLS
 7  CALL PrintLine
 8  END
 9
10  SUB PrintLine
11  '    Print a message on the screen
12
13      PRINT "Have a good day"
14  END SUB
```

```
Have a good day
```

PROGRAM 6.1   A program that demonstrates subprograms.

You execute a subprogram by writing its name in a CALL statement. In this program, we use a simplified form of the CALL statement; the complete form is discussed later. The CALL statement in line 7

```
CALL PrintLine
```

executes the PrintLine subprogram. When this CALL statement is executed, it transfers control to the SUB PrintLine statement in line 10. The PRINT statement in line 13 is executed, displaying the message

```
Have a good day
```

on the screen. The END SUB statement in line 14 transfers control back to the statement following the CALL statement. In Program 6.1, this is the END statement in line 8. Logically, the program behaves as though the PRINT statement in line 13 were inserted following line 7.

Typing a Subprogram

In Program 6.1, the subprogram is listed after the main module. (If two or more subprograms exist, they are listed in alphabetical order.) That is indeed how it looks when the program is printed, but when you are typing the program, you cannot simply type the main module and then type the subprogram. To type a subprogram, you first type the complete main module. (In Program 6.1, you would type lines 1 through 8.) You could proceed in two ways after that.

One way to type a subprogram is to move the cursor to the subprogram's name in the CALL statement—then use the New SUB command on the Edit menu (see Figure 3.2, page 79). QBasic presents you with the dialog box shown in Figure 6.1. The suggested name, in this case PrintLine, is the subprogram name that the cursor is on. When you press Enter (or click OK) to accept that name, QBasic presents you with the new View window shown in Figure 6.2. Notice that the title bar contains the name of the program (P06-01.BAS), followed by a colon and the name of the subprogram (PrintLine). The SUB and END SUB statements were already entered for you. You must type the remaining statements of the subprogram between the SUB and END SUB statements.

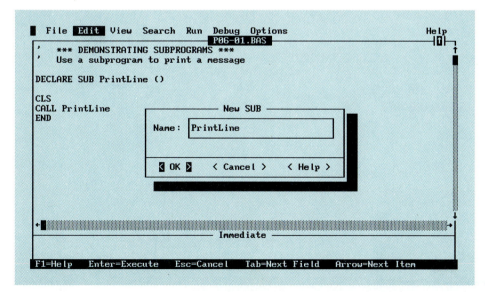

FIGURE 6.1
New SUB command dialog box.

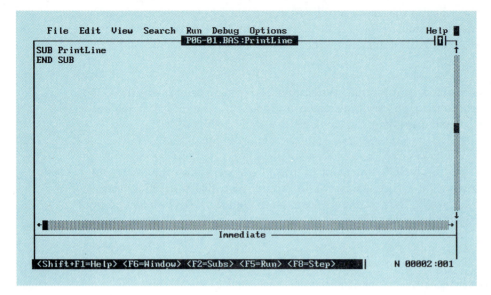

FIGURE 6.2
View window in which to type a subprogram.

The second method for typing a subprogram is to type a line containing the word SUB followed by the subprogram name, and then to press the Enter key. QBasic then presents you with the View window that you saw in Figure 6.2.

QBasic does not require that the statements in a subprogram be indented as they are in Program 6.1. However, just as it is a good idea to indent the lines in a loop to show the loop more clearly, it is also a good idea to indent the lines in a subprogram to show the subprogram more clearly.

To get back to the main module or to another subprogram, you can use the SUBs command from the View menu as shown previously in Figure 1.10, page 15. (The Reference bar reminds you that pressing F2 is the shortcut way to invoke the SUBs command.) When you do, QBasic presents you with the SUBs command dialog box shown in Figure 6.3. The list box shows the name of the main module, in capital letters, followed by the subprogram name(s). This program has only one subprogram, but if two or more subprograms exist, they are listed in alphabetical order. Highlight the subprogram you want to edit and either press the

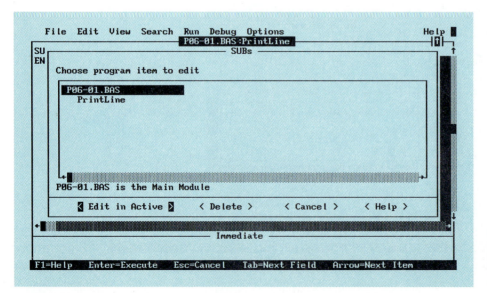

FIGURE 6.3
The SUBs command dialog box.

Enter key or click the Edit in Active button. QBasic displays the highlighted sub-program in the View window, with the cursor placed where it was the last time you edited this subprogram. You can use the Delete command button in the SUBs dialog box to delete the highlighted subprogram.

You can also cycle through the main module and procedures using Shift+F2 or Ctrl+F2. Shift+F2 cycles forward through the list of procedures, while Ctrl+F2 cycles backward through them.

You don't have to display the main module in order to execute the program. When you press Shift+F5, execution begins with the first statement in the main module—no matter which procedure is displayed.

Splitting the View Window

When you select the Split command on the View menu, the View window splits into two windows—as Figure 6.4 shows. Initially, the top window is active—but you can make the bottom window active by pressing F6 or by clicking the mouse anywhere in it. Pressing F6 again makes the Immediate window active, and pressing it once more makes the top window active again. Shift+F6 cycles through the windows in the reverse order. You can always tell which window is active because it contains the cursor, its title bar is highlighted and—if you have a mouse—the scroll bars are present. To return the View window to one window, select the Split command again.

Typically, you split the View window because you want to edit one subprogram (or the main module) while looking at another. To do so, decide which window you want to use and make it the active window. Then either select SUBs from the View window or use the shortcut key, F2. Highlight the subprogram you want to edit and press the Enter key—or click the Edit in Active command button. The highlighted subprogram is displayed in the active window, and the other window is not altered.

You can also change the size of the active window. Pressing Alt+Plus key increases the size by one line and pressing Alt+Minus key decreases it by one line. (You must use the Plus and Minus keys on the number keypad, and Num Lock must be off.) Pressing Ctrl+F10, or clicking the maximize button, expands the active window to fill the screen. Pressing Ctrl+F10 (or clicking the maximize button) again returns the active window to its former size. ■

```
   File  Edit  View  Search  Run  Debug  Options                    Help ■
                          ┌─────── P06-01.BAS ───────┐            ─┤0├─
   '   *** DEMONSTRATING SUBPROGRAMS ***                                 ↑
   '   Use a subprogram to print a message                               ▓
                                                                         ▓
   DECLARE SUB PrintLine ()                                              ▓
                                                                         ▓
   CLS                                                                   ▓
   CALL PrintLine                                                        ▓
   END                                                                   ↓
   +■░░░░░░░░░░░░░░░░░░░░░░░░░░░░░░░░░░░░░░░░░░░░░░░░░░░░░░░░░░░░░░░░░+→
   ──────────────── P06-01.BAS:PrintLine ────────────────          ─┤0├─
   SUB PrintLine
   '   Print a message on the screen

       PRINT "Have a good day"
   END SUB



   ───────────────────── Immediate ─────────────────────

   <Shift+F1=Help> <F6=Window> <F2=Subs> <F5=Run> <F8=Step>        N 00001:001
```

FIGURE 6.4
The View
window split.

Local Variables

Let's extend Program 6.1 to allow a user, George, to enter his name—and to print the name as well as the message. You might think that all you have to do is add an INPUT statement to accept a value for Name$, and add Name$ to the PRINT statement, as in Program 6.2. However, if you examine the output from Program 6.2, you'll see that the user's name was *not* printed.

The name was not printed because Program 6.2 really contains two variables called Name$. The variable Name$ in the main module and the variable Name$ in PrintLine refer to two different storage locations. Each variable gets its own storage location because these variables are local variables. A **local variable** is one that is known only in the main program or in the subprogram or function in which it is defined.

The string George, which the user entered in response to the INPUT statement, was assigned to the variable Name$ in the main module. But the PRINT statement refers to the variable Name$ in PrintLine. That variable was never assigned a value, so nothing was printed.

Your first thought might be that local variables are a lot of trouble, but in fact they are very convenient because they let you use subprograms and functions without knowing the names of the variables used inside them. For example, you don't know what variable names are used in the QBasic function UCASE$; all you have to know is that you give UCASE$ a string argument, and it returns the same string in capital letters. It would be annoying if you had to know the names of all the variables used in UCASE$ and avoid using them in your program. In a large programming project, many programmers can write the subprograms that are required. When the subprograms are combined into one large program, all you have to know is what the subprograms do and how to use them; you don't have to know what goes on inside them.

local variable
A variable that may be used only in the main module or procedure in which it is defined.

Passing Variables

The question remains: How can we modify Program 6.1 to print the user's name? To print the user's name, we must pass the variable Name$ from the main module to PrintLine.

```
1    '    *** DEMONSTRATING SUBPROGRAMS ***
2    '    Demonstrate local variables
3
4    DECLARE SUB PrintLine ()
5
6    CLS
7    INPUT "Enter your name: ", Name$
8    CALL PrintLine
9    END
10
11   SUB PrintLine
12   '    Print a message on the screen
13
14       PRINT "Have a good day "; Name$
15   END SUB
```

```
Enter your name: George
Have a good day
```

PROGRAM 6.2   A program that demonstrates local variables.

Program 6.3 shows how you change the CALL and SUB statements when you want to pass variables. The CALL statement in line 8

```
CALL PrintLine(Name$)
```

executes the PrintLine subprogram and passes to it the variable Name$. As with QBasic functions, the variables you pass to the subprogram are called arguments, and are written inside parentheses. If the subprogram uses two or more arguments, they are separated by commas.

The SUB statement in line 11

```
SUB PrintLine (Name$)
```

accepts the variable Name$. Name$ is now available in PrintLine, so the PRINT statement in line 14 prints the user's name as well as the message. The output in Program 6.3 shows that the user's name was printed.

Arguments and Parameters

In Program 6.3, the same variable name—Name$—was used in the main module and in PrintLine, but this is not necessary. Program 6.4, which calculates the average of three numbers, shows how you can use different names in the main module and in the subprogram. (QBasic added exclamation points to the end of the variable names in the DECLARE statement to indicate that these are single precision variables; you don't have to be concerned with these exclamation points.)

In Program 6.4, the calculation of the average is done in the subprogram Average. Assume that you wrote subprogram Average some time ago, and don't remember the variable names you used. To use Average, you only need to know that its first three arguments are the three numbers whose average you want to calculate, and its fourth argument is the average it calculates.

You are free to use A, B, and C as the names of the three numbers, even though Average uses X, Y, and Z to represent the three numbers. Furthermore, the program works even though the main module uses A as the name of one of the numbers, and Average uses A as the name for the average. To understand why this is so, we have to examine argument passing more carefully.

```
1    '    *** DEMONSTRATING SUBPROGRAMS ***
2    '    Pass an argument to a subprogram
3
4    DECLARE SUB PrintLine (Name$)
5
6    CLS
7    INPUT "Enter your name: ", Name$
8    CALL PrintLine(Name$)
9    END
10
11   SUB PrintLine (Name$)
12   '    Print a message on the screen
13
14       PRINT "Have a good day "; Name$
15   END SUB
```
```
Enter your name: George
Have a good day George
```

PROGRAM 6.3 A program that demonstrates passing an argument to a subprogram.

```
1  |  '    *** CALCULATING THE AVERAGE OF THREE NUMBERS ***
2  |  DECLARE SUB Average (X!, Y!, Z!, A!)
3  |  CLS
4  |
5  |  INPUT "Enter the first number, 0 to stop: ", A
6  |  DO UNTIL A = 0
7  |      INPUT "Enter second number: ", B
8  |      INPUT "Enter third number: ", C
9  |      CALL Average(A, B, C, Avg)
10 |      PRINT "The three numbers are"; A; B; C; "The average is"; Avg
11 |      INPUT "Enter the first number, 0 to stop: ", A
12 |  LOOP
13 |  END
14 |
15 |  SUB Average (X, Y, Z, A)
16 |      'Calculate average
17 |      'Receives three numbers, X, Y, and Z
18 |      'Returns average in A
19 |
20 |      Sum = X + Y + Z
21 |      A = Sum / 3
22 |  END SUB
```

```
Enter the first number, 0 to stop: 2
Enter second number: 5
Enter third number: 8
The three numbers are 2   5   8 The average is 5
Enter the first number, 0 to stop: 0
```

PROGRAM 6.4   A program that uses a subprogram to calculate the average of three numbers.

The CALL and SUB statements in Program 6.4 are

```
CALL Average(A, B, C, Avg)
SUB Average (X, Y, Z, A)
```

Recall that the variables in the CALL statement are called arguments; the variables in the SUB statement are called **parameters**.

Program 6.4 shows that the user entered 2 for A, 5 for B, and 8 for C. These values are shown in Figure 6.5(a). Parameters are not given their own storage locations. Rather, when the CALL statement is executed, QBasic associates each argument with its corresponding parameter so that they refer to the same storage location. This is how X is given the value of A, Y is given the value of B, and so on. (When the CALL statement is executed, we have not yet assigned a value to Avg, so it has the initial value 0.) Notice also that Sum (a local variable in Average) has its own storage location, which is not shared with the main module.

Because arguments and parameters refer to the same storage locations, if the subprogram changes the value of a parameter, the value of its associated argument automatically changes. As shown in Figure 6.5(b), when the LET statement in line 21 of Program 6.4 is executed, it assigns 5 to both A in subprogram Average, and Avg in the main module.

You can see that the order of the arguments and parameters must agree. For example, if the CALL statement in line 9 of Program 6.4 were

```
CALL Average(Avg, A, B, C)
```

incorrect results would be calculated.

parameter
A variable defined and used in a procedure; it is replaced by an argument when the procedure is executed.

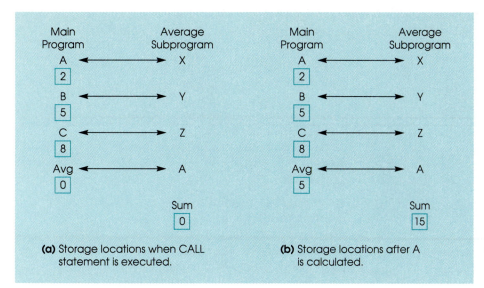

(a) Storage locations when CALL statement is executed.

(b) Storage locations after A is calculated.

FIGURE 6.5
Storage locations after A is calculated.

So you see that you do not have to use the same names for the arguments and parameters, but that they must be in the correct order. You must have the same number of arguments and parameters, and they must be the same type. That is, numeric arguments must correspond to numeric parameters, and string arguments must correspond to string parameters. (QBasic uses the DECLARE statement to check that the arguments in the CALL statement agree in number and type with the parameters in the SUB statement.) You can use a constant or even an expression for an argument, but parameters must be variables.

The syntax of the CALL statement is

```
CALL SubprogramName [(argumentlist)]
```

The square brackets show that the argument list is optional. The argumentlist is a list of the variables or constants passed to the subprogram, separated by commas.

The syntax of the SUB statement is

```
SUB SubprogramName [(parameterlist)] [STATIC]
```

The parameterlist is a list of the variables passed to the subprogram, separated by commas. If the optional parameter STATIC is coded, the local variables in the subprogram retain their values between calls to the subprogram. If STATIC is not coded, each time a subprogram is called, the numeric local variables are set to zero and the string local variables are set to the null string. You would use STATIC if you were using a local variable as an accumulator or as a counter.

The following examples illustrate the CALL and SUB statements.

ILLUSTRATIONS

CALL and SUB Statements	Effects
CALL Instructions	The CALL statement executes the subprogram Instructions. This is
SUB Instructions	similar to what we did in Program 6.1 (page 182), where the subprogram had no arguments.

(continued)

> **ILLUSTRATIONS**
>
> ```
> CALL Calc(6, X, Ans)
>
> SUB Calc (M, N, Result)
> ```
> The CALL statement executes the subprogram Calc. The parameter M is given the value 6, and the parameter N is given the value of the argument X. Upon return to the main module, the argument Ans will have the value of the parameter Result.
>
> ```
> CALL ChangeString(Test$, L)
>
> SUB ChangeString (S$, P)
> ```
> The CALL statement executes the subprogram ChangeString. The parameter S$ is given the value of the argument Test$, and the parameter P is given the value of the argument L. Presumably, ChangeString changes S$ in some way, and that change is reflected in Test$ upon return to the calling module.

Global Variables

In some problems, certain variables are used by almost all of the subprograms. Instead of including those variables in the argument lists of all the subprograms, those variables may be declared to be global variables. A **global variable** is one that is available to the main module and all the subprograms.

global variable
A variable that may be used anywhere in a program.

The simplest way to declare a variable to be a global variable is to include a COMMON SHARED statement in the main module before any executable statement. (The remark and DECLARE statements are the only ones we have studied that are not executable.) The syntax of the COMMON SHARED statement is

```
COMMON SHARED variablelist
```

For example, Program 6.2 (page 186) would work if we made Name$ a global variable by including the following statement at line 5:

```
COMMON SHARED Name$
```

You may think that you can save yourself the trouble of typing argument and parameter lists by declaring all variables to be global, but that is not a good idea. If a global variable is incorrect, to find the error, you must examine every procedure because it might have been changed in any of them. But if a variable is passed in argument lists, it could only have been changed in those few procedures that have access to it, which makes your debugging problem much easier. In fact, it is so easy to misuse the COMMON SHARED statement that many instructors forbid its use.

Syntax Summary

> **CALL Statement**
>
> Form: `CALL SubprogramName [(argumentlist)]`
> Example: `CALL Taxes(GrossPay, FedTax, StateTax, CityTax)`
> Explanation: QBasic executes the named subprogram, associating the arguments in the CALL statement with the parameters in the SUB statement.

SUB Statement

Form: `SUB SubprogramName [(parameterlist)] [STATIC]`
Example: `SUB Taxes (G, F, S, C)`
Explanation: Marks the first statement in a subprogram and lists the parameters used in the subprogram.

END SUB Statement

Form: `END SUB`
Example: `END SUB`
Explanation: Marks the end of a subprogram and returns control to the statement following the CALL statement that executed the subprogram.

COMMON SHARED Statement

Form: `COMMON SHARED variablelist`
Example: `COMMON SHARED TotalPay, AveragePay`
Explanation: Makes the listed variables global, so they are available to all subprograms without the need for passing arguments.

6.1 EXERCISES

1. ★a)   Write the statement to execute the subprogram named Sub1, which has no arguments. Write the statement to define Sub1.
   b)   Write the statement to execute the subprogram Sub2, whose arguments are a string variable and two numeric variables. Write the statement to define Sub2.

2.   The number of arguments in a CALL statement that executes a subprogram must be a) less than; b) equal to; or c) greater than the number of parameters in the SUB statement that defines that subprogram.

★3.   What output is produced by the following program?

```
CALL Sub1
CALL Sub2
END

SUB Sub1
    PRINT "RED"
    CALL Sub2
    PRINT "BLUE"
END SUB

SUB Sub2
    PRINT "YELLOW"
END SUB
```

4.   What output is produced by the following program?

```
Pay = 75
Bonus = 30
TotalPay = Pay + Bonus
CALL PrintAns
END
```

```
SUB PrintAns
    PRINT "The total pay is "; TotalPay
END SUB
```

5. Correct the errors in the following programs.

a)
```
A = 5
CALL PrintIt(A)
END

SUB PrintIt (Z)
    PRINT "The value of A is"; A
END SUB
```

b)
```
R = 23
S = 42
CALL Addem(R, S)
END

SUB Addem
    Sum = R + S
    PRINT "The sum is"; Sum
END SUB
```

★6. What output is produced by the following program?

```
CALL ConvertMoney("Mark", 5, .6165)
END

SUB ConvertMoney(Name$, Dollars, ConversionFactor)
    Money = Dollars * ConversionFactor
    PRINT Dollars; "Dollars is equal to"; Money; Name$;"s"
END SUB
```

7. What output is produced by the following program?

```
M = 5
N = 8
CALL CalcSum(M, N, Total)
PRINT M, N, Total
END

SUB CalcSum (Sum, A, B)
    Sum = A + B
END SUB
```

TOP-DOWN DESIGN

As your programs get more complex, you need more powerful tools to help you write them. Among the most powerful tools programmers use is top-down design. For our first example of designing a program using top-down design, we will write a program that calculates the area of several different geometric shapes.

EXAMPLE 2

A PROGRAM THAT USES SUBPROGRAMS TO CALCULATE AREAS

Problem Statement

Write a program that can calculate the area of a circle, a rectangle, and a triangle. The program should allow the user to select the shape whose area he or she wants calculated. It should then accept the dimensions of the shape, and calculate and print the area.

STEP 1 Variable Names

The variables in this problem are the following.

Variable	Variable Name
Input Variables	
User's choice	`Choice$`
Base of triangle	`TriangleBase`
Height of triangle	`Height`
Length of rectangle	`Length`
Width of rectangle	`RectangleWidth`
Radius of circle	`Radius`
Output Variable	
Area	`Area`

The variable Choice$ is used to indicate which shape the user wants to calculate the area of: C for a circle, R for a rectangle, T for a triangle, or Q to quit.

STEP 2 Algorithm

The algorithm we can use for this problem is

1. Execute steps 2 through 5 for each shape.
2. Display instructions for the user.
3. Input Choice$.
4. Input dimensions of selected shape.
5. Calculate and print the area.

Top-Down Design

To expand on this algorithm, we will use **top-down design** or **stepwise refinement**. When top-down design is used, the overall problem is divided into simpler tasks. Any tasks that are still complicated are further divided into their own tasks. This continues until all the tasks are so simple that they can be easily coded. This

top-down design or stepwise refinement
A method of developing an algorithm by breaking up a complex problem into a set of less complex problems.

"divide and conquer" technique is so easy that students often do not appreciate how powerful it is. Because it allows you to concentrate on one task at a time, it is one of the most powerful tools programmers have.

In this problem, the tasks are

1. Display instructions for the user.
2. Accept the user's input for Choice$.
3. Select subprogram for the selected shape.
4. Calculate and print the area of a circle.
5. Calculate and print the area of a rectangle.
6. Calculate and print the area of a triangle.
7. Display an error message if the user enters invalid data.
8. Pause after each case.

None of the tasks needs to be subdivided. At this point, we are not concerned with *how* these tasks are to be accomplished; we are just listing the tasks that must be done.

We next examine the list of tasks to decide which of them should be written as subprograms. We don't write every task as a subprogram because that would lead to a fragmented program, consisting of many one-statement subprograms. Tasks that are complex, or that involve more than just a few statements, are written as subprograms. Tasks that are not written as subprograms are performed in one of the other subprograms.

Deciding which tasks to write as subprograms is a matter of judgment and taste, and two experienced programmers might divide a program into subprograms differently. Beginners usually include too few subprograms, so if you can't decide whether a task should be a subprogram, it probably should. When you are deciding which tasks to write as subprograms, one rule to observe is that subprograms should perform one well-defined task. Subprograms that perform a single task are said to be "cohesive."

One advantage of using top-down design is that when you are developing the algorithm and the program, you needn't be concerned with all the details. For example, you may not know the formula for the area of a triangle. That doesn't stop you from drawing the top-down chart, or from drawing the flowchart for and writing the main module; the first time you need the correct formula is when you write the subprogram that calculates the area of a triangle. When you are debugging a program, you can even use dummy subprograms, which just return an arbitrary value. You can use these dummy subprograms to check the rest of the program. When the rest of the program is correct, you can then replace the dummy subprograms with correct ones.

When a problem is analyzed using top-down design, we often draw a **top-down chart**, which is also called a **hierarchy chart**. The top-down chart for this problem is shown in Figure 6.6. A top-down chart is drawn like an organization chart. The general statement of the problem—in this case, Calculate Areas—is at

top-down chart or hierarchy chart
A chart that shows the tasks required to solve a problem—and the relationship of these tasks.

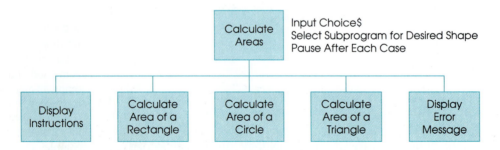

FIGURE 6.6   Top-down chart to calculate areas.

the top level. This is the main module. Below the main module are the subprograms into which the problem is divided. If any of these subprograms must be further divided, it is shown on the third level. In Figure 6.6, none of the subprograms has to be further divided. Good design dictates that a subprogram only executes another subprogram that is at a lower level. In Figure 6.6, this means that all the subprograms are executed from the main module.

The tasks that are not written as subprograms are listed next to the module in which they are performed. In Figure 6.6, the tasks Input Choice$, Select Subprograms for Desired Shape, and Pause After Each Case are performed in the main module.

Besides helping you to write your programs, top-down charts are excellent documentation because they show which subprograms execute which subprograms. It's hard for you to appreciate this yet, because our programs are relatively small. GORILLA.BAS, which is a game program that comes with DOS, is a large program that contains 22 subprograms. You can learn a lot about writing game programs in QBasic by studying GORILLA.BAS, but without a top-down chart, it is very difficult to understand the structure of the program.

A top-down chart is very different from a flowchart. A flowchart shows the logical structure of a program—the order in which statements are executed—and, when the program involves a decision, the conditions under which one group of statements is executed rather than a different group. The top-down chart shows which tasks must be performed, and which subprograms execute which subprograms, but not how or when the tasks are performed.

After you use top-down design and a top-down chart to identify the subprograms that must be written, you can use a flowchart or pseudocode to help plan the logic of these subprograms.

In this problem, only the main module is complicated enough to require a flowchart to help write it. The flowchart for the main module is shown in Figure 6.7. This flowchart uses the symbol for a subprogram—a rectangle with two vertical lines. The flowchart shows that Choice$ is tested in a SELECT CASE statement to execute the subprogram that calculates the area of the desired shape. If an invalid value is entered for Choice$, the DisplayErrorMsg subprogram is executed.

STEP 3   Hand-Calculated Answers

We have to calculate the area of a circle, a rectangle, and a triangle. The formulas and areas are shown in the following table.

Shape	Formula	Dimensions	Area
Circle	Area = π Radius^2	Radius = 20	1,256.64
Rectangle	Area = Length $\times$ Width	Length = 5 Width = 3	15
Triangle	Area = ½ Base $\times$ Height	Base = 10 Height = 5	25

In the formula for the area of a circle, π is the mathematical constant equal to 3.14159.

STEP 4   QBasic Program

The program to calculate areas is shown in Program 6.5. It does not contain any new QBasic statements. This program does not pass arguments between the main module and the subprograms; instead, it uses local variables. If all variables are local, you might wonder how CircleArea knows the value of Pi that it uses in line 52. The answer is that Pi is not a variable, but a symbolic constant—defined in the CONST statement in line 16. Symbolic constants defined in the main module are

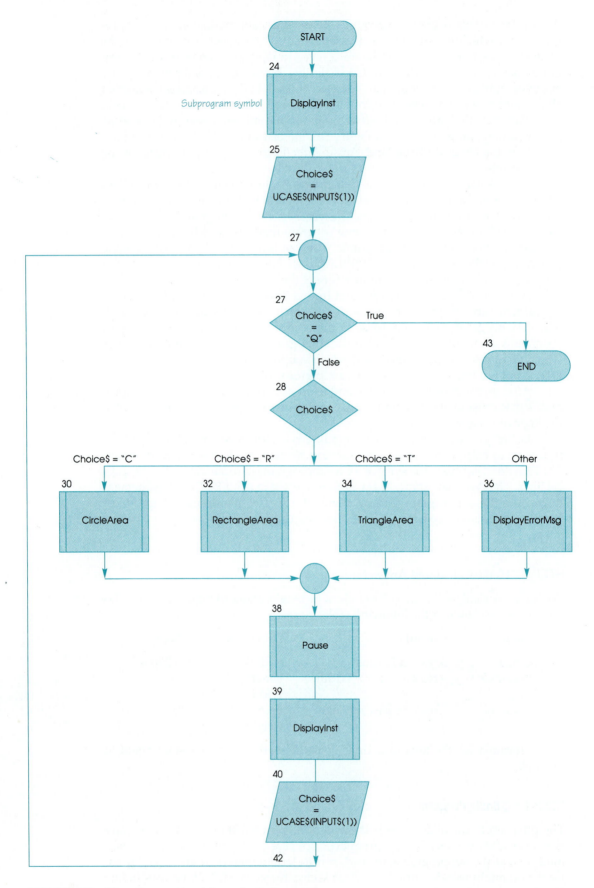

FIGURE 6.7 Top-down chart to calculate areas.

```
 1 | '     *** PROGRAM TO CALCULATE AREAS ***
 2 | '     Calculate area of a circle, rectangle, or triangle
 3 |
 4 | DECLARE SUB CircleArea ()
 5 | DECLARE SUB DisplayInst ()
 6 | DECLARE SUB RectangleArea ()
 7 | DECLARE SUB TriangleArea ()
 8 | DECLARE SUB DisplayErrorMsg ()
 9 | DECLARE SUB Pause ()
10 |
11 | '    Variables used
12 |
13 | '    Choice$          User's choice of shape (C, R, or T)
14 | '    Local variables defined in subprograms
15 |
16 | CONST Pi = 3.14159      'Constant, π, to calculate the area of a circle
17 |
18 | 'Process requests
19 | CALL DisplayInst
20 | Choice$ = UCASE$(INPUT$(1))
21 | PRINT Choice$
22 | DO UNTIL Choice$ = "Q"
23 |     SELECT CASE Choice$
24 |         CASE "C"
25 |             CALL CircleArea
26 |         CASE "R"
27 |             CALL RectangleArea
28 |         CASE "T"
29 |             CALL TriangleArea
30 |         CASE ELSE
31 |             CALL DisplayErrorMsg
32 |     END SELECT
33 |     PRINT
34 |     PRINT "Press any key when ready"
35 |     Dummy$ = INPUT$(1)
36 |     CALL DisplayInst
37 |     Choice$ = UCASE$(INPUT$(1))
38 |     PRINT Choice$
39 | LOOP
40 | END
41 |
42 | SUB CircleArea
43 | '    Calculate the area of a circle
44 |
45 | '    Local variables
46 |
47 | '    Area             Area of a circle
48 | '    Radius           Radius of a circle
49 |
50 |     PRINT
51 |     INPUT "Enter the radius of the circle: ", Radius
52 |     Area = Pi * Radius ^ 2
53 |     Fmt$ = "A circle with radius ## has area #,###.##"
54 |     PRINT USING Fmt$; Radius; Area
55 | END SUB
```

PROGRAM 6.5   A program that uses subprograms to calculate areas of geometric shapes. (continued on next page)

```
56  | SUB DisplayErrorMsg
57  | '    Beep speaker and print error message
58  |
59  |      BEEP
60  |      PRINT
61  |      PRINT "Please enter C, R, T, or Q"
62  | END SUB
63  |
64  | SUB DisplayInst
65  | '    Display instructions for user
66  |
67  |      CLS
68  |      PRINT "This program calculates the area of a circle, a triangle,"
69  |      PRINT "or a rectangle.  "
70  |      PRINT "Enter C to calculate the area of a circle"
71  |      PRINT "Enter R to calculate the area of a rectangle"
72  |      PRINT "Enter T to calculate the area of a triangle"
73  |      PRINT "Enter Q to quit."
74  |      PRINT
75  |      PRINT "Enter C, R, T, or Q: ";
76  | END SUB
77  |
78  | SUB RectangleArea
79  | '    Calculate the area of a rectangle
80  |
81  | '    Local variables
82  |
83  | '    Area            Area of a rectangle
84  | '    Length          Length of a rectangle
85  | '    RectangleWidth  Width of a rectangle
86  |
87  |      PRINT
88  |      INPUT "Enter the length of the rectangle: ", Length
89  |      INPUT "Enter the width of the rectangle: ", RectangleWidth
90  |      Area = Length * RectangleWidth
91  |      Fmt$ = "A rectangle with length ## and width ##, has area #,####"
92  |      PRINT USING Fmt$; Length; RectangleWidth; Area
93  | END SUB
94  | SUB TriangleArea
95  | '    Calculate the area of a triangle
96  |
97  | '    Local variables
98  |
99  | '    Area            Area of a triangle
100 | '    TriangleBase    The base of a triangle
101 | '    Height          Height of a triangle
102 |
103 |      PRINT
104 |      INPUT "Enter the base of the triangle: ", TriangleBase
105 |      INPUT "Enter the height of the triangle: ", Height
106 |      Area = (TriangleBase * Height) / 2
107 |      Fmt$ = "A triangle with base ## and height ## has area #,####.#"
108 |      PRINT USING Fmt$; TriangleBase; Height; Area
109 | END SUB
```

PROGRAM 6.5 *(continued)*

```
This program calculates the area of a circle, a triangle,
or a rectangle.
Enter C to calculate the area of a circle
Enter R to calculate the area of a rectangle
Enter T to calculate the area of a triangle
Enter Q to quit.

Enter C, R, T, or Q: T

Enter the base of the triangle: 30
Enter the height of the triangle: 10
A triangle with base 30 and height 10 has area   150

Press any key when ready
```

PROGRAM 6.5 *(continued)*

global—they may be used in all subprograms and functions in the program. (Incidentally, the symbol π, used in the remark in line 16, is typed by pressing and holding the Alt key while using the number pad to type 227—the ASCII code for π.)

Because the screen is cleared between cases, Program 6.5 shows the area calculated only for a triangle. However, the program was tested by calculating the area of a circle and a rectangle. An invalid value was also entered, and, as expected, the DisplayErrorMsg subprogram was executed.   ■

EXAMPLE 3

USING SUBPROGRAMS TO CALCULATE PAYROLL WITH OVERTIME

As a second example of using top-down design, consider again the Bat-O payroll program—but now, let's pay overtime.

Problem Statement

Write a payroll program for the Bat-O company that pays overtime. Employees are paid at their regular rate for the first 40 hours they work in a week. Employees who work more than 40 hours in a week are paid time-and-a-half for the hours over 40.

STEP 1   **Variable Names**

We begin by identifying and naming the variables in the problem. We can use the following names.

Variable	Variable Name
Input Variables	
Employee name	EmpName$
Pay rate	PayRate
Hours worked	Hours
Output Variables	
Regular pay	RegularPay
Overtime pay	OvertimePay
Gross pay	GrossPay

STEP 2   **Algorithm**

The algorithm for this problem is

1. Execute steps 2 through 6 for each employee.
2. Read EmpName$, PayRate for an employee.
3. Input Hours for that employee.
4. Determine whether this employee is entitled to overtime pay.
5. Calculate pay using the appropriate equations.
6. Print EmpName$, PayRate, Hours, RegularPay, OvertimePay, and GrossPay.

The top-down chart in Figure 6.8 shows the problem divided into three sub-programs: Print Headings, Calculate Overtime Pay, and Calculate Regular Pay. The tasks of reading EmpName$ and PayRate, accepting a value of Hours, calculating GrossPay, and printing the detail line are done in the main module.

The pseudocode for this problem is

Pay with Overtime

Main Module
Call PrintHeadings
Read EmpName$, PayRate
Do until trailer data is read
   Input Hours
   If Hours > 40 then
     Call Overtime
   Else
     Call Regular
   End if
   Calculate GrossPay
   Print EmpName$, PayRate, Hours, RegularPay, OvertimePay, GrossPay
   Read EmpName$, PayRate
End of loop
End Main Module

PrintHeadings
   Print headings
   Define Format$
End PrintHeadings

Overtime
   Calculate RegularPay
   Calculate OvertimePay
End Overtime

Regular
   Calculate RegularPay
   OvertimePay = 0
End Regular
End

STEP 3   **Hand-Calculated Answer**

Many students have difficulty writing the equations for this problem, so instead of simply presenting the hand-calculated answers, we will show how to develop the equations.

As in Chapter 5's parking lot problem, we begin with numerical calculations. The equations for the Regular subprogram are easier, so let's do those first.

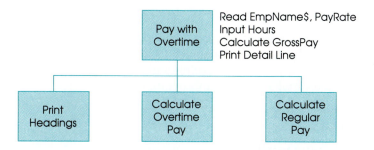

FIGURE 6.8   Top-down chart for payroll with overtime.

Suppose an employee earns $6 per hour and works 30 hours. For that employee, we have

RegularPay = 6 * 30 = 180

and

OvertimePay = 0

This employee's GrossPay is 180. Using these two statements as guides, we can write the LET statements required in the Regular subprogram:

```
RegularPay = PayRate * Hours
```

and

```
OvertimePay = 0
```

Notice that if we want overtime pay to be 0, we must include a LET statement that sets it equal to 0. If you think this statement is unnecessary because QBasic assigns 0 to uninitialized variables, be sure to do Exercise 3 at the end of this section.

The equations for the Overtime subprogram are somewhat more complicated. Given that employees are paid regular time for the first 40 hours, if an employee earns $6.75 per hour and works 50 hours, his regular pay is

RegularPay = 6.75 * 40 = 270

The employee is paid time and a half (1.5) for hours over 40, so his overtime pay is

OvertimePay = 1.5 * 6.75 * 10 = 101.25

In this equation, 10 represents the number of hours paid at the overtime rate and was calculated as the number of hours worked, 50, minus 40. Let's show that subtraction explicitly:

OvertimePay = 1.5 * 6.75 * (50 – 40) = 101.25

This employee's GrossPay is 371.25 (270 + 101.25). Using these two equations as guides, we can easily write the LET statements required for the Overtime subprogram:

```
RegularPay = PayRate * 40
```

and

```
OvertimePay = 1.5 * PayRate * (Hours - 40)
```

STEP 4 QBasic Program

The program is shown in Program 6.6. The equations we just developed show that the Regular and Overtime subprograms need the values of PayRate and Hours if they are to calculate RegularPay and OvertimePay. For the subprograms to access these variables, we must pass the variables to the subprogram when we call it. The CALL statement in line 27

```
CALL Overtime(PayRate, Hours, RegularPay, OvertimePay)
```

executes the Overtime subprogram and passes to it the variables it needs: PayRate and Hours. We include RegularPay and OvertimePay in the argument list so that the subprogram can return the values it calculates to the main module. The CALL statement in line 29, which executes the Regular subprogram, is similar.

The DATA statements are in lines 38 through 42. QBasic requires that the DATA statements be coded in the main module. If you code them in a procedure, when you save the program, QBasic moves them to the main module.

Notice the remark statements immediately after the SUB statements in lines 44 through 46, 53 through 55, and 68 through 70. These statements describe the function of the subprogram, which variables are passed to it, and which variables it returns to the calling program. These remark statements are very useful, and you should include such statements in your programs.

The output in Program 6.6 shows that the program's answers agree with our hand-calculated answer. ∎

```
 1  |  '    *** BAT-O PROGRAM WITH OVERTIME ***
 2  |  '    Calculate payroll, paying time and a half for hours over forty
 3  |
 4  |  DECLARE SUB PrintHeadings (Format$)
 5  |  DECLARE SUB Overtime (PayRate!, Hours!, RegularPay!, OvertimePay!)
 6  |  DECLARE SUB Regular (PayRate!, Hours!, RegularPay!, OvertimePay!)
 7  |
 8  |  '    Variables used
 9  |
10  |  '    EmpName$          Employee name
11  |  '    GrossPay          Gross pay
12  |  '    Hours             Hours worked
13  |  '    OvertimePay       Overtime pay
14  |  '    PayRate           Pay rate
15  |  '    RegularPay        Regular pay
16  |
17  |  CLS
18  |  CALL PrintHeadings(Format$)    'Print headings and define format string
19  |
20  |  '    Process employees
21  |  READ EmpName$, PayRate              'Data are at end of main program
22  |  DO UNTIL EmpName$ = "EOD"
23  |      PRINT "Enter hours for employee "; EmpName$;
24  |      INPUT ": ", Hours
25  |  '    Employees who work more than 40 hours get overtime
26  |      IF Hours > 40 THEN
27  |          CALL Overtime(PayRate, Hours, RegularPay, OvertimePay)
28  |      ELSE
29  |          CALL Regular(PayRate, Hours, RegularPay, OvertimePay)
30  |      END IF
31  |      GrossPay = RegularPay + OvertimePay
```

PROGRAM 6.6 A program that uses subprograms to calculate payroll with overtime. *(continued on next page)*

```
32        LPRINT USING Format$; EmpName$; PayRate; Hours; RegularPay; ↵
              OvertimePay; GrossPay
33        READ EmpName$, PayRate          'Data are at end of main program
34   LOOP
35   PRINT "Normal end of program"
36
37   '   *** Data used by program
38   DATA Joe Tinker, 6.75
39   DATA Joan Evers, 6.00
40   DATA Frank Chance, 5.75
41   DATA EOD, 0                              : REM Trailer data
42   END

43   SUB Overtime (PayRate, Hours, RegularPay, OvertimePay)
44   '   Calculate overtime pay for employees who work more than 40 hours
45   '     Receives PayRate and Hours
46   '     Returns RegularPay and OvertimePay
47
48       RegularPay = PayRate * 40
49       OvertimePay = 1.5 * PayRate * (Hours - 40)
50   END SUB
51
52   SUB PrintHeadings (Format$)
53   '   Print headings and define format string
54   '   No variables are received
55   '   Returns Format$
56
57    Title$ = "                    PAYROLL REPORT"
58    Head1$ = "              Pay          Regular  Overtime     Gross"
59    Head2$ = "   Name      Rate  Hours     Pay       Pay        Pay"
60    Format$ = "\            \  ##.##   ##    ###.##    ###.##   ###.##"
61    LPRINT Title$
62    LPRINT
63    LPRINT Head1$
64    LPRINT Head2$
65   END SUB
66
67   SUB Regular (PayRate, Hours, RegularPay, OvertimePay)
68   '   Calculate regular pay for employees who work less than 40 hours
69   '     Receives PayRate and Hours
70   '     Returns RegularPay and OvertimePay
71
72       RegularPay = PayRate * Hours
73       OvertimePay = 0
74   END SUB
```

```
Enter hours for employee Joe Tinker: 50
Enter hours for employee Joan Evers: 30
Enter hours for employee Frank Chance: 43
Normal end of program
```

```
                        PAYROLL REPORT

                 Pay          Regular  Overtime    Gross
   Name         Rate  Hours     Pay       Pay       Pay
Joe Tinker      6.75   50     270.00    101.25    371.25
Joan Evers      6.00   30     180.00      0.00    180.00
Frank Chance    5.75   43     230.00     25.88    255.88
```

PROGRAM 6.6 (continued)

6.2 EXERCISES

★**1.** Would Program 6.5 (pages 197–199) work if the variable Area in lines 52 and 54 were changed to CircleArea?

2. What answers would be printed for Joe Tinker if in Program 6.6 the CALL statement in line 27 were

```
CALL Overtime(Hours, PayRate, RegularPay, OvertimePay)
```

3. Since uninitialized variables are automatically given the value 0, many students don't understand the reason for line 73 in Program 6.6. Trace the program to determine the output it would produce if line 73 were deleted.

4. True or false: A top-down chart shows the order in which subprograms are executed.

6.3   FUNCTIONS

Recall that QBasic provides a second kind of procedure called a function. You have used some functions, like UCASE$, that are part of QBasic. The functions we will study now are similar to QBasic functions—but since you write them yourself, they can be customized for the problem you are working on.

You are already familiar with some function concepts because subprograms and functions share several features, such as local variables, arguments, and parameters. Functions are typed using the New FUNCTION command in the Edit menu, and they are edited using the SUBs command in the View menu.

But functions and subprograms differ in two important respects. First, to execute a subprogram, you CALL it—but to execute a function, you use its name anywhere you would use an expression. For example, in Program 6.5 (page 197), the QBasic function UCASE$ is used in line 20:

```
Choice$ = UCASE$(INPUT$(1))
```

Second, subprograms can perform any task. Recall that in Program 6.5, we used the subprogram DisplayInst to display instructions; in Program 6.6, we used subprograms to calculate RegularPay and OvertimePay. Functions, however, are designed to return a *single value*. Using UCASE$ as an example once more, it returns the upper case version of its argument string.

Names for functions follow the same rules as names for variables, and they must be different from any variable names and other procedure names in the program. In addition, function names may not start with FN. When you choose a function name, you must consider whether the function returns a number or a string. If a function returns a string, the function name must end with a $. That is why UCASE$ ends with a $.

EXAMPLE 4
USING A FUNCTION TO CALCULATE THE VOLUME OF A CONE

Problem Statement

Write a program that accepts a radius and height and calculates and prints the volume of a cone. Use a function in your program.

STEP 1   **Variable Names**

The variables in this problem are

Variable	Variable Name
Input Variables	
Radius	`Radius`
Height	`Height`
Output Variable	
Volume	`Volume`

STEP 2   **Algorithm**

The algorithm is

1. Execute steps 2 through 4 for all cones.
2. Input Radius and Height.
3. Calculate Volume.
4. Print Radius, Height, and Volume.

To calculate the Volume in step 4, we can use the equation:

$$Volume = \frac{\pi Radius^2 Height}{3}$$

where π is the mathematical constant 3.14159.

STEP 3   **Hand-Calculated Answer**

When Radius is 5 and Height is 10, the equation gives a Volume of 261.7992.

STEP 4   **QBasic Program**

Program 6.7 shows the QBasic program. It uses the function ConeVolume to calculate the volume of a cone. The main module accepts values for Radius and Height, and then line 20

```
Volume = ConeVolume(Radius, Height)
```

executes the ConeVolume function simply by using its name, with its arguments, on the right side of a LET statement. Control passes to line 26, and the volume is calculated and assigned to ConeVolume in line 31. Control is then returned to line 20, where the calculated volume is assigned to Volume.

In fact, line 20 is not necessary. Since a function reference may be used anywhere an expression may be used, we could omit line 20 and write the PRINT statement in line 21 as

```
PRINT "Volume ="; ConeVolume(Radius, Height)
```

The first statement in a function is a FUNCTION statement, as shown in line 26. The FUNCTION statement is similar to the SUB statement; it names the function and lists the parameters. The last statement in a function is an END FUNCTION statement (see line 32). An END FUNCTION statement is similar to an END SUB statement; it returns control to the statement that executed the function. Both the FUNCTION and END FUNCTION statements are supplied for you when you select the New FUNCTION command in the Edit menu.

You've seen the similarities between writing subprograms and functions, but one major difference exists. Somewhere in a function, you *must* assign a value to the function name. In function ConeVolume, line 31 assigns a value to ConeVolume. A function returns a value by having a value assigned to its name.

```
 1 | '    *** PROGRAM TO CALCULATE VOLUME OF A CONE ***
 2 | '    Calculate the volume of a cone given the radius and height
 3 |
 4 | DECLARE FUNCTION ConeVolume! (Radius!, Height!)
 5 |
 6 | '    Variables used
 7 |
 8 | '    Height       Height of cone
 9 | '    Radius       Radius of cone
10 | '    Volume       Volume of cone
11 |
12 | CONST Pi = 3.14159      'Constant, π , to calculate the area of a circle
13 |
14 | CLS
15 |
16 | '    Process cases
17 | INPUT "Enter radius, 0 to stop: ", Radius
18 | DO UNTIL Radius = 0
19 |     INPUT "Enter height: ", Height
20 |     Volume = ConeVolume(Radius, Height)
21 |     PRINT "Volume ="; Volume
22 |     INPUT "Enter radius, 0 to stop: ", Radius
23 | LOOP
24 | END
25 |
26 | FUNCTION ConeVolume (Radius, Height)
27 | '    Function to calculate volume
28 | '    Receives Radius and Height
29 | '    Returns volume of cone in ConeVolume
30 |
31 |     ConeVolume = (Pi * Radius ^ 2 * Height) / 3
32 | END FUNCTION
```

```
Enter radius, 0 to stop: 5
Enter height: 10
Volume = 261.7992
Enter radius, 0 to stop: 0
```

PROGRAM 6.7   A program that uses a function to calculate the volume of a cone.

Notice that in line 31, the arguments of ConeVolume are not included. The value assigned to ConeVolume is assigned to Volume when line 20 is executed.

You must understand one other subtle but vitally important point about functions. Inside a function, you may use the function's name *only* on the left side of a LET statement. For example, suppose we wanted to print a message if the cone's volume was greater than 100. You *cannot* use the following statement in the ConeVolume function:

```
IF ConeVolume > 100 THEN
    PRINT "Cone volume is greater than 100"
END IF
```

This statement does not test the value of the variable ConeVolume. Instead, it invokes another execution of the function ConeVolume. It is legal for a function to execute itself, but only under special conditions that are beyond the scope of this book. Those special conditions do not apply here, so this IF statement will cause an error.

One way to solve this problem is to use a local variable everywhere in the function, and assign the function name equal to the local variable just before the END FUNCTION statement. For example, we could use the local variable Volume, and write the function as follows:

```
Volume = (Pi * Radius ^ 2 * Height) / 3
IF Volume > 100 THEN
    PRINT "Cone volume is greater than 100"
END IF
ConeVolume = Volume
```

We can do anything we want with Volume, including testing it in an IF statement. In the last line of the function, we set ConeVolume equal to Volume.

The following are additional examples of FUNCTION statements. ■

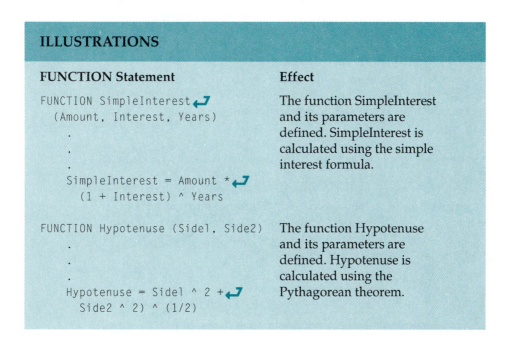

ILLUSTRATIONS

FUNCTION Statement	Effect

`FUNCTION SimpleInterest↵`
`   (Amount, Interest, Years)`
`      .`
`      .`
`      .`
`   SimpleInterest = Amount *↵`
`      (1 + Interest) ^ Years`
	The function SimpleInterest and its parameters are defined. SimpleInterest is calculated using the simple interest formula.

`FUNCTION Hypotenuse (Side1, Side2)`
`      .`
`      .`
`      .`
`   Hypotenuse = Side1 ^ 2 +↵`
`      Side2 ^ 2) ^ (1/2)`
	The function Hypotenuse and its parameters are defined. Hypotenuse is calculated using the Pythagorean theorem.

EXAMPLE 5 ▐
USING FUNCTIONS TO FIND THE LARGEST OF THREE NUMBERS

We can also use functions to resolve a problem we solved in Chapter 5—finding the largest of three numbers.

Problem Statement

Write a program that accepts three numbers and prints the largest. Assume that none of the numbers is equal to another.

STEP 1   Variable Names

We can use the same variable names we used in Chapter 5 (page 143). A, B, and C are the numbers; Largest is the largest of the three. In addition, we use a new variable Larger, which is the larger of A and B.

STEP 2 **Algorithm**

We use essentially the same algorithm used in Chapter 5; compare pairs of variables until you can conclude which variable is the largest.

STEP 3 **Hand-Calculated Answers**

As in Chapter 5, there are no answers to calculate by hand—but we will test the program with all six combinations of small, middle, and large.

STEP 4 **QBasic Program**

The program is shown in Program 6.8. The work is done by function Max, lines 31 through 41. Max compares its two arguments and returns the larger. Max is executed for the first time in line 15:

```
Larger = Max(A, B)
```

When Max is executed, it compares A and B and returns the larger. Line 15 assigns that value to Larger. Max is executed a second time in line 16:

```
Largest = Max(Larger, C)
```

This time, Max compares Larger and C and returns the larger of these two arguments. Line 16 assigns that value—which is the largest of A, B, and C—to Largest.
We could combine lines 15 and 16 into one statement:

```
Largest = Max(Max(A, B), C)
```

This statement shows that when you execute a function, you can use a function as an argument.
When we studied Program 6.4 (page 188), you learned that it is not necessary for arguments and parameters to have the same names. This program shows that sometimes it is *impossible* for the arguments and parameters to have the same names. Since Max is executed twice, with different arguments, it is not possible for the arguments and parameters to have the same names. ■

Syntax Summary

FUNCTION Statement

Form: FUNCTION FunctionName [(parameterlist)]
Example: FUNCTION PresentValue (Amount, Years, Rate)
Explanation: Declares the name of a function and lists parameters used in the function. Somewhere in the function definition, a value must be assigned to FunctionName.

END FUNCTION Statement

Form: END FUNCTION
Example: END FUNCTION
Explanation: Marks the end of a function and returns control to the statement that invoked the function.

```
 1 | '    *** FIND THE MAXIMUM OF THREE NUMBERS ***
 2 | '    Use a function twice to find the maximum of three numbers
 3 |
 4 | DECLARE FUNCTION Max! (X!, Y!)
 5 |
 6 | '    Variables used
 7 |
 8 | '    A, B, C        Three numbers
 9 | '    Larger         Larger of A and B
10 | '    Largest        Largest of the three numbers
11 |
12 | CLS
13 | READ A, B, C
14 | DO UNTIL A = 0
15 |     Larger = Max(A, B)
16 |     Largest = Max(Larger, C)
17 |     PRINT USING "The largest of ##  ##  ## is ##"; A; B; C; Largest
18 |     READ A, B, C
19 | LOOP
20 |
21 | '    *** Data used by program
22 | DATA 1, 2, 3
23 | DATA 1, 3, 2
24 | DATA 2, 1, 3
25 | DATA 2, 3, 1
26 | DATA 3, 1, 2
27 | DATA 3, 2, 1
28 | DATA 0, 0, 0                        : REM Trailer data
29 | END
30 |
31 | FUNCTION Max (X, Y)
32 | '    Function that determines the larger of its two arguments
33 | '    Receives two numbers X and Y
34 | '    Returns the larger in Max
35 |
36 |     IF X > Y THEN
37 |         Max = X
38 |     ELSE
39 |         Max = Y
40 |     END IF
41 | END FUNCTION
```

```
The largest of  1   2   3 is  3
The largest of  1   3   2 is  3
The largest of  2   1   3 is  3
The largest of  2   3   1 is  3
The largest of  3   1   2 is  3
The largest of  3   2   1 is  3
```

PROGRAM 6.8   A program that uses a function twice to find the largest of three numbers.

6.3 EXERCISES

★1.   Write a function that returns the product of its two parameters.

2.   Correct the errors in the following functions.

     a)
```
FUNCTION Sum (A, B)
     Total = A + B
END FUNCTION
```

     ★**b)**
```
FUNCTION Distance (Rate, Time)
     Distance (Rate, Time)= Rate * Time
END FUNCTION
```

3.   Write a function that returns the sum of its two parameters, except if the sum is greater than 100. If the sum is greater than 100, the function should return 0.

4.   Write a function that accepts a number from the keyboard, but does not return to the statement that invoked it until the user enters a number between 1 and 10 (end points included).

★5.   Would Program 6.8 produce correct answers if the order of the arguments in line 15 were reversed and written as:

```
Larger = Max(B, A)
```

6.   Show how you would extend Program 6.8 to print the largest of four variables named A, B, C, and D.

6.4   CONTROLLING THE SCREEN

In our work so far, we have treated the computer screen as though it were a piece of paper in a typewriter; each new line of output was printed on the next line. In fact, you can specify exactly where on the screen you want output printed and the colors to use when the output is printed. By taking advantage of these features, you make your programs look much more professional.

The LOCATE Statement

To design a screen, you again use a spacing chart. Figure 6.9 shows the design of a screen that displays a menu. We will use this menu for a program that calculates a customer's record store bill.

As the numbering at the left edge of Figure 6.9 shows, the screen is divided into 25 rows. The top row is row 1, and the bottom row is row 25. Rows are often called lines, so row 15 and line 15 are synonymous. Figure 6.9 also shows that the screen is divided into 80 columns. The leftmost column is column 1, and the rightmost column is column 80.

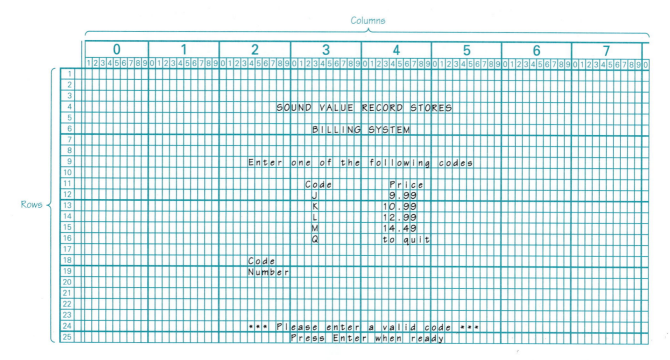

FIGURE 6.9   Screen layout chart for the Sound Value billing program.

After you fill out a spacing chart, you must instruct QBasic to display output in the appropriate row and column. To do so, use the LOCATE statement, which positions the cursor on the screen. The syntax of the LOCATE statement is

```
LOCATE [row] [,column] [,cursor]
```

where row specifies the row where you want to begin printing, and column specifies the column. After a LOCATE statement is executed, any output directed to the screen begins at the specified cursor position. The value chosen for cursor is used to make the cursor visible or invisible. If cursor is 1, the cursor is visible; if cursor is 0, it is invisible. When a program is run, the cursor is normally invisible. Because the INPUT statement makes the cursor visible, you may not have realized that it can also be invisible.

LOCATE is the first statement so far that uses arguments; in this case, row, column, and cursor. Notice that unlike the functions we studied, the arguments for the LOCATE statement are not enclosed in parentheses.

All three arguments in a LOCATE statement are optional. An omitted argument is not changed.

As an example of how you can use the LOCATE statement, consider Figure 6.9. This figure shows that we want to print the title, SOUND VALUE RECORD STORES, starting in row 4, column 28. The corresponding LOCATE statement is

```
LOCATE 4, 28
```

The LOCATE statement specifies only where printing is to begin; it does not itself cause anything to be printed. To print the title, we would use the statement

```
PRINT "SOUND VALUE RECORD STORES"
```

immediately after the LOCATE statement.

ILLUSTRATIONS

LOCATE Statement	Effect
`LOCATE Row, Column + 1`	This example shows that both row and column may be variables or expressions. In this statement, Row and Column are variables that must be assigned values before being used in the LOCATE statement. Row must have a value between 1 and 25, and Column must have a value between 0 and 79, so that Column + 1 has a value between 1 and 80.
`LOCATE , 60`	This example shows how you can omit an argument. The comma indicates that the row argument was omitted. By omitting the row argument, we tell QBasic to position the cursor at column 60 in the row in which the cursor is currently located.
`LOCATE , , 1`	Makes the cursor visible, without changing its position.

Using Color

In addition to position, you can also control the color of output on the screen. You can get the full range of colors if your computer has a color monitor. If your computer has a monochrome monitor, you can get only a limited range of colors, which are used for reverse video. **Reverse video** refers to displaying black characters on a white background—or, with an IBM monochrome monitor, on a green background. Your instructor will tell you the kind of monitor installed on your computer.

reverse video
A display in which black characters appear against a white background.

The COLOR Statement

When a character is printed on the screen, the color in which it is printed is called the **foreground color**, and the color against which it appears is called the **background color**. These colors may be specified using the COLOR statement. The syntax of the COLOR statement is

```
COLOR [foreground] [,background] [,border]
```

Here, foreground specifies the foreground color, background specifies the background color, and border specifies the color of the border that surrounds the screen.

If your computer has a color/graphics monitor, refer to Table 6.1 to find the values for foreground and the colors they represent. If your computer has a monochrome monitor, refer to Table 6.2 to find the values for foreground and the effects they produce. (For quick reference, Tables 6.1 and 6.2 are reproduced in Appendix B.) If you add 16 to the appropriate values for your monitor, the colors will blink. For example, a value of 20 gives blinking red on computers with color monitors, while a value of 17 gives blinking underlined white on computers with monochrome monitors.

For background, with a color/graphics monitor, you may use any value from 0 through 7. With the monochrome monitor, the only values you may use

foreground color
The color in which text is displayed.

background color
The color of the background against which text is displayed.

TABLE 6.1
Colors allowed for foreground in text mode with a color/graphics monitor

Number	Color	Number	Color
0	Black	8	Gray
1	Blue	9	Light blue
2	Green	10	Light green
3	Cyan	11	Light cyan
4	Red	12	Light red
5	Magenta	13	Light magenta
6	Brown	14	Yellow
7	White	15	High-intensity white

for background are 0 (black) and 7 (white), and 7 may be used only when foreground is 0 (black) or 16 (blinking black).

For border, with a color/graphics monitor, you may use values 0 through 15. The border feature is available only with a color/graphics monitor. The border argument is left over from the early days of computers; in most modern computers, border has no effect.

After a COLOR statement is executed, all characters sent to the screen thereafter are printed in the specified colors. Characters may be sent to the screen by a PRINT statement, or they may be entered at the keyboard in response to an INPUT statement. Any characters that were on the screen before the COLOR statement was executed retain their original colors. We will exploit this feature in the next program to print an error message in striking colors, while not affecting the rest of the output on the screen. A CLS statement executed after a COLOR statement is executed clears the whole screen to the background color.

Some examples may clarify how the COLOR statement is used.

ILLUSTRATIONS

COLOR Statement	Effect
COLOR 7, 0	Creates white (green on an IBM monochrome display) characters on a black background. This is the default setting.
COLOR 0, 7	Creates reverse video—black characters on a white (green on an IBM monochrome display) background.
COLOR 16, 7	Creates a blinking reverse video.
COLOR 0, 0	Creates black characters on a black background, making the characters invisible.
COLOR 7, 1	On machines with a color monitor, creates white characters on a blue background.

TABLE 6.2
Colors allowed for foreground in text mode with a monochrome monitor

Number	Color
0	Black
1	Underlined white characters
7	White
9	Underlined high-intensity white characters
15	High-intensity white

Any of the three arguments in a COLOR statement—foreground, background, or border—are optional. An omitted argument is not changed. For example,

```
COLOR 5
```

changes the foreground color to magenta, keeping the background color unchanged. The arguments may be constants (as in our examples), variables, or numeric expressions. So statements like

```
COLOR Red, White
```

are legal, providing that the variables Red and White are assigned legal values before the statement is executed. A common practice is to define the colors as constants, as shown in the following program. This makes the program self-documenting.

EXAMPLE 6
A PROGRAM THAT USES A MENU

We want to write a billing program for the Sound Value record store. The store established a coding system to indicate the price of items it sells:

Code	Price
J	9.99
K	10.99
L	12.99
M	14.49

Problem Statement

Write a program that displays a menu of codes and prices. The program should accept the code of an item and the number of those items a customer purchased, and use the preceding table to calculate and print the customer's bill.

STEP 1   **Variable Names**

We identify the following variables.

Variable	Variable Name
Input Variables	
Code of item	Code$
Number of items	Number

Output Variables

Price of item   `Price`
Bill   `Bill`

STEP 2   **Algorithm**

The algorithm for this problem is

1. Display the menu of codes and prices.
2. Execute steps 3 through 6 for all items purchased.
3.   Input Code$ and Number for the item.
4.   Use the Code$ to determine the Price of the item.
5.   Calculate the Bill, using the appropriate Price.
6.   Print Number, Code$, Price, and Bill.

Figure 6.10 shows a top-down chart for this problem. The problem is divided into three subprograms that display the menu, get the input, and set the price. The subprogram that gets the input does not return to the main module until the user enters a valid code. It executes a function that gets Code$ from the user; it also executes a subprogram that displays an error message if an invalid Code$ is entered.

The pseudocode for this problem is

Calculate Bills

Main Module
Set colors to white on blue
Call DisplayMenu
Call GetInput
Do until trailer data is entered
    Determine Price using function SetPrice
    Bill = Price * Number
    Print Bill
    Pause
    Call DisplayMenu
    Call GetInput
End of loop
End Main Module

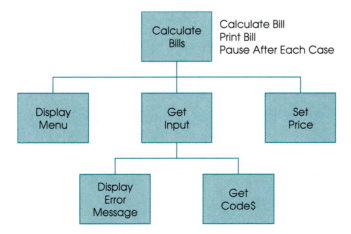

FIGURE 6.10   Top-down chart for a program that uses a menu.

```
DisplayMenu
    Clear the screen
    Display the menu
End DisplayMenu

GetInput
    Obtain Code$ using function GetCode$
    Do until a valid Code$ is entered
        Call DisplayErrMsg
        Obtain Code$ using function GetCode$
    End of loop
    If Code$ is not equal to Q then
        Input Number
    End if
End GetInput

GetCode$
    Get Code$ from user
End GetCode$

SetPrice
    Use Code$ to determine Price
End SetPrice

DisplayErrMsg
    Beep the speaker
    Set colors to blinking red on white
    Display error message
    Pause
    Erase error message
    Reset colors to white on blue
End DisplayErrMsg
End
```

STEP 3   Hand-Calculated Answer

We must calculate a bill for each of the four categories of items that the store sells. Using the price table given at the start of this example, we calculate the following bills.

Code	Price	Number	Bill
J	9.99	2	19.98
K	10.99	3	32.97
L	12.99	4	51.96
M	14.49	5	72.45

STEP 4   QBasic Program

The menu program is shown in Program 6.9. In the main program, lines 20 through 23 define four constants that are used to set the screen colors. Two of the constants are used in lines 30 and 57

```
COLOR White, Blue
```

to get white characters on a blue background. The other two constants are used in line 52

```
COLOR BlinkingWhite, Red
```

to display the error messages in blinking white on a red background.

The constants JPrice, KPrice, LPrice, and MPrice are used in the Display-Menu subprogram to produce the screen you see in Program 6.9's Output screen. They are also used in the SetPrice function to set the price depending on the code of the item that the user purchased. If the record store changes the price associated with a code, we need only change the constant. The new price is then automatically reflected in both the menu and the bills.

The main part of the program starts in line 33, which executes the Display-Menu subprogram. This subprogram, which starts at line 65, uses LOCATE and

```
1    '    *** SOUND VALUE BILLING PROGRAM ***
2    '    Calculate bills depending on category of item
3    '    and number bought
4
5    DECLARE SUB DisplayErrMsg ()
6    DECLARE SUB DisplayMenu ()
7    DECLARE FUNCTION GetCode$ ()
8    DECLARE SUB GetInput (Code$, Number!)
9    DECLARE FUNCTION SetPrice (Code$)
10
11   '    Variables used
12
13   '    Bill          Bill
14   '    Code$         Code of item
15   '    Number        Number purchased
16   '    Price         Price of item
17
18   '    Constants
19
20   CONST Blue = 1
21   CONST White = 7
22   CONST Red = 4
23   CONST BlinkingWhite = 31
24   CONST JPrice = 9.99
25   CONST KPrice = 10.99
26   CONST LPrice = 12.99
27   CONST MPrice = 14.49
28   CONST DetailFormat$ = "## code ! items at ##.## each total $###.##"
29
30   COLOR White, Blue                    'Set white characters on blue background
31
32   '    Process sales
33   CALL DisplayMenu
34   CALL GetInput(Code$, Number)
35   DO UNTIL Code$ = "Q"
36       Price = SetPrice(Code$)
37       Bill = Price * Number
38       LOCATE 21, 24
39       PRINT USING DetailFormat$; Number; Code$; Price; Bill
40       LOCATE 23, 24
41       PRINT "Press any key when ready ";
42       Dummy$ = INPUT$(1)
43       CALL DisplayMenu
44       CALL GetInput(Code$, Number)
45   LOOP
46   END
47
```

PROGRAM 6.9   A program that uses a menu. *(continued on next page)*

```
48  SUB DisplayErrMsg
49  '   Display error message when invalid Code$ is entered
50
51      BEEP
52      COLOR BlinkingWhite, Red             'Set blinking white on red
53      LOCATE 24, 24
54      PRINT "*** Please enter a valid code ***";   'Hanging ; prevents scrolling
55      LOCATE 25, 30
56      INPUT ; "Press Enter when ready", Dummy$      '; prevents scrolling
57      COLOR White, Blue                    'Reset standard colors
58      LOCATE 24, 24                        'Position cursor
59      PRINT SPACE$(33);               'Erase message on line 24 (33 is length↵
           of message)
60      LOCATE 25, 30                        'Position cursor
61      PRINT SPACE$(24);               'Erase message on line 25 (24 is length of↵
           message)
62      LOCATE 18, 31                        'Position cursor
63      PRINT SPACE$(1)                      'Erase previous code
64  END SUB

65  SUB DisplayMenu
66  '   Display menu
67
68      CLS
69      MenuFormat$ = "!            ##.##"
70      LOCATE 4, 28
71      PRINT "SOUND VALUE RECORD STORES"
72      LOCATE 6, 33
73      PRINT "BILLING SYSTEM"
74      LOCATE 9, 24
75      PRINT "Enter one of the following codes"
76      LOCATE 11, 32
77      PRINT "Code        Price"
78      LOCATE 12, 33
79      PRINT USING MenuFormat$; "J"; JPrice
80      LOCATE 13, 33
81      PRINT USING MenuFormat$; "K"; KPrice
82      LOCATE 14, 33
83      PRINT USING MenuFormat$; "L"; LPrice
84      LOCATE 15, 33
85      PRINT USING MenuFormat$; "M"; MPrice
86      LOCATE 16, 33
87      PRINT "Q           to quit"
88  END SUB
89
90  FUNCTION GetCode$
91  '   Get Code$ from user, using INPUT$
92
93      LOCATE 18, 24, 1              'Position cursor and make it visible
94      PRINT "Code   ";
95      Code$ = UCASE$(INPUT$(1))
96      PRINT Code$
97      GetCode$ = Code$
98  END FUNCTION
99
```

PROGRAM 6.9 *(continued)*

```
100 | SUB GetInput (Code$, Number)
101 | '    Get input from user
102 | '    No variables are received
103 | '    Returns a valid Code$ (J, K, L, M, or Q) and Number
104 |
105 |     Code$ = GetCode$
106 |     DO UNTIL (Code$ = "J" OR Code$ = "K" OR Code$ = "L" OR Code$ = "M" OR↵
        Code$ = "Q")
107 |         CALL DisplayErrMsg
108 |         Code$ = GetCode$
109 |     LOOP
110 |     IF Code$ <> "Q" THEN
111 |         LOCATE 19, 24
112 |         INPUT "Enter number purchased ", Number
113 |     END IF
114 | END SUB
115 |
116 | FUNCTION SetPrice (Code$)
117 | '    Determine price of item, depending on Code$ of item
118 | '    Receives Code$. Code$ is J, K, L, or M
119 | '    Returns price in SetPrice
120 |
121 |     SELECT CASE Code$
122 |         CASE "J"
123 |             SetPrice = JPrice
124 |         CASE "K"
125 |             SetPrice = KPrice
126 |         CASE "L"
127 |             SetPrice = LPrice
128 |         CASE "M"
129 |             SetPrice = MPrice
130 |     END SELECT
131 | END FUNCTION
```

```
                    SOUND VALUE RECORD STORES

                         BILLING SYSTEM


                 Enter one of the following codes

                      Code         Price
                       J            9.99
                       K           10.99
                       L           12.99
                       M           14.49
                       Q           to quit

            Code    W
```

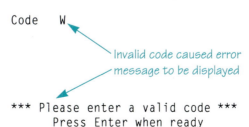

Invalid code caused error
message to be displayed

```
            *** Please enter a valid code ***
                  Press Enter when ready
```

PROGRAM 6.9 *(continued)*

PRINT statements to produce the menu. The CLS statement in line 68 clears the screen to the background color: blue.

Line 34 executes the GetInput subprogram, which is discussed shortly. The pretest UNTIL loop in lines 35 through 45 is executed until the user enters a Q for Code$. GetInput is designed to return only valid values of Code$. Therefore, without further testing, Code$ is used in line 36 as the argument to the SetPrice function, which uses Code$ in a SELECT CASE statement to determine the price. The Bill is calculated in line 37 and printed in line 39. The program then positions the cursor, prints a prompt, and pauses until the user presses any key. This pause gives the user time to read the bill.

GetInput, which starts at line 100, uses the GetCode$ function to get a value of Code$ from the user. To return only valid values of Code$ to the main module, GetInput uses a pretest UNTIL loop in lines 106 through 109. This loop is entered only if the user enters an invalid value for Code$. Inside the loop, the DisplayErrMsg subprogram is called to display an error message, and the Get-Code$ function is executed to get another value for Code$ from the user. The program stays in the loop until the user enters a valid value for Code$.

If the user enters any valid value for Code$ except Q, we want to get a value for Number. The IF statement in line 110 tests Code$; if it is not Q, the INPUT statement in line 112 gets a value for Number.

The DisplayErrMsg subprogram starts in line 48. Line 53 positions the cursor on row 24, column 24; line 54 prints an error message. We want to prevent scrolling, which would spoil the menu. To prevent scrolling, you must understand two things. First, any PRINT statement that writes on lines 24 or 25 must end with a hanging semicolon or comma. That is why the PRINT statement in line 54 ends with a hanging semicolon. Second, you must not print in column 80 of lines 24 or 25.

The LOCATE statement in line 55 positions the cursor to display the prompt of the following INPUT statement on row 25. The INPUT statement causes the program to pause. After reading and understanding the error message, the user can simply press the Enter key to continue. The Output screen in Program 6.9 shows the error message and prompt displayed.

If an INPUT statement prints a prompt on rows 24 or 25, when the user presses the Enter key to signal that all the data are typed, the screen will scroll. To prevent any scrolling, this INPUT statement (in line 56) uses a semicolon immediately following the word INPUT.

Because the COLOR statement affects only the colors of output generated after it is executed, only the text on rows 24 and 25 of the screen are printed in blinking white on red, as specified in the COLOR statement in line 52. The rest of the screen keeps its normal white characters on a blue background.

The SPACE$ Function

The LOCATE statements in lines 58, 60, and 62 position the cursor for the PRINT statements in lines 59, 61, and 63. These PRINT statements use the SPACE$ function to print spaces to erase the error message, the prompt, and the invalid Code$. The syntax of the SPACE$ function is

```
SPACE$(n)
```

where the argument, n, specifies the number of spaces to generate and may have any value between 0 and 32,767. In line 59, the argument is 33 because the error message is 33 characters long; similarly, the argument of the SPACE$ function in lines 61 and 63 is chosen to match the length of the string being erased. Unlike the SPC function, which may be used only in PRINT and LPRINT statements, the SPACE$ function may be used anywhere a string can be used.

Syntax Summary

LOCATE Statement

Form: `LOCATE [row] [,column] [,cursor]`
Example: `LOCATE 5, 30, 1`
Explanation: Positions the cursor on the screen for subsequent output.
               A value of 1 for cursor makes the cursor visible; a value of
               0 makes it invisible.

COLOR Statement

Form: `COLOR [foreground] [,background] [,border]`
Example: `COLOR 8, 3`
Explanation: Sets the colors used for subsequent output. The values that
               may be coded, and the colors they represent, are given in
               Tables 6.1 and 6.2 (pages 213–214).

6.4 EXERCISES

★**1.**   Write a statement or statements to print the message How many tickets
        please? in row 20 starting in column 10.

2.   Write LOCATE and INPUT statements that will print the prompt Enter
        your name: in row 6 starting in column 15.

★**3.**   Write a statement to print blue letters on a yellow background.

4.   Write a statement or statements to print 33 spaces starting at row 5,
        column 10.

5.   Program 6.10 is supposed to calculate the compound present value of an
        Amount that is to be paid Years from now, assuming an interest rate of
        InterestRate. If InterestRate is expressed as a percent, the present value is
        given by the equation

$$PresentValue = \frac{Amount}{\left(1 + InterestRate\,/\,100\right)^{Years}}$$

As the output shows, the program contains an error. Correct it.

```
1    '   *** CALCULATING PRESENT VALUE ***
2    '   Calculate present value given amount, years, and interest rate
3
4    DECLARE FUNCTION CalcPV! (Amount!, Years!, InterestRate!)
5
6    CLS
7    LPRINT "Amount", "Years", "Interest Rate", "Present Value"
8
```

PROGRAM 6.10   An incorrect program to calculate present value.
(continued on next page)

```
 9  |  '    Process cases
10  |  INPUT "Enter amount, 0 to stop: ", Amount
11  |  DO UNTIL Amount = 0
12  |      INPUT "Enter number of years: ", Years
13  |      INPUT "Enter interest rate (percent): ", InterestRate
14  |      PresentValue = CalcPV(Amount, Years, InterestRate)
15  |      LPRINT Amount, Years, InterestRate, PresentValue
16  |      INPUT "Enter amount, 0 to stop: ", Amount
17  |  LOOP
18  |  END
19  |
20  |  FUNCTION CalcPV (Amount, Years, InterestRate)
21  |  '    Calculate present value
22  |  '    Receives Amount, Years, and InterestRate
23  |  '    Returns present value in CalcPV
24  |
25  |      PresentValue = Amount / (1 + InterestRate / 100) ^ Years
26  |  END FUNCTION
```

```
Enter amount, 0 to stop: 1000
Enter number of years: 20
Enter interest rate (percent): 1
Enter amount, 0 to stop:

Amount          Years           Interest Rate Present Value
 1000            20             1                  0
```

PROGRAM 6.10 *(continued)*

WHAT YOU HAVE LEARNED

In this chapter, you learned that:

- Procedures are self-contained statements that perform a specific task, such as displaying a menu or calculating a value.
- Procedures simplify developing algorithms, drawing flowcharts, and writing and debugging programs. They also facilitate using top-down design.
- QBasic provides two kinds of procedures: subprograms and functions.
- Subprograms are a kind of procedure that may return more than one value and perform other general tasks.
- QBasic inserts DECLARE statements in programs that contain procedures.
- Subprograms are executed using the CALL statement.
- The New SUB command in the Edit menu is used to enter subprograms.
- The SUB command in the View menu is used to edit procedures.
- Selecting the Split command in the View menu divides the View window in two. Selecting the Split command again restores a single window.
- When you execute a procedure, the arguments passed to the procedure must match in type and number the parameters in the procedure definition.
- By default, all variables are local.

- The COMMON SHARED statement is used to declare global variables, and should be used sparingly.
- The SUB statement is used to indicate the first line in a subprogram, and lists the parameters used in the subprogram.
- The END SUB statement indicates the last line in a subprogram. It returns control to the statement following the CALL statement that executed the subprogram.
- Symbolic constants are global.
- Functions return one value.
- Functions are executed by using their name where you would use a variable name in an expression.
- The FUNCTION statement is used to indicate the first line in a function and lists the parameters used in the function.
- Somewhere in a function, you must assign a value to the function name.
- The END FUNCTION statement indicates the last line in a function and returns control to the statement that executed the function.
- The LOCATE statement is used to position output on the screen.
- The COLOR statement is used to specify the foreground and background colors of characters written to the screen.
- The SPACE$ function is used to generate spaces.

NEW QBASIC STATEMENTS

STATEMENT	EFFECT

CALL
`CALL DisplayMessage(Message$,`
`   Row, Column)`
	Transfers control to the subprogram DisplayMessage. The arguments Message$, Row, and Column are associated with the corresponding parameters in the SUB statement for DisplayMessage.

SUB `SUB DisplayMessage (Msg$, R, C)`	Marks the beginning of the subprogram DisplayMessage. The parameters Msg$, R, and C are associated with the corresponding arguments in the CALL statement that executes DisplayMessage.
END SUB `END SUB`	Marks the end of a subprogram, and returns control to the statement following the CALL statement that executed the subprogram.
COMMON SHARED `COMMON SHARED TotalSales, AverageSales`	Makes TotalSales and AverageSales global, so they may be used in any subprogram without argument passing.

FUNCTION

```
FUNCTION LetterGrade$ (Average)
```

Marks the beginning of the function LetterGrade$. The parameter Average is associated with the argument in the statement that executes the function.

END FUNCTION

```
END FUNCTION
```

Marks the end of a function, and returns control to the statement that executed the function.

LOCATE

```
LOCATE 10, 35
```

Positions the cursor on the screen so that subsequent output will start at row 10 and column 35.

COLOR

```
COLOR 0, 4
```

Sets the colors used for subsequent output on a color/graphics monitor to black on a red background.

KEY TERMS

background color	local variable	stepwise refinement
foreground color	parameter	top-down chart
global variable	procedure	top-down design
hierarchy chart	reverse video	

REVIEW EXERCISES

SELF-CHECK

1. When should you type the DECLARE statements?

2. What rules govern procedure names?

3. How do you execute a subprogram? How do you execute a function?

4. Is it legal to have a subprogram with no arguments?

5. List the steps to follow when you want to enter a new subprogram.

6. List the steps to follow if the main module is in a window and you want to edit a procedure.

7. True or false: Before executing a program, you should bring the main module into the View window.

8. How do you divide the View window into two parts?

9. What is a local variable? What is a global variable?

10. Which statement is used to define local variables? Which statement is used to define global variables?

11. What is the last line in a function?

12. Does the function Greeting$ return a number or a string?

13. What does the statement COLOR 1, 0 do if you are using a monochrome monitor? What does it do if you are using a color/graphics monitor?

14. True or false: A LOCATE statement may be used to display a message on the screen.

PROGRAMMING ASSIGNMENTS

Section 6.1

1. Write a program that could be used to help people learn about vitamins. Allow the user to enter A, B1, C, or D and have the program print the following information about the vitamins.

Vitamin A
Function: Promotes good eyesight.
Sources: Liver, carrots, sweet potatoes.
RDA: 1000 units.

Vitamin B1
Function: Used by the nervous system, heart, and liver.
Sources: Meat, fish, poultry, whole grains.
RDA: 1.5 mg.

Vitamin C
Function: Helps heal wounds and resist
          infections.
Sources: Citrus fruits, turnips, potatoes, cabbage.
RDA: 60 mg.

Vitamin D
Function: Important for bone development.
Sources: Sunlight, fortified milk, organ meats.
RDA: 7.5 units.

If the user does not enter one of these vitamins, print an error message. Use separate subprograms for each vitamin.

2. Write a program to print "Oh, Susanna!" The lyrics are given below. Simplify and shorten your program by using a subprogram to print the chorus.

I come from Alabama with
My banjo on my knee,
I'm going to Louisiana,
My Susanna for to see.

Chorus…

Oh, Susanna!
Oh, don't you cry for me,
For I come from Alabama with my banjo on my
    knee.

It rained all day the night I left
The weather was so dry,
The sun so hot I froze myself,
Susanna don't you cry.

Chorus (repeat three-line chorus)

I had a dream the other night,
When everything was still.
I thought I saw Susanna
A-coming down the hill.

Chorus (repeat three-line chorus)

The buckwheat cake was in her mouth,
The tear was in her eye,
Says I, 'I'm coming from the South.'
Susanna don't you cry.

Chorus (repeat three-line chorus)

Note: Apostrophes are used in place of quotation marks in the last verse because you don't know how to include quotation marks in a string yet.

3. Many people think that if a year is divisible by 4, it is a leap year. However, as mentioned in Chapter 5, the rules are more complicated than that. If a year is divisible by 100, then for it to be a leap year, it must be divisible by 400—not merely divisible by 4. This means, for example, that the year 1900 was not a leap year because 1900 is divisible by 100, but not divisible by 400. (Of course, divisible means *exactly* divisible, with a remainder of zero.) Write a program that accepts a year and determines if that year is a leap year. Use the MOD operator to determine if the year is exactly divisible by 400, 100, and 4. Use one subprogram to determine if a century year is a leap year, and a separate subprogram to determine if a regular year is a leap year.

Section 6.2

Now that you know about top-down design and top-down charts, you should use them when you develop your programs.

4. Write a program that can calculate the volume of a sphere, a cylinder, or a pyramid. The program should ask the user to enter an S, a C, or a P, to indicate the figure whose volume is to be calculated. If the user enters an S, the program should request the Radius of the sphere and calculate the volume of the sphere using the formula Vol = 4 * π * Radius ^ 3 / 3. If the user enters a C, the program should request the Radius and the Height of the cylinder, and calculate the volume of the cylinder using the formula Vol = π * Radius ^ 2 * Height. If the user enters a P, the program should request the Base and Height of the pyramid, and calculate the volume of the pyramid using the formula Vol = Base ^ 2 * Height / 3. In these formulas, π is the mathematical constant 3.14159.

If the user does not enter S, C, or P, the program should display an error message and request the user to enter a correct value. Use separate subprograms for each of the figures.

5. A college charges tuition depending on whether a student is a resident and on how many credits the student takes. If the student is a resident, the charges are

Less than 12 credits	$75 per credit
12 or more credits	$750

If the student is not a resident, the charges are

Less than 12 credits	$95 per credit
12 or more credits	$950

Write a program that calculates students' tuition bills. Use separate subprograms for residents and nonresidents.

Section 6.3

6. The area of a trapezoid whose parallel sides are *a* and *b*, and whose altitude is *h*, is

$$Area = \tfrac{1}{2} h(a+b)$$

Write a program that accepts values for *a*, *b*, and *h*, and that uses a function to calculate Area.

7. Write a program that accepts three numbers and prints the smallest one. Use a function that has three numbers as its arguments, and that returns the smallest value.

8. Write a program like Programming Assignment 5.21, but use functions to calculate the average grades and to assign letter grades.

9. Write a program that accepts a day of the week number and prints the day name. Let 1 be Sunday, 2 be Monday, and so on. Use a function to return the day name.

Section 6.4

10. Modify your solution to Programming Assignment 3.7, so the prompt that asks the user to enter a name is printed on a clear screen on row 5, starting in column 20. Then the screen should be cleared, the message Good Morning should be printed on row 10 starting in column 30, the name should follow (printed in reverse video), and the message Have a good day should be printed two rows down in blinking reverse video. (*Note:* To hold the display on the screen between cases, use an INPUT statement to cause a pause.)

11. The Beeline Travel Agency offers the following tours.

Code	Destination	Price
E	Europe	$3,500
H	Hawaii	$2,500
C	Caribbean	$2,000
A	Australia	$4,600
J	Japan	$4,800

Write a program that displays a menu of these choices, accepts a code and the number of people making the trip, and calculates and prints the total bill. If an invalid code is entered, print an error message in blinking blue on a white background.

ADDITIONAL PROGRAMMING ASSIGNMENTS

12. Write a program that accepts two numbers for variables A and B, and reverses the values. Use a subprogram named Switch to do the reversal.

13. In many situations, angles are measured in radians, rather than degrees. To convert from degrees to radians, you can use the formula

$$Radians = \frac{\pi}{180} Degrees$$

In this formula, π is the constant 3.14159. Write a program that uses a function to convert from degrees to radians. Use a symbolic constant for π.

14. Resolve Programming Assignment 2.15, using functions to calculate Time and Velocity.

15. Resolve Programming Assignment 2.18. Use a subprogram to obtain three numbers as input, and verify that the three numbers entered represent the sides of a triangle. Use a function to calculate the area.

16. A car rental agency has the following rates.

Number of Days Rented	Daily Charge Per Day	Mileage Charge Per Mile
>= 7	25.00	.10
< 7	30.00	.15

Write a program that accepts the number of days a car was rented and the number of miles driven, and that calculates the bill. Print the daily charge and the mileage charge, as well as the total bill. Use subprograms to calculate the daily and mileage charges.

17. Write a program that accepts a number (N) and a character (C$) and that prints a line consisting of N copies of C$. Use a subprogram to print the line.

BEYOND THE BASICS

18. Resolve Programming Assignment 2.20—but this time, accept the two durations and use a subprogram to convert seconds to minutes, and seconds and minutes to hours and minutes. Use one subprogram for both conversions.

19. Resolve Programming Assignment 5.35—but this time, use procedures in your solution of the quadratic equation.

20. Resolve Programming Assignment 5.36—but this time, verify that a valid date was entered. Also, use the complete rules for leap years, as given in Programming Assignment 6.3.

21. Write a program that accepts a three-digit number. Then, reverse the digits to generate a second number. For instance, if the entered number is 836, the second number becomes 638. Next, subtract the smaller number from the larger one to produce a new number. Reverse this new number and add the reverse number to its unreversed form. Print the sum. Continuing our

example, we would subtract 638 from 836 to get 198. When we reverse 198, we get 891. Adding 198 and 891 gives 1089. Run several cases, and see if you can draw any conclusions about the sum. Your program should use a function that returns the reverse of its argument. This function should call a subprogram. This subprogram should receive a number and return the right digit from that number, and the number remaining after the right digit is stripped from the original number.

22. Write a program that calculates grade point average (GPA). The program should accept a student's name. For each student, it should accept the name of a course, the number of credits, and the grade. Different students take different numbers of courses, so you will need trailer data to indicate that all the courses for a student were entered. You should verify that a valid grade was also entered. The grade point average is calculated using the formula

$$GPA = \frac{\sum C_i W_i}{\sum C_i}$$

In this equation, C_i is the number of credits of the ith course, and W_i is the weight of the ith course. The weights depend on the grade, as given in the following table.

Grade	Weight
A	4.0
A–	3.7
B+	3.3
B	3.0
B–	2.7
C+	2.3
C	2.0
C–	1.7
D+	1.3
D	1.0
D–	0.7
F	0.0

23. Write a program that draws a class schedule on the screen. Assume classes meet between 8 AM and 5 PM, Monday through Friday. The program should begin by printing Mon, Tue, Wed, Thu, and Fri across the screen; the times of 8, 9, 10, and so on should print down the screen. The program should next accept the name of a course and then ask for the day, hour, and room where the course will meet. The course name and room should be plotted in reverse video on the screen at the intersection of the day and hour. The program should continue to request a meeting day, hour, and room for a course until the user enters an X for the day, indicating that all the meetings for that course were entered. At that point, the program should request another course name and accept and plot the meetings for that course. Use EOD as the course name for trailer data.

24. Write a program that draws a tic-tac-toe board on the screen. The lines may be drawn using Xs, and the lines should be about 20 Xs long. *Hint:* Do not use more than four PRINT statements and consider the usefulness of statements of the form

```
Row = Row + 1
```

FOR...NEXT LOOPS AND QBASIC FUNCTIONS

LEARNING OBJECTIVES

After reading this chapter, you will be able to:

- Write programs that use counter-controlled loops.

- Use the QBasic statements FOR...NEXT, RANDOMIZE, MID$, and LINE INPUT.

- Use the QBasic numeric functions LOG, EXP, SQR, COS, SIN, TAN, ATN, SGN, ABS, FIX, INT, CINT, RND, and TIMER.

- Write programs that perform simulations.

- Use the QBasic string functions DATE$, TIME$, RTRIM$, LTRIM$, LCASE$, VAL, STR$, CHR$, ASC, STRING$, LEN, LEFT$, RIGHT$, MID$, and INSTR>.

In the problems studied so far, we used a DO loop to repeat QBasic statements. In many instances, however, we want to repeat statements a specified number of times. Although such loops can be written as DO loops, the FOR...NEXT statement is much more convenient.

In earlier chapters, you learned how to use some QBasic functions. In this chapter, we will discuss a great many more, including both numeric and string functions. You will learn how functions can be used to simulate systems that involve a random factor. You will also learn how to use string functions to solve interesting problems.

.7.1 THE FOR...NEXT LOOP

A loop that uses a counter to control the number of times it is executed is called a **counter-controlled loop.** The FOR and NEXT statements are used to create such loops. Like the DO and LOOP statements, the FOR and NEXT statements are always used together. They define a counter-controlled loop, with the FOR statement indicating the start of the loop and the NEXT statement indicating the end of the loop.

counter-controlled loop
A loop that uses a counter to control the number of times it is executed.

The following program uses the FOR and NEXT statements to print the numbers 1 through 10:

```
FOR Counter = 1 TO 10
    PRINT Counter
NEXT Counter
```

In this program, the FOR statement marks the top of a counter-controlled loop in which the variable Counter takes the values 1 through 10. The NEXT statement marks the end of the loop. All the statements between the FOR and the NEXT statements are executed with Counter equal to 1, 2, 3, and so on—up to 10. To keep this example simple, the only statement inside the loop is a PRINT statement, but you can have as many statements as you need. Notice that the PRINT statement is indented four spaces. QBasic doesn't require this indention, but the indents make it easier to see the beginning and end of the loop. You should follow the same convention.

The syntax of the FOR statement is

```
FOR counter-variable = initial-value TO final-value [STEP step-size]
```

In a FOR statement, counter-variable must be a numeric variable; initial-value and final-value may be constants, variables, or even expressions. The meaning of the optional STEP clause is discussed shortly.

The syntax of the NEXT statement is simply

```
NEXT counter-variable
```

where counter-variable must be the same as counter-variable in the FOR statement. As you will see later, a program may contain more than one FOR...NEXT loop. In such cases, QBasic pairs a NEXT statement with the FOR statement that has the same counter-variable.

The flowchart in Figure 7.1 shows how the FOR and NEXT statements work. (This flowchart assumes that step-size is positive. If step-size is negative, the relational operator in the decision box must be changed to <.) This flowchart shows that a FOR...NEXT loop is a pretest loop. It also shows that a counter-controlled loop contains three steps: **1)** the counter is initialized, **2)** the counter is tested, and

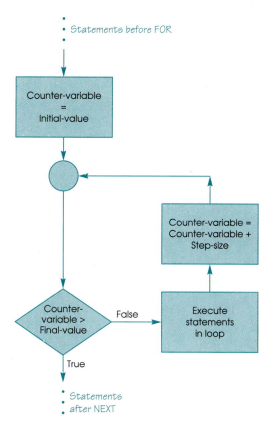

FIGURE 7.1   Flowchart for the FOR...NEXT statements with a positive step size.

3) the counter is incremented. We can use this flowchart to understand the sample program given previously.

The first time the FOR statement is executed, Counter is set to the initial value, which is 1. Then Counter is tested to see if it is greater than the final value, which is 10. Since the condition is false, the statement in the loop—PRINT Counter—is executed. This PRINT statement prints 1. When the NEXT statement is executed, Counter is incremented by the step size. You will learn more about the step size a little later; in this program, step size is 1, so Counter becomes 1 + 1 = 2. Then the FOR statement is executed again. It tests Counter once more to see if it is greater than 10. Since the condition is still false, the PRINT statement in the loop is executed again. This time, it prints 2. This procedure is repeated until the loop is executed with Counter equal to 10.

When Counter is 10 and the NEXT statement is executed, Counter is incremented to become 11. Now when Counter is tested, the condition is true. Instead of executing the loop again, the program exits from the loop by branching to the statement following the NEXT statement.

EXAMPLE 1 ▪▪▪▪▪▪▪▪▪▪▪▪▪▪▪▪▪▪

USING A FOR...NEXT LOOP TO CALCULATE POPULATION GROWTH

Now that you understand a bit about FOR and NEXT statements, let's use them to solve a problem.

Problem Statement

Write a program that accepts an initial population and growth rate, and that calculates the increase in population and the total population at the end of each of the next five years.

The clue that you should use a counter-controlled loop in this problem is that you will need to repeat the calculation for each of the next five years. Thus, you must set up a loop that is executed five times.

STEP 1   Variable Names

As always, you should begin by identifying the variables and assigning them names. Let's use the following.

Variable	Variable Name
Input Variables	
Population	`Population`
Growth rate	`Rate`
Output Variables	
Growth in population	`Growth`
Population	`Population`
Year counter	`Year`

STEP 2   Algorithm

The algorithm is

1. Input Population and Rate.
2. Repeat steps 3 through 5 for five Years.
3.   Calculate Growth.
4.   Add Growth to Population.
5.   Print Year, Growth, and Population.

The top-down chart for this problem is shown in Figure 7.2. The pseudocode is

Calculate Population Growth

Main Module
Call GetInput
Call PrintHeading
Call CalcGrowth
End Main Module

GetInput
    Input Population
    Input Rate
End GetInput

PrintHeading
    Print the heading
End PrintHeading

CalcGrowth
    For Year = 1 to 5
        Growth = Rate * Population
        Add Growth to Population
        Print Year, Growth, Population
    Next Year
End CalcGrowth
End

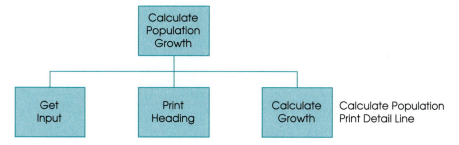

FIGURE 7.2   Top-down chart for population growth problem.

STEP 3   **Hand-Calculated Answers**

We now need to calculate answers by hand, but only for the first two years. If the computer-calculated answers for the first two years agree with our hand-calculated answers, we may assume the program is correct. Let's say that the town's current population is 40,000 and the growth rate is 10 percent. The results for the first two years are as follows.

Year	Growth	Population at End of Year
1	4,000	44,000
2	4,400	48,400

STEP 4   **QBasic Program**

Program 7.1 performs these same calculations. Notice that the first time line 28 is executed, a Population of 40000 is multiplied by a Rate of .10 and the result, 4000, is assigned to Growth. In line 29, this first year's Growth is added to the initial Population of 40000 to produce a new Population of 44000 at the end of the first year.

The second time line 28 is executed, the new Population of 44000 is multiplied by the Rate of .10 to give a Growth of 4400. Line 29 adds this Growth to the Population of 44000 to determine that Population equals 48400 at the end of the second year. As Program 7.1 shows, the loop repeats this procedure for years 3, 4, and 5. ■

```
 1 |  '    *** CALCULATE POPULATION GROWTH ***
 2 |  '   Calculate population growth for five years
 3 |
 4 |  DECLARE SUB GetInput (Population!, Rate!)
 5 |  DECLARE SUB CalcGrowth (Population!, Rate!, Format$)
 6 |  DECLARE SUB PrintHeading (Format$)
 7 |
 8 |  '    Variables used
 9 |
10 |  '    Format$          Format string for PRINT USING
11 |  '    Growth           Population growth in one year
12 |  '    Rate             Population growth rate
13 |  '    Population       Population
14 |  '    Year             Counter for years
15 |
```

PROGRAM 7.1   Using a FOR...NEXT loop to calculate population growth.
(continued on next page)

```
16 │ CLS
17 │ CALL GetInput(Population, Rate)
18 │ CALL PrintHeading(Format$)
19 │ CALL CalcGrowth(Population, Rate, Format$)
20 │ END
21 │
22 │ SUB CalcGrowth (Population, Rate, Format$)
23 │ '    Calculates growth and population in each year
24 │ '    Receives Population, Rate, and Format$
25 │ '    No variables are returned
26 │
27 │     FOR Year = 1 TO 5
28 │         Growth = Rate * Population
29 │         Population = Population + Growth
30 │         PRINT USING Format$; Year; Growth; Population
31 │     NEXT Year
32 │ END SUB
33 │
34 │ SUB GetInput (Population, Rate)
35 │ '    Gets input data
36 │ '    No variables are received
37 │ '    Returns Population and Rate
38 │
39 │     INPUT "Enter initial population: ", Population
40 │     INPUT "Enter growth rate: ", Rate
41 │ END SUB
42 │
43 │ SUB PrintHeading (Format$)
44 │ '    Prints the heading and defines format string
45 │ '    No variables are received
46 │ '    Returns Format$
47 │
48 │     PRINT "Year        Growth        Population"
49 │     Format$ = "  ##        #,###        ###,###"
50 │ END SUB
```

```
Enter initial population: 40000
Enter growth rate: .10

Year        Growth        Population
  1         4,000         44,000
  2         4,400         48,400
  3         4,840         53,240
  4         5,324         58,564
  5         5,856         64,420
```

PROGRAM 7.1 *(continued)*

7.1 EXERCISES

★**1.** Would the output of Program 7.1 be changed if lines 28 and 29 were interchanged? What if lines 39 and 40 were interchanged?

2. In every counter-controlled loop, the counter is initialized, tested, and incremented. Which of these operations is performed by the FOR...NEXT statement, and which must be separately coded by the programmer?

3. How many times will a FOR...NEXT loop that starts with the statement

```
FOR P = 1 TO 30
```

be executed?

7.2 VARIATIONS ON THE FOR...NEXT STATEMENT

We have used the simplest version of the FOR...NEXT statement. In this section, we will examine other ways to write the FOR statement.

Variable Starting and Ending Values

As we said earlier, both initial-value and final-value may be variables or expressions. Consider the following program:

```
INPUT "Enter initial value:~", Initial
INPUT "Enter final value: ", Final
FOR Counter = Initial TO Final
    PRINT Counter
NEXT Counter
```

This program prompts the user to enter values for Initial and Final, and then prints the numbers from Initial to Final.

The STEP Clause

In our examples so far, when the NEXT statement was executed, we calculated the next value of the counter variable by adding 1 to the old value. But you may not always want to go up in steps of 1. The STEP clause of the FOR statement lets you use any step size you like.

Like initial-value and final-value, step-size may be a number, a variable, or an expression. We did not have to use the STEP clause in our earlier problems because we were using a step size of 1. If you omit the STEP clause, QBasic uses a default step size of 1.

Suppose you want to print only the odd numbers from 1 through 10. The following program does that by adding a STEP clause to the FOR statement:

```
FOR Counter = 1 TO 10 STEP 2
    PRINT Counter
NEXT Counter
```

This program works like the earlier program that printed all the numbers from 1 to 10, except that when the NEXT statement is executed, Counter is incremented by adding 2 (the value of step-size). The loop is executed with Counter equal to 1, 3, 5, 7, and 9. After the loop is executed with Counter equal to 9, the NEXT statement adds 2 to Counter—making it 11. Since 11 is greater than the final value of 10, the program exits from the loop, and the statement that follows the NEXT statement is executed.

Noninteger and Negative Step Size

The step size doesn't have to be an integer; it doesn't even have to be positive. For example, the FOR statement

```
FOR X = 0 TO 1 STEP 0.25
```

causes X to have the values 0, 0.25, 0.50, 0.75, and 1. Nothing new is involved here; we still get the next X by adding the step size to the old X.

To show the use of a negative step size, consider the following program:

```
FOR Countdown = 10 TO 1 STEP -1
    PRINT Countdown
NEXT Countdown
```

This program prints the numbers 10, 9, 8, 7, 6, 5, 4, 3, 2, and 1. We still add the step size to the old Countdown to get the next Countdown, but when we add –1 to 10, we get 9—and when we add –1 to 9, we get 8, and so on—until we add –1 to 2 and get 1. When a negative step size is used, the program exits from the loop when the counter variable becomes *less* than the final value specified in the FOR statement. In this case, the program exits from the loop when the counter variable becomes 0. So for a negative step size to work properly, the final value must be less than or equal to the initial value.

FOR...NEXT Statement Rules

As you can see, using a FOR...NEXT loop is not difficult, but you should know a few rules. Inside a FOR...NEXT loop, you cannot change initial-value, final-value, or step-size. Even if you assign new values to these variables, the program uses the values that were in effect when the FOR statement was first executed. Also, inside a FOR...NEXT loop, you should not change the value of counter-variable. If you change the value of counter-variable, the loop will not be executed the correct number of times.

ILLUSTRATIONS

FOR...NEXT Statement	Effect

`FOR J = 11 TO 6 STEP -2`
`    PRINT J`
`NEXT J`
	The numbers 11, 9, and 7 are printed. The next J is obtained by adding the step size of –2 to the previous J.

`A = 13`
`B = 3`
`FOR J = A TO 2 * A STEP B`
`    PRINT J`
`NEXT J`
	The numbers 13, 16, 19, 22, and 25 are printed.

`FOR J = 1 TO 7 STEP 3`
`NEXT J`
`PRINT J`
	The number 10 is printed. The flowchart in Figure 7.1 (page 231) shows that when the program exits from the loop, the counter variable has the value that caused the exit. In this case, the loop is executed when J is 1, 4, and 7—and exited when J is 10.

`FOR J = 10 TO 5`
`    PRINT J`
`NEXT J`
	Nothing is printed. The flowchart in Figure 7.1 shows that if initial-value is greater than final-value, the loop is not executed at all.

Comparing FOR...NEXT Loops With DO Loops

Students are often confused about when they should use a FOR...NEXT loop and when they should use a DO loop. If you know the number of times you want to execute a loop, as we did in Program 7.1 (pages 233–234), use a FOR...NEXT loop. If you don't know how many times you want to execute a loop (such as when the loop is controlled by trailer data), use a DO loop. Similarly, when the loop is controlled by the value of a calculated variable, as it was in Program 4.5 (page 125) that calculated ozone loss, use a DO loop.

Syntax Summary

FOR...NEXT Statement

Form:
```
FOR counter-variable = initial-value TO
    final-value [STEP step-size]
    .
loop statements
    .
NEXT counter-variable
```

Example:
```
FOR J = 0 TO 10 STEP 2
    PRINT J
NEXT J
```

Explanation: When a FOR statement is executed, counter-variable is set equal to initial-value, and compared to final-value. If counter-value is less than or equal to final-value, the loop statements are executed. When the NEXT statement is executed, counter-variable is incremented by step-size. (If STEP is omitted, the increment is 1.) Control is transferred to the FOR statement, where counter-variable is again compared with final-value. If counter-variable is less than or equal to final-value, the loop statements are executed again. When counter-variable becomes greater than final-value, control is passed to the statement following the NEXT statement. If step-size is negative, the loop statements are executed until counter-variable becomes less than final-value.

7.2 EXERCISES

1.   Consider the following program:
```
FOR C = 11 TO 21 STEP 3
    PRINT C;
NEXT C
END
```

   ★a)   What output is produced?
   b)   What is the value of C when the END statement is executed?
   c)   What output is produced if the first line is changed to the following?
```
FOR C = 7 TO 8 STEP .2
```

    d) What output is produced if the first line is changed to the following?

```
FOR C = 30 TO 20 STEP -2
```

2. Consider the following program:

```
READ J, K, L
FOR I = J TO K STEP L
    PRINT I;
Missing statement
DATA 2, 10, 3
END
```

    ★**a)** What is the missing statement?
    b) What output is produced by this program?
    c) What output is produced if the second line is changed to the following?

```
FOR I = L TO K STEP J
```

3. What output is produced by the following program?

```
FOR K = 3 TO 8 STEP 2
NEXT K
PRINT K
END
```

4. What output is produced by the following program?

```
PRINT "1234567890"
FOR K = 1 TO 5
    PRINT SPACE$(6-K); "*"
NEXT K
END
```

★**5.** Will the following program print the numbers from 30 to 40? If it won't, show how to fix it.

```
FOR M = 30 TO 40
    PRINT M
    M = M + 1
NEXT M
END
```

7.3   NESTED FOR...NEXT LOOPS

Just as programs may contain more than one DO loop, they may also contain more than one FOR...NEXT loop. Figure 7.3(a) shows a simple example in which the A loop and the B loop are completely separate. When the program is executed, first the A loop is executed and then the B loop. FOR...NEXT loops used this way are called independent loops.

    Figure 7.3(b) also shows two FOR...NEXT loops—but in this case, the B loop is completely inside the A loop. You should recall from our discussion of DO loops in Chapter 4 that loops used this way are called nested loops. When loops are nested, the inner loop is completely executed on every pass through the outer loop. Although the figure shows two FOR...NEXT loops, you may nest as many as

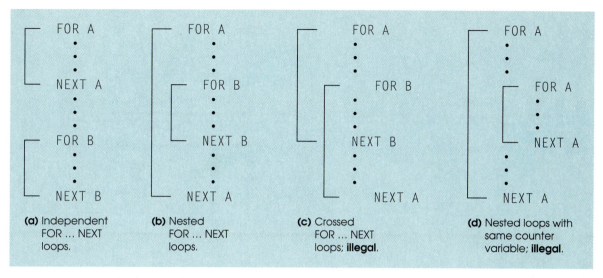

FIGURE 7.3   Arrangements of FOR...NEXT loops.

you like, as long as each inner loop is completely contained within the outer loop in which it starts.

Not all combinations of FOR...NEXT loops are legal in QBasic, however. The loops in Figure 7.3(c) are said to be *crossed* and are illegal. In addition, the counter variable in nested FOR...NEXT loops must be different in the two loops. Therefore, the nested loops shown in Figure 7.3(d) are also illegal.

To help you understand nested FOR...NEXT loops better, consider Program 7.2. When Program 7.2 is executed, the outer loop (the A loop) is executed 3 times. And in each execution, the inner loop (the B loop) is executed 2 times. Let's follow Figure 7.4 as we trace Program 7.2 to make these ideas clearer.

Line 3

```
FOR A = 1 TO 3
```

assigns 1 to A, and since A is not greater than 3, the outer loop is entered. Line 4

```
FOR B = 1 TO 2
```

```
1 |   '    *** NESTED FOR...NEXT LOOPS ***
2 | CLS
3 | FOR A = 1 TO 3
4 |     FOR B = 1 TO 2
5 |         C = A * B
6 |         PRINT USING "A = #   B = #   C = #"; A; B; C
7 |     NEXT B
8 | NEXT A
9 | END
```

```
A = 1   B = 1   C = 1
A = 1   B = 2   C = 2
A = 2   B = 1   C = 2
A = 2   B = 2   C = 4
A = 3   B = 1   C = 3
A = 3   B = 2   C = 6
```

PROGRAM 7.2   Illustration of nested FOR...NEXT loops.

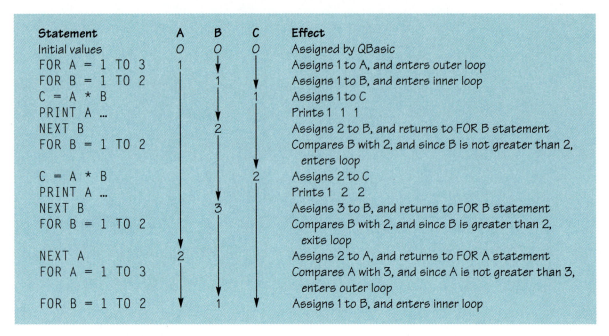

Statement	A	B	C	Effect
Initial values	0	0	0	Assigned by QBasic
FOR A = 1 TO 3	1			Assigns 1 to A, and enters outer loop
FOR B = 1 TO 2		1		Assigns 1 to B, and enters inner loop
C = A * B			1	Assigns 1 to C
PRINT A ...				Prints 1 1 1
NEXT B		2		Assigns 2 to B, and returns to FOR B statement
FOR B = 1 TO 2				Compares B with 2, and since B is not greater than 2, enters loop
C = A * B			2	Assigns 2 to C
PRINT A ...				Prints 1 2 2
NEXT B		3		Assigns 3 to B, and returns to FOR B statement
FOR B = 1 TO 2				Compares B with 2, and since B is greater than 2, exits loop
NEXT A	2			Assigns 2 to A, and returns to FOR A statement
FOR A = 1 TO 3				Compares A with 3, and since A is not greater than 3, enters outer loop
FOR B = 1 TO 2		1		Assigns 1 to B, and enters inner loop

FIGURE 7.4   Tracing Program 7.2.

assigns 1 to B, and since B is not greater than 2, the inner loop is entered. Line 5

```
C = A * B
```

multiplies 1 * 1, and assigns the answer, 1, to C. The PRINT statement in line 6

```
PRINT USING "A = #  B = #  C = #"; A; B; C
```

prints the first line of output, consisting of all 1s. Line 7

```
NEXT B
```

increments B, assigning it the value 2, and returns to the FOR B statement. Since the value of B is still not greater than 2, the inner loop is entered again. This time, line 5

```
C = A * B
```

assigns 1 * 2 = 2 to C. With these values of the variables, the PRINT statement prints the second line of output. Now when line 7

```
NEXT B
```

increments B, B is assigned the value 3. Control then returns to the FOR B statement. This time, B is greater than 2—so instead of executing the loop, the program branches to the NEXT A statement in line 8. This statement increments A, assigning it the value 2, and branches to the FOR A statement. The FOR A statement compares A with 3; since A is still not greater than 3, the outer loop is entered again. The FOR B statement in line 4 assigns B the value 1 and enters the inner loop. The program continues this way, eventually producing the output you see in Program 7.2.

EXAMPLE 2 ▌

PRINTING A BALANCE TABLE
To further illustrate nested FOR...NEXT loops, let's use them to solve a problem.

Problem Statement

Write a program that accepts an amount deposited in an account, and produces a table showing the balance in the account after 5, 10, 15, and 20 years, when the interest rates are 8, 10, and 12 percent.

STEP 1   **Variable Names**

We identify and name the following variables.

Variable	Variable Name
Input Variable	
Deposit	Deposit
Internal Variables	
Interest rate	Rate
Year counter	Year
Output Variable	
Balance	Balance

We can calculate the balance in the account using the compound interest formula:

```
Balance = Deposit * (1 + Rate) ^ Year
```

STEP 2   **Algorithm**

The algorithm for this problem is

1. Execute steps 2 through 4 for each Deposit of interest.
2. Repeat steps 3 and 4 for Year equal to 5, 10, 15, and 20.
3. Repeat step 4 for Rate equal to 8%, 10%, and 12%.
4. Calculate and print Balance.

The top-down chart for this problem is shown in Figure 7.5; the pseudocode is as follows.

Calculate a Balance Table

Main Module
Input Deposit
Do until trailer data is entered
    Call PrintHeadings
    Call PrintTable
    Input Deposit
End of loop
End Main Module

PrintHeadings
    Print headings
End PrintHeadings

PrintTable
    For Year = 5, 10, 15, and 20
        For Rate = 8%, 10%, and 12%
            Calculate Balance using the compound interest formula
            Print Balance
        Next Rate
    Next Year
End PrintTable
End

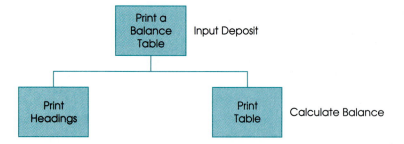

FIGURE 7.5   Top-down chart for printing a balance table.

STEP 3   Hand-Calculated Answer

Using a hand calculator and the compound interest formula, we find that $1000 deposited for 5 years at 10% interest grows to $1610.51.

STEP 4   QBasic Program

Just a few of the statements in Program 7.3, which is based on this algorithm, require discussion. The nested loops are shown in lines 41 through 48. In line 42, we print the value of Year so that each row in the table will be labeled with its year number. Line 42 and line 45, in which we print Balance, both use hanging semicolons. As noted in the discussion of Program 4.4 (page 122), if a print list ends with hanging punctuation, the next PRINT or PRINT USING statement executed continues printing on the same line. Using hanging semicolons in lines 42 and 45 causes Year and the three Balances that belong to that Year to be printed on one line, generating an attractive table. The empty PRINT statement in line 47 ensures that after Year and three Balances are printed on one line, the next Year and its three Balances will print on a new line. ■

```
 1  '    *** PRINTING A BALANCE TABLE ***
 2  '    Print a balance table for interest rates 8%, 10%, and 12%
 3  '    for 5, 10, 15, and 20 years
 4
 5  DECLARE SUB PrintHeadings ()
 6  DECLARE SUB PrintTable (Deposit!)
 7
 8  '    Variable used
 9
10  '    Deposit      Initial deposit
11
12  CLS
13  INPUT "Enter Deposit, 0 to stop: ", Deposit
14  DO UNTIL Deposit = 0
15      CALL PrintHeadings
16      CALL PrintTable(Deposit)
17      INPUT "Enter Deposit, 0 to stop: ", Deposit
18  LOOP
19  END
20
```

PROGRAM 7.3   Using nested FOR...NEXT loops to print a balance table. *(continued on next page)*

```
21 | SUB PrintHeadings
22 | '    Prints headings
23 | '    No variables received or returned
24 |
25 |     PRINT "              BALANCE  TABLE"
26 |     PRINT "               Interest Rate"
27 |     PRINT "Year      8%          10%          12%"
28 | END SUB
29 |
30 | SUB PrintTable (Deposit)
31 | '    Prints balance table
32 | '    Receives Deposit
33 | '    No variables are returned
34 |
35 | '    Local variables
36 |
37 | '    Balance      Balance in account at end of period
38 | '    Rate         Interest rate (decimal)
39 | '    Year         Counter for years
40 |
41 |     FOR Year = 5 TO 20 STEP 5           'Let Year be 5, 10, 15, and 20
42 |         PRINT USING " ##    "; Year;
43 |         FOR Rate = .08 TO .12 STEP .02
44 |             Balance = Deposit * (1 + Rate) ^ Year
45 |             PRINT USING "##,###.##   "; Balance;
46 |         NEXT Rate
47 |         PRINT
48 |     NEXT Year
49 | END SUB
```

```
Enter Deposit, 0 to stop: 1000

                BALANCE   TABLE
                Interest Rate
     Year      8%          10%          12%
       5    1,469.33    1,610.51    1,762.34
      10    2,158.93    2,593.74    3,105.85
      15    3,172.17    4,177.25    5,473.57
      20    4,660.96    6,727.50    9,646.29

Enter Deposit, 0 to stop: 0
```

PROGRAM 7.3 *(continued)*

7.3 EXERCISES

★**1.** Write the statements that are missing in the following program and then
   determine the output that it will produce.

```
FOR J = 3 TO 5
    FOR K = 1 to 3
        P = J + K
        PRINT P;
    Missing statement
Missing statement
END
```

2. What output is produced by the following program?

```
FOR A = 1 TO 2
    FOR B = 3 TO 1 STEP -1
        C = A * B
        PRINT C;
    NEXT B
NEXT A
END
```

3. What output is produced by the following program?

```
FOR A = 6 TO 10 STEP 2
    FOR B = A TO 3 * A STEP A
        C = A + B
        PRINT C;
    NEXT B
    PRINT
NEXT A
```

7.4   NUMERIC FUNCTIONS

QBasic provides many numeric functions in addition to those we examined earlier. Table 7.1 lists the functions we will examine in this chapter, and gives examples of how they are used. In this table, x represents a numeric expression.

The SQR function returns the square root of its argument, as long as the argument is positive or zero. For example, SQR(9) is 3. We could also calculate the square root by raising to the .5 power, as in 9 ^ .5, but the SQR function is about twice as fast.

The arguments of the trigonometric functions COS, SIN, and TAN must be in radians. To convert from degrees to radians, multiply the number of degrees by 0.01745329 (that is, $2\pi/360$). For example, if you want A to equal the sine of 30 degrees, you must code

```
A = SIN(30 * 0.01745329)
```

This statement assigns the sine of 30 degrees, which is 0.5, to A.

The ATN function returns the arctangent, in radians, of its argument. To convert from radians to degrees, multiply by 57.29578 (that is, $360/2\pi$). So if you want B to be the arctangent of 1, expressed in degrees, you must code

```
B = 57.29578 * ATN(1)
```

This statement assigns the arctangent of 1, which is 45, to B.

If you are not a math major, you may think you have no use for trigonometric functions. But as you will see in Chapter 12, such functions are important when creating graphics on your computer.

The SGN function is called the sign function. As Table 7.1 shows, if its argument is negative, the SGN function returns –1; if its argument is 0, it returns 0; and if its argument is positive, it returns +1. For example, SGN(34.9) is 1. You will see a use for this function shortly.

The ABS function returns the absolute value of its argument. The absolute value is always positive or zero. For example, both ABS(5.5) and ABS(–5.5) equal

TABLE 7.1
Numeric functions discussed in this chapter

Function	Purpose	Example	Value
ABS(x)	Returns the absolute value of x	ABS(5.5) ABS(-5.5)	5.5 5.5
ATN(x)	Returns the arctangent (in radians) of x	ATN(1)	.7854
CINT(x)	Returns x rounded to the nearest integer	CINT(9.7) CINT(-9.3)	10 –9
COS(x)	Returns the cosine of angle x, where x is in radians	COS(1)	.5403
EXP(x)	Returns e (2.71828) raised to the x power	EXP(2)	7.389
FIX(x)	Returns x truncated to an integer	FIX(8.95)	8
INT(x)	Returns the largest integer less than or equal to x	INT(9.7) INT(-9.7)	9 –10
LOG(x)	Returns the natural logarithm of x	LOG(7.389)	2
RND	Returns a random number between 0 and 1	RND	.54728*
SGN(x)	Returns –1 if x is negative, 0 if x is zero, and +1 if x is positive	SGN(-4.3) SGN(0) SGN(3.7)	–1 0 1
SIN(x)	Returns the sine of angle x, where x is in radians	SIN(.5)	.4794
SQR(x)	Returns the square root of x	SQR(9)	3
TAN(x)	Returns the tangent of angle x, where x is in radians	TAN(1)	1.557
TIMER	Returns the time, in seconds, according to the computer's internal clock	TIMER	32940.16*

*Value varies.

5.5. The ABS function is useful when you want to calculate the difference between two numbers, but you do not know which one is greater. That is, if you want to know the difference between M and N, the expression ABS(M - N) gives you the correct answer whether M is greater than, less than, or equal to N.

Three functions—FIX, INT, and CINT—are closely related. The FIX function discards digits to the right of its argument's decimal point. The INT function returns the largest integer that is less than or equal to its argument. The CINT function rounds its argument to the nearest integer. If the argument of the CINT function is outside the range –32,768 to 32,767, QBasic stops and displays the error message Overflow.

TABLE 7.2
Comparing the FIX, INT, and CINT functions

N	FIX(N)	INT(N)	CINT(N)
−9.3	−9	−10	−9
−9.5	−9	−10	−10
−9.7	−9	−10	−10
9.3	9	9	9
9.5	9	9	10
9.7	9	9	10

Table 7.2 compares the FIX, INT, and CINT functions for both negative and positive arguments.

You may think that you would never use some of these unusual functions, but they can be helpful in the most ordinary situations. Suppose you want a user to enter an integer in response to an INPUT statement. The condition in the following DO statement determines whether INT(M) is equal to M. If it is, then M is an integer; if it is not equal, M is not an integer, and the user is requested to enter a new value.

```
INPUT "Enter an integer: ", M
DO UNTIL INT(M) = M
     BEEP
     INPUT "Please enter an integer: ", M
LOOP
```

As another example, Programming Assignment 5.24 (page 177) asked you to calculate postage depending on the weight of the package. If you solved that problem, you probably multiplied the weight by the cost per ounce. But in fact, the U.S. Postal Service rounds the weight up to the next ounce. If your package weighs .3 ounces, you pay for 1 ounce; if it weighs 4.2 ounces, you pay for 5 ounces. If Weight is the weight of the package, the weight that should be used to calculate the postage is given by

```
EffectiveWeight = INT(Weight) + SGN(Weight - INT(Weight))
```

For example, if Weight is 4.2, INT(Weight) equals INT(4.2), which is 4; SGN(Weight − INT(Weight)), equals SGN(4.2 − 4), which equals SGN(.2), which is 1. So the EffectiveWeight is 4 + 1, or 5, which is the correct answer.

You can use the CINT function to round values. The following function uses CINT to round its argument N to P decimal positions.

```
FUNCTION RoundValue(N, P)
'      Receives N, the variable to be rounded,
'      and P, the number of decimal positions retained.
'      Returns N rounded to P decimal positions
       RoundValue = CINT(N * 10 ^ P) / 10 ^ P
END FUNCTION
```

If P is 1, RoundValue rounds to one decimal place; if P is 2, it rounds to two decimal places (for dollars and cents), and so on. If P is 0, it rounds to the nearest integer (0 decimal places).

The PRINT USING statement rounds printed values, but if the underlying values are not rounded, the printed values can look wrong. For example, suppose

A equals 23.186, B equals 45.327, and C equals A + B. If these three variables are printed using the numeric field ##.##, the output is

```
A    23.19
B    45.33
C    68.51
```

The arithmetic in the right column is wrong (9 + 3 = 12). If A and B were rounded *before* their addition, C would be correctly calculated and printed as 68.52.

Random Numbers

The RND function returns a **random number**; that is, a number that cannot be predicted. The RND function is used as follows:

```
A = RND
```

random number
A number that cannot be predicted.

Notice that the RND function does not need an argument. The RND function returns a random number between 0 and 0.9999999. (Because 0.9999999 is so close to 1, for convenience, we will often assume that the upper limit is 1.) All the numbers between 0 and 0.9999999 are equally likely to be returned. For example, if you executed the preceding LET statement three times, A might be assigned the values 0.469215, 0.917527, and 0.361473. Another time, A might be assigned three completely different values.

The RND function returns values between 0 and 0.9999999, but sometimes you will want a random integer chosen from a different interval. For example, suppose you want Number to be a random integer between 1 and 100. To get integers in the range from 1 to 100, you must first multiply the RND function by 100:

```
Number = 100 * RND
```

Since RND returns a value between 0 and 0.9999999, Number has a value between 0 and 99.99999. Next, use the INT function

```
Number = INT(100 * RND)
```

Now, Number has integer values between 0 and 99. Finally, to get Number to the range 1 to 100, add 1, producing the statement

```
Number = 1 + INT(100 * RND)
```

With this statement, Number has integer values between 1 and 100, and each integer is equally likely to be returned.

We can generalize this result. To get a variable, M, to have random integer values in the range LowerLimit to UpperLimit, use the statement

```
M = LowerLimit + INT((UpperLimit - LowerLimit + 1) * RND)
```

Although our definition of the RND function stated that it returns unpredictable random numbers, the numbers are not totally unpredictable. In any one run, the first time the RND function is executed, it starts with a number—called the random number seed—and performs some involved mathematical operations on the seed to generate the first random number. The RND function produces the second random number by operating on the first random number. Then it generates each succeeding random number by operating on the previous random number.

When the RND function is used without an argument, it always starts with the same seed; therefore, it generates the same series of "random" numbers every time it is used. It may seem pointless to generate the same series of "random" numbers; if they are always the same, they are predictable and not random. However, when you are debugging a program, you may find it easier to trace the program if the RND function returns the same series of "random" numbers each time.

After you debug a program, you can use the RANDOMIZE statement to make RND generate unpredictable random numbers. The RANDOMIZE statement causes the RND function to use a new seed. The customary way to use the RANDOMIZE statement is

```
RANDOMIZE TIMER
```

The TIMER function returns the time, according to the computer's internal clock, to the nearest hundredth of a second. TIMER thus returns one of hundreds of thousands of rapidly changing values. As a result, every time the program is executed, RND uses a different seed and generates a different, unpredictable sequence of random numbers.

The TIMER function can also be used on its own. For example, it can be used to determine how long a program takes to execute, as you will see in Programming Assignment 7.15.

You can also use the TIMER function to introduce a measured delay into a program. For example, the statements

```
Now = TIMER
DO WHILE TIMER < Now + 5
LOOP
```

cause a five-second delay.

EXAMPLE 3

USING RANDOM NUMBERS IN A GAME PROGRAM

Now that you know how to generate random numbers, let's write an easy game program that uses numeric functions.

Problem Statement

Write a program that randomly generates an integer between 1 and 100, and then asks a player to guess the integer. Each time the player enters a guess, the program should indicate whether the guess was correct, too high, or too low. If the player doesn't guess the integer in ten tries, the program should print the integer.

STEP 1   Variable Names

We identify and name the following variables.

Variable	Variable Name
Input Variable	
Number guessed	Guess
Internal Variables	
Number to be guessed	Number
Counter for guesses	Trial

STEP 2   Algorithm

The algorithm we can use is
1. Repeat steps 2 through 6 for each game.
2. Assign to Number a random integer between 1 and 100.
3. Repeat steps 4 and 5 10 times or until Guess equals Number.
4. Accept Guess.
5. If Guess equals Number, go to step 6. If Guess does not equal Number, print the appropriate message, either Too high or Too low.

6. If the user guessed Number, print a "Congratulations" message; otherwise print a "Sorry" message and Number.

STEP 3   Hand-Calculated Answers

This problem has no hand-calculated answers, but we will see later how to ensure that the program is correct.

STEP 4   QBasic Program

Program 7.4 plays "Guess the Number." The RANDOMIZE statement in line 15 supplies the RND function with a random seed. In the DO loop, line 18 assigns a random integer between 1 and 100 to Number, and line 19 calls the PlayGame subprogram. Trial is initialized to 0 in line 47. Then the program enters a DO loop, where it stays until a game ends. Line 49 increments Trial and line 50 accepts the user's guess. The SELECT CASE statement in lines 51 through 56 prints

```
Too high
```

if Guess is greater than Number, and

```
Too low
```

if Guess is less than Number.

The game is over if the user either guesses Number, or guesses ten times without guessing Number. If either of these events occurs, the condition on the LOOP statement in line 59

```
LOOP WHILE Guess <> Number AND Trial < 10
```

causes the program to exit from the loop and return to the main module.

Back in the main module, we have to determine if we returned because the user guessed Number, or if all 10 guesses were wrong. We determine that by comparing Guess with Number in line 24. If they are equal, the user guessed Number, and we print the "Congratulations" message. If they are not equal, the user made ten wrong guesses, and we print the "Sorry" message and Number.

To check this program, we could set a breakpoint at line 19. When the program stops, we could use the Immediate window to print Number. Knowing Number, we could verify that the program printed the correct responses to the user's guesses. ■

```
 1  |  '    *** GUESS THE NUMBER GAME ***
 2  |  '    Program selects a random number between 1 and 100,
 3  |  '    which the user has to guess in 10 tries
 4  |
 5  |  DECLARE SUB DisplayInst ()
 6  |  DECLARE SUB PlayGame (Number!, Guess!, Trial!)
 7  |
 8  |  '    Variables used
 9  |
10  |  '    Guess              Number guessed
11  |  '    Number             Number to be guessed
12  |  '    Response$          User's response to "play again?"
13  |  '    Trial              Counter for guesses
14  |
```

PROGRAM 7.4   Using random numbers in a game program. *(continued on next page)*

```
15    RANDOMIZE TIMER              'Seed random number generator
16    DO
17        CALL DisplayInst
18        Number = 1 + INT(100 * RND)          'Number is between 1 and 100
19        CALL PlayGame(Number, Guess, Trial)
20
21    '   Determine if program returned from PlayGame because
22    '   user guessed Number, or because 10 trials were used
23
24        IF Guess = Number THEN
25            PRINT "Congratulations, you took only "; Trial; "guesses"
26        ELSE
27            PRINT "Sorry, you used 10 guesses.  The number was"; Number
28        END IF
29
30        PRINT "Do you want to play again? (Y or N)"
31        Response$ = UCASE$(INPUT$(1))
32    LOOP UNTIL Response$ = "N"
33    END
34
35    SUB DisplayInst
36    '   Display instructions for user
37
38        CLS
39        PRINT "Guess the number between 1 and 100 the computer picked."
40        PRINT "You get 10 guesses - Good Luck!"
41    END SUB
42
43    SUB PlayGame (Number, Guess, Trial)
43    '   Play the game. Return when user guesses Number, or after 10 trials
44    '   Receives Number
45    '   Returns Guess and Trial
46
47        Trial = 0
48        DO
49            Trial = Trial + 1
50            INPUT "Guess : ", Guess
51            SELECT CASE Guess
52                CASE IS > Number
53                    PRINT "Too high"
54                CASE IS < Number
55                    PRINT "Too low"
56            END SELECT
57    '   Stay in loop while user has not guessed Number, and
58    '   has not used all 10 Trials
59        LOOP WHILE Guess <> Number AND Trial < 10
60    END SUB
```

```
Guess the number between 1 and 100 the computer picked.
You get 10 guesses - Good Luck!
Guess : 50
Too high
Guess : 25
Too high
Guess : 13
Too high
Guess : 6
Congratulations, you took only  4 guesses
Do you want to play again? (Y or N)
```

PROGRAM 7.4 *(continued)*

EXAMPLE 4

A SIMULATION PROGRAM

Numerical functions are also the basis for many simulation programs. **Simulation** programs attempt to recreate the behavior of a system on a computer. All kinds of systems may be simulated—for example, the national economy, telephone networks, and warehouse inventories.

Simulations allow users to experiment by varying particular factors and then studying the reaction of the system to those variations. Often, it is possible to perform such experiments on a computer when it would be impossible, dangerous, or too expensive to perform the same experiment on the system itself. Simulations allow users to ask "What if" questions. For example, a computer simulation of the national economy can enable economists to ask, "What if taxes were cut 10 percent?" The telephone company can get the answer to "What if telephone traffic increased 20 percent?" You can ask, "What if I use my favorite system playing the state lottery?" As the lottery example shows, simulations sometimes include random factors; such simulations are called **Monte Carlo simulations**.

simulation
Recreating the behavior of a system on a computer.

Monte Carlo simulation
A simulation that involves random elements.

Problem Statement

As an example of a Monte Carlo simulation, write a program that simulates tossing a coin 30 times.

STEP 1   Variable Names

We can use the following variable names.

Variable	Variable Name
Internal Variables	
A random number between 0 and 1	X
A counter for the number of tosses	Toss
Output Variables	
The number of heads that came up	Heads
The number of tails that came up	Tails

STEP 2   Algorithm

The algorithm we can use is

1. Initialize Heads and Tails to 0.
2. Repeat the following step 30 times.
3.   If a head comes up, print an H and increment Heads; otherwise, print a T and increment Tails.
4. Print Heads and Tails.

How do we decide whether the coin has come up heads or tails? A fair coin should come up heads about half the time and tails about half the time. Since half the numbers generated by the RND function are below .5 and half are .5 and above, we can consider any random number greater than or equal to .5 to mean that the coin came up heads, and any below .5 to mean that the coin came up tails.

STEP 3   Hand-Calculated Answers

As in the previous example, this problem has no hand-calculated answers. However, as you will see later, we still must check the program.

STEP 4 **QBasic Program**

The IF statement in lines 19 through 25 of Program 7.5 shows how a random number greater than .5 is counted as a head, and one less than or equal to .5 is counted as a tail. Program 7.5 also shows two executions of the program. These two executions illustrate an important fact about random simulations: Although on the average, we expect to get 15 heads and 15 tails, in any particular run, we may get substantial deviations from the expected results. In Program 7.5, the first execution gave 18 heads and only 12 tails; in the second execution, we got 13 heads and 17 tails.

Since this problem has no one "correct" answer, how can we know that the program is correct? We could set a breakpoint at line 26 and when the program halts, use the Immediate window to print X, Heads, and Tails. We could then verify that when X was greater than or equal to .5, an H was printed and Heads was incremented; when X was less than .5, a T was printed and Tails was incremented.

In Program 7.5, only 30 cases are simulated. In other problems where many more cases are simulated, if you print all the values calculated for all the cases, you will be overwhelmed by output. In those situations, it is a good idea to use a small number of cases while you are still debugging the program.

```
 1  '    *** SIMULATING A COIN TOSS ***
 2  '    Use random numbers to simulate tossing a coin
 3
 4  '    Variables used
 5
 6  '    Heads               The number of heads that came up
 7  '    Tails               The number of tails that came up
 8  '    Toss                A counter for the number of tosses
 9  '    X                   A random number between 0 and 1.0
10
11  CLS
12  RANDOMIZE TIMER
13  Heads = 0                'Initialize counters for Heads
14  Tails = 0                'and Tails
15
16  '    Simulate 30 tosses
17  FOR Toss = 1 TO 30
18      X = RND
19      IF X >= .5 THEN      'X greater than .5 means a head
20          PRINT "H ";
21          Heads = Heads + 1
22      ELSE
23          PRINT "T ";
24          Tails = Tails + 1
25      END IF
26  NEXT Toss
27  PRINT
28  PRINT USING "We have ## heads and ## tails"; Heads; Tails
29  END
```

```
T H H H H H H H T T T T H T T T H T H T H H H H H H H T T H H T
We have 18 heads and 12 tails

T T H H T H T H T T H T T H H T T T H H T H T T T T H H T H
We have 13 heads and 17 tails
```

PROGRAM 7.5   Using random numbers to simulate tossing a coin.

Alternatively, you can print periodically. Recall that Trial MOD 10 will equal 0 when Trial is 10, 20, 30, and so on. Therefore, the following statement

```
IF Trial MOD 10 = 0 THEN
    PRINT (any data you like)
END IF
```

prints every tenth trial.   ∎

Syntax Summary

> **RANDOMIZE Statement**
>
> Form: RANDOMIZE TIMER
> Example: RANDOMIZE TIMER
> Explanation: Supplies a random seed to RND, causing RND to generate a
>   series of unpredictable random numbers.

7.4 EXERCISES

1. What value is assigned to A in each of the following statements?
   a) `A = SGN(-4)`
   b) `A = ABS(-37.3)`
   ★c) `A = INT(17.9)`
   d) `A = INT(-17.9)`
   ★e) `A = FIX(17.9)`
   f) `A = FIX(-17.9)`
   g) `A = CINT(17.9)`
   h) `A = CINT(-17.9)`
   ★i) `A = SQR(36)`
   j) `A = SQR(225)`

2. Under what conditions will the following statements print the word EQUAL?
   ★a)
   ```
   IF ABS(X - Y) = ABS(Y - X) THEN
        PRINT "EQUAL"
   END IF
   ```

   b)
   ```
   IF X - Y = ABS(X - Y) THEN
        PRINT "EQUAL"
   END IF
   ```

3. Write the statements to calculate the following trigonometric functions.
   a) The cosine of 30 degrees.
   b) The tangent of 45 degrees.
   c) The arctangent, in degrees, of 0.5.

4. a) Write a statement to generate random integers between 5 and 30.
   ★b) Write a statement to generate random integers between 1 and 7.

5. What are the possible values of INT(RND)?

6. Modify Program 7.4 (page 249–50) so that it prints

   ```
   You only have 5 guesses left
   ```

   after the user enters the fifth wrong guess.

★7.   Modify Program 7.4 so that, in addition to printing

Too high

and

Too low

the program also prints

You are getting close

whenever the difference between the guess and the number is less than or equal to 5. (*Hint:* You will find the ABS function helpful.)

8.   What output would Program 7.5 generate if the relational operator in line 19 were < instead of >?

7.5   STRING FUNCTIONS

So far in this chapter, we have considered only numeric functions—but QBasic also provides a number of string-related functions. Table 7.3 lists the string functions we will explore in this chapter. In this table, x$ is a string or a **string expression**, which is a combination of string variables, constants, functions and operators that evaluates to a string. You will learn about the one string operator, concatenation, shortly. Just as the result of evaluating a numeric expression is a number, so the result of evaluating a string expression is a string. In the table, n and m are numeric expressions.

string expression
A combination of string variables, constants, and functions—and the concatenation operator—that evaluates to a string.

TABLE 7.3
String functions discussed in this chapter

Function	Purpose	Example	Value
ASC(x$)	Returns the ASCII code of the first character of x$	ASC("Star")	83, the ASCII code of S
CHR$(n)	Returns the character whose ASCII code is n	CHR$(83) ASCII	S, whose ASCII code is 83
DATE$	Returns the date, in the form mm-dd-yyyy	DATE$	03-21-1999*
INSTR(n, x$, y$)	Returns the position of y$ in x$—n specifies the position in x$ where the search is to begin	INSTR(1, "Star", "t") INSTR(1, "Star", "z") INSTR(3, "Star", "t")	2 0 0
LCASE$(x$)	Returns a copy of x$ with all the letters in lower case	LCASE$("MiXeD sTrInG")	mixed string

*Value varies

TABLE 7.3 *(continued)*

Function	Purpose	Example	Value
LEFT$(x$, n)	Returns the n leftmost characters of x$	LEFT$("Star", 3)	Sta
LELEN(x$)	Returns the length of x$	LEN("Star")	4
LTRIM$(x$)	Returns a copy of x$ with leading spaces removed	LTRIM$(" Star ")	"Star "
MID$(x$, n, m)	Returns m characters of x$ starting with the nth character	MID$("Violet", 2, 3)	iol
RIGHT$(x$, n)	Returns the n rightmost characters of x$	RIGHT$("Star", 3)	tar
RTRIM$(x$)	Returns a copy of x$ with trailing spaces removed	RTRIM$(" Star ")	" Star"
STR$(n)	Converts n to a string	STR$(14.7) STR$(-14.7)	" 14.7" "–14.7"
STRING$(n, m)	Returns a string of n characters, all consisting of the character whose ASCII code is m	STRING$(2, 36)	$$, because the character whose ASCII code is 36 is $
STRING$(n, x$)	Returns a string of n characters, all consisting of the first character of x$	STRING$(4, "Star")	SSSS
TIME$	Returns the time of day, in the form hh:mm:ss	TIME$	22:53:07*
UCASE$(x$)	Returns a copy of x$ with all the letters in upper case	UCASE$("MiXeD sTrInG")	MIXED STRING
VAL(x$)	Returns the numeric value of x$	VAL("4th of July") VAL("July 4th")	4 0

*Value varies

As you can see in the table, the functions whose names end with a $ return a string, while the others return a number. The most useful functions are discussed next.

The DATE$ function returns the date obtained from the system. For example, on March 21, 1999, the statement

```
PRINT DATE$
```

would print 03-21-1999.

Similarly, the TIME$ function returns the time obtained from the computer's internal clock. For example, at 10:53:07 P.M., the statement

```
PRINT TIME$
```

would print 22:53:07 (the computer uses a 24-hour clock). Thus, you might use the DATE$ and TIME$ functions to print the date and time on a report or letter.

The RTRIM$ function trims spaces from the right end (trailing spaces) of its string argument. If A$ = "It's a hot day   ", the statement

```
B$ = RTRIM$(A$)
```

assigns the string "It's a hot day" to B$.

The LTRIM$ function trims spaces from the left end (leading spaces) of its string argument. If A$ = "   It's a cold day", the statement

```
B$ = LTRIM$(A$)
```

assigns the string "It's a cold day" to B$.

You can use RTRIM$ and LTRIM$ together to trim spaces from both ends of a string in one statement. If A$ = "   It's a nice day   ", the statement

```
B$ = LTRIM$(RTRIM$(A$))
```

assigns the string "It's a nice day" to B$.

You have used the UCASE$ function since Chapter 4, and you know it converts its string argument to upper case. The LCASE$ function converts its string argument to lower case. So, if A$ = "New York, NY", the statement

```
B$ = LCASE$(A$)
```

assigns the string "new york, ny" to B$.

As you have learned, it is convenient for users if the INPUT$ function is used to obtain input, since then they do not have to press the Enter key. However, the INPUT$ function returns a string and sometimes we want to use INPUT$ to obtain numeric input. Fortunately, QBasic provides the VAL function to convert a string to a number.

The argument of VAL must be a string, but the value of the string should be a number. The argument may also contain leading spaces (spaces before the first character), a + or − sign, and a decimal point—all of which are considered numeric characters. So, for example, if A$ = "5280" the statement

```
X = VAL(A$)
```

assigns the value 5280 to X, because VAL converts the string "5280" to the number 5280. If the string contains a minus sign, as in

```
A$ = "-273.16"
```

then X will have the negative value −273.16. If A$ contains nonnumeric characters, as in

```
A$ = "4th of July"
```

X will have the value 4, because VAL stops converting when it reaches the first nonnumeric character. Finally, if

```
A$ = "July 4"
```

X will have the value 0, because VAL returns a 0 if the first character of its argument is nonnumeric.

The STR$ function is the counterpart of the VAL function and is used to convert a number to a string. If the argument of the STR$ function is positive, the string it returns contains a leading space. If the argument is negative, the string contains a leading minus sign. If the argument is not numeric, you'll get a Type mismatch error message.

The CHR$ function is used with a numeric argument, n, and returns the character whose ASCII code is n. The ASCII codes are listed in Appendix B and in the QBasic help system under Contents. You can use the CHR$ function to use characters that cannot be typed directly from the keyboard. For example, the following PRINT statement displays happy faces whose ASCII codes are 1 and 2 on the screen:

```
PRINT CHR$(1), CHR$(2)
```

(Unfortunately, while you can display these symbols on the screen, many printers will not print them.)

The CHR$ function can also be used to print a string that contains quotation marks. The ASCII code for the quotation mark is 34. Thus, to print the string

```
Mary said, "Use the CHR$ function".
```

you could code

```
CONST Quote$ = CHR$(34)
PRINT "Mary said, "; Quote$; "Use the CHR$ function"; Quote$; "."
```

Finally, the CHR$ function can be used to send special characters to the printer. The ASCII code for a form feed is 12, so the statement

```
LPRINT CHR$(12)
```

causes the printer to advance the paper to a new page. On IBM and some other printers, CHR$(15) causes the printer to produce compressed (small) letters, while CHR$(14) results in expanded letters. Unfortunately, these special characters are not standardized and are not recognized by all printers.

The ASC function is the opposite of the CHR$ function. It is used with a string argument and returns the ASCII code of the *first* character of the string. For example, the statement

```
Number = ASC("QBASIC")
```

assigns 81 to Number, because the ASCII code of Q is 81.

The STRING$ function has two forms that produce the same results. The statement

```
Asterisks$ = STRING$(30, "*")
```

assigns 30 asterisks to the variable Asterisks$. You can achieve the same result with the statement

```
Asterisks$ = STRING$(30, 42)
```

because the ASCII code for an asterisk is 42. Notice that the STRING$ function requires two arguments, which must be separated by commas. The first argument specifies the number of characters you want to generate. The second character is either the character you want to generate or the ASCII code of the character. The second argument may be longer than one character, but STRING$ uses only the first character.

The LEN function returns the length; that is, the number of characters in its argument. So if

```
A$ = "Hello, I Must Be Going"
```

LEN(A$) is equal to 22, because the comma and the spaces count as characters, but the quotation marks do not.

We will use the LEN function many times later in this chapter. For now, let's consider a simple application of it. If you are printing a report and want to center the title on a line 65 characters long, you could code the following statement:

```
LPRINT SPC((65 - LEN(Title$)) \ 2); Title$
```

In this case, the argument of the SPC function is the number of spaces that should be printed before the title, calculated as half the difference between 65 and the length of Title$.

The Substring Functions

Three functions—LEFT$, RIGHT$, and MID$—are used to extract parts of a string. When you extract part of a string, you create what is known as a **substring**. Let's consider the LEFT$ function first.

substring
Part of a string.

The LEFT$ Function

Using the LEFT$ function, the statement

```
B$ = LEFT$("Orange", 3)
```

assigns 3 characters of "Orange" starting from the left (that's how the function gets its name); that is, Ora is assigned to B$. The LEFT$ function requires two arguments. The first argument is the string or string expression from which a substring is to be extracted, and the second argument is the number of characters of the first argument that are to be extracted.

The RIGHT$ Function

The RIGHT$ function is similar to the LEFT$ function, except that it extracts characters starting from the right. So the statement

```
B$ = RIGHT$("Orange", 3)
```

assigns the string nge to B$.

The MID$ Function

Finally, the MID$ function extracts substrings from the middle of a string. For example,

```
B$ = MID$("Orange", 2, 3)
```

starts extracting at the second character of "Orange" and extracts 3 characters. Therefore, B$ equals ran. Note that if you omit the last argument—for example,

```
B$ = MID$("Orange", 2)
```

all the characters starting with the second will be assigned to B$—in this case, range.

The MID$ function is the most powerful string-extraction function because it can be used to perform the same functions as LEFT$ and RIGHT$. If MID$ is used with a starting position of 1, it functions exactly like the LEFT$ function. The statement

```
B$ = LEFT$(A$, N)
```

is equivalent to

```
B$ = MID$(A$, 1, N)
```

Similarly, the statement

```
B$ = RIGHT$(A$, N)
```

is equivalent to

```
L = LEN(A$)
B$ = MID$(A$, L - N + 1)
```

In fact, we can write these last two statements together as one more complicated statement:

```
B$ = MID$(A$, LEN(A$) - N + 1)
```

The MID$ Statement

Besides being used as a function, MID$ can also be used as a statement; that is, it can be used on the left side of an equals sign in a LET statement. The first argument of the MID$ statement is the string in which characters are to be replaced. The second argument specifies the position at which replacement is to start, and the third argument specifies the number of characters to be replaced.

The following statements use the MID$ statement to replace the hyphens the DATE$ function returns with slashes. The second line replaces the hyphen in position 3 with a slash, and the third line replaces the hyphen in position 6 with a slash.

```
Today$ = DATE$
MID$(Today$, 3, 1) = "/"
MID$(Today$, 6, 1) = "/"
PRINT Today$
```

If these statements are executed on March 21, 1999, they would print 03/21/99.

The INSTR Function

The INSTR function searches for the appearance of one string in another. For example, if A$ = "STRING PROCESSING", the statement

```
J = INSTR(1, A$, "R")
```

causes A$ to be searched, starting from position 1, for the string R. Since R appears in position 3 of A$, J is set equal to 3. Notice that the second R is ignored. INSTR stops searching as soon as it finds an R. This statement could also have been coded as

```
J = INSTR(A$, "R")
```

because if the first argument is not coded, INSTR automatically starts searching from position 1.

Next, consider the statement

```
J = INSTR(6, A$, "R")
```

This statement sets J to 9 because INSTR starts its search from position 6. Notice that J is the position of the R measured from the *start* of A$, not from the starting position of the search.

When INSTR does not find the string it is searching for, it returns a zero. So, for example, the statement

```
J = INSTR(11, A$, "R")
```

sets J equal to 0 because no R appears in A$ after the starting position, 11.

We can use the fact that INSTR returns 0 if the string is not found to simplify the condition on the DO statement in line 106 of Program 6.9 (pages 217–19). Recall that the statement was

```
DO UNTIL (Code$ = "J" OR Code$ = "K" OR Code$ = "L" OR Code$ ↵
    = "M" OR Code$ = "Q")
```

Using INSTR, that statement could be written in the simpler form

```
DO UNTIL INSTR(1, "JKLMQ", Code$) > 0
```

If Code$ is not J, K, L, M, or Q, INSTR(1, "JKLMQ", Code$) will equal 0, and the DO loop will be executed. When the user enters a valid Code$, the loop will be exited.

The INSTR function can also search for the appearance of strings of more than one character. Thus, the statement

```
J = INSTR(A$, "RING")
```

sets J equal to 3. Notice that J is set equal to the position in A$ where RING starts.

Concatenation

Unlike numeric variables or constants, string variables cannot be multiplied or divided. You can, however, "add" (put together) strings. The technical word for putting strings together is **concatenation**.

As an example of concatenation, consider the following QBasic statements:

concatenation
Combining strings or string variables.

```
A$ = "WATER"
B$ = "MELON"
F$ = A$ + B$
```

In the last line, the plus sign (+) is the string concatenation operator and indicates that A$ and B$ are to be concatenated, or put together, and the result assigned to F$. After that line is executed, F$ will contain WATERMELON. Notice that the two strings are put together end to end; no spaces are inserted between them.

Strings—as well as string variables—may be concatenated, and as many strings and string variables as you like may be concatenated in a single expression. So we can expand our example to the following statements:

```
A$ = "WATER"
B$ = "MELON"
C$ = "SWEET"
F$ = "RIPE " + C$ + " " + A$ + B$
```

After the last line is executed, F$ contains RIPE SWEET WATERMELON. Notice that to get a space between RIPE and SWEET, a space was included at the end of RIPE; to get a space between SWEET and WATERMELON, a string consisting of a single space was concatenated between C$ and A$.

7.5 EXERCISES

1. What value is assigned to A$ by the following statement?

   ```
   A$ = LTRIM$(RTRIM$("    So   many   spaces   "))
   ```

2. What value is assigned to A$ by the following statements?
   ★**a)**   `A$ = UCASE$(LCASE$("Up AnD dOwN"))`
   b)   `A$ = LCASE$(UCASE$("Up AnD dOwN"))`

3. Consider the statement

   ```
   J = VAL(P$)
   ```

   What value is assigned to J when P$ has the following values?
   ★**a)**   9
   b)   −1
   ★**c)**   Fourth of July
   d)   500 Fifth Avenue

4. What output is produced by the following statements?
   ★**a)**   `PRINT VAL("65")`
   b)   `PRINT STR$(65)`

★**c)** `PRINT ASC("65")`
  d) `PRINT CHR$(65)`

5. What output is produced by the following statements?
  a) `PRINT ASC(CHR$(90))`
  b) `PRINT CHR$(ASC("7"))`

★**6.** Simple Simon says the string

`Mary said, "Use the CHR$ function".`

could be coded as follows

`"Mary said, CHR$(34)Use the CHR$ function CHR$(34)."`

Comment.

7. What is the value of B$ after the following statements are executed?

```
B$ = LEFT$("BANANA", 3)
B$ = RIGHT$("BANANA", 3)
```

8. What is the value of W$ after each of the following statements is executed?
  a) `W$ = MID$("MISINFORMATION", 2, 3)`
★**b)** `W$ = MID$("MISINFORMATION", 3, 2)`
  c) `W$ = MID$("MISINFORMATION", 4, 6)`
  d) `W$ = MID$("MISINFORMATION", 6, 3)`

9. If the initial value of A$ is TIN, what will its value be after each of the following statements is executed?
  a) `MID$(A$, 1, 1) = "S"`
  b) `MID$(A$, 2, 1) = "A"`
★**c)** `MID$(A$, 2, 2) = "ED"`

10. Determine the value of J after each of the following statements is executed.
  a) `J = INSTR(1, "ANTISEPTIC", "T")`
★**b)** `J = INSTR(4, "ANTISEPTIC", "T")`
  c) `J = INSTR(9, "ANTISEPTIC", "T")`
  d) `J = INSTR(1, "ANTISEPTIC", "PIC")`
★**e)** `J = INSTR(1, "ANTISEPTIC", "SEP")`

11. What will the following statement print?

`PRINT STRING$(13, 47)`

7.6   USING STRING FUNCTIONS

Now that you understand string functions, let's use them to solve some interesting problems.

EXAMPLE 5

USING STRING FUNCTIONS TO REARRANGE NAMES

Problem Statement

Write a program that reads a name in the format

```
first-name space last-name
```

(example: Mark Twain) and prints it in the format

```
last-name comma space first-name
```

(example: Twain, Mark).

STEP 1   Variable Names

We begin by identifying and naming variables. Let's use the following.

Variable	Variable Name
Input Variable	
Name	NameIn$
Internal Variables	
Position of space (blank) in NameIn$	BlankPos
First name	FirstName$
Last name	LastName$
Output Variables	
Rearranged name	NameOut$

STEP 2   Algorithm

To solve this problem, we will use the following algorithm:

1. Repeat steps 2 through 6 for each name.
2. Read NameIn$.
3. Search NameIn$ for a blank.
4. If no blank is found, print an error message.
5. If a blank is found, extract the FirstName$ and LastName$ and rearrange them.
6. Print the rearranged name.

   Only steps 3 and 5 of this algorithm are complicated. We will discuss them in detail when we examine the program.

STEP 3   Hand-Calculated Answers

This problem has no hand-calculated answers, but we will verify that the program is correct when we examine the output.

STEP 4   QBasic Program

This algorithm produced Program 7.6. Step 3 of the algorithm is carried out in line 19

```
BlankPos = INSTR(NameIn$, " ")
```

where we use the INSTR function to search for a blank in NameIn$. In line 20, we use an IF statement to determine whether BlankPos is 0. If it is, then a blank was not found, and NameIn$ is not in the correct format. We then print an error message and READ the next name. The name in line 32, GeorgeSand, does not contain a blank, and the output shows the error message that was printed.

   If BlankPos is not 0, we have found a blank. We must then implement step 5 of the algorithm and extract the first and last names from NameIn$. We do that in the RearrangeName subprogram. The statement in line 48

```
FirstName$ = LEFT$(NameIn$, BlankPos - 1)
```

```
1  |  '     *** REARRANGING NAMES ***
2  |  '     Read Firstname Lastname, use INSTR to find space, and
3  |  '     print Lastname, Firstname
4  |
5  |  DECLARE SUB RearrangeName (NameOut$, NameIn$, BlankPos!)
6  |
7  |  '   Variables used
8  |
9  |  '   BlankPos     Position of blank in name
10 |  '   NameIn$      Original name
11 |
12 |  CLS
13 |  PRINT "   First Last         Last, First"
14 |  Fmt$ = "\                \    \                    \"
15 |
16 |  '   Process names
17 |  READ NameIn$
18 |  DO
19 |      BlankPos = INSTR(NameIn$, " ")          'Find space in name
20 |      IF BlankPos = 0 THEN
21 |          PRINT USING Fmt$; NameIn$; "No blank in name"
22 |      ELSE
23 |          CALL RearrangeName(NameIn$, BlankPos, NameOut$)
24 |          PRINT USING Fmt$; NameIn$; NameOut$
25 |      END IF
26 |      READ NameIn$
27 |  LOOP UNTIL NameIn$ = "EOD"
28 |
29 |  '     *** Data used in program
30 |  DATA "Mark Twain"
31 |  DATA "Lewis Carroll"
32 |  DATA "GeorgeSand"
33 |  DATA "Nelly Bly"
34 |  DATA "Isak Dinesen"
35 |  DATA  EOD
36 |  END
37 |
38 |  SUB RearrangeName (NameIn$, BlankPos, NameOut$)
39 |  '   Extract names
40 |  '   Receives NameIn$ and BlankPos
41 |  '   Returns NameOut$
42 |
43 |  '   Local variables
44 |
45 |  '   FirstName$      First name
46 |  '   LastName$       Last name
47 |
48 |      FirstName$ = LEFT$(NameIn$, BlankPos - 1)
49 |      LastName$ = MID$(NameIn$, BlankPos + 1)
50 |      NameOut$ = LastName$ + ", " + FirstName$
51 |  END SUB
```

PROGRAM 7.6   Using string functions to rearrange names. *(continued on next page)*

```
    First Last          Last, First
   Mark Twain          Twain, Mark
   Lewis Carroll       Carroll, Lewis
   GeorgeSand          No blank in name
   Nelly Bly           Bly, Nelly
   Isak Dinesen        Dinesen, Isak
```

PROGRAM 7.6 *(continued)*

extracts the first name from NameIn$. How does this statement work? Recall that when we execute this statement, BlankPos is equal to the position of the blank in NameIn$. We call BlankPos a **pointer** because it points to the blank. For example, if NameIn$ is equal to Mark Twain, BlankPos is equal to 5. Then the above statement assigns the BlankPos –1 = 5 –1 = 4 leftmost characters of NameIn$—that is, Mark—to FirstName$, which is exactly what we want.

Next, statement 49

```
LastName$ = MID$(NameIn$, BlankPos + 1)
```

extracts the last name from NameIn$. For Mark Twain, BlankPos + 1 = 5 + 1 = 6. Notice that the third argument of the MID$ function is not coded. Thus, this statement assigns all the characters beginning with the sixth character of NameIn$—that is, Twain—to LastName$, which again is exactly what we want.

Finally, in line 50, LastName$, a comma and space, and FirstName$ are concatenated and assigned to NameOut$. NameOut$ is printed when control is returned to the main module. ∎

pointer
A variable that indicates the location of an item of data.

EXAMPLE 6
USING STRING FUNCTIONS IN A WORD PROCESSING PROGRAM

String functions are also fundamental to word processing. In word processing, computers simplify creating and revising written materials—reports, stories, or even whole books. In fact, word processing is one of the most popular ways to use computers.

Problem Statement

Write a program that allows us to replace a string in some text with another string.

STEP 1   Variable Names

As usual, we begin by identifying and naming the variables. In this case, they are the following.

Variable	Variable Name
Input Variables	
A line of the text to be modified	Text$
String to be replaced	Original$
Replacement string	Replace$
Internal Variables	
Length of Original$	LenOriginal
Starting point for search of Original$ in Text$	Start
Position of start of Original$ in Text$	Position
Part of Text$	Part$

Output Variable
A line of new text   `NewText$`

STEP 2 Algorithm

We can use the following algorithm:

1. Accept Original$ and Replace$.
2. Repeat steps 3 through 7 for each line of text.
3. Read Text$.
4. Initialize NewText$ to the null string.
5. Repeat step 6 for all occurrences of Original$ in Text$.
6. Replace Original$ by Replace$ and assign the altered text to NewText$.
7. Print NewText$.

The only complicated part of this algorithm is step 6. We will discuss that step in detail as we examine the program.

STEP 3 Hand-Calculated Answers

This problem has no hand-calculated answers, but we will verify that the program is correct when we examine the output.

STEP 4 QBasic Program

In Program 7.7, which is based on this algorithm, the text in the DATA statements in lines 27, 28, and 29

```
       0         1         2         3         4         5
       1234567890123456789012345678901234567890123456789012345 67
DATA "In the theory of colour, there are three primary colours:"
DATA "red, blue and yellow.  Using these colours, we can create"
DATA "any colour we wish."
```

might be from a physics textbook. The numbers show the columns to help you follow the next discussion. The objective is to change the English spelling of colour to the American spelling of color.

In line 15, the program asks the user to enter the string to be replaced and assigns the string entered to Original$. In the example, Original$ is equal to colour. In line 16, the program asks for the replacement string and assigns the string entered to Replace$. In the example, Replace$ is equal to color. The DO loop is executed until the trailer data, XXX, is read. In the loop, the ReplaceText subroutine is executed and NewText$—which is returned by ReplaceText—is printed. The main work of the program is done in the ReplaceText subprogram.

In the subprogram, NewText$ is set to the null string in line 45. Recall that the null string is the string that contains no characters. It is represented in the program by two quotation marks next to each other. NewText$ is used as a string accumulator in line 53, and just as numeric accumulators must be initialized to 0, so must string accumulators be initialized to the null string.

In line 46, LenOriginal is set equal to the length of Original$, which in this case is the length of colour, or 6. Start is used in line 52 to extract part of Text$; the first time this line is executed, we want to start extracting from the first character. Therefore, in line 47, Start is set to 1.

In line 50,

```
Position = INSTR(Start, Text$, Original$)
```

the INSTR function is used to search for Original$ in Text$, starting from the first character of Text$ (recall that Start is 1). Position reports the position in Text$

```
 1 │  '   *** WORD PROCESSING PROGRAM ***
 2 │  '   Allow user to enter a string and a replacement string, and
 3 │  '   replace all occurrences of the string by the replacement string
 4 │
 5 │  DECLARE SUB ReplaceText (Text$, Original$, Replace$, NewText$)
 6 │
 7 │  '   Variables used
 8 │
 9 │  '   NewText$          Text after Original$ is replaced by Replace$
10 │  '   Original$         String to be replaced
11 │  '   Replace$          Replacement string
12 │  '   Text$             A line of text to be changed
13 │
14 │  CLS
15 │  INPUT "Enter text to be changed: ", Original$
16 │  INPUT "Enter replacement text: ", Replace$
17 │
18 │  '   Process all the lines of text
19 │  READ Text$
20 │  DO UNTIL Text$ = "XXX"
21 │      CALL ReplaceText(Text$, Original$, Replace$, NewText$)
22 │      PRINT NewText$
23 │      READ Text$
24 │  LOOP
25 │
26 │  '   *** Data used as text to be changed
27 │  DATA "In the theory of colour, there are three primary colours:"
28 │  DATA "red, blue and yellow.  Using these colours, we can create"
29 │  DATA "any colour we wish."
30 │  DATA XXX
31 │  END
32 │
```

PROGRAM 7.7   Using string functions in a word processing program. *(continued on next page)*

where Original\$ is found. If Position is 0, then Original\$ was not found in Text\$, and the DO loop is not executed. If Position is not zero, Original\$ was found in Text\$, and Position points to the character in Text\$ where Original\$ starts. In this case, the c of the first colour is the eighteenth character of Text\$, so Position is set to 18. All that needs doing now is to delete Original\$ from Text\$ and to insert Replace\$ in its place, which is done in the DO loop.

In line 52,

```
Part$ = MID$(Text$, Start, Position - Start)
```

Part\$ is assigned the value of the characters in Text\$ up to the first character of Original\$. Let's examine this statement closely. Start is 1, and Position – Start is 17, so this statement is equivalent to

```
Part$ = MID$(Text$, 1, 17)
```

This statement assigns 17 characters of Text\$, starting from the first character, to Part\$. Therefore, Part\$ contains "In the theory of ". In line 53, three items—NewText\$ (which contains the null string), Part\$, and Replace\$—are concatenated and assigned to NewText\$. NewText\$ now contains "In the theory of color".

In line 54, a new value of Start is calculated, equal to Position plus LenOriginal. In this case, Start becomes 18 + 6 = 24 and points to the comma following

```
33 | SUB ReplaceText (Text$, Original$, Replace$, NewText$)
34 | '    Replace all occurrences of Original$ in Text$ by Replace$
35 | '    Receives Text$, Original$, and Replace$
36 | '    Returns NewText$
37 |
38 | '    Local variables
39 |
40 | '    LenOriginal      Length of original string
41 | '    Part$            Part of Text$
42 | '    Position         Position of Original$ in Text$
43 | '    Start            Starting point for search of Original$ in Text$
44 |
45 |      NewText$ = ""                     'Initialize NewText$ to null string
46 |      LenOriginal = LEN(Original$)      'Needed to calculate new Start
47 |      Start = 1                         'Start at first character
48 |
49 | '    Find and replace all occurrences of Original$ in Text$
50 |      Position = INSTR(Start, Text$, Original$)
51 |      DO WHILE Position <> 0
52 |          Part$ = MID$(Text$, Start, Position - Start)
53 |          NewText$ = NewText$ + Part$ + Replace$
54 |          Start = Position + LenOriginal
55 |          Position = INSTR(Start, Text$, Original$)
56 |      LOOP
57 |      NewText$ = NewText$ + MID$(Text$, Start)
58 | END SUB
```

```
Enter text to be changed: colour
Enter replacement text: color

In the theory of color, there are three primary colors:
red, blue and yellow.  Using these colors, we can create
any color we wish.
```

PROGRAM 7.7 *(continued)*

colour. In line 55, the INSTR function searches for Original$ in the section of Text$ from character 24 to the end. The c of the second colour is the fiftieth character of Text$, so Position is set to 50. Since Position is not 0, the DO loop continues.

Let's study the second execution of line 52. Recall that Start is currently 24 and Position is 50, so line 52 is now equivalent to

```
Part$ = MID$(Text$, 24, 26)
```

This statement assigns 26 characters of Text$, starting from the twenty-fourth character, to Part$. Part$ is therefore ", there are three primary ". Then, in line 53, NewText$, Part$, and Replace$ are concatenated and assigned to NewText$. As a result, NewText$ becomes "In the theory of color, there are three primary color".

Start is updated in line 54 and becomes 56. When line 55 is executed, the INSTR function returns a 0, because colour does not occur beyond character 56 of Text$. Because Position is now 0, the program exits from the DO loop.

We are not quite finished with Text$, however, because NewText$ does not contain characters beyond the fifty-sixth character of Text$. Line 57 extracts the characters of Text$ from the fifty-sixth character to the end of Text$, concatenates them to NewText$, and assigns the whole string to NewText$. At this point, New-Text$ contains all of Text$, with every occurrence of colour replaced by color, so ReplaceText returns to the main module, where NewText$ is printed. ■

EXAMPLE 7

USING STRING FUNCTIONS TO MAKE A CODE

Some years ago, it was reported that within the federal government, the National Security Agency (NSA) made the greatest use of computers. Most governments use computer programs to put their messages into code and to break the codes of other countries. The programs used by governments are quite sophisticated, but you can write a rather simple QBasic program to encode a message.

Problem Statement

Write a program that accepts a message written in English, and then puts it into code. To keep the problem manageable, use a simple substitution code in which every letter in the original English message is replaced by a different letter in the coded message. Moreover, assume that the English message is written in capital letters.

STEP 1   Variable Names

We begin by identifying and naming the variables that we will use.

Variable	Variable Name
Input Variable	
English message	English$
Internal Variables	
Alphabet string	Alpha$
Translating string	Trans$
Current character	Char$
Character to replace Char$	Ch$
Pointer	Search
Counter variable	Change
Output Variable	
Coded message	Code$

STEP 2   Algorithm

We may then use the following algorithm:

1. Initialize Alpha$ to the alphabet, Trans$ to a translation string.
2. Accept a message for English$.
3. Initialize Code$ to the null string.
4. Repeat step 5 for each character in English$.
5.   Translate the character and concatenate it to Code$.
6. Print the coded message.

STEP 3   Hand-Calculated Answers

This problem has no hand-calculated answers.

STEP 4   QBasic Program

Look at Program 7.8, which is based on this algorithm. In line 14, Alpha$ is defined as a constant equal to the upper case letters of the alphabet, in their normal order. The translation string, Trans$, causes the letters in the English message to be replaced by different letters in the coded message. In line 15, Trans$ is defined as a constant equal to the letters of the alphabet in backward order. This Trans$ causes an A in the original English message to be changed to a Z in the coded message, a B to a Y, a C to an X, and so on—ending with a Z changed to an

```
 1  '    *** ENCODING A MESSAGE ***
 2  '    Encode a message using a substitution code.
 3
 4  DECLARE SUB MakeCode (English$, Code$)
 5
 6  '    Variables used
 7
 8  '    Alpha$        Alphabet string (global constant)
 9  '    Code$         Coded message
10  '    English$      English message
11  '    Trans$        Translating string (global constant)
12
13  CLS
14  CONST Alpha$ = "ABCDEFGHIJKLMNOPQRSTUVWXYZ"    'Initialize alphabet,
15  CONST Trans$ = "ZYXWVUTSRQPONMLKJIHGFEDCBA"    'and translate strings
16
17  LINE INPUT "English message:  ", English$      'Accept English string
18  CALL MakeCode(English$, Code$)
19  PRINT "Encoded message:  "; Code$              'Print coded message
20  END
21
22  SUB MakeCode (English$, Code$)
23  '    Encode English$
24  '    Receives English$
25  '    Returns Code$
26
27  '    Local variables
28
29  '    Ch$          Character from Trans$ to replace Char$
30  '    Char$        Character from English$
31  '    Change       Counter variable in FOR...NEXT loop
32  '    Search       Pointer for Char$ in Alpha$
33
34      Code$ = ""
35      FOR Change = 1 TO LEN(English$)            'Translate each character
36          Char$ = MID$(English$, Change, 1)      'Extract a character
37          Search = INSTR(Alpha$, Char$)          'Search for it in alphabet
38          IF Search = 0 THEN                     'If character not found,
39              Code$ = Code$ + Char$              'copy it,
40          ELSE                                   'otherwise
41              Ch$ = MID$(Trans$, Search, 1)      'get character from Trans$
42              Code$ = Code$ + Ch$                'and add it to Code$
43          END IF
44      NEXT Change
45  END SUB
```

English message: ONE IF BY LAND, TWO IF BY SEA
Encoded message: LMV RU YB OZMW, GDL RU YB HVZ

PROGRAM 7.8   Using string functions to encode a message.

A. You should understand, however, that the letters in Trans$ can be in any order. Different orders just produce different codes. The only requirement is that Trans$ contain every letter exactly once.

We obtain input in this program using the LINE INPUT statement in line 17. The LINE INPUT statement is fully discussed in the next section; for now, you can think of it as an ordinary INPUT statement.

All the work of encoding is done in the FOR...NEXT loop in the MakeCode subprogram. In line 34, Code$ is initialized to the null string. Code$ is used as a string accumulator in lines 39 and 42, and—as you learned when we examined Program 7.7 (pages 266–67)—string accumulators must be initialized to the null string. In line 36

```
Char$ = MID$(English$, Change, 1)
```

the MID$ function extracts a character from English$ and assigns it to Char$. When Change is 1, the first character of English$ is extracted; when Change is 2, the second character is extracted—and so on.

In line 37, the INSTR function is used to search Alpha$ for Char$. If Search is equal to 0, it means that Char$ does not appear in Alpha$ (it might be a space or a punctuation mark). In that case, in line 39, Char$ is concatenated to Code$. If Search is not 0, it points to the position in Alpha$ where Char$ appears.

The MID$ function in line 41

```
Ch$ = MID$(Trans$, Search, 1)
```

extracts the corresponding character from Trans$. To see exactly how this works, assume that Char$ equals E. When INSTR searches Alpha$ for Char$, it sets Search to 5 because E is the fifth character in Alpha$. Then in line 41, the fifth character of Trans$, V, is extracted from Trans$ and assigned to Ch$. In line 42, Ch$ is concatenated to Code$. In this way, the E in the original English message is changed to a V in the coded message.

When the FOR...NEXT loop is finished, all the characters in English$ are encoded, so MakeCode returns to the main module, where Code$ is printed.

The LINE INPUT Statement

The LINE INPUT statement allows a program to accept input that contains commas—without the user having to enclose the input in quotation marks. Furthermore, the input may even contain embedded quotation marks. The difference between a LINE INPUT statement and an ordinary INPUT statement is that the LINE INPUT statement reads a whole line at a time. That is, the LINE INPUT statement reads all the characters entered at the keyboard until the user presses the Enter key.

The syntax of the LINE INPUT statement is

```
LINE INPUT [;] ["prompt";] string-variable
```

Notice that only one string variable is coded; all the characters read are assigned to that one string variable. Like the optional semicolon in the INPUT statement, the optional semicolon that follows LINE INPUT prevents QBasic from scrolling the screen when the input is entered on line 24 or 25.   ∎

Syntax Summary

LINE INPUT Statement

Form:	`LINE INPUT [;] ["prompt";] string-variable`
Example:	`LINE INPUT "Enter the message to encode"; Code$`
Explanation:	Accepts a complete line of input from the keyboard—including commas and quotation marks—until the user presses the Enter key.

7.6 EXERCISES

1. How would you modify Program 7.6 (pages 263–64) so that a space is not printed after the comma?

2. In line 54 of Program 7.7 (pages 266–67), Start is calculated as Position + LenOriginal. How would the output change if Start were calculated as Position + 1?

3. Trace Program 7.7 when the second line of Text$ is processed.

★4. Trace Program 7.7, assuming that the value entered for Original$ is purple and the value entered for Replace$ is violet.

5. What output would Program 7.8 (page 269) produce if line 41 were changed to the following?

    ```
    Ch$ = MID$ (Alpha$, Search, 1)
    ```

★6. In Program 7.8, what would happen if a letter appeared twice in Trans$?

7. How would you change Program 7.8 if you wanted a space to be translated into a Z and a Z translated into a space?

★8. How would you change Program 7.8 to encode messages written in both upper and lower case letters?

9. Program 7.9 shows an incorrect solution to Programming Assignment 7.6. Find and correct the error.

```
1    '    CALCULATING THE SUM OF THE FIRST N INTEGERS
2    '    Calculate the sum 1 + 2 + ... + N
3
4    DECLARE FUNCTION Sum! (N!)
5
6    '    Variables used
7
8    '    N            Last number in sum
9    '    Sum          Function that calculates the sum of first N numbers
10
11   CLS
12   INPUT "Enter the final number, 0 to stop: ", N
13   DO UNTIL N = 0
14       PRINT "The sum from 1 to"; N; "is"; Sum(N)
15       INPUT "Enter the final number, 0 to stop: ", N
16   LOOP
17   END
18
19   FUNCTION Sum (N)
20   '    Calculate Sum = 1 + 2 + ... + N
21   '    Receives N, last term in series
22   '    Returns Sum
23
24   '    Local variables
25
26   '    J            Counter variable
27   '    TempSum      Holder for sum in function Sum
```

PROGRAM 7.9   A program that is supposed to calculate the sum of the first N integers. *(continued on next page)*

```
28  |
29  |       TempSum = 0                          'Initialize accumulator
30  |       FOR J = 1 TO N                       'For each number in range
31  |           TempSum = TempSum + N            'add it to accumulator
32  |       NEXT J
33  |       Sum = TempSum                        'Assign value to function
34  | END FUNCTION
```

```
Enter the final number, 0 to stop: 5
The sum from 1 to 5 is 25
Enter the final number, 0 to stop: 0
```

PROGRAM 7.9 *(continued)*

WHAT YOU HAVE LEARNED

In this chapter, you learned that:

- Loops that are executed a specified number of times are called counter-controlled loops.
- The FOR...NEXT statement is used to create counter-controlled loops.
- The STEP clause is used to set step sizes other than 1.
- Once inside a FOR...NEXT loop, you should not change the initial value, the final value, the step size or the counter variable.
- When two FOR...NEXT loops are separate, they are said to be independent. Independent loops may use the same counter variables.

- In nested FOR...NEXT loops, the inner loop must be completely inside the outer loop. Nested loops must use different counter variables.
- The RANDOMIZE TIMER statement supplies the RND function with a random seed.
- Simulation programs allow users to study the behavior of systems on a computer.
- The LINE INPUT statement accepts a complete line of input—including commas and quotation marks—until the user presses the Enter key.
- The QBasic functions discussed in this chapter are described in Tables 7.1, 7.2, and 7.3 (pages 245, 246, and 254 respectively).

NEW QBASIC STATEMENTS

STATEMENT	EFFECT
FOR...NEXT	

`FOR K = 2 TO 10 STEP 2`
`    PRINT K`
`NEXT K`
	Executes the statements between FOR and NEXT with K equal to 2, 4, 6, 8, and 10.

RANDOMIZE	
`RANDOMIZE TIMER`	Supplies the RND function with a random seed.
MID$	
`MID$(A$, 4, 2) = "PM"`	Replaces the fourth and fifth characters of A$ with PM.
LINE INPUT	
`LINE INPUT "Enter name"; Name$`	Accepts user input from the keyboard and assigns it to Name$.

KEY TERMS

concatenation
counter-controlled loop
Monte Carlo simulation

pointer
random number
simulation

string expression
substring

REVIEW EXERCISES

SELF-CHECK

1. When nested FOR...NEXT loops are used, is it necessary that the loops use the same or different variables for their counter variables?

2. Is the following a valid FOR statement?

   `FOR Z = 25 TO 35 STEP .1`

3. To have a FOR...NEXT loop work properly, if the step size is positive, the final value must be _____ the initial value. If the step size is negative, the final value must be _____ the initial value.

4. What step size is used if the STEP clause is omitted?

5. How many times will the following loop be executed?

```
FOR P = 16 TO 7
NEXT P
END
```

6. Why are systems simulated?

7. Explain the purpose of the RANDOMIZE statement.

8. How many variables may be listed in a LINE INPUT statement?

9. The RND function returns a random number between ____ and ____.

10. Match each function in the first column with its action listed in the second column.

A.	`LEFT$`	(1)	Returns the time in the form hh:mm:ss
B.	`TIMER`	(2)	Extracts a substring starting from the right
C.	`FIX`	(3)	Searches for one string in another
D.	`TIME$`	(4)	Extracts a substring starting from the left
E.	`MID$`	(5)	Discards digits to the right of the decimal point
F.	`CINT`	(6)	Returns a random number
G.	`INSTR`	(7)	Returns the length of its argument
H.	`INT`	(8)	Returns the largest integer less than or equal to its argument
I.	`RND`	(9)	Returns the time in seconds
J.	`RIGHT$`	(10)	Extracts an arbitrary substring
K.	`DATE$`	(11)	Returns the date
L.	`LEN`	(12)	Rounds its argument to the nearest integer

PROGRAMMING ASSIGNMENTS

Section 7.1

1. The Baker's Man sells rolls for $0.35 each. To help its salespeople, the company would like a table showing the cost of rolls for orders of 1 to 12 rolls. (*Hint*: This program does not require any input.)

2. Write a program to calculate the balance in a savings account at the Cache National Bank. The program should accept a deposit and interest rate, then calculate and print for each of the next 10 years the interest earned and the balance at the end of the year.

3. Program 7.1 (page 233) assumes that the growth rate stays constant. We might suppose that as the town grows, the new residents attract additional people, so that each year the growth rate increases by 5 percent. Write a program to calculate the population growth under this assumption.

4. a) One morning, Queen Doyenna set out from the castle and gave 1 ounce of gold to the first person she met, 2 ounces of gold to the second person she met, 3 ounces of gold to the third person, and so on—stopping when she had given 100 ounces of gold to the one hundredth person she met. How much gold did she give away?

   b) That same day, King Khan gave 1 pound of gold to the first person he met, ½ pound of gold to the second person he met, ⅓ pound of gold to the third person, and so on—stopping when he had given ¹⁄₁₀₀ of a pound of gold to the one hundredth person he met. How much gold did he give away?

Section 7.2

5. Write a program that uses a FOR...NEXT loop to print the numbers 4, 7, 10, 13, 16, and 19.

6. Write a program that accepts a number, N, and calculates and prints the sum $1 + 2 + \ldots + N$.

7. In 1626, Manhattan Island was sold for $24. Write a program that accepts today's year, then calculates and prints how much that $24 would be worth today if it had been deposited in a savings account paying 6 percent interest compounded annually instead. (*Hint*: Use a FOR...NEXT loop with an initial value of 1626.)

8. Write a program that uses a FOR...NEXT loop to print (all on one line):

```
10 - 9 - 8 - 7 - 6 - 5 - 4 -
   3 - 2 - 1 - Blastoff!
```

9. The factorial of a number, N, is defined as

```
1 * 2 * . . . * (N - 1) * N
```

Write a program that accepts a number between 1 and 30 and calculates and prints the factorial of that number.

Section 7.3

10. Every year, Harriet Stowe routinely Deposits a certain amount of money at a given interest Rate. At the end of Years, the Total in Harriet's account can be calculated by the following equation:

```
Total = Deposit * ((1 + Rate) ^↵
    Years - 1) / Rate
```

(*Note*: In this equation, Rate must be expressed as a decimal.) Write a program that will accept Deposit and print Total after 5, 10, 15, and 20 Years for Rates of 10, 12, and 14 percent.

11. The song "The Twelve Days of Christmas" speaks of the gifts "my true love gave to me." On the first day, the singer got a partridge in a pear tree; on the second day, two turtle doves and a partridge in a pear tree, for a total of three gifts; on the third day, three French hens, two turtle doves, and a partridge in a pear tree, for a total of six gifts; and so on. Write a program to determine the total number of gifts received in twelve days.

12. The relative damage done by an earthquake that measures Richter on the Richter scale at Distance miles from the center of the earthquake can be calculated by the following equation:

```
Damage = 0.8 * Richter ^ 3 /↵
   Distance ^ 2
```

Write a program that prints a table of Damage values. The table should have columns of Richter equal to 4, 5, 6, 7, and 8 and rows of Distance equal to 5, 10, 15, and 20 miles.

13. The cost of running an air conditioner depends on the temperature and humidity in the following way:

```
Cost = 1.5 * (Temperature - 68)↵
   / (120 - Humidity) ^ .5
```

Write a program that prints a table of Costs. The table should have columns of Humidity equal to 60, 70, 80, 90, and 100 percent, and rows of Temperatures equal to 70, 80, 90, and 100 degrees. If your program is correct, you should find that at 80 degrees and 70 percent humidity, the cost is $2.55.

Section 7.4

14. **a)** Write a program to help your kid brother improve his addition. The program should randomly select two integers between 1 and 10 and ask for their sum. For example, if the integers are 6 and 2, the program should print the message What is the sum of 6 and 2? The program should accept your brother's answer as input, check to see if his answer is correct, and print an appropriate message—either That's right or Sorry, the correct answer is 8. Use a FOR...NEXT loop to propose 10 problems and keep track of how many problems are answered correctly. After all 10 problems are answered, print the number that were answered correctly.

b) Use the TIMER function to determine how long it took to enter the answer. If the correct answer is entered, print the elapsed time, as well as the message That's right. If the incorrect answer is entered, do not print the elapsed time.

15. The TIMER function may be used to determine how long a program or a part of a program takes to execute. At the beginning of the program, add a statement like Start = TIMER, and at the end of the program, add a statement like Finish = TIMER. The difference Finish – Start gives the elapsed time in seconds. Use the TIMER function to verify that using the SQR function to calculate square roots is faster than raising to the .5 power. Use two FOR...NEXT loops to calculate the square roots of the integers between 1 and 1000. In one loop, use the SQR function; in the other, raise to the .5 power. Don't print the square roots; printing is so slow that it swamps the differences in calculation.

16. Write a program to play the following dice game. Two dice are thrown and your score is the higher number showing. If your score is a 5 or a 6, you win a dollar; otherwise, you lose a dollar. Start with $100, play 100 games, and print the amount of money you have left. Since a die may show any number from 1 to 6, you can simulate throwing a die by generating a random integer between 1 and 6. After 100 games, the original $100 should grow to about $110.

17. Write a program that plays the carnival game Chuck-a-luck with three dice. You bet on a number, and the dice are tossed. If none of the dice shows your number, you lose your bet. If one die shows your number, you win your bet. If two dice show your number, you win twice your bet; if all three dice show your number, you win three times your bet. Your program should start the player out with $100, then ask how much she wants to bet and which number she wants to bet on. If a player tries to bet more than she has, print a message and bet all her money. At the end of each play, display the three numbers that came up and the player's current money. If the player is bankrupt, end the game; otherwise, ask if the player wants to play again.

18. Some diskettes have 40 tracks. To read the data on a track, the arm must move to position the read/write head over the track. Assuming that all tracks are equally likely to be read, write a program that finds the average number of tracks that the arm must move for each read. Your answer should be near 13.3.

19. Write a program to play Sink the Sub. The program should place a submarine at a randomly chosen point on a grid in which X and Y run from 0 to 10. X runs east-west, with 0 being farthest west and 10 farthest east. Y runs north-south, with 0 being farthest south and 10 farthest north. Ask the player to enter the X and Y coordinates where the depth charge will be dropped. If the player enters the sub's coordinates, the sub is sunk, and the player wins. If the player misses the sub, have the program tell him in which direction he should move. For example, if Ysub = 5 and Xsub = 5, and the user guesses Y = 3, X = 7, the program should say Move North West. Give the user 5 tries; if the sub is still not sunk, announce its position. (*Hint*: You can analyze the Y and X guesses separately. For example, if Y is less than Ysub, you can tell the player to move north—independent of whether the X guess is too low, too high, or correct.)

Section 7.5

20. Write a program using the MID$ function to print the letters in HIPPOPOTAMUS in a triangle like the following:

```
        PO
       OPOT
      POPOTA
     PPOPOTAM
    IPPOPOTAMU
   HIPPOPOTAMUS
```

(Be sure to center the triangle on the screen or page.)

21. Write a program that accepts string input of up to 80 characters and displays it right-justified; that is, so the last character is displayed in column 80.

22. Write a program that accepts a word with up to 11 letters and prints the word down the screen, with each letter separated from the next lettter by two rows.

Section 7.6

23. You know that if in response to an INPUT prompt, you enter a nonnumeric character for a numeric variable, QBasic displays the infamous Redo from start error message. Nonprogrammers who see that message are likely to throw up their hands in frustration and turn the computer off. Write a polite program that uses a LINE INPUT statement to accept numeric data into a string. Check that the string contains onlythe digits 0 through 9, decimal points, and plus or minus signs. If the string contains any invalid characters, print a gentle message asking the user to reenter the data correctly.

24. Write a program to accept a string that includes a pair of parentheses with some characters inside them—as well as characters outside the parentheses. The program should delete the parentheses and the characters inside them and print the resulting string.

25. Stock prices are often quoted using fractions; that is, $37\frac{3}{8}$. In the fractions used, both the numerator and denominator have only one digit. Write a program that accepts a price in this form and prints it in dollars and cents.

26. A QBasic expression is balanced if **a)** it contains the same number of left and right parentheses and **b)** while it is scanned from left to right, the number of left parentheses is always greater than or equal to the number of right parentheses. Write a program that accepts an expression and reports whether it is balanced.

27. Write a program to read a phrase and print each word backward. For example, if your phrase is

HAPPY BIRTHDAY

your program should produce

YPPAH YADHTRIB

28. Write a program that accepts a string and changes a run of multiple spaces into a single space. For example, it should change

This   is a   test

to

This is a test.

29. The following message was encoded by Program 7.8:

DV SZEV NVG GSV VMVNB ZMW SV RH FH

Write a program that decodes this message.

ADDITIONAL PROGRAMMING ASSIGNMENTS

30. Write a program that accepts an integer, N. If N is odd, the program should calculate and print the sum $1 + 3 + 5 + \ldots + N$. If N is even, it should calculate and print the sum $2 + 4 + 6 + \ldots + N$.

31. The series of numbers

```
1, 1, 2, 3, 5, 8, 13, . . .
```

is known as the Fibonacci series. The first two terms in this series are 1, and the remaining terms are calculated by adding the preceding two terms. For example, 2 = 1 + 1, and 3 = 2 + 1. Write a program that prints the first 25 terms in the Fibonacci series.

32. In an ancient Chinese tale, a man who saved the emperor's life was told that he could ask anything for a reward. He requested a checkerboard. He then asked that one grain of rice be placed on the first square, two grains on the second square, four grains on the third square, and so on—doubling the number of grains on each square. A checkerboard contains 64 squares. Write a program that determines how many grains of rice were put on the last square and how many total grains were put on the man's checkerboard.

33. Mathematicians study a class of problems known as random walk problems, of which the following is an example. The bridge over the river Chi is 10 steps across and 6 steps wide. After having a few too many drinks at a nearby pub, Sherry Tipler tries to cross this bridge. Each time Sherry takes one step forward, she also lurches to the side. She lurches to the right and to the left with equal probability. Sherry steps on the bridge at the center line, but if she ever gets more than 3 steps from the center she falls in the river. If she manages to take 10 steps without falling in, she is safe. Simulate 100 attempted crossings of the bridge and keep track of how many times Sherry makes it across and how many times she falls in. (*Hint:* Use a FOR...NEXT loop to simulate the attempted crossings. Inside that loop, use a DO loop that continues executing as long as Sherry is on the bridge. You should find that she falls in about 35 percent of the time.)

34. Suppose you are waiting for your luggage to come off an airplane. If you are waiting for one piece of luggage, then on the average, half the luggage must come out of the plane before yours does. How many bags must come out if you are waiting for two pieces? Assume there are 120 pieces of luggage on the plane. You should find that you wait for about 80 bags.

35. Write a program that allows the user to enter a number with none, one, or numerous commas. Strip the commas from the number and print the original number and two times the number. Use the LINE INPUT statement to accept the number.

36. Write a program to perform the following operations. Start with any positive integer. Calculate the sum of the squares of its digits. For example, starting with 7639, we calculate 49 + 36 + 9 + 81 = 175. Now apply the same operation to 175. Keep repeating this procedure until you reach either the number 4 or the number 1. Print the values generated on the way to 4 or 1. Starting with 7639, the values are 175 75 74 65 61 37 58 89 145 42 20 4.

37. Write a program that searches for a string in some text. The program should accept a search string, read several lines of text from DATA statements, and display the text with the search string in blinking color. You may use the data in PA07-37.DAT—in which case, you should search for the string crooked and use XXX as the trailer data.

38. Write a program that encodes a message by interchanging the order of pairs of characters. For example, if the message is HAVE A GOOD DAY, the coded message is AHEVA G OO DADY. (Remember that a space counts as a character.)

BEYOND THE BASICS

39. The Slice of Life Pizza Parlor sells plain cheese pizza for $9.00. For additional toppings, its charges are as follows: mushrooms, $.50; anchovies, $.75; sausage, $1.25; and pepperoni, $1.50. Write a program that produces the following cost table.

Pepperoni	Sausage	Anchovies	Mushrooms	Price
No	No	No	No	9.00
No	No	No	Yes	9.50
No	No	Yes	No	9.75
No	No	Yes	Yes	10.25
No	Yes	No	No	10.25
No	Yes	No	Yes	10.75
No	Yes	Yes	No	11.00
No	Yes	Yes	Yes	11.50
Yes	No	No	No	10.50
Yes	No	No	Yes	11.00
Yes	No	Yes	No	11.25
Yes	No	Yes	Yes	11.75
Yes	Yes	No	No	11.75
Yes	Yes	No	Yes	12.25
Yes	Yes	Yes	No	12.50
Yes	Yes	Yes	Yes	13.00

40. A number, N, is classified as being deficient, perfect, or abundant—depending on whether the sum of the divisors of N is less than, equal to, or greater than N. In summing the divisors, 1 is included, but N itself is not. For example, the divisors of 4 are 1 and 2; since 1 + 2 = 3, 4 is a deficient number. The divisors of 6 are 1, 2, and 3; since 1 + 2 + 3 = 6, 6 is a perfect number. The divisors of 12 are 1, 2, 3, 4, and 6; since 1 + 2 + 3 + 4 + 6 = 16, 12 is an abundant number. Write a program that accepts a number and determines and prints its classification.

41. A particularly simple type of substitution code is known as a Caesar code, named after Julius Caesar, who supposedly used it. In terms of Program 7.8, the Trans$ string is in normal alphabetical order, but it is shifted to the left by an arbitrary number of letters. The letters that are pushed out of the front end of Trans$ are added to the back. For example, if we shifted Trans$ by four letters, it would be

```
Trans$ = "EFGHIJKLMNOPQRSTUVWXYZABCD"
```

With this Trans$, every letter in the original English message is replaced by the letter four letters after it in the alphabet. (We understand, for example, that the letter four letters "after" Z is D.) Since the shift can be any number from 1 to 25, there are 25 different Caesar codes.

Suppose you have found a coded message that was encoded using one of the Caesar codes—but of course, you don't know which one. Write a program that decodes the message by systematically trying all 25 Caesar codes. Practice your program on the following message:

```
JVUNYHABSHAPVUZ, FVB JHU HWWSF AV
    AOL UZH MVY H QVI
```

42. In spreadsheets, columns are named with letters. The sequence of letter names is A, B, C, . . . , Z, AA, AB, . . . , AZ, BA, BB, ... Many spreadsheets have 256 columns; therefore, the last column is named IV. Write a program that accepts a column's number, then determines and prints the column's name.

43. Write a program that accepts an English sentence and translates each word into pig Latin. If the first letter of the English word is a vowel, the word is translated into pig Latin by adding WAY to the end of the word. Thus, for example, APPLE becomes APPLEWAY.

If the first letter of the English word is not a vowel, the word is translated by moving the first letter of the word to the end of the word and adding AY to the end of the word. So, for example, PIG LATIN becomes IGPAY ATINLAY. (Consider only A, E, I, O, and U to be vowels.)

44. Write a program that accepts a number and displays that number in big digits on the screen. For example, if the user enters 468, the program should display

```
*   *      ****    ***
*   *    *           *   *
*****    ****      ***
    *    *   *   *   *   *
    *      ***     ***
```

45. Modify Program 7.5 (page 252) to plot the results on the screen. Draw the horizontal and vertical axes. After each toss, plot an asterisk one column to the right of the previous asterisk. If a head comes up, plot the asterisk one row higher than the last asterisk; if a tail comes up, plot it one row lower.

46. Write a program to play Hangman. The program should allow one player to enter a word, then erase the word and ask the second player to guess the word by entering one letter at a time. The program should print underscores to represent unknown letters. When a letter is guessed, the underscore should be replaced by the correct letter. If the letter occurs more than once, all occurrences should be shown. Give the player ten guesses and count only the wrong guesses.

8

ARRAYS

LEARNING OBJECTIVES

After reading this chapter, you will be able to:

- Explain what an array is.
- Process one- and two-dimensional arrays.
- Use the QBasic statements DIM and SWAP.
- Use the QBasic functions UBOUND and LBOUND.
- Sort an array.
- Search an array.

You know that the storage locations set up by QBasic to hold the value of a variable can hold only one value at a time. But some problems require us to have all the values of a variable stored in the computer.

For example, consider this problem: A program should accept students' names and test scores from the user, and calculate the average test score. Then the program should print each score and the difference between it and the average. Calculating the average test score presents no difficulties; we solved similar problems in Chapter 4. But to print the differences requires that all the original scores be available. However, each time the user enters a new test score, the previous test score is erased. Using only the QBasic you know now, you could not solve this problem—but it is easy to solve by using an array. In this chapter, you will learn how to use arrays and how to sort and search them.

8.1 UNDERSTANDING AND USING ONE-DIMENSIONAL ARRAYS

The DIM Statement

An **array** is a collection of storage locations that are accessed by the same variable name and that store the same kind of data—numeric or string. The individual storage locations are called **elements**. If you want to use an array in your program, you must indicate the number of storage locations you want associated with that variable. You do that by using a DIM statement.

DIM is short for "dimension," and specifies the size—that is, the number of storage locations—that should be reserved for each array. For example,

```
DIM Dwarfs$(1 TO 7), Gold(1 TO 12)
```

tells QBasic that you want Dwarfs$ and Gold to be arrays, not ordinary variables. Like ordinary variables, a $ at the end of an array name means that variable is a string variable array. The elements of the Dwarfs$ array are numbered from 1 to 7, and the elements of the Gold array are numbered from 1 to 12. These arrays are shown in Figure 8.1(a).

To use a particular element of an array, we specify a **subscript**. For example, to print the third element of the Dwarfs$ array, you need only write

```
PRINT Dwarfs$(3)
```

We say that Dwarfs$(3) is a subscripted variable and that 3 is the subscript. The subscript, which is always enclosed in parentheses immediately following the variable name, points to a particular element of the array.

array
A collection of storage locations that are accessed by the same variable name and that store the same kind of data—numeric or string.

elements
The individual components of an array.

subscript
A numeric constant, variable, or expression that specifies a particular element of an array.

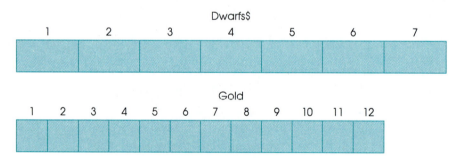

(a) Storage locations for the Dwarfs$ and Gold arrays.

(b) Dwarfs$ and Gold arrays with values assigned to the elements.

FIGURE 8.1   The Dwarfs$ and Gold arrays.

The syntax for a simple DIM statement is

```
DIM variable([lower TO] upper) [,...]
```

where variable is either a string or numeric variable and lower and upper are constants or numeric expressions. The subscript of the first element of the array is specified by lower, and upper specifies the subscript of the last element of the array. If you omit lower, QBasic uses a default value of 0.

This simple DIM statement defines an array that requires only one subscript to point to a particular element. This type of array is called a **one-dimensional array**. Later in this chapter, we will discuss the syntax of the full DIM statement.

As many variables as you want may be listed in a DIM statement, and you can have as many DIM statements as you want in a program, but (of course) you can dimension a particular array only once. The DIM statement must be executed before the first instruction that uses an array variable. It is therefore customary to put the DIM statement near the beginning of the program or in an initialization subprogram. Additional examples of DIM statements are as follows.

one-dimensional array
An array that requires one subscript to specify an element.

ILLUSTRATIONS

DIM Statement	Effect
`DIM Vowel$(1 TO 5)`	Reserves 5 storage locations, numbered 1 to 5, for the array Vowel$.
`DIM OddNumber(1 TO Num)`	Reserves Num storage locations for the array OddNumber. This example assumes that Num was previously assigned a value.
`DIM Accidents(1980 TO 1990)`	Reserves 11 storage locations, numbered 1980 through 1990, for the array Accidents. Accidents (1981) will reference the second element of the array. Presumably, the array will store data on accidents during the years 1980 through 1990. This example shows why you might want the first element of an array to have a number other than 1.
`DIM State$(1 TO 50), Area(1 TO 50)`	Reserves 50 storage locations, each (numbered 1 through 50) to the arrays State$ and Area.

As long as you specify a subscript, you may use an array variable anywhere that you could use an ordinary variable. The following example shows how you could use elements of the Gold array variable in a LET statement:

```
Amt = Gold(1) + Gold(12)
```

Suppose the values shown in Figure 8.1(b) were assigned to the elements of the Gold array. (For now, don't worry about how the values were assigned; you will see that later.) Before reading further, can you determine the value of Amt? The

LET statement is evaluated by adding the value of the 1st element of Gold—which is 5—and the 12th element of Gold—which is 6—and assigning the result—11—to Amt.

This example used constants as subscripts, but variables and even expressions may be used as subscripts. Consider the statements

```
J = 4
K = 11
X = Gold(K) + Gold(K - J)
```

To evaluate the last statement, the value of Gold(K) is required. Since the previous statement assigned 11 to K, Gold(K) is evaluated as Gold(11). Similarly, Gold(K − J) is evaluated as Gold(11 − 4) = Gold(7). Using the values for Gold(11) and Gold(7) in Figure 8.1(b), we see that X will be equal to 26 (9 + 17 = 26).

Notice especially that Gold(K − J) is not evaluated as Gold(K) − Gold(J). First the subscript K − J is evaluated, and then that element of the array is referenced. Similarly, Gold(K) + 1 is evaluated as Gold (11) + 1, which is equal to 9 + 1 = 10, while Gold(K + 1) is Gold(12), which is 6.

Assigning Values to an Array

Now that you know the fundamentals of arrays, let's consider how values are assigned to the elements of an array.

We could use READ and DATA statements to assign the values shown in Figure 8.1(b) to the Dwarfs$ array, as follows:

```
DIM Dwarfs$(1 TO 7)
READ Dwarfs$(1)
READ Dwarfs$(2)
READ Dwarfs$(3)
READ Dwarfs$(4)
READ Dwarfs$(5)
READ Dwarfs$(6)
READ Dwarfs$(7)
DATA Doc, Grumpy, Sleepy, Happy, Bashful, Sneezy, Dopey
```

But what if Dwarfs$ had 100 or 500 elements? Writing so many additional READ statements would be exhausting and lengthen our program significantly.

Instead, we could use a single READ statement inside a FOR...NEXT loop. For example,

```
DIM Dwarfs$(1 TO 7)
FOR J = 1 TO 7
    READ Dwarfs$(J)
NEXT J
DATA Doc, Grumpy, Sleepy, Happy, Bashful, Sneezy, Dopey
```

Let's trace these statements to see how they work. The first time the READ statement is executed, J is 1, so the statement READ Dwarfs$(J) is evaluated as READ Dwarfs$(1). The first value listed in the DATA statement, Doc, is assigned to Dwarfs$(1). The second time the READ statement is executed, J is 2, so the statement READ Dwarfs$(J) is evaluated as READ Dwarfs$(2). The second data value, Grumpy, is assigned to Dwarfs$(2). In this way, the loop assigns a value to all 7 elements of the Dwarfs$ array.

This is the fundamental idea behind the use of arrays: Write one or more statements that use subscripted variables (like the READ statement in this example), put these statements inside a FOR...NEXT loop, and use the counter variable of the FOR...NEXT loop as the subscript. The statements will be executed as many times as you need. Note that because a DIM statement may be executed only once, the DIM statement is not placed inside the FOR...NEXT loop. If you place a DIM statement inside the FOR...NEXT loop, the second time the DIM statement is executed, QBasic stops and displays the message Duplicate definition.

If we now change the upper bound of the Dwarfs$ array to 500, we would only have to change the final value of the FOR statement from 7 to 500 and add additional DATA statements. The program (excluding the DATA statements) remains the same length.

You can also use a PRINT statement inside a FOR...NEXT loop to print the values of an array—for example:

```
FOR K = 1 TO 7
    PRINT Dwarfs$(K)
NEXT K
```

Notice that this PRINT statement uses K for both the counter variable and the subscript, even though the READ statement in the previous example uses J. There is no connection between the variables J or K and the Dwarfs$ array; the value of the subscript is what's important. If J and K and a new variable ZZZ all have the value 5, then Dwarfs$(J), Dwarfs$(K), and Dwarfs$(ZZZ) all refer to the fifth element of the Dwarfs$ array.

We are not restricted to using READ and PRINT statements in FOR...NEXT loops; we can use any QBasic statement. Thus, we can add the corresponding elements of two arrays, as follows:

```
DIM A(1 TO 50), B(1 TO 50), C(1 TO 50)
FOR J = 1 TO 50
    C(J) = A(J) + B(J)
NEXT J
```

When the loop finishes executing, C(1) will equal A(1) + B(1), C(2) will equal A(2) + B(2), and so on.

Errors

When working with arrays, you may make some new kinds of errors. For example, students frequently write the statements to fill the Dwarfs$ array as

```
DIM Dwarfs$(1 TO 7)
READ Dwarfs$(J)
```

That is, they leave out the FOR and NEXT statements. You can avoid this kind of error if you remember that you want the READ statement to be executed seven times. This READ statement will be executed only once.

Another kind of error you might make is shown in the following example:

```
DIM Gold(1 TO 12)
K = 20
Gold(K) = 4
```

The upper value coded in a DIM statement for an array determines the maximum subscript you may use with that array. (Similarly, the lower value coded in a DIM statement determines the minimum subscript you may use with that array.) In this case, the LET statement tries to assign 4 to Gold(20). Since the maximum subscript that may be used with Gold is 12, Gold(20) doesn't exist. QBasic accordingly displays the message

```
Subscript out of range
```

and stops executing. This message indicates either that a DIM statement is wrong or that you assigned the subscript an incorrect value.

You must also remember to specify a subscript when using an array variable. For example, writing

```
PRINT Dwarfs$
```

is wrong. We reserved seven storage locations for Dwarfs$, but in this statement, we have not specified which one we want printed. In fact, it is legal—but poor practice—for a program to contain a subscripted variable and an ordinary variable with the same name. In executing this statement, QBasic would think we were referring to an ordinary variable named Dwarfs$. Since we never assigned a value to the ordinary variable Dwarfs$, QBasic would print the null string. Likewise, Gold(3) and Gold3 are completely different variables. Gold(3) refers to the third element of Gold, while Gold3 is an ordinary variable.

Now that you know something about arrays, we can use them to solve some problems.

EXAMPLE 1

USING ARRAYS TO PRINT THE DIFFERENCE FROM THE AVERAGE

Let's return to the problem mentioned at the beginning of this chapter.

Problem Statement

Write a program that accepts students' names and test scores, then calculates and prints the average test score. The program should also print each score—and the difference between that score and the average.

STEP 1   **Variable Names**

As always, we begin by identifying and naming the variables.

Variable	Variable Name
Input Variables	
Student names array	`Students$`
Test scores array	`Tests`
Number of students	`NumStudents`
Internal Variables	
Subscript	`Counter`
Test score accumulator	`Total`
Output Variables	
Average test score	`Average`
Difference, test score minus average	`Difference`

The Students$ and Tests arrays are called **parallel arrays** because of the correspondence between the data they contain. For instance, Students$(1) will contain a student's name, and Tests(1) will contain that student's test score.

STEP 2   **Algorithm**

We can use the following algorithm for this problem:

1. Input NumStudents.
2. Dimension Students$ and Tests with NumStudents elements.
3. Input a name and test score for each student.
4. Calculate and print Average.
5. Calculate and print Difference for each student.

parallel arrays
Two or more arrays in which the data stored in a particular element of one array correspond to data in the same element of the other(s).

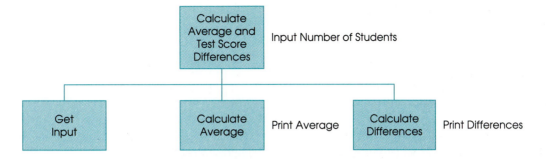

FIGURE 8.2   Top-down chart for a program that calculates the average test score and the differences from the average.

The top-down chart for this problem is shown in Figure 8.2. The three subprograms will get the names and test scores, calculate the average, and calculate and print the differences. For reasons that are explained when we examine the program, the task of inputting NumStudents is done in the main module.

The pseudocode for this problem is as follows:

Calculate Average and Differences from Average

```
Main Module
  Input NumStudents
  Call GetInput          → allow user to enter each student & grade
  Call CalcAverage
  Call CalcDiff
End Main Module

GetInput
  For each student
    Input student's name and test score
  Next student
End GetInput

CalcAverage
  For each test
    Add test score to accumulator
  Next test
  Calculate Average
  Print Average
End CalcAverage

CalcDiff
  For each student
    Calculate Difference
    Print Difference
  Next Student
End CalcDiff
End
```

Each subprogram consists of a FOR...NEXT loop. In the FOR...NEXT loop in GetInput, we input each student's name and test score. In the FOR...NEXT loop in CalcAverage, we accumulate the test scores. In the FOR...NEXT loop in CalcDiff, we calculate and print the differences.

STEP 3   **Hand-Calculated Answer**

To hand-calculate an answer, let's use the following data.

Student Name	Test Score
Melita	82
Benito	90
Angela	86
Mickey	74

From this data, we can quickly determine that the average test score is 83 and that Melita, Benito, Angela, and Mickey have grades that differ from this average by –1, 7, 3, and –9, respectively.

STEP 4   **QBasic Program**

Our algorithm and pseudocode produce Program 8.1. In line 18, the program uses an INPUT statement to accept a value for NumStudents. In line 19, a DIM statement is used to dimension Students$ and Tests with NumStudents elements. This way, each time the program is run, Students$ and Tests are dimensioned with the correct number of elements. The INPUT and DIM statements could have been coded in the GetInput subprogram. They were written in the main module because the DIM statement is so important that it should be one of the first statements seen by anyone who reads the program.

The CALL statements in lines 21, 22, and 23 show that to pass an array as an argument to a subprogram, you simply follow the array name by a pair of empty parentheses. For example,

```
CALL GetInput(Students$(), Tests())
```

executes the GetInput subprogram and passes to it the Students$ and Tests arrays.

The SUB statements in lines 26, 43, and 58 show that you use the same method to include an array name in a parameter list:

```
SUB CalcAverage (Tests(), Average)
```

You might expect that the final values of the FOR statements in lines 37, 53, and 67 should be NumStudents. Instead, it is UBOUND(Tests) in line 37 and UBOUND(Students$) in lines 53 and 67. UBOUND is a built-in QBasic function that returns the upper bound—that is, the highest subscript—that may be used with an array. In Program 8.1, UBOUND returns NumStudents. Using UBOUND saves us the trouble of passing NumStudents to the subprograms. UBOUND is also used in line 40, where we calculate Average by dividing Total by UBOUND(Tests).

QBasic has another function, LBOUND, that returns the lower bound—that is, the lowest subscript—that may be used with an array.

As mentioned earlier, usually when an array is passed as an argument, the variable name is followed by a pair of empty parentheses. But UBOUND and LBOUND are exceptions to that rule. As lines 37, 53, and 67 show, with these functions, you simply code the array name.

Notice that QBasic's answers agree with our hand-calculated answers.   ■

EXAMPLE 2 ▬▬▬▬▬▬▬▬▬▬▬▬▬▬▬

USING ARRAYS TO CALCULATE BILLS AND TOTALS

Arrays can also be used as accumulators and to simplify the logic of programs, as the following program shows.

```
 1  '   *** CALCULATE AVERAGE TEST SCORE AND DIFFERENCES FROM AVERAGE ***
 2  '   Calculate the average test scores, and print each student's
 3  '   score and difference from the average.
 4
 5  DECLARE SUB CalcAverage (Tests!(), Average!)
 6  DECLARE SUB CalcDiff (Students$(), Tests!(), Average!)
 7  DECLARE SUB GetInput (Students$(), Tests!())
 8
 9  '   Variables used
10
11  '   Average         Average test score
12  '   NumStudents     Number of students
13  '   Students$       Student names array
14  '   Tests           Test scores array
15
16  CLS
17
18  INPUT "Enter the number of students: ", NumStudents
19  DIM Students$(1 TO NumStudents), Tests(1 TO NumStudents)
20
21  CALL GetInput(Students$(), Tests())
22  CALL CalcAverage(Tests(), Average)
23  CALL CalcDiff(Students$(), Tests(), Average)
24  END
25
26  SUB CalcAverage (Tests(), Average)
27  '   Calculate and print average test score
28  '   Receives Tests()
29  '   Returns Average
30
31  '   Local variables
32
33  '   Counter         Subscript
34  '   Total           Test score accumulator
35
36      Total = 0                               'Initialize accumulator
37      FOR Counter = 1 TO UBOUND(Tests)
38          Total = Total + Tests(Counter)
39      NEXT Counter
40      Average = Total / UBOUND(Tests)
41      PRINT "Average test score is "; Average
42  END SUB
43
44  SUB CalcDiff (Students$(), Tests(), Average)
44  '   Calculate and print differences
45  '   Receives Students$(), Tests(), and Average
46  '   No variables are returned
47
48  '   Local variables
49
50  '   Counter         Subscript
51  '   Difference      Difference, test score minus average
52
53      FOR Counter = 1 TO UBOUND(Students$)
54          Difference = Tests(Counter) - Average
55          PRINT Students$(Counter), Tests(Counter), Difference
56      NEXT Counter
57
```

PROGRAM 8.1 Using arrays to calculate the average test score and the difference from the average. *(continued on next page)*

```
58 | SUB GetInput (Students$(), Tests())
59 | '    Get names and scores from user
60 | '    No variables received
61 | '    Returns Students$() and Tests()
62 |
63 | '    Local variable
64 |
65 | '    Counter          Subscript
66 |
67 |      FOR Counter = 1 TO UBOUND(Students$)
68 |          INPUT "Enter a student's name: ", Students$(Counter)
69 |          PRINT "Enter the test score for "; Students$(Counter);
70 |          INPUT ": ", Tests(Counter)
71 |      NEXT Counter
72 | END SUB
```

```
Enter the number of students: 4
Enter a student's name:  Melita
Enter the test score for Melita: 82
Enter a student's name:  Benito
Enter the test score for Benito: 90
Enter a student's name:  Angela
Enter the test score for Angela: 86
Enter a student's name:  Mickey
Enter the test score for Mickey: 74

Average test score is  83
Melita           82              -1
Benito           90               7
Angela           86               3
Mickey           74              -9
```

PROGRAM 8.1 *(continued)*

The No Bum Steer fast-food chain assigned a code number to each possible order, as follows.

Code No.	Order	Price
1	Hamburger	1.25
2	Fries	.90
3	Shake	1.00
4	Hamburger and Fries	2.00
5	Hamburger and Shake	2.15
6	Fries and Shake	1.75
7	Hamburger, Fries, and Shake	2.95
8	The customer's order is complete; print bill	
9	End of business day; print daily totals	

Problem Statement

Write a QBasic program that allows a clerk to enter the code numbers of a customer's order, and that uses the preceding table to calculate and print the customer's bill. When the clerk enters a 9, the program should print the number of customers who bought each of the seven different orders, and the income from each order. Finally, the program should print the total number of all orders sold and the total income from all orders.

STEP 1   Variable Names

As always, we begin by identifying and naming variables.

Variable	Variable Name
Input Variable	
Code number of the order	`Code`
Internal Variables	
Cost of orders array	`Cost`
Number of different orders on menu	`NumOrders`
Output Variables	
Customer's bill for one item	`Bill`
Total bill for a customer	`TotalBill`
Income from one kind of order	`Income`
Total daily income	`TotalIncome`
Total daily orders	`TotalOrders`
Name of orders array	`Order$`
Array to count the number of customers who bought each kind of order	`Counter`

STEP 2   Algorithm

We can use the following algorithm:

1. Initialize Counter array to 0, the Order$ array to the names of the orders, and Cost array to the costs of the orders.
2. Display the menu of orders and instructions.
3. Repeat steps 4 and 5 until clerk enters a 9.
4. Accept Code.
5. If Code is between 1 and 7, print Bill for that order, accumulate Bill into TotalBill, and count the order. If Code is 8, print TotalBill for this customer.
6. Calculate and print the number purchased and Income for each of the seven different orders.
7. Calculate and print TotalOrders and TotalIncome.

The top-down chart for this program is shown in Figure 8.3. The main program calls four subprograms: Initialize, DisplayMenu, ProcessOrders, and Print-Totals. In addition, ProcessOrders calls GetCode (which gets the input from the clerk) and DisplayError (which displays an error message if the clerk enters invalid data).

STEP 3   Hand-Calculated Answer

We will use the program to generate several bills and the daily total report, and then verify that they are correct.

STEP 4   QBasic Program

Program 8.2 is based on this algorithm. The main module dimensions the arrays, sets the colors to white on blue, clears the screen, and calls the four subprograms. All the work is done in the subprograms.

The Initialize subprogram starts at line 112. In the FOR...NEXT loop, the Counter array is initialized to 0, the Order$ array is initialized to the names of the orders, and the Cost array is initialized to the costs of the orders. The READ statement in line 119 uses the DATA statements in lines 35 through 41. When this subprogram returns to the main module, Cost(J) contains the cost of the Jth order.

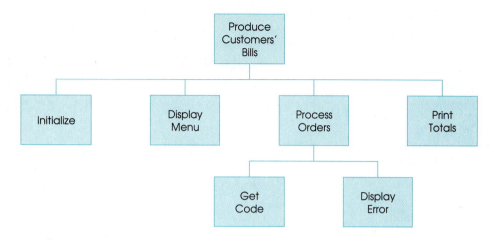

FIGURE 8.3 Top-down chart for a program that calculates bills for No Bum Steer.

That is, Cost(1) contains the cost of order number 1 (which is 1.25), Cost(2) contains the cost of order number 2 (which is .90), and so on. Similarly, Order$(1) contains the name of order number 1 (Hamburger), Order$(2) contains the name of order number 2 (Fries), and so on. You will see how the Cost and Order$ arrays are used soon.

The DisplayMenu subprogram begins at line 60. Line 65 sets the color to black on white, the default colors used by QBasic's menus. When the menu is displayed on the blue background color established by line 26, it looks just like one of QBasic's menus.

The rest of the subprogram uses LOCATE and PRINT statements to display the menu shown in Figure 8.4(a) (page 295). All the LOCATE statements position the cursor at column 13. The first LOCATE statement positions the cursor at row 1, the second at row 2, and so on. The LOCATE statement in the FOR...NEXT loop (lines 84 through 87) needs explaining. This loop prints the code, name, and price of the seven different orders. The counter variable, J, goes from 1 to 7—but when J is 1, we want to print at row 7. (The previous LOCATE statement, in line 82, positioned the cursor at row 6.) The LOCATE statement in line 85

```
LOCATE J + 6, 13
```

positions the cursor at row 7 when J is 1, at row 8 when J is 2, and so on.

Now that you understand the LOCATE statements, let's examine the PRINT statements. These PRINT statements use the CHR$ function to draw the double-line border and single horizontal lines in the menu. If you consult the ASCII table in Appendix B, you'll see that the code for the character that draws the top left corner, ╔, is 201; for the top right corner, ╗, 187; and for the horizontal lines, ═, 205. Line 73 prints the top line using the CHR$ and STRING$ functions with these codes. The ASCII code for the character that draws the vertical lines, ║, is 186. Line 66 sets the variable VertLn$ equal to CHR$(186). The PRINT statements between lines 75 and 95 draw the sides of the menu by including VertLn$ at the beginning and end of their print lists. Line 97 uses the CHR$ and STRING functions with ASCII codes 200, 205, and 188 to draw the bottom line of the menu.

The ProcessOrders subprogram uses the GetCode function to get the Code from the clerk. In GetCode, the LOCATE statement in line 106 positions the cursor inside the menu, next to the message Enter Code Number of Customer's Order. The INPUT$ function in line 107 accepts one character from the clerk, and the VAL function converts it to a number. Since INPUT$ does not echo the input

```
1   '    *** CUSTOMERS' BILLS FOR NO BUM STEER ***
2   '   Calculate bills for each customer and totals at the end of business
3
4   DECLARE SUB PrintTotals (Order$(), Cost!(), Counter!())
5   DECLARE SUB Initialize (Counter!(), Order$(), Cost!())
6   DECLARE SUB DisplayMenu (Order$(), Cost!())
7   DECLARE SUB DisplayError ()
8   DECLARE SUB ProcessOrders (Order$(), Cost!(), Counter!())
9   DECLARE FUNCTION GetCode! ()
10
11  '   Variables used
12
13  '   Cost            Cost of orders array
14  '   Counter         Array to count the number of customers
15  '                   who ordered each kind of order
16  '   NumOrders       Number of different orders on menu (global constant)
17  '   Order$          Name of orders array
18
19  CONST Black = 0
20  CONST Blue = 1
21  CONST Red = 4
22  CONST White = 7
23  CONST NumOrders = 7
24
25  DIM Counter(1 TO NumOrders), Cost(1 TO NumOrders), Order$(1 TO NumOrders)
26  COLOR White, Blue           'Set white on blue
27  CLS
28  CALL Initialize(Counter(), Order$(), Cost())
29  CALL DisplayMenu(Order$(), Cost())
30  CALL ProcessOrders(Order$(), Cost(), Counter())
31  CALL PrintTotals(Order$(), Cost(), Counter())
32
33  '   Data used by Initialize
34  '   The format is name of order, price of order
35  DATA Hamburger, 1.25
36  DATA Fries, .90
37  DATA Shake, 1.00
38  DATA Hamburger and Fries, 2.00
39  DATA Hamburger and Shake, 2.15
40  DATA Fries and Shake, 1.75
41  DATA "Hamburger, Fries, and Shake", 2.95
42  END
43
43  SUB DisplayError
44  '   Display error message
45  '   No variables received or returned.
46
47      BEEP
48      LOCATE 25, 16                               'On line 25
49      COLOR Red, White                            'Set red on white
50      PRINT "Enter a value between 1 and 9 please";  'Print message
51      Now = TIMER                                 'Pause
52      DO WHILE TIMER < Now + 1                    '1 second
53      LOOP
54      LOCATE 25, 16                               'Erase
55      COLOR White, Blue                           'error
56      PRINT SPACE$(36);                           'message
57      COLOR Black, White                      'Reset color for menu
58  END SUB
```

PROGRAM 8.2   Using arrays to display a menu and calculate bills and totals. *(continued on next page)*

```
59  |
60  |  SUB DisplayMenu (Order$(), Cost())
61  |  '    Display menu using ASCII graphics characters
62  |  '    Receives Order$() and Cost()
63  |  '    No variables are returned
64  |
65  |      COLOR Black, White          'Set black on white
66  |      VertLn$ = CHR$(186)         'Character used for vertical lines
67  |      MenuFmt$ = "!    #     \                    \    #.## !"
68  |        Title$ = "              WELCOME TO NO BUM STEER          "
69  |      Heading1$ = "  Enter the number that corresponds to order  "
70  |      Heading2$ = "  Code   Order                          Price "
71  |    Instruction$ = " Enter Code Number of Customer's Order        "
72  |      LOCATE 1, 13                                'Position cursor
73  |      PRINT CHR$(201); STRING$(46, 205); CHR$(187)  'Print top of menu
74  |      LOCATE 2, 13                                'Position cursor
75  |      PRINT VertLn$; Title$; VertLn$              'Print title
76  |      LOCATE 3, 13                                'Position cursor
77  |      PRINT VertLn$; STRING$(46, 196); VertLn$    'Print horizontal line
78  |      LOCATE 4, 13                                'Position cursor
79  |      PRINT VertLn$; Heading1$; VertLn$           'Print 1st heading
80  |      LOCATE 5, 13                                'Position cursor
81  |      PRINT VertLn$; SPACE$(46); VertLn$          'Print blank line
82  |      LOCATE 6, 13                                'Position cursor
83  |      PRINT VertLn$; Heading2$; VertLn$           'Print 2nd heading
84  |      FOR J = 1 TO NumOrders                      'Print all orders
85  |          LOCATE J + 6, 13                        'and costs
86  |          PRINT USING MenuFmt$; VertLn$; J; Order$(J); Cost(J); VertLn$
87  |      NEXT J
88  |      LOCATE 14, 13                               'Position cursor
89  |      PRINT VertLn$; "    8     For Customer's Bill "; SPACE$(17); VertLn$
90  |      LOCATE 15, 13                               'Position cursor
91  |      PRINT VertLn$; "    9     For Daily Totals    "; SPACE$(17); VertLn$
92  |      LOCATE 16, 13                               'Position cursor
93  |      PRINT VertLn$; STRING$(46, 196); VertLn$    'Print horizontal line
94  |      LOCATE 17, 13                               'Position cursor
95  |      PRINT VertLn$; Instruction$; VertLn$        'Print instructions
96  |      LOCATE 18, 13                               'Position cursor
97  |      PRINT CHR$(200); STRING$(46, 205); CHR$(188)  'Print bottom of menu
98  |  END SUB
99  |
99  |  FUNCTION GetCode
100 |  '    Gets Code from user, using INPUT$
101 |
102 |  '    Local variable
103 |
104 |  '    Code            Code number of order
105 |
106 |      LOCATE 17, 55, 1                            'Position cursor
107 |      Code = VAL(INPUT$(1))                       'Get new order number
108 |      PRINT Code                                  'Print new order number
109 |      GetCode = Code                              'Assign value to function
110 |  END FUNCTION
111 |
112 |  SUB Initialize (Counter(), Order$(), Cost())
113 |  '    Initialize Counter(), Order$(), and Cost()
114 |  '    No variables are received
115 |  '    Counter(), Order$(), and Cost() are returned
```

PROGRAM 8.2 *(continued)*

```
116 |
117 |        FOR J = 1 TO NumOrders
118 |            Counter(J) = 0                  'Initialize Counter() to 0
119 |            READ Order$(J), Cost(J)         'DATA statements are in main
120 |        NEXT J
121 | END SUB
122 |
123 | SUB PrintTotals (Order$(), Cost(), Counter())
124 | '    Print daily totals
125 | '    Receives Order$(), Cost(), and Counter()
126 | '    No variables are returned
127 |
128 | '    Local variables
129 |
130 | '    Income            Income from one kind of order
131 | '    TotalIncome       Total daily income
132 | '    TotalOrders       Total daily orders
133 |
134 |        TotalOrders = 0                      'Initialize accumulators for orders
135 |        TotalIncome = 0                      'and income
136 |
137 | '    Print headings
138 |        LPRINT "                    DAILY TOTALS"
139 |        LPRINT "                                      Number"
140 |        LPRINT "Code        Order            Purchased        Income"
141 |    OrderFmt$ = " # \                    \    ###          ###.##"
142 |    TotalFmt$ = "            Totals            ####        $#,###.##"
143 |
144 |        FOR J = 1 TO NumOrders
145 |            Income = Counter(J) * Cost(J)            'Accumulate
146 |            TotalOrders = TotalOrders + Counter(J)   'orders and
147 |            TotalIncome = TotalIncome + Income       'income
148 |            LPRINT USING OrderFmt$; J; Order$(J); Counter(J); Income
149 |        NEXT J
150 |        LPRINT USING TotalFmt$; TotalOrders; TotalIncome
151 | END SUB
152 |
153 | SUB ProcessOrders (Order$(), Cost(), Counter())
154 | '    Process customers' orders
155 | '    Receives Order$(), Cost()
156 | '    Returns Counter()
157 |
158 | '    Local variables
159 |
160 | '    Bill              Customer's bill for one item
161 | '    Code              Code number of the order
162 | '    TotalBill         Total bill for a customer
```

PROGRAM 8.2 (*continued*)

```
163 │ OrderFmt$ = "  Code  #  \                               \        $###.##"
164 │ TotalFmt$ = "                Your bill is ..................... $###.##"
165 │ TotalBill = 0
166 │ Code = GetCode
167 │ DO UNTIL Code = 9
168 │    SELECT CASE Code
169 │       CASE 1 TO NumOrders
170 │          Bill = Cost(Code)                        'Get bill for order
171 │          TotalBill = TotalBill + Bill             'Accumulate bill
172 │          Counter(Code) = Counter(Code) + 1    'Increment counter
173 │          LPRINT USING OrderFmt$; Code; Order$(Code); Bill
174 │       CASE 8                                    'Get total for customer
175 │          LPRINT USING TotalFmt$; TotalBill
176 │          LPRINT                             'Skip a line between bills
177 │          TotalBill = 0                      'Get set for next customer
178 │       CASE ELSE
179 │          CALL DisplayError
180 │    END SELECT
181 │    Code = GetCode
182 │ LOOP
183 │ END SUB
```

PROGRAM 8.2 *(continued)*

to the screen, line 108 prints Code. Line 109 assigns Code to GetCode, so the code entered can be returned to ProcessOrders.

In ProcessOrders, the program stays inside the DO loop until the clerk enters a 9. The SELECT CASE statement in lines 168 through 180 processes Code.

If Code is between 1 and 7, the bill for this order is calculated in line 170:

```
Bill = Cost(Code)
```

This statement is complicated, so make sure you understand how it works. If Code is 4, for example, QBasic interprets this statement as

```
Bill = Cost(4)
```

and assigns the correct value to Bill—2.00. Because of the way we initialized Cost, the correct value is assigned to Bill for all values of Code. If we weren't using an array to store the costs, to calculate Bill, we would have to use seven CASE clauses: one for each value of Code between 1 and 7.

Line 171 accumulates Bill into TotalBill, so we will be able to print this customer's bill when she finishes ordering.

Line 172

```
Counter(Code) = Counter(Code) + 1
```

counts this order. When Code is 4, this statement is interpreted as

```
Counter(4) = Counter(4) + 1
```

That is, if a customer chooses order number 4, then Counter(4) is incremented. Line 173 prints a line for this order on the customer's bill. It uses Order$(Code) to print the name of the order.

When the clerk enters an 8 (indicating that this customer is finished ordering), line 175 prints the total bill, line 176 prints a blank line to separate the customers' bills, and line 177 sets TotalBill back to 0 (to get ready for the next customer). A typical bill is shown in Figure 8.4(b). You can see that the bill was calculated correctly.

```
┌─────────────────────────────────────────────────────────┐
│                                                           │
│            WELCOME TO NO BUM STEER                        │
│         ─────────────────────────────────────            │
│     Enter the number that corresponds to order           │
│                                                           │
│     Code    Order                           Price         │
│      1      Hamburger                        1.25         │
│      2      Fries                            0.90         │
│      3      Shake                            1.00         │
│      4      Hamburger and Fries              2.00         │
│      5      Hamburger and Shake              2.15         │
│      6      Fries and Shake                  1.75         │
│      7      Hamburger, Fries, and Shake      2.95         │
│      8      For Customer's Bill                           │
│      9      For Daily Totals                              │
│         ─────────────────────────────────────            │
│     Enter Code Number of Customer's Order                 │
│                                                           │
└─────────────────────────────────────────────────────────┘
```

(a)   The menu for No Bum Steer.


```
   Code  4   Hamburger and Fries                $ 2.00
   Code  7   Hamburger, Fries, and Shake        $ 2.95
             Your bill is ....................  $ 4.95
```

(b)   A customer's bill.


```
                         DAILY TOTALS
                                    Number
   Code         Order              Purchased      Income
    1 Hamburger                        2            2.50
    2 Fries                            1            0.90
    3 Shake                            3            3.00
    4 Hamburger and Fries              1            2.00
    5 Hamburger and Shake              3            6.45
    6 Fries and Shake                  1            1.75
    7 Hamburger, Fries, and Shake      2            5.90
              Totals                  13       $   22.50
```

(c)   The Daily Total report.

FIGURE 8.4   Output from Program 8.2.

If Code is any value other than 1 through 9, line 179 in Program 8.2 calls the DisplayError subprogram, which starts at line 43. This subprogram beeps the speaker and displays an error message in red on white on row 25. Lines 52 and 53 cause a one-second delay, and then the error message is erased.

When the clerk enters a 9, indicating that the business day is over and that daily totals should be printed, the DO loop is exited, and control returns to the main program.

The main program calls PrintTotals to print the daily totals. PrintTotals uses a FOR...NEXT loop to print the number of each order purchased, and the income from each order. Line 145 calculates the income from order J by multiplying Counter(J), which contains the number of J orders sold, by Cost(J), which is the cost of each J order. Line 146 accumulates Counter(J) into TotalOrders, and line 147 accumulates Income into TotalIncome. Line 148 prints the daily totals for order J. Line 150 prints the daily totals for all the orders. Figure 8.4(c) shows the Daily Total report. You can check that the totals for each order and the totals for the day are calculated correctly. ■

Syntax Summary

DIM Statement (Simple Form)

Simple Form: `DIM variable([lower TO] upper), ...`
Example: `DIM States$(1 TO 50), Area(1 TO 50)`
Explanation: Reserves storage locations for array variables and specifies the minimum and maximum values that the subscripts may have.

8.1 EXERCISES

★**1.** Write a DIM statement to allocate 15 storage locations—numbered 1 to 15—to the array A. Write a DIM statement to allocate 10 storage locations—numbered 10 to 20—to the array B$.

2. Assume that the array StateName$ was dimensioned with 50 elements and that all 50 elements were assigned values. What is printed by the following statement?

`PRINT StateName$`

★**3.** Suppose that the array A was dimensioned with 10 elements and that the program contains a DATA statement with 10 values. Will the following statement assign values to all 10 elements?

`READ A(10)`

4. The array Days$ is defined to have seven elements—numbered 1 to 7—which have the values Sunday, Monday, Tuesday, Wednesday, Thursday, Friday, Saturday.
  a) What is printed by the following statement?

  `PRINT Days$(2), Days$(6)`

  b) What value is assigned to LongWeekend$ by the following statement?

  `LongWeekend$ = Days$(6) + ", " + Days$(7) + ", " + Days$(1)`

5. The array V is defined to have eight elements—numbered 1 to 8—whose values are 6, 2, 1, 7, 4, 3, 9, 6. Suppose J is equal to 3, K is equal to 4, and L is equal to 6. What value is assigned to A when each of the following LET statements is executed?
  ★**a)** `A = V(J) - V(K)`
  b) `A = V(L) * V(K - J)`
  ★**c)** `A = V(K) - V(J - K)`

  (*Hint*: Draw a set of numbered storage locations like those in Figure 8.1—page 280—and insert the values of V in sequence.)

6. What values are assigned to the array A—whose DIM statement is DIM A(1 TO 5)—by the following FOR...NEXT loops?

a)
```
FOR K = 1 TO 5
      A(K) = K
NEXT K
```

b)
```
FOR J = 1 TO 5
      A(J) = J
NEXT J
```

c)
```
FOR J = 1 TO 5
      A(6 - J) = J
NEXT J
```

d)
```
FOR J = 5 TO 1 STEP -1
      A(J) = J
NEXT J
```

e)
```
A(1) = 5
FOR J = 2 TO 5
      A(J) = J * A(1)
NEXT J
```

f)
```
A(1) = 5
FOR J = 2 TO 5
      A(J) = J * A(J - 1)
NEXT J
```

7. What output is produced by the following program?
```
DIM P(1 TO 5)
FOR J = 1 TO 5
     READ P(J)
NEXT J
FOR J = 5 TO 1 STEP -1
     PRINT P(J);
NEXT J
DATA 6, 4, 2, 9, 5
END
```

★8. Assume that array A was defined with 12 elements—numbered 1 to 12. Write the statements to add 1 to each element of A.

9. Consider the following program:
```
DIM X(1 TO 16)
FOR J = 1 TO 16
     X(J) = J
NEXT J
FOR J = 2 TO 4
     IF X(J) <> 0 THEN
          FOR K = 2 * J TO 16 STEP J
               X(K) = 0
          NEXT K
     END IF
NEXT J
FOR J = 1 TO 16
     IF X(J) <> 0 THEN
          PRINT X(J);
     END IF
NEXT J
END
```

★**a)**   What are the values of the elements of X when the first FOR...NEXT loop completes executing?

b)   What output is produced?

★**10.**   Simple Simon says that since the SELECT CASE statement in line 168 of Program 8.2 (pages 291–94) could be written

```
SELECT CASE Code$
```

the VAL function in line 107 is not needed. Why is he wrong?

11.   **a)**   How would you modify Program 8.2 to print the menu inside a box drawn with single lines instead of double lines? (*Hint*: Examine the table of ASCII codes in Appendix B.)

b)   In the menu drawn by Program 8.2, there is a small gap between the horizontal lines in rows 3 and 16 and the sides of the menu. How would you modify lines 77 and 93 to close that gap? (*Hint*: Examine the table of ASCII codes in Appendix B.)

8.2   THE BUBBLE SORT

Lists of data are often more useful if they are sorted—that is, arranged in numerical or alphabetical order. For example, a report consisting of student names and grade point averages is more useful if it is printed either in alphabetical order by student name or in numerical order by grade point average. When computer programs sort data, the data are often stored in arrays.

Many sorting techniques exist; in this section, you will learn a technique known as the **bubble sort**. This technique was so named because the elements of the array gradually move—that is, bubble—toward their final positions. Other sorting methods are faster than the bubble sort (see Programming Assignment 8.48 for one faster sorting method), but the bubble sort is easy to understand and program. Also, for small arrays, the differences in execution speed are not significant.

The elements of an array may be sorted into ascending or descending order. We will sort in ascending order. After the array is sorted, the first element will be less than or equal to the second element, the second will be less than or equal to the third, and so on. In the bubble sort, we compare adjacent elements of the array. If the first element is greater than the second element (that is, if the two elements are in the "wrong" order), we swap them. If the first element is less than or equal to the second element (that is, if the two elements are in the "right" order), we leave them alone. Every time we swap two elements, the array gets a little closer to being sorted; if we continue swapping long enough, eventually the array is sorted. We will discuss exactly how to determine when the array is completely sorted a little later.

Let's clarify this procedure by applying it to an actual example. Suppose we have an array, A, whose elements are in any mixed-up order, and we want to sort A so that its elements are in ascending order. The procedure works for both string and numeric arrays of any size. To keep this discussion to a reasonable length, however, let's assume that A contains only five elements and that initially they have the values shown in the left column of Figure 8.5(a).

We begin by comparing A(1) with A(2). Since 3 is less than 7, these elements are in the "right" order, so we leave them alone. After this comparison, the array

bubble sort
A method of sorting an array in which adjacent elements are compared and swapped if necessary, so that elements move slowly toward their final positions.

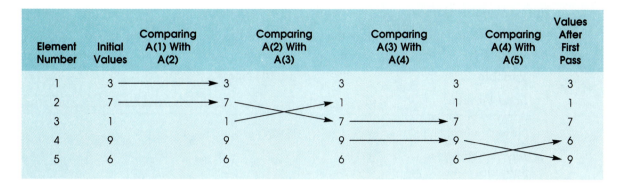

(a) First pass.

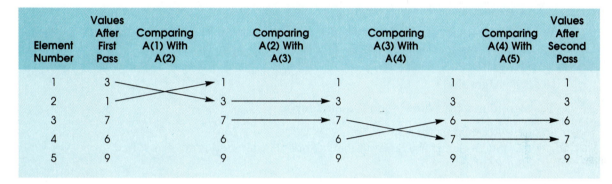

(b) Second pass.

FIGURE 8.5   Sorting using the bubble sort algorithm.

is unchanged, as shown in the third column of Figure 8.5(a). Next, we compare A(2) with A(3). Since 7 is greater than 1, these elements are in the "wrong" order, so we swap them. The array after this comparison is shown in the fourth column of Figure 8.5(a). We next compare the new A(3) with A(4). Since 7 is less than 9, these elements are in the "right" order, and so we leave them alone. The array after this comparison is shown in the fifth column of Figure 8.5(a). Finally, we compare A(4) and A(5). Since 9 is greater than 6, these elements are in the "wrong" order, so we swap them. After the first pass, the array A has the values shown in the last column of Figure 8.5(a).

It may seem that we have done a lot of work and have little to show for it, since array A is still pretty mixed up. But notice that the largest number, 9, is in the fifth element, which is where it belongs. If we repeat the procedure one more time, we get the results shown in Figure 8.5(b)—array A is now sorted. (Be sure you understand all the steps in Figure 8.5(b) before proceeding.) In this case, sorting array A required only two passes; in other cases, it might require one or many. The number of passes required to sort an array depends on two factors: the size of the array and how mixed up it is at the start.

EXAMPLE 3
PROGRAMMING A BUBBLE SORT

Problem Statement

Write a QBasic program that accepts a number representing the number of values to be sorted. The program should then accept that number of values into an array and sort the array in ascending order.

STEP 1 **Variable Names**

We begin by identifying and naming the variables. For this problem, we can use the following.

Variable	Variable Name
Input Variables	
Array to be sorted	A
Number of elements in array A	Number
Internal Variables	
Subscript	K
Flag to indicate the sort is finished	SortedFlag$
Output Variable	
Sorted array	A

We will discuss the variable SortedFlag$ later in this section. For now, let's examine the algorithm for this program.

STEP 2 **Algorithm**

The algorithm for the bubble sort is quite simple:

1. Accept data for array A.
2. Swap elements of array A that are out of order until array A is sorted.
3. Print array A.

This algorithm suggests that the program be divided into three subprograms: GetData, which gets the data to be sorted from the user; BubbleSort, which performs the sort; and PrintSortedArray, which prints the sorted array.

Flowchart

Figure 8.6 shows the flowchart for the BubbleSort program. (The GetInput and PrintSortedArray subprograms consist of simple FOR...NEXT loops, so to save space, their flowcharts are not shown.) In the main module, the program starts by accepting a value for Number (the number of elements of array A that are to be sorted) and dimensioning array A to have Number elements. After executing the GetInput subprogram that assigns values to the elements of array A, the program is ready to begin the actual sorting in subprogram BubbleSort.

The bubble sort requires that we compare adjacent elements of array A: A(1) with A(2), A(2) with A(3), and so on. How can we perform all these comparisons? Naturally, we don't want to write separate IF statements; if we did, our program would be much too complicated. We can use only one IF statement if we compare A(K) with A(K + 1), and put this IF statement inside a FOR...NEXT loop in which K is the counter variable. Then when K is 1, we compare A(1) with A(2). When K is 2, we compare A(2) with A(3), and so on. The FOR...NEXT loop is shown in flowchart symbols 33 through 38.

Notice, however, that the highest value K should have is Number − 1. If we allow K to have the value Number, we will try to compare A(Number) with A(Number + 1), and the highest subscript we can use with A is Number. Therefore, the final value of the FOR...NEXT loop should be Number − 1. We will use the UBOUND function in this program, as we did in Program 8.1 (pages 287–88), so the final value is shown on the flowchart as UBOUND(A) − 1.

Inside the loop, if the condition A(K) > A(K + 1) is true, we want to swap A(K) and A(K + 1). As you will see when we examine the program, QBasic has a special instruction named SWAP, which we will use to swap A(K) and A(K + 1). The reason for assignment symbol 36 is explained in the next section. If the condition A(K) > A(K + 1) is false, we do nothing.

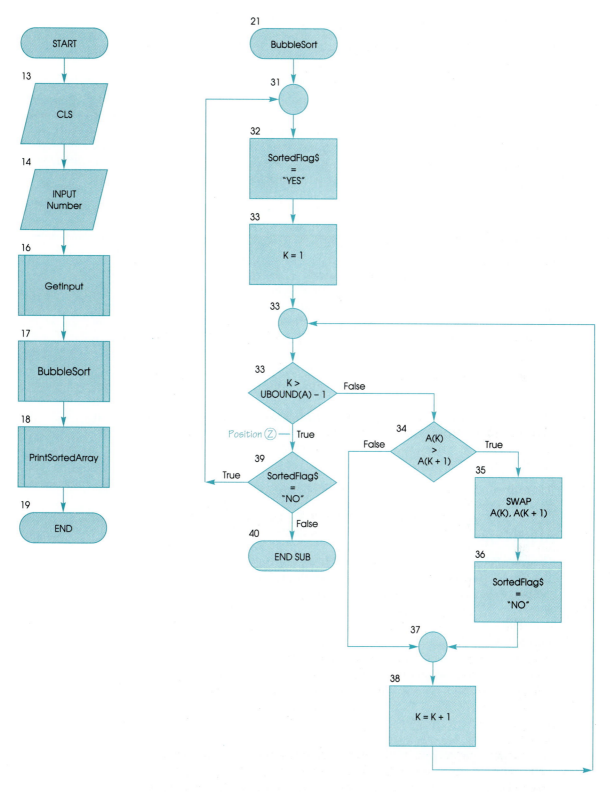

FIGURE 8.6   Flowchart for the BubbleSort program.

Using a Flag to Stop Sorting

We have one last problem to solve: How do we know when to stop? Suppose we completed the FOR...NEXT loop and are at position Ⓩ in Figure 8.6. If all the pairs of elements of array A are in the "right" order, we want to stop the sort and return to the main module.

How can we know when all the pairs of elements are in the "right" order? Clearly, if during a particular pass through array A, the condition $A(K) > A(K + 1)$ were never true, then all the pairs of elements would be in the "right" order, and the sort would be complete. To know that on the previous pass the condition was never true, we introduce a flag named SortedFlag$.

A **flag** is a variable introduced into a program for the sole purpose of controlling the execution of the program by indicating the presence or absence of some condition. That definition may sound complicated, but a flag is not very different from trailer data. When we use trailer data, we set one of the program's variables to a particular value to indicate that we reached the end of the input data. When we use a flag, we introduce a new variable and set it to a particular value to indicate some condition.

flag
A variable whose purpose is to control the execution of a program by indicating whether some condition has or has not occurred.

We will assign SortedFlag$ the value YES if the sort is finished and NO if it is not. As Figure 8.6 shows, we set SortedFlag$ to YES in assignment symbol 32, just before the FOR...NEXT loop, and we set it to NO in assignment symbol 36, in the "True" branch of the decision.

Suppose that on a pass through array A, the condition $A(K) > A(K + 1)$ is true—even once. Then the LET statement at symbol 36 sets SortedFlag$ to NO. When the FOR...NEXT loop is completed and we arrive at position Ⓩ, SortedFlag$ has the value NO. We must repeatedly execute the FOR...NEXT loop as long as, when we get to position Ⓩ, SortedFlag$ has the value NO. Obviously, we must put the FOR...NEXT loop in a DO loop, which is shown in symbols 31 through 39. Since we must always make at least one pass through the loop, we use a posttest loop. Even if A were originally sorted, we wouldn't know that until we made one pass through the loop.

Notice that this logic requires one additional pass after the array is sorted. It is this final pass that leaves SortedFlag$ equal to YES and ends the sort.

STEP 3 **Hand-Calculated Answers**

There are no answers to calculate by hand, but we must inspect the output to verify that the numbers are sorted.

STEP 4 **QBasic Program**

Program 8.3 shows the bubble sort in QBasic. The only new statement is in line 35: the SWAP statement, which interchanges the values of its two arguments. The syntax of the SWAP statement is quite simple:

```
SWAP variable1,variable2
```

When the SWAP statement is executed, the values of the two variables are exchanged. Any type of variables may be swapped, but the two variables must be of the same type: both numeric or both string.

The following examples show how the SWAP statement is used. ■

ILLUSTRATIONS

SWAP Statement	Effect
`SWAP P, Q`	Interchanges the values of P and Q.
`SWAP Name1$, Name2$`	Interchanges the values of Name1$ and Name2$.
`SWAP W, P(7)`	Interchanges the values of W and P(7).

The Output screen in Program 8.3 shows that the array was sorted.

```
1    '    *** BUBBLE SORT ***
2    '    Sort an array using the bubble sort algorithm
3
4    DECLARE SUB GetInput (A!())
5    DECLARE SUB BubbleSort (A!())
6    DECLARE SUB PrintSortedArray (A!())
7
8    '    Variables used
9
10   '    A                 Array. At start unsorted, at end sorted
11   '    Number            Number of elements in A
12
13   CLS
14   INPUT "Enter the number of numbers to be sorted: ", Number
15   DIM A(1 TO Number)
16   CALL GetInput(A())
17   CALL BubbleSort(A())
18   CALL PrintSortedArray(A())
19   END
20
21   SUB BubbleSort (A())
22   '    Sort A()
23   '    Receives A() unsorted
24   '    Returns A() sorted
25
26   '    Local variables
27
28   '    K                 Subscript
29   '    SortedFlags$      Flag to indicate the sort is finished
30
31       DO
32           SortedFlag$ = "YES"                'Set flag to sorted
33           FOR K = 1 TO UBOUND(A) - 1         'Examine all adjacent pairs
34               IF A(K) > A(K + 1) THEN        'If they are in wrong order
35                   SWAP A(K), A(K + 1)        'swap them
36                   SortedFlag$ = "NO"         'Set flag to not sorted
37               END IF
38           NEXT K
39       LOOP WHILE SortedFlag$ = "NO"  'Stay in loop while array is not sorted
40   END SUB
41
41   SUB GetInput (A())
42   '    Get values for A() from user
43   '    No variables are received
44   '    Returns A()
45
46   '    Local variable
47
48   '    K                 Subscript
49
50       PRINT "Enter the numbers to be sorted, one at a time"
51       FOR K = 1 TO UBOUND(A)
52           PRINT "Number";
53           INPUT ": ", A(K)
54       NEXT K
55   END SUB
```

PROGRAM 8.3　A program that performs a bubble sort. *(continued on next page)*

```
56
57   SUB PrintSortedArray (A())
58   '    Print sorted A()
59   '    Receives A()
60   '    No variables are returned
61
62   '    Local variable
63
64   '    K                    Subscript
65
66        FOR K = 1 TO UBOUND(A)
67             PRINT A(K);
68        NEXT K
69   END SUB
```

```
Enter the number of numbers to be sorted: 6
Enter the numbers to be sorted, one at a time
Number: 7
Number: 12
Number: 9
Number: 17
Number: 7
Number: 3
 3  7  7  9  12  17
```

PROGRAM 8.3 *(continued)*

EXAMPLE 4

SORTING PARALLEL ARRAYS

Program 8.3 sorts the single array A, but we often have to sort two or more parallel arrays simultaneously. For example, suppose we have two arrays: Student$ (which contains students' names) and GPA (which contains their grade point averages). We want to sort Student$ to put the names in alphabetical order—but while we are doing that, we must also move around the elements of GPA so that they stay in correspondence with the elements of Student$.

Problem Statement

Write a program that sorts the Student$ array, and that keeps the values in the GPA array in correspondence with the names in the Student$ array.

STEP 1   Variable Names

The variables are as follows.

Variable	Variable Name
Input Variables	
Array of GPAs	GPA
Array of student names	Student$
Internal Variables	
Subscript	K
Flag to indicate that the sort is finished	SortedFlag$
Output Variables	
Array of GPAs	GPA
Sorted array of student names	Student$

STEP 2   **Algorithm**

The algorithm and flowchart for this problem are very similar to those for sorting a single array, and so are not shown.

STEP 3   **Hand-Calculated Answers**

This problem has no hand-calculated answers.

STEP 4   **QBasic Program**

Program 8.4 sorts the Student$ array while keeping the elements of the GPA array in correspondence with the elements of the Student$ array. The only significant difference between this program and Program 8.3 (which sorts a single array) is the second SWAP statement in line 38:

```
SWAP GPA(K), GPA(K + 1)
```

This statement swaps the corresponding elements of the GPA array whenever we swap elements of the Student$ array.

The output shows that when the students' names were sorted, the elements of GPA were kept in correspondence with the elements of Students$. ∎

```
1    '    *** BUBBLE SORT OF PARALLEL ARRAYS ***
2    '    Sort on student's name, carrying along GPA
3
4    DECLARE SUB GetInput (Student$(), GPA!())
5    DECLARE SUB BubbleSort (Student$(), GPA!())
6    DECLARE SUB PrintSortedArrays (Student$(), GPA!())
7
8    '    Variables used
9
10   '    GPA             Array of GPAs
11   '    Number          Number of elements in GPA and Student$ arrays
12   '    Student$        Array of student names
13
14   CLS
15   INPUT "Enter the number of students: ", Number
16   DIM Student$(1 TO Number), GPA(1 TO Number)
17   CALL GetInput(Student$(), GPA())
18   CALL BubbleSort(Student$(), GPA())
19   CALL PrintSortedArrays(Student$(), GPA())
20   END
21
22   SUB BubbleSort (Student$(), GPA())
23   '    Sort Student$() and GPA() parallel arrays
24   '    Sort on Student$()
25   '    Receives unsorted Student$() and GPA()
26   '    Returns sorted Student$() and corresponding GPA()
27
28   '    Local variables
29
30   '    K               Subscript
31   '    SortedFlag$      Flag to indicate the sort is finished
32
```

(handwritten: Main module)

PROGRAM 8.4   *A program that sorts parallel arrays. (continued on next page)*

beginning of a pass

```
33          DO
34              SortedFlag$ = "YES"                    'Set flag to sorted
35              FOR K = 1 TO UBOUND(Student$) - 1    'Examine all adjacent pairs
36                  IF Student$(K) > Student$(K + 1) THEN  'If in wrong order
37                      SWAP Student$(K), Student$(K + 1)  'swap names,
38                      SWAP GPA(K), GPA(K + 1)            'and GPAs
39                      SortedFlag$ = "NO"                 'Set flag to not sorted
40                  END IF
41              NEXT K
42          LOOP WHILE SortedFlag$ = "NO" 'Stay in loop while array is not sorted
43      END SUB
```

1 pass thou the array

after a single pass (each pass)

```
44      SUB GetInput (Student$(), GPA())
45      '   Get students' names and GPAs from user
46      '   No variables received
47      '   Student$() and GPA() returned
48
49      '   Local variable
50
51      '   K                 Subscript
52
53          FOR K = 1 TO UBOUND(Student$)
54              INPUT "Enter a student's name: ", Student$(K)
55              PRINT "Enter GPA for "; Student$(K);
56              INPUT ": ", GPA(K)
57          NEXT K
58      END SUB
59
60      SUB PrintSortedArrays (Student$(), GPA())
61      '   Print sorted arrays
62      '   Receives Student$() and GPA()
63      '   No variables received
64
65      '   Local variable
66
67      '   K                 Subscript
68
69          PRINT "Student Name   GPA"
70          FOR K = 1 TO UBOUND(Student$)
71              PRINT USING "\          \   #.##"; Student$(K); GPA(K)
72          NEXT K
73      END SUB
```

```
Enter the number of students: 5
Enter a student's name: Rick
Enter GPA for Rick: 2.6
Enter a student's name: Ilsa
Enter GPA for Ilsa: 3.4
Enter a student's name: Victor
Enter GPA for Victor: 2.3
Enter a student's name: Louis
Enter GPA for Louis: 1.9
Enter a student's name: Sam
Enter GPA for Sam: 3.8

Student Name   GPA
Ilsa           3.40
Louis          1.90
Rick           2.60
Sam            3.80
Victor         2.30
```

PROGRAM 8.4 *(continued)*

Shuffling and Choosing From an Array

Sometimes, instead of sorting the elements of an array, we want to mix them up; that is, shuffle them. A subprogram that shuffles an array A, whose lower bound is 1, is

```
SUB Shuffle (A())
    Upper = UBOUND(A)
    FOR J = 1 TO UBOUND(A)
        K = 1 + INT(Upper * RND)
        SWAP A(J), A(K)
    NEXT J
END SUB
```

When this subprogram returns to the calling program, the elements of array A are completely shuffled. Of course, if your problem involves a string array, you would have to rewrite the subprogram—substituting A$ for A.

Another operation frequently performed is randomly choosing elements from an array. Suppose the debating club has 10 members and wants to randomly choose a member to be president. The 10 members' names could be entered into a Member$ array. Then a random number between 1 and 10 could be generated and used as the subscript for Member$ to choose the president. This process is straightforward—but now suppose the club wants to randomly choose 3 members to send to a debate. Following the procedure we used to choose the president, we might plan to generate three random numbers between 1 and 10 and use these numbers as subscripts for Member$. That would work, but with the complication that we must make sure we don't choose the same number more than once. We can avoid that complication by using the following subprogram:

```
SUB Choose (Pool$(), NumPick, Pick$())
    K = 1
    NumPool = UBOUND(Pool$)
    NumRemaining = NumPool
    FOR J = 1 TO NumPool
        IF RND < NumPick / NumRemaining THEN
            Pick$(K) = Pool$(J)
            K = K + 1
            NumPick = NumPick - 1
        END IF
        NumRemaining = NumRemaining - 1
    NEXT J
END SUB
```

Pool$ is the array that contains the elements we are choosing from (which is Member$ in our example) and NumPick is the number we are choosing (which is 3 in our example). When this subprogram returns to the calling program, the Pick$ array will contain NumPick elements randomly chosen from Pool$—with no element chosen more than once. As a bonus, if the elements of Pool$ are in order, then the elements of Pick$ are also in order. Of course, if your problem involves a numeric array, you have to rewrite the subprogram—substituting Pool and Pick for Pool$ and Pick$.

In the main program, Choose is called using the following statement:

```
CALL Choose(Members$(), (NumChoose), DebateTeam$())
```

What's unusual about this statement is that NumChoose is enclosed in parentheses. Normally, we expect a subprogram or function to change the arguments we pass to them. But we don't want NumChoose to be changed; on return from Choose, we want to use it, for example, as the final value in a FOR...NEXT loop to print DebateTeam$. When we enclose NumChoose in parentheses, the value of

NumChoose is passed to the parameter NumPick—but the changes that subprogram Choose makes to NumPick are not reflected in NumChoose.

Syntax Summary

SWAP Statement

Form: `SWAP variable1, variable2`
Example: `SWAP Sales(7), Sales(21)`
Explanation: The values of the two variables are exchanged.

8.2 EXERCISES

1. Suppose P = 15 and Q = 28. What are the values of these variables after executing the following statement?

    ```
    SWAP P,Q
    ```

2. The bubble sort in Program 8.3 (pages 303–04) sorts in ascending order. How would you change it to sort in descending order?

★3. How would you change Program 8.4 (pages 305–06) to sort by GPA, with the highest GPA printed first?

★4. Write the statements to swap elements A(K) and A(K + 1), without using the SWAP statement. *Hint:* The following two LET statements don't work:

    ```
    A(K) = A(K + 1)
    A(K + 1) = A(K)
    ```

5. What output would Program 8.4 produce if the SWAP statement in line 38 were omitted?

8.3   SEARCHING ARRAYS

As you saw, arrays are often used to store data for later use. For example, in Program 8.2 (pages 291–94), the Cost array stored the cost of the various orders. In that program, it was easy to extract the data we needed from the array because, for example, Cost(3) is the cost of order 3. But often, it is not so easy to extract the data we need; we must search the array. (Although we will discuss only the searching of string arrays, numerical arrays can also be searched.)

EXAMPLE 5
SEQUENTIAL SEARCH

Problem Statement

Write a program to translate English words into Spanish. The English words and their Spanish translations should be stored in parallel arrays.

STEP 1   **Variable Names**

As always, the first step is to identify and name the variables. We will use the following.

Variable	Variable Name
Input Variable	
Word to be translated	`EngWord$`
Internal Variables	
The number of words that can be translated	`NumWords`
Array that holds English words	`English$`
Array that holds Spanish words	`Spanish$`
Subscript	`J`
Output Variable	
Spanish translation of EngWord$	`SpanWord$`

In this algorithm, we use parallel arrays: English$ (which contains English words) and Spanish$ (which contains Spanish words). We will initialize the arrays so that Spanish$(J) contains the Spanish translation of English$(J). In other words, if English$(1) is BLACK, then Spanish$(1) is NEGRO, the Spanish translation of BLACK.

STEP 2   **Algorithm**

The algorithm for this problem may be stated quite simply:

1. Fill English$ and Spanish$ with the vocabulary words.
2. Repeat steps 3, 4, and 5 until trailer data is entered.
3.   Accept EngWord$.
4.   Search English$ for EngWord$.
5.   If EngWord$ was found in English$, display the corresponding word from Spanish$; otherwise, display an error message.

At the heart of this algorithm is step 4, the search, which we will examine soon. Notice, however, that in step 5, we allow for the possibility that the search was unsuccessful. This provides for misspelled English words and words beyond the translator program's vocabulary.

To save space, Figure 8.7 shows the flowchart only for the SequentialSearch subprogram. This search method is called a **sequential search** because it examines all the elements in order, one after the other.

The logic of a sequential search is straightforward. For reasons that are explained when we examine the DO loop, in symbol 66, we set SpanWord$ equal to the null string. We next set J to 1. J is the subscript for the search of the English$ array; since we want to examine every element of English$, we start with the first one.

Then, in a pretest WHILE loop that is shown in symbols 70 through 76, we compare each element of English$ with EngWord$. If for some J, English$(J) does not equal EngWord$, we increment J. On the next pass through the loop, we examine the next element of English$. If English$(J) does equal EngWord$, the search was successful and J contains the value for which the condition English$(J) = EngWord$ is true. We say that J *points to* the element of English$ that equals EngWord$. But recall that we created the English$ and Spanish$ arrays so that Spanish$(J) is the translation of English$(J). We therefore set SpanWord$ equal to Spanish$(J).

Finally, we must consider how to leave the DO loop. Actually, it is easier to understand the conditions under which to stay in the loop. We should stay in the loop if either we have not found a translation or if some elements in English$ still

sequential search
A method of searching an array in which the elements of the array are examined in sequence (one after the other).

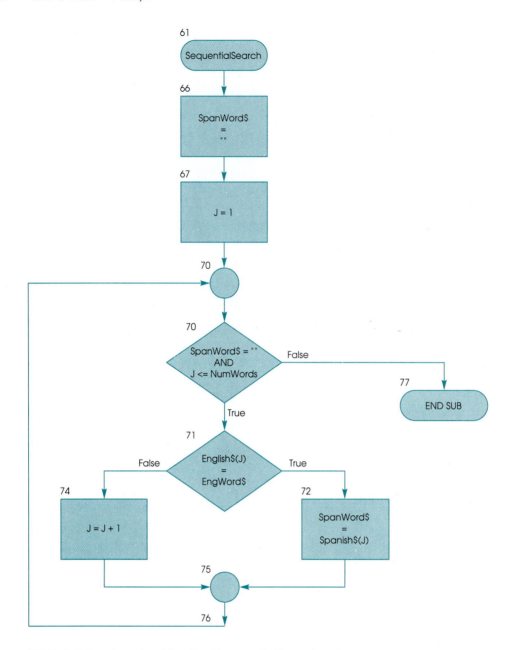

FIGURE 8.7 Flowchart for the SequentialSearch subprogram.

need examining. We know we have not found a translation if SpanWord$ equals the null string. We know some elements in English$ still need examining if J is less than or equal to NumWords. So we stay in the DO loop as long as the following condition is true.

```
SpanWord$ = "" AND J <= NumWords
```

STEP 3 Hand-Calculated Answer

We will run the program to verify that it correctly translates the words in its vocabulary, and that it prints an error message when asked to translate a word it doesn't know.

STEP 4   **QBasic Program**

Program 8.5 carries out the sequential search. The constant NumWords is defined in line 17. NumWords is used as the upper limit in the DIM statement in line 18, as the final value in the FOR statement in line 56, and in the condition in line 70. If we add more words to this program, all we have to do is add additional DATA statements for the new words and change the value of NumWords.

The DO statement in line 25 uses the null string as trailer data. When the user is finished with the program, he or she can exit from the program simply by pressing Enter when prompted for a word.

In the DO loop, the UCASE$ function is used to convert EngWord$ to upper case, and the SequentialSearch subprogram is called. When control returns from SequentialSearch, SpanWord$ is tested as though it were a flag. If it is not equal to the null string, it is printed as the translated word we are seeking; if it is equal to the null string, an error message is printed.

The SequentialSearch subprogram in lines 61 through 77 follows directly from the flowchart.

The Output screen shows that the words BLUE, YELLOW, and GREEN were translated correctly; however, when the user entered INDIGO, the error message printed.   ■

EXAMPLE 6 ▐▬▬▬▬▬▬▬▬▬▬▬▬▬▬▬▬▬▬▬▬▬▬▬▬▬

BINARY SEARCH

For small arrays, the sequential search is satisfactory. But for larger arrays that are arranged in numeric or alphabetical order, we can devise a much faster search method.

Problem Statement

Rewrite the previous example using a binary search to find EngWord$ in English$.

STEP 1   **Variable Names**

We can use the same variables as the previous example, but we must add two internal variables.

Variable	Variable Name
Internal Variables	
The subscript of the lowest element of English still in the search	Low
The subscript of the highest element of English still in the search	High

STEP 2   **Algorithm**

Imagine that you are looking for a name in a telephone book. If you sequentially searched for the name, you would start looking for it on page one and look at each page in turn until you found the name you were seeking. Of course, you would never do this; it is obviously too slow. What you would actually do is open the book about where you think the name might be. If you found that you over-shot the name, you would look closer to the front of the book; if you undershot the name, you would look closer to the back of the book. The reason this logic works is that the telephone book is arranged in alphabetical order. Similarly, a

```
1  |  '    *** TRANSLATING ENGLISH INTO SPANISH ***
2  |  '    Translate English words into Spanish by searching an array
3  |  '    of English words.
4  |
5  |  DECLARE SUB Initialize (English$(), Spanish$())
6  |  DECLARE SUB SequentialSearch (English$(), Spanish$(), EngWord$, SpanWord$)
7  |
8  |  '    Variables used
9  |
10 |  '    English$         English words array
11 |  '    EngWord$         Word to be translated
12 |  '    J                Subscript
13 |  '    NumWords         The number of words that can be translated
14 |  '    Spanish          Spanish words array
15 |  '    SpanWord$        Spanish word
16 |
17 |  CONST NumWords = 12
18 |  DIM English$(1 TO NumWords), Spanish$(1 TO NumWords)
19 |  CLS
20 |
21 |  CALL Initialize(English$(), Spanish$())
22 |
23 |  '    Translate words
24 |  INPUT "Enter word to be translated, Enter to end: ", EngWord$
25 |  DO UNTIL EngWord$ = ""
26 |      EngWord$ = UCASE$(EngWord$)
27 |      CALL SequentialSearch(English$(), Spanish$(), EngWord$, SpanWord$)
28 |      IF SpanWord$ <> "" THEN
29 |          PRINT EngWord$; " in Spanish is "; SpanWord$
30 |      ELSE
31 |          PRINT "Sorry, I cannot translate "; EngWord$
32 |      END IF
33 |      INPUT "Enter word to be translated, Enter to end: ", EngWord$
34 |  LOOP
35 |
36 |  '    Words used by Initialize
37 |  '    Format is English word, Spanish word
38 |  DATA BLACK, NEGRO
39 |  DATA BLUE, AZUL
40 |  DATA BROWN, PARDO
41 |  DATA GREEN, VERDE
42 |  DATA GREY, GRIS
43 |  DATA ORANGE, NARANJA
44 |  DATA PINK, ROSADO
45 |  DATA PURPLE, MORADO
46 |  DATA RED, ROJO
47 |  DATA TURQUOISE, TURQUESA
48 |  DATA WHITE, BLANCO
49 |  DATA YELLOW, AMARILLO
50 |  END
```

PROGRAM 8.5   A sequential search to translate English words into Spanish. *(continued on next page)*

binary search
A method of searching a sorted array in which half of the remaining array is eliminated from the search by each comparison.

binary search works only if the elements of the array being searched are arranged in alphabetical or numerical order.

Since the elements of English$ are in order, we can replace the sequential search in Program 8.5 with a binary search. To perform a binary search of English$ for GREEN, for example, you compare GREEN with a particular element. If

```
51 | SUB Initialize (English$(), Spanish$())
52 | '    Fill English$() and Spanish$() by reading DATA in main module
53 | '    No variables are received
54 | '    Returns English$(), and Spanish$()
55 |
56 |     FOR J = 1 TO NumWords
57 |         READ English$(J), Spanish$(J)
58 |     NEXT J
59 | END SUB
60 |
61 | SUB SequentialSearch (English$(), Spanish$(), EngWord$, SpanWord$)
62 | '    Perform a sequential of English$(), looking for EngWord$
63 | '    Receives English$(), Spanish$(), and EngWord$
64 | '    Returns SpanWord$
65 |
66 |     SpanWord$ = ""              'Null string serves as flag in main module
67 |     J = 1                       'Start with first word in array
68 | '    Stay in loop while match has not been found,
69 | '    and some words remain to be examined
70 |     DO WHILE SpanWord$ = "" AND J <= NumWords
71 |         IF English$(J) = EngWord$ THEN     'If word matches
72 |             SpanWord$ = Spanish$(J)        'we found translation
73 |         ELSE                               'otherwise
74 |             J = J + 1                      'look at next word
75 |         END IF
76 |     LOOP
77 | END SUB
```

```
Enter word to be translated, Enter to end: BLUE
BLUE in Spanish is AZUL
Enter word to be translated, Enter to end: INDIGO
Sorry, I cannot translate INDIGO
Enter word to be translated, Enter to end: YELLOW
YELLOW in Spanish is AMARILLO
Enter word to be translated, Enter to end: GREEN
GREEN in Spanish is VERDE
Enter word to be translated, Enter to end:
```

PROGRAM 8.5 *(continued)*

you overshoot—that is, if the element is greater than GREEN—you can eliminate all higher elements and look closer to the beginning of English$. If you undershoot—that is, if the element is less than GREEN—you can eliminate all lower elements and look closer to the end of English$.

Because each comparison eliminates part of the array, we use the variables Low and High to help us keep track of what part of the array is still in the search. Low is the subscript of the lowest element of English$ that is still in the search, and High is the subscript of the highest element still in the search. At the start, Low = 1 and High = NumWords, since the whole array must be searched. As in the sequential search, J is the subscript of the element compared to GREEN.

At each step, we compare GREEN with the element in the middle of the remaining array. You can calculate the subscript of the middle element of the remaining array using the equation

```
J = INT((Low + High) / 2)
```

If Low + High is an odd number, this equation makes J the lower of the two "middle" numbers.

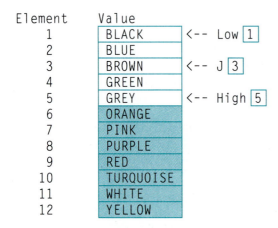

(a) First comparison.

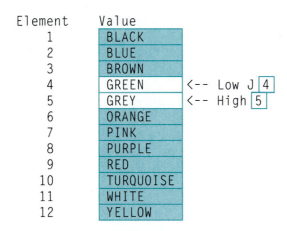

(b) Second comparison.

```
Element     Value
   1      | BLACK     |
   2      | BLUE      |
   3      | BROWN     |
   4      | GREEN     | <-- Low J 4
   5      | GREY      | <-- High 5
   6      | ORANGE    |
   7      | PINK      |
   8      | PURPLE    |
   9      | RED       |
  10      | TURQUOISE |
  11      | WHITE     |
  12      | YELLOW    |
```

(c) Third comparison.

FIGURE 8.8   Successful binary search for GREEN.

With Low = 1 and High = NumWords (which is 12), the equation makes J = 6. Figure 8.8 shows the pattern of elimination. In the first comparison, Figure 8.8(a), we see that GREEN is "less than" element J, ORANGE. Therefore, GREEN must be in the lower half of English$. With one comparison, we have eliminated half of English$!

Since we know that GREEN must be below J (if it is anywhere in the array), we move the upper limit, High, down to J – 1, or 5, as shown in Figure 8.8(b). With Low = 1 and High = 5, our equation gives the new J = 3. Comparing the third element of English$ (BROWN) to GREEN, we find that GREEN is "larger." Thus, GREEN must be between J + 1 and High.

To search this section of English$, we move the lower limit, Low, up to J + 1, or 4, as shown in Figure 8.8(c). With Low = 4 and High = 5, the equation gives J = 4. We compare GREEN to the fourth element of English$ and find a match. The search is over.

You may wonder what would happen if GREEN was not in the array English$. Suppose the fourth element of English$ were FUCHSIA instead of GREEN. When we got to the third comparison, we would have found GREEN "greater than" FUCHSIA. We then would have increased Low to J + 1, or 5. With High also at 5, the new J would be 5, and the new comparison—to GREY—would show GREEN "less than" GREY. But if we then decrease High to J – 1, or 4, High would be less than Low! This "crossing" of the upper and lower limits tells us that we have searched the complete array and that the word we seek is not in the array.

So the binary search ends either when we find a match (which means that the search was successful), or when the upper and lower limits cross (which means that the search was unsuccessful).

A flowchart that carries out this logic is shown in Figure 8.9. Notice that we stay in the DO loop while Low <= High and SpanWord$ = "". When either condition becomes false, we return to the main program. Just as we did in the sequential search, in the main program we will test SpanWord$ to determine if we returned because we found the word we were seeking or because the search was unsuccessful.

Perhaps you think that the binary search is quite complicated and *only* a little faster than the sequential search. Certainly, in the example we discussed, you're right. But if you were searching an array of 100, 1000, or 10,000 elements, a binary search is much faster. A sequential search of a 1000-element array requires an average of 500 comparisons; a binary search requires 10 or fewer comparisons!

Clearly, a binary search has advantages. However, it can be used *only* if your data are in order. If they are not, the binary search will likely report that the item you are seeking is not in the table—when the item actually is in the table, but not in its correct position. Also, when you search an array, you don't always look for an equality; sometimes, you look for a greater than or less than condition. Under those conditions, a binary search cannot be used and a sequential search must be performed.

STEP 3   Hand-Calculated Answer

As in the previous example, we must examine the output to verify that the program correctly translates the words in its vocabulary, and that it prints an error message when asked to translate a word it doesn't know.

STEP 4   QBasic Program

Program 8.6 shows a BinarySearch subprogram that could replace the Sequential-Search subprogram in Program 8.5 (pages 312–13). The only other change to Program 8.5 would be that line 27, which calls SequentialSearch, would be changed to call BinarySearch. This is a dramatic illustration of the advantages of using subprograms. To change the search method used in the program, we only had to replace the sequential search subprogram by the binary subprogram. The main program remains essentially the same; we simply call a different subprogram. ∎

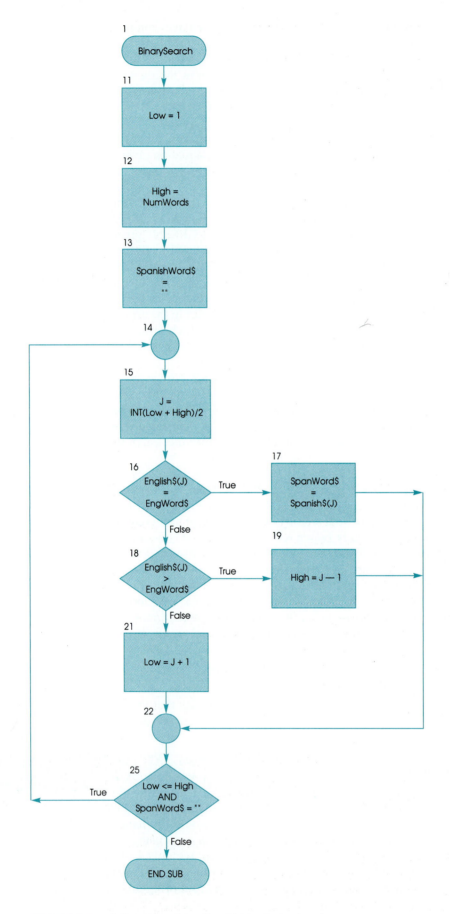

FIGURE 8.9   A flowchart for the BinarySearch subprogram.

```
 1  SUB BinarySearch (English$(), Spanish$(), EngWord$, SpanWord$)
 2  '    Perform a binary search of English$(), looking for EngWord$
 3  '    Receives English$(), Spanish$(), and EngWord$
 4  '    Returns SpanWord$
 5
 6  '    Local variables
 7
 8  '    Low                'Lowest element still in search
 9  '    High               'Highest element still in search
10
11       Low = 1                     'Initialize search
12       High = NumWords             'range
13       SpanWord$ = ""              'Null string serves as flag in main module
14       DO
15           J = INT((Low + High) / 2)          'Look at word in middle
16           IF English$(J) = EngWord$ THEN     'If it matches input word,
17               SpanWord$ = Spanish$(J)        'we found translation
18           ELSEIF English$(J) > EngWord$ THEN 'If it is higher than input,
19               High = J - 1                   'reduce upper limit
20           ELSE                               'If it is lower than input,
21               Low = J + 1                    'increase lower limit
22           END IF
23  '    Stay in loop while translation has not been found
24  '    and some words remain to be examined
25       LOOP WHILE SpanWord$ = "" AND Low <= High
26  END SUB
```

PROGRAM 8.6   A subprogram that performs a binary search to translate English words into Spanish.

8.3 EXERCISES

1. The words in English$ in Program 8.5 (pages 312–13) are in alphabetical order. Would the sequential search work properly if the words were not in alphabetical order?

2. Trace the binary search algorithm and show the values taken by Low, High, and J—using WHITE and ROSE as the search words.

★3. Since the words in English$ in Program 8.5 are in alphabetical order, we can improve the sequential search a little. If during the search we arrive at an element of English$ that is greater than EngWord$, the search ended unsuccessfully because EngWord$ cannot be any farther back in the English$ array. Modify the program to include this improvement.

8.4   TWO-DIMENSIONAL ARRAYS

Many real-life applications require arrays that have two subscripts. For example, a bowling team might want to keep track of each member's scores for each game that he or she bowls. If we let Scores be the array of scores, then Scores(3,2) could be the score of player number 3 for game number 2. Scores(1,4) could be the score of player number 1 in game number 4. Arrays that require two subscripts to point to a particular element are called **two-dimensional arrays** or **tables**. Arrays can have up to 255 dimensions, but arrays with more than three dimensions are not used very often.

Like one-dimensional arrays, two-dimensional arrays must be declared in a DIM statement. Up to now, we have used a simplified version of the DIM statement. The syntax of the complete DIM statement is

```
DIM variable ([lower1 TO] upper1 [,[lower2 TO] upper2] ...)
```

Notice that a comma is required to separate the two sets of dimensions. We refer to the elements of a two-dimensional array by row and column number, with the first subscript representing the row and the second representing the column. After a variable is dimensioned as a two-dimensional array, then whenever we use that variable, we must code two subscripts.

In our bowling applications, if the team has four members and we want to keep track of the scores for a five-game tournament, Scores is declared in the following DIM statement:

```
DIM Scores(1 TO 4, 1 TO 5)
```

In this DIM statement, the first subscript (which runs from 1 to 4) represents the players and the second subscript (which runs from 1 to 5) represents the games. The Scores array allocated by this DIM statement is represented by Figure 8.10(a),

two-dimensional array or table
An array that requires two subscripts to specify an element.

		Column		
	1	2	3	4	5

Row					
1	1, 1	1, 2	1, 3	1, 4	1, 5
2	2, 1	2, 2	2, 3	2, 4	2, 5
3	3, 1	3, 2	3, 3	3, 4	3, 5
4	4, 1	4, 2	4, 3	4, 4	4, 5

(a) The Scores array showing the subscripts used to point to each element.

		Game		
	1	2	3	4	5

Player					
1	1, 1 186	1, 2 174	1, 3 163	1, 4 191	1, 5 206
2	2, 1 158	2, 2 193	2, 3 168	2, 4 177	2, 5 181
3	3, 1 202	3, 2 226	3, 3 214	3, 4 258	3, 5 197
4	4, 1 136	4, 2 141	4, 3 157	4, 4 132	4, 5 154

(b) The elements of the Scores array, showing the players' scores.

FIGURE 8.10   The Scores array.

which also shows the subscripts used to point to each element. For example, the subscripts for the element in the first row and first column are 1, 1; the subscripts for the element in the third row and fourth column are 3, 4; and so on.

The DATA statements for the Scores array could be written as

```
DATA 186, 174, 163, 191, 206 : REM Scores for player 1
DATA 158, 193, 168, 177, 181 : REM Scores for player 2
DATA 202, 226, 214, 258, 197 : REM Scores for player 3
DATA 136, 141, 157, 132, 154 : REM Scores for player 4
```

The first line contains the first player's scores for all five games. The first number, 186, is the score for player 1 in game 1. The last number in the first line, 206, is the score for player 1 in game 5. Similarly, the first number in the last line, 136, is the score for player 4 in game 1; the last number in the last line, 154, is the score for player 4 in game 5.

We used FOR...NEXT loops to process one-dimensional arrays. Now we will use nested FOR...NEXT loops to process two-dimensional arrays. Thus, we can use the following nested FOR...NEXT loops to enter the previous data into the Scores array:

```
FOR Player = 1 TO 4
    FOR Game = 1 TO 5
        READ Scores(Player, Game)
    NEXT Game
NEXT Player
```

After executing these statements, the Scores array looks like Figure 8.10(b). As you can see, the score for the first player in the first game (186) is stored in element 1, 1; the score for the third player in the fifth game (197) is stored in element 3, 5; and so on.

EXAMPLE 7

THE BOWLING TOURNAMENT PROBLEM

We will illustrate two-dimensional arrays with a program that processes the Scores array.

Problem Statement

Write a program to calculate the average score of each player and the average score for each game in a bowling tournament.

STEP 1 Variable Names

We begin by identifying and naming the variables.

Variable	Variable Name
Input Variable	
Score array	Scores
Internal Variables	
Accumulator	TotalScore
Player subscript	Player
Game subscript	Game
Output Variable	
Average	Average

STEP 2 **Algorithm**

The algorithm we can use is

1. Read the scores into the Scores array.
2. Calculate and print the Average for each player.
3. Calculate and print the Average for each game.

Figure 8.11 shows a top-down chart for this problem. Each of the three tasks of reading the scores, calculating the player averages, and calculating the game averages is done in its own subprogram.

The pseudocode for this problem is the following.

Calculate Average Bowling Scores

```
Main Module
Call ReadScores
Call CalcPlayerAve
Call CalcGameAve
End Main Module

ReadScores
   FOR each player
      FOR each game
         READ Score
      NEXT game
   NEXT player
End ReadScores

CalcPlayerAve
   FOR each player
      Initialize TotalScore to 0
      FOR each game
         Accumulate Score into TotalScore
      NEXT game
      Calculate and print player average
   NEXT player
End CalcPlayerAve

CalcGameAve
   FOR each game
      Initialize TotalScore to 0
      FOR each player
         Accumulate Score into TotalScore
      NEXT player
      Calculate and print game average
   NEXT game
End CalcGameAve
End
```

STEP 3 **Hand-Calculated Answer**

Using the scores given in Figure 8.10(b), we can calculate the following averages.

Player	Average
1	184.0
2	175.4
3	219.4
4	144.0

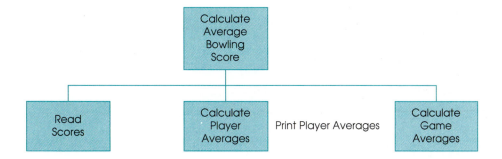

FIGURE 8.11   A top-down chart for the bowling tournament program.

Game	Average
1	170.5
2	183.5
3	175.5
4	189.5
5	184.5

STEP 4   **QBasic Program**

Program 8.7, which is based on this algorithm and pseudocode, consists of a main program and three subprograms. The main program simply calls the three subprograms. The first two subprograms, ReadScores and CalcPlayerAve, consist of a Game FOR...NEXT loop nested inside a Player FOR...NEXT loop. ReadScores, which starts at line 75, reads the data into Scores. CalcPlayerAve, which starts at line 51, has the same structure as ReadScores. The differences are that CalcPlayerAve has extra lines: Line 65 (which initializes the accumulator, TotalScore, to 0) and 69 and 70 (which calculate and print Average). Inside the inner loop, in line 67, the Scores array is accumulated one row at a time—instead of being read one row at a time, as it is in line 87 in ReadScores.

CalcGameAve, which starts at line 29, is entirely different. To calculate the average score for each game, we must process the Scores array by game, rather than by player. To do so, we must interchange the Player and Game loops, making the Game loop the outer loop and the Player loop the inner loop. Notice, however, that we do not interchange the subscripts on Scores. Player is still the first subscript, and Game is still the second subscript. ■

Using LBOUND and UBOUND With Two-Dimensional Arrays

LBOUND and UBOUND can be used with two-dimensional arrays, but you must specify which dimension of the array you want the bound for. The syntax for UBOUND is

```
UBOUND(array[,dimension])
```

The syntax for LBOUND is identical. For example,

```
UBOUND (Score, 1)
```

returns 4, the maximum subscript for the first dimension of Score, while

```
UBOUND (Score, 2)
```

returns 5, the maximum subscript for the second dimension of Score.

```
 1  |  '     *** AVERAGE BOWLING SCORES ***
 2  |  '     Calculate average bowling scores using two-dimensional arrays
 3  |
 4  |  DECLARE SUB ReadScores (Scores!())
 5  |  DECLARE SUB CalcPlayerAve (Scores!())
 6  |  DECLARE SUB CalcGameAve (Scores!())
 7  |
 8  |  '     Variable used
 9  |
10  |  '     Scores              Score array
11  |
12  |  CONST NumPlayers = 4
13  |  CONST NumGames = 5
14  |
15  |  DIM Scores(1 TO NumPlayers, 1 TO NumGames)
16  |  CLS
17  |  CALL ReadScores(Scores())
18  |  CALL CalcPlayerAve(Scores())
19  |  CALL CalcGameAve(Scores())
20  |
21  |  '   Data used by ReadScores
22  |  '   Format is Game 1, Game 2, Game 3, Game 4, Game 5
23  |  DATA 186,174,163,191,206           : REM Scores for player 1
24  |  DATA 158,193,168,177,181           : REM Scores for player 2
25  |  DATA 202,226,214,258,197           : REM Scores for player 3
26  |  DATA 136,141,157,132,154           : REM Scores for player 4
27  |  END
28  |
29  |  SUB CalcGameAve (Scores())
30  |  '     Calculate and print average for each game
31  |  '     Receives Scores()
32  |  '     No variables are returned
33  |
34  |  '     Local variables
35  |
36  |  '     Average           Average
37  |  '     Game              Game subscript
38  |  '     Player            Player subscript
39  |  '     TotalScore        Accumulator
40  |
41  |      GameFmt$ = "Average score for game # is ###.#"
42  |      FOR Game = 1 TO NumGames
43  |          TotalScore = 0
44  |          FOR Player = 1 TO NumPlayers
45  |              TotalScore = TotalScore + Scores(Player, Game)
46  |          NEXT Player
47  |          Average = TotalScore / NumPlayers
48  |          PRINT USING GameFmt$; Game; Average
49  |      NEXT Game
50  |  END SUB
```

PROGRAM 8.7   Using a two-dimensional array to calculate average bowling scores. *(continued on next page)*

```
51 | SUB CalcPlayerAve (Scores())
52 | '    Calculate and print average for each player
53 | '    Receives Scores()
54 | '    No variables are returned
55 |
56 | '    Local variables
57 |
58 | '    Average           Average
59 | '    Game              Game subscript
60 | '    Player            Player subscript
61 | '    TotalScore        Accumulator
62 |
63 |     PlayerFmt$ = "Average score for player # is ###.#"
64 |     FOR Player = 1 TO NumPlayers
65 |         TotalScore = 0
66 |         FOR Game = 1 TO NumGames
67 |             TotalScore = TotalScore + Scores(Player, Game)
68 |         NEXT Game
69 |         Average = TotalScore / NumGames
70 |         PRINT USING PlayerFmt$; Player; Average
71 |     NEXT Player
72 |     PRINT
73 | END SUB
74 |
75 | SUB ReadScores (Scores())
76 | '    Read scores
77 | '    No variables are received
78 | '    Returns Scores()
79 |
80 | '    Local variables
81 |
82 | '    Game              Game subscript
83 | '    Player            Player subscript
84 |
85 |     FOR Player = 1 TO NumPlayers
86 |         FOR Game = 1 TO NumGames
87 |             READ Scores(Player, Game)    'Data are in main module
88 |         NEXT Game
89 |     NEXT Player
90 | END SUB
```

```
Average score for player 1 is 184.0
Average score for player 2 is 175.4
Average score for player 3 is 219.4
Average score for player 4 is 144.0

Average score for game 1 is 170.5
Average score for game 2 is 183.5
Average score for game 3 is 175.5
Average score for game 4 is 189.5
Average score for game 5 is 184.5
```

PROGRAM 8.7 *(continued)*

Syntax Summary

> **DIM Statement**
>
> Form:
> ```
> DIM variable ([lower1 TO] upper1 [,[lower2 TO]↵
>     upper2] ...)
> ```
> Example: `DIM MostValuablePlayer$ (1950 TO 1990, 1 TO 2)`
> Explanation: Allocates area for array variables and specifies the minimum and maximum value that the subscripts may have. A two-dimensional array has two subscripts, and the subscripts are separated by commas.

8.4 EXERCISES

★1. In Figure 8.10 (page 318), what score did player 4 get in game 1? What score did player 1 get in game 4?

2. Assume that array A is dimensioned by the statement DIM A(5 TO 10, 20 TO 50). Write the statements to subtract 5 from every element of array A.

3. In Program 8.7, interchange lines 42 and 43. What value would be printed for the average score for the first game? What value would be printed for the average score for the second game?

4. Suppose in the bowling team problem, the data were given by game—rather than by player. In that case, the DATA statements are

```
DATA 186, 158, 202, 136 : REM Scores for first game
DATA 174, 193, 226, 141 : REM Scores for second game
DATA 163, 168, 214, 157 : REM Scores for third game
DATA 191, 177, 258, 132 : REM Scores for fourth game
DATA 206, 181, 197, 154 : REM Scores for fifth game
```

How would you modify Program 8.7 to accept the data in this form?

8.5 SIMULATION USING ARRAYS

Arrays can also be used in simulation programs, as the following example shows.

EXAMPLE 8

CHOCOLATE CHIP COOKIES

Every day, Chip Bloch bakes 1000 cookies, using 3000 chocolate chips. Although the average cookie obviously contains 3 chips (3000 chips ÷ 1000 cookies), Chip wants to know the percent of cookies that have 0 chips, 1 chip, 2 chips, and so on.

Problem Statement

Write a program that uses a Monte Carlo simulation to determine the distribution of chocolate chips in Chip Bloch's chocolate chip cookies.

STEP 1   **Variable Names**

We identify and name the following variables.

Variable	Variable Name
Internal Variables	
Array that counts the number of chips in each cookie	Cookie
Counter for chips	Chip
Number specifying a particular cookie	CookieNum
Output Variable	
Array used to count the number of cookies with 0, 1,...chips	Counter

STEP 2   **Algorithm**

The algorithm is simple:

1. Initialize Cookie and Counter arrays to 0.
2. Distribute 3000 chips randomly among 1000 cookies.
3. Count the number of cookies that contain 0, 1, 2, etc., chips.
4. Print the number of cookies that contain 0, 1, 2, etc., chips.

The top-down chart is shown in Figure 8.12. Each of the four tasks—initializing the arrays, distributing the chips, counting the cookies, and printing the results— is carried out in its own subprogram.

STEP 3   **Hand-Calculated Answer**

Like the Monte Carlo simulations in Chapter 7, the only way we can check this program is to use a breakpoint and step through the program—verifying that each step is logically and arithmetically correct.

STEP 4   **QBasic Program**

The algorithm is implemented in Program 8.8. The Cookie array represents the 1000 cookies—so in line 15, it is dimensioned with an upper limit of 1000. When the program is done, the value of Counter(J) will be the number of cookies with J chips. Since some cookies will have 0 chips, Counter is dimensioned with a lower limit of 0. Counter is dimensioned with a maximum subscript of 11 because experience shows that no cookies have four times the average number of chips.

When the program is done, the value of Cookie(J) will be the number of chips in cookie J. To reflect the fact that when we start the cookies contain zero

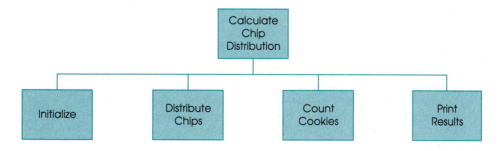

FIGURE 8.12   Top-down chart for calculating the distribution of chocolate chips in cookies.

```
 1  '    *** COOKIE PROGRAM ***
 2  '    Calculate chocolate chip distribution using a
 3  '    Monte Carlo simulation
 4
 5  DECLARE SUB Initialize (Cookie!(), Counter!())
 6  DECLARE SUB DistributeChips (Cookie!())
 7  DECLARE SUB CountCookies (Counter!(), Cookie!())
 8  DECLARE SUB PrintResults (Counter!())
 9
10  '    Variables used
11
12  '    Cookie          Array to represent the cookies
13  '    Counter         Array used to count the number of cookies
14  '                    with 0, 1, ...chips
15  DIM Cookie(1 TO 1000), Counter(0 TO 11)
16  CLS
17  RANDOMIZE TIMER                         'Random seed for RND
18  CALL Initialize(Cookie(), Counter())
19  CALL DistributeChips(Cookie())
20  CALL CountCookies(Counter(), Cookie())
21  CALL PrintResults(Counter())
22  END
23
24  SUB CountCookies (Counter(), Cookie())
25  '    Count the number of cookies that have 0, 1, 2, ... chips
26  '    Receives Cookie()
27  '    Returns Counter()
28
29  '    Local variable
30
31  '    CookieNum       Number specifying a particular cookie
32
33      FOR CookieNum = 1 TO 1000
34          IF Cookie(CookieNum) > 11 THEN  'If cookie has more than 11 chips
35              Cookie(CookieNum) = 11          'set chips to 11
36          END IF
37          Counter(Cookie(CookieNum)) = Counter(Cookie(CookieNum)) + 1
38      NEXT CookieNum
39  END SUB
40
41  SUB DistributeChips (Cookie())
42  '    Distribute the chips into the cookies
43  '    No variables are received
44  '    Returns Cookie()
45
```

PROGRAM 8.8   Using arrays to calculate the distribution of chocolate chips in cookies. *(continued on next page)*

chips, in Initialize we initialize the Cookie array to 0. Since the Counter array is used as a counter, it too is initialized to 0.

In DistributeChips, the FOR...NEXT loop simulates distributing 3000 chips in 1000 cookies. In line 52, a random number between 1 and 1000 is generated and assigned to CookieNum, where CookieNum is the number of the cookie that gets this chip. In line 53, the CookieNum element of Cookie is incremented to simulate adding a chip to that cookie. Line 53 functions like line 172 in Program 8.2 (pages 291–94). The program repeats this procedure for all 3000 chips.

```
46 |  '     Local variables
47 |
48 |  '     Chip                Counter for chips
49 |  '     CookieNum           Number specifying a particular cookie
50 |
51 |        FOR Chip = 1 TO 3000                    'For each chip, find out
52 |            CookieNum = 1 + INT(1000 * RND)     'which cookie it went into.
53 |            Cookie(CookieNum) = Cookie(CookieNum) + 1 'add it to cookie.
54 |        NEXT Chip
55 |  END SUB
56 |  SUB Initialize (Cookie(), Counter())
57 |  '     Initialize Cookie() and Counter()
58 |  '     Receives no variables
59 |  '     Returns Cookie() and Counter()
60 |
61 |        FOR J = 1 TO 1000
62 |            Cookie(J) = 0             'Initially, cookies contain no chips
63 |        NEXT J
64 |
65 |        FOR J = 0 TO 11               'Include zero element
66 |            Counter(J) = 0            'Initially, all counters are zero
67 |        NEXT J
68 |  END SUB
69 |
70 |  SUB PrintResults (Counter())
71 |  '     Print results
72 |  '     Receives Counter()
73 |  '     No variables are returned
74 |
75 |  PRINT "Chips    0    1    2    3    4    5    6    7    8    9    10   11+"
76 |        PRINT "Pct.  ";
77 |        FOR J = 0 TO 11
78 |            PRINT USING "##.# "; Counter(J) * 100 / 1000;
79 |         NEXT J
80 |  END SUB
```

```
Chips    0    1    2    3    4    5    6    7    8    9    10   11+
Pct.    5.2 14.4 22.0 23.9 15.2 11.7  4.5  1.8  0.8  0.4  0.1  0.0
```

PROGRAM 8.8 *(continued)*

In CountCookies, the FOR...NEXT loop counts the number of cookies that have 0, 1, 2,...chips. Line 37

```
Counter(Cookie(CookieNum)) = Counter(Cookie(CookieNum)) + 1
```

bears some study. The subscripted variable Cookie is used as a subscript for Counter, showing that a subscripted variable may be used as a subscript. But what does this complicated statement *mean*? Let's trace it. When CookieNum is 1, the statement is interpreted as

```
Counter(Cookie(1)) = Counter(Cookie(1)) + 1
```

Cookie(1) is the number of chips in the first cookie, but we don't know its value. Let's arbitrarily assume that the first cookie has 5 chips, so that Cookie(1) is 5. Then line 37 is interpreted as

```
Counter(5) = Counter(5) + 1
```

So the fifth element of Counter is incremented. Since the fifth element of Counter is supposed to contain the number of cookies with 5 chips, and since we just counted a cookie with 5 chips, the statement does what we want.

As mentioned earlier, the DIM statement for Counter specified an upper limit of 11 because we don't expect any cookies to have more than 11 chips. However, in a rare case, a cookie might have more than 11 chips. In that case, line 37 would cause a Subscript out of range error. To prevent that error, the IF statement in line 34 determines if a cookie has more than 11 chips. If any cookie does, line 35 sets the number of chips to 11. This means that in the output, the percent of cookies shown with 11 chips is actually the percent of cookies with 11 or more chips.

After all 1000 cookies are inspected, we are ready to print the results. This is done in PrintResults, which starts in line 70. Line 78 converts Counter(J) into a percent by dividing by 1000 (because there are 1000 cookies) and multiplying by 100 to convert the fraction into a percent. The results show that, as expected, no cookies had 11 or more chips. Only 5.2 percent of the cookies contain no chips. If you get a cookie with no chips, it just must be your unlucky day. ∎

8.5 EXERCISES

1. If we wanted to use 4000 chips instead of 3000, what changes must be made to Program 8.8? What changes must be made if we baked 500 cookies instead of 1000?

★2. Suppose CookieNum = 2 and Cookie(CookieNum) = 4. What does that mean?

3. Program 8.9 reads 12 monthly rainfalls, then calculates and prints the yearly total and each month's percentage of the total. After printing the heading, the program stopped, and QBasic displayed a Subscript out of range error message, with line 36 highlighted. Find and correct the error.

```
1  '    *** RAINFALL PERCENTAGES ***
2  '    Calculate percent of total rainfall in each month
3
4  DECLARE SUB ReadData (Rain!())
5  DECLARE SUB CalcPercent (Rain!(), Total!)
6  DECLARE FUNCTION CalcTotal! (Rain!())
7
8  '    Variables used
9
10 '    Rain         Monthly rainfall array
11 '    Total        Total rainfall for year
12
13 DIM Rain(1 TO 12)
14 CLS
15 CALL ReadData(Rain())
16 Total = CalcTotal(Rain())
17 PRINT USING "The total rainfall is ###.# inches"; Total
18 CALL CalcPercent(Rain(), Total)
```

PROGRAM 8.9 A program that incorrectly calculates rainfall percentages. *(continued on next page)*

```
19
20   '    Monthly rainfall data used by ReadData
21   DATA 2.3, 4.8, 3.3, 4.0, 5.2, 5.9, 5.3, 6.4, 4.7, 3.9, 2.1, 2.4
22   END
23
24   SUB CalcPercent (Rain(), Total)
25   '    Calculate monthly percentages
26   '    Receives Rain() and Total
27   '    No variables are returned
28
29   '    Local variable
30
31   '    Percent                       'Monthly percent of total rainfall
32
33        PRINT "Month    Rain    Percent"
34        Fmt$ = "   ##      ##.#      ##.#"
35        FOR K = 1 TO 12                            'For each month
36            Percent = 100 * Rain(J) / Total        'Calculate monthly percent
37            PRINT USING Fmt$; J; Rain(J); Percent  'Print monthly percent
38        NEXT K
39   END SUB
40
41   FUNCTION CalcTotal (Rain())
41   '    Sum the elements of Rain() to get Total
42   '    Receives Rain()
43   '    Returns Total in CalcTotal
44
45   '    Local variable
46
47   '    Total                        'Accumulator for rainfall
48
49        Total = 0                    'Initialize accumulator
50        FOR J = 1 TO 12              'For each month
51            Total = Total + Rain(J)  'Accumulate monthly rainfall
52        NEXT J
53        CalcTotal = Total            'Assign value to function
54   END FUNCTION
55
56   SUB ReadData (Rain())
57   '    Fill Rain() by reading data in main module
58   '    No variables are received
59   '    Returns Rain()
60
61        FOR J = 1 TO 12              'For each month
62            READ Rain(J)             'Read monthly rainfall (DATA in main)
63        NEXT J
64   END SUB
```

```
The total rainfall is   50.3 inches
Month     Rain     Percent
```

PROGRAM 8.9 *(continued)*

WHAT YOU HAVE LEARNED

In this chapter, you learned that:

- An array is a collection of storage locations that are accessed by the same variable name and that store the same kind of data—numeric or string. The individual parts of the array are called elements.
- The DIM statement is used to specify the highest and lowest values that the subscript can have.
- One subscript is used to reference the elements of a one-dimensional array, and two subscripts are used to reference the elements of a two-dimensional array.
- FOR...NEXT loops are used to process arrays: single loops for one-dimensional arrays, and nested loops for two-dimensional arrays.

- The bubble sort may be used to arrange the elements of an array in ascending or descending numerical or alphabetical order.
- The SWAP statement interchanges the values of two variables.
- To sort parallel arrays, SWAP the same elements of all the parallel arrays whenever you SWAP the elements of the array you are sorting.
- Arrays may be searched using a sequential search or a binary search. A binary search requires that an array first be sorted, but it is faster than a sequential search for large arrays.
- The UBOUND function returns the highest subscript that may be used with an array, and the LBOUND function returns the lowest subscript.

NEW QBASIC STATEMENTS

STATEMENT	EFFECT
DIM	
`DIM Sales(1980 TO 1994)`	Allocates 15 storage locations to the array Sales. The first storage location is referenced by the subscript 1980, the second by 1981, and the last by 1994.
SWAP	
`SWAP M, N`	Swaps the values of the variables M and N.

KEY TERMS

array	flag	subscript
binary search	one-dimensional array	table
bubble sort	parallel arrays	two-dimensional array
elements	sequential search	

REVIEW EXERCISES

SELF-CHECK

1. A binary search ends when either a match is found or _____.

2. Is the following DIM statement correct?

   `DIM A, B, C$`

3. True or false: The bubble sort may be used only to sort in ascending order.

4. Which statement is used to specify the highest and lowest subscripts that may be used with an array?

5. To specify a particular element of an array, you use a(n) _____.

6. If an array is not sorted, it must be searched using the _____ search.

7. In a LET statement, can subscripted variables be used on the left side only, on the right side only, or on either side of the equals sign?

8. What values do the UBOUND and LBOUND functions return?

9. For large arrays, is the sequential search faster or slower than the binary search?

10. Can the SWAP statement be used to swap numeric variables only, string variables only, or both numeric and string variables?

11. What two conditions must be satisfied if an array is to be searched using a binary search?

PROGRAMMING ASSIGNMENTS

Section 8.1

1. Write a program like Program 8.1 (pages 287–88), but have all scores greater than the average printed first, along with students' names—followed by scores less than or equal to the average, along with those students' names.

2. Write a program that accepts the number of different stocks an investor owns and then accepts the name, number of shares held, and price of each stock. Print a report that includes the input data and the value of each stock (number of shares multiplied by price) and the percent of total value contributed by each stock.

3. Write a program that allows a user to enter a number N and then N numbers—and then prints the numbers in reverse order.

4. Write a program that allows a user to enter a day number in the range 1 to 7 and prints the name of the day (day 1 is Sunday, day 2 is Monday, and so on). *Hint:* This program does not require an IF or SELECT CASE statement.

5. Write a program that can be used to score multiple-choice tests. The program should accept ten correct answers into a key array. The program should also accept a student's name and ten answers into an answer array. The key and answer arrays should be compared, and the student's grade calculated.

6. Solve Programming Assignment 6.11 once more—this time, using arrays to store the tour destinations and prices. Besides printing a bill for each client, print the daily totals of the number of clients who purchase each tour and the income from each tour. Also print the total number of tours sold and total income. Have the program display an attractive menu like the one in Figure 8.4(a).

7. Write a program that generates 1000 random integers in the range 1 to 10 and then prints the number of 1s generated, the number of 2s generated, and so on.

8. Write a program that reads some text and counts and prints the number of times each letter is used. To make the program interesting,

extend the text over several DATA statements and use a DATA statement containing the word XXX as trailer data. As an alternative, use the data in PA08-08.DAT. In either case, enter the text in all capital letters. (*Hint:* It is useful to set up an alphabet string, Alpha$, like the one used in Program 7.8. In addition, you should set up a counter array, Counter, with 26 elements—corresponding to the 26 letters. Examine the text, and whenever you find a letter in the text, add 1 to the corresponding element of Counter.)

9. Calculate the odds of getting each of the possible scores when two dice are tossed. Do not simulate tossing the dice; instead, use a nested FOR...NEXT loop to calculate the number of ways each of the scores can be obtained. You can calculate the odds of getting a particular score by dividing the number of ways that score can be obtained by 36 (the number of possible outcomes).

10. Write a program that allocates seats at a theater. The program should display a seating plan like the following:

```
*************************************************
*                GLOBE THEATRE                  *
*                                               *
*                                               *
* Orchestra    1  2  3  4  5  6  7  8  9  10 *
*             11 12 13 14 15 16 17 18 19 20 *
*                                               *
* Balcony      1  2  3  4  5  6  7  8  9  10 *
*             11 12 13 14 15 16 17 18 19 20 *
*             21 22 23 24 25 26 27 28 29 30 *
*************************************************
```

You should then ask which section and how many seats the customer wants. Customers may not request specific seats. Instead, the program should allocate seats sequentially, starting with the lowest numbered seat available in the desired section. As seats are allocated, the program should replace those seat numbers with Xs and then update the seating plan so that the screen always shows the current status of seats sold. (*Hint:* Use two string arrays—one for the orchestra seats and the other for the balcony seats—and initialize them with seat numbers. When a seat is sold, change the corresponding seat array element to X.)

Section 8.2

11. Write a program that finds and prints the median of a set of numbers. To find the median, the numbers must be sorted. If the number of numbers in the set is odd, the median is the

middle number; if the number of numbers is even, the median is the average of the two middle numbers.

12. Write a program that accepts a student's name and five test scores, then calculates the average score after dropping the lowest and highest test scores. (*Hint*: Sort the test scores.)

13. PA08-13.DAT contains the following data for each of the fifty states:

DATA Abbreviation, Area

Write a program that reads these data and prints a list in order by area, with the largest area first.

14. Unlike many computerized dating services, Chance Encounters, Inc., doesn't promise to match people according to their likes and dislikes—for example, chess players with chess players or hockey fans with hockey fans. Their only guarantee is that all dates will pair one woman and one man. To help them, read ten men's names into an array and ten women's names into a second array. Then shuffle each of the arrays and print ten pairs of names.

15. Sometimes parents have difficulty choosing names for a baby. It might be helpful to let the computer choose a name randomly. Write a program that allows a user to enter a number N and then N names. Have the program randomly select and print one of the names.

16. What's the Scoop ice cream parlor sells 12 different flavors of ice cream. Write a program that randomly selects three different flavors for a sundae.

Section 8.3

17. Solve Programming Assignment 5.22 again—but this time, use parallel arrays to hold both the names of the planets and the weight factors. When a user enters the name of a planet, search the planet array to find the position of the planet; then extract the weight factor from the corresponding element of the weight factor array.

18. Write a program like the one in Program 7.4—but this time, you pick the number and have the computer try to guess it using a binary search. Each time a guess is displayed, you must respond with an H if the guess is high, an L if it is low, and an E if it is equal to the number you picked.

19. PA08-19.DAT contains the following data for all 50 states:

DATA Ab, State Name

where Ab is a two-letter state abbreviation and State Name is the corresponding state name. The data are in order by abbreviation.
a) Write a program that accepts a two-letter state abbreviation and does a sequential search to find the state name.
b) Modify the program you wrote for part (a) to perform a binary search.

20. In one school, letter grades are assigned as follows.

Grade		
> = But <		Letter Grade
95	—	A
90	95	A–
87	90	B+
84	87	B
80	84	B–
77	80	C+
74	77	C
70	74	C–
67	70	D+
64	67	D
60	64	D–
0	60	F

Write a program that accepts a grade and prints the corresponding letter grade. (*Hint:* This problem shows that when you search an array, you don't always look for an equality. Set up a GradeBracket array containing the values 95, 90, 87, 84, . . . , 0 and the parallel array LetterGrade$ containing A, A–, B+, . . . , F. Next, perform a sequential search to find the first J that makes Grade >= GradeBracket(J). The letter grade is the corresponding element of LetterGrade$. Notice that because of the 0 in the twelfth element of GradeBracket, the search must always be successful.)

Section 8.4

21. Investors are planning to build a ski resort in Schussboom. They have three possible sites under study. Naturally, they are interested in the snowfall at these sites. They have collected data on the snowfall, in inches, for the three sites for each of the last five years. The data are as follows.

Site Number	Year Number				
	1	2	3	4	5
1	106	147	139	153	126
2	143	151	117	134	139
3	136	143	130	142	145

Write a program that calculates and prints the average snowfall over the past five years for each site. Also calculate and print the grand average snowfall for all three sites.

22. The Megaplex movie theater sells soda, candy, and popcorn. During one week, the sales were as follows.

Day	Soda	Candy	Popcorn
Sunday	234	112	93
Monday	187	94	98
Tuesday	170	101	43
Wednesday	194	92	71
Thursday	158	73	52
Friday	381	153	149
Saturday	423	189	172

Write a program that calculates and prints the total sales for each day; the total sales for the week for soda, candy, and popcorn (separately); and the total sales for the week for all items.

23. **a)** Write a program that assigns the following values to the two-dimensional array A:

1	2	3	4
5	6	7	8
9	10	11	12
13	14	15	16

(*Hint*: The following equation calculates these values.

```
Column + 4 * (Row - 1)
```

b) Write a program that assigns the rows of the two-dimensional array A of part (a) to the columns of the two-dimensional array B. B should have the following values:

1	5	9	13
2	6	10	14
3	7	11	15
4	8	12	16

24. The first six rows of a set of numbers known as Pascal's triangle are shown as follows:

```
          1
        1   1
      1   2   1
    1   3   3   1
  1   4   6   4   1
1   5   10   10   5   1
```

Notice that the first and last numbers in each row are 1s, that the *j*th row contains *j* numbers, and that each interior number is the sum of the two numbers above it. Write a program that prints the first 12 rows of the triangle. (*Hint*:

Create a two-dimensional array P and assign the value 1 to the elements that correspond to the exterior numbers. Then calculate the interior numbers.)

Section 8.5

25. Write a program that determines the expected sex distribution in four-children families. The program should simulate 500 four-children families and print the number of families with 0 boys and 4 girls, 1 boy and 3 girls, 2 boys and 2 girls, and so on. Assume that half the babies are boys and half are girls. (*Hint*: You do not need an array Families with 500 elements.)

26. Jack Cracker is collecting cards that come in a cereal box. There are five different cards, and you may assume that they are randomly distributed in the cereal boxes. Write a program that determines how many boxes on the average Jack must buy to get a complete set. (*Hint*: Set up an array Card$ with five elements and initialize the elements to "No". Generate a random integer between 1 and 5 to simulate getting a card and set the corresponding element of Card$ to "Yes". Jack has a complete set when all the elements of Card$ are "Yes".) To get a reliable average, simulate 50 trials.

27. Hard to believe (but mathematicians tell us it is true), but in a group of 23 people, the probability that two or more people have the same birthday is greater than 50 percent. (You might like to survey your class to test this assertion.) Write a program that accepts the size of a group and determines the probability that two people in it have the same birthday. Assume that all days are equally likely to be a birthday and ignore leap years. (*Hint*: Set up an array Day with 365 elements and initialize the elements to 0. Simulate birthdays by generating a random integer between 1 and 365 and set the corresponding element of Day to 1. When you generate an integer and find that the corresponding element of Day already contains a 1, you have found a match.) To get a reliable estimate, simulate 50 trials.

28. Write a program that simulates an epidemic. Start with N people and assume person number 1 has a cold. He sneezes on a randomly selected member of the group, which could even be himself. If the person he sneezes on is already sick, the epidemic stops spreading. If the person is not sick, that person catches the cold, and then it is his or her turn to sneeze on a randomly selected member of the group. This continues

until the epidemic stops spreading. Simulate 50 such epidemics and calculate the percentage of the group that catches cold.

ADDITIONAL PROGRAMMING ASSIGNMENTS

29. **a)** Write a program that accepts 10 numbers entered in numerical order and stores them in an array. Then allow the user to enter an eleventh number and store it in the array in its correct numerical position.
   b) Accept 10 numbers and store them as in part (a), but now let the eleventh number entered be the number that is deleted. Search the array to find that element and delete it. Move the elements with higher values to close the hole.

30. A number is a palindrome if it reads the same forward as backward. For example, 74347 is a palindrome. Write a program that accepts a number with up to 50 digits and determines whether it is a palindrome.

31. The following table gives the mileage between some American cities:

From	Atlanta	To Boston	Chicago
Atlanta	—	1068	730
Boston	1068	—	975
Chicago	730	975	—
Dallas	805	1819	936
Los Angeles	2197	3052	2095
New York	855	216	840

From	Dallas	To Los Angeles	New York
Atlanta	805	2197	855
Boston	1819	3052	216
Chicago	936	2095	840
Dallas	—	1403	1607
Los Angeles	1403	—	2915
New York	1607	2915	—

Write a program that accepts two cities' names and prints the mileage between them. The distances should be included in DATA statements. However, since the distance is the same in both directions (for example, the distance from Atlanta to Boston is the same as the distance from Boston to Atlanta), your program should contain only half the numbers in this table and should generate the other half. To solve this problem, you must search the array of city names for the starting city and then search the

same array of city names for the destination city. You should use one search subprogram.

32. Write a program that prints the words to "Old MacDonald Had a Farm." In case you forgot, MacDonald's farm had chicks, ducks, turkeys, pigs, cows, and horses; their sounds were cluck, quack, gobble, oink, moo, and neigh. Recall that each time a new animal is introduced, the sounds of the previous animals are repeated. If you exploit the repetitive nature of the song and use a nested FOR...NEXT loop, you will find that your program is less than 30 lines long. (*Hint:* Store the animal names in one array and their sounds in a second array.)

33. **a)** Write a program that converts an English message into Morse code. The Morse code is as follows.

A	· —	N	— ·
B	— · · ·	O	— — —
C	— · — ·	P	· — — ·
D	— · ·	Q	— — · —
E	·	R	· — ·
F	· · — ·	S	· · ·
G	— — ·	T	—
H	· · · ·	U	· · —
I	· ·	V	· · · —
J	· — — —	W	· — —
K	— · —	X	— · · —
L	· — · ·	Y	— · — —
M	— —	Z	— — · ·

You can use a period for a dot and a hyphen for a dash. In your output, separate the code for adjacent letters by a space.
   b) Write a program that converts Morse code into English. In your input, separate the code for adjacent letters by a space, and separate adjacent words by two spaces.

34. A prime number is an integer greater than 1 that is exactly divisible by only 1 and itself. For example, 2, 3, 5, and 7 are primes; however, 9, which is divisible by 3, is not a prime. One way of finding prime numbers is the Sieve of Eratosthenes. In terms of QBasic, it works like this: An array N is initialized so that N(J) = J for J from 2 to Max, where Max is the highest number you are interested in. Starting from 2, examine the elements of N. If the element is 0, nothing is done. If the element is not 0, then all the elements that are multiples of that element are set to 0. Continue in this way until you have examined all the elements up to and including the first element whose square is greater than or equal to Max. Those elements of N that are not 0 are prime. For example, the first element

examined is 2. It is not 0 (it was just initialized to 2), so elements 4, 6, 8, and so on are made 0. The next element examined is 3. It, too, is not 0, so elements 6, 9, 12, and so on are made 0. (We set element 6 to 0 twice, but that doesn't hurt anything.) We next examine element 4, but since it is 0, we do not do anything. Write a program to find the prime numbers less than 1000. (*Hint:* See Exercise 9 in Section 8.1 (pages 297–98).)

35. Allow a user to enter a number N and to input N numbers and store them in array A. Copy into a second array, B, only one of each of the numbers that occur in array A. For example, if A is 7, 3, 2, 5, 3, 9, 3, 5, then array B should contain 2, 3, 5, 7, 9.

36. The following data lists the world's longest rivers.

River	Length
Amazon	4,000
Amur	2,744
Chang	3,964
Congo	2,900
Huang	2,903
Lena	2,734
Nile	4,145
Ob-Irtysh	3,362

Write a program that reads these data and prints a list in order by length, with the longest river listed first.

37. Write a program that reads a tic-tac-toe board marked with Xs, Os, and spaces—and determines if a win occurs or not.

38. The Home Sweet Home Building Company offers houses at the following prices:

One bedroom	84,000
Two bedrooms	103,000
Three bedrooms	119,000

At extra cost, they also offer the following options:

Central air conditioning	3,400
Stone fireplace	2,700
Two-car garage	950
Finished basement	2,600
Deck	1,100
Pool	8,500

Write a program that displays a menu from which a customer may select a house and any options. The program should print a bill itemizing the cost of the house and the selected options—and the total cost of the house including options.

39. One state lottery selects 6 numbers from the numbers 1 through 48. Write a program that randomly selects the 6 numbers and then examines them to determine if they contain two (or more) consecutive numbers. For example, the set 4, 16, 23, 24, 38, 40 contains the pair 23-24. Simulate 100 such random selections to determine what percent of the lotteries contains a sequential pair.

40. Flip a coin 10 times and keep track of how many heads come up. Repeat the operation 500 times to get an accurate estimate of the number of times 0, 1, 2,…, 10 heads come up. (*Hint:* You will find a counter array like the one used in line 172 of Program 8.2 useful. And, like Program 8.8, this is one of those rare cases in which the zero element of the array is useful.)

BEYOND THE BASICS

41. Write a program that accepts an integer up to 1000 and finds its prime divisors.

42. Write a program that accepts an integer between 1 and 9999 and prints the number in words.

43. Write a program that accepts two dates in the twentieth century in the form month, day, year and that determines the number of days between the two dates. Use the program to determine how many days old you are.

44. Solve Programming Assignment 7.44 again— but this time, print the big numbers on the printer instead of on the screen.

45. Write a program that multiplies exactly two integers with up to 20 digits each to produce an answer that could have up to 40 digits.

46. Write a program that reads names and addresses and prints mailing labels three across, as shown here.

```
Mr. John Smith        Ms. Mary Jones       Mr. Harry Brown
146 Heights Road      13-21 7th Drive      34 Maple Avenue
Kansas City, KS 66122 New York, NY 11034   Dallas, TX 75268
```

Of course, you should not assume that the number of names to be printed is an exact multiple of three, so the last set you print may contain only one or two labels.

47. Write a program that plays the game of Concentration. This version of the game uses a deck of 40 cards that contains two 1s, two 2s, and so on—up to two 20s. Shuffle the deck and lay the cards face down in a table that contains 5 rows and 8 columns. Represent the cards by 40 asterisks. Two players take turns selecting a pair of cards by entering their row and column

numbers. Display the selected cards. If they match, give the player a point and keep the cards displayed. If the cards do not match, the player does not get a point, and the cards are replaced by asterisks. The game continues until all the cards are displayed; the player with the highest score wins. *Hint*: You can calculate a subscript based on the values the players enter for Row and Column using the formula

```
Subscript = Column + 8 * (Row - 1)
```

48. For large arrays, a sorting technique known as the Shell sort is many times faster than the bubble sort. Like the bubble sort, the Shell sort compares elements and swaps those that are in the wrong order. Unlike the bubble sort, which compares only adjacent elements, the Shell sort changes the distance between the elements that are compared. An example will make its operation clearer. Suppose we want to sort an array A, which contains 10 elements. Call the distance between the elements that are compared Gap. We start by making

```
Gap = 10 \ 2 = 5
```

and we compare A(1) and A(6), A(2) and A(7), and so on—finally comparing A(5) and A(10). If any pair of elements is in the wrong order, they are swapped. When all the pairs that are 5 elements apart are sorted, we calculate a new value for Gap, using the statement

```
Gap = Gap \ 2
```

and we sort the elements that are this distance apart. We continue this way as long as Gap is greater than or equal to 1. When the calculation of a new value of Gap gives a value less than 1, the whole array is sorted. Write a program that implements the Shell sort.

SEQUENTIAL FILES

LEARNING OBJECTIVES

After reading this chapter, you will be able to:

- Create, list, and update a sequential file.

- Use the QuickBASIC statements OPEN, WRITE #, CLOSE, INPUT #, TYPE, SHELL, PRINT #, PRINT # USING, and LINE INPUT #.

- Use the QBasic function EOF.

- Write programs that contain control breaks.

In previous chapters, we used READ and DATA statements to supply programs with "constant" data. For example, in Program 8.2 (pages 291–94), we used DATA statements for costs of the different orders at No Bum Steer; in Program 4.3 (pages 113–14), we used DATA statements for Bat-O's employees' names and pay rates. But often DATA statements are not suitable. For example, if Bat-O had thousands of employees, the number of DATA statements needed would make the program too big to fit in the computer's memory. Also, we sometimes need to use identical data in several different programs. We could copy the DATA statements from one program to another—but whenever data changed, we'd have to correct each statement separately in each program that used it, which is tedious and prone to errors.

To solve these problems, programs often use files instead of DATA statements as the source for their data. The files serve as central supply sources for any program that might need the data they contain. Furthermore, programs can modify the data stored in files, which makes files the ideal way to store relatively stable data (such as employee pay rates) that still must be changed occasionally.

Files can also be used to store the results of a program execution. For example, when a college calculates students' grade point averages, the results calculated at the end of one semester are used at the end of the next semester. Writing the results to a file provides this storage.

In this chapter, we will discuss how to create and read files. In addition, you will learn how to change the data in a file. Finally, you will learn what a control break is, and how to use control breaks to print subtotals throughout a report.

9.1 CREATING AND READING SEQUENTIAL FILES

In Chapter 1, we defined a file as a stored program. When you saved your programs, you were creating program files. In this chapter, you will learn how to create and use data files. Before you do so, however, you need to understand the parts of a data file.

File Organization

Let's begin with some definitions. A **field** is an item of data. A person's name, for example, would be stored in a field reserved for that information. Similarly, a social security number, a selling price, and a pay rate would each be stored in a field reserved for that item of data.

A **record** is a data structure that consists of one or more logically related fields. In Bat-O's payroll system, for example, a record might consist of three fields: one for the social security number, one for the employee's name, and one for the pay rate. Each record would contain data for one employee. Each record ends with two special characters: a carriage return (whose ASCII code is 13) and a line feed (whose ASCII code is 10). Figure 9.1 indicates how QBasic stores data records on a disk.

A data file is a collection of related records. In Bat-O's payroll system, the collection of all the employee records would be called the payroll file. Two different kinds of data files may be used with QBasic: sequential files (which are discussed in this chapter) and random-access files (which are discussed in the next chapter).

To use data from a file, you must be able to identify the record you want. You do so by singling out one of the fields to be the **key field**—or, more simply, the **key**. Then to refer to a particular record, you specify the key. Since you want the key to find only one record, the information in the key field must be different for each record. Thus for Bat-O, the social security number is a logical choice for the key field because no two employees can have the same social security number.

In a **sequential file**, the records are stored, read, and written in sequential order based on the value of the key. When a sequential file is read, the first record is read, then the second, then the third, and so on—until the last record is read. For our first problem, we will create a sequential file.

field
An item of data that is part of a record.

record
A data structure that consists of one or more logically related fields.

key (key field)
A field in a record used as the identifying field.

sequential file
A file in which records are stored, read, and processed in order—from the first record to the last.

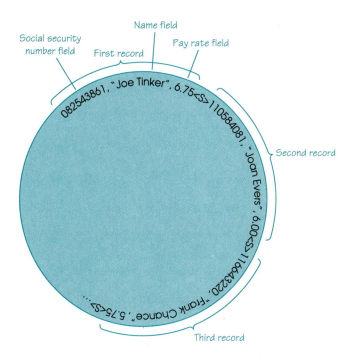

FIGURE 9.1   An indication of how a payroll file is stored on a diskette.
<S> represents the carriage return and line feed that are used to separate
records.

EXAMPLE 1

CREATING A SEQUENTIAL FILE

To give you a better idea of how a sequential file works, let's write a program to
create a file for Mr. Croesus, who wants to use a computer to keep track of his
stock holdings.

Problem Statement

Write a program that creates a sequential file to store stock holdings. Each record
will contain the stock name (which is the key field), the number of shares held,
and the price.

STEP 1   Variable Names

We start by identifying and choosing names for the variables. In this case we can
use the following.

Variable	Variable Name
Input and Output Variables	
Stock name	StockName$
Number held	NumHeld
Price	Price

We do not classify the variables as input or output because, as you will see
shortly, all of them are used for both input and output. We will name the file we
create STOCKS.SEQ.

STEP 2 **Algorithm**

The algorithm is quite simple:

1. Open STOCKS.SEQ for output.
2. Repeat steps 3 and 4 until the trailer data is read.
3.   Read StockName$, NumHeld, and Price.
4.   Write StockName$, NumHeld, and Price to STOCKS.SEQ.
5. Close STOCKS.SEQ.

STEP 3 **Hand-Calculated Answers**

There are no answers to calculate by hand, but we must verify that the file the program creates contains the correct data.

STEP 4 **QBasic Program**

Program 9.1, based on this algorithm, creates the stock file. The program simply reads the data and writes them to the disk in the form of a file. The information that this program uses to create the file is given in the DATA statements.

The OPEN Statement

Program 9.1 contains several new QBasic statements. Line 12 shows an OPEN statement

```
OPEN "STOCKS.SEQ" FOR OUTPUT AS #1
```

An OPEN statement *must* be executed for a file before any data may be read from or written to a file.

The syntax of the OPEN statement for sequential files is

```
OPEN "filename" FOR mode AS #filenumber
```

An OPEN statement associates a filename with a filenumber and specifies the processing mode. In line 12, filenumber is 1, filename is STOCKS.SEQ, and mode is OUTPUT.

Notice that the filename must be enclosed in quotation marks. The rules for data filenames are the same as the rules for program filenames. It's a good idea to use a filename extension like SEQ, since this helps you distinguish between sequential data files and program files (which, as you know, have the filename extension BAS) when you examine the names of the files on a disk.

You may use a string variable instead of a string to specify the filename. For example,

```
OPEN NewFile$ FOR OUTPUT AS #1
```

is legal, provided that NewFile$ was assigned a value before this OPEN statement is executed. If you don't want to use the default drive, you may include the device name as part of the filename; "B:STOCKS.SEQ" is an example of this.

In an OPEN statement for a sequential file, mode must be one of three choices: OUTPUT, INPUT, or APPEND. Their meanings are shown as follows:

OUTPUT   A file with the specified name will be created. The program will write data to the disk. *Warning*: If a file with that name already exists on the disk, the existing data will be *erased* and *replaced* by the new data.

```
 1 | '     *** CREATING THE STOCK FILE ***
 2 | '     Create the stock file by reading DATA statements and
 3 | '     writing to file
 4 |
 5 | '     Variables
 6 |
 7 | '     NumHeld        Number held
 8 | '     Price          Price
 9 | '     StockName$     Stock name
10 |
11 | CLS
12 | OPEN "STOCKS.SEQ" FOR OUTPUT AS #1
13 |
14 | '     Create file
15 | READ StockName$, NumHeld, Price
16 | DO UNTIL StockName$ = "EOD"
17 |     WRITE #1, StockName$, NumHeld, Price
18 |     READ StockName$, NumHeld, Price
19 | LOOP
20 | CLOSE #1
21 | PRINT "The Stock file has been created"
22 |
23 | '     Data to create file
24 | '     Format is Stock name, number held, price
25 | DATA Amer T&T, 300, 21.25
26 | DATA Bank Amer, 100, 19.25
27 | DATA DuPont, 200, 55
28 | DATA IBM, 125, 127
29 | DATA K Mart, 400, 33.25
30 | DATA Litton, 30, 66.25
31 | DATA Mobil, 100, 30
32 | DATA NCR, 350, 28.25
33 | DATA Pfizer, 250, 42.50
34 | DATA Texaco, 150, 36.125
35 | '     Trailer data follow
36 | DATA EOD, 0, 0
37 | END
```

```
The Stock file has been created
```

PROGRAM 9.1   Creating a sequential file.

INPUT   The file exists and will be read. If a file with the name
              you specify in the OPEN statement does not exist on
              your disk, QBasic displays an error message—File not
              found—and the program stops.

APPEND   The file exists and records will be added to the end of
              it. If a file that is opened with APPEND does not exist,
              QBasic creates it.

As noted previously, filenumber specifies the file number to be associated with the filename. You use the filename only in the OPEN statement. In all other statements that refer to that file, you must use the file number. Notice that a number sign, #, precedes the file number. Program 9.1 uses a filenumber of 1. In programs that use more than one file, every file must have a separate OPEN statement, and each file must have a different file number.

The OPEN statement also assigns a buffer to the file. A **buffer** is a part of the computer's memory where data are temporarily stored while they are being read from or written to a disk.

Before proceeding, make sure you understand how each of the following OPEN statements works.

buffer
A part of the computer's memory where data are temporarily stored while they are being read from or written to a disk.

ILLUSTRATIONS

OPEN Statement	Effect
`OPEN "PAYROLL.SEQ" FOR INPUT AS #1`	Opens the existing file PAYROLL.SEQ so it can be read and assigns file number 1 to it.
`OPEN "INVENTRY.SEQ" FOR APPEND AS #3`	Opens the file INVENTRY.SEQ and assigns file number 3 to it. If the file exists, new records will be added to the end of it. If the file does not exist, QBasic will create it.
`OPEN Filename$ FOR OUTPUT AS #2`	Opens and creates the file whose name was previously assigned to the variable Filename$ and assigns file number 2 to it.

The WRITE # Statement

A WRITE # statement, like the one in line 17,

```
WRITE #1, StockName$, NumHeld, Price
```

actually puts the data in a file. The syntax of the WRITE # statement is

```
WRITE #filenumber, expressionlist
```

where filenumber is the filenumber specified in a previous OPEN statement and expressionlist is a list of expressions whose values we want to write to the file, separated by commas. The WRITE # statement in line 17 of Program 9.1 writes StockName$, NumHeld, and Price to file number 1, which the OPEN statement specified is STOCKS.SEQ. Like the OPEN statement, the WRITE # statement uses the number sign before the file number.

As shown in Figure 9.1 (page 339), when the WRITE # writes the data to the disk, it automatically encloses strings in quotation marks, adds commas between fields, and adds a carriage return and line feed as a separator between records. It does this so that the data can later be read. Other examples of the WRITE # statement include the following statements.

ILLUSTRATIONS

WRITE # Statement	Effect
WRITE #1, Student$, Class$, Grade	Writes the values of the variables Student$, Class$, and Grade to the file that was previously opened as file number 1.
WRITE #3, SSNum$, Employee$, Pay	Writes the values of the variables SSNum$, Employee$, and Pay to the file that was previously opened as file number 3.

The CLOSE Statement

The purpose of the CLOSE statement in line 20

```
CLOSE #1
```

is to tell QBasic that you are finished with the file. The CLOSE statement ends the association between the filename and filenumber that was established with the OPEN statement. Executing a CLOSE statement for a file opened for OUTPUT also causes the final contents of the data buffer to be written to the file.

The syntax of the CLOSE statement is

```
CLOSE [#filenumber] [,#filenumber]...
```

As you can see, you may close several files with one CLOSE statement. For example,

```
CLOSE #1, #3
```

closes files associated with file numbers 1 and 3. If you type

```
CLOSE
```

and omit any filenumber, all open files are closed.

Finally, notice the sequence of operations in Program 9.1:

1. Open the file.
2. Process the file.
3. Close the file.

All of our file-processing programs will follow this sequence. In Program 9.1, the processing consists of writing to the file. In other programs, we might read the file. But no matter what the processing, we always open, process, and close.

Note that the OPEN statement is not placed inside the DO loop. If you place an OPEN statement inside the DO loop, the second time the OPEN statement is executed QBasic stops and displays the message: File already open.

Notice that while Program 9.1 is reading data from the DATA statements and writing to the file, it does not produce any output that is seen on the screen or printer. Thus, we include the PRINT statement in line 21 to tell the user that the program executed and created the file.

Even with the assurance of this message, you still have to verify that the data were correctly written to the file. To do so, you can use the File menu's Open command to retrieve the file. We previously used this command to retrieve only program files, but it can be used to retrieve sequential data files. Simply type the name of the file in the File Name text box and press the Enter key. ■

EXAMPLE 2 ■

READING A SEQUENTIAL FILE

While the Open command allows you to verify that the file was created correctly, Mr. Croesus wants a report showing the contents of the file.

Problem Statement

Write a program that reads the STOCKS.SEQ file and prints a report of its contents.

STEP 1 Variable Names

We can use the same variable names as in Program 9.1.

STEP 2 Algorithm

Our algorithm is as follows:

1. Open STOCKS.SEQ for input.
2. As long as records remain in the file, repeat steps 3 and 4.
3.   Read a record from the file.
4.   Print the record.
5. Close STOCKS.SEQ.

STEP 3 Hand-Calculated Answers

There are no hand-calculated answers for this problem, but we must confirm that the report contains the correct information.

STEP 4 QBasic Program

Program 9.2, which is based on our algorithm, reads and prints the STOCKS.SEQ file. Note that the OPEN and CLOSE statements in Program 9.2 perform the same functions as in Program 9.1 (page 341). However, this program uses 2 as the file number instead of 1, which was used in Program 9.1. The change was deliberate—to show that when you read a file, you don't have to use the same file number as was used when the file was created. (You don't even need to know what the original number was.) Also, although Program 9.2 uses the same variable names as when the file was created, that was not necessary, either. Any variable names—X$, Y, and Z, for example—would do, as long as we read string data into a string variable. The only name that must be the same is the filename, STOCKS.SEQ. And, of course, we must use file numbers and variable names consistently within this program.

The INPUT # Statement

The INPUT # statement in line 19

```
INPUT #2, StockName$, NumHeld, Price
```

```
1  |  '    *** READING AND PRINTING THE STOCK FILE ***
2  |  '    Read the stock file and print a report
3  |
4  |  '    Variables
5  |
6  |  '    Fmt$              Format string for PRINT USING
7  |  '    NumHeld           Number held
8  |  '    Price             Price
9  |  '    StockName$        Stock name
10 |
11 |  DECLARE SUB PrintHeadings (Fmt$)
12 |
13 |  CLS
14 |  OPEN "STOCKS.SEQ" FOR INPUT AS #2
15 |  CALL PrintHeadings(Fmt$)
16 |
17 |  '    Process file
18 |  DO WHILE NOT EOF(2)
19 |      INPUT #2, StockName$, NumHeld, Price
20 |      LPRINT USING Fmt$; StockName$; NumHeld; Price
21 |  LOOP
22 |  CLOSE #2
23 |  LPRINT "End of the Stock file"
24 |  END
25 |
26 |  SUB PrintHeadings (Fmt$)
27 |  '    Print headings
28 |  '    No variables are received
29 |  '    Fmt$ is returned
30 |
31 |      Fmt$ = "\          \    ####       ###.##"
32 |      LPRINT "     STOCK HOLDINGS"
33 |      LPRINT
34 |      LPRINT "Stock        Number      Closing"
35 |      LPRINT "Name          Held        Price"
36 |  END SUB
```

```
     STOCK HOLDINGS

Stock        Number     Closing
Name          Held       Price
Amer T&T      300       21.25
Bank Amer     100       19.25
DuPont        200       55.00
IBM           125      127.00
K Mart        400       33.25
Litton         30       66.25
Mobil         100       30.00
NCR           350       28.25
Pfizer        250       42.50
Texaco        150       36.13
End of the Stock file
```

PROGRAM 9.2   Reading a sequential file.

reads the data from the file and assigns the next three values in file number 2 (STOCKS.SEQ) to StockName$, NumHeld, and Price. The syntax of the INPUT # statement is

```
INPUT #filenumber, variablelist
```

Like the WRITE # statement, the INPUT # statement uses a # sign before filenumber. And as in the ordinary INPUT statement, the variables in variablelist are separated by commas—and you may list as many variables as you like. Before proceeding, be sure you understand how each of the following INPUT # statements works:

ILLUSTRATIONS

INPUT # Statement	Effect
`INPUT #1, Student$, Class$, Grade`	Reads the file that was previously opened as file number 1, and assigns the next three values from the disk to Student$, Class$, and Grade.
`INPUT #3, SSNum$, Employee$`	Reads the file that was previously opened as file number 3, and assigns the next two values from the disk to SSNum$ and Employee$.

The EOF Function

Line 18

```
DO WHILE NOT EOF(2)
```

in Program 9.2 uses the QBasic function EOF. The letters EOF stand for End Of File, and the EOF function indicates if all the data in the file (in this case, file number 2) was read. The EOF function returns a value of True when the last record in the file is read, and it returns a value of False if the last record was not read. Notice that the # symbol is not used before the file number in the parentheses following EOF.

Now we can understand how line 18 works. The statement causes the DO loop to keep executing while file 2 has not reached its end. When the INPUT # statement in line 19 reads the last record, the EOF(2) function returns a value of True. The next time EOF(2) is tested in line 18, the condition NOT EOF(2) is false, and the program exits from the DO loop.

You might be surprised that this program does not use a priming read. That is because when the INPUT # statement reads the last record, EOF is set to true. At that point, we still have to print the last record. If this program used a priming read and a second read at the end of the DO loop, the last record would not print.

The output produced by Program 9.2 agrees with the data listed in the DATA statements in Program 9.1, showing that both programs are correct. ■

Syntax Summary

OPEN Statement

Form: `OPEN "filename" FOR mode AS #filenumber`
Example: `OPEN "STUDENTS.SEQ" FOR INPUT AS #2`
Explanation: Opens a file so it may be processed and associates it with the
              file number filenumber. The mode must be one of the
              following: OUTPUT (which means the file will be created
              and written to), INPUT (which means the file exists and will
              be read), or APPEND (which means the file exists and new
              records will be added to the end of it).

WRITE # Statement

Form: `WRITE #filenumber, expressionlist`
Example: `WRITE #1, CardNum$, Price`
Explanation: Writes the values of the variables to the file that was
              previously opened with the file number of filenumber.

CLOSE Statement

Form: `CLOSE [#filenumber] [,#filenumber]...`
Example: `CLOSE #2`
Explanation: Closes the file associated with the file number of filenumber.
              If no filenumber is specified, all the open files are closed.

INPUT # Statement

Form: `INPUT #filenumber, variablelist`
Example: `INPUT #1, CaseNum$, Fee`
Explanation: Reads the file that was opened with the file number of
              filenumber and assigns values to the variables.

9.1 EXERCISES

1. Write an OPEN statement that could be used in a program that creates a file
    named EMPLOYEE.SEQ.

★2. The records in the EMPLOYEE.SEQ file contain five fields: employee num-
    ber, name, gender, year employed, and salary. Write a statement to put
    these data in the file.

3. Assume that the EMPLOYEE.SEQ file mentioned in Exercise 2 was created;
    write an OPEN statement that could be used in a program to print the con-
    tents of the file.

★4. Write a statement to read the data in the EMPLOYEE.SEQ file mentioned in
    Exercise 2.

5. Given the statement

    `OPEN "INVENTRY.DAT" FOR INPUT AS #1`

    write the DO WHILE statement that could be used to define a loop that exe-
    cutes until the end of INVENTRY.DAT is reached.

6. Modify Program 9.2 to print only those stocks whose current value—defined as the number of shares held times the price—is greater than $10,000.

UPDATING SEQUENTIAL FILES

We frequently have to update the data in sequential files. For example, Mr. Croesus wants to replace the old stock prices by new stock prices at the end of each week. This problem could be solved using three parallel arrays: one array each for the stock name, number held, and stock price. Instead, let's use this example to introduce QBasic's TYPE statement.

The TYPE Statement

The TYPE statement allows you to define a record. In this problem, we want to treat the stock's name, the number held, and the stock price together as a record. The TYPE statement

```
TYPE StockData
    Nam AS STRING * 9
    Held AS INTEGER
    Price AS SINGLE
END TYPE
```

defines this record. This TYPE statement defines a record whose name is StockData, which consists of three fields: Nam (Name is a reserved word and cannot be used as a variable name), Held, and Price.

Variable Types

In the TYPE statement, we must specify the characteristics of the fields. We want Nam to be a string—but contrary to our previous practice, we don't end its name with a $. Instead, as the example shows, we code AS STRING * 9. Although Nam is a string variable, it can't be the kind of string variable we have used so far. Those string variables had variable lengths. When the variable Animal$ contains Pig, its length is 3; when it contains Hippopotamus, its length is 12. A string variable used with TYPE statements must be a **fixed-length string variable**, which means that its length—the number of characters it contains—does not change. We indicate that Nam is a fixed-length string variable whose length is 9 by coding AS STRING * 9.

When you choose the length for a fixed-length string variable, you select a length that is large enough to hold the longest string that will be assigned to that variable. If you assign a string that is longer than the length you specified, QBasic discards the extra characters. If you assign a string that is shorter than the length you specified, QBasic left-justifies the string and fills the remaining characters with spaces. (This is similar to the way the PRINT USING statement prints strings.)

In the previous TYPE statement, AS INTEGER defines Held to be an **integer variable**. Variables that have values that are whole numbers between –32,768 and 32,767 can be defined as integer variables. Outside a TYPE statement, integer variables are defined by adding % to the end of their names, as in NumStudents%.

fixed-length string variable
A string variable whose length does not change.

integer variable
A variable that holds whole numbers in the range –32,768 to 32,767.

TABLE 9.1
QBasic's Numeric Types

Variable Type	Specified In a TYPE Statement	With a Suffix*	Minimum Value	Maximum Value
Integer	`INTEGER`	%	–32,768	32,767
Single-precision	`SINGLE`	!	±1.40129E–45	±3.402823E+38
Double-precision	`DOUBLE`	#	±4.94065E–324	±1.7976931E+308
Long-integer	`LONG`	&	–2,147,483,648	2,147,483,647

*By default, a variable name without a suffix is a single-precision variable.

The advantage of using integer variables is that they take less storage space and the computer is fastest when it does arithmetic on integer variables. But for our small programs, the time difference is insignificant—so in previous programs in this book, we did not use integer variables.

In the previous TYPE statement, AS SINGLE defines Price to be a **single-precision variable**. All the numeric variables used so far are single-precision variables, which is QBasic's default numeric variable type. Single-precision variables hold values with up to seven digits of accuracy.

In problems where round-off error is significant, **double-precision variables** may be used. Whereas single-precision variables store 7 digits, double-precision variables store 16. The trade-off for the greater accuracy is that double-precision variables take twice as much storage space as single-precision variables, and the computer performs arithmetic on them more slowly. In a TYPE statement, you indicate that a variable is a double-precision variable by coding AS DOUBLE. Outside a TYPE statement, double-precision variables are defined by adding # to the end of their names, as in NationalDebt#.

If a variable will have values that are whole numbers that are outside the range –32,768 to 32,767, but inside the range –2,147,483,648 to 2,147,483,647, you can use a **long-integer variable**. In a TYPE statement, you indicate that a variable is a long-integer variable by coding AS LONG. Outside a TYPE statement, long-integer variables are defined by adding & to the end of their names, as in Population&.

Table 9.1 summarizes this information about the variable types.

The syntax of the TYPE statement is

```
TYPE record-name
     field AS type
     field AS type
     .
     .
     .
     END TYPE
```

where record-name is the name of the record, field is the name of a field of this record, and type is SINGLE, INTEGER, LONG, DOUBLE, or STRING * n (n is the length of a fixed-length string variable). The names you select for the record and for the fields follow the usual QBasic rules for variable names, except that you do not use a name suffix to indicate a variable type. A TYPE statement must be executed before its record may be used in a program, so TYPE statements are usually

single-precision variable
A variable that holds values with up to seven digits of accuracy.

double-precision variable
A variable that holds values with up to 16 digits of accuracy.

long integer variable
A variable that holds whole numbers in the range –2,147,483,648 to 2,147,483,647.

placed near the beginning of the main program. Notice that the TYPE statement ends with END TYPE.

ILLUSTRATIONS

TYPE Statement	Effect
| ```
TYPE RiverData
    Nam AS STRING * 12
    Length AS SINGLE
END TYPE
``` | Defines a record named RiverData, which consists of Nam (a fixed-length string of length 12) and Length (a single-precision variable). |
| ```
TYPE BookRecord
    Title AS STRING * 40
    Author AS STRING * 30
    Pages AS INTEGER
    Cost AS SINGLE
END TYPE
``` | Defines a record named BookRecord, which consists of Title (a fixed-length string of length 40), Author (a fixed-length string of length 30), Pages (an integer), and Cost (a single-precision variable). |

Using Record Variables

The TYPE statement does not reserve any storage space for variables; it merely makes the record you defined available to your program. To actually use that record, you must define a variable to have that record's structure. Just as you use a DIM statement to tell QBasic that you want a variable to be an array, you also use a DIM statement to tell QBasic that you want a variable to have the structure defined in a TYPE statement. This is completely different from using the DIM statement to dimension arrays.

For example, in a program that contained the TYPE statement given in the previous Illustration that defines BookRecord, you could include the following statement:

```
DIM Book AS BookRecord
```

This makes Book not an ordinary variable, but a record variable that has the structure of BookRecord. Just as you need to be able to refer to individual elements of arrays, so do you need to be able to refer to the individual fields of Book. To refer to Title, you would code Book.Title. That is, you code the record variable name, Book (*not* BookRecord), followed by a period, followed by the field name. Similarly, to refer to the other fields of Book, you would code Book.Author, Book.Pages, and Book.Cost.

We are not quite finished: We can also define an array of records. Suppose we want the variable Rivers to be an array of 50 elements, each of which has the structure of the record RiverData, given in the preceding Illustration. We use a DIM statement as follows:

```
DIM Rivers(50) AS RiverData
```

Referring to the individual fields of Rivers is a little tricky. To print the Length of the 3rd river, for example, you would code

```
PRINT Rivers(3).Length
```

Notice that the subscript comes after the record variable name.

You can't use record variables in INPUT, READ, or PRINT statements. For example, the following statements are *wrong*:

```
INPUT Book
PRINT Rivers(5)
```

Instead, you must refer to the individual fields—such as Book.Title and Rivers(5).Nam. One place you can use record variables is in a LET statement. So, if Volume was defined to have the same structure as Book, the statement

```
Volume = Book
```

is legal. After this statement is executed, each field of Volume—Title, Author, Pages, and Cost—has the value of the corresponding field of Book. You can also use record variables in a SWAP statement.

EXAMPLE 3

UPDATING A SEQUENTIAL FILE

Problem Statement

Write a program that updates the Stocks file. The program should accept the new price of each stock, and calculate and print the percent change in price and the new value. The program should also print the total value of all the stocks.

STEP 1   **Variable Names**

This problem uses a record that consists of the stock name, the number held, and the price fields. So we will use the TYPE statement to define a record named StockData that contains the three fields Nam, Held, and Price. We will also define an array record variable named Stock to have the structure of StockData. The variable names are then as follows.

Variable	Variable Name
Input and Output Variables	
Stock name array	`Stock.Nam`
Number held array	`Stock.Held`
Price array	`Stock.Price`
Internal Variable	
Number of different stocks held	`NumStocks`
Output Variables	
Price last week	`OldPrice`
Percent change in price	`PercentChange`
Current value of a stock	`CurrentValue`
Total value of all stocks	`TotalValue`

STEP 2   **Algorithm**

We can use the following algorithm:

1. Print the headings.
2. Open STOCKS.SEQ for input.
3. Read STOCKS.SEQ into the Stock.Nam, Stock.Held, and Stock.Price arrays.
4. Close STOCKS.SEQ.
5. For each stock:
   Set OldPrice equal to Stock.Price.
   Enter new Stock.Price, calculate and print PercentChange and CurrentValue, and accumulate CurrentValue into TotalValue.

6. Print TotalValue.
7. Open STOCKS.SEQ for output.
8. Write the Stock.Nam, Stock.Held, and Stock.Price arrays to STOCKS.SEQ.
9. Close STOCKS.SEQ.

Notice that in one program, we will open a file for input, read it, close it, and then later open the same file for output and write to it.

In step 3 of the algorithm, we read the file into three arrays because we have to hold the whole file in memory. After updating the Price array, in step 8 we write the three arrays back to the file.

The top-down chart for this program is shown in Figure 9.2. The main module calls four subprograms to print the headings, read the file, update the prices, and rewrite the file.

STEP 3   Hand-Calculated Answers

The price of Amer T&T in the file is 21.25, and the new value is 23.50. This gives a percent change of 10.6 percent. The new value of the 300 shares Mr. Croesus owns is $7,050.

STEP 4   QBasic Program

The algorithm and top-down chart lead to Program 9.3. The main module uses CONST statements to define the format strings for the PRINT USING statements. This makes the format strings global, so they may be used in any subprogram. The main module defines the StockData record in lines 23 through 27, and the Stock array to have the structure of StockData in line 30. Notice that the record name StockData appears only in lines 23 and 30. Everywhere else in the program, the variable name Stock is used. The main module then calls on the four subprograms to do the rest of the work.

You might wonder why we bothered to define the record variable Stock. A glance at lines 33, 34, and 35 tells you why. The name of the stocks, the numbers held, and the prices are all contained in the record variable Stock. So we have to pass to the subprograms not the three fields, but only the record variable Stock. Notice that in the argument list, Stock is coded like an ordinary array, Stock().

Naturally, we have to let the subprograms know that the data they will receive has the structure of StockData. To do so, we code the parameter lists as

```
Stock() AS StockData
```

as you can see in lines 47, 62, and 74. When a parameter list contains a record variable, QBasic adds AS ANY to the DECLARE statements it generates; you can see this in lines 5, 6, and 7. The clause AS ANY means that type checking is not done.

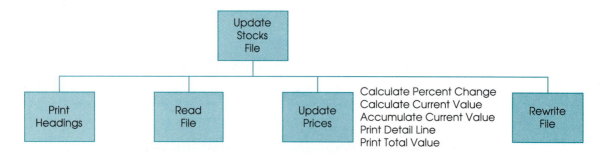

FIGURE 9.2   Top-down chart for a program that updates the Stocks file.

```
 1  '    *** STOCK SYSTEM - ENTERING NEW WEEKLY PRICES ***
 2  '    Update the stock file
 3
 4  DECLARE SUB PrintHeadings ()
 5  DECLARE SUB ReadFile (Stock() AS ANY, NumStocks!)
 6  DECLARE SUB UpdatePrices (Stock() AS ANY, NumStocks!)
 7  DECLARE SUB RewriteFile (Stock() AS ANY, NumStocks!)
 8
 9  '    Variables used
10
11  '    NumStocks        Number of different stocks held
12  '    Stock.Held       Number of stocks held array
13  '    Stock.Nam        Stock name array
14  '    Stock.Price      Stock price array
15
16  CLS
17
18  CONST Fmt1$ = "\          \    ####    ###.##       "
19  CONST Fmt2$ = "###.##       ###.#    ##,###.##"
20  CONST Fmt3$ = "TOTAL VALUE                         ###,###.##"
21
22  '    Define type for record
23  TYPE StockData
24      Nam AS STRING * 9
25      Held AS INTEGER
26      Price AS SINGLE
27  END TYPE
28
29  '    Define Stock as array of StockData type
30  DIM Stock(25) AS StockData
31
32  CALL PrintHeadings
33  CALL ReadFile(Stock(), NumStocks)
34  CALL UpdatePrices(Stock(), NumStocks)
35  CALL RewriteFile(Stock(), NumStocks)
36  END
37
38  SUB PrintHeadings
39  '    Print headings
40  '    No variables are received or returned
41
42      LPRINT "                    STOCK PERFORMANCE"
43      LPRINT
44      LPRINT "Stock        Number        Price        Percent    Current"
45      LPRINT "Name         Held  Last Week  This Week   Change     Value"
46  END SUB
47
48  SUB ReadFile (Stock() AS StockData, NumStocks)
48  '    Read stock file
49  '    No variables are received
50  '    Stock(), type StockData, and NumStocks returned
51
```

PROGRAM 9.3   Updating a sequential file. *(continued on next page)*

```
52 |        OPEN "STOCKS.SEQ" FOR INPUT AS #1
53 |        J = 0
54 |        DO WHILE NOT EOF(1)
55 |            J = J + 1
56 |            INPUT #1, Stock(J).Nam, Stock(J).Held, Stock(J).Price
57 |        LOOP
58 |        NumStocks = J
59 |        CLOSE #1
60 | END SUB
61 |
62 | SUB RewriteFile (Stock() AS StockData, NumStocks)
63 | '    Rewrite file
64 | '    Stock(), type StockData, and NumStocks received
65 | '    No variables returned
66 |
67 |        OPEN "STOCKS.SEQ" FOR OUTPUT AS #1
68 |        FOR J = 1 TO NumStocks
69 |            WRITE #1, Stock(J).Nam, Stock(J).Held, Stock(J).Price
70 |        NEXT J
71 |        CLOSE #1
72 | END SUB
73 |
74 | SUB UpdatePrices (Stock() AS StockData, NumStocks)
75 | '    Accept new closing prices and calculate percent changes
76 | '    Stock(), type StockData, and NumStocks received
77 | '    Updated Stock().Price returned
78 |
79 | '    Local variables
80 |
81 | '    CurrentValue     Current value of stock
82 | '    OldPrice         Price of stock last week
83 | '    PercentChange    Percent change of stock price
84 | '    TotalValue       Total value of all stocks
85 |
86 |        TotalValue = 0                    'Initialize accumulator
87 |        FOR J = 1 TO NumStocks            'Process all the stocks
88 |            OldPrice = Stock(J).Price
89 |            PRINT "Enter the closing price of "; Stock(J).Nam;
90 |            INPUT ": ", Stock(J).Price
91 |            PercentChange = (Stock(J).Price - OldPrice) * 100 / OldPrice
92 |            CurrentValue = Stock(J).Held * Stock(J).Price
93 |            TotalValue = TotalValue + CurrentValue
94 |            LPRINT USING Fmt1$; Stock(J).Nam; Stock(J).Held; OldPrice;
95 |            LPRINT USING Fmt2$; Stock(J).Price; PercentChange; CurrentValue
96 |        NEXT J
97 |        LPRINT USING Fmt3$; TotalValue
98 | END SUB
```

PROGRAM 9.3 *(continued)*

```
Enter the closing price of Amer T&T : 23.50
Enter the closing price of Bank Amer: 19.00
Enter the closing price of DuPont   : 56.875
Enter the closing price of IBM      : 129.25
Enter the closing price of K Mart   : 33.75
Enter the closing price of Litton   : 64.375
Enter the closing price of Mobil    : 29.25
Enter the closing price of NCR      : 29.50
Enter the closing price of Pfizer   : 41.00
Enter the closing price of Texaco   : 36.50
```

```
                       STOCK PERFORMANCE

Stock        Number         Price           Percent    Current
Name         Held     Last Week  This Week   Change      Value
Amer T&T      300       21.25      23.50       10.6     7,050.00
Bank Amer     100       19.25      19.00       -1.3     1,900.00
DuPont        200       55.00      56.88        3.4    11,375.00
IBM           125      127.00     129.25        1.8    16,156.25
K Mart        400       33.25      33.75        1.5    13,500.00
Litton         30       66.25      64.38       -2.8     1,931.25
Mobil         100       30.00      29.25       -2.5     2,925.00
NCR           350       28.25      29.50        4.4    10,325.00
Pfizer        250       42.50      41.00       -3.5    10,250.00
Texaco        150       36.13      36.50        1.0     5,475.00
TOTAL VALUE                                            80,887.50
```

PROGRAM 9.3 (continued)

The ReadFile subprogram opens the STOCKS.SEQ file for input, and reads it into the elements of the Stock array in a DO loop. When the loop is finished, the counter J is equal to the number of stocks—so in line 58, NumStocks is set equal to J. The STOCKS.SEQ file is then closed.

The UpdatePrices subprogram uses a FOR...NEXT loop to accept a new price for each stock from the user, and to calculate the percent change in the price. The results are printed in lines 94 and 95. Logically, only one LPRINT USING statement is needed—but with so many variables to be printed, that statement would be much longer than 80 characters. So the printing is done by two statements. By ending line 94 with a semicolon, we ensure that the two LPRINT USING statements produce just one line of output. Of course, the two format strings—Fmt1$ and Fmt2$—must be designed to work together (see lines 18 and 19).

Finally, the RewriteFile subprogram opens STOCKS.SEQ for output and rewrites the file using a FOR...NEXT loop. Notice that a file named STOCKS.SEQ is on the disk before Program 9.3 runs, and a file with the same name is on the disk after the program runs, *but these are two different files.* When STOCKS.SEQ is opened for OUTPUT in line 67, the original STOCKS.SEQ is erased and the new STOCKS.SEQ takes its place. Using the same name for the file is convenient, since STOCKS.SEQ will be the input file when Mr. Croesus figures stock price changes next week.

The report shows that the percent change in the price and the current value of the Amer T&T stock agrees with the hand-calculated answers. By adding all the current values, you can verify that the total value of all the stocks is correct. ■

The SHELL Statement

Every time you run Program 9.3, you change STOCKS.SEQ. When you are debugging the program, this can present problems. For example, if the OPEN statement in line 67 executes, but then because of some error the FOR…NEXT loop in lines 68 through 70 does not execute, the STOCKS.SEQ file will be empty. To continue your debugging of Program 9.3, you will have to rerun Program 9.1 (page 341) to recreate STOCKS.SEQ.

You will not have to rerun Program 9.1 if you have a backup file for STOCKS.SEQ. A **backup file** is a copy of a file that can be used to recreate the original. After STOCKS.SEQ is created, you can use the DOS command COPY to create a backup of the file; for example,

backup file
A copy of a file that can be used to recreate the original.

```
COPY STOCKS.SEQ STOCKS.BAK
```

You now have two versions of the stocks file: the original (named STOCKS.SEQ) and the backup (named STOCKS.BAK). After Program 9.3 runs and changes STOCKS.SEQ, you can execute the command

```
COPY STOCKS.BAK STOCKS.SEQ
```

to create a fresh copy of STOCKS.SEQ that can be used by Program 9.3. Since STOCKS.BAK was not changed, you can copy it as many times as you like.

You don't even have to exit from QBasic to execute the COPY command. Instead, you can use the QBasic statement SHELL to execute DOS commands from within QBasic.

The syntax of the SHELL command is

```
SHELL "DOS command"
```

SHELL temporarily exits from QBasic, executes the specified command, and then returns to QBasic. For example, to make a backup copy of STOCKS.SEQ, in the Immediate window you could execute the statement

```
SHELL "COPY STOCKS.SEQ STOCKS.BAK"
```

After STOCKS.SEQ is altered by Program 9.3, you can recreate a fresh copy by executing the command

```
SHELL "COPY STOCKS.BAK STOCKS.SEQ"
```

Since SHELL is an ordinary QBasic statement, it could also be included in Program 9.3. If this last statement were included at line 51, for example, every time Program 9.3 were executed, a fresh copy of STOCKS.SEQ would be created.

The PRINT # and PRINT # USING Statements

The PRINT # and PRINT # USING statements can be used to have a program print more than one report, even though only one printer is connected to the computer.

The syntaxes of the PRINT # and PRINT # USING statements are

```
PRINT #filenumber, expressionlist
```

and

```
PRINT #filenumber, USING formatstring; expressionlist
```

The output produced by the PRINT # and PRINT # USING statements is exactly the same as the output produced by the PRINT and PRINT USING statements, except that they write to a file instead of the screen. The WRITE # also writes data to a file, but the WRITE # separates the data with commas and encloses strings in quotation marks, so that the data may be later read by an INPUT # statement.

To see how the PRINT # and PRINT # USING statements can allow you to print more than one report—even though only one printer is connected to the computer—consider the following problem. A program is processing student records, and you want to print two reports—the first a list of students who made the Dean's List, and the second a list of students on probation. The Dean's List could be printed using the LPRINT and LPRINT USING statements we have used all along. The probation report could be printed to a file. You would first open the file for output:

```
OPEN "PROBTION.RPT" FOR OUTPUT AS #3
```

Every time you want to print a line to the probation report, you would use a statement like

```
PRINT #3, USING ProbationFmt$, Student$, Address$, GPA
```

or perhaps

```
PRINT #3, Student$, Address$, GPA
```

To print a blank line on the report, use the statement

```
PRINT #3,
```

The comma with nothing following it looks strange, but is correct. When the report is finished, close the file. At this point, the file could be imported into a word processing program, then edited and printed. Alternatively, staying in QBasic, the file could be opened for input:

```
OPEN "PROBTION.RPT" FOR INPUT AS #3
```

Then the file may be read and printed using a DO loop

```
DO WHILE NOT EOF(3)
    LINE INPUT #3, ProbationLine$
    LPRINT ProbationLine$
LOOP
```

The LINE INPUT # reads the lines from the disk file. The syntax of the LINE INPUT # statement is

```
LINE INPUT # filenumber, string-variable
```

Like the LINE INPUT statement, the LINE INPUT # statement ignores commas and quotation marks and reads a whole line. Thus, lines in the probation report may contain any characters you like, and the LINE INPUT # statement will read them. After the LINE INPUT # statement reads a line into the variable Probation-Line$, the LPRINT statement prints that line. This reading and writing process continues until PROBTION.RPT reaches its end and the DO loop also ends.

Syntax Summary

TYPE Statement

Form:
```
TYPE record-name
    field AS type
    field AS type
    .
    .
    .
END TYPE
```

(continued)

Example:
```
TYPE PatientData
     Last AS STRING * 20
     First AS STRING * 12
     Age AS INTEGER
     BloodPressure AS SINGLE
END TYPE
```

Explanation: Defines a record consisting of one or more fields.

SHELL Statement

Form: `SHELL "DOS Command"`

Example: `SHELL "COPY STUDENTS.BAK STUDENTS.SEQ"`

Explanation: Exits to DOS, executes the given command, and then returns to QBasic.

PRINT # Statement

Form: `PRINT #filenumber, expressionlist`

Example: `PRINT #2, Film$, Director$, Receipts`

Explanation: Writes the values of the expressions to the file previously opened with the file number specified as filenumber.

PRINT # USING Statement

Form:
```
PRINT #filenumber, USING formatstring; ↵
     expressionlist
```

Example:
```
PRINT #2, USING "\         \ $##.##"; Flower$, ↵
     Price
```

Explanation: Writes the values of the expressions to the file previously opened with the file number specified as filenumber, using the format specified in formatstring.

LINE INPUT # Statement

Form: `LINE INPUT #filenumber, string-variable`

Example: `LINE INPUT #1, WholeLine$`

Explanation: Reads a whole line from the file that was opened with the file number specified as filenumber and assigns its value to string-variable.

9.2 EXERCISES

★1. Write the statement that could be used to print the variables Author$, Title$, and Sales to SALES.RPT, which was opened as file number 2, using the format string named ReportLineFmt$.

2. Write the statements that could be used to read the lines in SALES.RPT referred to in Exercise 1, and print them on the printer. Assume that the file was opened as file number 1.

3. ★a) Write a TYPE statement to define a record named CityData that contains the name (a 20-character string), the area (a single-precision number), and the population (a long-integer variable).

   b) Write a statement to assign to a variable City the structure of CityData.

   ★c) Write a PRINT statement to print the name field of City.

d) Write a statement to define a variable Cities, which is an array of 50 elements that has the structure of CityData.

e) Write an INPUT statement to accept data for the population of the 24th element of Cities.

4. Write the statement that could be used to execute the DOS DIR command from within QBasic.

9.3 PRINTING REPORTS WITH SUBTOTALS

You saw how to write programs that print final totals. But businesses frequently require reports that print subtotals as well as final totals. Next, we will study how to write programs that print subtotals and final totals.

EXAMPLE 4

A SALES PROBLEM WITH SUBTOTALS

Problem Statement

A department store wants to keep track of its sales by department number. The management of the store wants a QBasic program that prints a report showing every sale and the total of all the sales. In addition, the program must print the subtotal of sales for each department. Allow for the possibility that the report may be longer than one page.

STEP 1   Variable Names

As always, we begin by identifying and naming the variables we will use.

Variable	Variable Name
Input Variables	
Employee's name	`Employee$`
Department number	`DeptNum`
Sales	`Sales`
Internal Variables	
Previous department number	`PrevDeptNum`
Line counter	`LineCntr`
Number of lines printed on a page	`PageSize`
Output Variables	
Total sales for a department	`DeptTotal`
Total sales for all departments	`FinalTotal`
Page number	`PageNum`

STEP 2   Algorithm

Assume that the program has to process the following data.

Employee Name	Department Number	Sales
Carol High	46	500
Reynolds English	46	234
Haideh Handjany	46	151
Stanley Thompson	46	77
Fabio Valdez	49	150
Maurice Butero	57	218
Yin Chen	57	600
Robert Amato	57	52
Mary Hannan	57	225
Michael Bergin	57	43

What is particularly significant about the data is that the number of sales for each department is variable. Notice that department 46 has four sales, department 49 has only one sale, and department 57 has five sales. How can a program know when it has processed all the sales for department 46 and is therefore ready to print the subtotal for that department? There is nothing special about the fourth record for department 46 to tell the program that it is the last record for that department. However, if the sales for each department are grouped together (as they are in our example), then a change in the department number means that the program must have finished reading the data for the previous department and that it should print the subtotal of its sales.

So we can use the following strategy: Each time the program reads a record, it compares that department number to the department number of the previous record. When it detects a change in department number, it knows that it should print the subtotal for the previous department. The change in department number is called a **control break**.

control break
A change in the value of an identifying variable, which means that some special processing—such as printing subtotals—should be performed.

Now that we understand what the program must do, we can use the following algorithm:

1. Set DeptTotal and FinalTotal to 0 and PageNum to 1.
2. Print headings.
3. Open the file for input.
4. While the file is not at its end, perform steps 5 through 9.
5.   Read a record.
6.   If DeptNum has changed, print the DeptTotal for the previous department.
7.   If the page is full, advance to a new page and print headings.
8.   Accumulate Sales into DeptTotal.
9.   Print Employee$, DeptNum, and Sales.
10. Print DeptTotal for the last department.
11. Print FinalTotal.

Let's look at steps 6 and 10 more closely. To perform step 6, the program must compare the DeptNum in the record it just read with the previous Dept-Num. Therefore, we will save the previous DeptNum in a variable named Prev-DeptNum.

You might also wonder why we need step 10 to print DeptTotal for the last department. Students often assume that this subtotal is already printed. But the program prints DeptTotal when it detects a change in DeptNum. When the program is working on the last department, it will reach the end of file, and Dept-Num will not change. Therefore, we must print the DeptTotal for the last department in step 10.

Figure 9.3 shows the top-down chart for this program. The upper-right corner of the Print Heading and Control Break subprograms are shaded to indicate that those subprograms are called from more than one place in the program. The main module calls Print Heading to print the headings on the first page. It calls

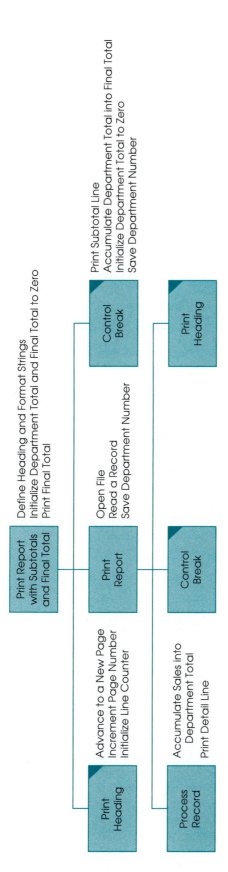

Control Break to print the DeptTotal for the last department. It calls Print Report to print the rest of the report.

Print Report calls Process Record to print the detail lines and to accumulate Sales into DeptTotal. It calls Control Break when it detects a change in DeptNum. It calls Print Heading when it determines that the current page is full.

The pseudocode for this program is as follows.

Print Report with Subtotals and a Final Total

```
Main Module
Define heading and format strings and PageSize
Set DeptTotal and FinalTotal to 0, and PageNum to 1
Call PrintHeading
Call PrintReport
Call ControlBreak
Print final total
End Main Module

PrintHeading
    Except for the first page, advance to a new page
    Print headings
    Set LineCntr to 4
    Increment PageNum
End PrintHeading

ControlBreak
    Print subtotal line
    Accumulate DeptTotal into FinalTotal
    Set DeptTotal to 0
    Save DeptNum in PrevDeptNum
    Increment LineCntr
End ControlBreak

ProcessRecords
    Accumulate Sales into DeptTotal
    Print detail line
    Increment LineCntr
End ProcessRecords
End
```

Instead of pseudocode for the PrintReport subprogram, Figure 9.4 shows a flowchart. As we said previously, the program prints DeptTotal when it detects that DeptNum is different from PrevDeptNum. But the first record must be handled differently, because when we read the first record, no PrevDeptNum exists. The flowchart shows that after we open the file, we read the first record in symbol 84. We save DeptNum from that record in PrevDeptNum, and then call Process-Record to process the first record.

At this point, the first record is processed, and the program enters a DO loop—where it stays until the file reaches its end. In the loop, the second and all subsequent records are read. The DeptNum of the just read record is compared with PrevDeptNum; if they are different, the ControlBreak subprogram is called. Then LineCntr is compared with PageSize to determine when to advance to a new page. (LineCntr is discussed more fully later, when we examine the program.) Finally, ProcessRecord is called to process the current record.

STEP 3   Hand-Calculated Answers

Using the data given in the previous step, we find that the total sales for department 46 are 962, for department 49 are 150, and for department 57 are 1,138. The grand total for all departments is 2,250.

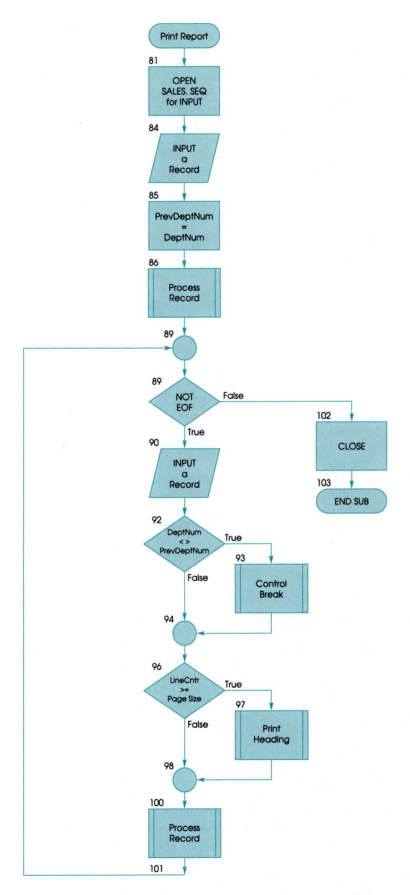

FIGURE 9.4 **Flowchart for the PrintReport subprogram.**

STEP 4   **QBasic Program**

The main module in Program 9.4 defines the heading and format strings, and PageSize. It initializes DeptTotal and FinalTotal to 0, and PageNum to 1. It then calls PrintHeading to print the headings on the first page.

The PrintHeading subprogram advances the printer to a new page by sending it a form feed character, CHR$(12), with the LPRINT statement in line 64. However, this LPRINT statement should not be executed for the first page. The IF statement on line 63 executes the LPRINT statement only if PageNum is greater than 1.

This execution of PrintHeading prints the heading on the first page. The question remains: How does the program know when to print the headings on subsequent pages? The answer is simple: The program keeps a running count of the lines already printed on a page. That is the function of the counter variable LineCntr. Since the heading fills four lines, LineCntr is initialized to 4 in line 72. Whenever detail lines are printed (as in lines 50 through 52 and line 111), LineCntr is incremented (as in lines 56 and 112). When LineCntr is equal to or greater than PageSize, the current page is full. The IF statement in line 96 executes the PrintHeading subprogram when LineCntr is equal to or greater than PageSize.

PageSize is given a value of 10 in line 27. In fact, 54 lines can fit on a standard 8½ × 11" page. The value of 10 for PageSize is used during testing so you can check that the heading logic works without needing a huge set of test data. When the program is working properly, PageSize can be set to the standard value of 54.

In line 51, the ControlBreak subprogram prints the subtotal. Note that this statement prints PrevDeptNum, not DeptNum. Why? Because PrevDeptNum contains the department number of the department whose total we are printing; DeptNum contains the department number of the current department—the one that caused the control break.

Besides printing the subtotal, the ControlBreak subprogram performs several other tasks. It accumulates DeptTotal into FinalTotal and resets DeptTotal to 0—to prepare to accumulate Sales for the new department. It saves the new Dept-Num in PrevDeptNum. Lastly, it increments LineCntr by 3, because it printed 3 lines.

In the output of Program 9.4, the dotted lines represent page breaks. You can see that the calculated answers agree with our hand-calculated answers.   ■

9.3 EXERCISES

★1. How would the output of Program 9.4 change if line 39 were deleted?

2. How would the output of Program 9.4 change if lines 53 and 54 were interchanged?

3. In a subprogram that prints headings, what do you do to the line counter variable? What do you do to the page counter variable?

4. Program 9.5 (page 368) shows the execution of a program that is supposed to print the contents of a file named CARS.SEQ. Instead, execution stopped at line 17 and QBasic displayed the error message Bad filename or number. Find and correct the error.

```
 1 | '    *** A REPORT WITH SUBTOTALS AND FINAL TOTAL ***
 2 | '    Produce a report with subtotals at Department Number breaks
 3 | '    and a final total at the end of the report
 4 |
 5 | DECLARE SUB ControlBreak (DeptNum!, DeptTotal!, LineCntr!, PrevDeptNum!, ↵
   |    FinalTotal!)
 6 | DECLARE SUB PrintReport (LineCntr, PageNum, PrevDeptNum, DeptTotal, FinalTotal)
 7 | DECLARE SUB PrintHeading (PageNum!, LineCntr!)
 8 | DECLARE SUB ProcessRecord (Employee$, DeptNum!, Sales!, LineCntr!, DeptTotal!)
 9 |
10 | '    Variables used
11 |
12 | '    DeptNum        Department number
13 | '    DeptTotal      Total sales for a department
14 | '    Employee$      Employee's name
15 | '    FinalTotal     Total sales for all departments
16 | '    LineCntr       Line counter
17 | '    PrevDeptNum    Previous department number
18 | '    Sales          Sales
19 |
20 | '    Define heading and format strings and page size
21 |         CONST Head$ = "              SALES REPORT         Page: ## "
22 |       CONST ColHead1$ = "    Employee            Dept"
23 |       CONST ColHead2$ = "      Name              Number      Sales"
24 | CONST DetailLineFormat$ = "\                 \      ##       #,###"
25 |  CONST DeptTotalFormat$ = "Total Sales for Department  ##      ##,###"
26 | CONST FinalTotalFormat$ = "Final Total for All Departments    ###,###"
27 | CONST PageSize = 10
28 |
29 | '    Initialize variables
30 | DeptTotal = 0                      'Department total
31 | FinalTotal = 0                     'Final total
32 | PageNum = 1                        'Page number
33 |
34 | CLS
35 | CALL PrintHeading(PageNum, LineCntr)      'Print headings on first page
36 | CALL PrintReport(LineCntr, PageNum, PrevDeptNum, DeptTotal, FinalTotal)
37 |
38 | '    Print break line for last department
39 | CALL ControlBreak(DeptNum, DeptTotal, LineCntr, PrevDeptNum, FinalTotal)
40 |
41 | '    Print final total line
42 | LPRINT USING FinalTotalFormat$; FinalTotal
43 | END
44 |
45 | SUB ControlBreak (DeptNum, DeptTotal, LineCntr, PrevDeptNum, FinalTotal)
46 | '    Process a control break
47 | '    DeptNum, DeptTotal, and LineCntr received
48 | '    PrevDeptNum and FinalTotal returned
49 |
50 |    LPRINT                                    'Print a blank line
51 |    LPRINT USING DeptTotalFormat$; PrevDeptNum; DeptTotal   'Print break line
52 |    LPRINT                                    'Print a blank line
53 |    FinalTotal = FinalTotal + DeptTotal       'Accumulate DeptTotal
54 |    DeptTotal = 0                             'Reset DeptTotal
55 |    PrevDeptNum = DeptNum                     'Save DeptNum
56 |    LineCntr = LineCntr + 3                   'Increment LineCntr
57 | END SUB
```

PROGRAM 9.4   A program that prints subtotals and a final total.
(continued on next page)

```
58   SUB PrintHeading (PageNum, LineCntr)
59   '    Advance to a new page and print headings
60   '    PageNum received
61   '    LineCntr returned
62
63        IF PageNum > 1 THEN                      'Except on page 1
64            LPRINT CHR$(12)                      'Advance to new page
65        END IF
66
67        LPRINT USING Head$; PageNum              'Print report heading
68        LPRINT                                   'Print a blank line
69        LPRINT ColHead1$                         'Print column
70        LPRINT ColHead2$                         'headings
71
72        LineCntr = 4                             'Initialize line counter
73        PageNum = PageNum + 1                     'Increment page number
74   END SUB
75
76   SUB PrintReport (LineCntr, PageNum, PrevDeptNum, DeptTotal, FinalTotal)
77   '    Print complete report
78   '    LineCntr received
79   '    DeptNum, DeptTotal, and FinalTotal returned
80
81        OPEN "SALES.SEQ" FOR INPUT AS #1
82
83   '    Process the first record
84        INPUT #1, Employee$, DeptNum, Sales                'Read first record
85        PrevDeptNum = DeptNum                              'Save DeptNum
86        CALL ProcessRecord(Employee$, DeptNum, Sales, LineCntr, DeptTotal)
87
88   '    Process rest of records
89        DO WHILE NOT EOF(1)
90            INPUT #1, Employee$, DeptNum, Sales                        'Read a record
91
92            IF DeptNum <> PrevDeptNum THEN                             'Did DeptNum change?
93                CALL ControlBreak(DeptNum, DeptTotal, LineCntr, PrevDeptNum, FinalTotal)
94            END IF
95
96            IF LineCntr >= PageSize THEN                               'Time for new page?
97                CALL PrintHeading(PageNum, LineCntr)
98            END IF
99
100           CALL ProcessRecord(Employee$, DeptNum, Sales, LineCntr, DeptTotal)
101       LOOP
102       CLOSE #1
103  END SUB
104
105  SUB ProcessRecord (Employee$, DeptNum, Sales, LineCntr, DeptTotal)
106  '    Process a record
107  '    Employee$, DeptNum, Sales, LineCntr received
108  '    DeptTotal returned
109
110       DeptTotal = DeptTotal + Sales                              'Accumulate sales
111       LPRINT USING DetailLineFormat$; Employee$; DeptNum; Sales
112       LineCntr = LineCntr + 1                                     'Increment LineCntr
113  END SUB
```

PROGRAM 9.4 (*continued*)

```
                SALES REPORT        Page:   1

        Employee           Dept
          Name             Number       Sales
Carol High                   46          500
Reynolds English             46          234
Haideh Handjany              46          151
Stanley Thompson             46           77


Total Sales for Department   46          962


--------------------------------------------------------

                SALES REPORT        Page:   2

        Employee           Dept
          Name             Number       Sales
Fabio Valdez                 49          150


Total Sales for Department   49          150


Maurice Butero               57          218
Yin Chen                     57          600
--------------------------------------------------------

                SALES REPORT        Page:   3

        Employee           Dept
          Name             Number       Sales
Robert Amato                 57           52
Mary Hannan                  57          225
Michael Bergin               57           43


Total Sales for Department   57        1,138


Final Total for All Departments      2,250
```

PROGRAM 9.4 *(continued)*

```
 1  '    *** READING AND PRINTING THE CARS FILE ***
 2  '    Read the cars file and print a report
 3
 4  DECLARE SUB PrintHeadings (Fmt$)
 5
 6  '    Variable names
 7
 8  '    CarName        Name of car
 9  '    Fmt$           Format string for PRINT USING
10  '    NumSold        Number of cars sold
11
12  CLS
13  OPEN "CARS.SEQ" FOR INPUT AS #1
14  CALL PrintHeadings(Fmt$)
15
16  '    Process file
17  DO WHILE NOT EOF(2)
18      INPUT #2, CarName$, NumSold
19      LPRINT USING Fmt$; CarName$; NumSold
20  LOOP
21  CLOSE #2
22  LPRINT "End of the Car file"
23  END
24
25  SUB PrintHeadings (Fmt$)
26  '    Print headings
27  '    No variables are received
28  '    Fmt$ is returned
29
30      Fmt$ = "\            \      ####"
31      LPRINT "       CARS SOLD"
32      LPRINT
33      LPRINT "Stock        Number     Closing"
34      LPRINT "Type                Sold"
35  END SUB
```

PROGRAM 9.5 An incorrect program to print the file named CARS.SEQ.

WHAT YOU HAVE LEARNED

In this chapter, you learned that:

- An OPEN statement must be executed before a file is read or written.
- The WRITE # statement writes to a sequential file.
- After a program is finished with a file, the CLOSE statement closes it.
- The INPUT # statement reads a sequential file.
- The EOF function tests for the end of a sequential file.
- The TYPE statement defines a record. The fields in the record may be defined to be fixed-length strings by coding AS STRING * n (where n is the length of the string), single-precision variables by coding AS SINGLE, double-precision variables by coding AS DOUBLE, integer variables by coding

AS INTEGER, and long-integer variables by coding AS LONG.

- The DIM statement is used to assign a record structure to a variable.
- The SHELL statement permits DOS commands to be executed from within QBasic.
- The PRINT # and PRINT # USING statements write a report to a disk file.
- The LINE INPUT # statement reads a line from a file.
- Using control breaks allows you to print subtotals.
- To print multi-page reports, use a variable that counts the number of lines printed on a page and a constant that specifies the number of lines on a page.

NEW QBASIC STATEMENTS

STATEMENT	EFFECT
OPEN	
`OPEN "AUCTION.SEQ" FOR INPUT AS #2`	Opens the file AUCTION.SEQ so it can be read, and associates file number 2 with it.
WRITE #	
`WRITE #2, Item$, Price`	Writes the values of Item$ and Price to the file that was previously opened as file number 2.
CLOSE	
`CLOSE #2`	Closes the file associated with file number 2.
INPUT #	
`INPUT #2, Item$, Price`	Reads the file that was opened as file number 2, and assigns values to Item$ and Price.
TYPE	

`TYPE PatientData`
`    Last AS STRING * 20`
`    First AS STRING * 12`
`    Age AS INTEGER`
`    BloodPressure AS SINGLE`
`END TYPE`
	Defines a record named PatientData, which consists of the fields Last, First, Age, and BloodPressure.

SHELL	
`SHELL "DIR"`	Exits to DOS, executes the DIR command, and returns to QBasic.
PRINT #	
`PRINT #2, Item$, Price`	Writes the values of Item$ and Price to the file opened as file number 2.

PRINT # USING

```
PRINT #2, USING Fmt$, Item$; Price
```
Writes the values of Item$ and Price, with the format specified by Fmt$, to the file opened as file number 2.

LINE INPUT

```
LINE INPUT #2, Record$
```
Reads a whole line from the file that was opened as file number 2.

KEY TERMS

backup file	field	long-integer variable
buffer	fixed-length string variable	record
control break	integer variable	sequential file
double-precision variable	key (key field)	single-precision variable

REVIEW EXERCISES

SELF-CHECK

1. When the end of a file is reached, the EOF function returns the value _____.

2. The _____ statement is used to read data from a sequential file.

3. The _____ statement must be executed before a file is read or written.

4. The _____ statement is used to execute a DOS command from within QBasic.

5. Explain the difference between the LINE INPUT # statement and the LINE INPUT statement.

6. What is the difference between the statements CLOSE #1 and CLOSE?

7. A file consists of a group of related _____.

8. Which statement is used to define a record?

9. Which QBasic statements are used to print to a file?

10. The OPEN statement for sequential files specifies three things. What are they?

11. How do you assign a type to a field defined in a TYPE statement?

12. The _____ statement is used to write data to a sequential file.

13. If, during execution, QBasic displays the error message

```
File not found
```

what is the most likely cause of the error?

14. What should a program do when a control break occurs?

15. Name the four types of numeric variables available in QBasic.

16. Which statement is used to assign a record structure to a variable ?

17. Choose the correct ending: The variables defined in a TYPE statement must be (a) string only; (b) numeric only; or (c) both string and numeric.

PROGRAMMING ASSIGNMENTS

Section 9.2

1. Write a program that allows Mr. Croesus to change the number of shares he owns of any stock simply by entering the name of the stock he wants to change and the number of shares he now owns.

2. The Molasses Delivery Service, Inc., has eight vans. The company keeps track of the total miles driven and gas used for each van so that it can calculate the miles per gallon (MPG). Write a program that creates a file in which each record contains the cumulative miles driven and gas used for a van. Then write a second program that accepts the current miles driven and gas used for each van. The program should update the file and print the current MPG and the cumulative MPG for each van, as well as the average values for all the vans.

3. Write two programs to create a home expenses system. The records in the file used by the

system should contain the name of an expense category and the year-to-date expenses in that category. Use the following categories: Auto, Clothing, Entertainment, Food, Insurance, Home, Savings, and Vacation. The first program should create this file, using zero for the year-to-date expenses. The second program should allow the user to enter category and expense data. The category should be indicated by a one-letter abbreviation (A, C, E, and so on). Each category may have several expenses, and the user should be permitted to enter the data in any order. When the user indicates that all the data are entered, the program should print the current and year-to-date expenses for each category and update the file.

4. Write three programs to create a student grades system. The first program should create a file that stores the students' names and leaves room for three test grades. The second program should allow the instructor to enter test grades for each student for a particular test. The third program—which should be executed only after grades for all three tests are entered—should calculate average grades and then print each student's name, grades, and average grade. Assume that no more than 40 students are ever in a class. (*Hint*: In the first program, accept students' names from the user and fill the students' names array. Create the file by writing the students' names array and a grades array, which is initially filled with zeros, to the file. In the second program, allow the user to enter the test number—1, 2, or 3—for which grades are entered. Display each student's name and allow the user to enter that student's grade. After all the grades are entered, rewrite the file.)

5. Write a file version of Programming Assignment 8.10. Write one program to create a SEATS.SEQ file to store the orchestra and balcony seats arrays. Then write a second program that reads SEATS.SEQ to initialize the orchestra and balcony seats arrays. This program should make the seat reservations as described in Programming Assignment 8.10. When the user indicates that a session is finished, save the two seat arrays back in SEATS.SEQ.

Section 9.3

6. The Sole Supplier Fish Market uses a computer to keep track of how much of each kind of fish— shrimp, clams, salmon, tuna, swordfish, flounder, monkfish, bluefish, and lobster—they sell. Their sales for one day were arranged in order by type of fish and recorded in DATA statements in PA09-06.DAT. The format of the DATA statements is

```
DATA fishname, weight
```

where fishname is a string and weight is a number. Write a program that reads and prints these data—and calculates and prints the total weight of each kind of fish.

7. A firm employs part time help. Some employees work every month, while others only work occasionally. Typical monthly earnings data for a given quarter might be as follows.

Employee	Monthly Earnings
Annette	385
Annette	260
Annette	250
Darlene	85
Darlene	85
Jimmy	45
Roy	225
Roy	260
Roy	115
Cubby	95

Write a program that accepts and prints these data—and calculates and prints the total earnings and average earnings per month for each employee, as well as a final total and average for all employees.

8. Frank Grinder uses a computer to track his school performance. Every time he takes a test, he records the name of the class and the test grade. Typical data might be as follows.

Class	Grade
English	76
English	84
Math	92
Psyc	71
Psyc	65
Psyc	54

Write a program that accepts and prints these data—and calculates and prints the average grade in each class.

ADDITIONAL PROGRAMMING ASSIGNMENTS

9. a) Wreck-A-Mended Service Station maintains a file of its customers' cars—named AUTO.SEQ—which contains four fields: the serial number (1–999), the make, the year, and the mileage when the car was last

serviced. Write a program to create this file with about 12 records.
b) Write a program that updates AUTO.SEQ. The program should accept a serial number and a mileage and update the corresponding record in the file. After all the update data are entered, the program should rewrite the file.
c) Write a program to read the AUTO.SEQ file and print a report of the cars with more than 25,000 miles. Print a heading on the report.

BEYOND THE BASICS

10. Write a program that allows Mr. Croesus to add or delete stocks from his list of holdings. If he wants to delete a stock, the program should ask him the name of the stock; after deleting it, the program should close up the gap in the arrays by moving the higher elements down. If he wants to add a stock, the program should request the name, number held, and price—then insert the stock in its alphabetical position.

11. Write a program that merges three files—FILE1.SEQ, FILE2.SEQ, and FILE3.SEQ—to produce a new file, FILE4.SEQ. The original files should be in order by key, and the merged file should also be in order by key. The records in the files can consist of only the key fields. To simplify the problem, create your files so that the same key does not appear in more than one input file. The simplest way to create the three input files is to use the DOS editor (available with DOS 5 and later versions). You can start the editor by typing the command EDIT at the DOS prompt. Then type the record keys, one key per line. Each line is read by QBasic as a record.

12. A file contains students' names and their GPAs. Write a program that prints the names of the students with the highest GPA. Your program must allow for ties, in which case the names of all the students tied for first place should be printed. Your program should read the file only once.

10

RANDOM-ACCESS FILES

LEARNING OBJECTIVES

After reading this chapter, you will be able to:

- Create, list, and maintain random-access files.
- Use the QBasic statements OPEN, PUT, GET, VIEW PRINT, and EXIT FOR.
- Create and maintain indexes for random-access files.
- Use the QBasic function LOF.

As you learned in Chapter 9, sequential files must be processed in order—from the first record to the last. To change one record in a sequential file, you must read and write every record. In some applications—for example, a payroll system—having to process every record is no problem, since you need to process every record (that is, pay every employee) anyway.

In many applications, however, processing every record is impractical. For example, in an airline reservation system, if you want to know whether seats are available for a particular flight, the program must be able to directly retrieve and display the record for that particular flight. If you buy a ticket, the program must be able to update the record for that flight and write it back to the file. Files that permit a record to be retrieved or written without processing all the preceding records are called **random-access files.** In this chapter, you will learn how to create and use random-access files.

random-access file
A file in which records can be retrieved or written without processing all the preceding records in the file.

Like sequential files, random-access files use a key to identify records. As you will see, in some applications you can use the record key as the record number. For example, the record whose key is 20 is the 20th record in the file. But in many situations, you may not use the record key as the record number, and you must create an index. We will discuss both kinds of applications in this chapter.

10.1 CREATING AND READING A RANDOM-ACCESS FILE

We begin by writing a program that creates a random-access file in which we can use the record key as the record number. You can think of this kind of file as a collection of pigeonholes. The record whose key is 1 is stored in the first pigeonhole, the record whose key is 2 is stored in the second pigeonhole, and so on.

EXAMPLE 1

CREATING A RANDOM-ACCESS FILE

Cuff's Department Store wants to use a computer to keep track of their charge account customers. Cuff's is a small store, with less than 1,000 charge account customers.

Problem Statement

Write a program to create a random-access file in which the key of the record is the record number. To keep this example simple, the records in this file contain only the customer's name and the balance owed. Assume that the file will contain no more than 999 records.

STEP 1 Variable Names

We start by identifying and naming the variables. The records in a random-access file *must* be defined using the TYPE statement. We will define a record named ChargeData that contains the fields Member and Balance. We will also define a record variable named Charge that has the structure of ChargeData.

Notice that even though the account number is used as the key, it is not part of the record. In this file, the account number *is* the record number. For example, the name and balance for account number 498 are stored in record number 498. When we want the name and balance for account number 498, we simply read record number 498. The variable names are then

Variable	Variable Name
Input and Output Variables	
Account number	`AcctNum`
Customer's name	`Charge.Member`
Balance in the account	`Charge.Balance`

The name of the file we will create is CHARGE.RND, where the extension RND is a reminder that this is a random-access file.

STEP 2   **Algorithm**

We can use the following algorithm:

1. Open CHARGE.RND.
2. Initialize every record.
3. Load the data into the file.
4. Close CHARGE.RND.

STEP 3   **Hand-Calculated Answers**

There are no hand-calculated answers—but after the file is created, we must verify that it contains the correct data.

STEP 4   **QBasic Program**

Program 10.1 creates CHARGE.RND. The TYPE statement in lines 15 through 18 defines the record ChargeData. ChargeData contains two fields: Member (which is a 20-character fixed-length string) and Balance (which is a single-precision numeric variable). The DIM statement in line 19 defines Charge to be a record variable that has the structure of ChargeData.

The OPEN Statement

Like sequential files, random-access files must be opened before they are processed. The OPEN statement for random-access files differs somewhat from that of sequential files. Its syntax is

```
OPEN "filename" FOR RANDOM AS #filenumber LEN = reclength
```

Here, filename and filenumber have the same meaning as they have with sequential files. But the OPEN statement for random-access files differs from that of sequential files in two ways.

1. The mode is not specified, because random-access files are opened for both input and output at the same time.
2. We must specify the record length, or number of characters in one record.

Fortunately, we don't have to calculate the length of the record. Instead, we can use QBasic's LEN function to return the length of the record variable. So, for example, in the OPEN statement for CHARGE.RND in line 22

```
OPEN "CHARGE.RND" FOR RANDOM AS #1 LEN = LEN(Charge)
```

the LEN function supplies the length of the record variable Charge to the OPEN statement.

In a random-access file, every record must be the same length. When you want to access a particular record, QBasic multiplies the record length by the record number to calculate how far the desired record is from the beginning of the file. It can then go directly to that record and retrieve it.

Additional OPEN statement examples are as follows.

ILLUSTRATIONS

OPEN Statement	Effect
`OPEN "PAYROLL.RND" FOR RANDOM`⏎ `AS #3 LEN = LEN(Payroll)`	Opens the file PAYROLL.RND for random processing, assigns it file number 3, and specifies that the record length is the length of the record variable Payroll.
`OPEN RandomFile$ FOR RANDOM`⏎ `AS #1 LEN = LEN(RecordVar)`	Opens the file whose name previously was assigned to the variable RandomFile$, assigns it file number 1, and specifies that the record length is the length of the record variable RecordVar.

After opening CHARGE.RND, the main program calls two subprograms. The first, InitializeFile, initializes the file; the second, LoadFile, puts the actual data into the file. To understand why random-access files must be initialized (recall that we did not have to initialize sequential files), you must know something about how QBasic allocates disk space for random-access files.

If this program did not initialize the file, the first record it would write would be record number 498, because that is the account number specified in the first DATA statement. (The order of writing records is explained in greater detail later.) Before QBasic writes that record, it will allocate space on the disk for records 1 through 497, but it will not write anything in the space. So, if the space allocated was at one time occupied by a file that was later deleted, the space will still contain left-over data from the old file. (When you delete a file, DOS does not erase the file's data—it simply erases the file's name from the disk's directory.) Later, when you read the new file, you may find left-over data mingled with new data. To avoid that problem, we must initialize the file.

The InitializeFile subprogram starts in line 55. We initialize the file by setting Charge.Member to 20 spaces in line 60, and Charge.Balance to 0 in line 61. The FOR...NEXT loop in lines 62 through 64 writes those data to every record in the file.

The PUT Statement

The PUT statement in line 63

```
PUT #1, J, Charge
```

actually writes the data to the file. Note that in a PUT statement, you do not list the individual fields that should be written to the file. Instead, you use the record variable; in this case, Charge. The PUT statement writes all the fields in the record—Charge.Member and Charge.Balance—to the file.

The syntax of the PUT statement is

```
PUT #filenumber, recordnumber, recordvariable
```

where filenumber (as usual) is the number assigned to the file in the OPEN statement, recordnumber is the record number that is to be written, and recordvariable is the record variable that is to be written.

```
1    '    *** CREATING THE RANDOM CHARGE ACCOUNT FILE ***
2    '    Read DATA and write to CHARGE.RND
3
4    DECLARE SUB InitializeFile (Charge AS ANY)
5    DECLARE SUB LoadFile (Charge AS ANY)
6
7    '    Variables used
8
9    '    AcctNum                   Account number
10   '    Charge record consisting of:
11   '        Charge.Member         Customer's name
12   '        Charge.Balance        Balance in the account
13
14   '    Define the ChargeData record
15   TYPE ChargeData
16       Member AS STRING * 20
17       Balance AS SINGLE
18   END TYPE
19   DIM Charge AS ChargeData
20
21   CLS
22   OPEN "CHARGE.RND" FOR RANDOM AS #1 LEN = LEN(Charge)
23   CALL InitializeFile(Charge)
24   CALL LoadFile(Charge)
25   CLOSE #1
26   PRINT "The Charge Account file has been created"
27
28   '    Data to create file
29   '    Format is Account number, Name, and Balance
30   DATA 498, "English, Reynolds", 8.59
31   DATA 786, "Lee, Bohyon", 25.71
32   DATA 537, "Thompson, Stanley", 47.51
33   DATA 849, "Valdez, Fabio", 13.85
34   DATA 175, "Mato, Robert", 33.07
35   DATA 562, "Rizzuto, James", 76.25
36   DATA 877, "Schwartz, Michael", 45.91
37   DATA 212, "Rufino, Carlos", 9.22
38   DATA 583, "Morley, John", 125.00
39   DATA 334, "Brevil, James", 108.42
40   DATA 604, "Martin, Kathleen", 16.37
41   DATA 146, "Falconer, Edward", 45.46
42   DATA 348, "Yeung, Suk", 26.17
43   DATA 626, "Paul, Marina", 42.85
44   DATA 397, "Fradin, Shirley", 56.84
45   DATA 659, "Burns, Jeffrey", 23.61
46   DATA 406, "Katz, Hal", 15.67
47   DATA 694, "Wright, Donna", 54.40
48   DATA 438, "Cuomo, Maria", 25.37
49   DATA 709, "Lopez, Anna", 19.26
50   DATA 474, "Alexander, Lisa", 52.36
51   DATA 753, "Goldberg, Lori", 15.87
52   '    Trailer data follow
53   DATA 9999,"XXX", 0
54   END
```

PROGRAM 10.1   Creating a random-access file: CHARGE.RND.
(continued on next page)

```
55 │ SUB InitializeFile (Charge AS ChargeData)
56 │ '    Initialize file
57 │ '    No variables received
58 │ '    Charge.Member and Charge.Balance returned
59 │
60 │     Charge.Member = SPACE$(20)        'Set Member equal to spaces
61 │     Charge.Balance = 0                'and Balance equal to zero
62 │     FOR J = 1 TO 999                  'Write to every record in the file
63 │         PUT #1, J, Charge
64 │     NEXT J
65 │ END SUB
66 │
67 │ SUB LoadFile (Charge AS ChargeData)
68 │ '    Load data into file
69 │ '    No variables received
70 │ '    Charge.Member and Charge.Balance returned
71 │
72 │ READ AcctNum, Charge.Member, Charge.Balance        'Priming read
73 │ DO UNTIL AcctNum = 9999
74 │     PUT #1, AcctNum, Charge                          'Write data to file
75 │     READ AcctNum, Charge.Member, Charge.Balance     'Read next DATA
76 │ LOOP
77 │ END SUB
```

The Charge Account file has been created

PROGRAM 10.1 *(continued)*

You can think of recordnumber as the number of the pigeonhole where the record is to be written.

In line 63, the recordnumber is J—so when J is 1, the PUT statement writes record number 1; when J is 2, it writes record number 2; and so on, until J is 999, when it writes the 999th record.

The PUT statement in line 63 writes the records in sequential order because that is the most convenient way to initialize a file. However, the PUT statement also allows us to write records in random order. This is fortunate because in on-line systems, the data may arrive in arbitrary order. To imitate an on-line system, the data in the DATA statements in lines 30 through 51 are *not* in order by AcctNum.

The actual data (as opposed to the initializing data) are written to CHARGE.RND in the LoadFile subprogram. In this subprogram, the READ statement assigns values to AcctNum, Charge.Member, and Charge.Balance. These data are written to CHARGE.RND by the PUT statement in line 74

```
PUT #1, AcctNum, Charge
```

The record number written by this statement depends on the value of AcctNum. In the first DATA statement (line 30), AcctNum is 498. Therefore, the first name (English, Reynolds) and the first balance (8.59) are written to record number (pigeonhole) 498. In the second DATA statement, AcctNum is 786, so the second record is written to record number 786—and so on. Additional examples of PUT statements are as follows.

ILLUSTRATIONS

PUT Statement	Effect
`PUT #1, RecNum, Student`	Writes the record variable Student to record number RecNum in the file opened as file number 1.
`PUT #3, 381, Stock`	Writes the record variable Stock to record number 381 in the file opened as file number 3.

After all the data are written to the file, control returns to the main program. In the main program, the file is closed in line 25. The CLOSE statement for random-access files is the same as the CLOSE statement for sequential files.

EXAMPLE 2

LISTING THE RECORDS IN A RANDOM-ACCESS FILE

As you learned in Chapter 9, the WRITE# statement—which is used to write records to a sequential file—adds a carriage return and line feed to the end of each record, thus separating records. But the corresponding statement for random-access files, the PUT statement, does not add any separator between records. Thus, you cannot simply use the Open command in the File menu to see if CHARGE.RND was created properly, as you can with sequential files. Instead, we need a separate QBasic program to list the file.

Problem Statement

Write a program that lists all the active records in the CHARGE.RND file.

STEP 1   Variable Names

We can use the same variable names that we used in Program 10.1.

STEP 2   Algorithm

The algorithm is simple:

1. Open CHARGE.RND.
2. Read every record in the file.
3. If the record is active, print it; otherwise, do nothing.
4. Close CHARGE.RND.

STEP 3   Hand-Calculated Answer

To check the program, we will compare the listing it produces against the data listed in Program 10.1's DATA statements.

STEP 4   QBasic Program

Program 10.2 lists the active records in the CHARGE.RND file. The TYPE, DIM, and OPEN statements are the same as they were when the file was created in Program 10.1 (pages 377–78).

```
1    '    *** READING THE RANDOM CHARGE ACCOUNT FILE ***
2    '    Read every record of CHARGE.RND, and print the active records
3
4    '    Variables used
5
6    '    AcctNum                  Account number
7    '    Charge record consisting of:
8    '        Charge.Member        Customer's name
9    '        Charge.Balance       Balance in the account
10
11   '    Define the ChargeData record
12   TYPE ChargeData
13       Member AS STRING * 20
14       Balance AS SINGLE
15   END TYPE
16   DIM Charge AS ChargeData
17
18   CLS
19   OPEN "CHARGE.RND" FOR RANDOM AS #1 LEN = LEN(Charge)
20   LPRINT "Account Number       Name                 Balance"
21   Fmt$ = "        ###         \                \     #,###.##"
22   FOR AcctNum = 1 TO 999
23       GET #1, AcctNum, Charge
24       IF Charge.Member <> SPACE$(20) THEN
25           LPRINT USING Fmt$; AcctNum; Charge.Member; Charge.Balance
26       END IF
27   NEXT AcctNum
28   LPRINT "End of Charge Account File"
29   CLOSE
30   END
```

Account Number	Name	Balance
146	Falconer, Edward	45.46
175	Mato, Robert	33.07
212	Rufino, Carlos	9.22
334	Brevil, James	108.42
348	Yeung, Suk	26.17
397	Fradin, Shirley	56.84
406	Katz, Hal	15.67
438	Cuomo, Maria	25.37
474	Alexander, Lisa	52.36
498	English, Reynolds	8.59
537	Thompson, Stanley	47.51
562	Rizzuto, James	76.25
583	Morley, John	125.00
604	Martin, Kathleen	16.37
626	Paul, Marina	42.85
659	Burns, Jeffrey	23.61
694	Wright, Donna	54.40
709	Lopez, Anna	19.26
753	Goldberg, Lori	15.87
786	Lee, Bohyon	25.71
849	Valdez, Fabio	13.85
877	Schwartz, Michael	45.91

End of Charge Account File

PROGRAM 10.2 Listing the active records in a random-access file (CHARGE.RND).

The GET Statement

The FOR...NEXT loop in lines 22 through 27 reads the file. The GET statement in line 23

```
GET #1, AcctNum, Charge
```

actually reads the data from the disk. Notice that just as with the PUT statement, you do not list the individual variables to be read with a GET statement. Instead, you use the record variable—in this case, Charge. Each time a GET statement is executed, a whole record is read and values are assigned to all the fields in the record.

The syntax of the GET statement is

```
GET #filenumber, recordnumber, recordvariable
```

As with the PUT statement, filenumber is the number assigned to the file in the OPEN statement, recordnumber is the record number to be read, and recordvariable is the record variable to be read.

In Program 10.2, every record from record number 1 through record number 999 is read. After each record is read, the IF statement in line 24 tests Charge.Member to determine whether it contains 20 spaces. If it does not, the record is active and is printed. Otherwise, the record is inactive and nothing is done.

The output produced by Program 10.2 agrees with the data listed in the DATA statements in Program 10.1, showing that both Programs 10.1 and 10.2 are correct.

Before proceeding, be sure you understand how the following GET statements work. ∎

ILLUSTRATIONS

GET Statement	Effect
`GET #2, StudentNum, Student`	Reads the record whose number is StudentNum from the file opened as file number 2 into the record variable Student.
`GET #1, 174, Stock`	Reads record number 174 from the file opened as file number 1 into the record variable Stock.

Syntax Summary

OPEN Statement
Form: `OPEN "filename" FOR RANDOM AS #filenumber ↵`
           `LEN = reclength`
Example: `OPEN "BOOKS.RND" FOR RANDOM AS #2 LEN = LEN(Books)`
Explanation: Opens a file for random processing and associates it with the file number specified by filenumber. The number of bytes in each record is specified by reclength.

(continued)

PUT Statement

Form: `PUT #filenumber, recordnumber, recordvariable`
Example: `PUT #2, BookNum, Book`
Explanation: Writes the record variable named recordvariable to the record number specified by recordnumber of the random access file opened as the file number specified by filenumber.

GET Statement

Form: `GET #filenumber, recordnumber, recordvariable`
Example: `GET #1, AcctNum, AcctRec`
Explanation: Reads the record number specified by recordnumber from the file that was opened as the file number specified by filenumber into the record variable named recordvariable.

10.1 EXERCISES

1. The first data listed in Program 10.1 are for account number 498 for English, Reynolds—but the first record listed by Program 10.2 is for account number 146 for Falconer, Edward. Why?

★2. Why must every record in a random-access file have the same length?

★3. The records in GPA.RND consist of the following fields: a student name (which is a string of length 25), the number of credits completed (which is an integer), and the student's GPA (which is a single-precision number).

   a) Write the TYPE statement to define a record structure named Student-Data that contains these fields. Name the fields Nam, Credits, and GPA.

   b) Write the statement to define a record variable named Student that has the structure of StudentData.

   c) Write the OPEN statement that could be used in a program that creates GPA.RND. Open the file as file number 1.

   d) Write the OPEN statement that could be used in a program that reads GPA.RND. Open the file as file number 1.

   e) Write the INPUT statements that could be used to accept data for the fields in Student.

   f) Write the statement to write a record to the file (StudentNum specifies the record to be written).

   g) Write the statement to read a record from the file (StudentNum specifies the record to be read).

4. The records in ADDRESS.RND consist of the following fields: Nam (stands for name, which is a string of length 20), Street (a string of length 25), City (a string of length 20), State (a string of length 2), and Zip (stands for zip code, which is a single-precision number).

   a) Write the TYPE statement to define a record structure named AddressData that contains these fields.

   b) Write the statement to define a record variable named Address that has the structure of AddressData.

   c) Write the OPEN statement that could be used in a program that creates ADDRESS.RND. Open the file as file number 1.

    d)   Write the OPEN statement that could be used in a program that reads ADDRESS.RND. Open the file as file number 1.

    e)   Write the INPUT statements that could be used to accept data for the fields in Address.

    f)   Write the statement to write a record to the file (RecordNumber specifies the record to be written).

    g)   Write the statement to read a record from the file (RecordNumber specifies the record to be read).

5. The records in PAYROLL.RND consist of the following fields: Nam (stands for name, which is a string of length 25), PayRate (a single precision number), Dependents (number of dependents, which is an integer), and YTDGross (year-to-date gross pay, which is a single-precision number).

    a)   Write a TYPE statement to define a record structure named PayrollData that contains these fields.

    b)   Write the statement to define a record variable named Payroll that has the structure of PayrollData.

    c)   Write the OPEN statement that could be used in a program that creates PAYROLL.RND. Open the file as file number 2.

    d)   Write the OPEN statement that could be used in a program that reads PAYROLL.RND. Open the file as file number 2.

    e)   Write the INPUT statements that could be used to accept data for the fields in Payroll.

    f)   Write the statement to write a record to the file (EmpNum specifies the record to be written).

    g)   Write the statement to read a record from the file (EmpNum specifies the record to be read).

10.2 MAINTAINING A RANDOM-ACCESS FILE

You may think that random-access files don't offer any advantages over sequential files since—just like sequential files—we had to read every record in the random-access file. In addition, we had to test Charge.Member to see if the record was active and should be printed, while sequential files contain no inactive records. Because Program 10.2 listed every active record, you have a misleading impression of random-access files. As you will discover, random-access files allow us to display only the record the user wants to see, which is not practical to do with sequential files.

EXAMPLE 3

MAINTAINING A RANDOM-ACCESS FILE

Cuff's needs a program that it can use to update its charge account file when the user makes a payment or incurs a new charge. It also must be able to add new customers and delete customers who close their accounts.

Problem Statement

Write a program that can be used to add, delete, update, and display records in Cuff's charge account file.

STEP 1 **Variable Names**

To solve this problem, we can use the same variables as in Programs 10.1 and 10.2, with the following additions.

Variable	Variable Name
Input Variables	
Code specifying operation to perform	`Code$`
Code specifying whether amount entered is a payment or a charge	`PaymentCode`
Amount paid or charged	`Amount`

STEP 2 **Algorithm**

When the program is run, the user enters a code indicating whether he or she wants to add, delete, update, or display a record—followed by the account number (record number) of the record. In addition, if a record is being updated, the user must enter the amount and a code indicating whether the amount is a payment or a charge. If a record is being added, the user must enter the name and initial balance.

Note that a request may be in error. You are not allowed to add a record with the same account number as a record already in the file—nor can you delete, update, or display a record that is not active.

These considerations lead to the following algorithm:

1. Open CHARGE.RND.
2. Display a menu.
3. Repeat steps 4 and 5 until the user wants to exit.
4.   Accept Code$ from the user.
5.   Perform the operation the user requested. If the requested operation is invalid, print an error message.
6. Close CHARGE.RND.

A top-down chart for this problem is shown in Figure 10.1. The main module calls seven subprograms. Three of these—Delete a Record, Update a Record, and Display a Record—in turn call Inactive Record if the record they are asked to process is not active. In addition, they—and Add a Record—call Pause to cause a timed pause of execution.

STEP 3 **Hand-Calculated Answer**

The easiest way to check this program is to add a record, and then display the added record to see if it was added correctly. Similarly, you can update a record—and then display it—to see if the update was done correctly. Finally, you can delete a record, and when you try to display it, the program should give you an error message instead.

STEP 4 **QBasic Program**

Program 10.3 produces the Output screen shown in Figure 10.2. The upper half of the screen shows the menu displayed by DisplayMenu; the lower half shows the results of processing the user's request—in this case, to update a record.

The TYPE, DIM, and OPEN statements in Program 10.3 are identical to the ones we used earlier. The main module calls the DisplayMenu subprogram to display the program's name and the menu on rows 3 through 9. The DisplayMenu subprogram then uses a VIEW PRINT statement to create a text viewport. A **viewport** is a section of the screen that functions like an independent screen. The VIEW PRINT statement in line 108

> **viewport**
> A section of the screen that functions like an independent screen.

```
VIEW PRINT 10 TO 25
```

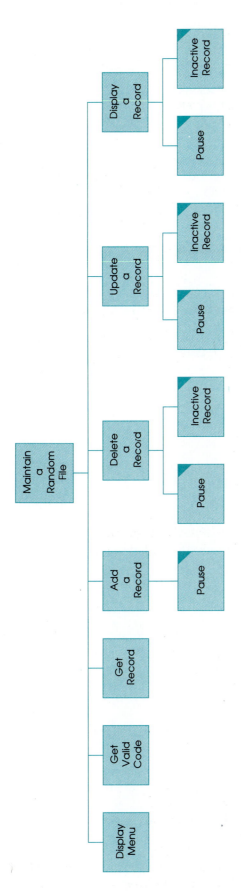

FIGURE 10.1   A top-down chart for a program that maintains a random-access file.

```
 1  '    *** MAINTAINING THE RANDOM CHARGE ACCOUNT FILE ***
 2  '   Add, delete, update, and display records from CHARGE.RND
 3
 4  DECLARE SUB AddRecord (AcctNum!, Charge AS ANY)
 5  DECLARE SUB DeleteRecord (AcctNum!, Charge AS ANY)
 6  DECLARE SUB UpdateRecord (AcctNum!, Charge AS ANY)
 7  DECLARE SUB DisplayRecord (AcctNum!, Charge AS ANY)
 8  DECLARE SUB Pause (Delay!)
 9  DECLARE SUB GetRecord (AcctNum!, Charge AS ANY)
10  DECLARE SUB InactiveRecord (AcctNum!)
11  DECLARE SUB DisplayMenu ()
12  DECLARE FUNCTION GetValidCode$ ()
13
14  '   Variables used
15
16  '   AcctNum                 Account number
17  '   Charge record consisting of:
18  '       Charge.Member       Customer's name
19  '       Charge.Balance      Balance in the account
20  '   Code$                   User input specifying operation to perform
21
22  CONST ErrorMsg1$ = "Please enter an account number between 1 and 999"
23  CONST ErrorMsg2$ = "Please enter a number between 1 and 5 "
24
25  '   Define the ChargeData record
26  TYPE ChargeData
27      Member AS STRING * 20
28      Balance AS SINGLE
29  END TYPE
30  DIM Charge AS ChargeData
31
32  OPEN "CHARGE.RND" FOR RANDOM AS #1 LEN = LEN(Charge)
33  CALL DisplayMenu
34
35  '   Process requests
36  Code$ = GetValidCode$
37  DO UNTIL Code$ = "5"
38      CALL GetRecord(AcctNum, Charge)
39      SELECT CASE Code$
40          CASE "1"
41              CALL AddRecord(AcctNum, Charge)
42          CASE "2"
43              CALL DeleteRecord(AcctNum, Charge)
44          CASE "3"
45              CALL UpdateRecord(AcctNum, Charge)
46          CASE "4"
47              CALL DisplayRecord(AcctNum, Charge)
48      END SELECT
49      CLS                                        'Clear lines 10 to 25
50      Code$ = GetValidCode$
51  LOOP
52  CLOSE
53  END
```

PROGRAM 10.3   Maintaining a random-access file. *(continued on next page)*

```
54 | SUB AddRecord (AcctNum, Charge AS ChargeData)
55 | '   Add records
56 | '   AcctNum and Charge record received
57 | '   No variables returned
58 |
59 |     IF Charge.Member <> SPACE$(20) THEN              'If record is active
60 |         BEEP                                         'can't add it
61 |         LOCATE 15, 20
62 |         PRINT AcctNum; "is currently assigned"
63 |     ELSE                                             'otherwise
64 |         LOCATE 14, 20                                'get
65 |         LINE INPUT "Enter name "; Charge.Member      'name,
66 |         LOCATE 15, 20
67 |         INPUT "Enter starting balance: ", Charge.Balance 'balance, and
68 |         PUT #1, AcctNum, Charge                       'add record
69 |         LOCATE 16, 20
70 |         PRINT "Record number "; AcctNum; "has been added"
71 |     END IF
72 |     CALL Pause(2)
73 | END SUB
74 |
75 | SUB DeleteRecord (AcctNum, Charge AS ChargeData)
76 | '   Delete records
77 | '   AcctNum and Charge record received
78 | '   No variables returned
79 |
80 |     IF Charge.Member = SPACE$(20) THEN               'If record is inactive
81 |         CALL InactiveRecord(AcctNum)                 'can't delete it
82 |     ELSE                                             'otherwise
83 |         Charge.Member = SPACE$(20)                   'Set name for inactive
84 |         Charge.Balance = 0                           'Set balance to 0
85 |         PUT #1, AcctNum, Charge                       'Write record
86 |         LOCATE 14, 20
87 |         PRINT "Record number "; AcctNum; "has been deleted"
88 |     END IF
89 |     CALL Pause(2)
90 | END SUB
91 |
92 | SUB DisplayMenu
93 | '   Display menu
94 |
95 |     CLS
96 |     LOCATE 3, 20
97 |     PRINT "CHARGE ACCOUNT MAINTENANCE MENU"
98 |     LOCATE 5, 28
99 |     PRINT "1  Add a record"
100|     LOCATE 6, 28
101|     PRINT "2  Delete a record"
102|     LOCATE 7, 28
103|     PRINT "3  Update a record"
104|     LOCATE 8, 28
105|     PRINT "4  Display a record"
106|     LOCATE 9, 28
107|     PRINT "5  Exit program"
108|     VIEW PRINT 10 TO 25
109| END SUB
```

PROGRAM 10.3 *(continued)*

```
110   SUB DisplayRecord (AcctNum, Charge AS ChargeData)
111   '    Display Record
112   '    AcctNum and Charge record received
113   '    No variables returned
114
115       IF Charge.Member = SPACE$(20) THEN              'If record is inactive
116           CALL InactiveRecord(AcctNum)               'can't display it
117           CALL Pause(2)
118       ELSE                                            'otherwise
119           LOCATE 15, 20                               'display it
120           PRINT "Account number     "; AcctNum
121           LOCATE 16, 20
122           PRINT "Name               "; Charge.Member
123           LOCATE 17, 20
124           PRINT USING "Current balance #,###.## "; Charge.Balance
125           LOCATE 18, 20
126           PRINT "Press any key to continue";
127           Dummy$ = INPUT$(1)
128       END IF
129   END SUB
130
131   SUB GetRecord (AcctNum, Charge AS ChargeData)
132   '    Get AcctNum from user, and retrieve record
133   '    AcctNum and Charge record returned
134   '    No variables received
135
136
137       LOCATE 13, 20
138       PRINT "Enter the three-digit account number ";
139       AcctNum = VAL(INPUT$(3))
140       PRINT AcctNum
141       DO WHILE AcctNum = 0                'Enter loop if is AcctNum is invalid
142           BEEP
143           LOCATE 15, 20
144           PRINT ErrorMsg1$                       'Print error message
145           AcctNum = VAL(INPUT$(3))           'Get a new account number
146           LOCATE 15, 20
147           PRINT SPACE$(LEN(ErrorMsg1$))   'Erase error message
148           LOCATE 13, 57
149           PRINT AcctNum
150       LOOP
151       GET #1, AcctNum, Charge                 'Retrieve desired record
152   END SUB
153   FUNCTION GetValidCode$
154   '    Get Code$ from user. Function does not return until
155   '    a valid Code$ has been entered.
156   '    No variables received
157   '    Code$ returned in GetValidCode$
158
159       LOCATE 10, 20
160       PRINT "Enter a number from 1 to 5: ";
161       Code$ = INPUT$(1)
162       PRINT Code$
163       DO UNTIL Code$ > "0" AND Code$ <= "5"   'Enter loop if Code$ is invalid
164           BEEP
165           LOCATE 15, 20
166           PRINT ErrorMsg2$;                          'Print error message
```

PROGRAM 10.3 (*continued*)

```
167              Code$ = INPUT$(1)
168              LOCATE 15, 20
169              PRINT SPACE$(LEN(ErrorMsg2$))        'Erase error message
170              LOCATE 10, 48
171              PRINT Code$
172         LOOP
173         GetValidCode$ = Code$                    'Return a valid Code$
174    END FUNCTION
175
176    SUB InactiveRecord (AcctNum)
177    '   Print error message when requested record is inactive
178    '   AcctNum received
179    '   No variables returned
180
181         BEEP
182         LOCATE 15, 20
183         PRINT AcctNum; "is currently inactive"
184    END SUB
185
186    SUB Pause (Delay)
187    '   Cause a pause of Delay seconds
188    '   Delay received
189    '   No variables returned
190
191         Later = TIMER + Delay         'Calculate time Delay seconds from now
192         DO WHILE TIMER < Later        'Loop for Delay seconds
193         LOOP
194    END SUB
195    SUB UpdateRecord (AcctNum, Charge AS ChargeData)
196    '   Update Record
197    '   AcctNum and Charge record received
198    '   No variables returned
199
200    '   Local variables
201
202    '   Amount                    Amount of payment or charge
203    '   PaymentCode$              Code specifying whether amount is
204    '                             a payment or a charge
205
206         IF Charge.Member = SPACE$(20) THEN          'If record is inactive
207             CALL InactiveRecord(AcctNum)            'can't update it
208         ELSE                                        'otherwise, update it
209             LOCATE 14, 20
210             PRINT USING "Current balance #,###.## "; Charge.Balance
211             LOCATE 15, 20
212             INPUT "Enter amount: ", Amount
213             LOCATE 16, 20
214             PRINT "Enter 1 for a charge, or 2 for a payment ";
215             PaymentCode$ = INPUT$(1)
216             PRINT PaymentCode$
217             IF PaymentCode$ = "1" THEN
218                 Charge.Balance = Charge.Balance + Amount   'Add charges
219             ELSE                                           'and
220                 Charge.Balance = Charge.Balance - Amount   'subtract payments
221             END IF
222             LOCATE 17, 20
223             PRINT USING "New balance #,###.## "; Charge.Balance
```

PROGRAM 10.3 *(continued)*

```
224 |          PUT #1, AcctNum, Charge                     'Write record
225 |          LOCATE 18, 20
226 |          PRINT "Record number "; AcctNum; "has been updated"
227 |       END IF
228 |       CALL Pause(2)
229 | END SUB
```

PROGRAM 10.3 *(continued)*

creates a viewport between rows 10 and 25. The advantage of using a viewport is that after a viewport is created, a CLS statement clears only the viewport. So after we process the user's request, the CLS statement in line 49 clears rows 10 through 25 (to get ready for the next request), without erasing the menu in rows 3 to 9.

After a viewport is established, all subsequent print output is restricted to the viewport. If you try to use a LOCATE statement to print outside the viewport, QBasic stops and displays an error message, Illegal function call.

The syntax of the VIEW PRINT statement is

```
VIEW PRINT [toprow TO bottomrow]
```

Both toprow and bottomrow must be between 1 and 25; also, bottomrow must be greater than toprow. A VIEW PRINT statement without any parameters reestablishes the whole screen as the text viewport.

The main module next invokes the GetValidCode$ function to get a Code$ from the user. GetValidCode$ does not return to the main module until the user enters a valid Code$—one between 1 and 5. If the user enters an invalid Code$, line 166 prints the constant ErrorMsg2$, which is defined in line 23. After the INPUT$ function in line 167 accepts another Code$, the PRINT statement in line 169

```
PRINT SPACE$(LEN(ErrorMsg2$))
```

uses the SPACE$ and LEN functions to print spaces to erase the error message.

```
              CHARGE ACCOUNT MAINTENANCE MENU

              1  Add a record
              2  Delete a record
              3  Update a record
              4  Display a record
              5  Exit program
         Enter a number from 1 to 5: 3


         Enter the three-digit account number   583
         Current balance    125.00
         Enter amount: 75
         Enter 1 for a charge, or 2 for a payment 2
         New balance       50.00
         Record number   583 has been updated
```

FIGURE 10.2
The update screen produced by Program 10.3.

The main module then enters a DO loop—where it remains until the user enters a Code$ of 5. Inside the loop, the main module calls the GetRecord subprogram to obtain a record. The GetRecord subprogram does not return to the main module until it reads a record. The GetRecord subprogram asks the user to enter the AcctNum of the desired record. In line 139, the INPUT$ function obtains three characters from the user, and the VAL function converts the string to a number. If an invalid value is entered, the VAL function returns 0. In that case, an error message is displayed, and the user is asked to enter a valid value. The error message is erased using the same technique described previously in GetValidCode$.

The GET statement in line 151

```
GET #1, AcctNum, Charge
```

reads the record whose record number is equal to AcctNum into the record variable Charge. This is the first time we have used the ability of the GET statement to read a specific record, so it is important that you understand how it works. For example, if the user enters 582 for AcctNum, this GET statement reads the data in record 582.

After the record is read, control returns to the main module. In the main module, Code$ is used in a SELECT CASE statement to determine which subprogram to call.

The AddRecord Subprogram

If the user enters a 1 for Code$, the main module calls the AddRecord subprogram. This subprogram begins by testing Charge.Member in line 59. If Charge.Member does not equal SPACE$(20), the account number is already assigned, so a new record with that account number may not be added. In that case, an error message is printed, and control returns to the main module.

If Charge.Member does equal SPACE$(20), we may add a new record. Lines 65 and 67 ask the user to enter the name and starting balance. Then the PUT statement in line 68 writes the record to the location specified by AcctNum. The PRINT statement in line 70 displays a success message.

Then line 72 calls Pause to cause a 2-second pause. The Pause subprogram, which begins at line 186, uses the TIMER function to cause a delay that depends on its argument. Control then returns to the main module. As mentioned earlier, the CLS statement in line 49 clears only the part of the screen under the menu.

The DeleteRecord Subprogram

If the user enters a 2 for Code$, the main module calls the DeleteRecord subprogram. As with AddRecord, we start by testing Charge.Member in line 80. Now, if Charge.Member *does* equal SPACE$(20), the record is inactive and cannot be deleted. Thus, InactiveRecord is called to print an error message. If Charge.Member does not equal SPACE$(20), we delete the record by setting Charge.Member to spaces in line 83 and Charge.Balance to 0 in line 84. The PUT statement in line 85 rewrites the record, and the PRINT statement in line 87 displays a success message.

The DisplayRecord subprogram is similar to the DeleteRecord subprogram. If the record is not active, an error message is displayed. If the record is active, its contents are displayed. Similarly, the UpdateRecord displays an error message if the record is not active. If the record is active, UpdateRecord asks the user to enter an amount and a code to indicate whether the amount is a payment or a charge. The Balance is updated, and the record is rewritten.

Finally, if the user enters 5 for Code$, the program exits from the DO loop. Line 52 closes the file. ■

Syntax Summary

> **VIEW PRINT Statement**
>
> Form: `VIEW PRINT [toprow TO bottomrow]`
> Example: `VIEW PRINT 4 TO 20`
> Explanation: Creates a text viewport between lines toprow and
>   bottomrow.

10.2 EXERCISES

★**1.** In Program 10.3, the INPUT$ function is used to obtain data in lines 139,
161, and 215. In all cases, numeric data are obtained. However, in line 139,
the VAL function is used to convert the string returned by INPUT$ into a
number—but in lines 161 and 215, the VAL function is not used. Why is the
VAL function used in line 139, but not in the other lines?

2. Simple Simon noticed that if a user enters an invalid code, the
GetValidCode$ subprogram in Program 10.3 prints an error message,
accepts a second value for Code$, and then erases the error message. He
says that if the user enters two invalid values in a row, the second invalid
value will be returned to the main module. Explain why he is wrong.

3. Write the VIEW PRINT statement to make the portion of the screen
between lines 14 and 21 a text viewport.

10.3   USING INDEXES WITH RANDOM-ACCESS FILES

At this point, you may think that random-access files are much simpler to use
than sequential files. Unfortunately, a serpent lurks in our Garden of Eden. So far,
we have used only a particularly simple example of a random-access file.

In the charge account example, we used the charge account number as the
record number, assuming that all charge account numbers were three-digit numbers in the range 1 to 999. When we created the file in Program 10.1 (pages
377–78), we created a file with 999 records: one for each of the possible charge
account numbers. It didn't matter that many of the records did not contain data,
since the wasted space was not large.

But the key field often cannot be used as the record number. For example, in
a payroll file, a social security number is the most logical choice for key field.
However, if we followed the example of our charge account program, we would
have to create a file with 999,999,999 records because social security numbers contain 9 digits. The result would be a very large file—too large to store on a disk.
Moreover, even if a firm had ten million employees, 99 percent of the file would
be empty. To use random-access files when the key field cannot be used as the
record number, we need indexes.

An **index** is an array that is used to locate records in a random-access file.
The array contains the keys and is constructed so that if we are given the value of
the key field, we can retrieve the record. The index array is stored on disk as a
separate sequential file.

index
An array used to
locate records in a
random-access file.

EXAMPLE 4
CREATING A RANDOM-ACCESS FILE WITH AN INDEX

The Bon Vivant Club wants a program that creates a membership file. This file will use the four-digit membership number as the key. The fields in the membership record are a four-digit membership number, last name, first name, title (Mr., Mrs., Ms., and so on), street address, city, state, zip code, annual dues, and amount paid.

Problem Statement

Write a program that creates the membership file of the Bon Vivant Club. Since the membership number (which is the key) cannot be used as the record number, the program should also create an index file.

STEP 1   Variable Names

As usual, we begin by identifying and choosing names for the variables. We will define a record named MemberData that contains the fields Number, Lname (last name), Fname (first name), Title, Street, City, State, Zip, Dues, and Paid. We will also define a record variable named Member. The variable names are then as follows.

Variable	Variable Name
Input and Output Variables	
Membership number	Member.Number
Last name	Member.Lname
First name	Member.Fname
Title	Member.Title
Street address	Member.Street
City	Member.City
State	Member.State
Zip code	Member.Zip
Annual dues	Member.Dues
Amount paid	Member.Paid
Internal Variables	
Record number being processed	RecNum
Number of records in the file	NumRecords
Output Variable	
Membership number array	MemNumIndex

The name of the membership file we will create is MEMBER.RND, and the name of the index file is MEMBER.IDX.

STEP 2   Algorithm

We can use the following algorithm:

1. Open MEMBER.RND.
2. Repeat steps 3 through 5 until the trailer data are read.
3.   Read the data into the record variables.
4.   Write a record to MEMBER.RND.
5.   Store the membership number in the index array.
6. Close MEMBER.RND.
7. Open MEMBER.IDX.
8. Write the index array to MEMBER.IDX.
9. Close MEMBER.IDX.

STEP 3   **Hand-Calculated Answers**

We will check this program when we run the next program we write, which displays selected records.

STEP 4   **QBasic Program**

Program 10.4 creates the membership file and the index. The TYPE statement in lines 25 through 36 defines the record MemberData. The membership numbers are all less than 9999, so Number is defined as an integer. Zip, Dues, and Paid are all single-precision numeric variables. The other fields are fixed-length strings. The DIM statement in line 38 defines the record variable Member to have the structure of MemberData. The index consists of the array MemNumIndex. In line 39, this array is dimensioned with 1000 elements because the exclusive Bon Vivant Club would never have more than 1000 members. Line 42 opens MEMBER.RND, and line 43 calls CreateFileAndIndex.

In the CreateFileAndIndex subprogram, which starts at line 83, RecNum is initialized to 0. Then in a loop, the data are read and written to MEMBER.RND. Logically, only one READ statement is required—but to keep the statement lengths under 80 characters, three READ statements are used. Similarly, in the main module, the data for each member are given in three DATA statements.

The PUT statement in line 98

```
PUT #1, RecNum, Member
```

actually writes the data to the file. In this statement, RecNum specifies the record number of the record that is being written. On each pass through the loop, RecNum is incremented in line 97. So the records are written as records 1, 2, 3, and so on.

Notice that the records are written in the order that they are read from the DATA statements. Thus, the data in the first three DATA statements are written as record number 1, the data in the second three DATA statements are written as record number 2, and so on. Since there is no meaning to the order in which the records are listed in the DATA statements, there is no meaning to the order in which the records are stored in the file. This was done deliberately to simulate an on-line system.

When the program reaches line 99, it has just written the record whose membership number is Member.Number as record number RecNum. To create the index, line 99 sets MemNumIndex(RecNum) equal to Member.Number. For example, if the record whose membership number is 3216 is stored as record number 7, then the seventh element of MemNumIndex is set equal to 3216. In later programs, we will search MemNumIndex to determine the record number of the record with a specified membership number.

The loop repeats until the trailer data are read. In line 102, NumRecords (which stands for the number of records in the file) is set equal to RecNum. Then MEMBER.RND is closed, and control returns to the main module.

At this point, MEMBER.RND is created, and the index array is filled with data. Figure 10.3 shows the contents of MemNumIndex. As you probably expected, the membership numbers are in the same order in this array as they are in Program 10.4's DATA statements. Remember that this is also the same order that the records occur in MEMBER.RND. The WriteIndex subprogram, which starts at line 106 in Program 10.4, writes the array to the disk file MEMBER.IDX, which is an ordinary sequential file.   ■

```
 1 | '    *** CREATING THE MEMBERSHIP FILE - WITH INDEX ***
 2 | '    Read DATA and create the membership file. Also create an index
 3 | '    to the membership file.
 4 |
 5 | DECLARE SUB WriteIndex (MemNumIndex!(), NumRecords!)
 6 | DECLARE SUB CreateFileAndIndex (Member AS ANY, MemNumIndex(), NumRecords)
 7 |
 8 | '    Variables used
 9 |
10 | '    Member record consisting of:
11 | '         Member.City          City
12 | '         Member.Dues          Annual dues
13 | '         Member.Fname         First name
14 | '         Member.Lname         Last name
15 | '         Member.Number        Membership number
16 | '         Member.Paid          Amount paid
17 | '         Member.State         State
18 | '         Member.Street        Street Address
19 | '         Member.Title         Title
20 | '         Member.Zip           Zip code
21 | '    MemNumIndex              Membership number array
22 | '    NumRecords               Number of records in the file
23 |
24 | '    Define the MemberData record
25 | TYPE MemberData
26 |     Number AS INTEGER
27 |     Lname AS STRING * 15
28 |     Fname AS STRING * 10
29 |     Title AS STRING * 10
30 |     Street AS STRING * 25
31 |     City AS STRING * 20
32 |     State AS STRING * 2
33 |     Zip AS SINGLE
34 |     Dues AS SINGLE
35 |     Paid AS SINGLE
36 | END TYPE
37 |
38 | DIM Member AS MemberData
39 | DIM MemNumIndex(1000)
40 |
41 | CLS
42 | OPEN "MEMBER.RND" FOR RANDOM AS #1 LEN = LEN(Member)
43 | CALL CreateFileAndIndex(Member, MemNumIndex(), NumRecords)
44 | CALL WriteIndex(MemNumIndex(), NumRecords)
45 | PRINT "Normal end of program"
46 | '    Data to create file - used by CreateFileAndIndex
47 | '    Three DATA statements make one record
48 | '    Format is Membership Number, Last Name, First Name, Title
49 | '    Street, City, State, Zip Code
50 | '    Dues, and Paid
51 | DATA 6057, Ripps, David, Dr. & Mrs.
52 | DATA 705 East 55 Street, New York, NY, 10028
53 | DATA 25, 25
54 | DATA 3168, Padilla, Rudy, Mr. & Mrs.
55 | DATA 4944 18 Place, Garrison, NY, 10524
```

PROGRAM 10.4   Creating a random-access file with an index. *(continued on next page)*

```
56    DATA 20, 10
57    DATA 3567, Carnes, Cecil, Mr.
58    DATA 2394 Welby Way, Los Alamos, NM, 87544
59    DATA 35, 35
60    DATA 4251, Lindauer, George, Dr. & Mrs.
61    DATA 2978 Ambleglen Court, Corydon, ID, 47122
62    DATA 25, 20
63    DATA 4232, Wardak, Henry, Mr. & Mrs.
64    DATA 130 Rover Road, Conoga Park, CA, 90047
65    DATA 50, 50
66    DATA 9751, Sanzeri, Philip, Mr. & Mrs.
67    DATA 39 Beechwood, Clearwater, FL, 33519
68    DATA 35, 25
69    DATA 3216, Mezquita, Fred, Mr.
70    DATA 8 Danbury Court, El Segundo, CA, 90245
71    DATA 25, 15
72    DATA 7257, Schoenwald, Richard, Dr. & Mrs.
73    DATA 709 Lincoln Ave, Pittsburgh, PA, 15206
74    DATA 35, 20
75    DATA 2792, Switzer, Steven, Mr. & Mrs.
76    DATA 8 Lequer Road, Port Washington, NY, 11050
77    DATA 50, 50
78    DATA 7349, Donner, Rachel, Ms.
79    DATA 147-16 92 Street, Forest Hills, NY, 11375
80    DATA 20, 10
81    '    Trailer data follow
82    DATA -9999, X, X, X

83    SUB CreateFileAndIndex (Member AS MemberData, MemNumIndex(), NumRecords)
84    '    Read DATA and create file and index
85    '    Member received - READs DATA statements in Main module
86    '    Returns MemNumIndex() and NumRecords
87
88    '    Local variable
89
90    '    RecNum                      Record number being processed
91
92        RecNum = 0                                    'Initialize record number
93        READ Member.Number, Member.Lname, Member.Fname, Member.Title
94        DO UNTIL Member.Number = -9999
95            READ Member.Street, Member.City, Member.State, Member.Zip
96            READ Member.Dues, Member.Paid
97            RecNum = RecNum + 1                       'Increment record number
98            PUT #1, RecNum, Member               'Write record
99            MemNumIndex(RecNum) = Member.Number  'Add data to index array
100           READ Member.Number, Member.Lname, Member.Fname, Member.Title
101       LOOP
102       NumRecords = RecNum
103       CLOSE #1
104   END SUB

106   SUB WriteIndex (MemNumIndex(), NumRecords)
107   '    Write index array to disk file
108   '    MemNumIndex() and NumRecords received
109   '    No variables returned
110
```

PROGRAM 10.4 *(continued)*

```
111 |     OPEN "MEMBER.IDX" FOR OUTPUT AS #1    'Open index file
112 |     FOR J = 1 TO NumRecords               'For every record
113 |         WRITE #1, MemNumIndex(J)          'write it to disk
114 |     NEXT J
115 |     CLOSE #1
116 | END SUB
```

Normal end of program

PROGRAM 10.4 *(continued)*

EXAMPLE 5
QUERYING A RANDOM-ACCESS FILE

Now that Bon Vivant's membership file is created, its treasurer wants to be able to check on a member's standing at any time.

Problem Statement

Write a program that accepts a membership number and displays the corresponding record. If an invalid membership number is entered, display an error message.

STEP 1 Variable Names

We can use the same variables we used when the file was created. In addition, we need the following internal variables.

Variable	Variable Name
Internal Variables	
Membership number entered by user	MemNumIn
Number of active elements in MemNumIndex	NumElements

STEP 2 Algorithm

We can use the following algorithm:

1. Open MEMBER.RND and MEMBER.IDX.
2. Read the MEMBER.IDX file and fill MemNumIndex.
3. Close MEMBER.IDX.
4. Repeat steps 5 through 8 while the user wants to continue.
5. Accept MemNumIn.

Element Number	Membership Number
1	6057
2	3168
3	3567
4	4251
5	4232
6	9751
7	3216
8	7257
9	2792
10	7349

FIGURE 10.3 The MemNumIndex array.

6. Perform a sequential search of MemNumIndex for MemNumIn.
7. If MemNumIn was found, read the corresponding record from the MEMBER.RND and display it.
8. If MemNumIn was not found, display an error message.
9. Close MEMBER.RND.

The top-down chart for this problem is shown in Figure 10.4. The main module calls LoadIndex (which loads the index array with data from the index file) and ProcessRequests (which handles the user's requests). ProcessRequests, in turn, calls one subprogram that gets the membership number from the user, and another that searches the index array for the entered membership number. If the entered membership number is found in the index array, a subprogram that displays the desired record is called. If the entered membership number is not found, a subprogram that displays an error message is called.

STEP 3 Hand-Calculated Answer

We will check this program by verifying that it displays the data listed in the DATA statements in Program 10.4 (pages 395–96). This will also verify that Program 10.4 created the file correctly.

STEP 4 QBasic Program

Program 10.5 queries the membership file. Figure 10.5 shows a typical screen produced by Program 10.5. This screen displays the fields for the record whose membership number is 9751. If you compare the displayed values with those listed in the DATA statements in lines 66 through 68 in Program 10.4, you will see that the displayed values are correct. This shows that both Programs 10.4 and 10.5 are correct.

In the main module, line 47 opens MEMBER.RND, and line 48 opens the membership number index file, MEMBER.IDX, for input. Then LoadIndex is called. In LoadIndex, the records of the index file—MEMBER.IDX—are read into the elements of MemNumIndex in a DO loop that continues until the end of file is

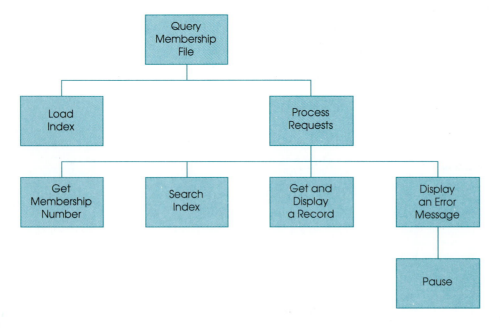

FIGURE 10.4 A top-down chart for a program that queries the membership file.

```
 1  '    *** QUERYING THE MEMBERSHIP FILE ***
 2  '    Display records from the membership file as requested
 3  '    by the user
 4
 5  DECLARE SUB ProcessRequests (Member AS ANY, MemNumIndex!(), NumElements!)
 6  DECLARE FUNCTION GetMemNum! ()
 7  DECLARE SUB GetAndDisplayRecord (Member AS ANY, RecNum!)
 8  DECLARE SUB DisplayErrorMsg (MemNumIn!)
 9  DECLARE SUB Pause (Delay)
10  DECLARE SUB LoadIndex (MemNumIndex!(), NumElements!)
11  DECLARE SUB SearchIndex (MemNumIndex!(), NumElements!, MemNumIn!, RecNum!)
12
13  '    Variables used
14
15  '    Member record consisting of:
16  '        Member.City          City
17  '        Member.Dues          Annual dues
18  '        Member.Fname         First name
19  '        Member.Lname         Last name
20  '        Member.Number        Membership number
21  '        Member.Paid          Amount paid
22  '        Member.State         State
23  '        Member.Street        Street Address
24  '        Member.Title         Title
25  '        Member.Zip           Zip code
26  '    MemNumIn                 Membership number entered by user
27  '    MemNumIndex              Membership number array
28  '    NumElements              Number of active elements in MemNumIndex
29  '    RecNum                   Record number being processed
30
31  TYPE MemberData
32      Number AS INTEGER
33      Lname AS STRING * 15
34      Fname AS STRING * 10
35      Title AS STRING * 10
36      Street AS STRING * 25
37      Town AS STRING * 20
38      State AS STRING * 2
39      Zip AS SINGLE
40      Dues AS SINGLE
41      Paid AS SINGLE
42  END TYPE
43  DIM Member AS MemberData
44  DIM MemNumIndex(1000)
45
46  CLS
47  OPEN "MEMBER.RND" FOR RANDOM AS #1 LEN = LEN(Member)
48  OPEN "MEMBER.IDX" FOR INPUT AS #2
49
50  CALL LoadIndex(MemNumIndex(), NumElements)
51  CALL ProcessRequests(Member, MemNumIndex(), NumElements)
52  CLOSE
53  END
```

PROGRAM 10.5   Querying a random-access file with an index.
(continued on next page)

```
54 | SUB DisplayErrorMsg (MemNumIn)
55 | '   Display error message
56 | '   MemNumIn received
57 | '   No variables returned
58 |
59 |     BEEP
60 |     LOCATE 25, 12
61 |     PRINT "Membership number"; MemNumIn; "is not in file ";
62 |     CALL Pause(2)
63 | END SUB
64 |
65 | SUB GetAndDisplayRecord (Member AS MemberData, RecNum)
66 | '   Get and display the record
67 | '   Receives Member and RecNum
68 | '   No variables are returned
69 |
70 |     GET #1, RecNum, Member               'Read record
71 |     LOCATE 10, 12                        'and display it
72 |     PRINT "Number"; Member.Number
73 |     LOCATE 11, 12
74 |     PRINT RTRIM$(Member.Title); " ";
75 |     PRINT RTRIM$(Member.Fname); " ";
76 |     PRINT RTRIM$(Member.Lname)
77 |     LOCATE 12, 12
78 |     PRINT Member.Street
79 |     LOCATE 13, 12
80 |     PRINT RTRIM$(Member.Town); ", ";
81 |     PRINT Member.State;
82 |     PRINT Member.Zip
83 |     LOCATE 14, 12
84 |     PRINT USING "Dues ###.##"; Member.Dues
85 |     LOCATE 15, 12
86 |     PRINT USING "Paid ###.##"; Member.Paid
87 | END SUB
88 |
89 | FUNCTION GetMemNum
90 | '   Get membership number from user
91 | '   No variables received
92 | '   Membership number returned in GetMemNum
93 |
94 |         LOCATE 8, 12
95 |         PRINT "Enter a 4-digit membership number (0000 to quit) ";
96 |         MemNumIn = VAL(INPUT$(4))
97 |         PRINT MemNumIn
98 |         GetMemNum = MemNumIn
99 | END FUNCTION
100 | SUB LoadIndex (MemNumIndex(), NumElements)
101 | '   Load MEMBER.IDX into MemNumIndex()
102 | '   No variables received
103 | '   MemNumIndex() and NumElements are returned
104 |
105 |     J = 0
106 |     DO WHILE NOT EOF(2)                  'Load index file
107 |         J = J + 1                        'into index
108 |         INPUT #2, MemNumIndex(J)         'array
109 |     LOOP
110 |     CLOSE #2
111 |     NumElements = J
112 | END SUB
```

PROGRAM 10.5 *(continued)*

```
113
114    SUB Pause (Delay)
115    '    Pause Delay seconds and clear screen
116    '    Delay received
117    '    No variables returned
118
119         Later = TIMER + Delay         'Calculate time Delay seconds from now
120         DO WHILE TIMER < Later        'Loop for Delay seconds
121         LOOP
122    END SUB
123
124    SUB ProcessRequests (Member AS MemberData, MemNumIndex(), NumElements)
125    '    Accepts user's input and processes it
126    '    Member, MemNumIndex(), and NumElements received
127    '    No variables returned
128
129         LOCATE 2, 20
130         PRINT "QUERY THE MEMBERSHIP FILE"
131         VIEW PRINT 3 TO 25
132         MemNumIn = GetMemNum
133         DO UNTIL MemNumIn = 0
134             CALL SearchIndex(MemNumIndex(), NumElements, MemNumIn, RecNum)
135             IF RecNum <> 0 THEN
136                 CALL GetAndDisplayRecord(Member, RecNum)
137                 LOCATE 24, 12
138                 PRINT "Press any key to continue";
139                 A$ = INPUT$(1)
140             ELSE
141                 CALL DisplayErrorMsg(MemNumIn)
142             END IF
143             CLS
144             MemNumIn = GetMemNum
145         LOOP
146    END SUB
147
147    SUB SearchIndex (MemNumIndex(), NumElements, MemNumIn, RecNum)
148    '    Sequential search of index array
149    '    MemNumIndex(), NumElements, and MemNumIn received
150    '    RecNum returned
151
152    '    On return, if RecNum is 0, the record was not found,
153    '    otherwise RecNum is the record number of the desired record
154    '    in MEMBER.RND
155
156         RecNum = 0
157         FOR J = 1 TO NumElements                 'Examine every element
158             IF MemNumIndex(J) = MemNumIn THEN    'If it equals input number
159                 RecNum = J                       'save subscript and
160                 EXIT FOR                         'exit from subprogram
161             END IF
162         NEXT J
163    END SUB
```

PROGRAM 10.5 *(continued)*

```
                  QUERY THE MEMBERSHIP FILE




Enter 4-digit membership number (0000 to quit)  9751

Number 9751
Mr. & Mrs. Philip Sanzeri
39 Beechwood
Clearwater, FL 33519
Dues  35.00
Paid  25.00




              Press any key to continue
```

FIGURE 10.5
The screen
displayed by
Program 10.5.

reached. In the DO loop, J serves as a subscript; it is incremented so that it always points to the next available element in MemNumIndex. When the program exits from the DO loop, J equals the number of elements in the array, so line 111 sets NumElements equal to J. Control returns to the main module, which calls ProcessRequests, which subsequently accepts the membership numbers and displays the records.

The ProcessRequests subprogram, starting at line 124, uses the GetMemNum function to obtain a membership number from the user. ProcessRequests then enters a DO loop, where it stays until the user enters a 0 for the membership number, which ends the session. In the DO loop, line 134 calls the SearchIndex subprogram to perform a sequential search of the MemNumIndex array.

This sequential search is programmed differently from the one you studied in Chapter 8. It uses a FOR...NEXT loop to examine each element of MemNumIndex. When it finds the element that is equal to MemNumIn, it uses an EXIT FOR statement to exit from the loop. An EXIT FOR statement transfers control to the statement following the NEXT statement; in this case, the END SUB statement.

Some authorities discourage the use of EXIT FOR statements because they violate one of the principles of structured programming: that a loop should have only one exit point. If your instructor prohibits the use of EXIT FOR statements, you can use the following adaption of the sequential search used in Chapter 8:

```
RecNum = 0
J = 1                                        'Start with first element
'Stay in loop while not found and
'some elements have not yet been examined
DO WHILE RecNum = 0 AND J <= NumElements
    IF MemNumIndex(J) = MemNumIN THEN        'If match is found
        RecNum = J                           'save subscript
    ELSE                                     'otherwise
        J = J + 1                            'increment subscript
    END IF
LOOP
```

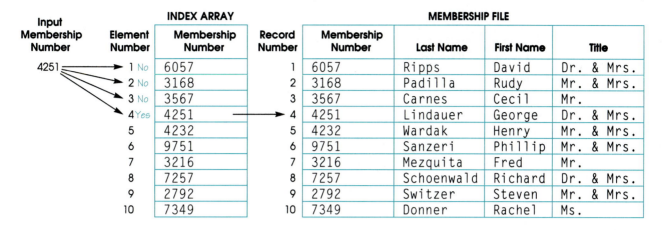

FIGURE 10.6   Searching the index array for the recordnumber of the record whose membership number is 4251.

Whichever search subprogram you use, the logic is the same. Suppose the user enters the membership number 4251. Figure 10.6 shows that 4251 is the membership number of record number 4, and because of the way we built MemNumIndex, 4251 is also the 4th element of MemNumIndex. The job of the SearchIndex subprogram is to make sure that when control is returned to ProcessRequests, RecNum is equal to 4.

Figure 10.6 shows how this is done. The search examines each element of MemNumIndex in turn. When J is 1, 2, and 3, the search finds that the first, second, and third elements of MemNumIndex do not equal 4251. When J is 4, however, the search finds that the fourth element of MemNumIndex is equal to 4251. The program sets RecNum equal to J (which is equal to 4), exits from the search, and returns to ProcessRequests. So you see that when the user enters a membership number that matches one in the file, SearchIndex returns the record number of the desired record in RecNum.

What happens if the user enters a membership number that does not match one in the file? In that case, when the program returns to ProcessRequests, RecNum will still have the value 0 that was assigned to it before the search began.

In ProcessRequests, line 135 tests RecNum. If RecNum does not equal 0, the search was successful, so line 136 calls the GetAndDisplayRecord subprogram. The GET statement in line 70 reads the record specified by RecNum, and the LOCATE and PRINT USING statements in lines 71 through 86 display the record. If RecNum equals 0, the search for the membership number was unsuccessful. In that case, line 141 calls the DisplayErrorMsg subprogram to print an error message.   ■

EXAMPLE 6 ▬▬▬▬▬▬▬▬▬▬▬▬▬▬▬▬

MAINTAINING A RANDOM-ACCESS FILE
Of course, Bon Vivant also needs a program to maintain its membership file.

Problem Statement

Write a program that can add, delete, and update records in the membership file. Print an error message if the user tries to add a record with a membership number equal to one already in the file, or if the user tries to delete or update a record that does not exist. The user should be allowed to update any field in the record except the membership number (since that is the key field).

STEP 1 **Variable Names**

We can use the same variables we used in Program 10.4 (pages 395–96), with the following additional internal variables.

Variable	Variable Name
Internal Variables	
Membership number entered by user	`MemNumIn`
User input to select from menu	`Code$`
Number of field to be updated	`UpdateFld`
Number of records in MEMBER.RND	`NumRecords`

STEP 2 **Algorithm**

The algorithm is as follows:

1. Open MEMBER.RND and MEMBER.IDX.
2. Read the MEMBER.IDX file and fill MemNumIndex.
3. Display a menu that allows users to add, delete, or update a record, or to exit.
4. Repeat steps 5, 6, and 7 until the user wants to exit.
5. To add a record:
    Accept the data for the new record.
    Write the record to the end of the file.
    Update MemNumIndex.
6. To delete a record:
    Accept the membership number of the record to be deleted.
    Delete the record by replacing that record's membership number with 0 in MemNumIndex.
7. To update a record:
    Accept the membership number of the record to be updated.
    Display the record and allow the user to change any field. When all the changes have been made, rewrite the record.
8. Close all the files.
9. Open MEMBER.IDX for output, and write MemNumIndex to MEMBER.IDX.
10. Close MEMBER.IDX.

The top-down chart for this problem is shown in Figure 10.7. This chart shows that the main module calls on separate subprograms to add, delete, and update records. These three subprograms in turn call on a subprogram to display an error message and to pause. In addition, the subprogram that adds records calls a subprogram to get the data for a record, and the subprogram that updates records calls a subprogram to update the individual fields.

The main module also calls subprograms to load the index array, display the menu, get a valid code (one that is between 1 and 4) from the user, get the membership number from the user, search the index array, and rewrite the index file.

STEP 3 **Hand-Calculated Answers**

The easiest way to check this program is to add a record, display it, and verify that it was added correctly. Similarly, we can update a record and then display it. Finally, we can delete a record and attempt to display it. In that case, the program should display an error message instead.

STEP 4 **QBasic Program**

The QBasic program that maintains the membership file is shown in Program 10.6. To conserve space, the DECLARE statements inserted by QBasic were deleted.

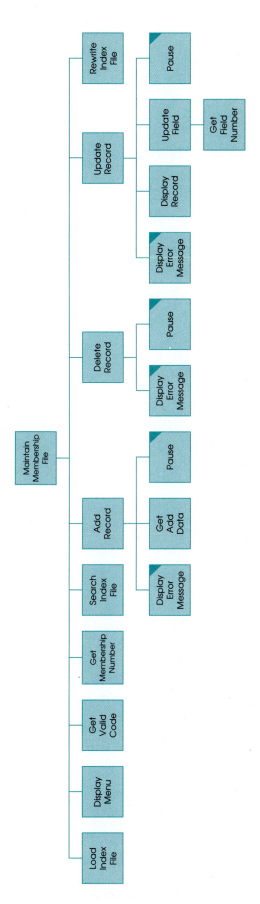

FIGURE 10.7 Top-down chart for a program that adds, deletes, and updates records in the membership file.

```
 1  '   *** MAINTAINING THE MEMBERSHIP FILE ***
 2  '   Add, delete, and update records from MEMBER.RND
 3
 4  '   The DECLARE statements, which are inserted here by
 5  '   QBasic, have been deleted to save space
 6
 7  '   Variables used
 8
 9  '   Code$                    User input to select from menu
10  '   Member record consisting of:
11  '       Member.City          City
12  '       Member.Dues          Annual dues
13  '       Member.Fname         First name
14  '       Member.Lname         Last name
15  '       Member.Number        Membership number
16  '       Member.Paid          Amount paid
17  '       Member.State         State
18  '       Member.Street        Street address
19  '       Member.Title         Title
20  '       Member.Zip           Zip code
21  '   MemNumIndex              Membership number array
22  '   NumRecords               Number of records in the file
23  '   RecNum                   Record number being processed
24  '   UpdateFld                User input specifying the number of field to be updated
25
26  TYPE MemberData
27      Number AS INTEGER
28      Lname AS STRING * 15
29      Fname AS STRING * 10
30      Title AS STRING * 10
31      Street AS STRING * 25
32      City AS STRING * 20
33      State AS STRING * 2
34      Zip AS SINGLE
35      Dues AS SINGLE
36      Paid AS SINGLE
37  END TYPE
38  DIM Member AS MemberData
39  CLS
40  DIM MemNumIndex(1000)
41  OPEN "MEMBER.RND" FOR RANDOM AS #1 LEN = LEN(Member)
42  NumRecords = LOF(1) / LEN(Member)         'Calculate number of records in MEMBER.RND
43  OPEN "MEMBER.IDX" FOR INPUT AS #2
44
45  CALL LoadIndex(MemNumIndex(), NumRecords)
46  CALL DisplayMenu
47
48  '   Process requests
49  Code$ = GetValidCode$
50  DO UNTIL Code$ = "4"
51      MemNumIn = GetMemNum
52      CALL SearchIndex(MemNumIndex(), NumRecords, MemNumIn, RecNum)
53      SELECT CASE Code$
54          CASE "1"
55              CALL AddRecord(Member, MemNumIndex(), NumRecords, MemNumIn, RecNum, ↵
                    Code$)
```

PROGRAM 10.6   Maintaining a random-access file with an index.
(continued on next page)

```
56                  CASE "2"
57                      CALL DeleteRecord(MemNumIndex(), MemNumIn, RecNum, Code$)
58                  CASE "3"
59                      CALL UpdateRecord(Member, MemNumIndex(), NumRecords, MemNumIn,↵
                          RecNum, Code$)
60          END SELECT
61          Code$ = GetValidCode$
62      LOOP
63      CALL RewriteIndexFile(MemNumIndex(), NumRecords)
64      END

65      SUB AddRecord (Member AS MemberData, MemNumIndex(), NumRecords, MemNumIn,↵
            RecNum, Code$)
66      '   Add a record
67      '   Member, MemNumIndex(), NumRecords, MemNumIn, RecNum, and Code$ received
68      '   No variables returned
69
70          IF RecNum <> 0 THEN                          'If member number is used
71              CALL DisplayErrorMsg(MemNumIn, Code$)    'no add
72          ELSE                                         'else
73              Member.Number = MemNumIn
74              CALL GetAddData(Member)                  'Get rest of data
75              NumRecords = NumRecords + 1              'Update number of records
76              PUT #1, NumRecords, Member               'Write record
77              MemNumIndex(NumRecords) = MemNumIn       'Update index array
78              LOCATE 25, 20
79              PRINT "Record"; MemNumIn; "added";
80          END IF
81          CALL Pause(2)
82          CLS
83      END SUB
84
85      SUB DeleteRecord (MemNumIndex(), MemNumIn, RecNum, Code$)
86      '   Delete a record
87      '   MemNumIndex(), MemNumIn, RecNum, and Code$ received
88      '   No variables returned
89
90          IF RecNum = 0 THEN                           'If member number not used
91              CALL DisplayErrorMsg(MemNumIn, Code$)    'no delete
92          ELSE                                         'else
93              MemNumIndex(RecNum) = 0                  'Update index array
94              LOCATE 25, 20
95              PRINT "Record"; MemNumIn; "deleted";
96          END IF
97          CALL Pause(2)
98          CLS
99      END SUB

100     SUB DisplayErrorMsg (MemNumIn, Code$)
101     '   Display error message
102     '   MemNumIn and Code$ received
103     '   No variables returned
104
105         BEEP
106         LOCATE 25, 20
107         SELECT CASE Code$               'Use Code$ to select error message to print
108             CASE "1"
```

PROGRAM 10.6 *(continued)*

```
109            PRINT "Membership number "; MemNumIn; " is in file, no add";
110         CASE "2"
111            PRINT "Membership number"; MemNumIn; " is not in file, no delete";
112         CASE "3"
113            PRINT "Membership number"; MemNumIn; " is not in file, no update";
114      END SELECT
115 END SUB
116
117 SUB DisplayMenu
118 '   Display menu
119 '   No variables received or returned
120
121      LOCATE 5, 20
122      PRINT "MEMBERSHIP MAINTENANCE MENU"
123      LOCATE 8, 26
124      PRINT "1     Add a record"
125      LOCATE 9, 26
126      PRINT "2     Delete a record"
127      LOCATE 10, 26
128      PRINT "3     Update a record"
129      LOCATE 11, 26
130      PRINT "4     Exit program"
131      VIEW PRINT 12 TO 25
132 END SUB

133 SUB DisplayRecord (Member AS MemberData)
134 '   Display a record
135 '   Member received
136 '   No variables returned
137
138      LOCATE 14, 1
139      PRINT SPACE$(79)
140      LOCATE 14, 10
141      PRINT USING " Membership number      ####"; Member.Number
142      LOCATE 15, 10
143      PRINT USING " 1. Last name           &"; Member.Lname
144      LOCATE 16, 10
145      PRINT USING " 2. First name          &"; Member.Fname
146      LOCATE 17, 10
147      PRINT USING " 3. Title               &"; Member.Title
148      LOCATE 18, 10
149      PRINT USING " 4. Street              &"; Member.Street
150      LOCATE 19, 10
151      PRINT USING " 5. City                &"; Member.City
152      LOCATE 20, 10
153      PRINT USING " 6. State               &"; Member.State
154      LOCATE 21, 10
155      PRINT USING " 7. Zip code            #####"; Member.Zip
156      LOCATE 22, 10
157      PRINT USING " 8. Dues                ###.##"; Member.Dues
158      LOCATE 23, 10
159      PRINT USING " 9. Paid                ###.##"; Member.Paid
160 END SUB

161 SUB GetAddData (Member AS MemberData)
162 '   Get rest of data for record to be added
163 '   No variables received
164 '   Member returned
165
```

PROGRAM 10.6 *(continued)*

```
166         LOCATE 15, 10
167         INPUT "Enter last name: ", Member.Lname
168         LOCATE 16, 10
169         INPUT "Enter first name: ", Member.Fname
170         LOCATE 17, 10
171         INPUT "Enter title: ", Member.Title
172         LOCATE 18, 10
173         INPUT "Enter street: ", Member.Street
174         LOCATE 19, 10
175         INPUT "Enter city: ", Member.City
176         LOCATE 20, 10
177         INPUT "Enter state: ", Member.State
178         LOCATE 21, 10
179         INPUT "Enter zip code: ", Member.Zip
180         LOCATE 22, 10
181         INPUT "Enter dues: ", Member.Dues
182         LOCATE 23, 10
183         INPUT "Enter paid: ", Member.Paid
184     END SUB

185     FUNCTION GetFldNum
186     '   Get number of field to update from user
187     '   No variables received
188     '   Field number returned in GetFldNum
189
190         LOCATE 25, 1
191         PRINT SPACE$(79);
192         LOCATE 25, 5, 1
193         PRINT "Enter 1 to 9 to update field, or 0 to end ";
194         UpdateFld = VAL(INPUT$(1))
195         PRINT UpdateFld;
196         DO UNTIL UpdateFld >= 0 AND UpdateFld <= 9
197             BEEP
198             LOCATE 25, 5
199             PRINT "Please enter a number between 0 and 9      ";
200             UpdateFld = VAL(INPUT$(1))
201             PRINT UpdateFld;
202         LOOP
203         GetFldNum = UpdateFld
204     END FUNCTION

205
206     FUNCTION GetMemNum
207     '   Get membership number from user
208     '   No variables received
209     '   Membership number returned in GetMemNum
210
211         LOCATE 14, 20
212         PRINT "Enter 4-digit membership number ";
213         MemNumIn = VAL(INPUT$(4))
214         PRINT MemNumIn
215         GetMemNum = MemNumIn
216     END FUNCTION

217     FUNCTION GetValidCode$
218     '   Get Code$ from user. Function does not return until
219     '   a valid Code$ has been entered.
220     '   No variables received
221     '   Code$ returned in GetValidCode$
222
```

PROGRAM 10.6 (continued)

```
223        LOCATE 12, 20
224        PRINT "Enter a number from 1 to 4: ";
225        Code$ = INPUT$(1)
226        PRINT Code$
227        DO UNTIL Code$ > "0" AND Code$ <= "4"
228            BEEP
229            LOCATE 15, 20
230            PRINT "Please enter a number between 1 and 4 ";
231            Code$ = INPUT$(1)
232            LOCATE 15, 20
233            PRINT SPACE$(39)
234            LOCATE 12, 48
235            PRINT Code$
236        LOOP
237        GetValidCode$ = Code$
238    END FUNCTION
239
240    SUB LoadIndex (MemNumIndex(), NumRecords)
241    '    Read MEMBER.IDX into MemNumIndex()
242    '    No variables received
243    '    MemNumIndex() and NumRecords returned
244
245        J = 0
246        DO WHILE NOT EOF(2)                     'Load index file
247            J = J + 1                           'into
248            INPUT #2, MemNumIndex(J)            'index array
249        LOOP
250        CLOSE #2
251    END SUB
252
252    SUB Pause (Delay)
253    '    Cause a pause of Delay seconds
254    '    Delay received
255    '    No variables returned
256
257        Later = TIMER + Delay         'Calculate time Delay seconds from now
258        DO WHILE TIMER < Later        'Loop for Delay seconds
259        LOOP
260    END SUB
261
262    SUB RewriteIndexFile (MemNumIndex(), NumRecords)
263    '    Rewrite the index array to the index file
264    '    MemNumIndex() and NumRecords received
265    '    No variables returned
266
267        CLOSE                                   'Close all files
268        OPEN "MEMBER.IDX" FOR OUTPUT AS #1     'Write updated
269        FOR J = 1 TO NumRecords                 'index array to
270            WRITE #1, MemNumIndex(J)            'index file
271        NEXT J
272        CLOSE                                   'Close all files
273    END SUB
274
275    SUB SearchIndex (MemNumIndex(), NumRecords, MemNumIn, RecNum)
276    '    Search index array for MemNumIn
277    '    MemNumIndex(), NumRecords, and MemNumIn received
278    '    RecNum returned
279
```

(continued)

```
280  '    On return, if RecNum is 0, the record was not found;
281  '    otherwise, RecNum is the record number of the desired record
282  '    in MEMBER.RND
283
284       RecNum = 0
285       FOR J = 1 TO NumRecords                    'Examine every element
286           IF MemNumIndex(J) = MemNumIn THEN      'If it equals input number
287               RecNum = J                         'save subscript and
288               EXIT FOR                           'exit from subprogram
289           END IF
290       NEXT J
291  END SUB

292  SUB UpdateField (Member AS MemberData)
293  '    Update fields
294  '    Member received
295  '    No variables returned
296
297       UpdateFld = GetFldNum               'Get a valid field number from user
298       DO UNTIL UpdateFld = 0
299           LOCATE 14 + UpdateFld, 32
300           PRINT SPACE$(25)
301           LOCATE 14 + UpdateFld, 32
302           SELECT CASE UpdateFld
303               CASE 1
304                   INPUT Member.Lname
305               CASE 2
306                   INPUT Member.Fname
307               CASE 3
308                   INPUT Member.Title
309               CASE 4
310                   INPUT Member.Street
311               CASE 5
312                   INPUT Member.City
313               CASE 6
314                   INPUT Member.State
315               CASE 7
316                   INPUT Member.Zip
317               CASE 8
318                   INPUT Member.Dues
319               CASE 9
320                   INPUT Member.Paid
321           END SELECT
322           UpdateFld = GetFldNum                'Get a valid field number from user
323       LOOP
324  END SUB

325  SUB UpdateRecord (Member AS MemberData, MemNumIndex(), NumRecords, MemNumIn, ↵
        RecNum, Code$)
326  '    Update a record
327  '    Member, MemNumIndex(), NumRecords, MemNumIn, RecNum, and Code$ received
328  '    No variables returned
329
330       IF RecNum = 0 THEN                         'If member number not used
331           CALL DisplayErrorMsg(MemNumIn, Code$)  'no update
332       ELSE                                       'else
333           GET #1, RecNum, Member                 'Get record
334           CALL DisplayRecord(Member)             'display it
```

PROGRAM 10.6 *(continued)*

```
335 |          CALL UpdateField(Member)              'update fields
336 |          PUT #1, RecNum, Member                'Rewrite updated record
337 |          LOCATE 25, 5
338 |          PRINT SPACE$(74);
339 |          LOCATE 25, 20
340 |          PRINT "Record"; MemNumIn; "updated";
341 |       END IF
342 |       CALL Pause(2)
343 |       CLS
344 | END SUB
```

PROGRAM 10.6 *(continued)*

The LOF Function

The main module opens MEMBER.RND and MEMBER.IDX. Line 42

```
NumRecords = LOF(1) / LEN(Member)
```

uses the LOF function to calculate the number of records in MEMBER.RND. The LOF (Length Of File) function returns the number of bytes allocated to a file. When we divide that number by the record length, LEN(Member), we get the number of records in the file—something we must know when we want to add records to the end of the file.

The main module next calls DisplayMenu to display the menu, and then starts to process the user's requests. It uses the function GetValidCode$ to obtain a Code$ between 1 and 4 from the user. The DO loop (lines 50 through 62) is executed until the user enters a 4 to end the session. In the loop, line 51 uses the GetMemNum function to obtain a membership number from the user. Then line 52 calls the SearchIndex subprogram. This subprogram—which searches MemNumIndex for MemNumIn—is identical to the SearchIndex subprogram in Program 10.5 (pages 399–401). It returns in RecNum the record number of the record whose membership number matches MemNumIn. If no record has a membership number that matches MemNumIn, the subroutine returns a 0 in RecNum.

Upon returning from SearchIndex, the SELECT CASE statement in lines 53 through 60 executes the appropriate subprogram, depending on the value the user entered for Code$.

The AddRecord Subprogram

The AddRecord subprogram starts by testing RecNum in line 70. Since we cannot add a record if the membership number is in use, if RecNum does not equal 0, the DisplayErrorMsg subprogram is called to display an error message. Otherwise, the GetAddData subprogram is called to obtain the rest of the data for the new record. Then—since we are adding a record—line 75 increments NumRecords, and the PUT statement in line 76 writes the new record to the NumRecords location. This PUT statement writes the new record at the end of MEMBER.RND. Lastly, the index array must be updated. Line 77 assigns the membership number of the added record to the NumRecords element of the index array.

The DeleteRecord Subprogram

The DeleteRecord subprogram also begins by testing RecNum. We cannot delete a record that isn't there, so if RecNum equals 0, the DisplayErrorMsg subprogram is called to display an error message. Otherwise, the record is deleted in line 93 by replacing the record's membership number in MemNumIndex with 0. To understand this statement, recall that RecNum points to the element of MemNumIndex that contains the record's membership number. Line 93 changes that element to 0. Notice that the record in MEMBER.RND is not erased—but since the membership number was erased from the index array, neither this program nor Program 10.5 can retrieve this record. We can consider the record logically deleted, even though it is not physically deleted. (This is analogous to the way DOS deletes files.)

The UpdateRecord Subprogram

Finally, let's consider the UpdateRecord subprogram. Because we don't have to update the index array, this subprogram is even easier than the others.

As usual, the subprogram begins by testing RecNum. We cannot update a record that isn't there, so if RecNum equals 0, the DisplayErrorMsg subprogram is called to display an error message. Otherwise, the record is read by line 333, and displayed by the DisplayRecord subprogram. The UpdateField subprogram is called to update one or more fields. Upon returning from UpdateField, the PUT statement in line 336 rewrites the updated record.

Figure 10.8 shows the screen with a displayed record, ready for updating. The user is not allowed to update the membership number since this field is the key, but all the other fields may be updated.

The UpdateField subprogram in Program 10.6 starts by executing the GetFldNum function to obtain from the user the number of the field to be updated. GetFldNum displays a message on line 25 on the screen that asks the user to enter the number of the field to be updated—1 to 9—or 0 to indicate that updating of this record is finished. The DO loop in lines 196 through 202 ensures that GetFldNum does not return to UpdateField until the user has entered a number between 0 and 9. In line 297, the value returned by GetFldNum is assigned to UpdateFld.

The DO loop in lines 298 through 323 updates the selected field. The program stays in this loop until the user enters a 0 for the number of the field to be updated.

```
          MEMBERSHIP MAINTENANCE PROGRAM


                1 to Add a record
                2 to Delete a record
                3 to Update a record
                4 to Exit program
          Enter a number from 1 to 4: 3

     Membership number      3216
        1. Last name        Mezquita
        2. First name       Fred
        3. Title            Mr.
        4. Street           8 Danbury Court
        5. City             ?
        6. State            CA
        7. Zip code         90245
        8. Dues              25.00
        9. Paid              15.00

     Enter 1 to 9 to update field, or 0 to end 5
```

FIGURE 10.8
A displayed record ready for updating.

```
Element      Membership
Number        Number

  1       6057
  2       3168
  3          0     ── Former position of 3567—deleted
  4       4251
  5       4232
  6          0     ── Former position of 9751—deleted
  7       3216
  8       7257
  9       2792
 10       7349
 11       5172     ── Record 5173 added at the end of the array
```

FIGURE 10.9   The MemNumIndex array after updating.

The LOCATE statement in line 299 and the PRINT statement in line 300 erase the current data in the field to be updated. The LOCATE statement in line 301 positions the cursor at the start of the field that is to be updated. In Figure 10.8, the user has entered a 5, and you can see the question mark positioned at the start of field 5.

Getting the cursor to the start of the field to be updated is not difficult. As you can see in the DisplayRecord subprogram (which starts at line 133), when the record is displayed, the first field that can be updated (Last Name) is displayed on line 15, the second field is displayed on line 16, and so on. This means that the field to be updated is displayed on line 14 + UpdateFld. All the fields are displayed starting at column 32. So the LOCATE statement in line 299 positions the cursor at row 14 + UpdateFld, column 32. The PRINT statement in line 300 prints 25 spaces to erase the current data, and the LOCATE statement in line 301 repositions the cursor to the start of the field.

The SELECT CASE statement in lines 302 through 321 uses the value of UpdateFld to select the INPUT statement from the set in lines 304 through 320 to update the desired field.

Figure 10.9 shows the index array after deleting records 3567 and 9751 and adding record 5173. Notice that record 5173 was added as record number 11, at the end of the file. ∎

Syntax Summary

EXIT FOR Statement

Form: EXIT FOR
Example: EXIT FOR
Explanation: Exits from a FOR...NEXT loop by branching to the statement
               following the NEXT statement.

10.3 EXERCISES

★1. If the record length of a file is 40, the file contains 20 records, and the file is opened as file number 1, what value is returned by LOF(1)?

2. If the record length of a file is 53 and the file is opened as file number 2, what is the statement to calculate the number of records in the file?

3. Why is it necessary in Program 10.1 to initialize the charge account file, but not necessary in Program 10.4 to initialize the membership file?

★4. In Program 10.5, why isn't a binary search used to search MemNumIndex?

5. In Program 10.6, the UpdateRecord subprogram does not update MemNum-Index, but both the AddRecord and DeleteRecord subprograms do. Why?

6. In Program 10.6, the AddRecord subprogram increases NumRecords, but the DeleteRecord subprogram does not decrease it. Why?

★7. In a program to list the membership file, would the following coding retrieve the deleted records?

```
FOR J = 1 TO NumRecords
    GET #1, J, Member
NEXT J
```

8. In Program 10.6, the user is not permitted to change the membership number. How would you correct the error if a record were stored with the wrong membership number?

9. Program 10.7 shows the execution of a program that was supposed to create A10-01.RND, described later in Programming Assignment 10.1. Execution stopped, QBasic highlighted line 44, and displayed the error message Bad record number. Find and correct the error.

```
1  |  '    *** PROGRAM FOR SECTION 10.3 Exercise 9 ***
2  |  '    Create A10-01.RND'
3  |
4  |  DECLARE SUB InitializeFile (Student AS ANY)
5  |  DECLARE SUB LoadFile (Student AS ANY)
6  |
7  |  '    Variables used
8  |
9  |  '    Student record consisting of
10 |  '         Student.Nam          Student's name
11 |  '         Student.Credits      Number of credits completed
12 |  '         Student.GPA          Student's GPA
13 |  '    StudentNum                Student's number
14 |
15 |  'Define the StudentData record
16 |  TYPE StudentData
17 |      Nam AS STRING * 25
18 |      credits AS INTEGER
19 |      GPA AS SINGLE
20 |  END TYPE
21 |  DIM Student AS StudentData
22 |
```

PROGRAM 10.7   An incorrect program to create A10-01.RND.
(continued on next page)

```
23  CLS
24  OPEN "A10-01.RND" FOR RANDOM AS #1 LEN = LEN(Student)
25  CALL InitializeFile(Student)
26  CALL LoadFile(Student)
27  CLOSE #1
28  PRINT "The Grade Point Average file has been created"
29  '    Data to create file
30  '    Format is Student number, name, credits, and GPA
31  DATA 429, "Quintano, Shelly", 56, 3.21
32  DATA 9999, X, 0, 0
33  END
34
35  SUB InitializeFile (Student AS StudentData)
36  '    Initialize file
37  '    No variables received
38  '    Student.Nam, Student.Credits, and Student.GPA returned
39
40      Student.Nam = SPACE$(25)         'Set name equal to spaces
41      Student.credits = 0              'Set credits equal to 0
42      Student.GPA = 0                  'Set GPA equal to 0
43      FOR J = 0 TO 999                 'Write every record in the file
44          PUT #1, J, Student
45      NEXT J
46  END SUB
47
48  SUB LoadFile (Student AS StudentData)
49  '    Load data into file
50  '    No variables received
51  '    Student record returned
52
53  READ StudentNum, Student.Nam, Student.credits, Student.GPA
54  DO UNTIL StudentNum = 9999
55      PUT #1, StudentNum, Student
56      READ StudentNum, Student.Nam, Student.credits, Student.GPA
57  LOOP
58  END SUB
```

PROGRAM 10.7 *(continued)*

WHAT YOU HAVE LEARNED

In this chapter, you learned that:

- The OPEN statement for a random-access file specifies the filename, the file number, and the record length.
- The PUT statement writes a record to a random-access file.
- The GET statement reads a record from a random-access file.
- The VIEW PRINT creates a text viewport.

- An index for a random-access file consists of an array that contains the keys. The order of the keys in the array is the same as the order of the records in the file. The index is stored as a separate sequential file.
- The EXIT FOR statement exits from a FOR ... NEXT loop by transferring control to the statement following the NEXT statement.
- The LOF function returns the number of bytes allocated to a file.

NEW QBASIC STATEMENTS

STATEMENT	EFFECT
OPEN	
`OPEN "STAMPS.RND" FOR RANDOM AS #1 ↵` `  LEN = LEN(Stamps)`	Opens the file STAMPS.RND so it can be processed and associates it with file number 1.
PUT	
`PUT #1, StampNum, Stamps`	Writes the record variable Stamps to the StampNum record of the file opened as file number 1.
GET	
`GET #1, StampNum, Stamps`	Reads the record number StampNum from the file opened as file number 1 into the record variable Stamps.
VIEW PRINT	
`VIEW PRINT 7 TO 15`	Creates a text viewpoint between rows 7 and 15.
EXIT FOR	
`EXIT FOR`	Exits from a FOR...NEXT loop by transferring control to the statement following the NEXT statement.

KEY TERMS

index
random-access file
viewport

REVIEW EXERCISES

SELF-CHECK

1. The _____ statement is used to read data from a random-access file.

2. Name two ways in which an OPEN statement for a random-access file differs from the OPEN statement for a sequential file.

3. The _____ statement is used to write data to a random-access file.

4. True or false: The LOF function returns the number of records in a file.

5. The _____ statement is used to define a text viewport.

6. The OPEN statement for random-access files specifies three things. What are they?

7. Choose the correct ending: If a text viewport was created, the CLS statement clears (a) the text viewport; (b) the area outside the text viewport; or (c) the whole screen.

8. The index array for a random-access file is stored as a(n) _____ file.

PROGRAMMING ASSIGNMENTS

In all of the programming assignments in this chapter, if your program to create the file fails, you should use the QBasic KILL command to delete the random-access file before you rerun the program. To do this, type and execute the following command in the immediate window:

```
KILL "filename.RND"
```

Section 10.1

1. The file PA10-01.RND contains the three fields described in Exercise 3 of Section 10.1. The student number is in the range 1 to 999. Write a program to list those students whose GPA is greater than 3.00. Include headings.

2. **a)** Write a program to create the ADDRESS.RND file described in Exercise 4 of Section 10.1. Assume that record number will be in the range 1 to 99.
   b) Write a second program to list the active records in ADDRESS.RND. Include headings in the report.

Section 10.2

3. Write a program to add, delete, update, and display records in the file PA10-01.RND, which was described in Programming Assignment 10.1. To

update GPA, ask the user to enter the number of credits completed this semester (CurrentCredits) and this semester's GPA (CurrentGPA), and calculate the updated GPA using the following equation:

$$NewGPA = \frac{OldGPA * OldCredits + CurrentGPA * CurrentCredits}{OldCredits + CurrentCredits}$$

4. Write a program to add, delete, update, and display records from the ADDRESS.RND file created in Programming Assignment 10.2.

Section 10.3

5. Write a program that could be used to print all the active records in the membership file.

6. **a)** Write a program to create a file that could be used in an inventory system. The fields in the records are the item number (key), which is a four-digit number; the item description, which is a 20-character string; the cost per unit; the price per unit; the reorder point; and the quantity on hand. The reorder point and quantity on hand will always be less than 10,000.
   b) Write a query program for the file created in (a).
   c) Write a program that adds, deletes, and updates the records in the file created in (a). The program should allow the user to change the item description, the cost and price per unit, and the reorder point. Also, the program should accept a quantity shipped and subtract that from the quantity on hand—and accept a quantity received and add that to the quantity on hand. If the quantity on hand falls below the reorder point, the program should print a message.

7. The file PA10-07.RND contains a four-digit StudentNum, which is the key, followed by the three fields described in Exercise 3 of Section 10.1. The index for the file is in PA10-07.IDX.
   a) Write a query program for this file.
   b) Write a program that adds, deletes, and updates the file. Update the GPA field as described in Programming Assignment 10.3.

ADDITIONAL PROGRAMMING ASSIGNMENTS

8. **a)** Write a program to create the PAYROLL.RND file described in Exercise 5 of Section 10.1. Assume that there will be no more than 99 employees.

b) Write a program to list the active records in PAYROLL.RND. Include headings in the report.

c) Write a program to add, delete, update, and display records in PAYROLL.RND. The program should allow the user to change the name, the pay rate, and the number of dependents. It should accept the weekly gross pay, and add that to year-to-date gross pay.

9. a) Write a program to create the PAYROLL.RND file described in Exercise 5 of Section 10.1, but add the social security number to the record and use it as the key. Name the file PAYROLL1.RND and the index PAYROLL1.IDX.

b) Write a query program for this file.

c) Write a maintenance program for this file. Update the file as described in Programming Assignment 10.8(c).

10. a) Write a program to create a file to store information about a stamp collection. The fields in the records are a four-digit catalog number, which is the key; the name of the stamp; the number owned; the total cost; and the current price. Use an index with this file.

b) Write a query program for this file. The program should display the fields in a record and calculate the total value of the displayed stamp. The total value of a stamp is the product of the number of the stamp owned and the current price. It should also calculate the profit (or loss) for the displayed stamp, which is the difference between the total value and the total cost.

c) Write a maintenance program for this file. The program should allow the user to change the name, the total cost, and the current price. It should also accept a number purchased and add that to the number owned—and accept a number sold and subtract that from the number owned.

BEYOND THE BASICS

11. Write a program to list the records in the membership file in order by membership number. (*Hint*: Sort MemNumIndex and remember the original order.)

12. a) Write a program that creates an index for the membership file based on last name.

b) Write a query program for the membership file that allows a record to be selected using either the membership number or the last name. You may assume that all the last names are unique.

11

DRAWING POINTS, LINES, AND CIRCLES

LEARNING OBJECTIVES

After reading this chapter, you will be able to:

- Understand the hardware required to execute graphics programs.

- Put the screen into a graphics mode.

- Use the QBasic statements SCREEN, COLOR, PSET, PRESET, LINE, PAINT, and CIRCLE.

- Draw and color points, lines, and circles.

- Use the DOS command GRAPHICS.

In earlier chapters, you learned how to use the computational capabilities of a personal computer—but in these two final chapters, you will learn how to use its extensive graphics capabilities. In this chapter, you will learn how to draw and color points, lines, boxes, and circles. In Chapter 12, you will learn how to draw graphs and charts and how to move figures around the screen.

11.1   INTRODUCTION TO GRAPHICS

To use the graphics features of your personal computer, it must have a graphics monitor. Also, the internal electronic components must be capable of generating graphics. If your computer does not have these components, you will not be able to execute the programs in this chapter or in Chapter 12. You do not need a color monitor—but if you have one, your graphics will be more interesting.

The Graphics Modes

In all our programs so far, we used QBasic in text mode. But QBasic also works in several graphics modes as well. We will discuss two of these modes: medium- and high-resolution graphics.

Whenever you start QBasic, it automatically begins in text mode. To change to a graphics mode, you must use the SCREEN statement. The syntax of the SCREEN statement is

```
SCREEN mode
```

A value of 0 for mode specifies text mode; a value of 1, medium-resolution graphics mode; and a value of 2, high-resolution graphics mode. If you try to execute a graphics command—like those we will study later in this chapter—without first executing a SCREEN statement to put the screen into a graphics mode, QBasic stops and displays an Illegal function call message.

The Coordinate Systems

Now that you know how to switch to the graphics modes, you may be wondering what they are and why there are more than one of them. In the graphics modes, you can draw a point anywhere on the screen. Thus, we say that in the graphics modes, the screen is **all points addressable**. To address any point on the screen, we must have a method of specifying that particular point. The method used is to give the point's **coordinates**, which are simply two numbers that permit QBasic to locate that point on the screen. Because the coordinates refer to specific physical points on the screen, we call them **physical coordinates**. One important way in which the graphics modes differ is in the physical coordinate systems they use.

As Figure 11.1 shows, in medium-resolution graphics mode, the screen is divided into 320 dots horizontally and 200 dots vertically. These dots are called **pixels** (a shortened version of picture elements). Pixels are numbered from 0 through 319 going from left to right, and from 0 through 199 going from top to bottom. The top edge of the screen is the X axis and the left edge is the Y axis. The horizontal coordinate of a pixel is called its X coordinate, and the vertical coordinate is called its Y coordinate.

Figure 11.1 shows that the pixel in the upper-left corner has an X coordinate of 0 and a Y coordinate of 0. The pixel in the lower-right corner has an X coordinate of 319 and a Y coordinate of 199. For convenience, the coordinates of a point are given in the form (X coordinate, Y coordinate). For example, the coordinates of the pixel in the lower-right corner are written as (319, 199). The coordinates of the pixel in the center of the screen are written as (160, 100).

Figure 11.2 shows that in high-resolution graphics mode, the physical coordinate system is similar—except that the X coordinates go from 0 through 639. In other words, the horizontal direction has twice as many pixels. As in medium-resolution graphics, the Y coordinate goes from 0 through 199. The coordinates of the pixel in the center of the screen are (320, 100).

all points addressable
Allowing the user to draw a point anywhere on the screen by means of a graphics instruction.

coordinates
A pair of numbers that locate a point on the screen.

physical coordinates
The coordinate system that refers to specific points on the screen.

pixel
A dot, or picture element, on the screen.

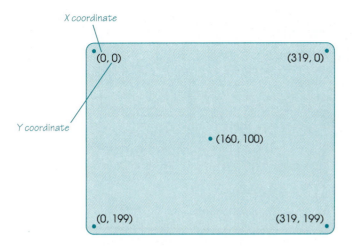

FIGURE 11.1   Medium-resolution coordinate system.

Because high-resolution mode has more pixels, you can draw figures with more detail. However, you must pay a price—you cannot use color. Medium-resolution mode allows you to use up to four colors at a time; in high-resolution mode, you can use only black and white.

Color

You studied the COLOR statement used in text mode in Chapter 6, but the COLOR statement in medium-resolution graphics mode is entirely different. (Since high-resolution mode does not support color, it is illegal to execute a COLOR statement in high-resolution.) The syntax of the COLOR statement in graphics mode is

```
COLOR background, palette
```

where background is a number or numeric expression with a value between 0 and 15, which specifies the background color. As you can tell from Table 11.1, background colors and numbers in graphics mode are the same as foreground colors and numbers in text mode (see Table 6.1, page 213). When you execute a COLOR statement, the screen changes to the background color. In the graphics modes, the border is the same color as the background.

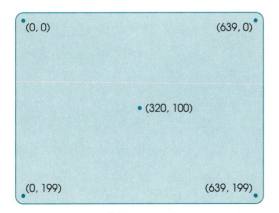

FIGURE 11.2   High-resolution coordinate system.

TABLE 11.1
Colors available as background in medium-resolution mode

Number	Color	Number	Color
0	Black	8	Gray
1	Blue	9	Light blue
2	Green	10	Light green
3	Cyan	11	Light cyan
4	Red	12	Light red
5	Magenta	13	Light magenta
6	Brown	14	Yellow
7	White	15	High-intensity white

To complete the COLOR statement, you also code a palette argument (a number or numeric expression with a value of either 0 or 1), which specifies one of two **palettes** (sets of four colors) that you may use. Table 11.2 shows the colors that correspond to the numbers 0 through 3 in the two palettes. (For your convenience, Tables 11.1 and 11.2 are reproduced in Appendix B.)

palette
A set of four colors that may be used to color figures.

With graphics statements like those we will study shortly, you specify the color you want to use by coding a number between 0 and 3. The colors that these numbers represent depend on the previously executed COLOR command. For example, the statement

```
COLOR 4, 1
```

makes color 4 (red) the background color, and palette 1 active. In subsequent graphics statements, Table 11.2 shows that you would code 0 to get the background color (red), code 1 to get cyan, code 2 to get magenta, and code 3 to get white. Notice that although in the COLOR statement, we coded a 4 to make red the background color (see Table 11.1 again), you code 0 to get red in subsequent graphics statements.

So you see that in medium-resolution graphics mode, you can have a maximum of four colors on the screen at one time. This situation is in marked contrast to text mode, where you can have 16 different colors on the screen at once.

In addition, there are limitations on the combinations you can have. Suppose, for example, you wanted to color a flag yellow, green, and red. Although yellow is not in either palette, you could get yellow by making it the background

TABLE 11.2
Colors in the medium-resolution palettes

Number	Palette 0	Palette 1
0	Background	Background
1	Green	Cyan
2	Red	Magenta
3	Brown	White

color, which Table 11.1 shows is color 14. Then to get green and red, you could specify palette 0. Thus, the color statement you would use is

```
COLOR 14, 0
```

However, you could not use a similar procedure to color an American flag. Since red is in palette 0, white is in palette 1, and blue is in neither palette, you cannot get the colors red, white, and blue on the screen at the same time.

If a COLOR statement is not executed, the default is

```
COLOR 0, 1
```

This statement specifies a background color of 0 (black) with palette 1.

ILLUSTRATIONS

Color Statement	Effect
COLOR 7, 0	Makes white the background color and palette 0 active.
COLOR 1, 1	Makes blue the background color and palette 1 active.

Drawing Points

Now that you know how to select colors, you are ready to learn how to draw figures. Let's start by drawing points.

PSET and PRESET

The simplest graphics statements are PSET and PRESET, which draw points. In medium-resolution the statements

```
PSET (100, 50), 2
```

and

```
PRESET (100, 50), 2
```

draw a point at the pixel whose coordinate is (100, 50), in color 2. Table 11.2 shows that color 2 is red if a previous COLOR statement made palette 0 the active palette, but color 2 is magenta if palette 1 is the active palette.

The syntaxes of the PSET and PRESET are

```
PSET (x, y)[,color]
PRESET (x, y)[,color]
```

where x and y are the coordinates of the pixel at which the point is to be drawn and may be a number or a numeric expression. If the coordinates of a point off the screen are coded—for example, (1000, 75)—no point is drawn, and no error message is printed.

In medium-resolution mode, you code color as a number between 0 and 3 to specify which color from the current palette will be used to draw the point.

In high-resolution mode (which offers only black and white), a color of 0 or 2 always produces black points and a color of 1 or 3 always produces white points.

The following illustrations assume that the screen is in medium-resolution mode, and that palette 0 is active.

ILLUSTRATIONS

PSET and PRESET Statements	Effect
`PSET (0, 199), 3` `PRESET (0, 199), 3`	Draws a point in the lower-left corner of the screen in color 3, which is brown.
`PSET (0, 0), 2` `PRESET (0, 0), 2`	Draws a point in the upper-left corner of the screen in color 2, which is red.
`PSET (160, 100), 0` `PRESET (160, 100), 0`	Draws a point in the center of the screen in the color that was specified as the background color in the COLOR statement.

These examples show that when you code the color argument, PSET and PRESET perform identically. But color is optional. If you omit it, PSET uses color 3 (brown or white, depending on which palette is active) in medium-resolution mode and color 1 (white) in high-resolution mode, while PRESET uses color 0 (the background color) in both modes. Drawing points in the background color makes them blend into the background—in effect, they disappear. Loosely speaking, then, we can say that when you use them without coding the color argument, PSET draws points and PRESET erases them.

EXAMPLE 1

A PROGRAM TO PLOT POINTS

Program 11.1 illustrates the PSET and PRESET statements. (Because this and other simple graphics problems require no variable names and only the simplest logic, our systematic procedure for developing the programs is not used in this chapter.) It may be difficult to see individual points, so Program 11.1 plots a cluster of four points at the center of the screen.

The SCREEN statement in line 4 sets the screen to medium-resolution, and the CLS statement in line 5 clears the screen. Since this program does not contain a COLOR statement, the default values—black background with palette 1—are used. Line 7 asks you to enter a value—1, 2, or 3—to be used for the color of the points. (Clr is used as the variable name because COLOR is a reserved word.) If you enter 0 by mistake, the points will be drawn in the background color, and you will be unable to see them. The PSET statement in line 9

```
PSET (160, 100), Clr
```

draws a point at the pixel whose coordinates are (160, 100)—the center of the screen—in the color specified by the value of Clr. The PSET statements in lines 10, 11, and 12 draw three more points in the same color at adjacent pixels.

Line 14 illustrates a technique that is useful when you are trying to understand a graphics program. When line 14 is executed, the program pauses—without disturbing the screen with a prompt or a question mark—and waits for you to enter a value to be assigned to A$. When you have examined the screen as long as you want, you can press any key and the program will continue.

```
 1 | '    *** DEMONSTRATING PSET AND PRESET ***
 2 | '    Draw points in specified color
 3 |
 4 | SCREEN 1                              'Set medium-resolution graphics
 5 | CLS                                   'Clear screen
 6 |
 7 | INPUT "Enter color, 1 to 3, (-1 to stop): ", Clr
 8 | DO UNTIL Clr = -1
 9 |     PSET (160, 100), Clr              'Plot four points
10 |     PSET (161, 100), Clr              'in center of
11 |     PSET (160, 101), Clr              'screen, in
12 |     PSET (161, 101), Clr              'specified color
13 |
14 |     A$ = INPUT$(1)                    'Pause
15 |     PRESET (160, 100)                 'Erase
16 |     PRESET (161, 100)                 'the
17 |     PRESET (160, 101)                 'four
18 |     PRESET (161, 101)                 'points
19 |     INPUT "Enter color, 1 to 3, (-1 to stop): ", Clr
20 | LOOP
21 | END
```

PROGRAM 11.1   Demonstrating the PSET and PRESET statements.

After you press a key to satisfy line 14, the PRESET statement in line 15

```
PRESET (160, 100)
```

is executed. Since this statement does not contain a color argument, it draws a point in the background color—erasing the point that was drawn by line 9. The PRESET statements in lines 16, 17, and 18 erase the points drawn by the PSET statements in lines 10, 11, and 12.

If you run this program, you will notice that the input prompt is printed in large white characters. Only 40 of these large characters fit on a line. All characters placed on the screen in medium-resolution are printed in this larger size. They are also displayed in color 3 from the current palette, which in this case is white.

After you have tried all the colors, you can enter –1 to stop execution and enter the following statement in the Immediate window:

```
COLOR 12, 0
```

This statement changes the background color to light red and the palette to palette 0. You will notice that the screen changes immediately from black to light red and that the color of any text on the screen changes from white to brown. In graphics mode, a COLOR statement instantly changes all the colors on the screen. This is in contrast to text mode, where (you should recall) a COLOR statement affects the colors only of text displayed after it is executed. You can then run the program to see the colors in palette 0.

Plotting Points in High-Resolution Mode

You can also run Program 11.1 in high-resolution mode by changing the SCREEN statement in line 4 to

```
SCREEN 2
```

When you run the program in high-resolution, you will see two differences. First, entering 1 for Clr gives you white points, while entering 2 gives you black points—which, since they are the same color as the background, are invisible. Second, the points appear one-quarter of the way across the screen—not in the center, as they were before. As you may recall, in high-resolution, there are 640 pixels in the *X* direction. Therefore, the pixels with *X* coordinates of 160 and 161 are only one-quarter of the way across the screen. The points are still halfway *down* the screen, however, since both medium-resolution and high-resolution have 200 pixels in the *Y* direction.

When you run the program in high-resolution, you will also notice that the input prompt is printed in white, standard 80-characters-per-line size. That is true of all characters placed on the screen in high-resolution. ■

Relative Coordinates

So far, we have specified the position of a pixel by giving its *X* and *Y* coordinates. *X* and *Y* are the **absolute coordinates** of the pixel. A second way of specifying position, in which the **relative coordinates** are specified, is sometimes more convenient. When relative coordinates are used, the position of a pixel is specified by giving its distance from a point mentioned earlier in the program. This point, called the **last point referenced**, differs according to the graphics statement executed. For PSET and PRESET, the last point referenced is the last point drawn. When the screen is first set to one of the graphics modes, the last point referenced is the center of the screen.

To use relative coordinates, you must include the word STEP in a graphics statement. STEP is used as follows:

```
STEP(x offset, y offset)
```

where x offset and y offset are the distances in the *X* and *Y* directions from the last point referenced. The x and y offsets may be positive or negative. Referring back to Figures 11.1 and 11.2 (page 423), you see that a positive value for x offset means move to the right, while a negative value means move to the left. A positive value for y offset means move down, while a negative value means move up. For example,

```
PSET STEP(20, 4)
```

means that the next point should be drawn 20 pixels to the right and 4 pixels down from the last point referenced.

EXAMPLE 2 ▮▮▮▮▮▮▮▮▮
A PROGRAM THAT USES RELATIVE COORDINATES

Program 11.2 illustrates relative coordinates. Like Program 11.1, it draws a cluster of four points. Line 4 defines the constant Magenta, which is used to specify colors in the PSET statements to make them easier to understand.

The PRESET statement in line 10

```
PRESET (50, 50)
```

uses absolute coordinates to draw a point in the background color at the pixel whose coordinates are (50, 50). Since the screen and the point are in the background color, the point is not visible; the purpose of the statement is to set the last

absolute coordinates
The expression of a pixel's location in terms of its *X* and *Y* coordinates.

relative coordinates
The expression of a pixel's location in terms of the *X* and *Y* distances from a point mentioned earlier in the program.

last point referenced
The point from which relative coordinates are measured.

```
1  │  '    *** DEMONSTRATING RELATIVE COORDINATES ***
2  │  '    Use STEP for relative coordinates
3  │
4  │  CONST Magenta = 2
5  │
6  │  SCREEN 1                          'Select medium-resolution graphics
7  │  COLOR 1, 1                        'Select blue background with palette 1
8  │  CLS                               'Clear screen
9  │
10 │  PRESET (50, 50)                   'Set last point referenced to 50, 50
11 │  PSET STEP(10, -5), Magenta        'Plot a point 10 pixels to the right and 5 up
12 │  PSET STEP(1, 0), Magenta          'Plot a point one pixel to the right
13 │  PSET STEP(-1, 1), Magenta         'You figure out where these
14 │  PSET STEP(1, 0), Magenta          'statements plot points
15 │  END
```

PROGRAM 11.2   *Demonstrating relative coordinates.*

point referenced to (50, 50). The PSET statements that follow use relative coordinates. Line 11

```
    PSET STEP(10, -5), Magenta
```

draws a Magenta point that is 10 pixels to the right and 5 pixels up from the last point referenced; that is, at (60, 45). This point then becomes the last point referenced. The PSET statement in line 12

```
    PSET STEP(1, 0), Magenta
```

draws a point 1 pixel to the right at the same vertical coordinate as (60, 45), which is (61, 45). Before you read further, figure out the coordinates of the points drawn by the statements in lines 13 and 14—and by the following statements.

ILLUSTRATIONS

PSET and PRESET Statements	Effect
`PSET STEP(30, -10), 2`	Draws a point 30 pixels to the right and 10 pixels up from the last point referenced in color 2 from the current palette.
`PRESET STEP(-5, 15)`	Draws a point 5 pixels to the left and 15 pixels down from the last point referenced in the background color.

As Program 11.2 shows, you may use both absolute and relative coordinates in the same program. This flexibility lets you use the coordinates that are most convenient for a particular statement.   ∎

Syntax Summary

SCREEN Statement

Form: `SCREEN mode`

Example: `SCREEN 1`

Explanation: Sets the screen mode. When mode is 0, the screen is set to text mode; when mode is 1, the screen is set to medium-resolution graphics mode; and when mode is 2, the screen is set to high-resolution graphics mode.

COLOR Statement (Graphics)

Form: `COLOR background, palette`

Example: `COLOR 10, 0`

Explanation: Sets colors in graphics mode: background (which must be in the range 0 through 15) selects the background color, and palette (which must be 0 or 1) selects the palette.

PSET Statement

Form: `PSET (x, y)[,color]`

Example: `PSET (125, 175), 2`

Explanation: Plots a point at the given coordinates using color from the current palette. In medium-resolution mode, if color is not coded, color 3 (brown or white) is used. In high-resolution, if color is not coded, white is used.

PRESET Statement

Form: `PRESET (x, y)[,color]`

Example: `PRESET (150, 25), 1`

Explanation: Plots a point at the given coordinates using color from the current palette. In medium-resolution mode, if color is not coded, color 0 (the background color) is used. In high-resolution, black is used.

11.1 EXERCISES

1. Draw a rectangle that represents the medium-resolution screen and locate the following points on it:
   a) (175, 50)
   b) (50, 175)
   c) (300, 100)
   d) (100, 160)

2. What are the approximate coordinates of the points shown if the following illustration represents a medium-resolution screen? What are the approximate coordinates of the points shown if the illustration represents a high-resolution screen?

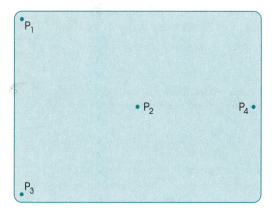

3. What is the color of the dots drawn by the PRESET statements in Program 11.1 (page 427)?

★4. Write the SCREEN statement that you would use to switch to medium-resolution mode.

5. Write the COLOR statement that you would use to select a cyan background color and palette 0.

★6. Write a COLOR statement that could be used in a program that draws a design colored red, magenta, and white.

7. Write a PSET statement to draw a point in color 1 that is 50 pixels to the left and 70 pixels up from the last point drawn.

11.2   DRAWING LINES

The LINE statement is used to draw lines and boxes. The full syntax of the LINE statement is

```
LINE [(x1, y1)]-(x2, y2)[,color][,B[F]]
```

This syntax is rather formidable, so let's begin with a simpler form. The simplest form of the LINE statement is

```
LINE (x1, y1)-(x2, y2)
```

This statement draws a line from the pixel at the first set of X and Y coordinates listed—(x1, y1)—to the pixel at the second set—(x2, y2). For example, in medium-resolution, the statement

```
LINE (319, 0)-(0, 199)
```

draws a line from the upper-right corner of the screen—(319, 0)—to the lower-left corner—(0, 199). The pixel (0, 199) then becomes the last point referenced. The order that you code the coordinates of the pixels doesn't matter, so the statement

```
LINE (0, 199)-(319, 0)
```

draws the same line, but it makes (319, 0) the last point referenced.

If your program specifies coordinates of a pixel that are off the screen, the line is drawn and "clipped" at the edge of the screen—a process known as **line clipping**. Thus,

line clipping
Cutting off a figure at the edge of the screen.

```
LINE (160, 100)-(400, 300)
```

draws a line that starts from the center of the screen—(160, 100)—and goes off the bottom of the screen. Line clipping is used by all the graphics statements.

Using the Immediate Window

You can examine the effect of any graphics statements by entering them in the Immediate window. First, put the screen in a graphics mode by executing the statement SCREEN 1 or SCREEN 2. Then you can enter a graphics statement, like the previous LINE statement, and watch what happens. You can even modify the statement and see the effects of the modifications. When the screen becomes too cluttered, you can clear it by executing the CLS statement and starting over again.

You can return the Output screen to 80-column text mode by executing the following statements in the Immediate window:

```
SCREEN 0
WIDTH 80
```

Drawing Connected Lines

Another form of the LINE statement omits the first pair of coordinates:

```
LINE -(x2, y2)
```

This statement draws a line from the last point referenced to the point whose coordinates are (x2, y2). Consider the statements

```
LINE (10, 100)-(200, 100)
LINE -(120, 20)
```

In medium-resolution, the first statement draws a horizontal line from near the left edge of the screen—(10, 100)—to about the center of the screen—(200, 100). The second statement draws a line from pixel (200, 100)—which became the last point referenced when the first statement was executed—to the pixel (120, 20).

Since each line starts where the previous line ended, this method of specifying coordinates automatically draws connected lines. To draw a closed figure, all you have to do is make the coordinates of the last statement the same as the first statement's first coordinates. For example, the following statements

```
LINE (90, 25)-(190, 80)
LINE -(120, 150)
LINE -(90, 25)
```

draw a triangle because the coordinates of the last statement—(90, 25)—are the same as the first coordinates of the first statement.

Using Relative Coordinates

Don't confuse this method of specifying coordinates with relative coordinates. The coordinates given in the previous example's second LINE statement are the *absolute* coordinates of the pixel to which the line will be drawn. Relative coordinates can be used only when the word STEP is coded.

Either or both of the coordinates in a LINE statement may be given in the relative form, however. The statement

```
LINE STEP(10, -5)-(20, 0)
```

draws a line starting 10 pixels to the right and 5 pixels up from the last point referenced, to the pixel (20, 0). The statement

```
LINE (100, 100)-STEP(50, 10)
```

draws a line from pixel (100, 100) to pixel (150, 110). Notice that when the relative form is used for the second pair of coordinates, they are relative to the first pair of coordinates. You can also use relative coordinates when the first pair of coordinates is omitted. For example,

```
LINE -STEP(50, 10)
```

draws a line from the last point referenced to the pixel 50 pixels to the right and 10 pixels down.

Finally, the relative form may be used for both coordinates. Thus,

```
LINE STEP(100, 50)-STEP(30, 40)
```

draws a line that starts 100 pixels to the right and 50 pixels down from the last point referenced. The end point of the line is 30 pixels to the right and 40 pixels down from the starting point.

Using Color

Now that you understand part of the syntax of the LINE statement, let's look at the other arguments.

All the lines we've drawn so far are in the default color. As we said when discussing PSET and PRESET, in high-resolution, the default color is color 1 (white). And in medium-resolution, the default color is color 3, which is brown for palette 0 and white for palette 1. If we wish to draw lines in other colors, we can do so by including the color number after the second pair of coordinates, as shown in the syntax of the LINE statement. In medium-resolution, we can use colors 0 through 3. For example, the statement

```
LINE (10, 10)-(300, 190), 2
```

draws a line in color 2. In high-resolution, we can use color 0 (black) or 1 (white).

Drawing Boxes

If you look again at the syntax of the LINE statement, you'll see that we can include the letter B or the letters BF after the color argument. The letter B means that a box (a rectangle) should be drawn, and the letters BF (box fill) mean that the box should be filled with the specified color. The statement

```
LINE (40, 180)-(100, 80), 1, B
```

draws a box in color 1, with one corner at pixel (40, 180) and the opposite corner at pixel (100, 80). This box is shown in Figure 11.3(a), but not in the colors you will see on the screen.

You can draw the same box by specifying the two other opposite corners, as in the statement

```
LINE (40, 80)-(100, 180), 1, B
```

You draw the same box no matter which set of coordinates you specify first. So the statement

```
LINE (100, 180)-(40, 80), 1, B
```

draws the same box as the two previous statements.

If the last argument in these statements were BF instead of B, the box would be filled with color 1, as shown in Figure 11.3(b). (Note: Again, this is not in the

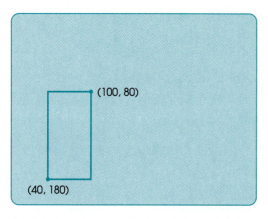

(a) Drawing a box with the LINE statement, using the B argument.

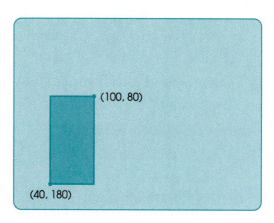

(b) Drawing a box with the LINE statement, using the BF argument.

FIGURE 11.3 Drawing boxes.

color that you will see on your screen.) When the B or BF argument is used, the box drawn always has its sides parallel to the sides of the screen.

The following LINE statements assume that the screen is in medium-resolution mode.

ILLUSTRATIONS

LINE Statement	Effect
`LINE (0, 0)-(319, 199), 2`	Draws a line from the upper-left corner of the screen—(0, 0)—to the lower-right corner—(319, 199)—in color 2 from the current palette.
`LINE -(160, 100), 1`	Draws a line from the last point referenced to the center of the screen—(160, 100)—in color 1 from the current palette.
`LINE STEP(20, -5)-STEP(-30, 10)`	Draws a line that starts 20 pixels to the right and 5 pixels up—STEP(20, –5)—from the last point referenced. The end point of the line is 30 pixels to the left and 10 pixels down—STEP(–30, 10)—from the starting point. The line is drawn in the default color.
`LINE (190, 20)-(240, 140), 2, BF`	Draws and fills a box in color 2 from the current palette. The upper-left corner of the box is at (190, 20), and the lower-right corner is at (240, 140).

EXAMPLE 3 ▰▰▰▰▰▰▰▰▰▰▰

A PROGRAM THAT DEMONSTRATES THE LINE STATEMENT

Program 11.3 uses many of the graphics features you have learned so far to draw several arrows. The PRESET statement in line 11 uses the X and Y values entered in response to lines 8 and 10 to set the last point referenced, which becomes the upper-left corner of the shaft of the arrow. Line 12

```
LINE -STEP(30, 10), , B
```

draws a box, which is the shaft of the arrow. One corner of the rectangle is at (X, Y), which line 11 established as the last point referenced, and the opposite corner is 30 pixels to the right and 10 pixels down.

Lines 13 through 16 draw the point of the arrow. Line 13

```
LINE -STEP(0, 10)
```

draws a vertical line 10 pixels down from the lower-right corner of the shaft. Line 14

```
LINE -STEP(12, -15)
```

draws a diagonal line 12 pixels to the right and 15 pixels up. Line 15

```
LINE -STEP(-12, -15)
```

draws a second diagonal line 12 pixels to the left and 15 pixels up. Line 16

```
LINE -STEP(0, 10)
```

draws a second vertical line 10 pixels down. Finally, line 17 draws a line in color 0, the background color—erasing the right edge of the box that was drawn by line 12.

Notice in Program 11.3's output that only part of the last arrow that lies within the screen is drawn. This is an example of line clipping, which was mentioned earlier. ▰

Aspect Ratio

You would expect that the statement

```
LINE (120, 60)-STEP(80, 80), , B
```

would draw a square 80 pixels high and 80 pixels wide. But if you enter it, you will see that it draws a rectangle that is taller than it is wide. The sides are 80 pixels long, but they have different physical lengths. To understand why, you need to understand **aspect ratio**.

Aspect ratio is defined as the horizontal distance between pixels divided by the vertical distance between pixels. To calculate aspect ratio, assume that a screen is 12 inches wide. On most screens, the vertical dimension is three-quarters of the horizontal dimension. So if the screen is 12 inches wide, it will be 9 inches tall. (The actual dimensions do not matter; only the ratio is important.) Recall that medium-resolution has 320 pixels horizontally and 200 pixels vertically. The distances between pixels are

Horizontal distance = 12 inches / 320 pixels = 0.0375 inches
Vertical distance   = 9 inches / 200 pixels = 0.045 inches

Again, the absolute values of these distances are not important; what is important is their ratio, which is

$$\text{Aspect Ratio} = \frac{\text{Horizontal distance}}{\text{Vertical distance}} = \frac{0.0375}{0.045} = 0.833$$

aspect ratio
The ratio of the horizontal distance between pixels to the vertical distance between pixels (horizontal distance ÷ vertical distance).

```
 1  |  '    *** DEMONSTRATING THE LINE STATEMENT ***
 2  |  '    Using the LINE statement to draw arrows
 3  |
 4  |  SCREEN 1                              'Select medium-resolution graphics
 5  |  COLOR 4, 1                            'Select red background with palette 1
 6  |  CLS                                   'Clear screen
 7  |
 8  |  INPUT "Enter x coordinate, 0 to end: ", X
 9  |  DO UNTIL X = 0
10  |      INPUT "Enter y coordinate: ", Y
11  |      PRESET (X, Y)                     'Set last point referenced to X, Y
12  |      LINE -STEP(30, 10), , B           'Draw shaft of arrow
13  |      LINE -STEP(0, 10)                 'Draw
14  |      LINE -STEP(12, -15)               'point
15  |      LINE -STEP(-12, -15)              'of
16  |      LINE -STEP(0, 10)                 'arrow
17  |      LINE -STEP(0, 10), 0              'Erase extra line
18  |      INPUT "Enter x coordinate, 0 to end: ", X
19  |  LOOP
20  |  END
```

```
Enter x coordinate, 0 to end: 50
Enter y coordinate: 125
Enter x coordinate, 0 to end: 100
Enter y coordinate: 150
Enter x coordinate, 0 to end: 150
Enter y coordinate: 175
Enter x coordinate, 0 to end: 200
Enter y coordinate: 200
Enter x coordinate, 0 to end: ■
```

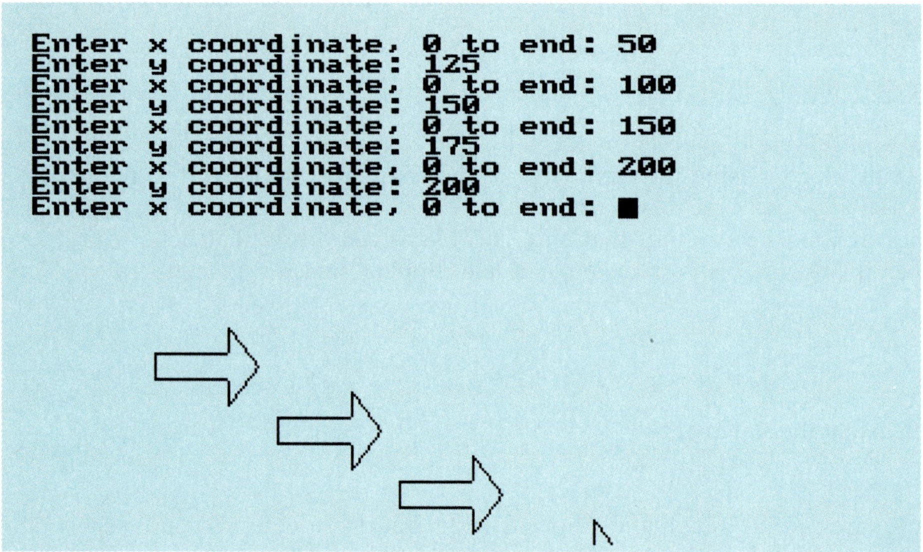

PROGRAM 11.3   Demonstrating the LINE statement.

The aspect ratio of 0.833 is usually expressed as the fraction ⅚. This calculation shows, then, that the horizontal distance between pixels is only ⅚ as great as the vertical distance. In other words, the distance spanned by 6 pixels in the horizontal direction is equal to the distance spanned by 5 pixels in the vertical direction. Not all screens have an aspect ratio of exactly ⅚—but for most screens, the aspect ratio is close to ⅚.

To draw a square on a standard screen, we must make the number of pixels in the horizontal (that is, the X) direction ⅚ times the number of pixels in the vertical (that is, the Y) direction. If we want a square with a side that is 80 pixels in the Y direction, the side in the X direction must be

X pixels $= \frac{6}{5} \times 80 = 96$

Therefore, the statement

```
LINE (120, 60)-STEP(96, 80), , B
```

draws the desired square.

Performing this calculation every time you want to draw a complicated figure is quite tedious, so you may want to use a graphics layout form. In fact, when writing graphics programs, such a layout form often proves more useful than a flowchart. Figure 11.4 shows a form for medium-resolution graphics. On this form, the distances between pixels in the X and Y directions are in the same ratio as they are on a standard screen. You can reproduce this form (enlarged, if possible), draw the figure you want to create, and read the coordinates of the pixels from the form. When you read the coordinates from the form, you can use the numbers along the axes, which mark the spaces that represent the pixel positions. However, you should realize that because of space constraints, only every fourth pixel is labeled.

In high-resolution, there are twice as many pixels in the horizontal direction as there are in medium-resolution, so the horizontal distance between pixels is half as great. There are the same number of pixels in the vertical direction, so the vertical distance between pixels is the same. This means that the aspect ratio in high-resolution is half what it is in medium-resolution, or $5/12$. You can use the graphics layout form in Figure 11.5 to design figures to be drawn in high-resolution. Because this figure is even more crowded than the medium-resolution one, only every eighth pixel is labeled in the horizontal position.

Whether enlarged or not, you may find reading the graphics layout form difficult to read. If so, you may prefer to use the following equations for any row or column in both medium- and high-resolution graphics.

Coordinate of first pixel
 in *column* (or *row*) $\quad = 8 \times column$ (or *row*) number $- 8$

Coordinate of last pixel
 in *column* (or *row*) $\quad = 8 \times column$ (or *row*) number $- 1$

Coordinate of middle pixel
 in *column* (or *row*) $\quad = 8 \times column$ (or *row*) number $- 4$

For example, for column 10, these equations give

Coordinate of first pixel in column 10 $= 8 \times 10 - 8 = 72$
Coordinate of last pixel in column 10 $= 8 \times 10 - 1 = 79$
Coordinate of middle pixel in column 10 $= 8 \times 10 - 4 = 76$

To calculate the row or column number when you know the coordinate, you need only one equation:

Row or column number = Coordinate / 8 + 1

Notice that this equation uses integer division.

Printing a Graphics Screen

While it is great fun to produce images on the screen, you may sometimes need to print your output (when doing homework problems, for example). If you have an IBM, Hewlett-Packard, or other compatible printer, you can use the DOS GRAPHICS command. To use the GRAPHICS command, while you are still in DOS and before you start QBasic, type the command

```
GRAPHICS type
```

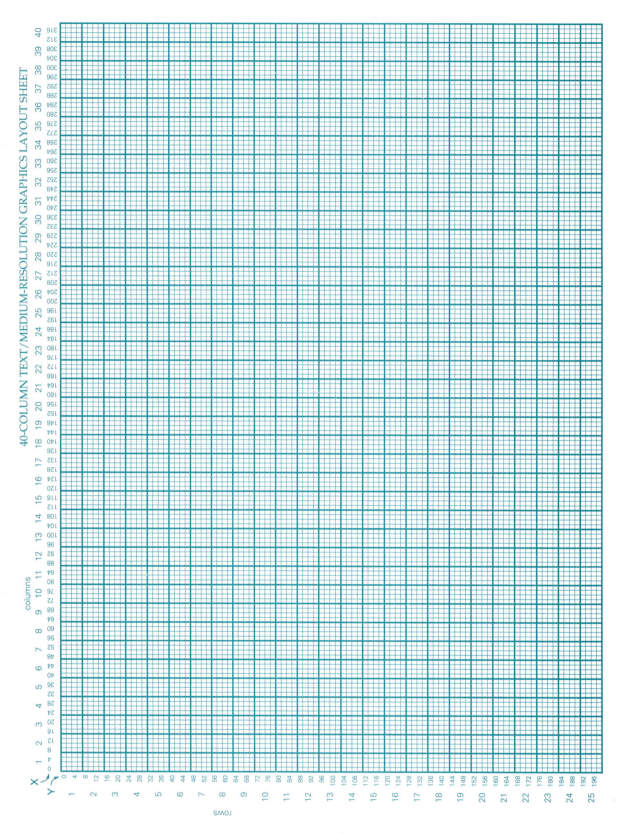

FIGURE 11.4 Medium-resolution graphics layout form. The aspect ratio is included in the form's design. To program a figure, simply draw it exactly as you want it to appear and use the resulting coordinates. Note that each box represents 2 pixels in both the X and Y directions.

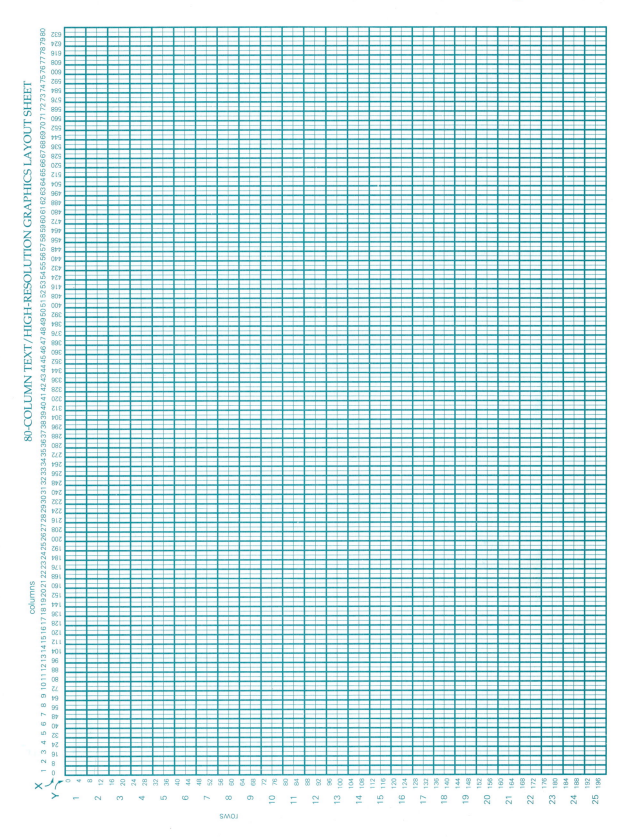

FIGURE 11.5 High-resolution graphics layout form. The aspect ratio is included in the form's design. To program a figure, simply draw it exactly as you want it to appear and use the resulting coordinates. Note that each box represents 4 pixels in both the *X* and *Y* directions.

where type indicates the type of printer you are using. Some values for type are graphics (for an IBM Graphics Printer) and laserjet (for a Hewlett-Packard Laser-Jet printer). The DOS manual lists many other values for type; your instructor will tell you the correct value to use in your lab.

The GRAPHICS command loads a screen-printing program into memory. Then you can start QBasic and execute programs that create graphics screens. Whenever you want to print a screen, you simply use the Print Screen key—just as you would if you were printing a text mode screen.

Syntax Summary

LINE Statement
Form: `LINE[(x1, y1)]-(x2, y2)[,color][,B[F]]`
Example: `LINE (25, 100)-(280, 15), 3, BF`
Explanation: Draws a line from the pixel whose coordinates are (x1, y1) to the pixel whose coordinates are (x2, y2), in the color specified by color, selected from the current palette. If B is coded, a box is drawn with the given coordinates as the opposite corners. If BF is coded, the box is filled with the color.

11.2 EXERCISES

★1. Write a LINE statement to draw a line from the center of the medium-resolution screen to the upper-right corner. Would the statement be different for a high-resolution screen? If so, what would be the correct statement?

2. We developed the LINE statement that draws a square whose Y dimension is 80 pixels. Write the LINE statement that draws a square whose X dimension is 80 pixels and whose upper-left corner is at (120, 60).

★3. Note that the following statement uses absolute coordinates:

```
LINE (20, 10)-(60, 60)
```

Rewrite the statement, expressing the second set of coordinates in relative form.

4. Which point is the last point referenced by the following statement?

```
LINE (100, 160)-(5, 10)
```

5. Given two LINE statements that draw two sides of a triangle,

```
LINE (80, 40)-(180, 140)
LINE -(250, 100)
```

write a LINE statement that draws the third side of the triangle.

6. What is the distance, in pixels, from the left end of the shaft to the point of the arrow in Program 11.3 (page 436)?

7. In medium-resolution, which is longer: a vertical line 100 pixels long or a horizontal line 115 pixels long?

You learned that using the BF argument of the LINE statement fills a box with color. But the BF argument cannot be used to color an irregular shape, such as the arrow in Program 11.3. In contrast, the PAINT statement may be used to color a figure of any shape.

The Paint Statement

The syntax of the PAINT statement is

```
PAINT (x, y)[,paint][,boundary]
```

where x and y are the coordinates of any pixel inside the enclosed area that is to be painted, paint is the color used to paint that area, and boundary is the color of the edges of the area.

The PAINT statement is easier to understand if we start with a simple example. Suppose we draw a box with the following statement:

```
LINE (100, 160)-(220, 80), 1, B
```

This statement draws a box in color 1. If a previously executed COLOR statement selected palette 1, the outline of this box is cyan. We could have filled the box with cyan by coding BF instead of B, but let's use the following PAINT statement to fill it with white instead:

```
PAINT (110, 150), 3, 1
```

In this statement, x is 110, y is 150, paint is 3, and boundary is 1. This statement paints in color 3 (white), starting at pixel (110, 150)—which is a point inside the box—moving in all directions until pixels of color 1 (cyan) are encountered.

The PAINT statement is always used this way:

1. Outline an area in a particular color.
2. Select any point within the area.
3. Execute a PAINT statement in which you code the coordinates of that point as the starting point, any color you want as paint, and the color that was used to draw the outline as boundary.

ILLUSTRATIONS

PAINT Statement	Effect
`PAINT (200, 100), 2, 1`	Paints color 2, starting from the pixel (200, 100) and going in all directions until a boundary of color 1 is encountered.
`PAINT (XInside, YInside), Clr, Bdry`	Paints color Clr, starting from the pixel (XInside, YInside) and going in all directions until a boundary of color Bdry is encountered.

Warning: When you paint an area, be careful that the area is completely surrounded by an outline of boundary color. If you leave a gap, the paint will "leak out."

In medium-resolution, paint and boundary may be 0 through 3. In high-resolution, they may be either 0 or 1. Because high-resolution has only two colors, it doesn't make sense for paint to be different from boundary. You can paint the screen white only until a white outline is reached, or black until a black outline is reached. (Think about painting the screen black until a white outline is reached. Since the outline is white, the area must have been black already!)

If paint is not coded, it defaults to color 3 in medium-resolution and color 1 in high-resolution. If boundary is not coded, it defaults to the value of paint. The position of the starting point may be given in either absolute or relative coordinates. When it finishes executing, PAINT makes the starting point the last point referenced.

EXAMPLE 4

USING LINE AND PAINT STATEMENTS TO DRAW A HOUSE

Program 11.4 shows the easiest way to construct and paint a house (although not in the colors that you will see on your screen). CONST statements define Green, Red, and Brown, which are used to specify colors in the graphics statements.

The SCREEN statement changes to medium-resolution graphics mode, the COLOR statement selects a background color of blue with palette 0, and the CLS statement clears the screen. Lines 13, 14, and 15

```
LINE (100, 80)-(160, 30), Brown
LINE -(220, 80), Brown
LINE -(100, 80), Brown
```

draw the triangle that forms the outline of the roof in brown. Lines 16 and 17

```
LINE (140, 70)-(150, 55), Brown, B
LINE (170, 70)-(180, 55), Brown, B
```

draw the two rectangles that form the two attic windows—also in brown. Line 18

```
PAINT (160, 70), Brown, Brown
```

starts painting at (160, 70)—which is a point inside the roof—in brown until a boundary of brown is reached. Lines 19 and 20

```
PAINT (145, 60), Green, Brown
PAINT (175, 60), Green, Brown
```

paint the two attic windows green.

The same procedure is used in lines 23 through 35 to draw and paint the body of the house. Notice that it is not necessary to paint the lower windows since they are in the background color. Lines 38 and 39 are straightforward; they draw and paint the grass.

The LOCATE and PRINT statements in lines 40 and 41 show that it is possible to have both text and graphics on the same screen. The graphics statements have no effect on where output produced by PRINT statements is placed on the screen. To put the output where we want it, we use the LOCATE statement—just as we do in text mode. The row and column indications on the graphics layout forms in Figures 11.4 and 11.5 (pages 438 and 439) are helpful in choosing the values of row and column for the LOCATE statement. In medium-resolution mode, the characters placed on the screen by a PRINT statement are the large 40-character-per-line size, and are in color 3. In high-resolution mode, the characters are in the standard 80-character-per-line size, and are white. ∎

Syntax Summary

PAINT Statement
Form: `PAINT (x, y),[paint][,boundary]`
Example: `PAINT (160, 100), 1, 3`
Explanation: Paints the color specified by paint in all directions, starting
             from the pixel (x, y) until an outline of the color specified by
             boundary is encountered.

```
1  |  '    *** DRAW AND PAINT A HOUSE ***
2  |  '   Demonstrating the LINE and PAINT statements
3  |
4  |  CONST Green = 1
5  |  CONST Red = 2
6  |  CONST Brown = 3
7  |
8  |  SCREEN 1                              'Medium-resolution graphics
9  |  COLOR 1, 0                            'Blue background with palette 0
10 |  CLS                                   'Clear screen
11 |
12 |  '    *** Draw and paint roof
13 |  LINE (100, 80)-(160, 30), Brown           'Draw
14 |  LINE -(220, 80), Brown                    'the
15 |  LINE -(100, 80), Brown                    'roof
16 |  LINE (140, 70)-(150, 55), Brown, B        'Draw two
17 |  LINE (170, 70)-(180, 55), Brown, B        'windows
18 |  PAINT (160, 70), Brown, Brown             'Paint roof
19 |  PAINT (145, 60), Green, Brown             'Paint
20 |  PAINT (175, 60), Green, Brown             'windows
21 |
22 |  '    *** Draw and paint body of house
23 |  LINE (100, 160)-(220, 80), Red, B         'Draw body
24 |  LINE (120, 110)-STEP(20, -25), Red, B     'Draw three
25 |  LINE (150, 110)-STEP(20, -25), Red, B     'second-floor
26 |  LINE (180, 110)-STEP(20, -25), Red, B     'windows
27 |  LINE (120, 155)-STEP(20, -25), Red, B     'Draw two first-
28 |  LINE (180, 155)-STEP(20, -25), Red, B     'floor windows
29 |  LINE (150, 160)-STEP(0, -30), Red         'Draw
30 |  LINE -STEP(10, -10), Red                  'the
31 |  LINE -STEP(10, 10), Red                   'door
32 |  LINE -STEP(0, 30), Red                    'with
33 |  LINE -STEP(-20, 0), Red                   'peak
34 |  PAINT (110, 150), Red, Red                'Paint body
35 |  PAINT (160, 140), Brown, Red              'Paint the door
36 |
37 |  '    *** Draw and paint the grass
38 |  LINE (0, 160)-(320, 160), Green           'Draw boundary between grass and sky
39 |  PAINT (10, 170), Green, Green             'Paint grass
40 |  LOCATE 23, 14
41 |  PRINT "Home Sweet Home"
42 |  A$ = INPUT$(1)                            'Pause
43 |  END
```

PROGRAM 11.4   Using the LINE and PAINT statements to draw and paint a house.
(continued on next page)

PROGRAM 11.4 *(continued)*

11.3 EXERCISES

1. Suppose an area was drawn with a white outline. Write the PAINT statement to paint the area magenta. *Note:* Assume the point (160, 100) is inside the area.

★2. Explain what the following PAINT statement does:

```
PAINT (40, 70), 3, 2
```

3. In Program 11.4, could line 18 (which paints the roof) be placed before lines 16 and 17 (which draw the two attic windows)?

11.4 DRAWING CIRCLES

The CIRCLE statement permits us to draw circles and parts of circles as easy as pi (pun intended). The syntax of the CIRCLE statement is

```
CIRCLE (x, y), radius[,color][,start][,end][,aspect]
```

Like the LINE statement, the full syntax of the CIRCLE statement is rather intimidating, so let's start with a simpler form:

```
CIRCLE (x, y), radius[,color]
```

where x and y are the coordinates of the center of the circle and may be given in either absolute or relative form, radius is the radius of the circle, and color is the color in which the circle should be drawn. The color argument in the CIRCLE statement works the same way as it does in the LINE statement, except that it cannot fill the inside of the circle with color, the way the BF argument does with the LINE statement. The statement

```
CIRCLE (100, 50), 20, 1
```

draws a circle of radius 20 pixels in color 1, centered at pixel (100, 50). The center of the circle then becomes the last point referenced.

Make sure you understand how the following CIRCLE statements work before proceeding.

ILLUSTRATIONS

CIRCLE Statement	Effect
`CIRCLE STEP(50, 90), 30, 2`	Draws a circle with a radius of 30 pixels, in color 2, centered at the pixel that is 50 pixels to the right and 90 pixels down from the last point referenced.
`CIRCLE (200, 150), Radius, Clr`	Draws a circle with a radius of Radius pixels, in the color specified by Clr, centered at pixel (200, 150).

EXAMPLE 5

A PROGRAM THAT DRAWS TWO CIRCLES

Program 11.5 draws and paints two circles (although the colors that you see on your screen will be different). The SCREEN statement changes to medium-resolution graphics mode, the COLOR statement selects a background color of black with palette 1, and the CLS statement clears the screen.

Line 12

```
CIRCLE (160, 100), 50, White
```

draws the inner circle with its center at (160, 100), its radius 50 pixels, and its outline White. The PAINT statement in line 13

```
PAINT STEP(0, 0), Cyan, White
```

paints the inner circle Cyan. This statement uses relative coordinates—STEP(0, 0)—to specify the starting point for painting. Since the last point referenced by the CIRCLE statement is the center of the circle, this PAINT statement uses 0 for both the x and y offsets to start painting at the center of the circle. The last point referenced by the PAINT statement is the starting pixel: (160, 100).

Line 14

```
CIRCLE STEP(0, 0), 75, White
```

draws the outer circle. It too uses relative coordinates—STEP(0, 0)—to make the center of the circle (160, 100). The radius of the circle is 75 pixels, and its outline is White. The PAINT statement in line 15

```
PAINT STEP(60, 0), Magenta, White
```

uses relative coordinates—STEP(60, 0)—to start painting at X coordinate 160 + 60 = 220, and Y coordinate 100 + 0 = 100, which is inside the outer circle. The painting is done in Magenta.

```
1   '    *** DEMONSTRATING THE CIRCLE STATEMENT ***
2   '    Draw two concentric circles
3
4   CONST Cyan = 1
5   CONST Magenta = 2
6   CONST White = 3
7
8   SCREEN 1                          'Medium-resolution graphics
9   COLOR 0, 1                        'Black background with palette 1
10  CLS                               'Clear the screen
11
12  CIRCLE (160, 100), 50, White      'Draw inner circle in white
13  PAINT STEP(0, 0), Cyan, White     'Paint circle cyan
14  CIRCLE STEP(0, 0), 75, White      'Draw outer circle in white
15  PAINT STEP(60, 0), Magenta, White 'Paint doughnut magenta
16  A$ = INPUT$(1)                    'Pause
17  END
```

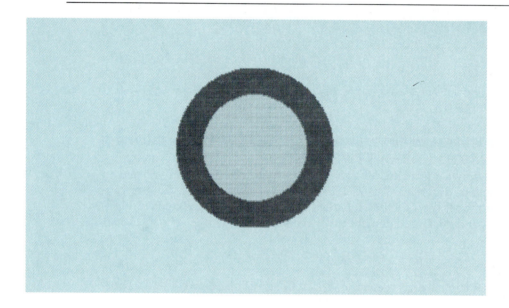

PROGRAM 11.5   Demonstrating the CIRCLE statement.

In the output of Program 11.5, the circles look squashed. On the screen, they look more like circles, but circles are often distorted when they are printed.   ■

Drawing Parts of Circles

The CIRCLE statement also allows us to draw an arc—that is, just part of a circle. When we draw part of a circle, we must specify where to start drawing and where to stop. The start and end arguments are used for this purpose. Before you can learn how to use start and end, though, you must understand how QBasic measures angles.

Degrees and Radians

If you have a Ph.D. in mathematics, fine. If you hated every minute of high school algebra, don't despair. The following section is easier than it sounds.

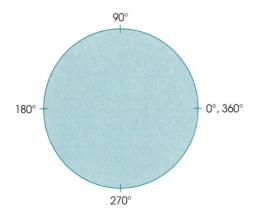

FIGURE 11.6 *Dividing a circle into 360 degrees.*

A circle is divided into 360 degrees. As Figure 11.6 shows, 0 degrees is at "3 o'clock." Mathematicians and QBasic use radians instead of degrees to measure the size of angles. Most of us, however, find it is easier to think in terms of degrees. So we need an easy way to convert degrees to radians.

A full circle contains 360 degrees. It also contains $2 \times \pi$ radians, where π is the numeric constant discussed previously (see Chapter 6) that equals 3.14159. Since 360 degrees = $2 \times \pi$ radians, it follows that 1 degree = $(2 \times \pi)/360$ radians. Therefore, if you include in your programs the following two statements,

```
CONST Pi = 3.14159
CONST Deg2Rad = (2 * Pi) / 360
```

then whenever you need to use radians, you can just multiply the number of degrees by Deg2Rad (degrees to radians). For example,

```
Deg2Rad * 45
```

converts 45 degrees into radians. If you use these equations, you don't need to know how many radians there are in 45 degrees; the program does the conversion for you.

Coding the Start and End Arguments

Now that you understand about radians, coding the start and end arguments is easy. You use start to specify the angle where the drawing of the arc should begin, and end to specify the angle where the drawing of the arc should end. For example, if Deg2Rad was defined in a program, then the statement

```
CIRCLE (200, 75), 25, 1, Deg2Rad * 270, Deg2Rad * 90
```

draws an arc from 270 degrees to 90 degrees in color 1, as shown here.

This statement illustrates that it is legal for start to be greater than end. If start or end are omitted, as they were in all the examples before this section, QBasic uses default values of 0 degrees for start and 360 degrees for end. In other words, it draws the whole circle. If start or end are outside the range of 0 to 360 degrees, the program stops and QBasic displays the error message Illegal function call.

You can also draw a line from the center of the circle to an arc. To do this, you precede start or end with a minus sign. For example, the statement

```
CIRCLE (80, 150), 30, , -Deg2Rad * 90, -Deg2Rad * 180
```

draws the following wedge in the default color, color 3.

(As usual, if we omit an argument—in this case, color—and code a later argument, we must code a comma to indicate the missing argument.)

You might think that coding –Deg2Rad * 0 or –0 for start or end would draw a line from the center of the circle to 0 degrees, but that doesn't work. Instead, to draw a wedge that begins or ends at 0 degrees, you must code some small angle in place of 0; for example, –Deg2Rad * .01. Other examples of drawing wedges with the CIRCLE statement include the following.

ILLUSTRATIONS

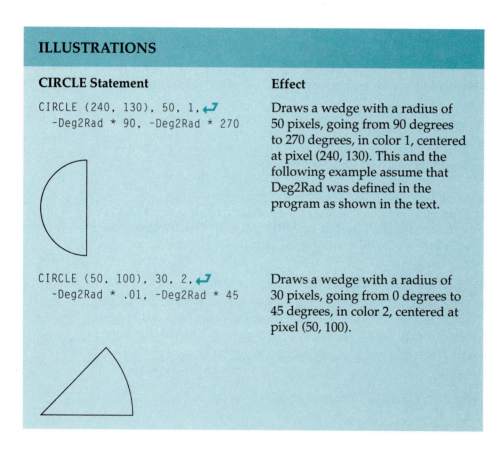

CIRCLE Statement	Effect
`CIRCLE (240, 130), 50, 1, ↵` `  -Deg2Rad * 90, -Deg2Rad * 270`	Draws a wedge with a radius of 50 pixels, going from 90 degrees to 270 degrees, in color 1, centered at pixel (240, 130). This and the following example assume that Deg2Rad was defined in the program as shown in the text.
`CIRCLE (50, 100), 30, 2, ↵` `  -Deg2Rad * .01, -Deg2Rad * 45`	Draws a wedge with a radius of 30 pixels, going from 0 degrees to 45 degrees, in color 2, centered at pixel (50, 100).

EXAMPLE 6 ▌▬▬▬▬▬▬▬▬▬▬

USING GRAPHICS STATEMENTS TO DRAW PAC-MAN
Program 11.6 uses CIRCLE, PAINT, and PSET statements to draw a Pac-Man-like figure. The CONST statements define Cyan and Brown—which are used in the graphics statements to specify colors—and the conversion factor Deg2Rad.

```
1    '    *** DRAWING PAC-MAN ***
2    '    Using CIRCLE, PAINT, and PSET statements to draw figure
3
4    CONST Cyan = 0
5    CONST Brown = 3
6    CONST Pi = 3.14159                  'Numeric constant π
7    CONST Deg2Rad = (2 * Pi) / 360      'Conversion factor, degrees to radians
8
9    SCREEN 1                            'Medium-resolution graphics
10   COLOR 3, 0                          'Cyan background with palette 0
11   CLS                                 'Clear screen
12
13   '    Draw the face
14   CIRCLE (160, 100), 60, Brown, -Deg2Rad * 45, -Deg2Rad * 335  'Draw outline
15   PAINT STEP(-10, 0), Brown, Brown          'Paint face
16   CIRCLE (140, 74), 5, Cyan                 'Draw eye
17   PAINT STEP(0, 0), Cyan, Cyan              'Paint eye
18   PSET STEP(0, 0), Brown                    'Draw eye pupil
19   CIRCLE (160, 65), 5, Cyan                 'Draw second eye
20   PAINT STEP(0, 0), Cyan, Cyan              'Paint second eye
21   PSET STEP(0, 0), Brown                    'Draw second eye pupil
22   A$ = INPUT$(1)                            'Pause
23   END
```

PROGRAM 11.6   Using graphic statements to draw Pac-Man.

Line 14

```
CIRCLE (160, 100), 60, Brown, -Deg2Rad * 45, -Deg2Rad * 335
```

draws the outline of the face as a wedge starting at 45 degrees and ending at 335 degrees. This leaves the gap from 335 degrees to 45 degrees as the mouth. The last point referenced is the center of the circle: (160, 100).

The PAINT statement in line 15

```
PAINT STEP(-10, 0), Brown, Brown
```

starts painting at an X coordinate of $160 - 10 = 150$ and a Y coordinate of $100 + 0 = 100$—not at $(160, 100)$, which is the center of the circle. When only part of a circle is drawn, as it is in Program 11.6, the center of the circle is on the boundary of the figure. And painting must start *inside* the area that is to be painted. Any number of points could have served as the starting point; here, we arbitrarily use a point 10 pixels to the left of the center of the circle.

When you want to write a program to draw a complex figure like this one, you should first draw the figure on the graphics layout form and then convert the drawing into graphics statements. Some adjustments will be required to get the figure exactly the way you want it. Clever programming can help in making any adjustments. For example, it was necessary to try several sets of coordinates for the CIRCLE statements that draw the eyes (lines 16 and 19):

```
CIRCLE (140, 74), 5, Cyan
CIRCLE (160, 65), 5, Cyan
```

to find the best ones: $(140, 74)$ and $(160, 65)$. Using relative coordinates for the PAINT and PSET statements that follow these CIRCLE statements (lines 17, 18, 20, and 21):

```
PAINT STEP(0, 0), Cyan, Cyan
PSET STEP(0, 0), Brown
```

avoids having to change the coordinates of the PAINT and PSET statements every time the coordinates of CIRCLE statements change.   ■

Coding Aspect

The final argument of the CIRCLE statement is aspect, which is related—but not identical—to the aspect ratio we discussed earlier. Coding aspect in a CIRCLE statement lets you draw ellipses (ovals). To draw an ellipse, we must specify two radii: the X radius (which is measured along the X axis) and the Y radius (which is measured along the Y axis). In the CIRCLE statement, aspect is the ratio of Y radius to X radius, where both radii are measured in pixels.

When a CIRCLE statement without aspect is coded, QBasic uses the default value of $5/6$ in medium-resolution and $5/12$ in high-resolution. These default values compensate for the aspect ratio of the medium- and high-resolution screens and ensure that when a CIRCLE statement without aspect is executed, a circle—a figure in which the physical lengths of the X radius and Y radius are equal—is drawn. By coding aspect, we can create the "stretched circles" known as ellipses.

EXAMPLE 7 ▬▬▬▬▬▬▬▬▬▬▬▬▬▬▬▬▬▬▬▬▬▬

A PROGRAM THAT DRAWS ELLIPSES
Program 11.7 draws ellipses with various values of aspect. Note that while all these circles have the same radius—75—they have different shapes because of the different values assigned to aspect. The circles on the left side of the output have values of aspect of 1 or more, and those on the right have values of 1 or less.
Lines 8, 9, and 10

```
CIRCLE (80, 100), 75, , , , 1
CIRCLE (80, 100), 75, , , , 2
CIRCLE (80, 100), 75, , , , 3
```

draw the three circles on the left. These three circles all have the same center—(80, 100)—and the same radius—75—but aspect ratios of 1, 2, and 3.

```
 1 | '    *** DEMONSTRATING ASPECT PARAMETER ***
 2 | '    Draw circles with different aspects
 3 |
 4 | SCREEN 1                              'Medium-resolution graphics
 5 | COLOR 0, 1                            'Black background with palette 1
 6 | CLS                                   'Clear screen
 7 |
 8 | CIRCLE (80, 100), 75, , , , 1         'Aspect
 9 | CIRCLE (80, 100), 75, , , , 2         '1 and
10 | CIRCLE (80, 100), 75, , , , 3         'greater
11 |
12 | CIRCLE (240, 100), 75, , , , 1        'Aspect
13 | CIRCLE (240, 100), 75, , , , .5       '1 and
14 | CIRCLE (240, 100), 75, , , , .25      'smaller
15 | A$ = INPUT$(1)                        'Pause
16 | END
```

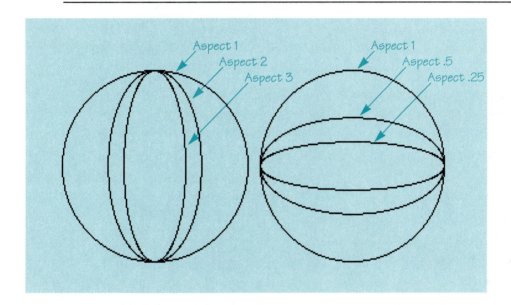

PROGRAM 11.7   Demonstrating the aspect argument.

If aspect is greater than or equal to 1, QBasic uses the radius coded in the CIRCLE statement as the Y radius and calculates the X radius using the equation

X radius = Y radius / aspect

In Program 11.7, the three circles on the left all have the same Y radius of 75, but three different X radii.

Lines 12, 13, and 14

```
CIRCLE (240, 100), 75, , , , 1
CIRCLE (240, 100), 75, , , , .5
CIRCLE (240, 100), 75, , , , .25
```

draw the three circles on the right. These three circles all have the same center—(240, 100)—and the same radius—75—but aspect ratios of 1, .5, and .25.

If aspect is less than 1, QBasic uses the radius coded in the CIRCLE statement as the X radius and calculates the Y radius using the equation

Y radius = X radius × aspect

In Program 11.7, the three circles on the right all have the same X radius of 75, but three different Y radii.

Before proceeding, be sure you understand how the following CIRCLE statements produce oval shapes.

ILLUSTRATIONS

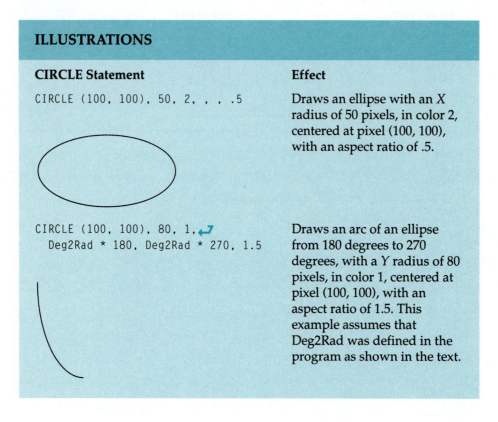

CIRCLE Statement	Effect
CIRCLE (100, 100), 50, 2, , , .5	Draws an ellipse with an X radius of 50 pixels, in color 2, centered at pixel (100, 100), with an aspect ratio of .5.
CIRCLE (100, 100), 80, 1,↵ Deg2Rad * 180, Deg2Rad * 270, 1.5	Draws an arc of an ellipse from 180 degrees to 270 degrees, with a Y radius of 80 pixels, in color 1, centered at pixel (100, 100), with an aspect ratio of 1.5. This example assumes that Deg2Rad was defined in the program as shown in the text.

When you draw an ellipse on the graphics layout chart, you can determine the value of aspect to code in the CIRCLE statement by dividing the Y radius by the X radius, where both radii are measured in pixels. Then code the CIRCLE statement, using the larger radius as radius. ∎

Syntax Summary

CIRCLE Statement
Form: CIRCLE (x, y),radius[,color][,start][,end][,aspect]
Example: CIRCLE (175, 90), 50, 3, Deg2Rad * 180, Deg2Rad *↵
                 270, 1.5
Explanation: Draws a circle (or ellipse if aspect is coded) that is centered at (x, y) and has a radius of radius pixels in the color specified by color. The start and end arguments specify the starting and ending angles of the curve, and aspect specifies the ratio of the Y radius to the X radius (both are measured in pixels).

11.4 EXERCISES

★**1.** Write the CIRCLE statement to draw a circle in cyan that is centered at pixel (100, 80) and has a radius of 60 pixels. Write the PAINT statement to paint the circle white.

2. What output would Program 11.5 (page 446) produce if the coordinates in line 12 were changed to (200, 50), and no other coordinates were changed?

3. Write the CIRCLE statement to draw the following wedge, centered at (160, 100) with a radius of 90 pixels.

PAINT the wedge green.

4. The PAINT statement in line 15 of Program 11.6 (page 449) starts painting at a point 10 pixels to the left of the center of the circle drawn by line 14. Could the PAINT statement begin 10 pixels to the right?

★**5.** Suppose a circle is drawn using the statement

```
CIRCLE (160, 100), 80, , , , 2
```

What is the X radius of this circle? What is the Y radius?

6. Program 11.8 shows a program that is supposed to draw a half-circle wedge. When the program was executed, QBasic stopped on the CIRCLE statement and displayed the error message Illegal function call. Find and correct the error.

```
1  '    *** DRAWING A HALF-CIRCLE WEDGE ***
2  '    Using the start and end arguments to draw part of a circle
3
4  CONST Pi = 3.14159                    'Constant π
5  CONST Deg2Rad = (2 * Pi) / 360        'Conversion factor degrees to radians
6
7  COLOR 12, 0                           'Light red background with palette 0
8  CLS                                   'Clear screen
9
10 '    Draw the wedge
11 CIRCLE (160, 100), 75, 3, -Deg2Rad * 90, -Deg2Rad * 270 'Draw wedge
12 A$ = INPUT$(1)                        'Pause
13 END
```

PROGRAM 11.8 A program that is supposed to draw a half-circle wedge.

WHAT YOU HAVE LEARNED

In this chapter, you learned that:

- To execute graphics programs, your computer must be equipped with a graphics monitor.
- Among the graphics modes you can use are medium-resolution and high-resolution.
- The SCREEN statement is used to change the screen from text mode to one of the graphics modes.
- In medium-resolution mode, the X coordinates run from 0 to 319; in high-resolution mode, they run from 0 to 639. In both modes, the Y coordinates run from 0 to 199.
- In graphics mode, the COLOR statement specifies a background color and a palette.
- When coded with the color argument, PSET and PRESET perform identically. When coded with-out the color argument, the PSET statement draws points and the PRESET statement erases them.
- You can specify position using either absolute or relative coordinates. To use relative coordinates, you must include the word STEP in a graphics statement.
- The LINE statement draws lines and boxes.
- In medium-resolution, the aspect ratio is $5/6$; in high-resolution, it is $5/12$.
- The DOS command GRAPHICS allows you to print a graphics screen.
- The PAINT statement colors a figure.
- The CIRCLE statement draws circles, ellipses, and parts of circles and ellipses.

NEW QBASIC STATEMENTS

STATEMENT	EFFECT
SCREEN	
SCREEN 1	Sets the screen mode, which may be text (0), medium-resolution graphics (1), or high-resolution graphics (2).
COLOR	
COLOR 5, 1	Sets the background color to 5 (magenta) with palette 1.
PSET	
PSET (275, 25), 3	Plots a point at (275, 25) in color 3.
PRESET	
PRESET (35, 180), 1	Plots a point at (35, 180) in color 1.
LINE	
LINE (10, 10)-(50, 50), 2, BF	Draws a box whose opposite corners are (10, 10) and (50, 50), and fills it with color 2.
PAINT	
PAINT (30, 40), 1, 2	Paints in color 1 in all directions, starting at (30, 40) and stopping when color 2 is encountered.
CIRCLE	
CIRCLE (200, 125), 25, 3	Draws a circle in color 3, centered at (200, 125), with a radius of 25.

KEY TERMS

absolute coordinates
all points addressable
aspect ratio
coordinates

last point referenced
line clipping
palette

physical coordinates
pixel
relative coordinates

REVIEW EXERCISES

SELF-CHECK

1. If aspect is not coded with a CIRCLE statement, what value is used? Is the same value used in both medium-resolution and high-resolution?

2. What is the last point referenced after a CIRCLE statement is executed?

3. What are the coordinates of the four corner points in medium-resolution and in high-resolution?

4. What is the default color number used by the PRESET statement?

5. Explain the difference between coding B and coding BF with a LINE statement.

6. True or false: On a medium-resolution screen, the PRINT statement always produces white characters.

7. What colors are available with palette 0?

8. What are the differences between the medium- and the high-resolution graphics modes?

9. What is the default color number used by the LINE statement?

10. What is the cause of the error if, during execution, a program stops at a PSET statement and displays the error message Illegal function call?

11. How do you specify relative coordinates in a graphics statement?

PROGRAMMING ASSIGNMENTS

Section 11.1

1. Write a program that draws a cluster of four magenta points in the upper-right corner of the medium-resolution screen. Use both absolute and relative coordinates to specify the position.

2. Write a program that draws a cluster of four points in the lower-left corner of the high-resolution screen. Use both absolute and relative coordinates to specify the position.

3. Use the fact that a COLOR statement changes all the colors on the screen in a program that tests reflexes. The program should present instructions in white characters on a red background. The instructions should explain that a short time after the test starts, the screen will turn blue—after which the user should press the space bar as quickly as possible. Allow the user to indicate that he or she is ready to start the test by pressing the Enter key. (*Hint*: Use the RND function to generate a random delay before turning the screen red; use the TIMER function to measure the interval between the time that the screen turns red and when the user presses the space bar. The RND and TIMER functions were explained in Chapter 7.)

Section 11.2

4. Write a program to draw an arrow like the one in Program 11.3, but facing left.

5. Write a program to draw this flag:

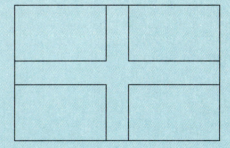

6. Write a program to draw a rocket:

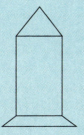

7. Write a program to draw three nested boxes on a red background. The common center of all three boxes should be the center of the medium-resolution screen. The largest box should have sides of 120 pixels and be colored cyan, the next box should have sides of 60 pixels and be colored magenta, and the innermost box should have sides of 30 pixels and be colored white. Your figure should look like the one that follows, except that yours should be in the appropriate colors.

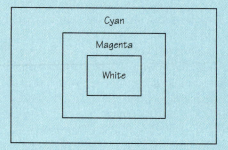

Section 11.3

8. Modify the program you wrote for Programming Assignment 11.4 to paint the left-facing arrow cyan.

9. Modify the program you wrote for Programming Assignment 11.5 to paint the flag. The background should be blue, the cross white, the upper-left and lower-right sections cyan, and the lower-left and upper-right sections magenta.

10. Add a red chimney to the house drawn in Program 11.4. The fire code requires that the chimney be higher than the peak of the roof. Since it is difficult to determine the exact coordinates where the chimney meets the roof, you may outline the chimney in brown and then paint it red.

Section 11.4

11. Write a program that draws a face like the one in Program 11.6, but have the face turned to the left.

12. Write a program that draws a happy face like the one that follows. The face should be cyan, the mouth white, and the eyes black.

13. Write a program that draws the following truck. Make the wheels a different color from the body.

14. Write a program that divides the screen into four quadrants. In the upper-left quadrant, draw a cyan circle on a blue background. In the upper-right quadrant, draw a magenta circle on a cyan background. In the lower-right quadrant, draw a white circle on a magenta background. In the lower-left quadrant, draw a blue circle on a white background.

ADDITIONAL PROGRAMMING ASSIGNMENTS

15. Write a program to draw a crescent moon:

16. Write a program to draw a pizza with a slice removed:

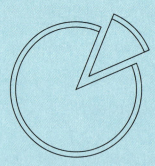

17. Write a program to draw 100 circles randomly on the screen. For each circle, the X coordinate of the center should be a random number between 0 and 319, the Y coordinate should be a random number between 0 and 199, and the radius should be a random number between 5 and 25. Paint the circle with a random color chosen from the four available colors.

18. Write a program to draw the following church. Use color 0 for the windows and the belfry, color 1 for the building, and color 2 for the doors and the steeple peak.

19. Write a program to draw this football field:

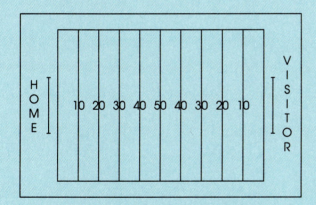

20. Write a program to draw the Star of David:

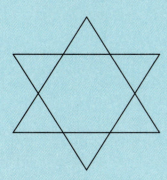

21. Write a program to draw a stop sign. The sign should be red and the letters white. Use any color other than red or white for the background.

22. Write a program to draw this valentine:

23. Write a program to draw this pail:

24. Write a program to draw the following design. Paint the center portion in color 3 and the other portions as indicated.

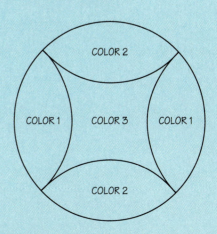

BEYOND THE BASICS

25. Write a program to draw the following checker-board. The board squares should be color 1 and color 2. One set of checkers should be color 0, and the second set should be color 3.

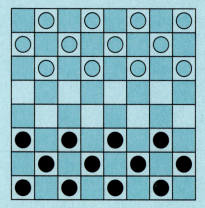

26. Write a graphics version of the random walk problem presented in Programming Assignment 7.33. Make the bridge 100 pixels long and 60 pixels wide. Each time Sherry takes a step, she walks 10 pixels along the length of the bridge and lurches 10 pixels to the side. Plot her progress. If she falls in, print SPLASH! near where she fell in. If she makes it safely, print SAFE! near her arrival point. Then ask whether the user wants to see another walk.

27. Write a graphics version of the Hangman program presented in Programming Assignment 7.46. Begin by drawing a gallows. Then, every time the user enters a wrong letter, draw part of a figure. Also, display the wrong letters in alphabetical order on row 25, leaving spaces for correct and not-yet-guessed letters. For example:

D H JK N   R U   Y

12

GRAPHS, CHARTS, AND ANIMATION

LEARNING OBJECTIVES

After reading this chapter, you will be able to:

- Draw line and bar graphs and pie charts.
- Use the QBasic statements VIEW, WINDOW, GET, and PUT.
- Achieve animation.

In Chapter 11, you learned how to use graphics statements to draw pictures. In this chapter, you will learn how to use these statements to draw line and bar graphs and pie charts.

To help you draw graphs, you will learn how to define a graphics viewport, similar to the text viewport you used earlier. You will also learn how to define coordinates that are relevant to your problem, which makes drawing graphs much easier.

In this chapter, you will also find out how to move figures around the screen. To do so, you will learn how to capture a figure and how to later display it.

12.1   ESSENTIALS FOR DRAWING GRAPHS AND CHARTS

Two graphics statements, VIEW and WINDOW, are useful in programs that draw graphs and charts.

The VIEW Statement

The VIEW statement lets you define a graphics viewport, which is similar to the text viewport that the VIEW PRINT statement creates. We will discuss how graphics viewports work after we examine the syntax of the VIEW statement.

The syntax of the VIEW statement is

```
VIEW [(x1, y1)-(x2, y2)][,color][,boundary]
```

where (x1, y1) and (x2, y2) are the coordinates of diagonally opposite corners of the viewport. The color argument specifies the color that the viewport should be painted and works the same way as color works in the other graphics statements. If you do not code color, the viewport is not painted. The boundary argument specifies the color to be used to draw a boundary line around the viewport. In medium-resolution mode, boundary may be 0 through 3. In high-resolution mode, boundary may be either 0 or 1. If you do not code boundary, no boundary is drawn. If you code a VIEW statement with no arguments, you reestablish the whole screen as one viewport.

Figure 12.1 shows a viewport that was established by the statement

```
VIEW (50, 25)-(250, 175), 1, 1
```

The coordinates of the upper-left corner of the viewport are (50, 25), and those of the lower-right corner are (250, 175). You get the same viewport if you use the coordinates of the lower-left and upper-right corners:

```
VIEW (50, 175)-(250, 25), 1, 1
```

In either case, the result is that an X (vertical) line at 50 forms the left boundary of the viewport and an X line at 250 the right boundary, while a Y (horizontal) line at 25 forms the upper boundary and a Y line at 175 the lower boundary.

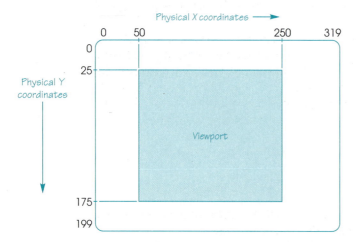

FIGURE 12.1   A viewport (shown in gray) created by the statement
VIEW (50, 25)–(250, 175), 1, 1.

Before proceeding, be sure you understand how each of the following VIEW statements works.

ILLUSTRATIONS

VIEW Statement	Effect
VIEW (70, 30)-(270, 130), 3, 1	Establishes a viewport painted in color 3 with a border of color 1 whose upper-left corner is at (70, 30) and whose lower-right corner is at (270, 130).
VIEW (150, 90)-(170, 110)	Establishes a viewport whose upper-left corner is at (150, 90) and whose lower-right corner is at (170, 110). The viewport is not painted, and the boundary is not drawn.
VIEW	Reestablishes the whole screen as one viewport.

EXAMPLE 1
DEMONSTRATING THE VIEW STATEMENT

Program 12.1 shows how the VIEW statement works. Note that in this program, all three circles were drawn by the same CIRCLE statement—the one in line 32:

```
CIRCLE (45, 40), 30
```

Let's see how one CIRCLE statement could draw three different circles.

The first circle is drawn when the CALL DrawCircle statement in line 13 is executed. This circle (labeled NO VIEW) looks exactly as you would expect: Its center is at (45, 40), and its radius is 30. Next, the VIEW statement in line 16

```
VIEW (200, 20)-(300, 90), , 1
```

is executed. This statement defines the section of the screen between pixels (200, 20) and (300, 90) as a viewport. Now when the CALL DrawCircle statement in line 19 is executed, the CIRCLE statement in line 32 draws a circle in the viewport labeled VIEW 1.

How did the circle get in the viewport? After you create a viewport, the coordinates of the upper-left corner of the viewport are automatically added to the coordinates specified in any graphics statements. In the VIEW statement in line 16, the coordinates of the upper-left corner of the viewport are (200, 20). When the CIRCLE statement in line 32 was executed, these values were added to the coordinates specified in the statement, so that the statement was effectively

```
CIRCLE (45+200, 40+20), 30
```

or

```
CIRCLE (245, 60), 30
```

This is the statement that drew the circle labeled VIEW 1. A viewport has no effect on the output produced by LOCATE and PRINT statements.

The second viewport, which is created in line 22, is similar to the first, except that it is too small to contain the circle. As you can see from the circle labeled VIEW 2, only that portion of the circle that fits in the viewport is drawn. After a

```
1   '    *** DEMONSTRATING THE VIEW STATEMENT ***
2   '   Drawing circles in viewports
3
4   DECLARE SUB DrawCircle ()
5
6   SCREEN 1                        'Medium-resolution graphics
7   COLOR 0, 1                      'Black background with palette 1
8   CLS                             'Clear screen
9
10  '    Draw circle without a viewport
11  LOCATE 1, 3                     'Locate and print
12  PRINT "NO VIEW"                 'label
13  CALL DrawCircle                 'Draw circle
14
15  '    Draw circle in first viewport
16  VIEW (200, 20)-(300, 90), , 1   'Establish viewport 1
17  LOCATE 4, 29                    'Locate and print
18  PRINT "VIEW 1"                  'label
19  CALL DrawCircle                 'Draw circle in viewport
20
21  '    Draw circle in second viewport
22  VIEW (200, 100)-(250, 170), , 2 'Establish viewport 2
23  LOCATE 14, 26                   'Locate and print
24  PRINT "VIEW 2"                  'label
25  CALL DrawCircle                 'Draw circle in viewport
26
27  A$ = INPUT$(1)                  'Pause
28  END
29
30  SUB DrawCircle
31      '    *** Subprogram to draw circle
32      CIRCLE (45, 40), 30
33  END SUB
```

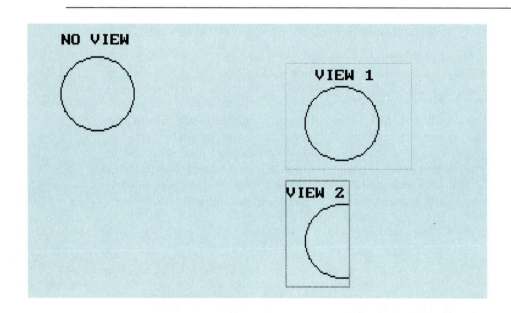

PROGRAM 12.1   Demonstrating the VIEW statement.

viewport is created, QBasic behaves as though the rest of the screen does not exist. Figures are drawn relative to the viewport and—because of line clipping—parts of figures that would fall outside the viewport are not drawn.

If you have several viewports, you can treat them as independent screens. The CLS statement clears only the most recently created viewport. You can clear the whole screen by executing a CLS statement with the argument 0: CLS 0. ■

The WINDOW Statement

The WINDOW statement changes the coordinates of the screen. You change the coordinates so that the coordinates of the screen match the coordinates of your problem. For example, suppose you want to plot a graph in which X goes from 0 to 10 and Y goes from 100 to 500. You could use the statement

```
WINDOW (0, 100)-(10, 500)
```

to assign the coordinates (0, 100) to the lower-left corner of the screen, and (10, 500) to the upper-right corner. We call the coordinates specified by a WINDOW statement **world coordinates**, in contrast to the usual physical coordinates you learned about in Chapter 11. If a WINDOW statement is executed after a VIEW statement, the new coordinates apply to the viewport. The syntax of the WINDOW statement is

world coordinates
A coordinate system established by the user to fit a given problem.

```
WINDOW [SCREEN][(x1, y1)-(x2, y2)]
```

where (x1, y1) and (x2, y2) are the coordinates you want to use. Normally, (x1, y1) are the coordinates of the lower-left corner, and (x2, y2) are the coordinates of the upper-right corner. If you include the SCREEN argument in the WINDOW statement, the coordinates will be reversed. That is, (x1, y1) will be the coordinates of the upper-left corner and (x2, y2) will be the coordinates of the lower-right corner.

If you execute a WINDOW statement with no arguments, the coordinate system created by a previously executed WINDOW statement is abolished, and the screen returns to the usual physical coordinates.

Check your understanding of the WINDOW statement against the following examples.

ILLUSTRATIONS

WINDOW Statement	Effect
WINDOW (0, 0)-(10, 100)	Assigns (0, 0) as the coordinates of the lower-left corner and (10, 100) as the coordinates of the upper-right corner of a previously defined viewport. If a viewport was not previously defined, the coordinates apply to the whole screen.
WINDOW SCREEN (-1, -1)-(1, 1)	Assigns (-1, -1) as the coordinates of the upper-left corner and (1, 1) as the coordinates of the lower-right corner of a previously defined viewport. If a viewport was not previously defined, the coordinates apply to the whole screen.

(continued)

WINDOW	Abolishes any previously established world coordinate system and returns the screen to the usual physical coordinates.

EXAMPLE 2

DEMONSTRATING THE WINDOW STATEMENT

Problem Statement

Write a program that draws a graph of a line that goes through the points (100, 1000) and (500, 1500). Use the VIEW and WINDOW statements to create a viewport with the appropriate coordinates.

STEP 1 Variable Names

This program does not use any variables.

STEP 2 Algorithm

The algorithm is

1. Define the viewport.
2. Define the world coordinates.
3. Print the coordinates and labels along the X and Y axes.
4. Draw the line.

STEP 3 Hand-Calculated Answers

This problem has no hand-calculated answers.

STEP 4 QBasic Program

Program 12.2 draws the desired graph. The VIEW statement in line 8

```
VIEW (50, 25)-(250, 175), , 1
```

defines the viewport shown in Figure 12.2. The WINDOW statement in line 9

```
WINDOW (0, 1000)-(500, 2000)
```

defines the world coordinate system for that viewport, which is also shown in Figure 12.2. That figure shows that (0, 1000) is the coordinate of the lower-left corner and (500, 2000) is the coordinate of the upper-right corner. Notice that in this coordinate system, *Y* increases as we move toward the top of the screen. As you might expect, this orientation makes it much easier to draw graphs.

The LOCATE and PRINT statements in lines 12 through 25 label the *Y* and *X* axes. The LINE statement in line 28

```
LINE (100, 1000)-(500, 1500)
```

draws a line between pixels (100, 1000) and (500, 1500). Although no pixels have these physical coordinates, the WINDOW statement allows us to define the screen with the coordinates we want. QBasic translates our world coordinates into physical coordinates and draws the line where it should be.

Figure 12.3 shows the output produced by Program 12.2. ■

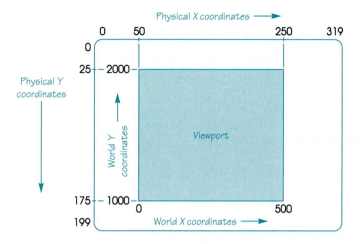

FIGURE 12.2   A viewport with world coordinates.

```
 1 |  '    *** DEMONSTRATING THE WINDOW STATEMENT ***
 2 |  '    Drawing a line graph in a viewport with world coordinates
 3 |
 4 |  SCREEN 1                       'Medium-resolution graphics
 5 |  COLOR 0, 1                     'Black background with palette 1
 6 |  CLS                            'Clear screen
 7 |
 8 |  VIEW (50, 25)-(250, 175), , 1  'Create viewport
 9 |  WINDOW (0, 1000)-(500, 2000)   'Establish coordinates
10 |
11 |  '      Print Y coordinates
12 |  LOCATE 4, 3
13 |  PRINT "2000"
14 |  LOCATE 13, 5
15 |  PRINT "Y"
16 |  LOCATE 22, 3
17 |  PRINT "1000"
18 |
19 |  '      Print X coordinates
20 |  LOCATE 24, 7
21 |  PRINT "0";
22 |  LOCATE 24, 20
23 |  PRINT "X";
24 |  LOCATE 24, 31
25 |  PRINT "500";
26 |
27 |  '      Draw line
28 |  LINE (100, 1000)-(500, 1500)
29 |  A$ = INPUT$(1)
30 |  END
```

PROGRAM 12.2   Demonstrating the WINDOW statement.

Aspect Ratio

We have to modify the definition of aspect ratio for a viewport with world coordinates. In such a viewport, the definition of aspect ratio is the physical length of a line one unit long in the X direction divided by the physical length of a line one unit long in the Y direction.

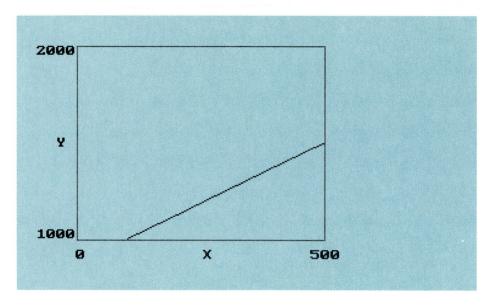

FIGURE 12.3
Output
produced by
Program 12.2.

If we let L_x be the length in pixels of the viewport in the X direction, L_y be the length in the Y direction, R_x be the range of coordinates in the X direction, and R_y be the range of coordinates in the Y direction—then in the medium-resolution screen, the aspect ratio of the viewport is given by

$$a = 0.833 \times \frac{L_x / R_x}{L_y / R_y}$$

In the high-resolution screen, the same equation is used, but the constant is 0.417. This aspect ratio is used by the CIRCLE statement as the default value for aspect to draw a circle in a viewport with world coordinates. Similarly, this is the definition you must use with a LINE statement to draw a square in a viewport with world coordinates.

As an example of applying this equation, line 8 in Program 12.2 shows that $L_x = 250 - 50 = 200$ and $L_y = 175 - 25 = 150$. Line 9 shows that $R_x = 500 - 0 = 500$, and $R_y = 2000 - 1000 = 1000$. Substituting these values into the equation gives

$$a = 0.833 \times \frac{200 / 500}{150 / 1000} = 2.22$$

as the aspect ratio of this viewport.

You will see an application of this definition of aspect ratio when we draw a pie chart later in this chapter.

Syntax Summary

VIEW Statement

Form: VIEW [(x1, y1)-(x2, y2)][,color][,boundary]
Example: VIEW (60, 50)-(260, 150), 2, 1
Explanation: Defines a viewport that is painted in the color specified by color, with a border specified by boundary. (x1, y1) and (x2, y2) are diagonally opposite corners of the viewport.

WINDOW Statement

Form: WINDOW [SCREEN][(x1, y1)-(x2, y2)]
Example: WINDOW (1980, 0)-(2000, 1000)
Explanation: Establishes world coordinates. If SCREEN is omitted, (x1, y1) are the coordinates of the lower-left corner of the viewport, and (x2, y2) are the coordinates of the upper-right corner. If SCREEN is coded, these assignments are reversed, with (x1, y1) the coordinates of the upper-left corner and (x2, y2) the coordinates of the lower-right corner. If a viewport was previously defined, the world coordinates apply to the viewport.

12.1 EXERCISES

★1. Code a VIEW statement to establish a viewport whose left boundary is the line X = 120, whose right boundary is the line X = 200, whose upper boundary is the line Y = 100, and whose lower boundary is the line Y = 190.

2. A viewport was established by the statement

    ```
    VIEW (40, 10)-(300, 120)
    ```

    Write a VIEW statement to define the same viewport using the other two corners.

3. Suppose a viewport was established between (250, 100) and (300, 150). Describe the line drawn by the statement

    ```
    LINE (0, 0)-(50, 50)
    ```

★4. Suppose a program contains the following statements:

    ```
    VIEW (30, 30)-(100, 100)
    WINDOW (0, 0)-(10, 10)
    PSET (0, 0)
    ```

    What are the physical coordinates of the point drawn by the PSET statement?

5. A homework assignment requires students to define a viewport whose lower-left corner has world coordinates of (0, 0) and whose upper-right corner has coordinates of (100, 100). One student uses the statement

    ```
    VIEW (0, 0)-(100, 75)
    ```

    to define the viewport. Code the WINDOW statement for this student. A second student uses the statement

    ```
    VIEW (100, 100)-(200, 175)
    ```

    to define the viewport. Code the WINDOW statement for this student.

12.2 DRAWING DIFFERENT TYPES OF GRAPHS AND CHARTS

It is remarkably easy to draw graphs and charts using QBasic; as you will see, the hardest part is printing the labels and coordinates for them.

EXAMPLE 3
DRAWING A LINE GRAPH

Problem Statement

Write a program that plots the inflation rate versus years for 16 years, beginning with a year that the user specifies. The layout of the graph is shown in Figure 12.4. The starting year, maximum inflation rate, and 16 annual inflation rates will be given in DATA statements.

STEP 1   Variable Names

We begin by choosing variable names.

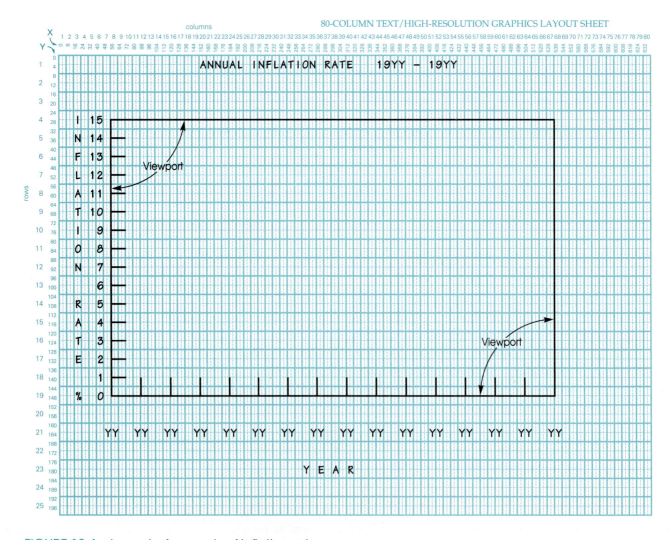

FIGURE 12.4   Layout of a graph of inflation rates.

Variable	Variable Name
Input Variables	
Starting year for graph	`FirstYear`
Maximum inflation rate for *Y* coordinate	`MaxRate`
Input and Output Variables	
A character	`Char$`
Inflation rate	`InflationRate`
Year	`Year`
Internal Variables	
Counter variable	`J`
X coordinate of end of tick line	`EndTick`

STEP 2   Algorithm

The algorithm is

1. Print the coordinates and labels along the X and Y axes.
2. Define the viewport.
3. Define the world coordinates.
4. Plot the data.

STEP 3   Hand-Calculated Answers

There are no answers to calculate by hand—although after the graph is drawn, you should check it to make sure that the points are plotted where they should be.

STEP 4   QBasic Program

Since this graph does not have color, we will use the high-resolution mode to take advantage of the extra detail available in high-resolution. Program 12.3 draws the graph.

In the main module, the SCREEN 2 statement in line 14 sets the mode to high-resolution graphics, and the CLS statement clears the screen. The READ statement in line 18 reads FirstYear and MaxRate. MaxRate is the value of the largest *Y* coordinate. It must, of course, be greater than or equal to the highest inflation rate that will be plotted. By changing the values in the DATA statements in lines 26 and 32, the graph can plot the inflation rate for any 16-year period.

Next, the SetUpGraph subprogram is called to draw the coordinates, print the labels, set up the viewport, and define the world coordinates. In the SetUpGraph subprogram, let's consider first how the *X* (horizontal) coordinates are printed. The FOR...NEXT loop in lines 93 through 96 prints the years. Line 94

```
LOCATE 21, 4 * Year + b
```

specifies that Year should be printed in row 21 and column 4 * Year + b. We will use this kind of expression frequently in this chapter, so it is important that you understand how to derive it.

We want the first year to print in columns 7 and 8, and the second year to print in columns 11 and 12. So when the year increases by 1, the column number increases by 4. For that to happen, we must use the expression 4 * Year in the column parameter of the LOCATE statement.

The value of b is determined by calculating the value it must have to make any one Year come out in the correct column. Since we want to print FirstYear starting in column 7, we can use the equation for column number to calculate b:

```
7 = 4 * FirstYear + b
```

```
1   '   *** DRAWING A LINE GRAPH ***
2   '   Draw a line graph of inflation versus year in a viewport
3   '   with world coordinates. The graph covers 16 years, starting
4   '   with the year given in a DATA statement.
5
6   DECLARE SUB SetUpGraph (FirstYear!, MaxRate!)
7   DECLARE SUB PlotData (FirstYear!)
8
9   '   Variables used
10
11  '   FirstYear       Starting year for graph
12  '   MaxRate         Maximum inflation rate for Y coordinate
13
14  SCREEN 2                                'High-resolution graphics
15  CLS                                     'Clear screen
16
17  '   Read values used to setup graph and coordinates
18  READ FirstYear, MaxRate
19
20  CALL SetUpGraph(FirstYear, MaxRate)     'Draw axes and coordinates
21  CALL PlotData(FirstYear)                'Plot the data
22  a$ = INPUT$(1)                          'Pause
23
24  '   The following data are FirstYear and MaxRate
25  '   Note: MaxRate must be <= 17
26  DATA 78, 15
27
28  '   Data for READ in SetUpGraph
29  DATA I, N, F, L, A, T, I, O, N, " ", R, A, T, E, " ", %
30
31  '   Inflation rate for READ in PlotData
32  DATA 7.7,11.3,13.5,10.4,6.1,3.2,4.2,4.4,2.3,4.4,5.3,4.7,3.5,4.7,3.5,4.3
33  END
34
35  SUB PlotData (FirstYear)
36  '   Plot data
37  '   FirstYear received
38  '   No variables returned
39
40  '   Local variables
41
42  '   InflationRate   Inflation rate
43  '   Year            Year
44
45  '   Read first inflation rate and plot first point
46      READ InflationRate
47      PSET (FirstYear, InflationRate)
48
49  '   Read and plot remaining points
50      FOR Year = FirstYear + 1 TO FirstYear + 15
51          READ InflationRate
52          LINE -(Year, InflationRate)
53      NEXT Year
54  END SUB
```

PROGRAM 12.3   Drawing a line graph. *(continued on next page)*

```
55  | SUB SetUpGraph (FirstYear, MaxRate)
56  | '    Set up graph
57  | '    FirstYear and MaxRate received
58  | '    No variables returned
59  |
60  | '    Local variables
61  |
62  | '    Char$            A character; used to print Y label
63  | '    EndTick          X coordinate of end of tick line
64  | '    InflationRate    Inflation rate
65  | '    Year             Year
66  |
67  | '    Locate and print heading
68  |      LOCATE 1, 20
69  |      Title$ = "ANNUAL INFLATION RATE    19## - 19##"
70  |      PRINT USING Title$; FirstYear; FirstYear + 15
71  |
72  | '    Print Y label
73  |      FOR J = 1 TO 16
74  |          READ Char$
75  |          LOCATE J + 3, 3
76  |          PRINT Char$
77  |      NEXT J
78  |
79  | '    Print Y coordinates
80  |      FOR InflationRate = 0 TO MaxRate
81  |          LOCATE -InflationRate + 19, 5
82  |          PRINT USING "##"; InflationRate
83  |      NEXT InflationRate
84  |
85  | '    Print X label
86  |      LOCATE 23, 34
87  |      PRINT "Y E A R"
88  |
89  | '    Print X coordinates
90  | '    Calculate b, used in following LOCATE statement,
91  | '    to print FirstYear in column 7
92  |      b = 7 - 4 * FirstYear
93  |      FOR Year = FirstYear TO FirstYear + 15
94  |          LOCATE 21, 4 * Year + b
95  |          PRINT USING "##"; Year
96  |      NEXT Year
97  |
98  | '    0 Inflation rate is at Y = 148, so MaxRate is at
99  | '    148 - 8 * MaxRate (8 pixels per row)
100 |      VIEW (55, 148)-(535, 148 - 8 * MaxRate), , 1        'Define viewport
101 |      WINDOW (FirstYear, 0)-(FirstYear + 15, MaxRate)    'Define coordinates
102 |
103 |      FOR Year = FirstYear TO FirstYear + 15             'Draw
104 |          LINE (Year, 0)-(Year, 1)                       'tick marks
105 |      NEXT Year                                          'along X axis
106 |
107 | '    Draw tick marks .5 year long along Y axis
108 |      EndTick = FirstYear + .5
109 |      FOR InflationRate = 0 TO MaxRate
110 |          LINE (FirstYear, InflationRate)-(EndTick, InflationRate)
111 |      NEXT InflationRate
112 | END SUB
```

PROGRAM 12.3 *(continued)*

which solves for b to give

```
b = 7 - 4 * FirstYear
```

which is the LET statement used in line 92 to calculate b. In Program 12.3, FirstYear is equal to 78, so this equation makes b equal to –305.

Recall that the LOCATE statement in line 94 uses the expression 4 * Year + b to specify the column to print Year. When Year is 78, this expression makes the column 4 * 78 – 305, which equals 7. When Year is 79, this expression makes the column 4 * 79 – 305, which equals 11. Figure 12.4 shows that these are the columns in which the first and second years should print, so you can see that our LOCATE statement is correct.

The Y coordinates are printed in the FOR…NEXT loop in lines 80 through 83. The LOCATE statement in line 81

```
LOCATE -InflationRate + 19, 5
```

specifies that InflationRate should be printed in column 5 and in row –InflationRate + 19. The expression –InflationRate + 19 was derived as follows: Figure 12.4 shows that when InflationRate increases by 1, we want the row number to decrease by 1. To get that to happen, InflationRate is multiplied by –1. Figure 12.4 also shows that InflationRate of 0 should print in row 19. To get that to happen, 19 is added to –InflationRate, giving the final expression –InflationRate + 19.

To verify this expression, notice that it prints an InflationRate of 10 in row 9, where Figure 12.4 shows that it should be printed.

The FOR…NEXT loop in lines 73 through 77 prints the Y label, Inflation Rate %. The LOCATE statement in line 75

```
LOCATE J + 3, 3
```

specifies that the label should be printed in column 3, and that the Jth character should be printed in row J + 3. The expression J + 3 was derived as follows: Figure 12.4 shows that successive characters are printed in successive rows. For that to happen, J is multiplied by +1. Also, the first character, I, is printed in row 4. For that to happen, the LOCATE statement must specify a row number of J + 3.

Defining the Viewport and Coordinates

Now that we have printed the X and Y coordinates, we must make sure that when we plot the points, their positions agree with the coordinates. We do that by defining a viewport and world coordinates to go with it. The VIEW statement is in line 100:

```
VIEW (55, 148)-(535, 148 - 8 * MaxRate), , 1
```

You can determine the coordinate values for this statement from the graphics layout form as follows.

FirstYear is printed in columns 7 and 8. We want the viewport to start at the last pixel in column 7, which has an X coordinate of 55—so in the VIEW statement, we make x1 = 55. Similarly, we make y1 = 148, which is the Y coordinate of the middle of row 19. We always plot 16 years of data, so the viewport ends at the last pixel in column 67, which has an X coordinate of 535. So in the VIEW statement, we make x2 = 535. The highest inflation rate is MaxRate. Since each row contains 8 pixels, we calculate the value of y2 in the VIEW statement as

```
148 - 8 * MaxRate
```

Notice that this VIEW statement includes a value of 1 for the boundary argument. This causes the boundary of the viewport to be drawn in color 1, white. The boundary of the viewport serves as the X and Y axes of the graph.

Now that the viewport is created, the WINDOW statement in line 101

```
WINDOW (FirstYear, 0)-(FirstYear + 15, MaxRate)
```

defines the coordinates to go with it. Specifying the arguments for the WINDOW statement is easy; we want X to go from FirstYear to FirstYear + 15, and Y to go from 0 to MaxRate.

The FOR...NEXT loop in lines 103 through 105 uses these world coordinates to draw vertical tick marks on the X axis. Line 104

```
LINE (Year, 0)-(Year, 1)
```

draws vertical lines between InflationRate of 0 and 1 for each value of Year between FirstYear and FirstYear + 15.

Similarly, the FOR...NEXT loop in lines 109 through 111 draws horizontal tick marks on the Y axis. First, line 108 assigns the value FirstYear + .5 to EndTick. EndTick is used in line 110

```
LINE (FirstYear, InflationRate)-(EndTick, InflationRate)
```

to draw horizontal lines between FirstYear and EndTick for each value of InflationRate between 0 and MaxRate.

Plotting the Data

With the viewport and its coordinates defined, the main module next calls the PlotData subprogram, which draws the graph. Line 46 reads the first inflation rate. Line 47 uses a PSET statement to plot the first point with the coordinates (FirstYear, InflationRate).

The FOR...NEXT loop in lines 50 through 53 draws the graph. Line 51 reads the remaining inflation rates, and line 52 draws a line from the last point referenced to the point (Year, InflationRate). The first time this LINE statement executes, the last point referenced is the point plotted by the PSET statement. Every other time the LINE statement executes, the last point referenced is the end of the line drawn the previous time the LINE statement was executed. In this way, the program connects one point on the graph to the next.

Figure 12.5 shows the graph produced by Program 12.3. ■

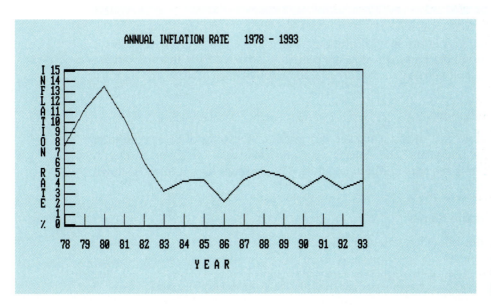

FIGURE 12.5
Graph produced
by Program 12.3.

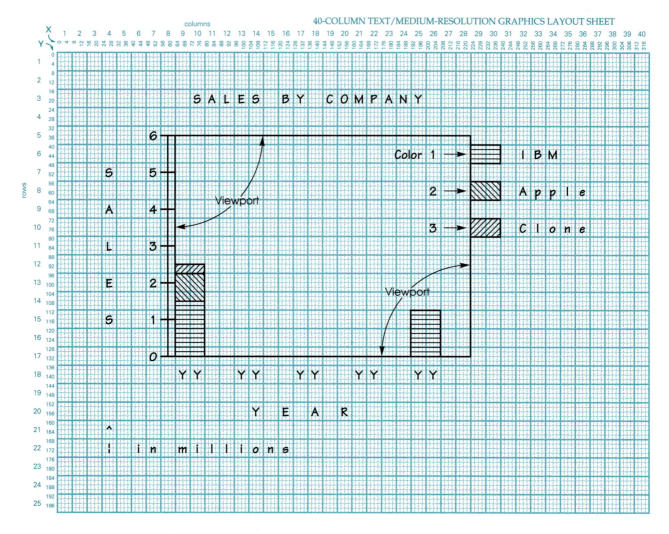

FIGURE 12.6   Layout of a bar graph of sales.

EXAMPLE 4

DRAWING A BAR GRAPH

Sometimes bar graphs are more useful than line graphs, especially when color is used. In the usual bar graph, the data are plotted as adjacent bars. In a stacked bar graph, data are plotted as bars that are placed on top of each other.

Problem Statement

Write a program that draws a stacked bar graph of the sales of three computer companies for five years. The starting year and sales data are given in DATA statements. Draw the bars in different colors. The graphics layout form is shown in Figure 12.6.*

STEP 1   Variable Names

We will use the following variable names.

---

*The data used in this graph were invented and should not be interpreted as giving past or future sales.

Variable	Variable Name
Input and Output Variables	
A character	`Char$`
Starting year for graph	`FirstYear`
IBM sales	`IBM`
Apple sales	`Apple`
Clone sales	`Clone`
Internal Variable	
Counter variables	`Sales, Year`

STEP 2 **Algorithm**

1. Print the coordinates and labels along the X and Y axes.
2. Define the viewport.
3. Define the world coordinates.
4. Plot the data.

STEP 3 **Hand-Calculated Answers**

This problem has no hand-calculated answers.

STEP 4 **QBasic Program**

Program 12.4 draws the bar graph. Like Program 12.3 (pages 470–71), the main module calls SetUpGraph to draw the coordinates and print the labels, and calls PlotData to draw the bars.

In SetUpGraph, printing the title, the X and Y labels and coordinates, and drawing the axes involve techniques that we discussed in connection with Program 12.3. The FOR…NEXT loop in lines 87 through 90 prints the Y coordinates and uses hyphens to draw the tick marks on the Y axis. Lines 115, 119, and 123 use the LINE statement with the BF argument to draw the legend as three small boxes, with three different colors (although the output seen in this book does not display these colors).

Unlike Program 12.3, the viewport should not coincide with the axes in this program. The first year is printed in columns 9 and 10. In order to draw the bars, we need the coordinate of the first pixel in column 9, which has an X coordinate of 64, to be FirstYear. Therefore, in the VIEW statement in line 128

```
VIEW (64, 36)-(224, 132)
```

we make x1 = 64. The WINDOW statement in line 131

```
WINDOW (FirstYear, 0)-(FirstYear + 5, 6)
```

makes the X coordinates start at FirstYear.

Determining the right vertical boundary of the viewport is a little tricky. The graph should show 5 years of data. The last year—FirstYear + 4—is printed in columns 25 and 26. Therefore, the first pixel in column 25, whose X coordinate is 192, must have a coordinate of FirstYear + 4. However, we want to draw the bar for that year in columns 25 and 26; that is, between pixels 192 and 207. If we make the right vertical boundary of the viewport pixel 192, we won't be able to draw anything beyond pixel 192. So we have to make the right vertical boundary of the viewport somewhere beyond pixel 192. How far should we extend it? It's easiest to extend it to some pixel whose coordinates we know. We are using four columns (that is, 32 pixels) for each year. The coordinate of pixel 192 is FirstYear + 4, so the coordinate of pixel 192 + 32 = 224 is FirstYear + 5. So even though we won't draw anything beyond pixel 207, in the VIEW statement, we make x2 = 224.

```
1    '    *** DRAWING A BAR GRAPH ***
2    '    Draw a bar graph of computer sales by company and year
3    '    The graph covers 5 years, starting with the year
4    '    given in a DATA statement
5
6    DECLARE SUB SetUpGraph (FirstYear)
7    DECLARE SUB PlotData (FirstYear)
8
9    '    Variables used
10
11   '    FirstYear        Starting year for graph
12
13   SCREEN 1                    'Medium-resolution graphics
14   COLOR 0, 1                  'Black background with palette 1
15   CLS                         'Clear screen
16
17   READ FirstYear
18
19   CALL SetUpGraph(FirstYear)  'Draw axes and coordinates
20   CALL PlotData(FirstYear)    'Plot the data
21   a$ = INPUT$(1)              'Pause
22
23   '    The following data is FirstYear
24   DATA 89
25
26   '    Data for READ in SetUpGraph
27   DATA S, A, L, E, S
28
29   '    Data for READ in PlotData
30   '    Format is IBM, Apple, Clone sales
31   DATA .2, .3, .28           : ' First year Sales
32   DATA .58, .70, .38         : ' Second year Sales
33   DATA 1.16, 1.05, .55       : ' Third year Sales
34   DATA 1.73, 1.38, .81       : ' Fourth year Sales
35   DATA 2.50, 1.79, 1.19      : ' Fifth year Sales
36   END
37
38   SUB PlotData (FirstYear)
39   '    Plot data
40   '    FirstYear received
41   '    No variables returned
42
43   '    Local variables
44
45   '    Apple          Apple sales
46   '    IBM            IBM sales
47   '    Clone          Clone sales
48   '    Year           Counter variable
49
50   FOR Year = FirstYear TO FirstYear + 4
51   '        Read sales for the three companies
52           READ IBM, Apple, Clone
53
54   '        Draw IBM bar
55           LINE (Year, 0)-(Year + .5, IBM), 1, BF
56
57   '        Draw Apple bar on top of IBM bar
58           LINE (Year, IBM)-(Year + .5, IBM + Apple), 2, BF
```

PROGRAM 12.4 Drawing a bar graph. *(continued on next page)*

```
59  '        Draw Clone bar on top of Apple bar
60           LINE (Year, IBM + Apple)-(Year + .5, IBM + Apple + Clone), 3, BF
61    NEXT Year
62
63  END SUB
64
65  SUB SetUpGraph (FirstYear)
66  '   Set up graph
67  '   FirstYear received
68  '   No variables returned
69
70  '   Local variables
71
72  '   Char$           A character; used to print Y label
73  '   Sales           Counter variable; used to print Y coordinates
74  '   Year            Counter variable
75
76  '   Print title
77      LOCATE 3, 10: PRINT "SALES BY COMPANY"
78
79  '   Print Y label - S A L E S
80      FOR J = 1 TO 5
81          READ Char$
82          LOCATE 2 * J + 5, 4
83          PRINT Char$
84      NEXT J
85
86  '   Print Y coordinates
87      FOR Sales = 0 TO 6
88          LOCATE -2 * Sales + 17, 6
89          PRINT USING "##!"; Sales; "-"
90      NEXT Sales
91  '   Print legend
92      LOCATE 21, 4
93      PRINT "^"
94      LOCATE 22, 4
95      PRINT "| in millions"
96
97  '   Print X label
98      LOCATE 20, 14
99      PRINT "Y E A R"
100
101 '   Print X coordinates
102 '   Calculate b, used in following LOCATE statement,
103 '   to print FirstYear in column 9
104     b = 9 - 4 * FirstYear
105     FOR Year = FirstYear TO FirstYear + 4
106         LOCATE 18, 4 * Year + b
107         PRINT USING "##"; Year
108     NEXT Year
109
110 '   Draw X and Y axes
111     LINE (60, 30)-(60, 132)
112     LINE (60, 132)-(208, 132)
113
```

PROGRAM 12.4 *(continued)*

```
114  '     Draw legends
115        LINE (223, 39)-(239, 47), 1, BF
116        LOCATE 6, 32
117        PRINT "IBM"
118
119        LINE (223, 55)-(239, 63), 2, BF
120        LOCATE 8, 32
121        PRINT "Apple"
122
123        LINE (223, 71)-(239, 79), 3, BF
124        LOCATE 10, 32
125        PRINT "Clone"
126
127  '     Define viewport
128        VIEW (64, 36)-(224, 132)
129
130  '     Define coordinates
131        WINDOW (FirstYear, 0)-(FirstYear + 5, 6)
132  END SUB
```

PROGRAM 12.4 *(continued)*

Then, in the WINDOW statement, we make the *X* coordinate corresponding to that pixel FirstYear + 5.

The bars are drawn in the PlotData subprogram that starts in line 37. In a FOR...NEXT loop, the program reads the data for one year and uses three LINE statements with the BF argument to draw three boxes. The first box, which is drawn by line 54

```
LINE (Year, 0)-(Year + .5, IBM), 1, BF
```

starts at the point (Year, 0) and extends up to the point (Year + .5, IBM). Since we are using four columns per year, using a coordinate of Year + .5 draws a box that is two columns wide. The height of the box is determined by the size of IBM's sales. The other two boxes are drawn by lines 57

```
LINE (Year, IBM)-(Year + .5, IBM + Apple), 2, BF
```

and 60

```
LINE (Year, IBM + Apple)-(Year + .5, IBM + Apple + Clone), 3, BF
```

Each box is drawn on top of the previous box. The loop continues until the bars for all the years are drawn.

Figure 12.7 shows the bar graph produced by Program 12.4.   ■

EXAMPLE 5

DRAWING A PIE CHART

Finally, let's develop a program to draw a pie chart.

Problem Statement

Write a program that draws a pie chart. The program should accept the name of the chart and the data to draw it from the user. The segments of the chart should be drawn in four different colors. Draw a legend showing the names of the segments and their colors.

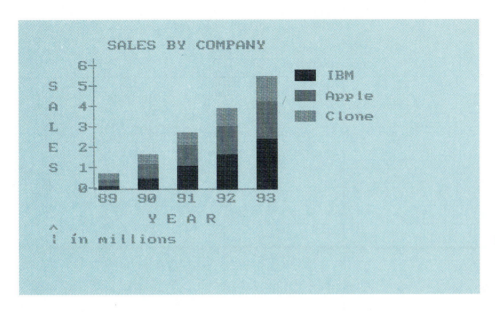

FIGURE 12.7
Bar graph
produced by
Program 12.4.

The graphic layout form is shown in Figure 12.8. The first segment of the pie chart starts at 3 o'clock, and the segments are plotted counterclockwise—to agree with the way degrees are measured—as we showed in Figure 11.6 (page 447).

STEP 1   **Variable Names**

We will use the following variable names.

Variable	Variable Name
Input Variables	
Amount of each category array	`Amt`
Name array	`Label$`
Number of categories	`Number`
Name of chart	`ChartName$`
Internal Variables	
Angular size of wedge	`Angle`
Color to paint wedge	`Clr`
Coordinates for painting	`XPaint and YPaint`
Ending angle of wedge	`EndAngle`
Middle angle of wedge	`MidAngle`
Percentage array	`Percent`
Starting angle of wedge	`StartAngle`
Subscript	`J`
Total of amounts	`Total`

STEP 2   **Algorithm**

The algorithm is

1. Accept the chart name, the number of categories, and the name and amount of each category.
2. Calculate the percentage of the total for each category.
3. Print the chart name and draw the legend.
4. Draw the pie chart.

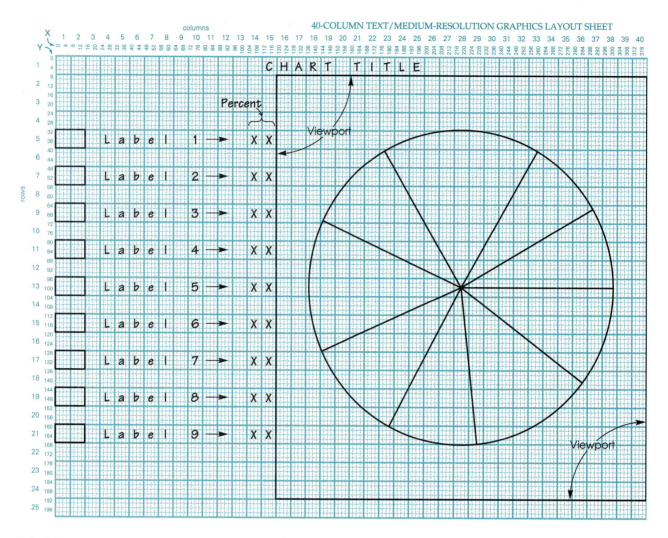

FIGURE 12.8   Layout of a pie chart.

STEP 3   Hand-Calculated Answers

This problem has no hand-calculated answers.

STEP 4   QBasic Program

In Program 12.5, the main module calls four subprograms: GetData, Draw-Legend, SetUpCoordinates, and DrawChart.

    To make the program general, the title, the number of categories, and the name and amount of each category are obtained using INPUT statements in the GetData subprogram. Next, in the FOR...NEXT loop (lines 109 through 111), the percentage of the total for each category is calculated and stored in the Percent array. The Percent array is used to draw the pie chart.

    The DrawLegend subprogram, which starts at line 63, prints the title and the legend. In the legend, each category is identified by a box with its color, its name, and its percentage.

Drawing the Wedges

The SetUpCoordinates subprogram, which starts in line 114, defines the viewport and coordinates. The VIEW statement in line 119

```
VIEW (119, 8)-(319, 191)
```

makes that part of the screen that is not used for the legend or title into one large viewport. The WINDOW statement in line 122

```
WINDOW (-1.1, -1.1)-(1.1, 1.1)
```

establishes a coordinate system in which both *X* and *Y* run from –1.1 to 1.1. These coordinates were chosen so that a circle whose radius is 1 would fill the viewport. Notice that this choice makes the coordinates of the center of the viewport (0, 0).

The DrawChart subprogram starting in line 33 consists primarily of a FOR...NEXT loop that draws the wedge for each category. Since we don't have to specify the size of angles directly, it is convenient to work with radians. A circle contains 2 * Pi radians, where the constant Pi is defined in line 17 to be equal to 3.14159. Therefore, in line 50

```
Angle = Percent(J) * 2 * Pi
```

we calculate the Angle of the wedge for the *J*th category by multiplying Percent(J) by 2 * Pi. For example, if a category accounts for 25 percent of the total, its wedge is 25 percent of the circle.

Now we know how big the wedge should be—but to draw it, we have to specify where it starts and where it ends. The first wedge will, of course, start at 0 degrees—which is why StartAngle is initialized to 0 in line 48. In line 51, we add the Angle calculated in line 50 to StartAngle in order to find EndAngle. Line 53 calculates the middle angle of the wedge as the average of the starting and ending angles. The middle angle is used later to paint the wedge.

```
 1    '    *** DRAWING A PIE CHART ***
 2
 3    DECLARE SUB SetUpCoordinates ()
 4    DECLARE SUB GetData (ChartName$, Number!, Label$(), Percent!())
 5    DECLARE SUB DrawLegend (ChartName$, Number!, Label$(), Percent!())
 6    DECLARE SUB DrawChart (Number!, Percent!())
 7
 8    '    Variables used
 9
10    '    ChartName$          Name of chart
11    '    Label$              Name array
12    '    Number              Number of categories
13    '    Percent             Percentage array
14
15    DIM Label$(9), Percent(9)                'Maximum number of categories is 9
16
17    CONST Pi = 3.14159                       'Constant π
18    SCREEN 0                                 'Text mode to accept data
19    CLS                                      'Clear screen
20
21    '    Get data from user
22    CALL GetData(ChartName$, Number, Label$(), Percent())
23
24    SCREEN 1                                 'Graphics mode to draw chart
25    CLS                                      'Clear screen
26    COLOR 0, 1                               'Black background with palette 1
27
28    CALL DrawLegend(ChartName$, Number, Label$(), Percent())
29    CALL SetUpCoordinates
30    CALL DrawChart(Number, Percent())
31    A$ = INPUT$(1)                           'Pause
32    END
```

PROGRAM 12.5   *Drawing a pie chart. (continued on next page)*

```
33 | SUB DrawChart (Number, Percent())
34 | '   Draw pie chart
35 | '   Number and Percent() received
36 | '   No variables returned
37 |
38 | '   Local variables
39 |
40 | '   Angle              Angular size of wedge
41 | '   Clr                Color to paint wedge
42 | '   EndAngle           Ending angle of wedge
43 | '   MidAngle           Middle angle of wedge
44 | '   StartAngle         Starting angle of wedge
45 | '   XPaint             X coordinate for painting
46 | '   YPaint             Y coordinate for painting
47 |
48 |     StartAngle = 0                          'Initialize start angle
49 |     FOR J = 1 TO Number                     'Draw wedge for each category
50 |         Angle = Percent(J) * 2 * Pi         'Size of wedge as % of circle
51 |         EndAngle = Angle + StartAngle       'End of wedge
52 |         'Calculate MidAngle as average of StartAngle & EndAngle
53 |         MidAngle = (StartAngle + EndAngle) / 2
54 |         CIRCLE (0, 0), 1, 3, -StartAngle - .001, -EndAngle   'Draw wedge
55 |         XPaint = .5 * COS(MidAngle)          'Calculate X and
56 |         YPaint = .91 * .5 * SIN(MidAngle)    'Y coordinates for paint
57 |         Clr = J MOD 4                        'Calculate color
58 |         PAINT (XPaint, YPaint), Clr, 3       'Paint wedge
59 |         StartAngle = EndAngle                'Start of next wedge
60 |     NEXT J
61 | END SUB
62 |
63 | SUB DrawLegend (ChartName$, Number, Label$(), Percent())
64 | '   Print title and draw legend
65 | '   ChartName$, Number, Label$(), and Percent() received
66 | '   No variables returned
67 |
68 | '   Local variable
69 |
70 | '   Clr                Color to paint wedge
71 |
72 | '   Start at line 1 column 1 and print title in center of screen
73 |     LOCATE 1, 1
74 |     PRINT SPC((40 - LEN(ChartName$)) \ 2); ChartName$
75 |
76 | '   Draw legend for each category
77 |     FOR J = 1 TO Number
78 |         LINE (0, 16 * J + 15)-STEP(16, 8), 3, B  'Draw box,
79 |         Clr = J MOD 4                            'calculate color, and
80 |         PAINT (8, 16 * J + 19), Clr, 3           'paint it
81 | '       Locate and print label
82 |         LOCATE 2 * J + 3, 4
83 |         PRINT USING "\       \ ##"; Label$(J); 100 * Percent(J)
84 |     NEXT J
85 | END SUB
```

PROGRAM 12.5 *(continued)*

The CIRCLE statement in line 54

```
CIRCLE (0, 0), 1, 3, -StartAngle - .001, -EndAngle
```

actually draws the wedge. In this statement, the center of the circle is at (0, 0). The wedge goes from StartAngle to EndAngle, and we outline it by including minus

```
 86 | SUB GetData (ChartName$, Number, Label$(), Percent())
 87 | '   Get data and calculate percentages
 88 | '   No variables received
 89 | '   ChartName$, Number, Label$(), and Percent() returned
 90 |
 91 | '   Local variables
 92 |
 93 | '   Amt                     Amount of each category array
 94 | '   Total                   Total of amounts
 95 |
 96 |     DIM Amt(9)                               'Maximum of 9 categories
 97 |     Total = 0                                'Initialize Total
 98 |
 99 |     INPUT "Enter the name of the chart: ", ChartName$
100 |     INPUT "Enter number of categories (< 10): ", Number
101 |
102 |     FOR J = 1 TO Number                      'For each category
103 |         INPUT "Enter name: ", Label$(J)      'Get name
104 |         PRINT "Enter value for "; Label$(J);  'Get amount
105 |         INPUT ": ", Amt(J)
106 |         Total = Total + Amt(J)               'Accumulate amount into total
107 |     NEXT J
108 |
109 |     FOR J = 1 TO Number                      'For each category
110 |         Percent(J) = Amt(J) / Total          'Calculate percent
111 |     NEXT J
112 | END SUB
113 |
114 | SUB SetUpCoordinates
115 | '   Create viewport and establish coordinates
116 | '   No variables received or returned
117 |
118 | '   Make the right half of the screen a viewport
119 |     VIEW (119, 8)-(319, 191)
120 |
121 | '   Make coordinates run from -1.1 to +1.1 for both X and Y
122 |     WINDOW (-1.1, -1.1)-(1.1, 1.1)
123 | END SUB
```

```
Enter the name of the chart: SQUIRREL NUT CO.
Enter number of categories (< 10): 6
Enter name: PEANUTS
Enter value for PEANUTS: 47
Enter name: WALNUTS
Enter value for WALNUTS: 38
Enter name: CASHEWS
Enter value for CASHEWS: 35
Enter name: ALMONDS
Enter value for ALMONDS: 26
Enter name: PECANS
Enter value for PECANS: 20
Enter name: FILBERTS
Enter value for FILBERTS: 16
```

PROGRAM 12.5 *(continued)*

signs in front of both of these angles. However, in drawing these wedges, we must keep two considerations in mind: 1) as we mentioned in Chapter 11, coding −0 does not draw a line from the center to the arc; and 2) the final value of End-Angle must not be greater than 2 * Pi. The simplest way to satisfy these two conditions and still draw the wedge as it should look is to subtract a small value (in line 54, we use .001) from StartAngle.

Finding a Point Inside the Wedge

Next we must paint the wedge, which requires that we start at a point inside the wedge. To find the coordinates of a point inside the wedge, we must use a little trigonometry.

Figure 12.9 shows that if the coordinates of one end of a line are at $(0, 0)$, and if the line is L units long and makes an angle A with the X axis, then the X and Y coordinates of the end point of the line are given by the two equations

```
Xt = L * cos(A)
Yt = L * sin(A)
```

These values are called X_t and Y_t because they represent the values calculated by trigonometric equations. Before we can use them in our program, they must be corrected for the aspect ratio of the viewport. The equation we derived earlier in this chapter gives an aspect ratio of .91 for this viewport. We calculate XPaint and YPaint in lines 55 and 56

```
XPaint = .5 * COS(MidAngle)
YPaint = .91 * .5 * SIN(MidAngle)
```

In these lines, L is set equal to 0.5 and A is set equal to MidAngle. If you recall that the radius of the pie chart is 1, you will realize that these values represent a point in the center of the wedge. XPaint is simply set equal to the trigonometric value, but YPaint is calculated by multiplying the trigonometric value by the aspect ratio of the viewport, 0.91. If the aspect ratio were greater than 1, YPaint would be set equal to the trigonometric value, and XPaint would be calculated by dividing the trigonometric value by the aspect ratio.

Line 57

```
Clr = J MOD 4
```

calculates the color to paint the wedge. When J goes through the values 1 to Number, this statement generates colors 1, 2, 3, 0—and then repeats. (The same equation is used in line 79 to calculate the color to paint the legend.) The PAINT statement in line 58

```
PAINT (XPaint, YPaint), Clr, 3
```

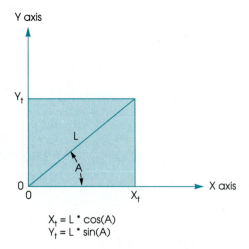

$$X_t = L * \cos(A)$$
$$Y_t = L * \sin(A)$$

FIGURE 12.9   Finding the coordinates of the end point of a line.

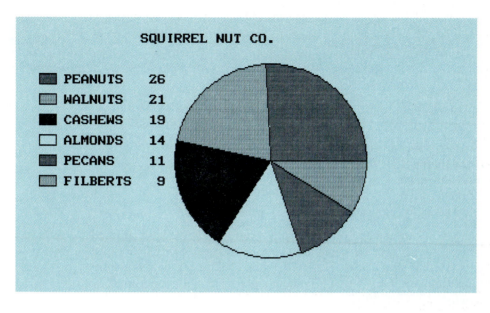

FIGURE 12.10
Pie chart
produced by
Program 12.5.

paints the wedge in color Clr. Line 59 sets StartAngle for the next wedge equal to
EndAngle for the previous wedge, and the whole process is repeated for the next
category.

Figure 12.10 shows the pie chart produced by Program 12.5.   ■

12.2 EXERCISES

★1. Code the statements that could be added to Program 12.3 (pages 470–71) to
print tick marks along the right Y axis. Where would the statements be
inserted?

2. Suppose we want to draw a graph in which the Y coordinates run from 0 to
9 and are printed in column 16. The Y coordinate of 0 should be printed in
row 21, the coordinate of 1 in row 19, and so on. Write the statements to
print the Y coordinates.

3. Suppose we want to draw a graph in which the X axis represents the 12
months. We will print the X coordinates in row 23 and print a J (for Janu-
ary) in column 4, an F in column 7, and so on. Write the statements to print
the X coordinates.

4. Program 12.3 draws a graph starting in FirstYear—but the starting value of
the FOR statement in line 50 is FirstYear + 1. Explain why.

★5. Figure 12.7 (page 479) would be easier to read if the Y axis tick marks were
continued across the graph as a series of dotted horizontal lines. Write the
code to draw these dotted lines. (*Hint*: The PSET statement can be used to
draw a dotted line.)

6. In Program 12.5 (pages 481–83), if the number of categories is 5 or 9, then
the last category is painted the same color as the first, making it difficult to
read the chart. Show how you would change the program to avoid this
problem.

12.3 SCREEN ANIMATION

Now that you have learned how to draw figures on the screen, let's discuss how you can move them. To move a figure on the screen, five steps are necessary:

1. Draw the figure.
2. Save the figure.
3. Display the figure.
4. Erase the figure.
5. Display the figure at a new location.

For the first step, you can use any of the graphics commands we have studied (such as LINE or CIRCLE). For the remaining steps, you must use the GET and PUT statements we will study now. These GET and PUT statements are completely different from the GET and PUT statements used with random files, which were discussed in Chapter 10.

The GET Statement

The GET statement reads the colors of the pixels in a rectangular section of the screen and saves them in a numeric array. The syntax of the GET statement for graphics is

```
GET (x1, y1)-(x2, y2), arrayname
```

where (x1, y1) are the coordinates of one corner of the rectangle and (x2, y2) are the coordinates of the opposite corner. Note that (x1, y1) and (x2, y2) define the same rectangle in the GET statement that they do in the LINE statement with the B argument. The colors of the pixels inside this rectangle are saved in the array named arrayname. The GET and PUT statements refer to the whole array and are the *only* statements in which it is legal to code the name of an array without including a subscript.

For example, the GET statement

```
GET (150, 90)-(170, 110), Picture
```

stores the colors of the pixels in the rectangle whose upper-left corner is at (150, 90) and whose lower-right corner is at (170, 110) in the array Picture. Before proceeding, make sure you understand how each of the following GET statements works.

ILLUSTRATIONS

GET Statement	Effect
`GET (225, 10)-(250, 20), Figure`	Stores the colors of the pixels in the rectangle whose upper-left corner is at (225, 10) and whose lower-right corner is at (250, 20) in the array Figure.
`GET (0, 0)-(319, 199), SaveScreen`	Stores the whole screen in the array SaveScreen.

Calculating the Size of the Array

Now that you know a bit about the GET statement, you next must learn how to calculate the dimension of the array coded in the GET statement. You can calculate the proper size for the array used with a GET statement by implementing the following equations, which are adapted from the QBasic help system. First, calculate the number of bytes needed, using the equation

```
Number of bytes = 4 + Ly × INT((Lx × B + 7)/8)
```

In this equation, L_x and L_y are the X and Y lengths in pixels of the rectangle, and B equals 2 in medium-resolution and 1 in high-resolution. In the example GET statement cited earlier,

```
GET (150, 90)-(170, 110), Picture
```

L_x is calculated as $170 - 150 + 1 = 21$, and L_y is $110 - 90 + 1 = 21$ (the length is one more than the difference between the ending and starting pixels). Assuming this GET statement is used in medium-resolution, B is 2. The equation gives

$$
\begin{aligned}
\text{Number of bytes} &= 4 + 21 \times \text{INT}((21 \times 2 + 7)/8) \\
&= 4 + 21 \times \text{INT}(49/8) \\
&= 4 + 21 \times \text{INT}(6.125) \\
&= 4 + 21 \times 6 \\
&= 4 + 126 \\
&= 130
\end{aligned}
$$

So 130 bytes are required to store the figure.

Next, find the number of elements required in the array, using the equation

Number of elements = Number of bytes/F

where F equals 2 for integer arrays, 4 for single-precision arrays, and 8 for double-precision arrays. Assuming that we use a single-precision array, the number of elements required is

Number of elements = $130/4 = 32.5$

which must be rounded up to 33.

If you try to save an image in an array that is too small, the program will stop and display the message Illegal function call. On the other hand, an array that is too large does not cause any trouble.

The PUT Statement

The PUT statement displays a graphic image saved by a GET statement on the screen. For example, the PUT statement

```
PUT (50, 30), Picture
```

displays the graphic image saved in the Picture array on the screen. The upper-left corner of the image is at (50, 30).

The syntax of the PUT statement is

```
PUT(x, y), arrayname
```

where (x, y) are the coordinates at which the upper-left corner of the rectangle is to be placed and arrayname is the name of the array that contains the figure. Other examples of the PUT statement are as follows.

ILLUSTRATIONS

PUT Statement	Effect
PUT(30, 50), Store	Puts the image stored in array Store on the screen, with its upper-left corner at (30, 50).
PUT(0, 0), SaveScreen	Puts the image stored in array SaveScreen on the screen, with its upper-left corner at (0, 0).

If a graphic image is PUT upon itself, it is erased. Recall that at the beginning of this section, we said that one of the steps necessary to achieving animation is erasing the image. We will erase a graphic image by PUTting it on itself.

EXAMPLE 6

DEMONSTRATING THE GET AND PUT STATEMENTS

We can now write a program that demonstrates the GET and PUT statements.

Problem Statement

Write a program that moves a circle across the screen.

STEP 1 Variable Names

Variable	Variable Name
Internal Variables	
NumBytes	Number of bytes required in array that saves the circle
SaveCircle	Array used to save the circle
X1 and X2	X coordinates of rectangle saved by GET
Y1 and Y2	Y coordinates of rectangle saved by GET

STEP 2 Algorithm

The algorithm is

1. Display a circle.
2. Save the circle.
3. Erase the circle.
4. Repeat steps 5, 6, and 7 for values of X of 0, 10, 20, and so on, stopping when X equals 290.
5. Display the circle with its upper-left corner at coordinate (X, 100).
6. Pause.
7. Erase the circle.

STEP 3 Hand-Calculated Answers

This problem has no hand-calculated answers.

STEP 4 QBasic Program

Program 12.6 moves the circle across the screen. It uses the function ArraySize to calculate the size of the array needed to store the graphic image, and the subprogram Pause to cause the program to pause a specified time.

```
1    '   *** DEMONSTRATING THE GET AND PUT STATEMENTS ***
2    '   Use GET and PUT to move a circle across the screen
3
4    DECLARE SUB Pause ()
5    DECLARE FUNCTION ArraySize! (X1!, X2!, Y1!, Y2!)
6
7    '   Variables used
8
9    '   NumBytes          Number of bytes required in array that saves
10   '                     the circle
11   '   SaveCircle        Array used to save the circle
12   '   X1, X2            X coordinates of rectangle saved by GET
13   '   Y1, Y2            Y coordinates of rectangle saved by GET
14
15   CONST Delay = .2                       'Length of pause, .2 seconds
16   SCREEN 1                               'Medium-resolution graphics
17   COLOR 0, 1                             'Black background with palette 1
18   CLS                                    'Clear screen
19
20   '   Use ArraySize function to calculate size of array used to
21   '   store circle. Rectangle saved by GET goes from 0 to 20
22   '   in both X and Y directions
23   DIM SaveCircle(1 TO ArraySize(0, 20, 0, 20))
24
25   CIRCLE (10, 10), 10, 2                  'Draw circle
26   PAINT (10, 10), 1, 2                    'Paint it
27   GET (0, 0)-(20, 20), SaveCircle        'Save it
28   a$ = INPUT$(1)                          'Pause
29
30   PUT (0, 0), SaveCircle                  'Erase circle
31   a$ = INPUT$(1)                          'Pause
32
33   FOR X = 0 TO 290 STEP 10                'Step across the screen
34       PUT (X, 100), SaveCircle           'Display circle
35       CALL Pause                         'Pause
36       PUT (X, 100), SaveCircle           'Erase circle
37   NEXT X
38   END
39   FUNCTION ArraySize (X1, X2, Y1, Y2)
40   '   Calculate size of a single-precision array used to store rectangle
41   '   saved with a GET statement in medium-resolution screen
42   '   X1, X2, Y1, Y2 are received
43   '   One corner of the rectangle has coordinates (X1, Y1), and
44   '   opposite corner has coordinates (X2, Y2)
45   '   Size of array is returned in ArraySize
46   '   The formulas used are adapted from the QBasic help system
47
48       NumBytes = 4 + (Y2 - Y1 + 1) * INT(((X2 - X1 + 1) * 2 + 7) / 8)
49
50   '   Add 1 to calculated size to round up
51       ArraySize = INT(NumBytes / 4) + 1
52   END FUNCTION
```

PROGRAM 12.6   Demonstrating the GET and PUT statements. *(continued on next page)*

```
53
54    SUB Pause
55    '    Pause for Delay seconds
56    '    Delay is a global constant defined in the main module
57
58         Now = TIMER
59         DO WHILE TIMER < Now + Delay
60         LOOP
61    END SUB
```

PROGRAM 12.6 *(continued)*

Line 25

```
CIRCLE (10, 10), 10, 2
```

draws a circle with a magenta outline. The center of the circle is at (10, 10), and the radius of the circle is 10. Line 26 paints the circle cyan. The GET statement in line 27

```
GET (0, 0)-(20, 20), SaveCircle
```

saves the circle in the array SaveCircle. Actually, the GET statement saves a rectangle that includes the circle. The upper-left corner is at (0, 0), and the lower-right corner is at (20, 20).

The SaveCircle array is dimensioned in line 23

```
DIM SaveCircle(1 TO ArraySize(0, 20, 0, 20))
```

This statement invokes the ArraySize function to calculate the upper subscript. It passes to ArraySize the coordinates of the upper-left and the lower-right corners of the rectangle.

ArraySize, which begins at line 39, uses these coordinates in the equations we discussed earlier to calculate the required size of the array.

The INPUT$ statement in line 28 halts execution until you press a key, giving you time to study the screen. When you press a key, the PUT statement in line 30

```
PUT (0, 0), SaveCircle
```

displays the image stored in SaveCircle on the screen, with its upper-left corner at (0, 0). Because this coordinate is the same as the upper-left corner of the GET statement that saved the image, the circle is erased. The INPUT$ statement in line 31 causes another pause so that you can see the erasure.

After you press a key to satisfy line 31, the FOR...NEXT loop in lines 33 through 37 causes the circle to move across the screen. The PUT statement in line 34

```
PUT (X, 100), SaveCircle
```

displays the circle; the PUT statement in line 36 (which is identical) erases it. On each pass through the loop, a larger value of X is used in these two PUT statements, so that the circle moves from left to right across the screen. Using a larger step size in line 33 makes the circle move faster; using a smaller step size makes the circle move slower.

To make the animation realistic, each image must be displayed just long enough for its position to register with the user. Therefore, line 35 calls the Pause subprogram to cause a pause of Delay seconds. The best value to use for the Delay depends on the size of the image and the characteristics of the monitor, but it is always small. Notice that in line 15, Delay is set to only .2—meaning two-tenths of a second. There are no rules for calculating the duration of the pause; the best value is found by trial and error.

Since the rectangle saved by the GET statement in line 27 measures 21 pixels in both the *X* and *Y* directions, when we PUT the rectangle, the *X* coordinate must not be greater than 298, and the *Y* coordinate must not be greater than 178. If these limits are exceeded, part of the figure will fall outside of the screen. When that happens, the program stops and QBasic displays the message Illegal function call. ■

Congratulations! You have come a long way in your study of QBasic. You now know how to perform calculations, program loops, make decisions, execute subprograms, use arrays, manipulate files, and draw and animate figures. You have developed a strong foundation for your studies of other programming languages, such as Visual Basic, C, and C++.

A lack of space prevents us from discussing several advanced statements that can enhance your programs. The PLAY statement allows you to play musical notes; the DRAW statement allows you to draw odd-shaped figures; and the INKEY$ statement allows your program to respond when the user presses special keys like the arrow or function keys. You can use the QBasic help system to learn how these statements work and use them in your programs.

Syntax Summary

GET Statement (for graphics)

Form: `GET (x1, y1)-(x2, y2), arrayname`
Example: `GET (20, 20)-(100, 30), SavePic`
Explanation: Saves the rectangular portion of the screen defined by (x1, y1) and (x2, y2) in the array named arrayname.

PUT Statement (for graphics)

Form: `PUT(x, y), arrayname`
Example: `PUT(160, 100), SaveArray`
Explanation: Displays the image stored in the array named arrayname on the screen, with its upper-left corner at (x, y).

12.3 EXERCISES

★**1.** Modify Program 12.6 to make the circle move down the screen.

2. In Program 12.6, what would happen if the final value in line 33's FOR statement were changed from 290 to 300?

3. Explain why the GET statement requires two sets of coordinates, but the PUT statement requires only one.

4. A medium-resolution graphics program contains the statement

`GET (0, 0)-(40, 50), SaveFig`

Calculate the number of elements that SaveFig needs.

★**5.** Write the GET statement to save a circle whose center is at (100, 100) and whose radius is 50, in the array BigCircle. Assuming that the program uses medium-resolution graphics, calculate the number of elements BigCircle needs.

6. Write the PUT statement to display the circle saved in BigCircle (see Exercise 5) so that the center of the circle is at the center of the screen.

7. Program 12.7 shows the execution of a program that is supposed to draw a circle inside a viewport in the center of the screen. Only the viewport was drawn, with no sign of the circle. No error message was displayed. Find and correct the error.

```
 1  |  '    *** DRAWING A CIRCLE IN A VIEWPORT
 2  |  '    Draw a circle inside a viewport that has world coordinates
 3  |
 4  |  SCREEN 1                            'Medium-resolution graphics
 5  |  COLOR 0, 1                          'Black background with palette 1
 6  |  CLS                                 'Clear screen
 7  |
 8  |  VIEW (120, 60)-(200, 140), , 1      'Establish viewport
 9  |  WINDOW (-1, -1)-(1, 1)              'Establish coordinates
10  |  CIRCLE (160, 100), 1, 2             'Draw circle
11  |  A$ = INPUT$(1)                      'Pause
12  |  END
```

PROGRAM 12.7   A program that is supposed to draw a circle inside a viewport.

WHAT YOU HAVE LEARNED

In this chapter, you learned that:

- The VIEW statement defines a graphic viewport.
- The WINDOW statement creates a coordinate system chosen by the user.
- Animation requires that a figure be displayed, that it be erased, and that it then be displayed at a new location.

- The GET statement saves a figure on the screen in an array.
- The PUT statement displays a previously saved figure.

NEW QBASIC STATEMENTS

STATEMENT	EFFECT
VIEW	
`VIEW (30, 100)-(200, 10), 2, 3`	Defines a viewport whose lower-left corner is at (30, 100) and whose upper-right corner is at (200, 10). The viewport is painted color 2, and has a border of color 3.
WINDOW	
`WINDOW (0, 5)-(1, 10)`	Establishes world coordinates. The coordinates of the lower-left corner of the viewport are (0, 5), and the coordinates of the upper-right corner are (1, 10).
GET	
`GET (0, 0)-(160, 100), Pic`	Saves the rectangle between (0, 0) and (160, 100) in the array Pic.
PUT	
`PUT (160, 100), Pic`	Displays on the screen the graphic image stored in Pic, with its upper-left corner at (160, 100).

KEY TERMS

world coordinates

REVIEW EXERCISES

SELF-CHECK

1. True or false: If the array named in a GET statement is too small for the specified rectangle, only part of the rectangle is saved.

2. The WINDOW statement establishes the (physical/world) coordinate system.

3. Describe the viewport created by the statement
   `VIEW (160, 100)-(319, 199)`

4. How can you abolish a coordinate system established by a WINDOW statement?

5. True or false: If a figure is PUT upon itself, it is erased.

6. True or false: If a VIEW statement is coded without the boundary argument, the boundary is drawn in the foreground color.

7. What is the most likely cause of the error if, during execution, QBasic stops at a PUT statement and displays the error message Illegal function call? What is the most likely cause of the error if QBasic stops at a GET statement?

PROGRAMMING ASSIGNMENTS

Section 12.1

1. Write a program that creates a viewport whose upper-left corner is at (100, 60) and whose lower-right corner is at (200, 140). Paint the viewport color 1 and outline it in color 2. Use a WINDOW statement to assign coordinates of (0, 0) to the lower-left corner of this viewport and (10, 10) to the upper right corner. Use a LINE statement to draw a box in color 3—two of whose corners are (1, 1) and (9, 9).

2. Write a program that plots a sine wave for angles between 0 and 360 degrees, in steps of 5 degrees. It will be helpful to establish a viewport with coordinates (0, -1) and (360, 1). Use a LINE statement to draw a horizontal line through (0, 0) to represent the X axis and a PSET statement to plot the points. Remember that the argument of the SIN function must be in radians.

Section 12.2

3. Write a program to draw a line graph of the following average monthly precipitation data for Miami:

Month	Jan	Feb	Mar	Apr	May	Jun
Inches	2.2	2.0	2.1	3.6	6.1	9.0

	Jul	Aug	Sep	Oct	Nov	Dec
	6.9	6.7	8.7	8.2	2.7	1.6

4. Modify Program 12.4 to draw the bars next to each other, instead of on top of each other. Make the bars one column wide.

5. The data in the following table show the profit, in millions of dollars, that Monolith, Inc., made from three geographical areas over five years. Write a program to draw a bar graph that displays these data.

Source of Profit	Year				
	1989	1990	1991	1992	1993
USA	16	18	22	23	26
Europe	6	8	9	10	11
Japan	2	3	6	11	14

6. Write a program that draws a pie chart in which, for emphasis, the first wedge is displaced from the center of the chart, as shown in the following figure:

Section 12.3

7. Write a program to move the arrow drawn in Program 11.3 across the screen.

8. Write a program to move the following sailboat across the screen. Draw a horizontal line to represent the water surface, and sail the boat on the surface. Paint the hull color 1, the sail color 2, and the pennant color 3.

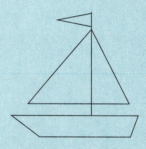

9. Write a program to move Tom's delivery truck, which was drawn in Programming Assignment 11.13, across the screen. Draw a horizontal line to represent a highway and drive the truck on the highway.

ADDITIONAL PROGRAMMING ASSIGNMENTS

10. Cheap Skates, Inc., had the following annual sales (in millions of dollars). Write a program to draw a line graph of these data.

Year	1984	1985	1986	1987	1988
Sales	6.9	6.3	5.8	4.9	4.2

	1989	1990	1991	1992	1993
	5.3	7.4	7.7	8.3	8.6

11. The following data show the percent of families in the Kingdom of Serendip with incomes in the specified ranges for the years 1970, 1980, and 1990.

Family Income	1970	1980	1990
Above $25,000	18.9	37.6	39.2
$15,001–$25,000	33.4	31.0	27.7
$0–$15,000	47.7	31.4	33.1

Write a program that draws a bar graph to display these data.

12. Modify Program 7.5 to perform 5 trials of 30 coin tosses each and plot a bar graph of the number of heads and the number of tails in each trial. (*Hint*: Store the number of heads and tails in each trial in an array.)

13. Write a program to "pass" a football from one goalpost to the other on the football field you drew in Programming Assignment 11.19. You can draw an acceptable football using a CIRCLE statement with a radius of 16 and an aspect ratio of 0.4. Your program will be more impressive if the ball follows a long arc, rather than a straight line. A reasonable arc is a semicircle with an aspect ratio of 0.4. To calculate X and Y coordinates, you can adapt the technique used in Program 12.5 to calculate XPaint and YPaint.

14. Bezier curves are widely used in computer graphics. A Bezier curve is described by four points, the coordinates of which we can write as (x_1, y_1), (x_2, y_2), (x_3, y_3), and (x_4, y_4). The points on the Bezier curve are calculated using the following equations:

$$x(t) = (1-t)^3 x_1 + 3t(1-t)^2 x_2 + 3t^2(1-t)x_3 + t^3 x_4$$

$$y(t) = (1-t)^3 y_1 + 3t(1-t)^2 y_2 + 3t^2(1-t)y_3 + t^3 y_4$$

In these equations, t is a parameter that goes from 0 to 1. As these equations show, the Bezier curve goes through only the first (x_1, y_1) and last (x_4, y_4) points. The figure will be more interesting if, in addition to the Bezier curve, you draw straight lines between (x_1, y_1) and (x_2, y_2) and between (x_3, y_3) and (x_4, y_4). Write a program that allows a user to enter the coordinates of four points and then draws the Bezier curve described by them. Since you cannot know what values the user will enter for the coordinates of the four points, your program will have to determine the minimum and maximum values of x and y and establish a coordinate system for a viewport that accommodates these values. One set of data that gives an interesting figure is $(0, 0)$, $(4, 2)$, $(-2, -2)$, and $(2, 0)$.

15. The following is a common statistics problem: Given a set of data points (x_i, y_i), $i = 1, 2, \ldots, n$,

find the equation of the straight line that best represents these data. The equation of the straight line is

$$y = mx + b$$

where m and b are calculated by the equations

$$m = \frac{\sum y_i x_i - (\sum y_i)(\sum x_i)/n}{\sum x_i^2 - (\sum x_i)^2 / n}$$

and

$$b = \frac{\sum y_i - m \sum x_i}{n}$$

Write a program that accepts n followed by n data points and calculates m and b. Plot the data points and the line. Since you cannot know the range of values of the data, your program will have to determine the minimum and maximum values of x and y and establish a coordinate system for a viewport that accommodates these values. It is not necessary to label the graph with the X and Y coordinates.

You may use the following test data:

X   5.0, 4.2, 4.3, 3.8, 4.4, 5.2, 6.0, 6.5, 5.9, 4.0
Y   2.0, 3.0, 3.2, 4.0, 3.6, 2.1, 1.7, 1.2, 1.8, 2.4

These data give $m = -0.841$, and $b = 6.64$.

BEYOND THE BASICS

16. Write a program that draws two Pac-Man-like faces: one with its mouth open (like the one in Program 11.6) and one with its mouth closed. Move these two faces across the screen—displaying first one and then the other face—so that the face looks as though it is eating as it moves. (*Hint*: The animation will be more effective if the faces are about half the size of the face in Program 11.6.)

17. When characters are displayed by a PRINT statement, they may be placed only at a specified row and column. However, if characters are displayed by a PRINT statement and then saved by a GET statement, a subsequent PUT statement can place them anywhere on the screen. To save a character with a GET statement, you should know that characters are displayed in a square that is 8 pixels on each side. Use this technique to draw and label the following pitcher on a medium-resolution screen. The pitcher should be 41 pixels wide by 69 pixels high.

18. Write a program to draw the birthday cake that follows. Outline the cake in color 3. Use color 1 for the candles. Draw an ellipse for each flame; outline the flames in color 3 and paint them in color 2. You should ask the user's age and display the appropriate number of candles. You should then ask the user to blow out the candles—and after a short delay, the program should erase the flames.

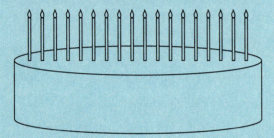

19. Write a program that accepts a time, in hours and minutes. It should then draw a clock face, like the following one, displaying that time. To get the numbers displayed correctly, you will have to use a PUT statement—as explained in Programming Assignment 12.17.

20. Demonstrate your mastery of QBasic by creating the following design. (*Hint:* Display the message and GET it. Then reverse the direction of the *Y* coordinate and PUT the message.)

```
I AM A QBASIC EXPERT
I AM A QBASIC EXPERT
```

ANSWERS TO SELECTED EXERCISES

CHAPTER 1

1.1 EXERCISES

2. Central Processing Unit.
4. Soft copy output. Hard copy output.

1.2 EXERCISES

1. Press and release the Alt key; press R (or use the left and right arrow keys to highlight the Run menu) and press Enter; select the Start command. Alternatively, use the shortcut keys: Shift+F5. With a mouse, click on the Run menu and then click on the Start command.
3. If a program is not saved, when you exit from QBasic—or when you turn off the computer—the program is lost. If you want to use that program again, you must reenter it, which wastes time and can introduce new errors.

CHAPTER 2

2.1 EXERCISES

1. d) Illegal—a name may not contain a hyphen.
   f) Illegal—Width is a reserved word.
2. a) Illegal—a numeric constant may not contain a $.
   b) Legal.
3. a) Incorrect—remove the comma: B = 6500
   c) Correct.
4. c) B will be 9.
8. The program is incorrect. To correct it, interchange the third and fourth lines.
11. The output will be the same: 156.25.
14. The output will be: 6   8   14   −2.
17. If your program contains a logic error, the answers produced by the program do not agree with the hand-calculated answers.

2.2 EXERCISES

1. b) The expression contains one too many left parentheses. A right parenthesis must be added, but where it should be added cannot be determined.
2. c) 3.5
   d) 7

3. **a)** 3
   c) 4
4. **b)** `G = (B + 2 * C + 3 * D) / (6 * E)`
   c) `T = D * ((1 + R) ^ N - 1) / R`

CHAPTER 3

3.1 EXERCISES

1. **b)** Legal.
   e) Illegal—Left$ is a reserved word.
3. **b)** Incorrect—add a dollar sign to ZipCode: ZipCode$ = "10050" or remove the quotation marks: ZipCode = 10050
   d) Incorrect—add quotation marks around Rose: Flower$ = "Rose"

3.2 EXERCISES

1. **a)** Add quotation marks around the prompt:
   `INPUT "Enter number sold: ", Sold`

3. **a)** `INPUT "Enter the amount of the check: ", Amount`

3.3 EXERCISES

2. **a)** The output would be: Joe Tinker   6.75   40   0
4. The output is the letter A.

3.4 EXERCISES

2. `PRINT TAB(40); "Please enter your name"`

4. The output is: Peachesbbbbbbb$b1.35 (b = blank space)

8. **a)** `CONST OvertimeLimit = 40`

3.5 EXERCISES

1. Press any cursor control key.
4. When you choose the Find and Verify command, QBasic stops each time it finds the specified text and asks if it should be changed. When you choose the Change All command, all the occurrences of the specified text are changed.

CHAPTER 4

4.1 EXERCISES

1. **b)** False.
2. **a)** False.
   d) True.

4.2 EXERCISES

3. **a)** As written, Hello will not be printed. To print Hello once, change the condition to A = 10.
   b) This program prints Hello forever.
4. **b)** This program does not print Goodbye. To print it five times, change the condition to B > 5 and add the statement B = B + 1 to the loop.
5. The output is 4 8 16 32 and 64.
6. **a)** Only the first line of output will be printed.
7. QBasic would display the Redo from start error message.

4.3 EXERCISES

1. a) `READ Runner$, Time`
3. Only the second DATA statement will cause an error.
4. a) 19
 b) 23
6. `TotalArea = TotalArea + Area`
8. a) The program prints 15, which is the correct answer.

4.4 EXERCISES

1. a) `DO WHILE LossRate <> 0`
3. a) The program prints 3   3 on the first line and 5   10 on the second line.

4.5 EXERCISES

1. That statement is the next to be executed.
4. The statement is executed as soon as you press the Enter key.

CHAPTER 5

5.1 EXERCISES

1.
```
IF A > B THEN
    PRINT "A is greater"
ELSE
    PRINT "A is not greater"
END IF
```

4.
```
IF Year MOD 4 = 0 THEN
    PRINT "Election Year"
END IF
```

5.2 EXERCISES

1. a) The statement prints: Red Yellow Green White
3.
```
IF Temp > 90 AND Humidity > 90 THEN
    PRINT "Lousy Day"
END IF
```

4. a)
```
IF A > B THEN
    C = A - B
    IF C = D THEN
        A = A - 1
    ELSE
        B = B - 1
    END IF
ELSE
    C = A + B
    A = A + 1
END IF
```

7. a) True.
 c) False.

5.3 EXERCISES

2. Yes, the program would give the same results.
5. `Section$ = INPUT$(4)`

5.4 EXERCISES

```
3. SELECT CASE Wpm
      CASE IS > 60
          Grade$ = "Excellent"
      CASE 40 TO 60
          Grade$ = "Good"
      CASE < 40
          Grade$ = "Weak"
   END SELECT

5. SELECT CASE Day$
      CASE "SUN"
          PRINT "Sunday"
      CASE "MON"
          PRINT "Monday"
      CASE "TUE"
          PRINT "Tuesday"
      CASE "WED"
          PRINT "Wednesday"
      CASE "THU"
          PRINT "Thursday"
      CASE "FRI"
          PRINT "Friday"
      CASE "SAT"
          PRINT "Saturday"
      CASE ELSE
          PRINT "Invalid"
   END SELECT
```

CHAPTER 6

6.1 EXERCISES

1. **a)** To execute Sub1, use the statement: CALL Sub1
      To define Sub1, use the statement: SUB Sub1
3. This program prints RED YELLOW BLUE YELLOW, with each word on a separate line.
6. The program prints: 5 Dollars is equal to 3.0825 Marks

6.2 EXERCISES

1. The program would not work because the subroutine is named CircleArea, and you can't have a variable and subroutine with the same name.

6.3 EXERCISES

```
1. FUNCTION Prod (X, Y)
   '    Calculates the product of its two arguments
   '    Receives X and Y
   '    Returns the product in Prod

        Prod = X * Y
   END FUNCTION
```
2. **b)** Change the LET statement to: Distance = Rate * Time
5. The program would produce the correct answers.

6.4 EXERCISES

1. `LOCATE 20,10`
   `PRINT "How many tickets please?"`

3. `COLOR 1, 14`

CHAPTER 7

7.1 EXERCISES

1. The output would be changed if lines 28 and 29 were interchanged. The output would *not* be changed if lines 39 and 40 were interchanged.

7.2 EXERCISES

1. a) The output is: 11 14 17 20
2. a) The missing statement is: NEXT I
5. The program shown does not work. To fix it, delete the LET statement.

7.3 EXERCISES

1. The first missing statement is NEXT K, and the second is NEXT J. With these statements, the program prints: 4 5 6 5 6 7 6 7 8

7.4 EXERCISES

1. c) 17
   e) 17
   i) 6
2. a) This statement always prints EQUAL.

4. b) `N = 1 + INT(7 * RND)`

7. Add the following IF statement after line 56:

```
IF ABS(Guess - Number) <= 5 THEN
    PRINT "You are getting close"
END IF
```

7.5 EXERCISES

2. a) UP AND DOWN
3. a) 9
   c) 0
4. a) 65
   c) 54
6. Simple Simon is wrong. Because CHR$ is inside the quotation marks, QBasic considers it part of the string—rather than an execution of the CHR$ function.
8. b) SI
9. c) TED
10. b) 8
   e) 5

7.6 EXERCISES

4. Since purple does not occur in Text$, in line 50 Position will be set to 0, the loop will therefore not be executed, and in line 57 all of Text$ will be assigned to NewText$.

6. Two different letters in English$ would be translated into the same letter in Code$. If that happened, Code$ could not be decoded.

8. Just extend Alpha$ and Trans$ to include the lower case letters.

CHAPTER 8

8.1 EXERCISES

1.
```
DIM A(1 TO 15)
DIM B$(10 TO 20)
```

3. No. This statement reads one value and assigns it to A(10).

5. a) −6

   c) This statement generates a negative subscript, and will cause a Subscript out of range error.

7. The output is: 5 9 2 4 6

8.
```
FOR J = 1 TO 12
     A(J) = A(J) + 1
NEXT J
```

9. a) X(1) = 1, X(2) = 2, and so on—with X(16) = 16

10. Simple Simon is wrong because the input value is used as a subscript (in line 170, for example), and subscripts must be numeric variables.

8.2 EXERCISES

3. Change line 36 to: `IF GPA(K) < GPA(K+1) THEN`

4. The following statements swap A(K) and A(K+1):

```
Temp = A(K)
A(K) = A(K+1)
A(K+1) = Temp
```

8.3 EXERCISES

3. Add the following condition to the DO statement in line 70:

```
AND English$(J) <= EngWord$
```

8.4 EXERCISES

1. In game 1, player 4 scored 136. In game 4, player 1 scored 191.

8.5 EXERCISES

2. Cookie number 2 contains 4 chips.

CHAPTER 9

9.1 EXERCISES

2. `WRITE #1, EmpNum, EmpName$, Gender$, Year, Salary`

4. `INPUT #1, EmpNum, EmpName$, Gender$, Year, Salary`

9.2 EXERCISES

1. `PRINT #2, USING ReportLineFmt$; Author$, Title$, Sales`

3. a)
```
TYPE CityData
     Nam AS STRING * 20
     Area AS SINGLE
     Population AS LONG
END TYPE
```

c) `PRINT City.Nam`

9.3 EXERCISES

1. The subtotal for the last department would not be printed.

CHAPTER 10

10.1 EXERCISES

2. When QBasic retrieves a specific record, it uses the constant record length together with the record number to determine the location of the record on the disk.

3. a)
```
TYPE StudentData
     Nam AS STRING * 25
     Credits AS INTEGER
     GPA AS SINGLE
END TYPE
```

b) `DIM Student AS StudentData`

c) `OPEN "GPA.RND" FOR RANDOM AS #1 LEN = LEN(Student)`

d) Same as part **c)**.

e)
```
INPUT "Enter student's name: ", Student.Nam
INPUT "Enter number of credits: ", Student.Credits
INPUT "Enter GPA: ", Student.GPA
```

f) `PUT #1, StudentNum, Student`

g) `GET #1, StudentNum, Student`

10.2 EXERCISES

1. Line 139 obtains values for AcctNum, which is used in the GET statement in line 151 to specify the record to be read, and must therefore be numeric. The other INPUT$ statements obtain values for Code$ and PaymentCode$, which do not have to be numeric.

10.3 EXERCISES

1. LOF(1) returns 800.
4. The data in MemNumIndex are not in sequential order, so a binary search cannot be used.
7. The coding would retrieve all the records—including the deleted records—because deleted records are still in the file, and the coding reads every record.

CHAPTER 11

11.1 EXERCISES

4. `SCREEN 1`

6. `COLOR 4, 1`

11.2 EXERCISES

1. In medium-resolution: `LINE(160, 100)-(319, 0)`
In high-resolution: `LINE(320, 100)-(639, 0)`

3. `LINE(20, 10)-STEP(40, 50)`

11.3 EXERCISES

2. It paints an area outlined in color 2 with color 3, starting at pixel (40, 70).

11.4 EXERCISES

1. `CIRCLE(100, 80), 60, 1`
`PAINT(100, 80), 3, 1`

5. The *Y* radius is 80, and the *X* radius is 40.

CHAPTER 12

12.1 EXERCISES

1. `VIEW(120, 100)-(200, 190)`
4. The physical coordinates are (30, 100).

12.2 EXERCISES

1. Add the following statements between lines 108 and 109:

```
LastYear = FirstYear + 15
StartTick = LastYear - .5
```

Add the following statement between lines 110 and 111:

```
LINE (StartTick, InflationRate)-(LastYear, InflationRate)
```

5. Add the following lines between lines 131 and 132 in Program 12.4:

```
FOR Sales = 1 TO 6
    FOR Year = FirstYear TO FirstYear + 4.5 STEP .1
        PSET(Year,Sales)
    NEXT Year
NEXT Sales
```

12.3 EXERCISES

1. Replace lines 33 through 37 with the following statements:

```
FOR Y = 0 TO 170 STEP 10
    PUT(160, Y), SaveCircle
    CALL Pause
    PUT(160, Y), SaveCircle
NEXT Y
```

5. An acceptable answer is

```
GET(50, 50)-(150, 150), BigCircle
```

where BigCircle has 658 elements. Alternatively, if the default aspect of $\frac{5}{6}$ is considered, the statement can be written as

```
GET(50, 58)-(150, 142), BigCircle
```

where BigCircle has only 554 elements.

ASCII CODES

ASCII Value	Character	ASCII Value	Character
000	(nul)	039	'
001	☺	040	(
002	☻	041	)
003	♥	042	*
004	♦	043	+
005	♣	044	,
006	♠	045	-
007	• (beep)	046	.
008	◘	047	/
009	○ (tab)	048	0
010	◙ (line feed)	049	1
011	♂ (home)	050	2
012	♀ (form feed)	051	3
013	♪ (carriage return)	052	4
014	♫	053	5
015	☼	054	6
016	►	055	7
017	◄	056	8
018	↕	057	9
019	‼	058	:
020	¶	059	;
021	§	060	<
022	▬	061	=
023	↨	062	>
024	↑	063	?
025	↓	064	@
026	→	065	A
027	←	066	B
028	∟ (cursor right)	067	C
029	↔ (cursor left)	068	D
030	▲ (cursor up)	069	E
031	▼ (cursor down)	070	F
032	(space)	071	G
033	!	072	H
034	"	073	I
035	#	074	J
036	$	075	K
037	%	076	L
038	&	077	M

ASCII Value	Character	ASCII Value	Character
078	N	132	ä
079	O	133	à
080	P	134	å
081	Q	135	ç
082	R	136	ê
083	S	137	ë
084	T	138	è
085	U	139	ï
086	V	140	î
087	W	141	ì
088	X	142	Ä
089	Y	143	Å
090	Z	144	É
091	[	145	æ
092	\	146	Æ
093	]	147	ô
094	^	148	ö
095	_	149	ò
096	`	150	û
097	a	151	ù
098	b	152	ÿ
099	c	153	Ö
100	d	154	Ü
101	e	155	¢
102	f	156	£
103	g	157	¥
104	h	158	₧
105	i	159	ƒ
106	j	160	á
107	k	161	í
108	l	162	ó
109	m	163	ú
110	n	164	ñ
111	o	165	Ñ
112	p	166	ª
113	q	167	º
114	r	168	¿
115	s	169	⌐
116	t	170	¬
117	u	171	½
118	v	172	¼
119	w	173	¡
120	x	174	«
121	y	175	»
122	z	176	▒
123	{	177	▓
124	¦	178	█
125	}	179	│
126	~	180	┤
127	⌂	181	╡
128	Ç	182	╢
129	ü	183	╖
130	é	184	╕
131	â	185	╣

ASCII Value	Character	ASCII Value	Character
186	‖	221	▌
187	╗	222	▐
188	╝	223	▀
189	╜	224	α
190	╛	225	β
191	╗	226	Γ
192	╚	227	π
193	╩	228	Σ
194	╦	229	σ
195	╠	230	μ
196	─	231	τ
197	╬	232	Φ
198	╞	233	Θ
199	╟	234	Ω
200	╚	235	δ
201	╔	236	∞
202	╩	237	Ø
203	╦	238	∈
204	╠	239	∩
205	═	240	≡
206	╬	241	±
207	╧	242	≥
208	╨	243	≤
209	╤	244	⌠
210	╥	245	⌡
211	╙	246	÷
212	╘	247	≈
213	╒	248	°
214	╓	249	·
215	╫	250	•
216	╪	251	√
217	╛	252	^{n}
218	╒	253	^{2}
219	█	254	▪
220	▄	255	(blank)

Colors allowed for foreground in text mode and as background in
medium-resolution mode with a color/graphics monitor

Number	Color	Number	Color
0	Black	8	Gray
1	Blue	9	Light blue
2	Green	10	Light green
3	Cyan	11	Light cyan
4	Red	12	Light red
5	Magenta	13	Light magenta
6	Brown	14	Yellow
7	White	15	High-intensity white

Colors allowed for foreground in text mode
with a monochrome monitor

Number	Color
0	Background
1	Underlined white characters
7	White
9	Underlined high-intensity white characters
15	High-intensity white

Colors in the medium-resolution palettes

Number	Palette 0	Palette 1
0	Background	Background
1	Green	Cyan
2	Red	Magenta
3	Brown	White

MENU COMMANDS, SHORTCUT KEYS, AND FUNCTION KEY USAGE

Menu Commands and Shortcut Keys

Command	Shortcut Key	Action
File Menu		
New		Removes currently loaded file from memory
Open		Loads new file into memory
Merge*		Inserts specified file into current module
Save		Saves current file
Save As		Saves current file with specified name
Save All*		Writes all currently loaded modules to files on disk
Create File*		Creates a module, include file, or document; retains loaded modules
Load File*		Loads a module, include file, or document; retains loaded modules
Unload File*		Removes a loaded module, include file, or document from memory
Print		Prints specified text
DOS Shell*		Temporarily suspends Quick-BASIC and invokes DOS Shell
Exit		Exits QBasic and returns to DOS

---

*Available only in QuickBASIC
†Available only in QBasic

Command	Shortcut Key	Action
Edit Menu		
Undo*	Alt+Bksp	Restores current edited line to its original condition
Cut	Shift+Del	Deletes selected text and copies it to clipboard
Copy	Ctrl+Ins	Copies selected text to clipboard
Paste	Shift+Ins	Inserts clipboard contents at current location
Clear	Del	Deletes selected text without copying it to clipboard
New SUB		Opens a window for a new subprogram
New FUNCTION		Opens a window for a new FUNCTION procedure
View Menu		
SUBS	F2	Displays a loaded SUB or FUNCTION
Next SUB*	Shift+F2	Displays next SUB or FUNCTION procedure in the active window
Split		Divides screen into two View windows
Next Statement*		Displays next statement to be executed
Output Screen	F4	Displays output screen
Include Files*		Displays include file for editing
Include Lines*		Displays include file for viewing only (not for editing)
Search Menu		
Find		Finds specified text
Selected Text*	Ctrl+\	Finds selected text
Repeat Last Find	F3	Finds next occurrence of text specified in previous search
Change		Finds and changes specified text
Label*		Finds specified line label
Run Menu		
Start	Shift+F5	Runs current program
Restart		Clears variables in preparation for restarting single stepping
Continue	F5	Continues execution after a break

Command	Shortcut Key	Action
Modify COMMAND$*		Sets string returned by COMMAND$ function
Make EXE File*		Creates executable file on disk
Make Library*		Creates Quick library and stand-alone (.LIB) library on disk
Set Main Module*		Makes the specified module the main module

Debug Menu

Command	Shortcut Key	Action
Step[†]	F8	Executes next program statement
Procedure Step[†]	F10	Executes next program statement, tracing over procedure calls
Add Watch*		Adds specified expression to the Watch window
Instant Watch*	Shift+F9	Displays the value of a variable or expression
Watchpoint*		Causes program to stop when specified expression is TRUE
Delete Watch*		Deletes specified entry from Watch window
Delete All Watch*		Deletes all Watch window entries
Trace On		Highlights statement currently executing
History On*		Records statement execution order
Toggle Breakpoint	F9	Sets/clears breakpoint at cursor location
Clear All Breakpoints		Removes all breakpoints
Break on Errors*		Stops execution at first statement in error handler
Set Next Statement		Makes the statement at the cursor the next statement to execute

Calls Menu*

Command	Shortcut Key	Action
procedure		Displays active procedure calls, moves cursor to procedure call line

Options Menu

Command	Shortcut Key	Action
Display		Changes display attributes
Help Path[†]		Sets search path for Help files
Set Paths*		Sets default search paths
Right Mouse*		Changes action of right mouse click
Syntax Checking		Turns editor's syntax checking on or off

Command	Shortcut Key	Action
Full Menus*		Toggles between Easy and Full Menu usage
Help Menu		
Index		Displays help index
Contents		Displays help table of contents
Topic:	F1	Displays information about the Basic keyword that the cursor is on
Using Help	Shift+F1	Displays information about how to use online Help
About†		Displays product version and copyright information

INTRODUCTION TO DOS

DOS, which stands for Disk Operating System, is a collection of programs. Some of these programs control the computer—the CPU, RAM, disk drives, keyboard, monitor, and printer. Other programs, called "utility" programs, make it easier for you to use the computer. DOS programs that control the computer include MSDOS.SYS and IO.SYS (on IBM computers, these are named IBMDOS.COM and IBMBIO.COM), and COMMAND.COM. A diskette that contains these control programs is called a DOS or system diskette and may be used to start the computer.

When you either turn on the computer or perform a warm boot, the program in ROM reads MSDOS.SYS and IO.SYS (or their IBM counterparts) from the diskette in drive A into RAM. That is why, if you are using a diskette system, you must insert your DOS diskette into drive A before you turn on the computer. With a hard-disk system, if no diskette is in drive A, the ROM program will read MSDOS.SYS and IO.SYS from the hard disk into RAM. They, in turn, read COMMAND.COM into RAM. These programs work behind the scenes without any intervention from the user.

In addition to these programs that control the computer, DOS includes 20–40 "utility" programs that make it easier to use the computer. You get these programs (usually called "commands") and a 660-page manual (which explains them) when you buy DOS from Microsoft Corporation, IBM, or from the computer's manufacturer. In this appendix, we will explain only a few of the most useful DOS commands.

Using Utility Commands

The DOS utility commands can be divided into two groups: internal and external. Internal commands—such as COPY, DEL, and DIR—are part of COMMAND.COM and are always available after COMMAND.COM is read into RAM. In a diskette system, external commands such as DISKCOPY and FORMAT are stored on a diskette, and the diskette must be in a disk drive for these commands to be executed. In a hard-disk computer, all the DOS commands are usually copied to the hard disk, and are therefore always available. Both internal and external DOS commands may be entered in either upper or lower case.

The Default Drive

If you are using a diskette system, after you turn on the computer, you may be asked to enter the date and time. You will then see the DOS prompt—A>—on the screen. What happens with hard-disk systems depends on how they were set up. On some, you will see the DOS prompt C:\DOS>. (In this prompt, DOS means that the default directory is named DOS. Directories are discussed later.) On others, you will see a menu. If you choose Command Prompt from the menu, you will see the C:\DOS> prompt. The letter A or C in the DOS prompt indicates which drive is the DOS default drive. Unless you specify otherwise, the default drive is the one that is used when you execute a DOS command.

You can change the default drive by typing a letter followed by a colon. For example, to change the default drive to A, type the command A: (do *not* put a space between the A and the :).

The FORMAT Command

Before a new diskette can be used to store files, it must be formatted using the FORMAT command. A diskette needs to be formatted only once, before its first use. Formatting a diskette erases all the data stored on it, so you must be very careful that you don't accidentally format a diskette that contains files you want to keep. Since FORMAT is an external command, in a diskette system you would usually have a diskette that contains the FORMAT program in drive A and the diskette to be formatted in drive B. To format the diskette in drive B, make A the default drive, and use the command

    FORMAT B:

On a hard-disk system, you usually format new diskettes in drive A, so the appropriate command is

    FORMAT A:

In either case, the FORMAT program is loaded into RAM, and you are told to insert a new diskette into the appropriate drive and then to press the Enter key.

As you learned in Chapter 1, diskettes have various storage capacities. The 5¼-inch diskettes can store either 360K or 1.2M, while the 3½-inch diskettes can store either 720K, 1.44M, or 2.88M. You should buy diskettes that match the capacity of the disk drive you will be using. (Your instructor will tell you the capacity of the disk drives in your laboratory.) If your diskette doesn't match the capacity of the drive, you can use a switch as part of the FORMAT command. A switch is a parameter that is used with a DOS command to modify its action. Switches always begin with a slash. The /F:size switch directs DOS to format the disk with the capacity specified by size. For example, the command

    FORMAT A:/F:720

formats the 3½-inch disk in drive A with a capacity of 720K.

This kind of formatting is fine if your intention is to prepare a diskette to store program files, but not if you want to create a DOS diskette that can be used to start the computer. To format a diskette so that it may be used as a DOS diskette, use the /S switch. For example, the command

    FORMAT A:/S

formats the diskette in drive A, and then copies the DOS control programs to it. You can mix switches, as in

    FORMAT A:/S/F:720

to create a DOS diskette with a capacity of 720K. In this command, the order of the switches doesn't matter.

When the formatting is complete, you are asked to enter a volume label. As explained later, the volume label is displayed when you execute a DIR command. The volume label can be up to 11 characters long. It's a good idea to enter your name as the volume label.

Directories

Disks can store hundreds—even thousands—of files. So that you can find a particular file when you want it, files are stored in directories and subdirectories. Although directories and subdirectories are mostly used with hard disks, they can also be used with diskettes. When you format a disk, it initially contains only one directory, which is called the root directory. When you are in the root directory, the prompt is C:\>, where the backslash (\) represents the root directory.

Hard disks are organized with each major application in its own directory. For example, DOS, your word processor, and your spreadsheet would each have its own directory. You would create one or more subdirectories to store the files associated with each application. Under your word processor directory, you might create one subdirectory to store your letters, a second to store your book reports, and so on. The following is the structure of a hard disk with only a few directories and subdirectories.

As you can see, DOS, spreadsheet (SS), and word processor (WP) are directories that branch off the root. SS has two subdirectories: BUDGET and EXPENSES. WP also has two subdirectories: HOMEWORK and REPORTS.

```
Root

    ── DOS

    ── SS

            ── BUDGET
            ── EXPENSES

    ── WP

            ── HOMEWORK

            ── REPORTS
```

Next, we will study how to create subdirectories, move in and out of them, and delete them when they are no longer needed.

You create a new directory with the command MD (make directory). For example, the command

```
MD WP
```

makes the directory named WP. Directory names follow the same rules as filenames, but directory names usually do not have filename extensions. Although we created a directory named WP, we are still in the root directory. The CD (change directory) command is used to move between directories. For example, to move to the WP directory, use the command

```
CD WP
```

This command makes the WP directory the default directory. After this command is executed, the prompt changes to C:\WP>.

Two periods next to each other represent the parent (one level up) of the current directory. So if you are in the WP directory, and execute the command

```
CD ..
```

you will move to the parent of the WP directory, which is the root directory.

Once you are in the WP directory, you can make subdirectories below it. For example, the command

```
MD HOMEWORK
```

creates the subdirectory HOMEWORK under the WP directory. If you then move into the HOMEWORK subdirectory, the prompt becomes C:\WP\HOMEWORK.

When you no longer need a directory, you can delete it using the command RD (remove directory). For example, the command

```
RD HOMEWORK
```

deletes the HOMEWORK directory. To delete a directory, it must not contain any files. (You will learn how to delete files later.) Furthermore, the directory you are trying to delete must not be the default directory.

The DIR Command

The DIR command lists the contents of a disk or directory. To display the contents of the default drive or directory, simply type DIR and press the Enter key. For example, when the DIR command is used with the DOS/QBasic diskette used at Queensborough Community College, it produces the following output:

```
Volume in drive A is QBASIC
Volume Serial Number is 5A1B-040A
Directory of A:\

COMMAND  COM     52925 03-10-93  12:00p
QBASIC   HLP    130881 03-10-93  12:00p
QBASIC   EXE    194309 03-10-93  12:00p
QBASIC   INI        50 08-25-93  11:16a
GRAPHICS COM     19694 03-10-93  12:00p
GRAPHICS PRO     21232 03-10-93  12:00p
AUTOEXEC BAT       357 08-25-93   2:14p
         7 file(s) 477024 bytes
                 177934 bytes free
```

The columns in this listing show the filename and extension, the size of the file in bytes, and the date and time the file was created or last changed. The last two lines show the number of files listed and the number of unused bytes available on the diskette. The filenames and numbers you will see if you apply the DIR command to your diskette will differ, depending on the type of diskette and the version of DOS you are using.

Notice that MSDOS.SYS and IO.SYS are not included in this listing. These two files are on the diskette, but they are "hidden," which means that their names do not appear when the DIR command is used.

When the DIR command is used to show the contents of a directory, the output is similar, but it includes two additional lines. One line shows the filename as a single period, and the second shows the filename as two periods. The single period represents the current directory, and the two periods represent the parent directory. In addition, any subdirectories that belong to the current directory are identified with the label <DIR> in the column that lists the size of files.

To obtain a listing of the contents of a diskette or directory that is not the DOS default, simply include the name of the drive and directory in the DIR command. For example, the command

```
DIR C:\DOS
```

produces a listing of the contents of the DOS directory in drive C.

If a disk contains many files, they cannot all be displayed on the screen at the same time. You can use the /P switch with the DIR command to cause the screen to pause when it is full. For example,

```
DIR C:\WP/P
```

A full screen of filenames will be displayed, with the prompt

```
Press any key to continue
```

on the last line.

You can also use the asterisk to stand for part of a filename, as explained in Chapter 1. So to see the names of only your QBasic programs in the default directory, use the command

```
DIR *.BAS
```

The COPY Command

The COPY command is used to copy files from one directory to another. The directories may be on the same disk or on different disks. Assuming that drive A is the default drive, to copy the file named PA3-4.BAS from the diskette in drive A to the directory named PROGRAMS in drive C, use the command

```
COPY PA3-4.BAS C:\PROGRAMS
```

You can also use an asterisk to represent part of the filename, as explained in the DIR command section. So to copy all the QBasic programs from the diskette in default drive A to the PROGRAMS directory in drive C, use the command

```
COPY *.BAS C:\PROGRAMS
```

To copy all of the files from the diskette in default drive A to the PROGRAMS directory in drive C, use the command

```
COPY *.* C:\PROGRAMS
```

Note that since the files MSDOS.SYS and IO.SYS are hidden, they are not copied. Therefore, you cannot use the COPY command to create a DOS diskette.

The DISKCOPY Command

The DISKCOPY command allows you to make an exact copy of a diskette to a diskette of the same storage capacity. The contents of the target diskette will be destroyed, so make sure that it does not contain any files you wish to keep. If the target diskette is not formatted, DISKCOPY will format it as it makes the copy.

To make a copy of a diskette, type the command

```
DISKCOPY A: B:
```

The DISKCOPY program is loaded into RAM, and then you are prompted to insert the source diskette in drive A and the target diskette in drive B. Follow these instructions and press any key when you are ready. On a computer that contains only one diskette drive, you will be prompted alternately to insert the source and target diskettes.

DISKCOPY makes an exact copy of the source diskette, including the hidden files MSDOS.SYS and IO.SYS—so if the source diskette is a DOS diskette, the target diskette will also be a DOS diskette.

The DEL or ERASE Command

The DEL command—or its identical twin, the ERASE command—allows you to delete files from a disk. It is equivalent to the QBasic KILL command (see the programming assignments in Chapter 10). The command

```
DEL PA3-5.BAS
```

deletes the file PA3-5.BAS from the default directory.

You can use asterisks to delete a family of files with one command. The command

```
DEL *.BAS
```

deletes all the QBasic files from the default directory. The command

```
DEL *.*
```

deletes all the files from the default directory. Since that is such a drastic step, DOS asks you

```
Are you sure (Y/N)
```

before it executes the command. If you type Y and press the Enter key, DOS deletes all the files. But before you execute this command, you should execute a DIR command first. The files listed by the DIR command are those that will be deleted by the DEL *.* command. You can then examine the DIR output to verify you are deleting only files that you really want to delete.

SUMMARY OF STATEMENTS, FUNCTIONS, AND COMMANDS

Statement	Purpose
`BEEP`	Sounds the speaker
`CALL SubprogramName [(argumentlist)]`	Executes the named subprogram
`CIRCLE(x,y),radius[,color][,start][,end][,aspect]`	Draws a circle
`CLOSE [#filenum][,#filenum]...`	Closes open files
`CLS`	Clears the screen
`COLOR background,palette` **(Graphics mode)**	Selects colors
`COLOR [foreground][,background][,border]` **(Text mode)**	Selects colors
`COMMON SHARED variablelist`	Makes the listed variables global, so they can be shared between subprograms
`CONST ConstantName = expression`	Defines a symbolic constant
`DATA constant1 [, constant2]...`	Provides data for READ statements
`DIM variable([lower1 TO] upper1 [,[lower2 TO] upper2]...)`	Specifies the size of an array
`DO [{WHILE	UNTIL} condition]`	Marks the top of a loop that is ended with a LOOP statement
`END`	Stops execution of a program
`END FUNCTION`	Marks the end of a function and returns control to the statement that invoked the function
`END SUB`	Marks the end of a subprogram and returns control to the statement following the CALL statement that executed the subprogram
`EXIT FOR`	Exits from a FOR…NEXT loop by branching to the statement following the NEXT statement
`FOR counter = start TO end [STEP increment]`	Marks the top of a FOR…NEXT loop
`FUNCTION FunctionName [(parameterlist)]`	Declares the name of a function and lists parameters used in the function
`GET #filenum, recordnum, recordvariable`	Reads a record from a random file
`GET(x1,y1)-(x2,y2),arrayname` **(Graphics mode)**	Saves the colors of the pixels in an area of a graphics screen

```
IF condition1 THEN
    statements executed if condition1 is true
[ELSEIF condition2 THEN
    statements executed if condition2 is true]
[ELSE
    statements executed if all the conditions ↵
      are false]
END IF
```
Evaluates conditions and executes the statements associated with the condition that is true

```
INPUT #filenum, expressionlist
```
Reads data from a sequential file

```
INPUT [;]["prompt"{; | ,}] variablelist
```
Accepts data entered at the keyboard

```
[LET] variable = expression
```
Assigns a value to a variable

```
LINE INPUT #filenum, string variable
```
Reads a line of data from a file

```
LINE INPUT [;]["prompt";] string variable
```
Reads a line of data entered at the keyboard

```
LINE [(x1,y1)]-(x2,y2)[,color][,B[F]]
```
Draws a line

```
LOCATE [row][,column][,cursor]
```
Positions the cursor

```
LOOP [{WHILE | UNTIL} condition]
```
Marks the bottom of a loop whose top is indicated by a DO statement

```
LPRINT expressionlist
```
Prints values on the printer

```
LPRINT USING format-string; expressionlist
```
Prints values on the printer using the specified format

```
MID$(string variable,n,m) = string expression
```
Replaces characters in a string variable

```
NEXT counter
```
Marks the end of a FOR...NEXT loop

```
OPEN "filename" FOR mode AS #filenum
```
(Sequential files)

Opens a sequential file

```
OPEN "filename" FOR RANDOM AS #filenum ↵
   LEN=reclength
```
(Random files)

Opens a random file

```
PAINT(x,y)[,paint][,boundary]
```
Colors an area of the screen

```
PRESET(x,y)[,color]
```
Draws a point of the specified color

```
PRINT expressionlist
```
Prints values on the screen

```
PRINT #filenum, expressionlist
```
Writes data to a sequential file

```
PRINT #filenum USING format-string; expressionlist
```
Writes data to a file using the specified format

```
PRINT USING format-string; expressionlist
```
Prints values on the screen using the specified format

```
PSET(x,y)[,color]
```
Draws a point of the specified color

```
PUT #filenum, recordnum, recordvariable
```
Writes a record to a random file

```
PUT(x,y),arrayname
```
(Graphics mode)

Writes colors onto an area of a graphics screen

```
RANDOMIZE [n] or RANDOMIZE TIMER
```
Reseeds the random number generator

```
READ variablelist
```
Assigns to the variables in variablelist values read from a DATA statement

```
REM any comment you like or
' any comment you like
```
Allows documentation in a program

```
RESTORE
```
Causes the next READ statement to obtain its values from the first values in the data bank

`SCREEN mode`	Sets the screen mode

`SELECT CASE testexpression`
   `CASE test1`
      `statements to be executed if test1 is true`
   `[CASE test2`
      `statements to be executed if test2 is true]`
   `[CASE ELSE`
      `statements to be executed if all tests are false]`
`SELECT END`
	Executes one of several groups of statements, depending on which test matches testexpression

`SHELL "DOS command"`	Permits DOS commands to be executed from within QBasic
`SUB SubprogramName [(parameterlist)] [STATIC]`	Marks the first statement in a subprogram, and lists the parameters used in the subprogram
`SWAP variable1, variable2`	Exchanges the values of two variables

`TYPE record name`
   `field AS type`
`END TYPE`
	Defines a record consisting of one or more fields

`VIEW [(x1,y1)-(x2,y2)][,color][,boundary]`	Establishes a viewport
`VIEW PRINT [toprow TO bottomrow]`	Establishes a text viewport between lines toprow and bottomrow
`WIDTH size`	Sets the number of characters in a line on the screen
`WINDOW [SCREEN][(x1,y1)-(x2,y2)]`	Establishes world coordinates
`WRITE #filenum, expressionlist`	Writes data to a sequential file in a form that can be read by an INPUT # statement

Function	**Purpose**
`ABS(x)`	Returns the absolute value of x
`ASC(x$)`	Returns the ASCII code of the first character of x$
`ATN(x)`	Returns the arctangent (in radians) of x
`CHR$(n)`	Returns the character whose ASCII code is n
`CINT(x)`	Returns x rounded to the nearest integer
`COS(x)`	Returns the cosine of angle x, where x is in radians
`DATE$`	Returns the date, in the form mm-dd-yyyy
`EOF(n)`	Returns true if the end of file n has been reached, and false if the end of file n has not been reached
`EXP(x)`	Returns e (2.71828…) raised to the x power
`FIX(x)`	Returns x truncated to an integer
`INPUT$(n)`	Returns a string of n characters read from the keyboard

`INSTR(n,x$,y$)`	Returns the position of y$ in x$; n specifies the position in x$ where the search is to begin
`INT(x)`	Returns the largest integer less than or equal to x
`LCASE(x$)`	Returns x$ with all the letters in lower case
`LEFT$(x$,n)`	Returns the n left-most characters of x$
`LEN(x$)`	Returns the length of x$
`LOF(n)`	Returns the length in bytes of the file opened as file number n
`LOG(x)`	Returns the natural logarithm of x
`LTRIM$(x$)`	Returns x$ with leading spaces removed
`MID$(x$,n,m)`	Returns m characters of x$ starting with the nth character
`RIGHT$(x$,n)`	Returns the n right-most characters of x$
`RND`	Returns a random number between 0 and 1
`RTRIM$(x$)`	Returns x$ with trailing spaces removed
`SGN(x)`	Returns −1 if x is negative, 0 if x is 0, and +1 if x is positive
`SIN(x)`	Returns the sine of angle x, where x is in radians
`SPACE$(n)`	Returns a string of n spaces
`SPC(n)`	Skips n spaces in a PRINT statement
`SQR(x)`	Returns the square root of x; x must be $>= 0$
`STR$(n)`	Returns n converted to a string
`STRING$(n,m)`	Returns a string of n characters, all consisting of the character whose ASCII code is m
`STRING$(n,x$)`	Returns a string of n characters, all consisting of the first character of x$
`TAB(n)`	Tabs to column n in a PRINT statement
`TAN(x)`	Returns the tangent of angle x, where x is in radians
`TIME$`	Returns the time of day, in the form hh:mm:ss
`TIMER`	Returns the time, in seconds, from the PC's clock
`UCASE$(x$)`	Returns x$ with all the letters in upper case
`VAL(x$)`	Returns the numeric value of x$

Command (Entered in the Immediate window)	Purpose
`KILL filename`	Deletes the specified file from a diskette
`NAME filename1 AS filename2`	Renames filename1 to filename2

GLOSSARY

absolute coordinates   The expression of a pixel's location in terms of its X and Y coordinates.

accumulator   A variable used to obtain the sum of the values of another variable.

algorithm   A step-by-step procedure to solve a problem.

all points addressable   Allowing the user to draw a point anywhere on the screen by means of a graphics instruction.

argument   A constant, variable, or expression supplied to a function—and used by the function to determine a result.

array   A collection of storage locations that are accessed by the same variable name and that store the same kind of data—numeric or string.

ASCII code   American Standard Code for Information Interchange. The code used to store data in the computer.

aspect ratio   The ratio of the horizontal distance between pixels to the vertical distance between pixels (horizontal distance / vertical distance).

background color   The color of the background against which text is displayed.

backup file   A copy of a file that can be used to recreate the original.

binary search   A method of searching a sorted array in which half of the remaining array is eliminated from the search by each comparison.

bit   Binary digit.

booting   Reading DOS from a disk into RAM.

breakpoint   A statement in a program where execution pauses.

bubble sort   A method of sorting an array in which adjacent elements are compared and swapped, if necessary, so that elements move slowly toward their final positions.

buffer   A part of the computer's memory where data are temporarily stored while they are being read from or written to a disk.

bugs   Errors in a program.

byte   The unit of storage, consisting of eight bits, that can store one character.

central processing unit (CPU)   The computer component that executes program instructions, such as adding two numbers or printing results.

clicking   Pressing and quickly releasing a mouse button.

clipboard   A temporary storage area that holds text you are copying or moving.

compiler   A program that translates a program into machine language before any statements are executed.

compound condition   A set of two or more simple conditions joined by the reserved words AND or OR.

computer   An electronic device that can accept data, process the data according to your instructions, and display results.

computer program   A set of instructions followed by a computer to solve a problem.

concatenation   Combining strings or string variables.

condition   A logical expression in which two numeric or two string expressions are compared. A condition is either true or false.

constant   A value—either a number or a string—that does not change when a program is executed.

control break   A change in the value of an identifying variable, which means that some special processing—such as printing subtotals—should be performed.

coordinates   A pair of numbers that locate a point on the screen.

counter   A variable that is used to keep track of some number, such as the number of times that a loop is executed.

counter-controlled loop   A loop that uses a counter to control the number of times it is executed.

cursor   A short flashing line that indicates where the next character you type will appear on the screen.

data   Values in the form of numbers or words that the computer processes.

debugging   Eliminating errors (bugs) in a program.

default   The value you get automatically (used if you don't specify a different value).

detail line   A line that is printed for each case or record processed.

dialog box   A box that QBasic displays when it needs additional information to execute a command.

diskette drive   A secondary storage device that can read and write data on diskettes.

diskette (floppy disk)   A magnetic-coated plastic disk that is used to store programs and data.

disk operating system (DOS)   A collection of programs that control the PC and make it easier for you to use it.

documenting   Adding comments to a program to explain what the program does and how it does it.

double-precision variable   A variable that holds values with up to 16 digits of accuracy.

drag   To move the mouse pointer to an object, press the left mouse button, and move the mouse pointer while holding down the button.

elements   The individual components of an array.

endless loop   A loop that doesn't stop executing.

exponentiation   Raising a numeric value to a power.

expression   A combination of variables, numbers, and arithmetic operation symbols that can be evaluated to produce a number.

field   An item of data that is part of a record.

file   A program, or other data, stored on a diskette or hard disk. A data file is a collection of related records.

filename   The name of a file. Can be up to eight characters and is composed of letters, digits, and selected special characters.

filename extension   One to three characters that may be added to the end of a filename. QBasic automatically uses BAS as the filename extension.

fixed-length string variable   A string variable whose length does not change.

flag   A variable whose purpose is to control the execution of a program by indicating whether some condition has or has not occurred.

flowchart   A pictorial representation of an algorithm that shows its logical structure more clearly.

foreground color   The color in which text is displayed.

format string   A string that specifies the placement and format of output produced by a PRINT USING or LPRINT USING statement.

function   A part of QBasic that operates on one or more arguments and returns a value.

function keys   Any of the keys labeled F1 through F12.

global variable   A variable that may be used anywhere in a program.

hanging punctuation   A comma or a semicolon that is coded after the last variable in a PRINT or LPRINT statement.

hard copy   Printed output.

hard disk   A high-capacity, fast-access, secondary storage device.

hardware   The physical components of a computer system—the parts of the computer you can physically touch.

hierarchy of operations   The order in which the operations are performed when expressions are evaluated.

hyperlink   A term that may be used as an entry point into the QBasic help system.

Immediate window   The area of the QBasic screen where statements are executed when they are entered.

index   An array used to locate records in a random-access file.

initialize   To assign a variable a value at the start of a program or a loop.

input unit   The component of a computer system that allows you to enter data and instructions into the computer.

integer division   Division that yields as its answer only the integer (whole number) part of the quotient. Specified by the backslash: \.

integer variable   A variable that holds whole numbers in the range –32,768 to 32,767.

interpreter   A program that translates a program into machine language one statement at a time.

kilobyte (K)   1024 bytes.

key (key field)   A field in a record used as the identifying field.

last point referenced   The point from which relative coordinates are measured.

left-justified   Printed as far to the left in a field as possible.

line clipping   Cutting a figure at the edge of the screen.

local variable   A variable that may be used only in the main module or procedure in which it is defined.

logical operator   In this book, one of the reserved words AND, OR, and NOT.

logic error   An error in a program that lets the program execute—but it produces a wrong answer.

long integer variable   A variable that holds whole numbers in the range –2,147,483,648 to 2,147,483,647.

loop   A set of statements that is executed repeatedly.

megabyte (M)   Approximately 1 million bytes (exactly 1,048,576 bytes).

machine language   The only language the computer understands without translation.

menu   A list of choices from which you make a selection.

Menu bar   The bar at the top of the QBasic screen that contains the names of the menus.

modulo arithmetic   Arithmetic in which the answer is the integer that is the remainder of an integer division. Specified by the operator MOD.

monitor   A television-like display device.

Monte Carlo simulation   A simulation that involves random elements.

mouse   A device that you roll around on the desktop in order to move a pointer on the screen.

mouse pointer   The rectangle that moves around the screen when you roll the mouse around the desktop.

multiple-alternative decision   A decision in which more than two choices exist.

nested IF statement   An IF statement that contains another IF statement in either its true or false branches.

nested loops   Loops in which an inner loop is enclosed inside an outer loop.

null string   The string that contains no characters.

numeric variable   A variable whose value is a number.

one-dimensional array An array that requires one subscript to specify an element.

output unit The component of a computer system that displays the computer's results.

palette A set of four colors that may be used to color figures.

parallel arrays Two or more arrays in which the data stored in a particular element of one array correspond to data in the same element of the other(s).

parameter A variable defined and used in a procedure; it is replaced by an argument when the procedure is executed.

personal computer (PC) A single-user computer made by IBM (and many other companies).

physical coordinates The coordinate system that refers to specific points on the screen.

pixel A dot, or picture element, on the screen.

pointer A variable that indicates the location of an item of data.

posttest loop A loop in which the condition is tested after the statements in the loop are executed. In QBasic, such loops are coded by including a condition on the LOOP statement.

pretest loop A loop in which the condition is tested before the statements in the loop are executed. In QBasic, such loops are coded by including a condition on the DO statement.

primary storage (main memory) The computer component in which data and instructions that are being processed are stored.

priming read The INPUT statement that accepts the first value. It is coded before the start of the loop.

procedure Self-contained statements that perform a specific task—such as displaying a menu or calculating a value.

prompt A message displayed by the computer indicating that it is waiting for you to enter instructions or data.

pseudocode A language somewhere between English and QBasic that is used to develop the algorithm for a program.

QBasic A modern version of the BASIC language, QBasic is distributed with DOS versions 5.0 and later.

random-access file A file in which records can be retrieved or written without processing all the preceding records in the file.

random access memory (RAM) The part of primary storage that stores programs and data while the computer is working on them. The contents are erased when the computer is turned off (temporary storage).

random number A number that cannot be predicted.

read only memory (ROM) The part of primary storage with contents that cannot be changed (permanent storage).

record A data structure that consists of one or more logically related fields.

Reference bar The bar at the bottom of the QBasic screen that shows the operations that the function keys will perform, the keyboard status, and the cursor position.

relational operator One of the six symbols =, <, >, <=, >=, and <> used in writing conditions.

relative coordinates The expression of a pixel's location in terms of the X and Y distances from a point mentioned earlier in the program.

reserved word A word that has a special meaning in QBasic.

reverse image A display in which black characters appear against a white background.

right-justified Printed as far to the right in a field as possible.

round-off errors A small numerical error that sometimes occurs in a computer-calculated answer because of the way the computer stores numbers.

run-time error   An error that causes QBasic to stop execution.

scientific notation   A method of printing very large and very small numbers.

scrolling   To move text up, down, right, and left so that you can see parts that aren't visible.

secondary storage device   A computer component, such as a diskette drive, that supplements primary storage—allowing data and programs to be stored permanently.

sentinal value   *See* trailer data.

sequential file   A file in which records are stored, read, and processed in order—from the first record to the last.

sequential search   A method of searching an array in which the elements of the array are examined in sequence (one after another).

simulation   Recreating the behavior of a system on a computer.

single-precision variable   A variable that holds values with up to seven digits of accuracy.

soft copy   Output displayed on the monitor's screen.

software   The instructions that the computer follows.

spacing chart   A chart used to design printed reports and screens.

statement   An instruction to the computer.

string   A sequence of letters, numbers, or other characters.

string expression   A combination of string variables, constants, and functions—and the concatenation operator—that evaluates to a string.

string variable   A variable whose value is a string.

subscript   A numeric constant, variable, or expression that specifies a particular element of an array.

substring   Part of a string.

syntax   The rules that must be followed when writing a statement.

syntax error   A violation of the rules for writing QBasic statements.

system unit   The case that houses the CPU, primary storage, hard disk, and diskette drives.

table   *See* two-dimensional array.

toggle   A key that alternately turns on and off when pressed.

top-down chart or hierarchy chart   A chart that shows the tasks required to solve a problem—and the relationship of these tasks.

top-down design or stepwise refinement   A method of developing an algorithm by breaking up a complex problem into a set of less complex problems.

tracing   Executing a program by hand, line by line, and keeping track of the changing values of the variables.

trailer data   Extra data entered after all the real data to indicate that all the real data were entered. Also called sentinel values.

two-dimensional array   An array that requires two subscripts to specify an element. Also called a table.

uninitialized variable   A variable to which a value was not assigned.

variable name   The name of a storage location in primary storage where data are stored.

View window   The area of the QBasic screen where you type your programs.

viewport   A section of the screen that functions like an independent screen.

warm boot   An action equivalent to turning the computer off and then on. Accomplished by pressing the Ctrl+Alt+Delete keys.

world coordinates   A coordinate system established by the user to fit a given problem.

INDEX